Bihar Higher Secondary School Teacher

Physics

Latest Edition
Practice Kit

10 Tests
10 Mock Test

Based On Real Exam Pattern

✓ Thoroughly Revised and Updated
✓ Detailed Analysis of all MCQs

<table>
<tr><td>Title</td><td>: Bihar Higher Secondary School Teacher Physics</td></tr>
<tr><td>Author Name</td><td>: Mr. Rohit Manglik</td></tr>
<tr><td>Published By</td><td>: EduGorilla Community Pvt. Ltd.</td></tr>
<tr><td>Publishers Address</td><td>: 12/651, First Floor Opp. Arvindo Park, Near Jama Masjid, Indira Nagar, Lucknow, Uttar Pradesh-226016, India</td></tr>
</table>

Copyright EduGorilla

Disclaimer EduGorilla

ROHIT MANGLIK
CEO, EduGorilla

Dear Applicants,

People say *"Success comes to those who work hard."* But I've seen people working hard for their exams day in and day out for marginal success. While others succeed in their examinations by putting in just half the work. So are they God Gifted? No! I believe that it's because they work *smart* and not just *hard*. Similarly, for your exams, you should strategize your preparation so as to increase the likelihood of success. Well with EduGorilla get ready to increase your *chances of selection* in your exam by *16x*.

EduGorilla helps you in not only working *hard* but also working in a *smart and strategic* manner. With EduGorilla's preparation package, you get a chance to make your exam preparation easy, and a fun learning path towards selection. Finding the right path to your preparations can be difficult if you don't know in which direction to head. Don't worry, we have you covered! EduGorilla will be your guide to success in your journey. With our Preparation Package, you can prepare strategically and beat the exam in just one attempt.

EduGorilla's Preparation Package includes-

- **Test Series**
- **Books**

Our preparation package is handcrafted as per the latest changes, expert opinions, and students' discretion. Thus, enabling you to get through each stage of the selection process for your exam.

Our Books are designed by the teachers and experts of the respective exam with a combined 150+ years of experience; to provide you with easy, efficient, and effective learning. Our books are smart, in the sense that not only do they give you the answers to the questions but also provide similar questions for practice.

EduGorilla's competent Test Series gives you real-time experience and confidence through which you can clear your offline or online exam in just one attempt. We currently host 93,000+ mock tests for 1,480+ competitive and academic exams.

Thus, EduGorilla misses no chance to assist you in your preparation and covers all stages of the exam, so that you don't have to look anywhere else.

We provide complete preparation packages for defense, banking, teaching, and other National & State-Level exams. Hence, it doesn't matter which exam you aspire to because you will reach your success.

ALL THE BEST !
Let EduGorilla be your Guide to Success.

Rohit Manglik,
Founder and CEO, EduGorilla

INTRODUCTION

EduGorilla focuses on guiding students to succeed in their examinations. With that in mind, our book, titled "Bihar Higher Secondary School Teacher : Physics", has been drafted through the collective efforts of our distinguished experts with 150+ years of combined experience. This book consists of questions that are created following the latest changes in the syllabus and exam pattern. We compiled the book on the basis of questions that are most likely to appear in the Bihar Higher Secondary Teacher : Physics. Through EduGorilla's "Bihar Higher Secondary School Teacher : Physics" your chances of success will increase 16x.

EduGorilla does this through our Complete Preparation Package. This package consists of well-conceptualized and structured content in the form of questions that are tailor-made according to your needs and will help you practice for exams in a smart way by pinpointing all the necessary information. It also provides hints and solutions, along with a smart answer sheet for your self-evaluation. You can assess your shortcomings and work accordingly on areas that may require more of your attention.

EduGorilla promises to help you succeed in your examination and accomplish your dream goals. We believe in our aspirants and see them at the top of the merit list. And the first step towards the top is to start preparing with us. EduGorilla's "Bihar Higher Secondary School Teacher : Physics" includes the following attributes.

➤ Well-Researched Content

➤ Top-Notch Quality

➤ Detailed Answers and Analysis

➤ Smart Answer Sheet

➤ Exam Relevant Questions

Therefore, EduGorilla fortifies your preparation and makes it durable enough to help you stand tall and beat the examination.

Bihar Higher Secondary Teacher : Physics
Scan QR code for Eligibility, Exam Pattern, Syllabus and more.

Book ID: 1304

TABLE OF CONTENTS

1. Dimensions of coefficient of viscosity is:
   (a) $[MT^2]$
   (b) $[ML^{-3}\,T^{-4}]$
   (c) $[ML^{-1}\,T^{-2}]$
   (d) $[ML^{-1}\,T^{-1}]$

2. The percentage error in the measurement of mass and speed are 2% and 3% respectively. The error in the estimate of kinetic energy obtained by measuring mass and need will be:
   (a) 12%
   (b) 10%
   (c) 8%
   (d) 2%

3. The position of a particle at any time t is given by the relation $x(t) = \frac{v}{A}\left(1 - e^{-At}\right)$ where v is the velocity. Then what will be the dimension of A ?
   (a) $[T^{-1}]$
   (b) $[T^2]$
   (c) $[L^1]$
   (d) $[L^{-2}]$

4. Which of these relations is wrong?
   (a) $1\text{cal} = 4.18$ J
   (b) $1\,\text{Å} = 10^{-10}$ m
   (c) $1\text{MeV} = 1.6 \times 10^{-13}$ J
   (d) $1\,\text{Newton} = 10^{-5}$ dyne

5. A person travels along a straight road for the first half time with a velocity v_1 and for the second half time with a velocity v_2. The mean velocity $'V'$ is given by
   (a) $V = \frac{v_1 + v_2}{2}$
   (b) $\frac{1}{V} = \frac{1}{v_1} + \frac{1}{v_2}$
   (c) $V = \sqrt{v_1 v_2}$
   (d) $V = \sqrt{\frac{v_2}{v_1}}$

6. A body moving in a straight line with an initial velocity of 5 ms^{-1} and a constant acceleration covers a distance of 30 m in the $3rd$ second. How much approx distance will it cover in the next 2 seconds?
   (a) 70 m
   (b) 80 m
   (c) 36 m
   (d) 100 m

7. Which of the following remain constant for a projectile fired from the earth?
   (a) Horizontal component of velocity
   (b) Vertical component of velocity
   (c) Velocity of projection
   (d) Acceleration of projected

8. A body 'X' is dropped from vertically from the top of a tower. If another identical body 'Y' is thrown horizontally from the same point at the same instant, then _________.
   (a) X will reach the ground earlier
   (b) Y will reach the ground earlier than X
   (c) Both 'X' and 'Y' will reach the ground simultaneously
   (d) Depends on external factors

9. Two vectors have a resultant equal to either. The angle between them is _________.
   (a) 60°
   (b) 120°
   (c) 90°
   (d) 100°

10. Work energy theorem is the "Work done by _______ force acting on the particle is equal to change in kinetic energy".
    (a) Only Conservative
    (b) Only Non-conservative
    (c) Net
    (d) None of these

11. A cricket bat is cut at the location of its center of mass as shown. Then,

    (a) The bottom piece will have a greater mass
    (b) The two pieces will have same mass
    (c) The handle piece will have a greater mass
    (d) The mass of the handle piece will be double the mass of the bottom piece

12. What is the value acceleration due to gravity of a black hole?
    (a) $g = \frac{GM}{R^2}$
    (b) $g = \infty$
    (c) $g = 0$
    (d) $g = \sqrt{\frac{GM}{R^2}}$

13. If the orbital velocity of the satellite revolving around the earth is 7 km/sec, then its escape velocity will be:
    (a) 11.2 km/sec
    (b) 8 km/sec
    (c) 9.9 km/sec
    (d) 10.2 km/sec

14. Which of the following laws says that "Every object in the universe attracts every other object with a force which is proportional to the product of their masses and inversely proportional to the square of the distance between them?"
    (a) Universal Law of gravitation
    (b) Kepler's Law
    (c) Newton's third Law of motion
    (d) Newton's first Law of motion

15. The value of acceleration due to gravity is:
    (a) Same at equator and poles
    (b) Increased from pole to equator
    (c) Least at equator
    (d) Least at poles

16. If the horizontal velocity given to a satellite is greater than the critical velocity but less than the escape velocity, then the satellite will _______.
    (a) Revolve in a circular orbit
    (b) Will strike the earth along a parabolic path
    (c) Start revolving in an elliptical orbit
    (d) It will disappear in the outer space

17. In an experiment, brass and steel wires of length 1 m each with areas of cross $1mm^2$ section are used. The wires are connected in series and one end of the combined wire is connected to a rigid support and other end is subjected to elongation. The stress requires to produced a new elongation of 0.2 mm is: [Given, the Young's Modulus for steel and brass are respectively $120 \times 10^9 N/m^2$ and $60 \times 10^9 N/m^2$]
    (a) $8 \times 10^6 N/m^2$
    (b) $4.0 \times 10^6 N/m^2$
    (c) $1.2 \times 10^6 N/m^2$
    (d) $0.2 \times 10^6 N/m^2$

18. The elastic limit of brass is $379 MPa$. What should be the minimum diameter of a brass rod if it is to support

a $400N$ load without exceeding its elastic limit?
(a) $1.00mm$
(b) $1.16mm$
(c) $0.90mm$
(d) $1.36mm$

19. If a force is applied to an elastic wire of the material of Poisson's ratio 0.2 there is a decrease of the cross-sectional area by 1%. The percentage increase in its length is:
(a) 1%
(b) 5%
(c) 2.5%
(d) 1.5%

20. If a soap bubble expands, the pressure inside the bubble:
(a) Remains the same
(b) Is equal to the atmospheric pressure
(c) Decreases
(d) Increases

21. A body floats in a liquid contained in a beaker. If the whole system falls under gravity, them the upthrust on the body due to liquids is:
(a) Equal to the weight of the body in air
(b) Equal to the weight of the body in liquid
(c) Zero
(d) Equal to the weight of the immersed part of the body

22. The working of venturimeter is based on:
(a) Torricelli's law
(b) Pascal's law
(c) Bernoulli's theorem
(d) Archimede's principle

23. A rectangular vessel when full of water, takes 10 min to be emptied through an orifice in its bottom. How much time will take to be emptied when half-filled with water?
(a) 9 min
(b) 7 min
(c) 5 min
(d) 3 min

24. The scale of temperature in which the temperature is only positive is:
(a) Farenheit
(b) Celcius
(c) Kelvin
(d) Reaumur

25. "Good absorber of heat is good radiator of heat also" is:
(a) Stefan's law
(b) Kirchhof's law
(c) Plank's law
(d) Wien's law

26. Water in an electric kettle becomes hot due to __________.
(a) Conduction
(b) Convection
(c) Radiation
(d) Motion of its molecules

27. Which law of thermodynamics defines the concept of temperature?
(a) First Law of Thermodynamics
(b) Second Law of Thermodynamics
(c) Zeroth Law of Thermodynamics
(d) Third Law of Thermodynamics

28. A geyser heats water flowing at the rate of 3.0 litres per minute from $27°C$ to $77°C$. If the geyser operates on a gas burner, what is the rate of consumption of the fuel if its heat of combustion is $4.0 \times 10^4 J/g$?

(a) $4.0 \times 10^4 J/g$
(b) $1.0 \times 10^4 J/g$
(c) $4.0 \times 10^{-8} J/g$
(d) $5.0 \times 10^5 J/g$

29. A cylinder with a movable piston contains 3 moles of hydrogen at standard temperature and pressure. The walls of the cylinder are made of a heat insulator, and the piston is insulated by having a pile of sand on it. By what factor does the pressure of the gas increase if the gas is compressed to half its original volume?
(a) 2.666
(b) 3.656
(c) 2.639
(d) None of the above

30. What happens when a gas expands adiabatically?
(a) No energy is needed for expansion
(b) Law of conservation of energy is inapplicable
(c) Energy is needed and comes from the wall of the gas's container
(d) Internal energy of the gas is used in doing work

31. $ABCDA$ is a cyclic process explaining the thermodynamic process. What is the work done by the system in the cycle?

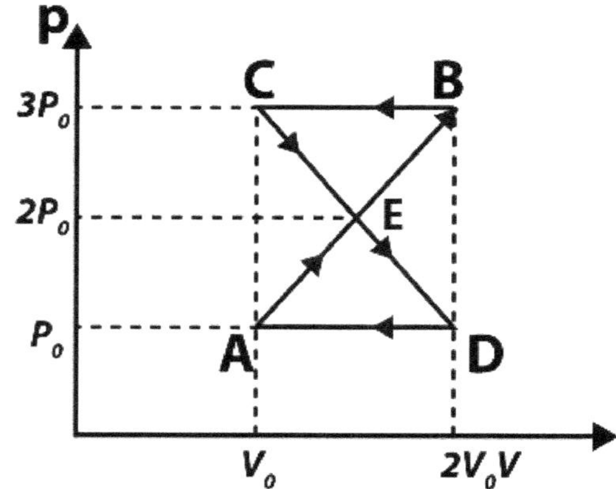

(a) 0
(b) $\dfrac{\rho_0 V_0}{2}$
(c) $\rho_0 V_0$
(d) $2\rho_0 V_0$

32. A flask contains argon and chlorine in the ratio of $2 : 1$ by mass. The temperature of the mixture is $27°C$. The ratio of average kinetic energies of two gases per molecule is:
(a) $2 : 1$
(b) $3 : 1$
(c) $1 : 1$
(d) $6 : 1$

33. Find the kinetic energy of 5 liters of a gas at STP, given the standard pressure, is $1.013 \times 10^5 \text{ N/m}^2$.
(a) 9.597×10^2 J
(b) 2.597×10^2 J
(c) 6.597×10^2 J
(d) 7.597×10^2 J

34. If α moles of a monoatomic gas are mixed with β moles of a polyatomic gas and mixture behaves like diatomic gas, then:
[Neglect the vibrational mode of freedom]
(a) $2\alpha = \beta$
(b) $\alpha = 2\beta$
(c) $\alpha = -3\beta$
(d) $3\alpha = -\beta$

35. A balloon contains 1500 m^3 of helium at $27°C$ and 4 atmospheric pressure. The volume of helium at $-3°C$ temperature and 2 atmospheric pressure will be:
(a) 2700 m^3
(b) 1900 m^3
(c) 1700 m^3
(d) 1500 m^3

36. Find the minimum attainable pressure of an ideal gas in process $T = T_0 + \alpha V^2$, where T_0 and α are positive constants and V is the volume of one mole of gas assuming $\dfrac{d^2P}{dT^2} = +ve$.

(a) $2R\sqrt{\alpha T_0}$ (b) $3R\sqrt{\alpha T_0}$

(c) $3R$ (d) $3R\sqrt{\dfrac{\alpha T_0}{2}}$

37. In the following reaction product P is:

$$R - \underset{\underset{O}{\|}}{C} - Cl \xrightarrow[Pd-BaSO_4]{H_2} P$$

(a) RCH_2OH (b) RCOOH

(c) RCHO   (d) RCH_3

38. Polarization in acrolein can be described as:

(a) $\overset{+\delta}{CH_2} = CH - \overset{+\delta}{CHO}$ (b) $\overset{-\delta}{CH_2} = CH - \overset{+\delta}{CHO}$

(c) $\overset{-\delta}{CH_2} = CH - \overset{+\delta}{CHO}$ (d) $\overset{+\delta}{CH_2} = CH - \overset{-\delta}{CHO}$

39. Among the following compounds, the strongest base is:

(a) $NH_2 - \underset{\underset{O}{\|}}{C} - NH_2$ (b) $NH_2 - \underset{\overset{\|}{NH}}{C} - NH_2$

(c) $C_6H_5 - NH_2$ (d) $CH_3 - NH - CH_3$

40. $2Ag^+(aq) + Cu(s) \rightleftharpoons Cu^{2+}(aq) + 2Ag(s)$

The standard potential E° for this reaction is 0.46 V. Which change will increase the potential the most?

(a) Doubling the $\left[Ag^+\right]$

(b) Halving the $\left[Cu^{2+}\right]$

(c) Doubling the size of the $Cu(s)$ electrode

(d) Decreasing the size of the Ag electrode by one-half

41. The equilibrium constant for the disproportionation of $HgCl_2$ into $HgCl^+$ and $HgCl_3^-$ is,

Given,

$HgCl^+ + Cl^- \rightleftharpoons HgCl_2; K_1 = 3 \times 10^6$

$HgCl_2 + Cl^- \rightleftharpoons HgCl_3^-; K_2 = 9.0$

(a) 27×10^6 (b) 3.3×10^{-7}

(c) 3.3×10^{-6} (d) 3×10^{-6}

42. What is the force between two small charged spheres of charges $2 \times 10^{-7}C$ and $3 \times 10^{-7}C$ placed 30 cm apart in the air?

(a) $5 \times 10^3\,N$ (b) $4 \times 10^{-13}\,N$

(c) $6 \times 10^{-3}\,N$ (d) None of the above

43. The magnitude of the force on a charge Q in the electric field E is:

(a) $\dfrac{E}{Q}$ (b) $\dfrac{Q}{E}$

(c) EQ (d) E^2Q

44. Coulombs force between two point charges varies with distance ' r ' in relation to _______.

(a) r   (b) $\dfrac{1}{r}$

(c) r^2 (d) $\dfrac{1}{r^2}$

45. Which of the following statements is true/false regarding charged particle?

A. An ion is a charged particle and can be negatively or positively charged. A negatively charged ion is called an anion and a positively charged ion, a cation

B. An ion is a charged particle and can be negative or positively charged. A negatively charged ion is called a cation. And a positively charged ion, an anion.

(a) A and B are both false

(b) Only A is true

(c) A and B are both true

(d) Only B is true

46. An infinite line charge produces a field of $9 \times 10^4 N/C$ at distance of 2 cm. Calculate the linear charge density.

(a) $10^{-6}\,C/m$ (b) $10^{-7}\,C/m$

(c) $10^{-8}\,C/m$ (d) $10^{-1}\,C/m$

47. Which one of the following is the dimensional formula for ϵ_0 ?

(a) $\left[M^{-2}L^{-4}T^4A^2\right]$ (b) $\left[M^{-3}L^{-2}T^4A^4\right]$

(c) $\left[M^{-2}L^{-3}T^5A^2\right]$ (d) $\left[M^{-1}L^{-3}T^4A^2\right]$

48. How many coulombs of charge do 25×10^{31} electrons possess?

(a) $80 \times 10^{12}C$ (b) $4 \times 10^{12}C$

(c) $40 \times 10^{12}C$ (d) $8 \times 10^{12}C$

49. A uniformly charged conducting sphere of 2.4 m diameter has a surface charge density of $80.0\mu C/m^2$. What is the total electric flux leaving the surface of the sphere?

(a) $1.3 \times 10^8\,Nm^2/C$ (b) $1.6 \times 10^5\,Nm^3/C$

(c) $2.5 \times 10^8\,Nm^2/C$ (d) $1.6 \times 10^8\,Nm^2/C$

50. In the potentiometer circuit shown in the figure, the balance point with $R = 10\Omega$ when switch S_1 is closed and S_2 is open is $50cm$, while that when S_2 is closed and S_1 is open is $60cm$. What is the value of X?

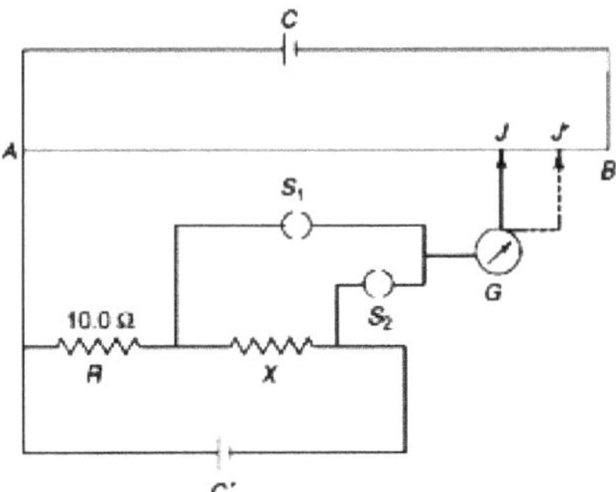

(a) 1Ω (b) 2Ω

(c) 3Ω (d) 4Ω

51. The figure below shows a network of eight resistors numbered 1 to 8 each equal to 2Ω, connected to a $3V$ battery of negligible internal resistance. The current I in the circuit is:

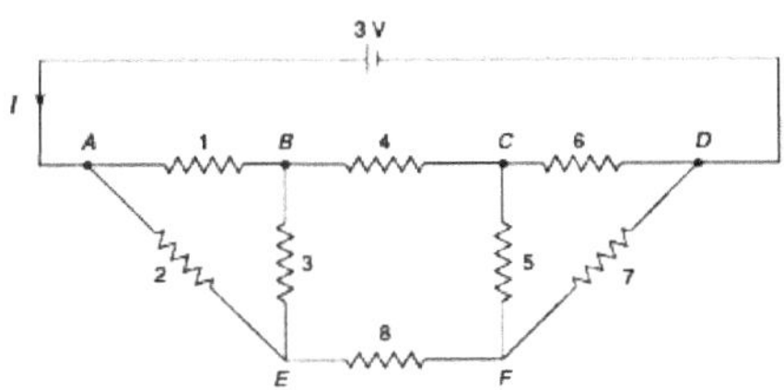

(a) $0.25A$ (b) $0.5A$

(c) $0.75A$ (d) $1.0A$

52. Assume that each atom of copper contributes one free electron. Density of Cu is $9\,\text{g/cm}^3$ and atomic weight is $63\,\text{g}$. If current flowing through a Cu wire of $1mm$ diameter is $1.1A$, drift velocity of electrons will be:

(a) $0.1\,\text{mm/s}$ (b) $0.2\,\text{mm/s}$

(c) $0.3\,\text{mm/s}$ (d) $0.5\,\text{mm/s}$

53. Specific resistance of ali metals is mostly affected by ________.

(a) Temperature   (b) Pressure

(c) Magnetic field   (d) Volume

54. A bar of diamagnetic material placed in an external magnetic field will __________ field.

(a) pull in the field lines and move from high to low

(b) repel out the field lines and move from low to high

(c) pull in the field lines and move from low to high

(d) repel out the field lines and move from high to low

55. Two small bar magnets are placed in a line with like poles facing each other at a certain distance d apart. If the length of each magnet is negligible as compared to d, the force between them will be inversely proportional to:

(a) d (b) d^2

(c) $\frac{1}{d^2}$ (d) d^4

56. If in a vertical wire the current is flowing upward then the direction of magnetic field on the left side of the wire will be:

(a) Perpendicular to the paper and outward

(b) Perpendicular to the paper and inward

(c) Vertically upward

(d) Vertically downward

57. Electromagnets are used in ________.

(a) Electric bells   (b) Loudspeakers

(c) Both (A) and (B)   (d) None of these

58. When a hole is cut at the center of the bar magnet, then the pole strength of the bar magnet will________.

(a) Increase   (b) Decrease

(c) Remain unchanged   (d) None of these

59. A short bar magnet placed with its axis at $30°$ with an external field of 800 G experiences a torque of 0.016 Nm. What is the magnetic moment of the magnet?

(a) $0.40\,\text{A m}^2$ (b) $0.20\,\text{A m}^2$

(c) $1.40\,\text{A m}^2$ (d) $0.70\,\text{A m}^2$

60. A solenoid has a core of a material with relative permeability 400. The windings of the solenoid are insulated from the core and carry a current of 2 A. If the number of turns is 1000 per metre, calculate the magnetic field.

(a) 1.8 T   (b) 1.5 T

(c) 2 T   (d) 1.0 T

61. A closely wound solenoid of 800 turns and area of cross section $2.5 \times 10^{-4}\,\text{m}^2$ carries a current of 3.0 A. What is its associated magnetic moment?

(a) 1.6JT^{-1} (b) 0.6JT^{-1}

(c) 2.6JT^{-1} (d) 0.9JT^{-1}

62. The magnetic moment of an electron with orbital angular momentum J will be:

(a) $\frac{\text{eJ}}{\text{m}}$ (b) $\frac{\text{eJ}}{2\,\text{m}}$

(c) $\frac{2\,\text{m}}{\text{e}\vec{J}}$ (d) 0

63. Which of the following is correct regarding eddy currents in the coil?

(a) Eddy currents flow in straight lines, like a wire.

(b) Eddy current helps in generating electrical energy.

(c) By making use of a laminated core, eddy currents are increased.

(d) Eddy currents converts useful energy into heat and waste it.

64. A stepdown transformer reduces the voltage of a transmission line from 2200 V to 220 V. The power delivered by it is 880 W and its efficiency is 88%. The input current is:

(a) $4.65A$ (b) $0.45A$

(c) $\backslash(0.0465\,\text{A}\backslash$ (d) $4.65mA$

65. The induced emf is given by:

(a) $E = -N\frac{d\phi}{dt}$ (b) $E = -N\frac{dB}{dt}$

(c) $E = -\frac{dH}{dt}$ (d) $E = +\frac{dH}{dt}$

66. A plane electromagnetic wave is incident on a material surface. The wave delivers momentum p and energy E :

(a) $p = 0, E \neq 0$ (b) $p \neq 0, E = 0$

(c) $p \neq 0, E \neq 0$ (d) $p = 0, E = 0$

67. A plane Electromagnetic Wave of frequency 30 MHz travels in free space along the x - direction. The electric field component of the wave at a particular point of space and time $E = 6\,\text{vm}^{-1}$ along y -direction. Its magnetic field component B at this point would be:

(a) 2×10^{-8} T along z -direction

(b) 6×10^{-8} T along x -direction

(c) 2×10^{-8} T along y -direction

(d) 6×10^{-8} T along z -direction

68. The flux of electric field through closed conducting plate changes with time as $\phi_E = \left(50t^2 + 10t + 2\right)Vm$ then, the value of displacement current into medium of ϵ_0 at $t = 2$ sec is:

(a) $210\epsilon_0$ (b) $100\epsilon_0$

(c) $110\epsilon_0$ (d) $50\epsilon_0$

69. Speed of electromagnetic waves is the same:

(a) For all wavelengths   (b) In all media

(c) For all intensities   (d) For all frequencies

70. If the kinetic energy of an electron gets doubled, its de Broglie wavelength will become ________.

(a) Doubled   (b) $\left(\frac{1}{\sqrt{2}}\right)$ times

(c) $\sqrt{3}$ times   (d) $\sqrt{2}$ times

71. How does retarding potential vary with the frequency of light causing photoelectric effect?

(a) Infinite   (b) Zero

(c) Decreases   (d) Increases

72. In a Rutherford scattering experiment, when a projectile of charge z_1 and mass M_1 approaches a target nucleus of charge z_2 and mass M_2, the distance of the closest approach is r_0. The energy of the projectile is:

(a) Directly proportional to $z_1 z_2$

(b) Inversely proportional to z_1

(c) Directly proportional to mass M_1

(d) Directly proportional to $M_1 \times M_2$

73. When the number of nucleons in nuclei increases, the binding energy per nucleon:

(a) Increases continuously with mass number

(b) Decreases continuously with mass number

(c) Remains constant with mass number

(d) First increases and then decreases with increase of mass number

74. Which of the following curves may represent the speed of the electron in a Hydrogen atom as a function of the principal quantum number n ?

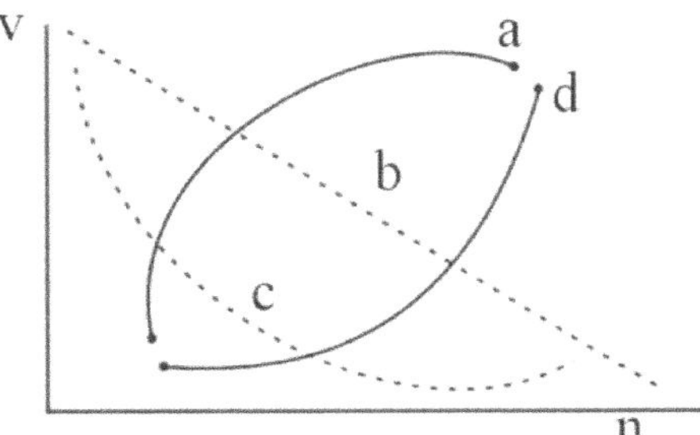

(a) a

(b) b

(c) c

(d) d

75. If λ is the wavelength of a hydrogen atom from the transition $n = 3$ to $n = 1$, then what is the wavelength for doubly ionized lithium-ion for the same transition?

(a) $\dfrac{\lambda}{3}$

(b) 3λ

(c) $\dfrac{\lambda}{9}$

(d) 9λ

76. How is the resistance of semiconductor classified?

(a) High resistance

(b) Positive temperature co-efficient

(c) Negative temperature co-efficient

(d) Low resistance

77. The depletion layer in a $p - n$ junction diode is $10^{-6}\ m$ wide and its knee potential is $0.5\ V$. What is the inner electric field in the depletion region?

(a) $5 \times (10)^6\ \dfrac{V}{m}$

(b) $5 \times (10)^{-7}\ \dfrac{V}{m}$

(c) $5 \times (10)^5\ \dfrac{V}{m}$

(d) None of these

78. The energy band gap is maximum in which of the following?

(a) Metals

(b) Superconductors

(c) Insulators

(d) Semiconductors

79. How are charge carriers produced in intrinsic semiconductors?

(a) By pure atoms

(b) By electrons

(c) By impure atoms

(d) By holes

80. If the electrical conductivity of a semiconductor increases when electromagnetic radiation of a wavelength shorter than 2480 nm is incident on it. What is the bandgap (in eV) for the semiconductor?

(a) 0.9 eV

(b) 0.7 eV

(c) 0.5 eV

(d) 1.1 eV

// Smart Answer Sheet //

Correct — Percentage of students who answered correctly.

Skipped — Percentage of students who skipped.

Q.	Ans.	Correct / Skipped	Q.	Ans.	Correct / Skipped	Q.	Ans.	Correct / Skipped
1	D	45.65% / 1.14%	2	C	87.76% / 0.0%	3	A	32.8% / 4.81%
4	D	44.13% / 1.03%	5	A	89.28% / 0.0%	6	C	69.98% / 1.08%
7	A	69.09% / 1.14%	8	C	89.4% / 0.0%	9	B	68.47% / 1.15%
10	C	66.36% / 1.65%	11	A	80.45% / 0.0%	12	B	48.29% / 1.69%
13	C	42.64% / 1.1%	14	A	66.43% / 1.37%	15	C	50.86% / 1.77%
16	C	78.41% / 0.0%	17	A	60.94% / 1.64%	18	B	52.17% / 1.17%
19	C	50.0% / 1.45%	20	C	49.3% / 1.18%	21	A	61.11% / 1.26%
22	C	50.06% / 1.41%	23	B	45.85% / 1.15%	24	C	85.38% / 0.0%
25	B	42.28% / 1.72%	26	B	44.2% / 1.0%	27	C	89.06% / 0.0%
28	A	64.51% / 1.35%	29	C	18.73% / 3.47%	30	D	80.14% / 0.0%
31	A	13.96% / 4.51%	32	C	57.76% / 1.45%	33	D	54.62% / 1.23%
34	A	42.59% / 1.47%	35	A	21.6% / 3.96%	36	A	22.37% / 3.8%
37	C	55.27% / 1.43%	38	D	63.31% / 1.37%	39	A	46.2% / 1.89%
40	A	32.87% / 3.63%	41	D	64.98% / 1.63%	42	C	55.04% / 1.22%
43	C	89.46% / 0.0%	44	D	89.94% / 0.0%	45	B	19.03% / 4.43%
46	B	76.12% / 0.0%	47	D	65.73% / 1.46%	48	C	66.57% / 1.32%
49	D	16.19% / 3.93%	50	B	25.56% / 3.26%	51	D	48.8% / 1.35%
52	A	41.58% / 1.04%	53	A	22.36% / 3.51%	54	D	49.04% / 1.37%
55	D	18.88% / 3.43%	56	A	21.83% / 3.03%	57	C	79.78% / 0.0%
58	C	45.62% / 1.43%	59	A	43.35% / 1.73%	60	D	47.4% / 1.22%
61	B	65.6% / 1.69%	62	B	79.29% / 0.0%	63	D	45.99% / 1.38%
64	B	67.1% / 1.64%	65	A	46.26% / 1.28%	66	C	60.2% / 1.42%
67	A	62.31% / 1.28%	68	A	40.82% / 1.12%	69	C	59.16% / 1.4%
70	B	86.61% / 0.0%	71	D	59.61% / 1.97%	72	A	64.86% / 1.23%
73	D	65.69% / 1.97%	74	C	47.49% / 1.02%	75	C	57.89% / 1.21%
76	C	40.73% / 1.63%	77	C	57.04% / 1.76%	78	C	50.32% / 1.32%
79	C	63.71% / 1.28%	80	C	57.35% / 1.1%			

// Hints and Solutions //

1(D). As we know,

Coefficient of viscosity, $\eta = \dfrac{F}{A\frac{dv}{dx}}$

Then,

$[F] = [\,\text{Force}\,] = MLT^{-2}$

$[\,A\,] = [\,\text{Area}\,] = L^2$

$\left[\dfrac{dv}{dx}\right] = [\,\text{Velocity gradient}\,] = \dfrac{LT^{-1}}{L}$

$= T^{-1}$

$\therefore [\eta] = \dfrac{MLT^{-2}}{L^2\,T^{-1}} = [ML^{-1}\,T^{-1}]$

Hence, the correct option is (D).

2(C). Given,

The percentage error in the measurement of mass,

$\dfrac{\Delta m}{m} \times 100 = 2\%$

The percentage error in the measurement of speed,

$\dfrac{\Delta v}{v} \times 100 = 3\%$

The kinetic energy of the particle is given by

$KE = \dfrac{mv^2}{2}$

The percentage error in kinetic energy will be,

$= \dfrac{\Delta m}{m} \times 100 + 2\dfrac{\Delta v}{v} \times 100$

$= 2 + 6$

$= 8\%$

3(A). Given,

$x(t) = \dfrac{v}{A}\left(1 - e^{-At}\right)$

As we know that $(1 - e^{-At})$ is a constant value and will have no dimension.

Thus, the dimension of $\dfrac{v}{A}$ will be equal to the dimension of x.

Dimension of position, $x = \left[M^0 L^1 T^0\right]$

The dimension of velocity, $v = \left[M^0\,L^1\,T^{-1}\right]$

$\Rightarrow x = \dfrac{v}{A}$

$\Rightarrow \left[M^0 L^1 T^0\right] = \dfrac{\left[M^0 L^1 T^{-1}\right]}{A}$

$\Rightarrow A = \left[T^{-1}\right]$

4(D). As we know,

1 kg = 1000 gm

1 m = 100 cm

1 Newton = 1 kg m/s^2

1 Newton = 1000 gm $\times$ 100 cm/s^2

1 Newton = 10^5 gm cm/s^2

1 gm cm/s^2 = 10^{-5} Newton

As we know,

1 dyne = 1 gm cm/s^2

Then,

1 Newton = 10^5 dyne

5(A). Total displacement $= \left(v_1 \times \dfrac{t}{2}\right) + \left(v_2 \times \dfrac{t}{2}\right)$

$= (v_1 + v_2)\dfrac{t}{2}$

Mean velocity $= \dfrac{\text{Total displacement}}{\text{Total time}}$

$= \dfrac{\left[(v_1 + v_2)\frac{t}{2}\right]}{t}$

$= \dfrac{(v_1 + v_2)}{2}$

Mean velocity of man is $\dfrac{(v_1 + v_2)}{2}$

6(C). Let's review the 4 fundamental kinematic equations of motion for constant acceleration:

$s = ut + \dfrac{1}{2}at^2$

$v^2 = u^2 + 2as$

$v = u + at$

$s = (u + v)\dfrac{t}{2}$

Where, s is distance, u is initial velocity, v is final velocity, a is acceleration and t is time.

In this case,

we know that, $u = 5m/s, s = 30m, t = 3s$

So, we find a from $s = ut + \dfrac{1}{2at^2}$

$30 = 5 + \dfrac{1}{2a}$

So, $a = \dfrac{15}{4.5} = 3.333\ m/s^2$

Then, $v = u + at = 5 + 3.333 = 15\ m/s$

And this is used as initial velocity in $s = ut + \dfrac{1}{2}at^2$,

where, $t = 2s$

$s = 15(2) + \dfrac{1}{2}(3.333)$

$s = 30 + 6.667 = 36.667$

The distance traveled in the next $2s$ is $36.667m$.

7(A). Projectile motion is the motion of an object projected into the air, under only the acceleration of gravity. The object is called a projectile, and its path is called its trajectory. The horizontal component of projectile motion is not affected by the force of gravity. The initial velocity can be given as x components and y components.

There is horizontal velocity component and it is always constant because there is no acceleration in the horizontal direction.

$u_x = u\cos\theta =$ horizontal component at maximum height

So, Horizontal component of velocity remains constant for a projectile fired from the earth.

8(C). Both 'X' and 'Y' have zero initial velocity and cover the same height under the acceleration due to gravity. Both 'X' and 'Y' will reach the ground simultaneously. 'X' and 'Y' differ in horizontal velocity but vertical motion of both of them is same, with no initial velocity and 'g' as acceleration, so the time taken by both of them will be the same.

$t = \sqrt{\dfrac{2h}{g}}$

Where, h = height of tower(height is same in both case),

g = acceleration due to gravity,

t = time taken

9(B). We know that,

Resultant force $R = \sqrt{(P^2 + Q^2 + 2PQ\cos\theta)}$

or $R^2 = P^2 + Q^2 + 2PQ\cos\theta$

Two equal vectors have a resultant equal to either of them

Therefore $R = P = Q$

$Q^2 = Q^2 + Q^2 + 2Q^2\cos\theta$

$\Rightarrow -Q^2 = 2Q^2\cos\theta$

$\Rightarrow \cos\theta = -\dfrac{1}{2} = \cos 120°$

$\Rightarrow \theta = 120°$

So, if wo vectors have a resultant equal to either then the angle between the vector will be $120°$.

10(C). Work energy theorem: Work done by net force acting on the particle is equal to change in kinetic energy So,

Work done $= (KE)_{\text{final}} - (KE)_{\text{initial}} = \Delta KE$

From the above definition it is clear that work done by net force is the reason to change the kinetic energy of particle.

11(A). As there is more material near the bottom end of the bat, the centre of mass of the bat is nearer the bottom end of the bat. The bat will balance horizontally on a knife-edge placed at the centre of mass. Centre of the mass is the point about which the rigid body can be balanced. The centre of mass of the handle piece and the bottom piece are at distances d_1 and d_2 respectively from the centre of mass of the entire bat.

For the rotational equilibrium, we have $M_1 d_1 = M_2 d_2$ where M1 and M_2 are the masses of the handle piece and the bottom piece respectively. The distance d_1 is greater than d_2 since the handle piece has thinner regions compared to the bottom piece.

Therefore, $M_2 > M_1$

12(B). Blackhole is a very dense body where the gravitational field is so strong that it absorbs all the radiation flowing from near it.

Blackhole is just like any other star but because of its high density and small radius it exerts huge force due to gravity hence acceleration due to gravity on its surface will be very large.

This was proved experimentally, that the value acceleration due to gravity of a black hole is infinity i.e., $g = \infty$

13(C). Given, $v_\circ = 7 \ km/sec$

We know that the relation between the orbital velocity and the escape velocity is given as,

$v_e = \sqrt{2}v_\circ$

Where $v_e =$ escape velocity and $v_\circ =$ orbital speed of the satellite

So the escape velocity of the satellite is given as,

$v_e = \sqrt{2}v_\circ$

$v_e = \sqrt{2} \times 7$

$v_e = 9.9 \ km/sec$

14(A).
- The universal law of gravitation was proposed by Sir Isaac Newton In the year 1686.
- Newton's law of gravitation: Every particle in the universe attracts every other particle with a force, which is directly proportional to the product of their masses and inversely proportional to the square of the distance between them.

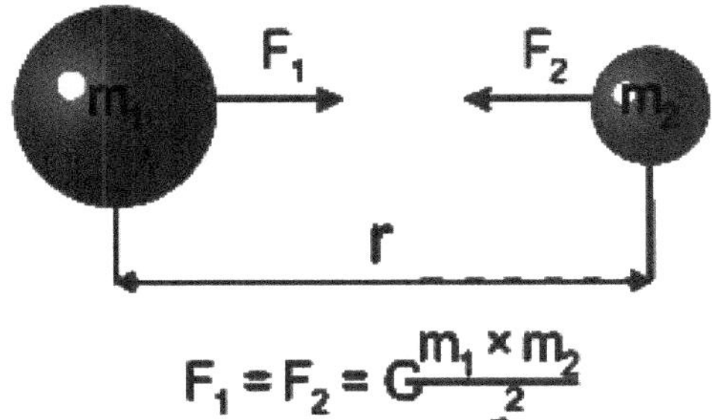

- If two bodies with mass m_1 and m_2 , where r be the distance between two masses, then gravitational force,

$F_1 = F_2 = F \propto \dfrac{m_1 m_2}{r^2}$

Where, $F =$ force of attraction, $G = 6.67 \times 10^{11} \ N - m^2/kg^2$ (gravitational constant) m_1 and $m_2 =$ mass of bodies, $r =$ distance between them.

Universal Law of gravitation says that "Every object in the universe attracts every other object with a force which is proportional to the product of their masses and inversely proportional to the square of the distance between them".

15(C). Acceleration due to gravity (g):

- The force of attraction exerted by the earth on a body is called gravitational pull or gravity.
- We know that when a force acts on a body, it produces acceleration.
- Therefore, a body under the effect of gravitational pull must accelerate.
- Acceleration due to gravity at the surface of the earth is given by:

$\Rightarrow g = \dfrac{GM}{R^2}$

- As Earth is elliptical in shape i.e., it is flattened at the poles and bulged out at the equator, due to which the equatorial radius is about 21 km longer than the polar radius.
- As the polar radius is smaller than the equatorial radius, therefore the acceleration due to gravity is maximum at poles and **minimum at the equator.**

16(C). If the horizontal velocity given to a satellite iS greater than the critical velocity but less than the escape velocity, then the satellite will start revolving in an elliptical orbit.

If the velocity of the projection is less than the critical velocity then the satellite moves in elliptical orbit, but the point of projection is apogee and in the orbit the satellite comes closer to the earth with its perigee point lying at $180°$.

17(A). In given experiment, a composite wire is stretched by a force F .

Net elongation in the wire = elongation in brass wire + elongation in steel wire … (i)

Now, Young's modulus of a wire of cross-section (A) when some force (F is applied,

$Y = \dfrac{FI}{A\Delta I}$

We have,

$\Delta I =$ elongation $= \dfrac{FI}{AY}$

So, from relation (i), we have

$\Delta I_{net} = \Delta I_{brass} + \Delta I_{steel}$

$\Rightarrow \Delta I_{net} = \left(\dfrac{FI}{AY}\right)_{brass} + \left(\dfrac{FI}{AY}\right)_{steel}$

As wires are connected in series and they are of same area of cross-section, length and subjected to same force, so

$\Delta I_{net} = \dfrac{F}{A}\left(\dfrac{I}{Y_{brass}} + \dfrac{I}{Y_{steel}}\right)$

Here,

$\Delta I_{net} = 0.2 \ mm$

$= 0.2 \times 10^{-3} \ m$

and $I = 1 \ m$

$Y_{brass} = 60 \times 10^9 Nm^{-2}$

$Y_{steel} = 120 \times 10^9 Nm^{-2}$

On putting the values, we have

$0.2 \times 10^{-3} = \dfrac{F}{A}\left(\dfrac{1}{60\times 10^9} + \dfrac{1}{120\times 10^9}\right)$

$\Rightarrow$ Stress $= \dfrac{F}{A} = 8 \times 10^6 Nm^{-2}$

18(B). Given,

Elastic limit of brass, $\sigma = 379 MPa$

Load, $P = 400 \ N$

We know that,

$P = \sigma A$

Where, Area of cross section, $A = \dfrac{1}{4}\pi r^2$

$\Rightarrow P = \sigma \dfrac{1}{4}\pi r^2$

$400 = 379 \times \left(\dfrac{1}{4} \times 3.14 \times r^2\right)$

$r^2 = \dfrac{400}{379} \times \dfrac{4}{3.14}$

$r^2 = 1.34$

$r = 1.15 \ mm$

Therefore, the minimum diameter of a brass rod if it is to support a $400\ N$ load without exceeding its elastic limit is approx $1.16\ mm$.

19(C). The cross-sectional area,
$A = \pi r^2$
$\Rightarrow \dfrac{dA}{A} = 2\dfrac{dr}{r}$
Decrease of the cross-sectional area $= \dfrac{dA}{A} = 1\%$
$\Rightarrow \dfrac{dr}{r} = 0.5\%$
Poisson's ratio as,
$\sigma = \dfrac{\frac{-dr}{r}}{\frac{dl}{l}}$
$\Rightarrow \dfrac{dl}{l} = 2.5\%$

20(C). In a liquid drop, we have only one surface but in the air bubble we have two surfaces and a mathematical expression of the excess pressure inside an air bubble and inside the liquid drop by using the concept of surface tension is written as:
$P_i - P_o = \dfrac{4T}{r}$
Here, P_i and P_o are the pressure inside and outside, T is the temperature and r is the radius.
When the soap bubble expands the radius of the soap bubble will increase, therefore from equation (1) we see that the change in pressure is inversely proportional to the radius of the soap.
$\therefore$ soap bubble expands the radius will increases and inside pressure will decrease.

21(A). Upthrust is independent of all factors of the body such as its mass, size, density, etc, except the volume of the body inside the fluid. Fraction of volume immersed in the liquid $V_{in} = \left(\dfrac{\rho}{\sigma}\right)V$ i.e., it depends upon the densities of the block and liquid. So, there will be no change in it if the system moves upward or downward with constant velocity or some acceleration. Therefore, the upthrust on the body due to liquid is equal to the weight of the body in the air.

22(C). When fluid flows in a pipe, where the pipe is thin (ie, where the velocity of the fluid is high), the pressure of the fluid decreases, it is called venturi effect. The effect is named after the Italian physicist Giovanni Batista Venchuri. Its working is based on the theorem of Bernoulli. We find the rate of flow of water from a venturimeter.

23(B). If A_0 in the area orifice at the bottom below the free surface and A that of vessel, then time t taken to be emptied the tank is given as,
$t = \dfrac{A}{A_0}\sqrt{\dfrac{2H}{g}}$
$\therefore \dfrac{t_1}{t_2} = \sqrt{\dfrac{H_1}{H_2}}$
$\Rightarrow \dfrac{t}{t_2} = \sqrt{\dfrac{H_1}{\frac{H_1}{2}}}$
$\Rightarrow \dfrac{t}{t_2} = \sqrt{2}$
$\therefore t_2 = \dfrac{t}{\sqrt{2}} = \dfrac{10}{\sqrt{2}}$
$= 5\sqrt{2} = 7$ min

24(C). Since the absolute zero temperature is 0 Kelvin. Below this temperature, we can't measure in kelvin scale.
So the Kelvin scale of temperature is only positive.
The freezing point and boiling point of water at different temperature scales are:

Scale	Freezing Point	Boiling Point
Centigrade ($0°C$)	$0°C$	$100°C$
Fahrenheit ($°F$)	$32°F$	$212°F$
Kelvin (K)	$273K$	$373K$
Reaumur ($0°R$)	$0°R$	$80°R$

25(B). "Good absorber of heat is good radiator of heat also" is kirchhof's law.
Kirchhoff's Radiation Law: For any arbitrary body emitting and absorbing thermal radiation in thermodynamic equilibrium, the emissivity is equal to absorptivity.
A black body is an example of a good absorber of heat as well as a good emitter of heat. The ease with which a black body can absorb a photon is the reverse process of emitting the one. This entire cycle takes place because of the number of transitions that are associated with the EM field.

26(B). Water in an electric kettle becomes hot by convection. It is the process of transfer of heat by mass motion of a fluid such as water when the heated fluid is caused to move away from the source of it and carrying energy with it.

27(C). Zeroth Law of Thermodynamics defines the concept of temperature.
The First Law of Thermodynamics tells us about the concept of internal energy.
The Second Law of Thermodynamics tells us that some form of energy gets lost whenever energy is transferred or transformed.
The Third Law of Thermodynamics tells us about the concept of entropy.

28(A). It is given that,
Water flows at a rate of 3.0 litre $/min = 3 \times 10^{-3} m^3/min$
Density of water, $\rho = 10^3 kg/m^3$.
Clearly, mass of water flowing per minute $= 3 \times 10^{-3} \times 10^3 kg/min = 3kg/min$
The geyser heats the water, raising the temperature from $27°C$ to $77°C$.
Initial temperature, $T_1 = 27°C$
Final temperature, $T_2 = 77°C$
Thus, rise in temperature,
$\Delta T = T_2 - T_1$
$\Delta T = 77°C - 27°C$
$\Delta T = 50°C$
Now, heat of combustion $= 4 \times 10^4 J/g = 4 \times 10^7 J/kg$
Specific heat of water $= 4.2 J/g°C$
It is known that total heat used, $\Delta Q = mc\Delta T$
$\Delta Q = 3 \times 4.2 \times 10^3 \times 50$
$\Delta Q = 6.3 \times 10^5 J/min$
Now, consider $m kg$ of fuel to be used per minute.
Thus, the heat produced $= m \times 4 \times 10^7 J/min$
However, the heat energy taken by water $=$ heat produced by fuel
Thus, equating both the sides,
$\Rightarrow 6.3 \times 10^5 = m \times 4 \times 10^7$
$\Rightarrow m = \dfrac{6.3 \times 10^5}{4 \times 10^4}$
$\Rightarrow m = 15.75 g/min$
Clearly, the rate of consumption of the fuel when its heat of combustion is $4.0 \times 10^4 J/g$ supposing the geyser operates on a gas burner is $15.75 g/min$.

29(C). Here, the cylinder is said to be completely insulated from its neighbourhood. As a result, no heat gets exchanged between the system (cylinder) and its neighbourhood. Clearly, the process turns out to be adiabatic.

Now, consider:
Final pressure inside the cylinder $= P_2$
Initial volume inside the cylinder $= V_1$
Final volume inside the cylinder $= V_2$
Ratio of specific heats, $\gamma = 1.4$
For an adiabatic process, it is known that $P_1 V_1^{\gamma} = P_2 V_2^{\gamma}$.

Also, the final volume is compressed to half of its initial volume. $\Rightarrow V_2 = \dfrac{V_1}{2}$

Thus,
$$\Rightarrow P_1 V_1^{\gamma} = P_2 \left(\dfrac{V_2}{2}\right)^{\gamma}$$
$$\Rightarrow \dfrac{P_2}{P_1} = \dfrac{V_1^{\gamma}}{\left(\dfrac{V_1}{2}\right)^{\gamma}}$$
$$\Rightarrow \dfrac{P_2}{P_1} = 2^{\gamma} = 2^{1.4} = 2.639$$

Clearly, the pressure rises by a factor of 2.639.

30(D). An adiabatic expansion has less work done and no heat flow, thereby a lower internal energy comparing to an isothermal expansion which has both heat flow and work done. For an adiabatically expanding ideal monatomic gas which does work on its environment (W is positive), internal energy of the gas should decrease.

31(A). In a cyclic process work done is equal to the area under the cycle and is positive if the cycle is clockwise and negative if anticlockwise.

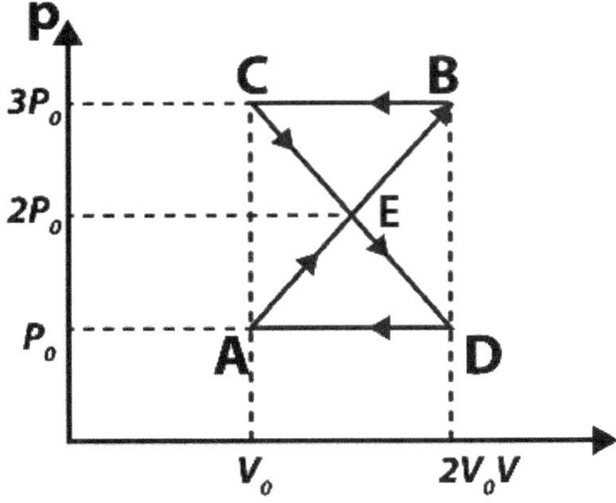

$W_{AEDA} = +$ Area of $\triangle AED = +\dfrac{1}{2}P_0V_0$

$W_{BCEB} = -$ Area of $\triangle BCE = -\dfrac{1}{2}P_0V_0$

The net work done by the system is:
$W_{net} = W_{AEDA} + W_{BCEB}$
$= +\dfrac{1}{2}P_0V_0 - \dfrac{1}{2}P_0V_0 = 0$

32(C). The average translational kinetic energy (per molecule) of any (ideal) gas (be it monatomic like argon, diatomic like chlorine or polyatomic) is always equal to $\dfrac{3}{2}k_B T$. It depends only on temperature and is independent of the nature of the gas. Since argon and chlorine both have the same temperature in the flask, the ratio of average kinetic energy (per molecule) of the two gases is $1:1$.

33(D). Given,
$P = 1.013 \times 10^5 \text{ N/m}^2$

$V = 5 \text{ litres} = 5 \times 10^{-3} \text{ m}^3$
The kinetic energy is given by,
$E = \dfrac{3}{2}PV$
$\Rightarrow E = \dfrac{3}{2}\left(1.013 \times 10^5 \text{ N/m}^2\right)\left(5 \times 10^{-3} \text{ m}^3\right)$
$\Rightarrow E = 7.5 \times 1.013 \times 10^2 \text{ J}$
$\Rightarrow E = 7.597 \times 10^2 \text{ J}$

34(A). Given,
Moles of monoatomic gas $= \alpha$
Moles of diatomic gas $= \beta$
The mixture is behaving as diatomic gas. If we neglect the vibrational mode of freedom then degree of freedom (f_{mix}) of mixture is 3 (for translational) + 2 (for rotational) = 5
We know that,
$f_{mix} = \dfrac{f_1 n_1 + f_2 n_2}{n_1 + n_2}$
$\Rightarrow 5 = \dfrac{3\alpha + 6\beta}{\alpha + \beta}$
$\Rightarrow 5\alpha + 5\beta = 3\alpha + 6\beta$
$\therefore 2\alpha = \beta$

35(A). Given,
$P_1 = 4 \text{ atm}$
$T_1 = 27°C = 27 + 273 = 300K$
$T_2 = -3°C = 273 - 3 = 270 \text{ K}$
$V_1 = 1500 m^3$
$P_2 = 2 \text{ atm}$
According to ideal gas equation,
$\dfrac{P_1 V_1}{T_1} = \dfrac{P_2 V_2}{T_2}$ ....(i)
Where P_1, V_1, P_2, V_2 are pressure and volume at temperatures, T_1 and T_2, respectively.
From equation (i), we get
$V_2 = \dfrac{P_1 V_1}{T_1} \times \dfrac{T_2}{P_2}$
$\Rightarrow V_2 = \dfrac{4 \times 1500}{300} \times \dfrac{270}{2}$
$\Rightarrow V_2 = 2700 \text{ m}^3$

36(A). Given,
$T = T_0 + \alpha V^2$ ... (i)
For 1 mole of a gas,
$PV = RT$
$\Rightarrow V = \dfrac{RT}{P}$
Substituting this value in equation (i), we get
$T = T_0 + \alpha\left(\dfrac{RT}{P}\right)^2$
$\Rightarrow T = T_0 + \alpha\dfrac{R^2 T^2}{P^2}$
$\Rightarrow TP^2 = T_0 P^2 + \alpha R^2 T^2$
$\Rightarrow P = \sqrt{\alpha}RT(T - T_0)^{\frac{-1}{2}}$ ... (ii)
After differentiating, we get
$\dfrac{dP}{dT} = \sqrt{\alpha}R\left[(T - T_0)^{\frac{-1}{2}} - \dfrac{1}{2}T(T - T_0)^{\frac{-3}{2}}\right]$
For minimum pressure,
$\dfrac{dP}{dT} = 0$
$\therefore 0 = \sqrt{\alpha}R\left[(T - T_0)^{\frac{-1}{2}} - \dfrac{1}{2}T(T - T_0)^{\frac{-3}{2}}\right]$
After solving, we get
$T = 2T_0$
From equation (ii), we get
$P_{min} = \sqrt{\alpha}R2T_0(2T_0 - T_0)^{\frac{-1}{2}}$
$= 2R\sqrt{\alpha T_0}$
At $T = 2T_0$
$P = 2R\sqrt{\alpha T_0}$

37(C). This is Rosenmund reaction. The Rosenmund reaction is a hydrogenation process where molecular hydrogen reacts with the acyl chloride in the presence of catalyst – palladium on barium sulfate.

$$R - \underset{\underset{O}{\|}}{C} - Cl \xrightarrow[\text{Pd–BaSO}_4]{\text{H}_2} \underset{P}{RCHO}$$

$BaSO_4$ prevents the aldehyde from being reduced and acts as a poison to the palladium catalyst in this reaction.

38(D). O-atom is ore electronegative than C-atom, therefore O-atom bears partial negative charged, and C-atom to which it is attached bear partial positive charge. Polarization in acrolein can be described by the below-given reaction:

$$CH_2\!=\!CH - C\!=\!O \longleftrightarrow \overset{\oplus}{C}H_2 - CH\!=\!C - \overset{\ominus}{O}$$

39(A). Option (A) (Guanidine) is the strongest base because its conjugate acid is highly stable due to delocalization. It has 3 equivalent resonating structures.

40(A). According to the given reaction, we can write

$$E = E^\circ - \frac{0.059}{2}\log\frac{\left[Cu^{2+}\right]}{\left[Ag^+\right]^2}$$

The cell potential will increase the most by doubling the concentration of Ag^+ ion.

41(D). For the first reaction,

$$K_1 = \frac{[HgCl_2]}{[HgCl^+][Cl^-]}$$

For the second reaction,

$$K_2 = \frac{[HgCl_3]}{[HgCl_2][Cl^-]}$$

Finally,

$$K_3 = \frac{[HgCl^+]\left[HgCl_3^-\right]}{\left[HgCl_2\right]^2}$$

$$\Rightarrow K_3 = \frac{K_2}{K_1}$$

$$\Rightarrow K_3 = \frac{9}{3\times 10^6}$$

$$\Rightarrow K_3 = 3 \times 10^{-6}$$

42(C). Repulsive force of magnitude $(F) = 6 \times 10^{-3}$ N
Charge on the first sphere $(q_1) = 2 \times 10^{-7}$C
Charge on the second sphere $(q_2) = 3 \times 10^{-7}$C
Distance between the two spheres $(r) = 30cm = 0.3m$
Electrostatic force between the two spheres is given by Coulomb's law as $(F) = \frac{1}{4\pi\varepsilon_0} \times \frac{q_1 q_2}{r^2}$
Where, ε_0 is the permittivity of free space and $\frac{1}{4\pi\varepsilon_0} = 9 \times 10^9 Nm^2/C^2$
Now on substituting the given values, Coulomb's law becomes.

$$F = \frac{9\times 10^9 \times 2\times 10^{-7}\times 3\times 10^{-7}}{(0.3)^2}$$

$$F = \frac{54\times 10^9 \times\times 10^{-14}}{0.09}$$

$$F = 6 \times 10^{-3} \text{ N}$$

Therefore, we found the electrostatic force between the given charged spheres to be $F = 6 \times 10^{-3}$ N . Since the charges are of the same nature, we could say that the force is repulsive.

43(C). The magnitude of electric force experienced by a charged particle in an electric field is given as
$F = Eq_0$
Where E = electric field intensity,
q_0 = charge on the particle.
Therefore when a charge Q is placed in the electric field E, the magnitude of the force on the charge Q will be:
$F = EQ$

44(D). Coulomb's law: When two charged particles of charges q_1 and q_2 are separated by a distance r from each other then the electrostatic force between them is directly proportional to the multiplication of charges of two particles and inversely proportional to the square of the distance between them.

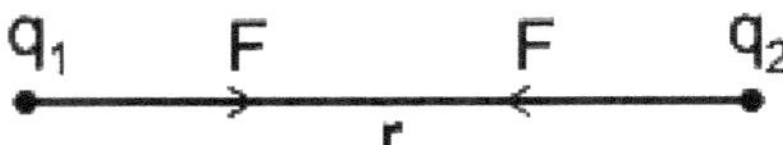

Force $(F) \propto q_1 \times q_2$
$F \propto \frac{1}{r^2}$
$F = K \times \frac{q_1 \times q_2}{r^2}$
Where K is a constant and it is equal to $= 9 \times 10^9 Nm^2/C^2$
From the above, it is clear that Coulomb's force between two point charges varies with distance ' r ' in relation to $\frac{1}{r^2}$.

45(B). An ion is an atom or a group of atoms that does not equal the number of electrons to the number of protons. Electrons have a negative charge, whereas there is a positive charge for protons. This results in a negative charge when an atom gains electrons. An anion is called this form of ion. This results in a positive charge when an atom loses electrons. A cation is considered a positively-charged ion. Usually, positive ions are metals or behave like metals. Just like atoms may lose electrons to become cations, others can absorb electrons and become anions that are negatively charged.

46(B). Given,
Electric field, $E = 9 \times 10^4 N/C$
Distance, $r = 2 \times 10^{-2}m$
Using the formula of electric field for uniformly charged wire
$$E = \frac{\lambda}{2\pi r\varepsilon_0}$$
$\therefore \lambda = E \times 2\pi r\varepsilon_0$
where, λ is a linear charge density,
and, $\epsilon_0 = 8.854 \times 10^{-12}$
Then,
$\lambda = 9 \times 10^4 \times 2\pi \times 2 \times 10^{-2} \times 8.854 \times 10^{-12}$
$\lambda = 18 \times 10^4 \times 2 \times 3.14 \times 10^{-2} \times 8.854 \times 10^{-12}$
$\lambda = 10^3 \times 10^{-10}$
$\Rightarrow \lambda = 10^{-7}$
Therefore,
Linear charge density, $\lambda = 10^{-7} \, C/m$

47(D). We know that:
Permittivity of free space is given by:
$$\epsilon_0 = \frac{q_1 q_2}{4\pi F r^2}$$
Dimensions of $[F] = \left[MLT^{-2}\right]$
where, M means mass, L means length, T means time.
Here, Dimension of q_1 = Dimension of q_2
Dimensions of $(q_1) = AT$
Dimensions of $(q_2) = AT$

Dimensions of $(r) = [L]$

Thus, dimensional formula of $[\epsilon_0] = \dfrac{[AT][AT]}{[MLT^{-2}][L^2]}$

$\Rightarrow [\epsilon_0] = \left[M^{-1}L^{-3}T^4A^2\right]$

48(C). Given,
No. of electrons $= 25 \times 10^{31}$
We know that:
Charge of one electron $= 1.6 \times 10^{-19}$ Coulomb.
Therefore,
Charge of 25×10^{31} electrons will be:
$Q = $ No. of electrons $\times$ Charge of one electron
$Q = 25 \times 10^{31} \times 1.6 \times 10^{-19}$
$Q = 40 \times 10^{12} C$

49(D). Given,
Diameter of the sphere $= 2.4$
$\therefore$ Radius of sphere, $r = \dfrac{2.4}{2} = 1.2m$
Surface charge density of conducting sphere,
$\sigma = 80 \times 10^{-6} C/m^2$
Therefore,
Charge on sphere will be:
$q = \sigma A = \sigma 4\pi r^2$
$q = 80 \times 10^{-6} \times 4 \times 3.14 \times (1.2)^2$
$q = 1.45 \times 10^{-3} C$
Then, the total electric flux leaving the surface of the sphere will be calculated using the gauss formula, i.e.,
$\phi = \dfrac{q}{\varepsilon_0}$
$\phi = \dfrac{1.45 \times 10^{-3}}{8.854 \times 10^{-12}}$ $\left(\because \epsilon_0 = 8.854 \times 10^{-12}\right)$
$\phi = 1.6 \times 10^8 Nm^2/C$

50(B). Let K be the potential gradient of the potentiometer wire due to current cell E and be the current from cell E and be the current through resistance 10Ω and $x\Omega$ due to cell E'.
Potential difference across $10\Omega = I \times 10$ volt
Potential difference across $x\Omega = I \times x$
When switch S_1 is closed and S_2 is open, the potential difference across 10Ω is balanced across length $50\,cm$ is $I \times 10 = K \times 50$
When switch S_2 is closed and S_1 is open, the potential difference across $(10 + x)\Omega$ is balanced across length $60\,cm$ is
$I(10 + x) = K \times 60$
Now, $10 + \dfrac{x}{10} = \dfrac{60}{50}$
$= \dfrac{6}{5}$ or $x = 2\Omega$

51(D).

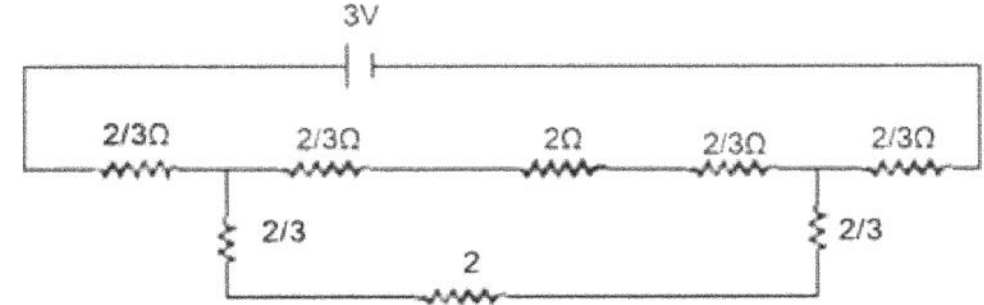

Using delta star conversion for ABC&CDF ,
hence each resistance will be $\left(\dfrac{2}{3}\right)\Omega$
Hence $\left(\dfrac{2}{3}\right) + 2 + \left(\dfrac{2}{3}\right) = \left(\dfrac{4}{3}\right) + 2 = \left(\dfrac{10}{3}\right)\Omega$
also $\left(\dfrac{2}{3}\right) + 2 + \left(\dfrac{2}{3}\right) = \left(\dfrac{10}{3}\right)\Omega$
hence

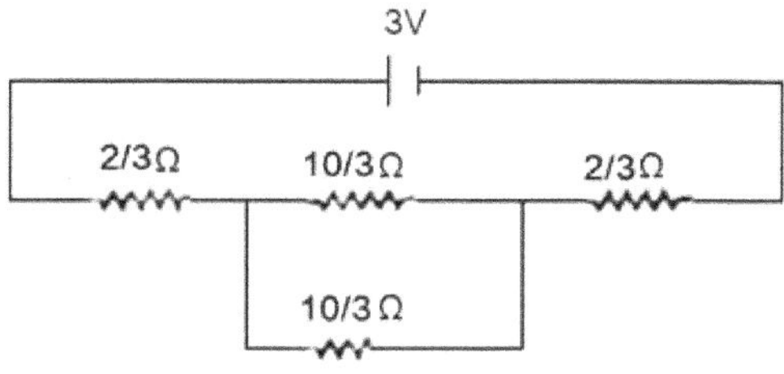

$\therefore$ Equivalent R $= \left(\dfrac{2}{3}\right) + \left(\dfrac{2}{3}\right) + \left[\left(\dfrac{10}{3}\right)\|\left(\dfrac{10}{3}\right)\right]$
$= \left(\dfrac{4}{3}\right) + \left(\dfrac{5}{3}\right) = 3\Omega$
$\therefore 1 = \left(\dfrac{3}{R}\right) = \left(\dfrac{3}{3}\right) = 1$ A

52(A). Given:
Each atom of copper contributes 1 free electron
Density of copper $= 9$ g/cm^3
Diameter of copper wire $= 1$ mm
Current flowing from the wire $= 1.1$ A
Number of atoms $63g$ of copper will be
$= 6.023 \times 10^{23}$
We know that density is equals to mass per unit volume. So
Volume $= \dfrac{\text{mass}}{\text{density}}$
$\dfrac{63}{9} = 7$ cm^3 $= 7 \times 10^{-6}$ m^3
So n will be $= \dfrac{6.023 \times 10^{23}}{7 \times 10^{-6}}$
$= 0.86 \times 10^{29}$
Area $= \pi r^2 = 3.14 \times \left(0.5 \times 10^{-3}\right)^2$
$= 0.785 \times 10^{-6}$
We know that drift velocity $(v_d) = \dfrac{I}{neA}$, where I is current, A is area.
By substituting the values we get-
$v_d = \dfrac{1.1}{0.86 \times 10^{29} \times 1.6 \times 10^{-19} \times 0.785 \times 10^{-6}}$
$v_d = 0.1$ mm s^{-1}

53(A). Specific resistance of ali metals is mostly affected by temperature.
Specific resistance of metal at temperature T, $\quad \rho_T = \rho_0(1 + \alpha\Delta T)$
Specific resistance of metal depends on the temperature of the metal and it increases with increase in temperature. Also specific resistance of metals does not vary with volume of substance, pressure and applied magnetic field.

54(D). A bar of diamagnetic material placed in an external magnetic field will repel out the field lines and move from high to low field.
Diamagnetic Substances: The substances which are weekly magnetized when placed in an external magnetic field, in a direction opposite to the applied field are called diamagnetic substances.
Example: Copper, lead, gold, silver, zinc, antimony, bismuth, etc.
Properties:
- These substances are repelled by a magnet.
- Atomic orbitals of these substances are completely filled.
- It develops weak magnetization in a direction opposite to the direction of the applied magnetic field.
- As soon as the magnetizing field removed, it loses its magnetization.
- When placed in a non-uniform magnetic field, it tends to move from stronger to weaker regions of the magnetic field.
- When placed in a uniform magnetic field, it

aligns itself perpendicular to the direction of the magnetic field.
- Magnetic susceptibility is a small negative value.
- Relative permeability is close to one and always less than 1.
- Magnetic permeability is slightly less compared to free space.

55(D). A bar magnet is a magnetic dipole. It is analogous to an electric dipole which is a system of two equal and opposite equal charges. Isolated magnetic charges or magnetic monopoles do not exist in nature. Even if a bar magnet is broken down to the atomic level, the north and south poles can never be separated.
Use the formula of force between two bar magnets.
$$F = \frac{\mu_0}{4\pi} \frac{6M_1M_2}{r^4}$$
Here,
F is force between two bar magnets.
M $_1$ and M $_2$ are magnetic moments.
r is the distance between bar magnets.
μ_0 is the permeability of free space.
If the length of the bar magnets is negligible compared then $r = d$
Thus, the force acting between them will be proportion to $\frac{1}{d^4}$.

56(A). By the right-hand thumb rule, we can say that if in a vertical wire the current is flowing upward then the direction of the magnetic field on the left side of the wire will be perpendicular to the paper and outward because when the thumb of the right hand is kept in the direction of the current the direction of the fingers on the left side is perpendicular to the paper and outward.

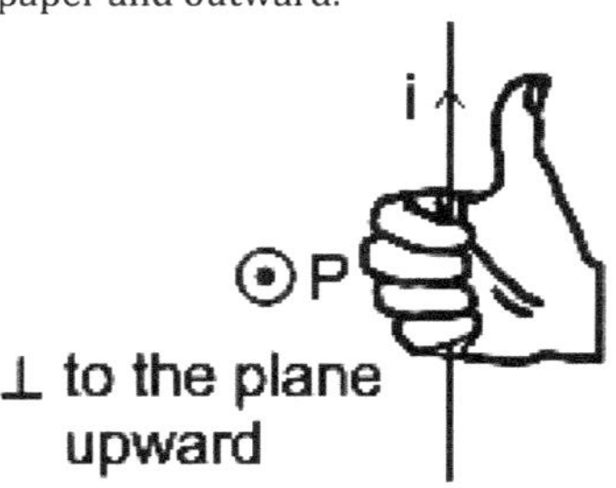

57(C). Electromagnets are used in electric bells, loudspeakers, and telephone diaphragms.
- An electromagnet is a type of magnet in which the magnetic field is produced by an electric current.
- Electromagnets usually consists of wire wounds into a coil.
- The magnetism of the electromagnets can be increased by placing a soft iron rod inside the solenoid.
- The core of electromagnets is made of ferromagnetic materials which have high permeability and low retentivity.
- Giant electromagnets are used in cranes to lift machinery, and bulk quantities of iron and steel.

58(C). When a hole is cut at the center of the bar magnet, then the pole strength of the bar magnet will remain unchanged.
- The point on the magnet which has maximum attraction property is called the poles of the magnet.
- The poles of the magnet lie slightly inside from the end.

- When a hole is cut at the center of the bar magnet its end remains unaffected where the poles of the magnet lie.

59(A). Given,
$\theta = 30°$
Magnetic field, $B = 800$ G
Torque, $\tau = 0.016$ Nm
As we know,
Magnetic moment of the magnet
$\tau = mB\sin\theta$
$0.016 = m \times \left(800 \times 10^{-4}\ \text{T}\right) \times (\sin 30)$
$0.016 = m \times \left(800 \times 10^{-4}\ \text{T}\right) \times (\frac{1}{2})$
$m = 160 \times \frac{2}{800} = 0.40\ \text{A m}^2$

60(D). Given,
Relative permeability, $\mu_r = 400$
Current $I = 2$ A
$\mu_0 = 4\pi \times 10^{-7}$
The field H is dependent of the material of the core, and is
$H = nI$
$= 1000 \times 2.0$
$= 2 \times 10^3$ A/m
The magnetic field B is given by,
$B = \mu_r\mu_0 H$
$= 400 \times 4\pi \times 10^{-7} \times 2 \times 10^3$
$= 1.0$ T

61(B). Given,
$n = 800$
$A = 2.5 \times 10^{-4}\ \text{m}^2$
$I = 3.0$ A
A magnetic field develops along the axis of the solenoid. Therefore current-carrying solenoid acts like a bar magnet.
Associated magnetic moment,
$m = nIA$
$= 800 \times 3 \times 2.5 \times 10^{-4}$
$= 0.6\text{JT}^{-1}$

62(B). As we know,
Angular momentum $J = m\omega r^2 \ldots (1)$
where ω is the angular velocity, r is the radius of the orbit.
As we know,
Magnetic moment $\mu = i$ A
$= \frac{e\omega}{2\pi}\pi r^2 \ldots (2)$
By dividing equation (1) and (2), we get
$$\therefore \frac{\mu}{J} = \frac{\frac{e\omega}{2\pi}\pi r^2}{m\omega r^2} = \frac{e}{2m}$$
$$\Rightarrow \mu = \frac{eJ}{2\ \text{m}}$$

63(D). "Eddy currents converts useful energy into heat and waste it" is correct regarding eddy currents in the coil.
Eddy Current is the loops of electrical current induced within conductors by changing magnetic fields in the conductor are called eddy currents. Eddy currents transform useful energy, into heat, which isn't generally useful. Eddy currents cause a loss of energy because they have the tendency to oppose.

64(B). Given,
Input Voltage, $V_i = 2200$ V
Output Volatge, $V_o = 220$ V
$P_{\text{output}} = 880$ W
Efficiency $(\eta) = 88\%$

$$= \frac{88}{100}$$
$$= 0.88$$
$$\eta = \frac{P_{\text{output}}}{P_{\text{input}}}$$
$$\Rightarrow 0.88 = \frac{880}{P_{\text{input}}}$$
$$\Rightarrow P_{\text{input}} = 1000 \text{ W}$$
Now,
Power, $P = VI$
$$\Rightarrow I = \frac{P}{V}$$
$$\Rightarrow I_{\text{input}} = \frac{P_{\text{input}}}{V_i}$$
$$\Rightarrow \frac{1000}{2200}$$
$$\Rightarrow 0.45 \text{ A}$$

65(A). The induced emf is given by $E = -N\frac{d\phi}{dt}$.

According to faraday's second law of electromagnetic induction, the induced emf in a coil is equal to the rate of change of flux linked with the coil.

i.e., $E = -N\frac{d\Phi}{dt}$

Where, N = number of turns, $d\phi$ = change in magnetic flux and E = induced e.m.f.

The negative sign says that it opposes the change in magnetic flux which is explained by Lenz law.

For N turns, the emf will be:

$$E = -N\frac{d\phi}{dt}$$

66(C). When an electromagnetic wave strikes a material surface, it transports the momentum, as well as the energy, to the surface. The striking electromagnetic wave exerts pressure on the surface. The total energy transferred to the surface by the electromagnetic wave is given by $E = pc$. Therefore, $p \neq 0, E \neq 0$.

67(A). Given,

The frequency of Electromagnetic wave along y - direction

$\nu = 30 \text{ MHz}$

The electric field component of the wave along y - direction.

$E = 6 \text{ vm}^{-1}$

The speed of light in vacuum $c = 3 \times 10^8 \text{ m/sec}$

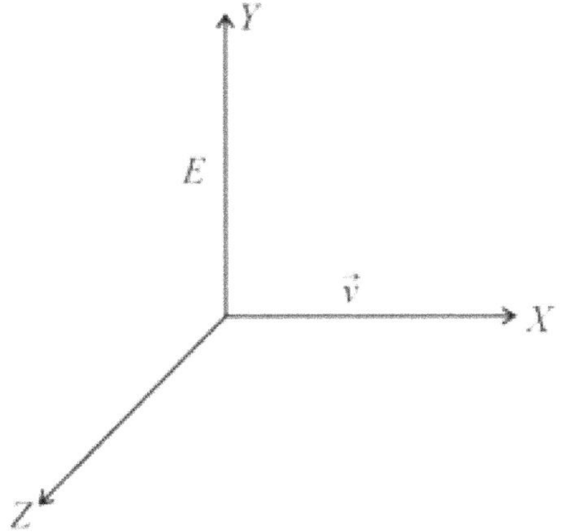

In Electromagnetic, the ratio of the amplitudes of electric and magnetic field is always constant and it is equal to velocity of the Electromagnetic Waves.

$$\frac{E}{B} = c$$
$$B = \frac{E}{c} = \frac{6}{3\times10^8}$$
$$B = 2 \times 10^{-8} \text{ T}$$

68(A). Given:

$$\phi_E = \left(50t^2 + 10t + 2\right)Vm$$

We know that:

The expression for displacement current is given by,

$$i_d = \epsilon_0 \frac{d\phi_E}{dt}$$
$$= \epsilon_0 \frac{d\left(50t^2+10t+2\right)}{dt}$$
$$= \epsilon_0(100t + 10)$$

For $t = 2$ sec,

$$i_d = \epsilon_0(100 \times 2 + 10)$$
$$= \epsilon_0(200 + 10) = 210\epsilon_0$$
$$= 210\epsilon_0 A$$

69(C). The speed will be the same for all intensities in a given medium will be same.

All electromagnetic waves, regardless of frequencies, travels through a vacuum at the speed of light i.e. $c = vx\,\lambda$, Where v is the frequency, λ is the wavelength and c is the speed of light.

The relation between speed and intensity of a wave is given by $I = \frac{1}{2}\epsilon_o E_o^2 c$ where ϵ_o is the electric permittivity of free space (vacuum) and is equal to $8.85 \times 10^{-12} C^2 N^{-1} m^{-2}$, c is the speed of wave and E_o is the amplitude of the electric field.

For a medium: $\lambda \times v = v$, thus the speed will be not the same for all frequencies and wavelengths, hence option (A) and (D) are incorrect.

As we know that when wave travels from one medium to another, its speed changes so option (B) is incorrect.

70(B). Given that,

Kinetic Energy, $(K.E.) = E_2 = 2E_1$

From de-Broglie wavelength formula, we know that

$$\lambda = \frac{h}{p} = \frac{h}{\sqrt{2m(K.E.)}}$$

Therefore,

$$\lambda_1 = \frac{h}{\sqrt{2mE_1}} \qquad \ldots\ldots (i)$$
$$\lambda_2 = \frac{h}{\sqrt{2mE_2}} \qquad \ldots\ldots (ii)$$

Dividing equation (i) by equation (ii), we get

$$\frac{\lambda_1}{\lambda_2} = \sqrt{\frac{E_2}{E_1}} = \sqrt{\frac{2E_1}{E_1}}$$
$$\frac{\lambda_2}{\lambda_1} = \sqrt{\frac{1}{2}}$$
$$\lambda_2 = \lambda_1 \left(\frac{1}{\sqrt{2}}\right)$$

71(D). The stopping potential is directly proportional to the frequency of light. Hence, the stopping potential increases with an increase in the frequency of the incident light.

72(A). According to Rutherford scattering experiment, the energy of the projectile is equal to the potential energy at the closest approach.

$$KE = \frac{1}{4\pi\varepsilon_0}\frac{z_1 z_2}{r_0}$$

Therefore, energy $\propto z_1 z_2$.

73(D).

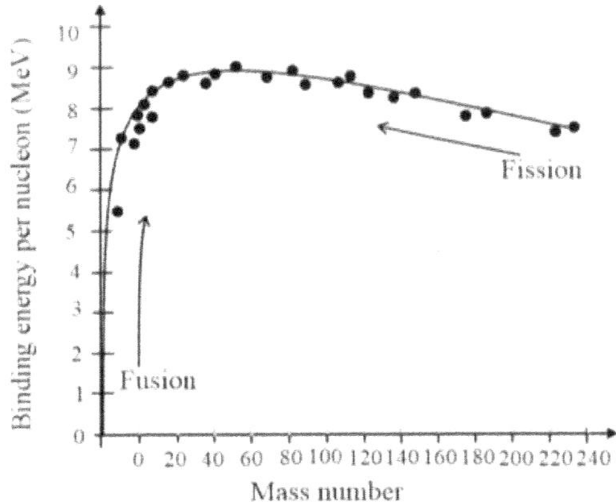

Above diagram is binding energy per nucleon versus mass number graph. From the graph, we can see that the binding energy per nucleon first increase and then decreases with mass number.

74(C). The speed of an electron as a function of principle quantum number n is given by,

$$v = \left(2.17 \times 10^7 \text{ m s}^{-1}\right) \times \frac{Z}{n}$$

Then,

$$v \propto \frac{1}{n}$$

The graph between speed and principal quantum number is a rectangular hyperbola represented by graph c .

75(C). As given, λ is the wavelength of a hydrogen atom from the transition $n = 3$ to $n = 1$.

For wavelength,

$$\frac{1}{\lambda} = RZ^2 \left(\frac{1}{n_1^2} - \frac{1}{n_2^2}\right)$$

Here, transition is same.

So, $\lambda \propto \dfrac{1}{Z^2}$

$$\frac{\lambda_{\text{H}}}{\lambda_{\text{Li}}} = \frac{\left(Z_{\text{Li}}\right)^2}{\left(Z_{\text{H}}\right)^2}$$

$$\frac{\lambda_{\text{H}}}{\lambda_{\text{Li}}} = \frac{(3)^2}{(1)^2} = 9$$

$$\lambda_{\text{Li}} = \frac{\lambda_{\text{H}}}{9} = \frac{\lambda}{9}$$

76(C). Semiconductors have negative temperature co-efficient. The reason for this is, when the temperature is increased, a large number of charge carriers are produced due to the breaking of covalent bonds and hence these electrons move freely and gives rise to conductivity.

77(C). In both forward biasing and reverse biasing, applied potential establishes an internal electric field which acts against or towards the potential barrier. This internal electric field is weakened or stronger at the junction. In forward biasing knee voltage is the forwards voltage at which the current through the junction starts to increase rapidly. Once the applied forward voltage exceeds the knee voltage, the current starts increasing rapidly.

In forward biasing condition, the inner electric field is given by $E = -\dfrac{\Delta V}{\Delta r}$

or

$$|E| = \frac{\Delta V}{\Delta r} = \frac{0.5}{10^{-6}}$$

$$= \frac{5 \times 10^{-1}}{10^{-6}}$$

$$= 5 \times 10^5 \ \frac{V}{m}$$

78(C). The energy bandgap is maximum in insulators. This makes it difficult for electrons to move to the conduction band. This is contrary to metals and superconductors, which has minimum band gaps facilitating the movement of electrons.

79(C). Impure semiconductors in which the charge carriers are produced due to impurity atoms are called extrinsic semiconductors. They are obtained by doping an intrinsic semiconductor with impurity atoms. Electric current flows through "free" electrons and "holes", also called charge carriers. Doping is done by adding elements such as phosphorus or boron to a semiconductor such as silicon, which substantially increases the amount of free electrons or holes available in the semiconductor.

80(C). We know that, Speed of light $(c) = 3 \times 10^8$ ms $^{-1}$

$h = 6.6 \times 10^{-34}$ js

Given,

Wavelength $(\lambda) = 2480$ nm

$= 2480 \times 10^{-9}$ m $\qquad (\because 1 \text{ nm} = 10^{-9} \text{ m})$

Band gap $(E_g) = ?$

Band gap, $E_g = \dfrac{hc}{\lambda}$ j

$$= \frac{\left(6.63 \times 10^{-34}\right)\left(3 \times 10^8\right)}{2480 \times 10^{-9} \times 1.6 \times 10^{-19}} \text{ eV}$$

$$= 0.5 \text{ eV}$$

1. Unit of electric power may also be expressed as:
   (a) Volt Ampere
   (b) Kilowatt hour
   (c) Watt second
   (d) Joule second

2. If there is a positive error of 50% in the measurement of velocity of a body, then the error in the measurement of kinetic energy is :
   (a) 25%
   (b) 50%
   (c) 100%
   (d) 125%

3. The quantity that does not have mass in its dimension is:
   (a) Electrical potential
   (b) Electrical resistance
   (c) Specific heat
   (d) Magnetic flux

4. The unit of which of the following is meter?
   (a) Light year
   (b) Wavelength
   (c) Displacement
   (d) All of the above

5. The graph shows the dependence of velocity on time for a body that is restricted to move in one dimension, along the x-axis. At t = 0, the body is at rest at x = 0.

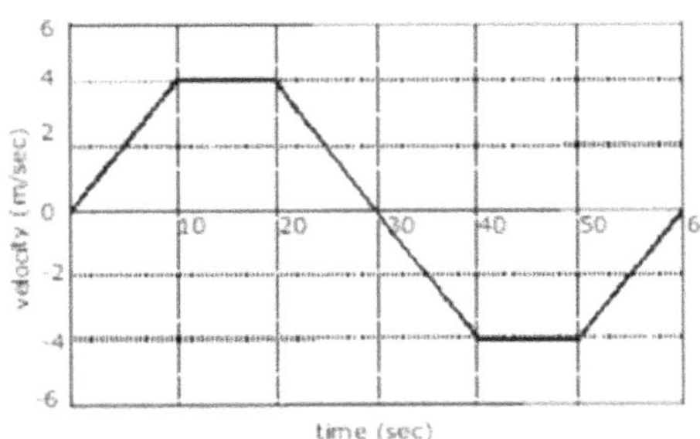

At t = 60 sec, the body is located at
   (a) x = 0 m
   (b) x = 40 m
   (c) x = 6 m
   (d) x = -60 m

6. A passenger train moving at a speed of 5 ms^{-1} is followed by an express train moving on the same track at a speed of 30 ms^{-1}. The rear side of the passenger train is at some distance. The driver of the express train applies brakes to avoid a collision. If the retardation due to brakes is 4 ms^{-2}, then find the time in which the accident is avoided after the application of brakes.
   (a) 4.25 s
   (b) 5.25 s
   (c) 6.25 s
   (d) 7.25 s

7. A moving particle of mass m, makes a head-on elastic collision with another particle of mass $2m$, which is initially at rest. The percentage loss in energy of the colliding particle on collision is close to:
   (a) 50%
   (b) 66.7%
   (c) 90%
   (d) 100%

8. The total path length is always ________ to the magnitude of the displacement vector of a particle.
   (a) equal
   (b) greater than or equal
   (c) less than
   (d) None of the above

9. An object thrown from an aeroplane is an example of __________.
   (a) projectile motion
   (b) resolution of forces
   (c) composition of vectors
   (d) addition of vectors

10. What will be the angular velocity of flywheel making 420 revolutions per minute?
    (a) 42 radian per second
    (b) 12 radian per second
    (c) 56 radian per second
    (d) 44 radian per second

11. A liquid flows through pipes of different diameters. Velocity of liquid is 2 ms^{-1}. At the point where the diameter of the pipe is 6 cm. The velocity of liquid at a point where the diameter of the pipe is 3 cm will be
    (a) 1 ms^{-1}
    (b) 4 ms^{-1}
    (c) 8 ms^{-1}
    (d) 16 ms^{-1}

12. An electric pump is used to fill an overhead tank of capacity 9 m^3 kept at a height of 10 m above the ground. If the pump takes 5 minute to fill the tank by consuming 10 kW of power, the efficiency of the pump should be (Take $g = 10 \text{ ms}^{-2}$)
    (a) 60%
    (b) 40%
    (c) 30%
    (d) 20%

13. A body of density ρ is dropped from rest from a height h into a lake of density $\sigma(\sigma > \rho)$. The maximum depth the body sinks inside the liquid is (neglect viscous effect of liquid):
    (a) $\dfrac{h}{\sigma - \rho}$
    (b) $\dfrac{h\rho}{\sigma}$
    (c) $\dfrac{h\rho}{\sigma - \rho}$
    (d) $\dfrac{h\sigma}{\sigma - \rho}$

14. On heating, solid is directly converted into a gaseous state. This process is called ______.
    (a) Sublimation
    (b) Evaporation
    (c) Diffusion
    (d) Condensation

15. The heat given to a substance during the phase change is called __________.
    (a) Specific heat
    (b) Latent heat
    (c) Thermal capacity
    (d) None of these

16. What temperature are Fahrenheit and Celsius equal?
    (a) $-40°$
    (b) 574.59
    (c) 40
    (d) -574.59

17. The ice point of water in Kelvin scale is ______.
    (a) $273.15K$
    (b) $373.15K$
    (c) $0K$
    (d) $-273.15K$

18. What amount of heat must be supplied to $2.0 \times 10^{-2} kg$ of Nitrogen (at room temperature) to raise its temperature by $45°C$ at constant pressure? (Molecular mass of $N_2 = 28; R = 8.3 J mol^{-1} K^{-1}$.)
    (a) $773.38 J$
    (b) $933.38 J$
    (c) $903.28 J$
    (d) $900.38 J$

19. "Heat cannot by itself flow from a body at a lower temperature to a body at a higher temperature"- the statement is which of the following?
    (a) First law of thermodynamics
    (b) Conservation of mass
    (c) Conservation of momentum

(d) Second law of thermodynamics

20. What is the ratio of $\dfrac{C_p}{C_v}$ for gas if the pressure of the gas is proportional to the cube of its temperature and the process is an adiabatic process?

(a) $\dfrac{4}{3}$ (b) $\dfrac{5}{7}$

(c) $\dfrac{3}{2}$ (d) $\dfrac{7}{9}$

21. An ideal refrigerator has a freezer at a temperature of $-13^\circ C$. The coefficient of performance of the engine is 5. The temperature at which heat is rejected will be:

(a) $30.5^\circ C$ (b) $32.5^\circ C$

(c) $39^\circ C$ (d) $38^\circ C$

22. Two vessels A and B, thermally insulated, contain an ideal monoatomic gas. A small tube fitted with a valve connects these vessels. Initially the vessel A has 2 litres of gas at $300\,K$ and $2 \times 10^5\,N/m^2$ pressure while vessel B has 4 litres of gas at $350\,K$ and $4 \times 10^5\,N/m^2$ pressure. The valve is now opened and the system reaches equilibrium in pressure and temperature. Calculate the new pressure and temperature.

(a) $T = 338.71\,K$, $P = 3.3 \times 10^5 N/m^2$

(b) $T = 328.7\,K$, $P = 3.4 \times 10^5 N/m^2$

(c) $T = 238.7\,K$, $P = 3.4 \times 10^5 N/m^2$

(d) $T = 368.71\,K$, $P = 3.4 \times 10^5 N/m^2$

23. C_V and C_P denote the molar specific heat capacities of a gas at constant volume and constant pressure, respectively. Then:

(a) $C_P - C_V$ is larger for a diatomic ideal gas than for a monoatomic ideal gas

(b) $C_P + C_V$ is larger for a diatomic ideal gas than for a monoatomic ideal gas

(c) $C_P \cdot C_V$ is smaller for a diatomic ideal gas than for a monoatomic ideal gas

(d) Both (B) and (C)

24. Hydrogen gas is filled in a balloon at $20^\circ C$. If the temperature is made $40^\circ C$, pressure remaining same, what fraction of hydrogen will come out?

(a) 0.07   (b) 0.25

(c) 0.5   (d) 0.75

25. A certain amount of an ideal gas is contained in a closed vessel. The vessel is moving with a constant velocity v. The molecular mass of gas is M. The rise in temperature of the gas when the vessel is suddenly stopped is $\left(\gamma = \dfrac{C_p}{C_v}\right)$.

(a) $\dfrac{Mv^2(\gamma-1)}{2R(\gamma+1)}$ (b) $\dfrac{Mv^2(\gamma-1)}{2R}$

(c) $\dfrac{Mv^2}{2R(\gamma+1)}$ (d) $\dfrac{Mv^2}{2R(\gamma-1)}$

26. The equation of state of a gas is given by, $\left(P + \dfrac{aT^2}{V}\right)V^c = (RT + b)$, where, a, b, c and R are constants. The isotherms can be represented by $P = AV^m - BV^n$, where, A and B depend only on temperature:

(a) $m = -c$ & $n = -1$ (b) $m = c$ & $n = 0$

(c) $m = -1$ & $n = c$ (d) $m = c$ & $n = 1$

27. A simple pendulum has a time period of T, if the mass of the bob is made one fourth, then the time period of the pendulum will become:

(a) $2T$ (b) $\sqrt{2}T$

(c) $\dfrac{1}{\sqrt{2}}T$ (d) T

28. In which type of motion the restoring force is proportional to the displacement of the body:

(a) Uniform circular motion

(b) Periodic motion

(c) Simple Harmonic Motion

(d) Elliptical motion

29. The phase difference between displacement and acceleration of a particle in a simple harmonic motion is:

(a) π radian   (b) $\dfrac{3\pi}{2}$ radian

(c) $\dfrac{\pi}{2}$ radian   (d) zero

30. The string of a musical instrument is 90 cm long and has a fundamental frequency of 124 Hz. The distance x from one end of the string where it should be pressed to produce a fundamental frequency of 186 Hz.

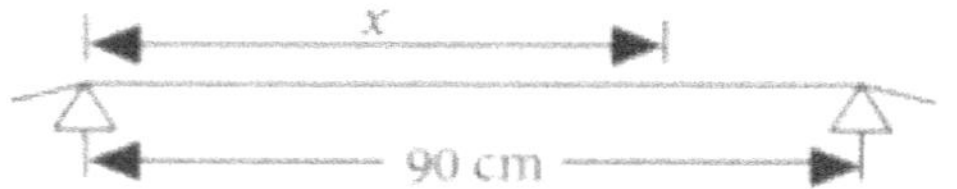

(a) 60 cm   (b) 50 cm

(c) 45 cm   (d) 75 cm

31. A sinusoidal wave with amplitude y is traveling with speed v on a string with linear density ρ. The angular frequency of the wave is ω. The following conclusions are drawn. Mark the one which is correct. (in particular option if we are changing one quantity assume others are kept constant)

(a) Doubling the frequency doubles the rate at which energy is carried along the string

(b) If the amplitude were doubled, the rate at which energy is carried would be halved

(c) If the amplitude were doubled, the rate at which energy is carried would be doubled

(d) The rate at which energy is carried is directly proportional to the velocity of the wave

32. Which among the following is not related to the conservation of charge?

(a) Charge can be created in a body.

(b) Charge can be transferred from one object to another.

(c) Net charge of the system remains constant.

(d) Charge can neither be created nor be destroyed.

33. Two small charged spheres A and B have charges $10\mu C$ and $940\mu C$, respectively, and are held at a separation of 90 cm from each other. At what distance from A would the electric intensity be zero?

(a) 22.5 cm   (b) 18 cm

(c) 36 cm   (d) 30 cm

34. When we rub a glass rod with silk then the charge on the glass rod will be:

(a) Positive   (b) Negative

(c) Neutral   (d) None of the above

35. A point charge $+q$ is placed at a distance d from an isolated conducting plane. The field at a point P on the other side of the plane is:

    (a) Directed perpendicular to the plane and away from the plane

    (b) Directed perpendicular to the plane but towards the plane

    (c) Directed radially away from the point charge

    (d) Directed radially towards the point charge

36. Calculate the Coulomb force between 2 alpha particles separated by $3.2 \times 10^{-15} m$.

    (a) $60N$ (b) $50N$

    (c) $90N$ (d) $70N$

37. The electric field at a point is:

    (a) Always continuous.

    (b) Continuous if there is no charge at that point.

    (c) Discontinuous if there is a charge at that point.

    (d) Both (B) and (C)

38. A point charge $+10\mu C$ is at a distance of $5cm$ directly above the centre of a square of side $10cm$, as shown in Fig. What is the magnitude of the electric flux through the square? (Hint: Think of the square as one face of a cube with edge $10cm$).

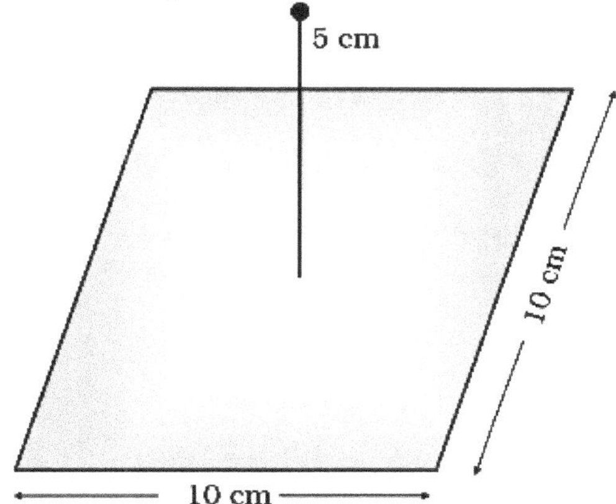

    (a) $1.88 \times 10^5 Nm^2 C^{-1}$ (b) $2.90 \times 10^5 Nm^2 C^{-1}$

    (c) $1.52 \times 10^5 Nm^2 C^{-1}$ (d) $3.2 \times 10^5 Nm^2 C^{-3}$

39. A dielectric slab of thickness 1.0 cm and dielectric constant 5 is placed between the plates of a parallel plate capacitor of plate area 0.01 m ^{2} and separation 2.0 cm. Calculate the change in capacity on introduction of dielectric.

    (a) 4.425×10^{-13} Farad   (b) 5.436×10^{-12} Farad

    (c) 2.95×10^{-12} Farad   (d) 5.436×10^{-13} Farad

40. A transformer having efficiency of 90% is working on $200\ V$ and $3\ kW$ power supply. If the current in the secondary coil is $6\ A$, the voltage across the secondary coil and the current in the primary coil respectively are:

    (a) $300V,\ 15\ A$ (b) $450V,\ 15\ A$

    (c) $450V,\ 13.5\ A$ (d) $600V,\ 13.5\ A$

41. The specific resistance of a rod of copper as compared to that of thin wire of copper is __________.

    (a) Less

    (b) More

    (c) Same

    (d) Depends upon the length and area of cross-section of the wire

42. Estimate the average drift speed of conduction electrons in a copper wire of cross-sectional area 1.0×10^{-7} m^2 carrying a current of 1.5 A. Assume that each copper atom contributes roughly one conduction electron. The density of copper is 9.0×10^3 kg/m^3 , and its atomic mass is $63.5\ u$.

    (a) 3.1×10^{-3} ms^{-1} (b) 1.1×10^{-3} ms^{-1}

    (c) 4.1×10^{-3} ms^{-1} (d) 2.1×10^{-3} ms^{-1}

43. When $5\ V$ potential difference is applied across a wire length $0.1\ m$, the drift velocity of electron is $2.5 \times 10^{-4}\ ms^{-1}$. If the electron density in the wire is $8 \times 10^{28}\ m^{-3}$, the resistivity of the material is close to:

    (a) $1.6 \times 10^{-8} \Omega m$ (b) $1.6 \times 10^{-7} \Omega m$

    (c) $1.6 \times 10^{-6} \Omega m$ (d) $1.6 \times 10^{-5} \Omega m$

44. A plane electromagnetic wave, has frequency of $2.0 \times 10^{10}\ Hz$ and its energy density is $1.02 \times 10^{-8}\ J/m^3$ in vacuum. The amplitude of the magnetic field of the wave is close to $\left(\frac{1}{4\pi\epsilon_0} = 9 \times 10^9\ \frac{Nm^2}{C^2} \right.$ and speed of light $= 3 \times 10^8\ ms^{-1}$):

    (a) $160nT$ (b) $180nT$

    (c) $190nT$ (d) $150nT$

45. A magnetic field does not interact with a __________.

    (a) Moving electric change

    (b) Moving permanent magnet

    (c) Stationary electric charge

    (d) Stationary permanent magnet

46. The magnetic field at the centre of current carrying coil is B_0 If its radius is reduced to half keeping current the "same then magnetic field at its centre become:

    (a) B_0 (b) $2\,B_0$

    (c) $4\,B_0$ (d) $\frac{B_0}{2}$

47. For a series LCR circuit, the Root mean square (RMS) values of voltage across various components are $V_L = 90$ V, $V_C = 60$ V and $V_R = 40$ V .
The RMS value of the voltage of the circuit is:

    (a) 190 V   (b) 110 V

    (c) 70 V   (d) 50 V

48. During an experiment, the properties of the different types of magnetic materials studied, where a ferromagnetic material was heated at a temperature above its Curie temperature. Which statement is true for the condition?

    (a) The domains get arranged randomly

    (b) No effect on the domains

    (c) The ferromagnetic material becomes paramagnetic

    (d) The domains get arranged perfectly

49. A magnetic needle has magnetic moment $6.7 \times 10^{-2} Am^2$ and moment of inertia $I = 7.5 \times 10^{-6}$ kg m^2 . It performs 10 complete oscillations in 6.70 s . What is the magnitude of the magnetic field?

    (a) 0.01 T   (b) 0.1 T

    (c) 0.07 T   (d) 0.5 T

50. What is the magnitude of the equatorial and axial fields due to a bar magnet of length 5.0 cm at a distance of 50 cm from its mid-point? The magnetic moment of the bar magnet is 0.40 A m^2.
    (a) 0.2×10^{-7} T and 6.4×10^{-7} T
    (b) 1.2×10^{-7} T and 6.4×10^{-7} T
    (c) 3.2×10^{-7} T and 6.4×10^{-7} T
    (d) 2.2×10^{-7} T and 6.4×10^{-7} T

51. The earth's magnetic field at the equator is approximately 0.4G . Estimate the earth's dipole moment.
    (a) 3×10^{23} Am^2 (b) 1×10^{23} Am^2
    (c) 1.05×10^{23} Am^2 (d) 2.05×10^{23} Am^2

52. In the magnetic meridian of a certain place, the horizontal component of the earth's magnetic field is 0.26G and the dip angle is $60°$. What is the magnetic field of the earth at this location?
    (a) 0.62G   (b) 2G
    (c) 0.52G   (d) 1.52G

53. The core of the transformer is laminated because:
    (a) The weight of the transformer may be reduced
    (b) Rusting of the core may be prevented
    (c) The ratio in primary and secondary may increase
    (d) Energy losses due to eddy currents may be minimised

54. If the frequency of the applied AC potential is increased in the R-L circuit, then the impedance of the circuit will:
    (a) Increase   (b) Decrease
    (c) Remain same   (d) None of these

55. In an ac circuit an alternating voltage $e = 200\sqrt{2}\sin 100t$ volts is connected to capacitor of capacity $1\mu F$. The r.m.s. value of the current in the circuit is:
    (a) $20mA$ (b) $10mA$
    (c) $100mA$ (d) $200mA$

56. If n_R and n_V denote the number of photons emitted by a red bulb and violet bulb of equal power in a given time, then:
    (a) $n_R = n_V$ (b) $n_R > n_V$
    (c) $n_R < n_V$ (d) $n_R \geq n_V$

57. The magnetic field in a plane electromagnetic wave is given by $B_y = \left(2 \times 10^{-7}\right) \sin \left(0.5 \times 10^3 x + 1.5 \times 10^{11}t\right) T$. This electromagnetic wave is:
    (a) Visible light   (b) Infrared
    (c) Microwave   (d) Radiowave

58. Structure of solids is investigated by using ________ :
    (a) γ-rays   (b) X-rays
    (c) Cosmic rays   (d) Infrared radiation

59. Wavelength of X-ray is of the order:
    (a) 10^{-10} m   (b) 10^{-10} cm
    (c) 10^{10} m   (d) 10^{10} cm

60. Which of the following is the correct statement regarding an astronomical telescope?

    (a) The focal length of eyepiece of an astronomical telescope is larger than the focal length of its objective.
    (b) The aperture of objective lens of telescope is larger than the aperture of the eyepiece.
    (c) The aperture of objective lens of telescope is smaller than the aperture of the eyepiece.
    (d) The magnification of an astronomical telescope increases with the decrease in focal length of its objective.

61. If a glass rod is immersed in a liquid of same refractive index, then it will appear ______.
    (a) Bent   (b) Longer
    (c) Shorter   (d) Invisible

62. The property of light used in optical fibers is __________.
    (a) Dispersion
    (b) Interference
    (c) Total internal reflection
    (d) Diffraction

63. If an equivalent lens is made of two convex lenses of focal length 10 cm and 20 cm. Find the equivalent focal length ______.
    (a) 20 cm   (b) -20 cm
    (c) -6.67 cm   (d) $+6.67$ cm

64. In Young's double slit experiment, if the distance between the slits and the screen is doubled and the separation between the slits is reduced to half, the fringe width
    (a) Is doubled   (b) Becomes four times
    (c) Is halved   (d) Remains unchanged

65. Interference proves:
    (a) Transverse nature of a wave
    (b) Longitudinal nature of wave
    (c) Wave nature
    (d) Particle nature

66. Light is polarized to the maximum when it is incident on a glass surface at an angle of incidence:
    (a) $57°$ (b) $67°$
    (c) $53°$ (d) $37°$

67. According to de Broglie, Which of the following statements is true about the wavelength of a moving particle?
    (a) It is never large enough to measure
    (b) It is proportional to the speed of the particle
    (c) It is inversely proportional to the momentum of the particle
    (d) It is equal to Planck's constant

68. De Broglie relation is true for __________.
    (a) all particles
    (b) charged particles only
    (c) negatively charged particles only
    (d) massless particles like photons only

69. What is the de Broglie wavelength associated with an electron, accelerated through a potential differnece of 100 volts?
    (a) $0.123\ nm$ (b) $1.123\ nm$

(c) $0.223\ nm$ (d) $0.423\ nm$

70. The energy flux of sunlight reaching the surface of the earth is $1.388 \times 10^3 Wm^{-2}$. The photons in the sunlight have an average wavelength of $550\ nm$. How many photons per square metre are incident on the earth per second?

(a) 4×10^{21} (b) 4×10^{34}

(c) 4×10^{31} (d) 4×10^{28}

71. A 100 W sodium lamp radiates energy uniformly in all directions. The lamp is located at the centre of a large sphere that absorbs all the sodium light which is incident on it. The wavelength of the sodium light is $589\ nm$. The number of photons delivered per second to the sphere is:

(a) 3×10^{15} (b) 3×10^{10}

(c) 3×10^{20} (d) 3×10^{19}

72. If first excitation potential of a hydrogen-like atom is V electron volt, then the ionization energy of this atom will be:

(a) V electron volt

(b) $\dfrac{3V}{4}$ electron volt

(c) $\dfrac{4V}{3}$ electron volt

(d) Cannot be calculated by given information

73. What should be the velocity of an electron so that its momentum becomes equal to that of a photon of wavelength $5200\ Å$?

(a) $700\ \text{m s}^{-1}$ (b) $1000\ \text{m s}^{-1}$

(c) $1400\ \text{m s}^{-1}$ (d) $2800\ \text{m s}^{-1}$

74. What is the energy needed to ionize H-atom from its second excited state if the energy of the ground state of H-atom is 13.6 eV?

(a) 3.4 eV   (b) - 1.51 eV

(c) 12.1 eV   (d) 13.6 eV

75. Particles which can be added to the nucleus of an atom without changing its chemical properties are called________.

(a) Neutrons   (b) Electrons

(c) Protons   (d) Alpha particles

76. Which of the following gates serve as building blocks in digital circuits?

(a) OR and AND gates

(b) AND and NOT gates

(c) OR and NOT gates

(d) NAND and NOR gates

77. Which of the following is known as indirect band gap semiconductors?

(a) Germanium   (b) Nickel

(c) Platinum   (d) Carbon

78. Two ideal junction diodes D_1 and D_2 are connected to a battery as shown in the figure. What is the current supplied by the battery if its terminals are interchanged?

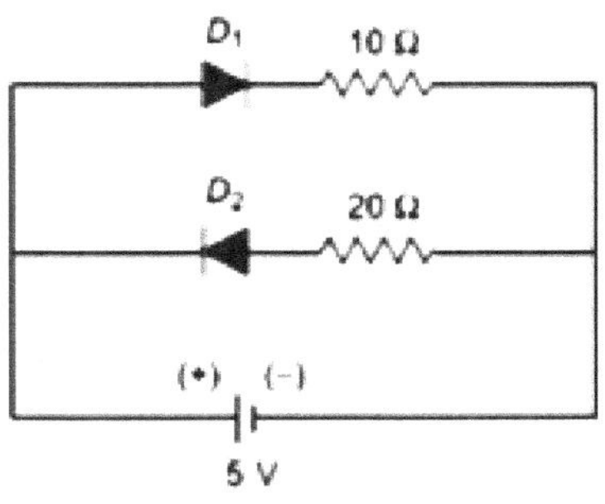

(a) 0.25 A   (b) 0.5 A

(c) 0.75 A   (d) zero

79. In a pure semiconductor crystal, if current flows due to breakage of crystal bonds, then what is the semiconductor called?

(a) Acceptor

(b) Donor

(c) Intrinsic semiconductor

(d) Extrinsic semiconductor

80. In a p-n-p transistor, working as a common base amplifier, the current gain is 0.96 and the emitter current is 7.2 mA. The base current is:

(a) 0.20 mA   (b) 0.36 mA

(c) 0.30 mA   (d) 0.45 mA

// Smart Answer Sheet //

Correct — Percentage of students who answered correctly.

Skipped — Percentage of students who skipped.

Q.	Ans.	Correct / Skipped	Q.	Ans.	Correct / Skipped	Q.	Ans.	Correct / Skipped
1	A	85.36% / 0.0%	2	C	17.55% / 3.8%	3	C	43.58% / 1.87%
4	D	85.39% / 0.0%	5	A	66.09% / 1.16%	6	C	81.2% / 0.0%
7	C	56.88% / 1.54%	8	B	89.67% / 0.0%	9	A	86.2% / 0.0%
10	D	61.63% / 1.24%	11	C	86.3% / 0.0%	12	C	83.55% / 0.0%
13	C	43.84% / 1.37%	14	A	42.98% / 1.93%	15	B	89.04% / 0.0%
16	A	53.06% / 1.97%	17	A	65.22% / 1.9%	18	B	14.53% / 3.7%
19	D	84.39% / 0.0%	20	C	41.71% / 1.7%	21	C	66.09% / 1.88%
22	A	60.36% / 1.68%	23	D	41.33% / 1.6%	24	A	69.37% / 1.76%
25	B	41.81% / 1.82%	26	A	56.69% / 1.22%	27	D	64.95% / 1.37%
28	C	48.64% / 1.24%	29	A	44.76% / 1.34%	30	A	63.76% / 1.63%
31	D	47.4% / 1.6%	32	A	48.32% / 1.62%	33	D	69.71% / 1.86%
34	A	83.17% / 0.0%	35	A	46.87% / 1.79%	36	C	12.05% / 3.51%
37	D	87.97% / 0.0%	38	A	14.47% / 4.69%	39	C	46.05% / 1.93%
40	B	63.46% / 1.95%	41	C	59.59% / 1.12%	42	B	68.28% / 1.96%
43	D	14.8% / 3.86%	44	A	32.14% / 4.04%	45	C	82.22% / 0.0%
46	B	41.72% / 1.05%	47	D	11.87% / 3.52%	48	C	32.02% / 3.25%
49	A	29.39%	50	C	12.26%	51	C	48.95%

		3.71%			4.63%			1.16%
52	C	48.75% / 1.69%	53	D	55.78% / 1.3%	54	A	58.0% / 1.22%
55	A	64.6% / 1.98%	56	B	68.93% / 1.43%	57	C	53.88% / 1.88%
58	B	44.27% / 1.09%	59	A	76.95% / 0.0%	60	B	25.53% / 4.98%
61	D	56.0% / 1.47%	62	C	68.19% / 1.17%	63	D	88.51% / 0.0%
64	B	48.1% / 1.73%	65	C	86.23% / 0.0%	66	A	61.38% / 1.93%
67	C	47.04% / 1.95%	68	A	79.93% / 0.0%	69	A	46.49% / 1.57%
70	A	27.59% / 3.45%	71	C	16.63% / 3.45%	72	C	63.44% / 1.13%
73	C	52.82% / 1.86%	74	B	53.91% / 1.84%	75	A	56.07% / 1.92%
76	D	77.68% / 0.0%	77	A	88.09% / 0.0%	78	A	10.1% / 4.37%
79	C	42.13% / 1.94%	80	C	56.55% / 1.6%			

// Hints and Solutions //

1(A). The unit of electric power may also be expressed as Volt Ampere.

The rate at which electric energy is dissipated or consumed in an electric circuit is termed as electric power.

The power P is given by, $P = VI$.

The SI unit of electric power is watt (W) or Volt Ampere. It is the power consumed by a device that carries $1\,A$ of current when operated at a potential difference of $1\,V$.

2(C). Given,

The percentage error in velocity $= \frac{\Delta v}{v} \times 100$

Kinetic energy $\text{K.E.} = \frac{1}{2}mv^2$

Percentage error in the kinetic energy,

$\frac{\Delta \text{K.E.}}{\text{K.E.}} \times 100 = m \times 2\frac{\Delta v}{v} \times 100$

$\Rightarrow \frac{\Delta \text{K.E.}}{\text{K.E.}} \times 100 = 2 \times 50\%$

$\Rightarrow \frac{\Delta \text{K.E.}}{\text{K.E.}} \times 100 = 100\%$

Thus, the error in the measurement of kinetic energy is 100%.

3(C). Specific heat: $\left[L^2\, T^{-2}\, K^{-1} \right]$

Electrical potential: $\left[M^1 L^2 T^{-3} A^{-1} \right]$

Electrical resistance: $\left[M^1\, L^2\, T^{-3}\, A^{-2} \right]$

Magnetic flux: $\left[M^1\, L^2\, T^{-2}\, A^{-1} \right]$

From the above information, it is clear that the specific heat does not have mass in its dimension.

4(D). The unit of light year is meter. A light year is the distance traveled by light in one year. and wavelength is the distance between two consecutive vertices or descents. The unit of wavelength is also the meter. The minimum distance covered by an object in a certain direction with respect to a reference point is called displacement. The unit of displacement is also the meter.

5(A). From the graph, as it seems the body at t = 60 sec, the body is located at x = 0 m. The body first constantly increases its velocity and then decreases it. Therefore, clearly, the answer will be 0.

6(C). The initial relative velocity of the express train w.r.t the passenger train,

$u_{ep} = u_e - u_p$

$= 30 - 5$

$= 25\ ms^{-1}$

The final relative velocity of the express train w.r.t the passenger train,

$v_{ep} = 0$ (because the express train comes to rest relative to the passenger train)

From the first equation of motion,

$v_{eq} = u_{ep} - at$

$\Rightarrow 0 = 25 - 4t$

$\Rightarrow 4t = 25$

$\Rightarrow t = 6.25\ s$

7(C). According to the question,

Fractional decrease in kinetic energy of mass m.

$= 1 - \left(\frac{m_2 - m_1}{m_2 + m_1} \right)^2$

$= 1 - \left(\frac{2-1}{2+1} \right)^2$

$= 1 - \left(\frac{1}{3} \right)^2$

$= 1 - \frac{1}{9}$

$= \frac{8}{9}$

Percentage loss in energy $= \frac{8}{9} \times 100 \simeq 90\%$

8(B). Total path length is a scalar quantity, whereas displacement is a vector quantity. Therefore, the total path length is always greater than the magnitude of displacement. It becomes equal to the magnitude of displacement only when a particle is moving in a straight line.

9(A). An object thrown from an aeroplane is an example of projectile motion. When a particle is projected obliquely near the earth's surface, it moves simultaneously in the direction of horizontal and vertical without being propelled by an engine or fuel. The motion of such a particle is called projectile motion. The path followed by a projectile is called its trajectory.

10(D). Given:

No. of revolutions $(N) = 420$

Total time taken $(t) = 1$ minute $= 60$ seconds

We have to find Angular velocity.

We know that,

Angular velocity $(\omega) = 2 \times \pi \times \frac{N}{t}$

$(\omega) = 2 \times \frac{22}{7} \times \frac{420}{60}$

$(\omega) = 2 \times 22 \times \frac{60}{60}$

$(\omega) = 44$ radian per second

So, the angular velocity of flywheel $(\omega) = 44$ radian per second.

11(C). According to the principle of continuity,

$A_1 V_1 = A_2 V_2$

$\Rightarrow V_2 = \frac{A_1 V_1}{A_2}$

$\therefore V_2 = \left[\frac{\pi(3)^2}{\pi(1.5)^2} \right] \times 2 = 8\,\text{ms}^{-1}$

12(C). Given,

The volume of water to be raised $= 9\,\text{m}^3$

Since we know that

Density of water $= 1000 \text{kgm}^{-3}$

So, mass of water to be raised

$\text{Mass} = 1000 \times 9$

$\text{Mass} = 9000\ \text{kg}$

So, the potential energy change for 9000 kg of water to be raised to a height of 10 m above the ground is given by;

$PE = 9000 \times 10 \times 10$

$PE = 9 \times 10^5 J$

Since,

$$\text{Power} = \frac{\text{energy}}{\text{time}}$$

So, output power $= \frac{9 \times 10^5}{t}$

It is given that time taken to raise the water is 5 minute, converting the time in S.I. unit (seconds), we get;

Time $= 5 \times 60$

$t = 300\text{sec}$

Thus, output power is given by,

$$p = \frac{9 \times 10^5}{300}$$

$= 3000 \text{ W}$

Given,

Input power $= 10kW = 10 \times 10^3 W$

Hence, efficiency of pump $= \frac{\text{output}}{\text{input}}$

$e = \frac{3000}{10000}$

$e = 0.3$

$e = 0.3 \times 100$

$= 30\%$

13(C). Velocity of the ball as it reaches water surface is $\sqrt{2gh}$

Net upward force acting on the body

$F = \sigma V g - \rho V g$

$\Rightarrow ma = \sigma V g - \rho V g$

$\Rightarrow (\rho V)a = V g (\sigma - \rho)$

$\Rightarrow a = g \left(\frac{\sigma - \rho}{\rho} \right)$ in upward direction

Lets say it sinks to the depth H, at this instant final velocity becomes $v = 0$, so we have,

$0 = (\sqrt{2gh})^2 - 2 \times g \left(\frac{\sigma - \rho}{\rho} \right) \times H \quad \because v^2 = u^2 + 2as$

$\Rightarrow H = \left(\frac{h\rho}{\sigma - \rho} \right)$

14(A). The conversion of a solid directly into vapors is called sublimation.

Sublimation: It is the conversion of a solid directly into vapors. Sublimation takes place when the boiling point is less than the melting point.

The heat required to change a unit mass of solid directly into vapors at a given temperature is called the heat of sublimation at that temperature.

15(B). The heat given to the substance during the phase change is called latent heat. It can be either the latent heat of fusion or the latent heat of vaporization depending upon the phase change.

These are some important terms used related to latent heat:
- Liquid to solid: Latent heat of solidification
- Liquid to vapour: Latent heat of evaporation/ vaporization (CD)
- Vapour to liquid: Latent heat of condensation

16(A). Concept:

Temperature: It is the measure of the degree of hotness and coldness of a body. The SI unit of temperature is Kelvin (K).

Fahrenheit and Celsius are measurements of temperature and are related to each other as follows:

$$C = (F - 32) \times \frac{5}{9}$$

Where C is the temperature in Celsius and F is the temperature in Fahrenheit.

Calculation:

Since we need temperature in fahrenheit and celsius to be equal:

Now, let $C = F = x$

So,

$x = (x - 32) \times \frac{5}{9}$

or, $9x = 5x - 160$

or, $4x = -160$

or, $x = -40$

Therefore, $-40°C = -40°F$

17(A). Concept:

Temperature: It is the measure of the degree of hotness and coldness of a body. The SI unit of temperature is Kelvin (K). The major temperature scales are:

Celsius scale: It is also known as the centigrade scale and the most commonly used scale. It is defined from assigning $0°C$ to $100°C$ of freezing and boiling point of water at 1 atmospheric pressure.

Kelvin scale: It is the base unit of temperature, denoted with K. There are no negative numbers on the Kelvin scale as the lowest is $0K$.

The relation between Celsius and Kelvin is given by:

$°C + 273.15 = K$

Given:

The ice point of water $= 0°C$

Temperature $(T) = 0°C$

$°C + 273.15 = K$

$\Rightarrow K = 273.15K$

18(B). Given that,

Mass of Nitrogen, $m = 2.0 \times 10^{-2} kg = 20g$.

Rise in temperature, $\Delta T = 45°C$.

Molecular mass of N_2, $M = 28$

Universal gas constant, $R = 8.3 J \, \text{mol}^{-1} K^{-1}$

Number of moles, $n = \frac{m}{M}$

$n = \frac{2 \times 10^{-2} \times 10^3}{28}$

$n = 0.714$

Now, molar specific heat at constant pressure for nitrogen,

$C_p = \frac{7}{2}R$

$C_p = \frac{7}{2} \times 8.3$

$C_p = 29.05 J mol^{-1} K^{-1}$

The total amount of heat to be supplied is given by the relation:

$\Delta Q = nC_p \Delta T$

$\Delta Q = 0.714 \times 29.05 \times 45$

$\Delta Q = 933.38 J$

Clearly, the amount of heat to be supplied is $933.38 J$.

19(D). In physics, the second law of thermodynamics says that heat flows naturally from an object at a higher temperature to an object at a lower temperature, and heat doesn't flow in the opposite direction of its own.

20(C). Given,

$p \propto T^3 \quad \ldots (i)$

In an adiabatic process,

$T^\gamma p^{1-\gamma} = \text{constant} \left[\text{as } \gamma = \frac{C_p}{C_v} \right]$

$T \propto \frac{1}{p^{\frac{(1-\gamma)}{\gamma}}}$

$T^{\left(\frac{\gamma}{\gamma - 1} \right)} \propto p \quad \ldots (ii)$

Comparing Eqs. (i) and (ii),

Since the pressure is same in both the condition, equating the powers of temperature from both sides we get,

$3\gamma - 3 = \gamma$ or $2\gamma = 3$

$\frac{C_p}{C_v} = \gamma = \frac{3}{2}$

21(C). Given that, the temperature of freezer,

$T_2 = -13°C$

$\Rightarrow \quad T_2 = -13 + 273 = 260K$

Coefficient of performance, $\beta = 5$

The coefficient of performance is defined as,

$\beta = \frac{T_2}{T_1 - T_2}$

$= 5 = \frac{260}{T_1 - 260}$

$= T_1 - 260 = \frac{260}{5}$

$= T_1 - 260 = 52$

$T_1 = (52 + 260)K = 312K$

$T_1 = (312 - 273)°C$

$T_1 = 39°C$

22(A). Given,

$P_1 = 2 \times 10^5 \ N/m^2$

$P_2 = 4 \times 10^5 \ N/m^2$

$V_1 = 2 \ L$

$V_2 = 4 \ L$

$T_1 = 300 \ K$

$T_2 = 350 \ K$

For ideal gas,

$U = \frac{3}{2}nRT = \frac{3}{2}PV$

$\Rightarrow \frac{3}{2}P_1V_1 + \frac{3}{2}P_2V_2 = \frac{3}{2}PV$

$\Rightarrow P = \frac{P_1V_1 + P_2V_2}{V}$

On putting the values, we get

$P = \frac{2 \times 2 \times 10^5 + 4 \times 4 \times 10^5}{2 + 4}$

$P = 3.3 \times 10^5 \ N/m^2$

Number of moles will be conserved.

$n = n_1 + n_2$

$\therefore \frac{P_1V_1}{RT_1} + \frac{P_2V_2}{RT_2} = \frac{PV}{RT}$

$\Rightarrow \frac{2 \times 10^5 \times 2}{300} + \frac{4 \times 10^5 \times 4}{350} = \frac{10 \times 10^5 \times 6}{3\,T}$

$\Rightarrow \frac{4}{300} + \frac{16}{350} = \frac{20}{T}$

$\Rightarrow T = 338.71 \ K$

23(D). As we know,

Molar heat capacity when volume is constant,

$C_V = \frac{f}{2}R$ ....(i)

Molar heat capacity when pressure is constant,

$C_P = \left(\frac{f}{2} + 1\right)R$ ....(ii)

Where, R is Ideal gas constant and its value is $8.31432 \times 10^3 \ N \cdot m \cdot kmol^{-1} \cdot K^{-1}$.

f = 3 (for monoatomic gas) = 5 (for diatomic gas)

(B) By adding equation (i) and (ii), we get

$C_P + C_V = (f + 1)R$

For monoatomic ideal gas, f = 2

$C_P + C_V = (3 + 1)$

$= 4R$

For diatomic gas, f = 5

$C_P + C_V = (5 + 1)$

$= 6R$

Thus, $C_P + C_V$ is larger for a diatomic ideal gas than for a monoatomic ideal gas.

(C) By multiplying equation (i) and (ii), we get

$C_P \cdot C_V = \frac{f}{2}\left(\frac{f}{2} + 1\right)R^2$

$= \left(\frac{f^2}{4} + \frac{f}{2}\right)R^2$

For monoatomic gas, f = 3

$C_P \cdot C_V = \frac{15R^2}{4}$

For diatomic gas, f = 5

$C_P \cdot C_V = \frac{35R^2}{4}$

24(A). Given that, temperature is increased from $20°C$ to $40°C$.

Then, $T_1 = 20°C$

$= 20 + 273$

$= 293 \ K$

$T_2 = 40°C$

$= 40 + 273$

$= 313 \ K$

Since, here pressure is constant so applying Charle's Law,

$V \propto T$

$\therefore \frac{V_1}{T_1} = \frac{V_2}{T_2}$

$\Rightarrow V_2 = \left(\frac{T_2}{T_1}\right) \times V_1$ ...(i)

Fraction of hydrogen that comes out $= \frac{V_2 - V_1}{V_1}$

Putting value of V_2 from (i), we get

$\frac{V_2 - V_1}{V_1} = \frac{\left(\frac{313}{293}\right)V_1 - V_1}{V_1}$

$= \frac{313V_1 - 293V_1}{293V_1}$

$= \frac{20}{293}$

$= 0.07$

25(B). If m is the total mass of the gas, then its kinetic energy $= \frac{1}{2}mv^2$.

When the vessel is suddenly stopped, disordered kinetic energy will increase the temperature of the gas (because the process will be adiabatic).

Then, by the energy of the conservation,

$\frac{1}{2}mv^2 = nC_v\Delta T$

$\because n = \frac{m}{M}$

Where,

n = Total number of Gas molecular

m = Total mass of the gas

M = Molecular mass

$\frac{1}{2}mv^2 = \frac{m}{M}C_v\Delta T$

$\because C_v = \left(\frac{R}{\gamma - 1}\right)$

$\Rightarrow \frac{m}{M}\frac{R}{\gamma - 1}\Delta T = \frac{1}{2}mv^2$

$\Rightarrow \Delta T = \frac{Mv^2(\gamma - 1)}{2R}$

26(A). Given,

$\left(P + \frac{aT^2}{V}\right)V^c = (RT + b)$

$\Rightarrow P = (RT + b)V^{-c} - (aT^2)V^{-1}$ .....(i)

As we know,

$P = AV^m - BV^n$ ....(ii)

Comparing equation (i) and equation (ii), we get

$m = -c \ \& \ n = -1$

27(D). Given: $m_2 = \frac{1}{4}m_1$

The time period of the simple pendulum is given as,

$\Rightarrow T = 2\pi\sqrt{\frac{l}{g}}$ .....(i)

Where, T = Time period of oscillation, l = length of the pendulum, and g = gravitational acceleration

Since the time period of the simple pendulum does not depend on the mass of the bob, so the change in mass of the bob will not affect the time period of the pendulum.

28(C). Simple Harmonic Motion:
- It is a special type of periodic motion, in which a particle moves to and fro repeatedly about a mean position.
- In linear S.H.M. a restoring force that is always directed towards the mean position and its magnitude at any instant is directly proportional to the displacement of the particle from the mean position at that instant

i.e. Restoring force Displacement of the particle from the mean position.

F -x F = -kx

Where k is known as force constant.

29(A). Displacement of the particle executing SHM,

$x = A\sin(\omega t + \phi)\ldots(i)$

$\dfrac{dx}{dt} = A\omega\cos(\omega t + \phi)$

As we know,

Acceleration $(a) = \dfrac{d^2x}{dt^2}$

$a = -\omega^2 A\sin(\omega t + \phi)$

$\Rightarrow a = \omega^2 A\sin(\omega t + \phi + \pi)\ldots(ii)$

Thus, phase difference between displacement and acceleration of the particle is π radian.

30(A). The velocity of the travelling wave remains a constant.

Initially for fundamental mode, the length of the string is half the wavelength.

$\lambda = 180$ cm

$\nu = 124$Hz

The new frequency is given by,

$\nu_2 = 186$ Hz

$\nu\lambda = $ constant

$\nu_1\lambda_1 = \nu_2\lambda_2$

By putting the values, we get

$\lambda_2 = 120$ cm

The midpoint of this would be the node (where the string needs to be plucked). The string needs to be plucked at 60 cm.

31(D). Given,

A sinusoidal wave with amplitude y is traveling with speed v on a string with linear density ρ. The angular frequency of the wave is ω.

As we know the rate of energy of the wave is equal to the average power transmitted by a wave.

Energy per wavelength,

$E_\lambda = \frac{1}{2}\mu\omega^2 A^2\lambda$

$P_{avg} = \dfrac{E_\lambda}{\text{time}}$

$= \frac{1}{2}\mu\omega^2 A^2\dfrac{\lambda}{t}$

$v = \dfrac{\lambda}{t}$

Where,

$\lambda \to$ wavelength

$t \to$ time

$v \to$ velocity

$= \frac{1}{2}\mu\omega^2 A^2 v$

Pavg $\propto \omega^2$

It means that doubling the angular frequency will make 4 times the energy rate.

Pavg $\propto A^2$

It means that doubling the amplitude will make 4 times the energy rate.

Pavg $\propto v$

Power energy or the rate at which energy is carried, is directly proportional to the velocity of the wave.

32(A). **Law of conservation of charge:**

The total charge of an isolated system remains constant. The electric charges can neither be created nor destroyed, they can only be transferred from one body to another. The law of conservation of charge is obeyed both in large-scale and microscopic processes. In fact, charge conservation is a global phenomenon i.e., the total charge of the entire universe remains constant.

From the above, it is clear that charge can neither be created nor be destroyed, but it can be transferred from one object to another by using some methods like induction and conduction. Therefore option (A) is incorrect and options (B) and (D) is correct.

If the charges are distributed in a system, then the net charge of the system remains constant. Therefore option (C) is correct.

33(D).

Here, $AB = r = 90$ cm $= 0.9$ m

$q_A = 10\mu C = 10 \times 10^{-6}C$

$q_B = 40\mu C = 40 \times 10^{-6}C, AC =?$

At point $C, E_A = E_B$

$\dfrac{q_A}{4\pi\varepsilon_0(AC)^2} = \dfrac{q_B}{4\pi\varepsilon_0(BC)^2}$

$\dfrac{q_A}{(AC)^2} = \dfrac{q_B}{(r-AC)^2}$

$\dfrac{10\times10^{-6}}{(AC)^2} = \dfrac{40\times10^{-6}}{(0.9-AC)^2}$

$\dfrac{1}{(AC)^2} = \dfrac{4}{(0.9-AC)^2}$

$\dfrac{1}{AC} = \dfrac{2}{(0.9-AC)}$

$0.9 - AC = 2AC$

$3AC = 0.9$

$AC = 0.3$ m $= 30$ cm

So at 30 cm distance from A the electric intensity will be zero.

34(A). When we rub a glass rod with silk then the charge on the glass rod will be positive. When we rub a glass rod with silk, some of the electrons from the rod are transferred to the silk cloth. Thus the rod gets positively charged and the silk gets negatively charged.

35(A). When a point charge +q is placed at a distance (d) from an isolated conducting plane, some negative charge develops on the surface of the plane towards the charge and an equal positive charge develops on the opposite side of the plane. Hence, the field at a point P on the other side of the plane is directed perpendicular to the plane and away from the plane as shown in figure:

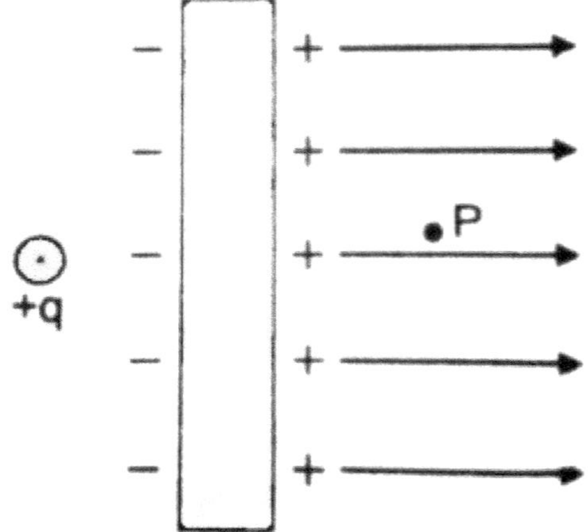

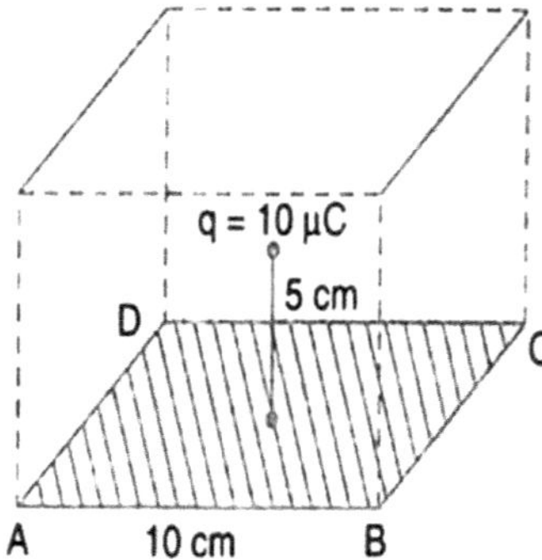

36(C). Given,
Charge on an alpha particle, $q_1 = q_2 = +2e$
Distance between the particles, $r = 3.2 \times 10^{-15} m$
We know that:
Charge on an electron, $e = 1.6 \times 10^{-19}$
and, $\frac{1}{4\pi\epsilon_0} = 9 \times 10^9$
Now, using coulomb's law, we get,
Force acting on the particles is given by,
$F = \frac{1}{4\pi\epsilon_0} \times \frac{q_1 q_2}{r^2}$
$F = \frac{9\times10^9 \times 2\times1.6\times10^{-19}\times2\times1.6\times10^{-19}}{3.2\times10^{-15}\times3.2\times10^{-15}}$
$F = \frac{36\times10^9 \times 2.56\times10^{-19}\times10^{-19}}{3.2\times10^{-15}\times3.2\times10^{-15}}$
$F = 90 N$

37(D). The electric field at a point is continuous if there is
no charge at that point and discontinuous if there
is a charge at that point.
Electric field is a region of space in which an
electric charge experiences a force. The direction of
the electric field at a point in space is the direction
in which a positive test charge moves if placed at
that point.
The electric field at a point is continuous only when
there is no negative or positive charge in its vicinity
that affects its pathway. If there is no other charge
in the medium, The electric field because of any
charge will be continuous. It will be discontinuous
if there is a charge at that viable point.
Charged particles tend to change the emergence
and divergence of continuous electric field lines.

38(A). Let us assume that the charge $q = 10\mu C = 10^{-5} C$ is
placed at a distance of $5cm$ from the square $ABCD$
of each side $10cm$. The square $ABCD$ can be
considered as one of the six faces of a cubic Gaussian
surface of each side $10cm$.
Now, the total electric flux through the faces of the
cube as per Gaussian theorem:
$\phi = \frac{q}{\epsilon_0}$
Therefore, the total electric flux through the square
$ABCD$ will be:

$\phi_E = \frac{1}{6} \times \phi$
$= \frac{1}{6} \times \frac{q}{\epsilon_0}$
$= \frac{1}{6} \times \frac{10^{-5}}{8.854\times10^{-12}} \quad (\because \epsilon_0 = 8.854 \times 10^{-12})$
$= 1.88 \times 10^5 Nm^2 C^{-1}$

39(C). Given,
Thickness of the dielectric slab, $t = 1cm = 10^{-2} m$
Dielectric constant, $\varepsilon_\tau = K = 5$
Area of the plates of the capacitor,
$A = 0.01 m^2 = 10^{-2} m^2$
Distance between parallel plates of the capacitor,
$d = 2$ cm $= 2 \times 10^{-2} m$
We know that:
Capacity with air in between the plates,
$C_0 = \frac{\epsilon_0 A}{d}$
Where, $\epsilon_0 = 8.854 \times 10^{-12}$
$= \frac{8.85\times10^{-12}\times10^{-2}}{2\times10^{-2}}$
$C_0 = 4.425 \times 10^{-12}$ Farad
Capacity with dielectric slab in between the plates,
$C = \frac{\epsilon_0 A}{d - t\left(1 - \frac{1}{K}\right)}$
$= \frac{8.85\times10^{-12}\times10^{-2}}{\left(2\times10^{-2}\right) - 10^{-2}\left(1 - \frac{1}{5}\right)}$
$C = 7.375 \times 10^{-12}$ Farad
Increase in capacity on introduction of dielectric:
$C - C_0 = \left(7.375 \times 10^{-12}\right) - \left(4.425 \times 10^{-12}\right)$
$= 2.95 \times 10^{-12}$ Farad

40(B). Here,
Efficiency of the transformer
$\eta = 90\%$
Input power, $P_{in} = 3\ kW = 3 \times 10^3\ W = 3000\ W$
Voltage across the primary coil,
$V_p = 200\ V$
Current in the secondary coil, $I_s = 6\ A$
As $P_{in} = I_p V_p$
$\therefore$ Current in the primary coil,
$I_p = \frac{P_{in}}{V_p} = \frac{3000\ W}{200\ V} = 15\ A$
Efficiency of the transformer,
$\eta = \frac{P_{out}}{P_{in}} = \frac{V_s I_s}{V_p I_p}$
$\therefore \frac{90}{100} = \frac{6V_s}{3000}$ or
$V_s = \frac{90\times3000}{100\times6}$
$= 450\ V$

41(C). The specific resistance of a rod of copper as
compared to that of thin wire of copper is same.
Specific resistance of a conductor depends on the
nature of material but is independent of the
dimension of the conductor. Thus specific
resistance of rod of copper as compared to that of

thin wire of copper is same.

42(B). The direction of the drift velocity of conduction electrons is opposite to the electric field direction, i.e., electrons drift in the direction of increasing potential.

The drift speed v_d is,

$$v_d = \frac{I}{neA}$$

Now,

$e = 1.6 \times 10^{-19} C, A = 1.0 \times 10^{-7}\, m^2, I = 1.5\, A$.

The density of conduction electrons, n is equal to the number of atoms per cubic metre (assuming one conduction electron per Cu atom as is reasonable from its valence electron count of one). A cubic metre of copper has a mass of $9.0 \times 10^3 kg$. Since 6.0×10^{23} copper atoms have a mass of $63.5 g$

$$n = \frac{6.0 \times 10^{23}}{63.5} \times 9.0 \times 10^6$$
$$= 8.5 \times 10^{28}\ \text{m}^{-3}$$

which gives,

$$v_d = \frac{1.5}{8.5 \times 10^{2n} \times 1.6 \times 10^{-10} \times 1.0 \times 10^{-7}}$$
$$= 1.1 \times 10^{-3} ms^{-1}$$

43(D). According to the question,

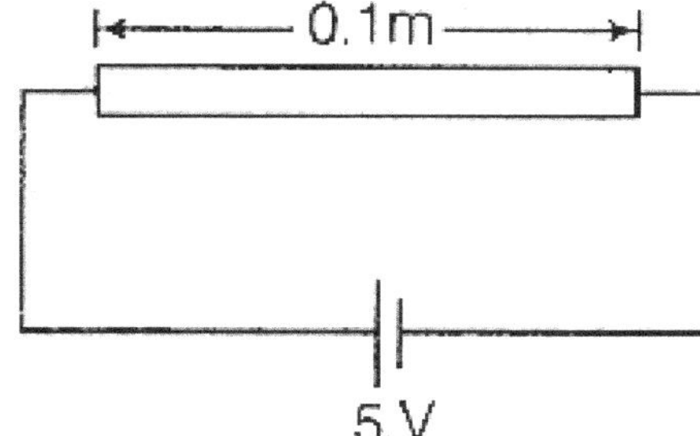

Given:
$v_d = 2.5 \times 10^{-4}\, m/s$
$\Rightarrow n = 8 \times 10^{28}\, m^{-3}$
$L = 0.1\, m$
$p = 5\, V$

We know that,

$J = nev_d$ or $l = nev_d A$

Where symbols have their usual meaning.

$J = $ electron density
$v_d = $ drift velocity
$p = $ Electric Potential
$L = $ length of wire

Now,

$$\frac{V}{R} = nev_d A$$

or $\dfrac{V}{\frac{pL}{A}} = nev_d A$

or $\dfrac{V}{pL} = nev_d$

or $\rho = \dfrac{V}{nev_d L}$

$$= \frac{5}{8 \times 10^{28} \times 16 \times 10^{-19} \times 25 \times 10^{-4} \times 0.1}$$

$\rho = 16 \times 10^{-5} \Omega m$

44(A). Given:
$\mu = 9 \times 10^9$
$U = 1.02 \times 10^{-8}\, J/m^2$

Energy density $(U) = \dfrac{B_0^2}{2\mu_0}$ ... (1)

And $C = \dfrac{1}{\sqrt{\mu_0 \epsilon_0}}$ ... (2)

$\mu_0 = \dfrac{1}{C^2 \varepsilon_0}$

$B = \sqrt{U \times 2\mu_0}$

$$B = \sqrt{1.02 \times 10^{-8} \times 2 \times \frac{1}{9 \times 10^{16}} \times 4\pi \times 9 \times 10^9}$$
$$= 160 nT$$

45(C). A magnetic field does not interact with a stationary electric charge.

Magnetic Force acting on a charged particles moving with velocity v in magnetic field B is given as

$F = qV \times B$

-This force does not change the speed but changes the direction of the charged particle.

-If the speed $v = 0$, the force is zero. So, if there is no speed of the charge with respect to the given magnetic field, no magnetic force will be applied to it.

In the case of Electromagnetic induction, if there is relative motion between the magnetic field and current-carrying conductor, or there is a change in the magnetic field only then the current is induced. In any case, the relative change between electric charge flow or magnetic field will only produce any related change.

46(B). Let B_0 be the initial magnetic field and $B = $ New magnetic field after changing the radius.

The magnetic field at the center of the circular loop before changing the radius is given by

$$B_0 = \frac{\mu_0 I}{2\pi R}$$

After changing the radius into half the new magnetic field can be written as,

$$B = \frac{\mu_0 I}{2\pi \frac{R}{2}}$$

$$\Rightarrow B = 2\frac{\mu_0 I}{2\pi R}$$

$$\Rightarrow B = 2B_0$$

47(D). Given,
$V_R = 40\ \text{V}; V_L = 90\ \text{V}; V_C = 60\ \text{V}$

We know that,

$$iZ = \sqrt{i^2 R^2 + i^2 \left(\frac{1}{\omega C} - \omega L\right)^2}$$

$$E = \sqrt{V_R^2 + (V_C - V_L)^2}$$

Where E is the emf, V_R is the potential drop across the resistor, V_L is the potential drop across the inductance, and V_R is the potential drop across the capacitance.

$$E = \sqrt{V_R^2 + (V_C - V_L)^2}$$

$$E = \sqrt{40^2 + (60 - 90)^2}$$

$E = 50V$

48(C). On heating a ferromagnetic material above its Curie temperature, different domains have net magnetization in them which are randomly distributed. Thus the net magnetization of the substance due to various domains decreases to a minimum. And the ferromagnetic material becomes paramagnetic material.

49(A). Given,
Magnetic moment of a magnetic needle,
$m = 6.7 \times 10^{-2} \text{Am}^2$
Moment of inertia $I = 7.5 \times 10^{-6}\ \text{kg m}^2$
Magnetic needle performs 10 complete oscillations in 6.70 s.

The time period of oscillation is,

$$T = \frac{6.70}{10} = 0.67\ \text{s}$$

As we know, magnetic field is,

$$B = \frac{4\pi^2 I}{mT^2}$$
$$= \frac{4\times(3.14)^2\times7.5\times10^{-6}}{6.7\times10^{-2}\times(0.67)^2}$$
$$= 0.01 \text{ T}$$

50(C). Given,
The magnetic moment of the bar magnet, $m = 0.40$ A m^2
A distance from its mid-point, $r = 50$ cm $= 0.5$ m
$\frac{\mu_0}{4\pi} = 10^{-7}$
As we know,
The magnitude of the equatorial field due to a bar magnet,
$$B_E = \frac{\mu_0 m}{4\pi r^3}$$
$$= \frac{10^{-7}\times0.4}{(0.5)^3}$$
$$= \frac{10^{-7}\times0.4}{0.125} = 3.2 \times 10^{-7} \text{ T}$$
The magnitude of the axial field due to a bar magnet,
$$B_A = \frac{\mu_0 2m}{4\pi r^3}$$
$$B_A = \frac{10^{-7}\times2\times0.40}{(0.5)^3}$$
$$= 6.4 \times 10^{-7} \text{ T}$$

51(C). Given,
$B_E = 0.4\text{G} = 4 \times 10^{-5}$ T
The radius of the earth $r = 6.4 \times 10^6$ m
The equatorial magnetic field is,
$$B_E = \frac{\mu_0 m}{4\pi r^3}$$
$$m = \frac{4\times10^{-5}\times\left(6.4\times10^6\right)^3}{\frac{\mu_0}{4\pi}}$$
As we know,
$\frac{\mu_0}{4\pi} = 10^{-7}$
$$= \frac{4\times10^{-5}\times\left(6.4\times10^6\right)^3}{10^{-7}}$$
$$= 4 \times 10^2 \times \left(6.4 \times 10^6\right)^3$$
$$= 1.05 \times 10^{23} \text{ Am}^2$$

52(C). Given,
The horizontal component of the earth's magnetic field, $H_E = 0.26$G
The dip angle, $\theta = 60°$
As we know,
$$B_E = \frac{H_E}{\cos\theta}$$
$$B_E = \frac{H_E}{\cos 60°}$$
$$= \frac{0.26}{\left(\frac{1}{2}\right)} = 0.52\text{G}$$

53(D). The core of the transformer is laminated because energy losses due to eddy currents may be minimised.
The core of the transformer is laminated to reduce these to a minimum as they interfere with the efficient transfer of energy from the primary coil to the secondary one. The eddy currents cause energy to be lost from the transformer as they heat up the core - meaning that electrical energy is being wasted as heat.

54(A). If the frequency of the applied AC potential is increased in the R-L circuit, then the impedance of the circuit will increase.
We know that,
The reactance of the inductor coil is:
$X_L = 2\pi f L \quad \dots (i)$

And, the impedance of the R-L circuit is:
$Z = \sqrt{R^2 + X_L^2} \quad \dots (ii)$
By equation (i) and equation (ii),
We get,
$Z = \sqrt{R^2 + (2\pi f L)^2} \quad \dots (iii)$
By equation (iii) it is clear that if the frequency of the applied AC potential is increased in the R-L circuit, the impedance of the circuit will increase.

55(A). Given,
The voltage $(e) = 200\sqrt{2}\sin 100t$,
Capacitance $(C) = 1\mu\text{F} = 1 \times 10^{-6}$ Farads,
Angular Velocity $(\omega) = 100$ rads/sec,
$V_0 = 200\sqrt{2}$
The RMS voltage is:
$$V_{rms} = \frac{V_0}{\sqrt{2}}$$
$$\Rightarrow V_{rms} = \frac{200\sqrt{2}}{\sqrt{2}}$$
$$\Rightarrow V_{rms} = 200$$
The impedance in the circuit is:
$$Z = \frac{1}{C\omega}$$
$$\Rightarrow Z = \frac{1}{1\times10^{-6}\times100}$$
$$\Rightarrow Z = 10^4 \Omega$$
The current in the circuit is:
$$I = \frac{V_{rms}}{Z}$$
$$I = \frac{200}{10^4}$$
$$= 20 \times 10^{-3}$$
$$= 20 \text{ mA}$$

56(B). Energy possessed by a photon is given by,
$$E = hv = \frac{hc}{\lambda}$$
If power of each photon is P then energy given out in t second is equal to Pt. Let, the number of photons be n, then
For red light, $n_R = \frac{Pt\lambda_R}{hc}$
For violet light, $n_V = \frac{Pt\lambda_V}{hc}$
$\therefore \frac{n_R}{n_V} = \frac{\lambda_R}{\lambda_V}$
As, $\lambda_R > \lambda_V$
So, $n_R > n_V$

57(C). The magnetic field in a plane of the electromagnetic wave is given by,
$B = 2 \times 10^{-7} \sin\left(0.5 \times 10^3 x + 1.5 \times 10^{11}t\right)$
Comparing this equation with the standard wave equation:
$B_y = B_0 \sin[Kx + \omega t]$
From the above equation, $K = \mathbf{0.5} \times 10^3 = $ propagation constant
$K = \frac{2\pi}{\lambda}$ where, $\lambda = $ wavelength of wave
$\lambda = \frac{2\times3.14}{0.3\times10^3}$
$\lambda = 1.256 \times 10^{-2}$ m
$\lambda = 1.256$ cm
The wavelength range of microwaves is 10^{-3} m to 0.3 m. The wavelength of this wave lies between $10^{-3}m$ to $0.3m$, so the equation represents microwaves.

58(B). X-rays have wavelength of order of inter-atomic spacing of atoms of solid crystals. So X-rays are most suited for investigating solid structure.

59(A). Since, 1 nm = 10^{-9} m

The wavelength (λ) range of X-rays: 0.01 nm to 10 nm

So $\lambda = (0.01 \times 10^{-9})$ m to (10×10^{-9}) m = 10^{-11} m to 10^{-8} m

Thus, the Wavelength of the X-ray is of the order: 10^{-10} m.

60(B). Since the focal length of the objective lens of the telescope is larger than the focal length of their eyepiece lens. So option (A) is not correct.

The aperture of the objective lens of the telescope is larger than the aperture of the eyepiece so that the objective lens should receive more light from the object placed at far away and form a bright image of that object. So option (B) is correct and option (C) is incorrect.

Magnification of a telescope is $M = \dfrac{f_0}{f_e}$ so magnification decreases with a decrease in focal length of the objective. So option (D) is not correct.

61(D). When the glass rod has the same refractive index as a liquid, therefore the light rays are not bent at all. So glass rod in liquid appears invisible. The refraction of light takes place on going from one medium to another because the speed of light is different in the two media. The greater the difference in the speeds of light in the two media, the greater will be the amount of refraction. A medium in which the speed of light is more is known as an optically rarer medium and a medium in which the speed of light is less is known as an optically denser medium.

62(C). The property of light used in optical fibers is total internal reflection. Optical fibres are designed in such a way that the high refractive index of the inner core and lower refractive index of outer core causes the total internal reflection of the light ray. Therefore, optical fibre works on the principle of total internal reflection.

63(D). We know that,
$$\dfrac{1}{F_{eq}} = \dfrac{1}{f_1} + \dfrac{1}{f_2}$$
Here, $f_2 = +20$ cm and $f_1 = +10$ cm
Now,
$$\dfrac{1}{F_{eq}} = \dfrac{1}{20} + \dfrac{1}{10}$$
$$\Rightarrow \dfrac{1}{F_{eq}} = \dfrac{3}{20}$$
$$\Rightarrow F_{eq} = +6.67 \text{ cm}$$

64(B). Fringe width $\beta = \dfrac{D\lambda}{d}$

where D is the distance between slits and screen and d is the distance between the slits.

Thus, From question $D' = 2D$ and $d' = \dfrac{d}{2}$

When D is doubled and d is reduced to half, then the fringe width becomes
$$\beta' = \dfrac{\lambda 2D}{\left(\dfrac{d}{2}\right)}$$
$$= \dfrac{4\lambda D}{d}$$
$$= 4\beta$$

Thus, when the double slit experiment the distance between the slits and the screen is doubled and the separation between the slits is reduced to half, the fringe width becomes four times.

65(C). The wave theory of light was first demonstrated by Thomas Young in 1801 through Young's double-slit experiment.

This experiment shows that the observed pattern of interference occurs due to the superposition of light waves which proves the wave nature of light. In this experiment, two narrow slits that are close to each other, are illuminated by a monochromatic light source.

The two slits are responsible for the production of two different wavefronts which then superimpose on a screen forming the definite interference pattern.

For two coherent sources s_1 and s_2, the resultant intensity at some point p is given by:
$$I = I_1 + I_2 + 2\sqrt{I_1 I_2} \cos\phi$$
Thus, interference proves wave nature.

66(A). The angle of incidence at which a beam of unpolarized light falling on a transparent surface is reflected as a beam of completely plane polarised light is called polarising or Brewster angle. It is denoted by i_P.

Brewster's law: It states that when a ray is passed through some transparent medium having refractive index μ at any particular angle of incidence, the reflected ray is completely polarized; and the angle between reflected and refracted ray is $90°$.

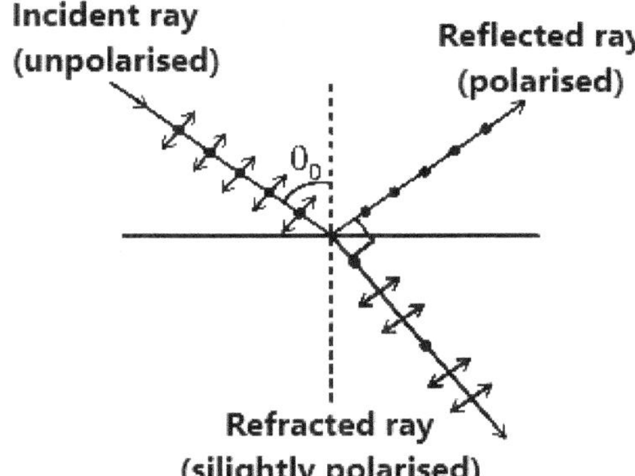

$\mu = \tan\theta_B$

Where μ = refractive index and θ_B is Brewster's angle or polarizing angle (i_p).

Given that:

The light is incident on the glass.

The refractive index of glass $(\mu) = \dfrac{3}{2}$

The angle of incidence $(i_p) = ?$

$$\dfrac{3}{2} = \tan\theta$$
$$\Rightarrow \theta = \tan^{-1}\left(\dfrac{3}{2}\right)$$
$$\Rightarrow \theta = 56.30° \approx 57°$$

67(C). De Broglie wavelength associated with the particle:
$$\lambda = \dfrac{h}{p}$$
$$\Rightarrow \lambda \propto \dfrac{1}{p}$$
Where h is the Planck's constant.

Thus de Broglie wavelength is inversely proportional to the momentum of the particle.

68(A). De Broglie proposed that as light exhibits both wave-like and particle-like properties, matter to exhibit wave-like and particle-like properties. This nature was described as dual behaviour of matter. For any particle of mass m moving with velocity v has a de Broglie wavelength given as:
$$\lambda = \dfrac{h}{p}$$
This is true for all material particle.

69(A). The de-Broglie wavelength of an electron is given by,
$$\lambda = \frac{h}{\sqrt{2}\, m_e v}$$
Here λ is the wavelength of an electron.
$h = 6.63 \times 10^{-34}$
m_e = mass of an electron
v = potential difference
We know that,
Plancks constant $(h) = 6.63 \times 10^{-34}$
Volt $= 100\, v$
Mass of electron $(m_e) = 9.1 \times 10^{-31}$
Putting all these values in $\lambda = \dfrac{h}{\sqrt{2}\, m_e \mathbf{v}}$
$$= \frac{6.63 \times 10^{-34}}{\sqrt{2} \times 9.1 \times 10^{-31} \times 100}$$
$= 0.123\, nm$

70(A). Given,
$I = 1.388 \times 10^3 Wm^{-2}$
$\lambda = 550 \times 10^{-9}\, m$
$h = 6.63 \times 10^{-34} Js$
As we know,
$$E = \frac{hc}{\lambda}$$
Number of photos incident on earth's surface per second per square metre is,
$$n = \frac{I}{E}$$
$$= \frac{I\lambda}{hc}$$
$$= \frac{1.388 \times 10^3 \times 550 \times 10^{-9}}{6.63 \times 10^{-34} \times 3 \times 10^{-8}}$$
$= 4 \times 10^{21}$

71(C). Given,
$\lambda = 589 \times 10^{-9}\, m$
$h = 6.63 \times 10^{-34} Js$
$P = 100\, W$
Energy of a photon,
$$E = \frac{hc}{\lambda}$$
$$= \frac{6.63 \times 10^{-34} \times 3 \times 10^8}{589 \times 10^{-9}}$$
$= 3.38 \times 10^{-19}$
Number of photons deliverved per second,
$$n = \frac{P}{E}$$
$$= \frac{100}{3.38 \times 10^{-19}} = 3 \times 10^{20}$$

72(C). First   excitation   potential
$= Rhc \left(\frac{1}{1^2} - \frac{1}{2^2} \right) = Rhc \frac{3}{4}$
$\therefore \frac{3}{4} Rhc = V$ electron volt...(i)
Ionization energy
$n = 1 \to n = \infty$
$E = Rhc \left[1 - \frac{1}{-\infty^2} \right]$
$E = Rhc$ ....(ii)
From equation (i) and (ii)
$\frac{3}{4} E = V$
$E = \frac{4V}{3}$
$\therefore Rhc = \frac{4V}{3}$ electron volt

73(C). As given, its momentum is equal to that of a photon of wavelength $5200\, \mathring{A}$.
According to De Broglie's equation Momentum,
$$p = \frac{h}{\lambda}$$
या $v = \dfrac{h}{m\lambda}$
$$\Rightarrow v = \frac{6.62 \times 10^{-34}}{9.1 \times 10^{-31} \times 5.2 \times 10^{-7}}$$

$\Rightarrow v = 1.4 \times 10^3$ m s^{-1} = 1400 m s^{-1}

74(B). As we know,
Second excited state corresponds to n $= 3$
$\therefore E = -\dfrac{13.6}{n^2}$
$\Rightarrow E = -\dfrac{13.6}{(3)^2}$ eV
$\Rightarrow E = -\dfrac{13.6}{9}$ eV $= -1.51$ eV

75(A). Particles which can be added to the nucleus of an atom without changing its chemical properties are called neutrons.
When neutrons are added to nucleus of an atom its chemical properties remains unchanged because atomic number of particle remains same. But when electron, proton or alpha particles are added atomic number changes so chemical properties changes.

76(D).

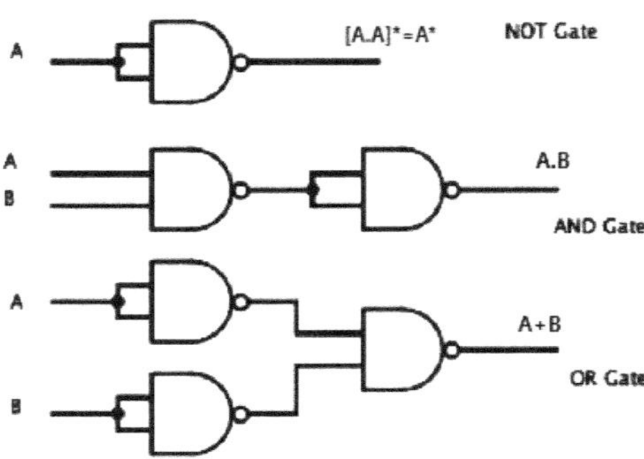

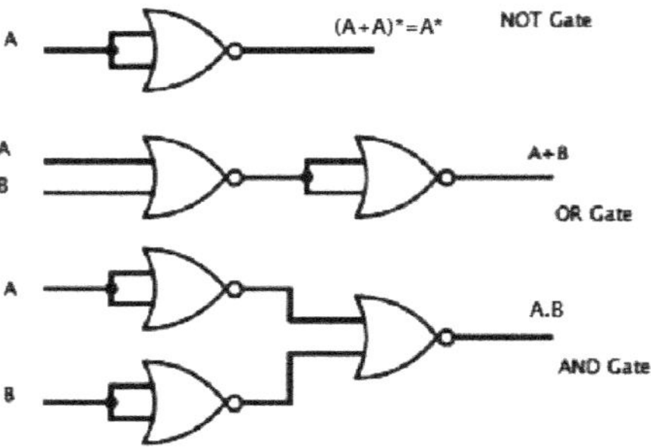

NAND and NOR gates are known as universal gates. Any one of these gates can be used to implement any kind of logic gate. This kind of feasibility does not exist with other gates ie any other gate cannot solely implement all logic gates. For example (AND) gate cannot be implemented using an (OR) gate and (vice- versa). The implementation of (NAND) and (NOR) gates to generate other logic gates is shown above.

77(A). The elemental semiconductor is made up of a single element from the fourth column elements such as Germanium. Here recombination takes place takes place via traps. It is called indirect band gap semiconductors.
Germanium (Ge) is a group- IV indirect band gap semiconductor but the difference between its direct and indirect band gap is only $140 meV$.

78(A). When the terminals are interchanged, then D_1 is reverse biased through which no current will flow, so the resistance 10 Ω will not be calculated. Since, now D_2 is forward biased, only the resistance of 20 Ω will be calculated.

We know that, $i = \dfrac{V}{R}$

Therefore the current is equal to $\dfrac{5}{20} = 0.25\ A$.

79(C). In a pure semiconductor crystal, if current flows due to the breaking of crystal bonds, the semiconductor is called intrinsic semiconductor. An intrinsic (pure) semiconductor, also called an undoped semiconductor or I-type semiconductor, is a pure earth conductor in which no significant dopant species is present. Therefore the number of charge carriers is determined by the properties of the material rather than by the amount of impurities. In intrinsic semiconductors the number of excited electrons and the number of holes are equal: n = p This can happen even after doping the conductor, although only Only when it is doped with both donors and acceptors alike. In this case, n = p still holds, and the semiconductor remains intrinsic, though doped.

80(C). Current gain $= \dfrac{I_C}{I_B}$

I_C = collector current

I_B = base current

I_E = Emitter current

So, $I_B = \dfrac{I_C}{\text{current gain}}$

$= \dfrac{7.2}{0.96}$ mA

$= 7.5$ mA

As $I_E = I_B + I_C$

So, $I_B = I_E - I_C$

$= (7.5 - 7.2)$ mA

$= 0.30$ mA

1. For a rectangle, if length $l = 16.2$ cm and breadth $b = 10.1$ cm, then find the percentage uncertainty in the area of this rectangle.
   (a) 1.6%
   (b) 1.0%
   (c) 1.9%
   (d) 2.6%

2. Which of the following is not a fundamental unit?
   (a) Meter
   (b) Kilogram
   (c) Ampere
   (d) Volt

3. The distance of the planet from the earth is measured by ________.
   (a) Direct method
   (b) Directly by metre scale
   (c) Spherometer method
   (d) Parallax method

4. What is an astronomical unit defined as?
   (a) What is an astronomical unit defined as?
   (b) The average distance between the center of the Sun and the center of the Moon
   (c) Average distance between the center of the earth and the pole star
   (d) Average distance between the center of the Earth and the center of the Sun

5. The velocity-time $(v - t)$ graph for a moving object is shown in the figure. The total displacement of the object during the time interval when there is non-zero acceleration and retardation is:

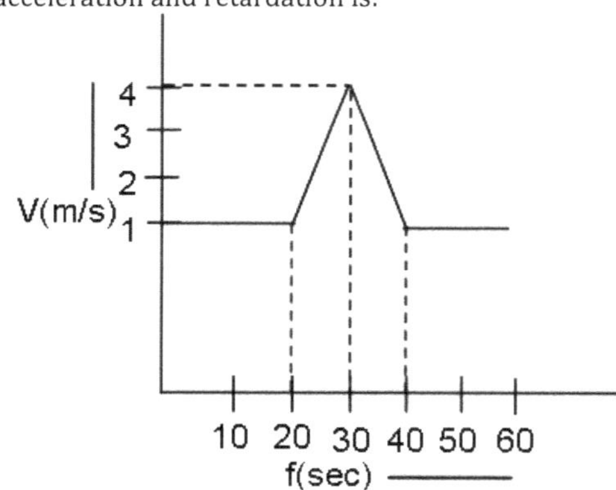

   (a) 60 m
   (b) 50 m
   (c) 40 m
   (d) 30 m

6. For a body moving with uniform acceleration a, initial and final velocities in a time interval t are u and v respectively. Then, its average velocity in the time interval t is:
   (a) $\left(v + \frac{at}{2}\right)$
   (b) $\left(v - \frac{at}{2}\right)$
   (c) $(v - at)$
   (d) None of these

7. A body covers a distance of 20 m in 7th sec. and 24 m in the 9th sec. How much shall it cover in 15 sec.?
   (a) 32 m
   (b) 36 m
   (c) 45 m
   (d) 35 m

8. Rain is falling vertically with a speed of $30\,\text{m/s}$. A woman rides a bicycle with a speed of $10\,\text{m/s}$ in the north to south direction. What is the direction in which she should hold her umbrella?
   (a) $45°12'$
   (b) $30°20'$
   (c) $14°45'$
   (d) $18°26'$

9. Find the magnitude of the centripetal acceleration of a particle on the tip of a fan blade, 0.30 m metre in diameter, rotation at 1200 revolutions per minute.
   (a) $4397.5\ \text{m/s}^2$
   (b) $2366.30\ \text{m/s}^2$
   (c) $4737.6\ \text{m/s}^2$
   (d) $2034.5\ \text{m/s}^2$

10. An aeroplane flying horizontally with a speed of 360 km/h releases a bomb at a height of 490 m from the ground. If $g = 9.8\ \text{m/s}^2$, then at how much distance it will strike the ground?
    (a) 10 km
    (b) 5 km
    (c) 1 km
    (d) 16 km

11. A machine gun is mounted on a 2000 kg car on a horizontal frictionless surface. At some instant the gun fires bullets of mass 10gm with a velocity of 500 m/sec with respect to the car. The number of bullets fired per second is ten. The average thrust on the system is:
    (a) 550 N
    (b) 50 N
    (c) 250 N
    (d) 250 dyne

12. Two perpendicular forces of 8 Newton and 6 Newton are applied on a body of mass 5.0 kg. Find the magnitude of the acceleration of the body.
    (a) $9m/s^2$
    (b) $3m/s^2$
    (c) $2m/s^2$
    (d) $4m/s^2$

13. The driver of an auto-rickshaw moving at a speed of 36 km/h, seeing a child standing in the middle of the road, stops his vehicle in exactly 4.0 seconds and saves the child. If the auto-rickshaw stops immediately near the child, what is the average damping force on the vehicle? The mass of auto-rickshaw and driver is 400 kg and 65 kg respectively.
    (a) 3.162×10^3 Newton
    (b) 1.162×10^4 Newton
    (c) 2.162×10^3 Newton
    (d) 1.162×10^3 Newton

14. A scooter of mass 120 kg is moving with a uniform velocity of 108 km/h. The force required to stop the vehicle in 10 sec:
    (a) 720 N
    (b) 180 N
    (c) 1200 N
    (d) 360 N

15. For one dimensional motion, the force F(x) and the potential energy U(x) are related as:
    (a) $F(x) = \frac{-dU(x)}{dx}$
    (b) $F(x) = \frac{dU(x)}{dx}$
    (c) $U(x) = \frac{dF(x)}{dx}$
    (d) $U(x) = \frac{-dF(x)}{dx}$

16. In an elastic collision, the kinetic energy of the system ______.
    (a) Decreases
    (b) Increases
    (c) Remains constant
    (d) First decreases then increases

17. The kinetic energy k of a particle moving along a circle of radius R depends on the distance covered s as $k = as^2$ where a is a constant. The force acting on the particle is:
    (a) $\frac{2as^2}{R}$
    (b) $2as\sqrt{1 + \left[\frac{s}{R}\right]^2}$

(c) 2as

(d) $\dfrac{2a\mathrm{R}^2}{\mathrm{s}}$

18. In which of the following cases will the work done be maximum? The body is moved through a distance S on the ground.

(a)

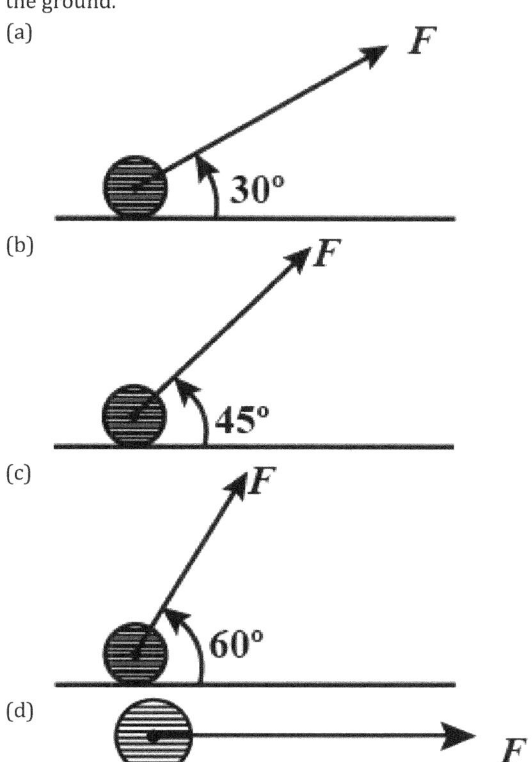

(b)

(c)

(d)

19. A disc of radius r is rotating about its center with an angular speed ω_0 it is gently placed on a rough horizontal surface. After what time it will be in pure rolling?

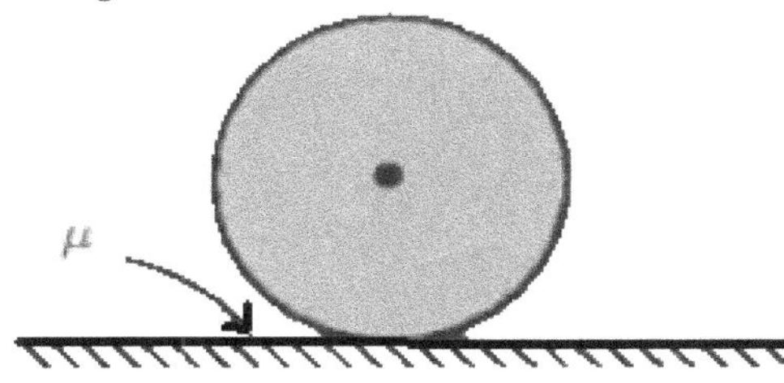

(a) $\dfrac{\omega_0 r}{2\mu g}$

(b) $\dfrac{\omega_0 r}{3\mu g}$

(c) $\dfrac{\omega_0 r}{\mu g}$

(d) $\dfrac{3}{2}\dfrac{\omega_0 r}{\mu g}$

20. From a circular ring of mass 'M' and radius 'R' an arc corresponding to a $90°$ sector is removed. The moment of inertia of the remaining part of the ring about an axis passing through the centre of the ring and perpendicular to the plane of the ring is 'K' times 'MR^2'. Then the value of $'K'$ is:

(a) $\dfrac{1}{8}$

(b) $\dfrac{3}{4}$

(c) $\dfrac{7}{8}$

(d) $\dfrac{1}{4}$

21. A uniform rod of length $200\,\mathrm{cm}$ and mass $500\,\mathrm{g}$ is balanced on a wedge placed at $40\,\mathrm{cm}$ mark. A mass of $2\,\mathrm{kg}$ is suspended from the rod at $20\,\mathrm{cm}$ and another unknown mass 'm' is suspended from the rod at

$160\,\mathrm{cm}$ mark as shown in the figure. Find the value of 'm' such that the rod is in equilibrium. $(g = 10\,\mathrm{m/s^2})$

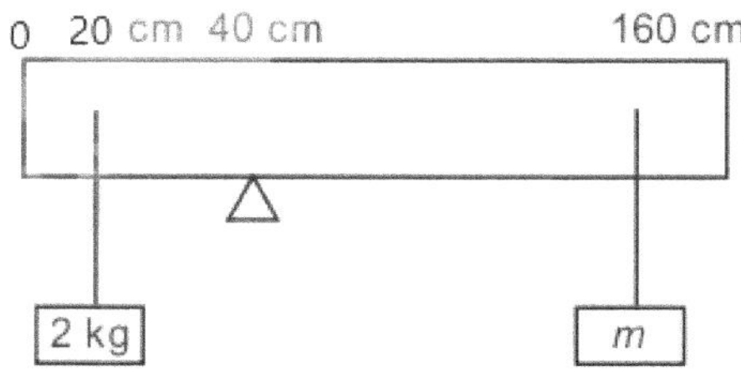

(a) $\dfrac{1}{12}$ kg

(b) $\dfrac{1}{2}$ kg

(c) $\dfrac{1}{3}$ kg

(d) $\dfrac{1}{6}$ kg

22. Two identical spherical masses are kept at some distance as shown. Potential energy when a mass m is taken from the surface of one sphere to the other:

(a) Increases continuously

(b) Decreases continuously

(c) First increases then decrease

(d) First decreases then increase

23. An astronaut on a strange planet finds that acceleration due to gravity is twice as that on surface of Earth. Which of the following could explain this?

(a) Both the mass and radius of the planet are twice as that of Earth.

(b) Mass of the planet is half as that of Earth, but radius is same as that of Earth.

(c) Both the mass and radius of the planet are half as that of Earth.

(d) Radius of the planet is half as that of Earth, but the mass is the same as that of Earth.

24. How many times a two stage rocket should be fired to launch a satellite in its proper orbit?

(a) One

(b) Two

(c) Three

(d) Four

25. If gravitational mass of a body on the moon be denoted by M_m and that on the earth be M_e, then:

(a) $M_m = \dfrac{1}{6}M_e$

(b) $M_m = M_e$

(c) $M_m = 2M_e$

(d) $M_m = 6M_e$

26. The gravitational force between two objects is F. If masses of both objects are halved without changing distance between them, then the gravitational force would become _______.

(a) F/4

(b) F/2

(c) F

(d) 2 F

27. The radius of an air bubble at the bottom of a lake is r and it becomes $2r$ when the air bubble rises to the top surface of the lake. If P cm of water is the atmospheric pressure, what is the depth of the lake?

(a) $2P$

(b) $8P$

(c) $4P$

(d) $7P$

28. Fluids offer resistance to motion due to internal friction, this property is called _______.

(a) viscosity

(b) buoyancy

(c) specific gravity   (d) continuity

29. A metal plate of area 10^3 cm^2 rests on a layer of oil 6 mm thick. A tangential force of 10^2 N is applied on it to move it with a constant velocity of 6 cm s^1 . The coefficient of viscosity of the liquid is
(a) 0.1 poise   (b) 0.5 poise
(c) 0.7 poise   (d) 0.9 poise

30. A capillary tube of radius r is immersed in water and water rises in it to a height h . The mass of the water in the capillary is 5 g . Another capillary tube of radius $2r$ is immersed in water. The mass of water that will rise in this tube is:
(a) 2.5 g (b) 5.0 g
(c) 10.0 g (d) 20.0 g

31. Outdoors on the winter, why does a piece of metal feel colder than piece of wood?
(a) Metal is a good conductor of heat than wood
(b) Wood is a good conductor of heat than metal
(c) Wood conducts heat faster than metal
(d) Both the metals and wood are bad conductors of heat

32. 200° Celsius = ________ Fahrenheit.
(a) $-73°F$ (b) $-328°F$
(c) $392°F$ (d) $73°F$

33. The heat transfer in the light bulb takes place due to:
(a) Conduction   (b) Convection
(c) Radiation   (d) None of these

34. Why the surface of a lake is frozen in severe winters, but the water at its bottom is still at liquid state?
(a) The density of water is maximum of $3°C$
(b) Since the surface of the lake is at the same temperature as the air, no heat is lost
(c) Ice is a bad conductor of heat
(d) None of these

35. A thermodynamic system is taken through the cycle $ABCD$ as shown in the figure. Heat rejected by the gas during the cycle is:

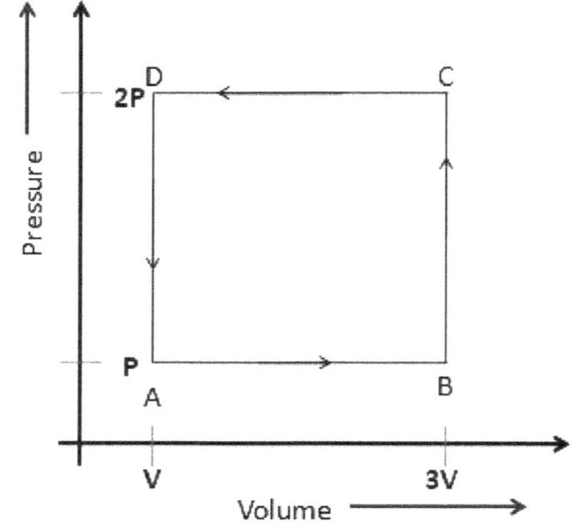

(a) PV (b) $2PV$
(c) $4PV$ (d) $\frac{1}{2}PV$

36. The iron blade has a ring in which the wooden handle is fixed. The ring is slightly smaller in size than a wooden handle. The ring is heated. When the ring cools, it __________ and tightly fits on the handle.
(a) Contracts   (b) Expands
(c) Evaporates   (d) Condenses

37. __________ factor that affects the heat of reaction which is based on Kirchoff's equation.
(a) Molecularity   (b) Temperature
(c) Pressure   (d) Volume

38. Two bodies in contact are said to be in thermal equilibrium when:
(a) No work is done by the bodies
(b) When one of the body has a higher temperature
(c) No heat flow occurs between the two bodies
(d) All of the above

39. An ideal gas is enclosed in a cylinder at pressure of 2 atm and temperature, 300 K . The mean time between two successive collisions is 6×10^{-8} s . If the pressure is doubled and temperature is increased to 500 K , the mean time between two successive collisions will be close to:
(a) 0.5×10^{-8} s   (b) 2×10^{-7} s
(c) 3×10^{-6} s   (d) 4×10^{-8} s

40. One kg of a diatomic gas is at a pressure of $8 \times 10^4 \, N/m^2$. The density of the gas is $4 \, kg/m^3$. What is the energy of the gas due to its thermal motion?
(a) 3×10^4 J   (b) 5×10^4 J
(c) 6×10^4 J   (d) 7×10^4 J

41. A plotting compass is placed near the south pole of a bar magnet. The pointer of plotting compass will:
(a) Point away from the south pole
(b) Point parallel to the south pole
(c) Point at right angles to the south pole
(d) Point at right angles to the south pole

42. Induced current in a coil can be generated by changing-
(a) Electric field
(b) Magnetic field
(c) Gravitational field
(d) Change in any field can generate induced current

43. Two long conductors, separated by a distance d carry currents I_1 and I_2 in the same direction. They exert a force F on each other. Now the current in one of them is increased to two times and its direction is reversed. The distance is also increased to 3 times. The new value of the force between them is:
(a) $-2F$ (b) $\frac{F}{3}$
(c) $\frac{-2F}{3}$ (d) $\frac{-F}{3}$

44. Curie temperature is the temperature above which:
(a) A paramagnetic material becomes ferromagnetic.
(b) A ferromagnetic material becomes paramagnetic.
(c) A paramagnetic material becomes diamagnetic.

(d) A ferromagnetic material becomes diamagnetic.

45. A circular coil of radius R having N number of turns carries a steady current I. The magnetic induction at the centre of the coil is 0.1 tesla. If the number of turns is doubled and the radius is halved, which one of the following will be the correct value for the magnetic induction at the centre of the coil?

(a) 0.05 tesla   (b) 0.2 tesla

(c) 0.4 tesla   (d) 0.8 tesla

46. _________ are those which gets strongly magnetised when placed in an external magnetic field.

(a) Ferromagnetic substances

(b) Diamagnetic substances

(c) Paramagnetic substances

(d) All of above

47. A domain in ferromagnetic iron is in the form of a cube of side length $1\mu m$. Estimate the number of iron atoms in the domain and the maximum possible dipole moment and magnetisation of the domain. The molecular mass of iron is $55\ g/mole$ and its density is $7.9\ g/cm^3$. Assume that each iron atom has a dipole moment of $9.27 \times 10^{-24}\ A\ m^2$:

(a) $7.0 \times 10^5 Am^{-1}$ (b) $7.0 \times 10^3 Am^{-1}$

(c) $6.0 \times 10^4 Am^{-1}$ (d) $8.0 \times 10^5 Am^{-1}$

48. The effective length of a magnet is 31.4 cm and its pole strength is 0.8Am. The magnetic moment, if it is bent in the form of a semicircle is _______ Am^2.

(a) 1.2   (b) 1.6

(c) 0.16   (d) 0.12

49. On heating a ferromagnetic substance above Curie temperature ___________.

(a) becomes paramagnetic

(b) becomes diamagnetic

(c) remains ferromagnetic with constant magnetic susceptibility

(d) becomes electromagnetic

50. The electric current of an electromagnet is switched off then the magnetic property of the electromagnet will:

(a) Remain for few moment

(b) Vanish instantly

(c) Will decrease with time for long

(d) Will increase with time for long

51. The magnetic flux linked with a coil varies as $\phi = 3t^2 + 4t + 9$. The magnitude of the emf induced at $t = 2$ sec is:

(a) $8V$ (b) $16V$

(c) $32V$ (d) $64V$

52. In the series LCR circuit, the power dissipation is through:

(a) R   (b) L

(c) C   (d) Both L and C

53. The concept of displacement current was proposed by:

(a) Faraday   (b) Biot-Savart

(c) Ampere   (d) Maxwell

54. Light with an energy flux of $18w/m^2$ of Wm^{-2} falls on a non-reflecting surface at normal incidence. If the surface has an area of $20\ cm^2$. The average force exerted on the surface during 30 minutes is:

(a) $6.48 \times 10^5 N$ (b) $3.60 \times 10^2 N$

(c) $1.2 \times 10^{-6} N$ (d) $2.16 \times 10^{-3} N$

55. The electric field of a plane electromagnetic wave varies with time of amplitude $2\ V\ m^{-1}$ propagating along z-axis. The average energy density of the magnetic field is (in Jm^{-3}):

(a) 13.29×10^{-12} (b) 8.86×10^{-12}

(c) 17.71×10^{-12} (d) 4.43×10^{-12}

56. What is the velocity of light in a diamond if the refractive index of the diamond with respect to vacuum is 2.5?

(a) $1.2 \times 10^8 m/s$ (b) $5 \times 10^8 m/s$

(c) $1.2 \times 10^{10} m/s$ (d) $2.5 \times 10^8 m/s$

57. A lens has focal length $+20\ cm$. Its power will be _______.

(a) $\frac{1}{20}$ dioptre   (b) $\frac{1}{500}$ dioptre

(c) $\frac{1}{5}$ dioptre   (d) 5 dioptre

58. In a compound microscope, the objective and the eyepiece have focal lengths of 5 cm and 9.5 cm, respectively, and both are kept at a distance of 20 cm. If the final image is formed at the least distance of 25 cm from the eyepiece, find the total magnification.

(a) 19.6   (b) 89

(c) 6   (d) 1.2

59. In a photoelectric experiment, if both the intensity and frequency of the incident light are doubled, then the saturation photoelectric current:

(a) Remains constant   (b) Is halved

(c) Is doubled   (d) Becomes four times

60. How will the image formed by a convex lens be affected if the central portion of the lens is wrapped in black paper, as shown in the figure?

(a) No image will be formed by the remaining portion of the lens.

(b) The central portion of the image will be absent.

(c) A full image will be formed, but it will be less bright.

(d) There will be two images, one due to each exposed half.

61. A parallel beam of light strikes a piece of transparent glass having cross section as shown in the figure below. Correct shape of the emergent wavefront will be (figures are schematic and not drawn to scale)

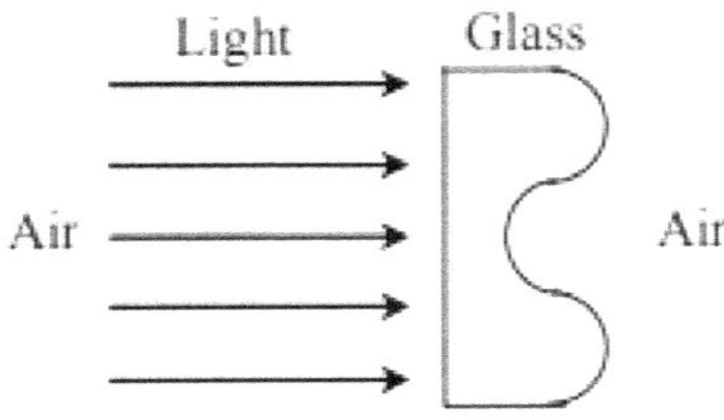

62. Linearly polarized wave:
- (a) Travels in a straight line
- (b) Has a field vector in one direction
- (c) Field oscillations are in x -direction
- (d) None of these

63. The phenomenon of sound propagation in the air is:
- (a) Isothermal process
- (b) Isobaric process
- (c) Adiabatic process
- (d) None of these

64. Ratio of energies of two photons whose wavelengths are $600 \mathring{A}$ and $400 \mathring{A}$ is:
- (a) $2:3$
- (b) $3:2$
- (c) $1:5$
- (d) $5:1$

65. Photoelectric effect occurs only if:
- (a) Frequency of incident light is lesser than threshold frequency
- (b) Frequency of incident light is greater than threshold frequency
- (c) Frequency of incident light is equal to threshold frequency
- (d) Frequency of incident light is is equal to or greater than threshold frequency

66. Radiation of frequency ν is incident on photosensitive metal. Maximum kinetic energy of the photoelectrons is E. If the frequency of incident radiation is doubled, find out the maximum kinetic energy of photoelectrons.
- (a) 2E
- (b) $\dfrac{E}{2}$
- (c) $E + h\nu$
- (d) $E - h\nu$

67. Which of the following statements is true regarding the photoelectric experiment?
- (a) The stopping potential increases with the increase in the intensity of incident light.
- (b) The photocurrent increases with the intensity of light.
- (c) The photocurrent increases with the increase in frequency

68. Two photons of energy twice and thrice the work function of the metal is incident on the metal surface. The ratio of maximum velocities of the photoelectrons emitted in the two cases, respectively, is:
- (a) $\sqrt{2}:1$
- (b) $\sqrt{3}:\sqrt{3}$
- (c) $\sqrt{3}:\sqrt{2}$
- (d) $1:\sqrt{2}$

69. Two free protons are separated by a distance of 1 Å. If they are released, the kinetic energy of each proton when at infinite separation is:
- (a) 5.6×10^{-19} J
- (b) 11.5×10^{-19} J
- (c) 23.0×10^{-19} J
- (d) 46.0×10^{-19} J

70. The half-life of $^{238}_{92}\text{U}$ undergoing α -decay is 4.5×10^9 years. What is the activity of 1 g sample of $^{238}_{92}\text{U}$?
- (a) 9.00×10^4 Bq
- (b) 1.23×10^4 Bq
- (c) 4.23×10^4 Bq
- (d) 5.23×10^4 Bq

71. Which one of the following statements is correct?
- (a) Rutherford's alpha-particle scattering experiment led to the discovery of electrons.
- (b) J J Thomson suggested that the nucleus of an atom contains protons.
- (c) The atomic number of an electron of an element is the same as the number of protons of its atom.
- (d) The mass number of an atom is equal to the number of electrons in its shells.

72. When a uranium isotope $_{92}\text{U}^{235}$ is bombarded with a neutron, it generates $_{36}\text{Kr}^{89}$ three neutrons and:
- (a) $_{56}\text{Ba}^{144}$
- (b) $_{40}\text{Zr}^{91}$
- (c) $_{36}\text{Kr}^{101}$
- (d) None of the above

73. The resistance of a wire at room temperature $30°C$ is found to be 10Ω. Now, to increase the resistance by 10% the temperature of the wire must be [The temperature coefficient of resistance of the material of wire is $0.002°C$].
- (a) $36°C$
- (b) $83°C$
- (c) $63°C$
- (d) $33°C$

74. If a full-wave rectifier circuit is operating from 50 Hz mains, then the fundamental frequency in the ripple will be
- (a) 70.7 Hz
- (b) 100 Hz
- (c) 25 Hz
- (d) 59 Hz

75. Pure silicon at 300 K has equal electron (n_e) and hole (n_h) concentration of $1.5 \times 10^{16} m^{-3}$. Doping by indium increases n_h to $4.5 \times 10^{22} m^{-3}$. The n_e in the doped silicon is:
- (a) 3×10^9 m $^{-3}$
- (b) 4×10^9 m $^{-3}$
- (c) 5×10^9 m $^{-3}$
- (d) 6×10^9 m $^{-3}$

76. The increase in the width of the depletion region in a $p - n$ junction diode is due to:
- (a) Forward bias only
- (b) Reverse bias only
- (c) Both forward bias and reverse bias
- (d) Increase in forward current

77. For transistor action, which of the following statements is correct?

(d) All of the above

    (a)   Base, emitter and collector regions should have same doping concentrations

    (b)   Base, emitter and collector regions should have same size

    (c)   Both emitter junction as well as the collector junction are forward biased

    (d)   The base region must be very thin and lightly doped

78. A wire of length 2 m is made from 10 cm^3 of copper. A force F is applied so that its length increases by 2 mm . Another wire of length 8 m is made from the same volume of copper. If the force F is applied to it, its length will increase by:

    (a) 0.8 cm   (b) 1.6 cm

    (c) 2.4 cm   (d) 3.2 cm

79. The breaking stress of a wire depends upon:

    (a)   The length of the wire

    (b)   The radius of the wire

    (c)   The material of the wire

    (d)   The shape of the cross-section

80. A wire of length L , area of cross-section A is hanging from a fixed support. The length of the wire changes to L_1 when mass M is suspended from its free end. The expression for Young's modulus is:

    (a) $\dfrac{MgL_1}{AL}$ (b) $\dfrac{Mg(L_1 - L)}{AL}$

    (c) $\dfrac{MgL}{AL_1}$ (d) $\dfrac{MgL}{A(L_1 - L)}$

// Smart Answer Sheet //

Correct	Percentage of students who answered correctly.
Skipped	Percentage of students who skipped.

Q.	Ans.	Correct / Skipped	Q.	Ans.	Correct / Skipped	Q.	Ans.	Correct / Skipped
1	A	41.92% / 1.7%	2	D	47.98% / 1.94%	3	D	56.87% / 1.17%
4	D	54.53% / 1.42%	5	B	56.42% / 1.99%	6	B	41.65% / 1.07%
7	B	64.99% / 1.27%	8	D	64.19% / 1.81%	9	B	48.8% / 1.09%
10	C	44.37% / 1.07%	11	B	51.06% / 1.27%	12	C	53.99% / 1.25%
13	D	63.56% / 1.96%	14	D	65.37% / 1.64%	15	A	89.4% / 0.0%
16	C	67.51% / 1.4%	17	B	11.79% / 3.85%	18	D	42.3% / 1.72%
19	B	42.2% / 1.14%	20	B	87.77% / 0.0%	21	A	31.96% / 4.67%
22	C	83.94% / 0.0%	23	C	50.17% / 1.26%	24	B	81.17% / 0.0%
25	B	87.47% / 0.0%	26	A	87.58% / 0.0%	27	D	51.87% / 1.33%
28	A	81.22% / 0.0%	29	A	54.93% / 1.34%	30	C	52.24% / 1.8%
31	A	51.2% / 1.4%	32	C	58.5% / 1.62%	33	C	78.52% / 0.0%
34	C	40.58% / 1.12%	35	B	19.46% / 4.29%	36	B	45.95% / 1.07%
37	B	64.16% / 1.81%	38	C	79.91% / 0.0%	39	D	41.74% / 1.98%
40	B	56.47% / 1.55%	41	C	22.6% / 3.87%	42	B	78.48% / 0.0%
43	C	24.12% / 4.94%	44	B	52.29% / 1.87%	45	C	28.42% / 3.02%

Q.	Ans.	Correct / Skipped	Q.	Ans.	Correct / Skipped	Q.	Ans.	Correct / Skipped
46	A	76.93% / 0.0%	47	D	20.79% / 4.61%	48	C	53.66% / 1.52%
49	A	65.44% / 1.39%	50	A	45.41% / 1.29%	51	B	48.45% / 1.83%
52	A	79.56% / 0.0%	53	D	53.34% / 1.07%	54	C	62.97% / 1.74%
55	B	43.78% / 1.61%	56	A	66.63% / 1.54%	57	D	81.67% / 0.0%
58	A	20.24% / 4.85%	59	C	86.76% / 0.0%	60	C	44.39% / 1.32%
61	A	82.04% / 0.0%	62	B	86.21% / 0.0%	63	C	41.42% / 1.49%
64	A	56.29% / 1.12%	65	B	77.59% / 0.0%	66	C	43.71% / 1.79%
67	B	51.66% / 1.46%	68	D	69.81% / 1.58%	69	B	18.65% / 4.97%
70	B	45.55% / 1.5%	71	C	63.07% / 1.19%	72	A	56.1% / 1.6%
73	B	65.23% / 1.63%	74	B	66.41% / 1.08%	75	C	46.75% / 1.28%
76	B	41.04% / 1.29%	77	D	45.84% / 1.89%	78	D	89.5% / 0.0%
79	C	67.97% / 1.5%	80	D	57.61% / 1.97%			

// Hints and Solutions //

1(A). Given,

Length $l = 16.2$ cm

Breadth $b = 10.1$ cm

We can write with least count,

$l = 16.2 \pm 0.1$ cm

Now, percentage uncertainty in length $= \dfrac{0.1}{16.2} \times 100$

$= 0.617 \approx 0.6\%$

Similarly, we can write with least count,

$b = 10.1 \pm 0.1$ cm

The percentage uncertainty in breadth $\dfrac{0.1}{10.1} \times 100$

$= 0.990099 \approx 1\%$

Now we can write,

$l = 16.2$ cm $\pm 0.6\%$

$b = 10.1$ cm $\pm 1\%$

Area of a rectangle $= l \times b$

$= 16.2 \pm 0.6\% \times 10.1 \pm 1\%$

$= 163.62$ cm^2 $\pm 1.6\%$

Thus, the percentage uncertainty in the area of this rectangle $= 1.6\%$

2(D). The fundamental units are the base units defined by International System of Units. These units are not derived from any other unit, therefore they are called fundamental units. The seven base units are:

- Meter (m) for Length
- Second (s) for Time
- Kilogram (kg) for Mass
- Ampere (A) for Electric current
- Kelvin (K) for temperature
- Mole (mol) for Amount of substance
- Candela (cd) for Luminous intensity

Volt is not a fundamental unit, it is a derived unit.

3(D). The distance of the planet from the earth is measured by parallax method. Parallax is a displacement or difference in the apparent position of an object viewed along two different lines of sight, and is measured by the angle or semi-angle of inclination between those two lines. Parallax Method is used for large distances.

4(D). An astronomical unit is defined as the average distance between the center of the Earth and the center of the Sun. The astronomical unit is the unit of length, which is approximately 150 million kilometers and is based on the distance from the Earth to the Sun.

1 astronomical unit $(1AU) = 1.496 \times 10^{11}$ m

5(B). Between time intervals $20 sec$ to $40 sec$, there is non-zero acceleration and retardation.

Hence distance travelled during this interval

= Area between time interval $20 sec$ to $40 sec$

= area of triangle + area of rectangle, below the triangle

= distance during interval = area under the triangle

$= \frac{1}{2} \times 20 \times 3 + 20 \times 1$

$= 30 + 20 = 50 m$.

6(B). We know, Average velocity can be calculated using the formula,

Average velocity

$= \dfrac{\text{Total displacement}}{\text{Total Time}} = \dfrac{ut + \frac{1}{2}at^2}{t}$

Average velocity $= u + \frac{1}{2}$ at

From equations of motion $v = u + at$

Using this equation we can write $u = v - at$

Substitute $u = v - at$ in the above equation obtained for Average velocity we get

Average velocity $= v - at + \frac{1}{2}$ at $= v - \frac{1}{2}$ at.

7(B). Let u is initial velocity and a is acceleration

$\Rightarrow s_{n^{th}} = u + \frac{1}{2}a(2n - 1)$

$\Rightarrow 20 = u + \frac{1}{2}a(14 - 1) = u + \frac{13a}{2}$

$\Rightarrow 2u + 13a = 40$ ... (i)

$2u = u + \frac{1}{2}a(18 - 1)$

$\Rightarrow 2u + 17a = 48$ ... (ii)

Subtracting equation (i) from (ii) we get

$4a = 8 \Rightarrow a = 2m/s^2$

From equation (i)

$2u + 13 \times 2 = 40$

$\Rightarrow 2u = 40 - 26 = 14$

$\Rightarrow u = 7m/s$

$\Rightarrow s_{15} = u + \frac{1}{2}a(2 \times 15 - 1)$

$= 7 + \frac{1}{2} \times 2(29)$

$= 7 + 29 = 36 m$

8(D). The described situation is shown in the given figure.

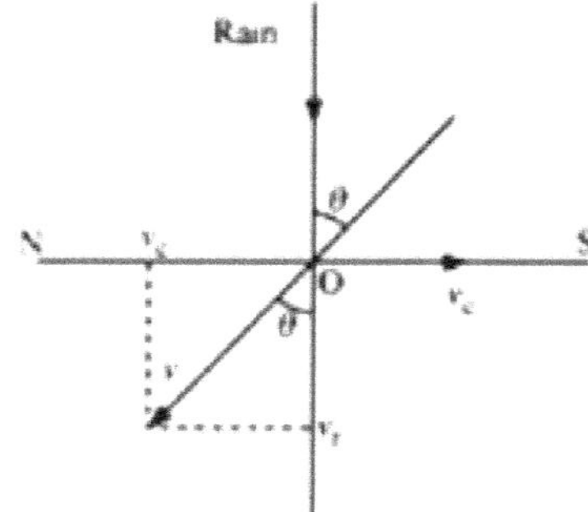

Here,

v_c = Velocity of the cyclist

v_r = Velocity of falling rain

In order to protect herself from the rain, the woman must hold her umbrella in the direction of the relative velocity (v) of the rain with respect to the woman.

$v = v_r + (-v_c)$

$= 30 + (-10) = 20$ m/s

$\tan\theta = \frac{v_c}{v_r} = \frac{10}{30}$

$\theta = \tan^{-1}(\frac{1}{3})$

$= \tan^{-1}(0.3333) = 18°26'$

Therefore, the woman should hold her umbrella at $18°26'$ south of vertical direction.

9(B). Given,

Diameter = 0.30 m

then radius, $(r) = \frac{0.30}{2} = 0.15$ m

and Frequency $(n) = 1200$ revolution per minute

$= \frac{1200}{60} = 20$ revolution per second

$\therefore$ Angular velocity, $(\omega) = 2\pi n = 2\pi \times 20 = 40\pi$ radian per second

Therefore, centripetal acceleration, $a_c = \omega^2 r$

$\Rightarrow a_c = 0.15 \times (40\pi)^2$

$\Rightarrow a_c = 2366.30$ m/s^2

So, the magnitude of the centripetal acceleration of a particle on the tip is 2366.30 m/s^2 .

10(C). Time taken by the bomb to fall through a height of 490 m

$t = \sqrt{\dfrac{2 h}{g}}$

$= \sqrt{\dfrac{2 \times 490}{9.8}} = 10 sec$

The distance at which the bomb strikes the ground

= horizontal velocity $\times$ time

$= 360 \times 10$

$= 360 \times (\frac{10}{3600})$

$= 36 \times (\frac{1}{36})$

$= 1$ km

So, the bomb will strike the ground at $= 1$ km distance.

11(B). Given,

Mass of car, $M = 2000$ kg

Mass of bullet, $m = 10 \times 10^{-3}$ kg

Velocity of bullet, $u = 500$ m/sec

The number of bullets fired per second is ten. Then,

$\frac{N}{t} = 10$

$F_{avg} = \dfrac{\Delta P}{\Delta t}$

$= \dfrac{Nm(v_2 - v_1)}{t}$

$= 10 \times 10 \times 10^{-3} \times 5 \times 10^2$

$= 50$ N

12(C). Given,

Mass of the body, $m = 5.0$ kg

Magnitude of forces,

$\left|\overrightarrow{F_1}\right| = 8$ Newton

$\left|\overrightarrow{F_2}\right| = 6$ Newton

The magnitude of the resultant force of these forces,

$F = \sqrt{\left|\overrightarrow{F_1}\right|^2 + \left|\overrightarrow{F_2}\right|^2}$

$= \sqrt{[8^2 + 6^2]}$

$= \sqrt{(64 + 36)}$

$= \sqrt{100} = 10$ Newton

Magnitude of acceleration,

$a = \dfrac{F}{M}$

$= \dfrac{10}{5.0}$

$= 2 m/s^2$

13(D). Given,
The initial speed of the auto rickshaw, $u = 36$ km/h
$= 36 \times (\frac{5}{18})$ m/s $= 10$ m/s
The final speed of the auto rickshaw when it stops,
$v = 0$
Time taken to stop, $t = 4.0$ sec
From the first equation of motion,
$v = u + at$
$0 = 10 + a \times 4$
$a = -(\frac{10}{4})$
$a = -2.5$ m/s^2
The mass of the system (auto-rickshaw + driver),
$M = 400 + 65 = 465$ kg
$\therefore$ Average retarding force, $F = M \times a$
$= 465 \times (2.5)$
$= 1,162.5$
$= 1.162 \times 10^3$ Newton

14(D). Given,
Mass of a scooter, $m = 120$ kg
Velocity $v = 108$ km/h $= 108 \times \frac{5}{18} = 30$ m/s
Time taken to stop $t = 10$ sec
Final velocity, $v = 0$ m/s
From the first equation of motion,
$v = u + at$
$0 = 30 + a \times 10$
$a = -\frac{30}{10} = -3$ m/s^2
Since force cannot be negative we will use a positive value for acceleration.
Force, $F = ma$
$= 120 \times 3 = 360$ N

15(A). The potential energy is equal to negative work done in shifting an object from some reference point to a given position for conservative force.
In mathematical form, it is given as,
$dU(x) = -F(x)dx$
$\therefore F(x) = \dfrac{-dU(x)}{dx}$
where F is the force in newton and $\dfrac{dU}{dx}$ is change in potential energy per unit length.

16(C). In an elastic collision, the kinetic energy of the system remains constant. In the elastic collision, both momentum and kinetic energy are conserved. Since in the elastic collision kinetic energy of the system is conserved, it will remain constant.

17(B). Given:
$\frac{1}{2}mv^2 = as^2$
$\Rightarrow v = s\sqrt{\frac{2a}{m}}$
So $a_R = \dfrac{v^2}{R} = \dfrac{2as^2}{mR}$ ......(i)
Further more as $a_t = \dfrac{dv}{dt} = \dfrac{dv}{ds} \cdot \dfrac{ds}{dt} = v\dfrac{dv}{ds}$ .... (ii)
From equation (i) i.e. $v = s\sqrt{\frac{2a}{m}}$ yields
$a_t = \left[s\sqrt{\frac{2a}{m}} \right]\left[\sqrt{\frac{2a}{m}} \right] = \dfrac{2as}{m}$ ....(iii)
So, that $a = \sqrt{a_R^2 + a_t^2}$
$= \sqrt{\left[\frac{2as^2}{mR}\right]^2 + \left[\frac{2as}{m}\right]^2}$
Thus $a = \dfrac{2as}{m}\sqrt{1 + [\frac{s}{R}]^2}$
$\therefore F = ma = 2as\sqrt{1 + [\frac{s}{R}]^2}$

18(D). Work done is given by dot product of force and displacement.
$W = F.S$
Both force and displacement are vector component and their dot product is scalar quantity and given by $|\vec{F}| \cdot |\vec{S}| \cos\theta$.
Where θ is the angle between the force and displacement. As the body is moved along the ground with the same magnitude of displacement and force and then force having the least angle with horizontal will be the highest work, as $\cos\theta$ is maximum as θ goes towards zero.

19(B). The acceleration due to friction is given as, $a = \dfrac{f}{m}$
$= \dfrac{\mu mg}{m}$
$= \mu g$
Angular acceleration due to friction is given as,
$\alpha = \dfrac{\tau}{I}$
$= \dfrac{fR}{\frac{1}{2}mR^2} = \dfrac{2f}{mR} = \dfrac{2ma}{mR}$
$= \dfrac{2\mu g}{R}$
The final angular velocity is given as, $\omega = \omega_0 - \alpha$
$\omega = \omega_0 - \dfrac{2\mu gt}{R}$
The final velocity is given as,
$v = at$
$v = \mu gt$
we know that,
$v = R\omega$
$\mu gt = R\left(\omega_0 - \dfrac{2\mu gt}{R}\right)$
$t = \dfrac{\omega_0 R}{3\mu g}$
Thus, the time is $\dfrac{\omega_0 R}{3\mu g}$ after that the disc will be in pure rolling.

20(B). Given that,
Mass of Ring $= M$; Radius of Ring $= R$
Now 90°arc is removed from circular ring, then mass removed $= \dfrac{M}{4}$

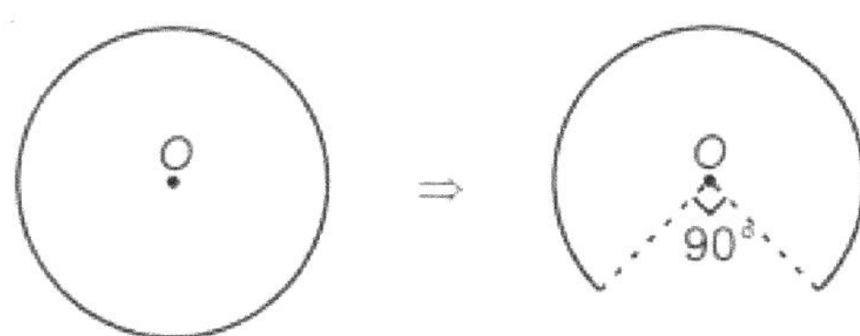

Mass of remaining portion $= \dfrac{3M}{4}$
Moment of inertia of remaining part $= \int dmr^2$
$\Rightarrow I = R^2 \int dm \quad (\because r = R)$
$\Rightarrow I = \dfrac{3MR^2}{4}$.
So, the value of K is $\dfrac{3}{4}$.

21(A). Given that:
Mass of rod = 500 g; Length of rod = 200 cm

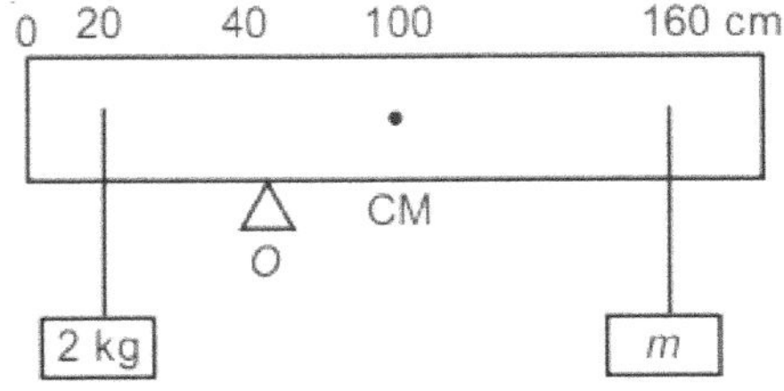

Rod will be in equilibrium, when net torque about point O will be zero.

Torque at point O due to 2 kg mass

$\vec{\tau} = \vec{r} \times \vec{F} = rF \sin\theta(\hat{n})$

$\tau_1 = 20 \times 20 \times 10^{-2} \times \sin 90°(\hat{k})$

$= 4 \text{ N m}(\hat{k})$

Torque due to mass of rod:

$\tau_2 = 5 \times 60 \times 10^{-2} \times \sin 90°(-\hat{k})$

$= 3 \text{ N m}(-\hat{k})$

Torque due to mass m

$\tau_3 = mg \times 120 \times 10^{-2} \times \sin 90°(-\hat{k})$

$= 12 \text{ N m}(-\hat{k})$

Net torque about point O will be zero.

So $\vec{\tau_1} + \vec{\tau_2} + \vec{\tau_3} = 0$

$\Rightarrow 4 - 3 - 12m = 0$

$\Rightarrow 12m = 1$

$m = \frac{1}{12} \text{ kg}$

22(C). Let the mass m is at distance r from one of the spheres and the mass of spheres is M

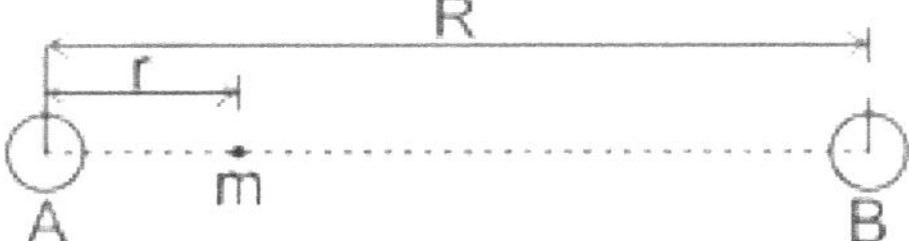

Then the total potential energy of the system is,

$U = -\dfrac{GM^2}{R} - \dfrac{GMm}{r} - \dfrac{GMm}{(R-r)}$

Now at $r = \dfrac{R}{4}$, the potential energy of the system is,

$U_1 = -\dfrac{GM^2}{R} - \dfrac{GMm}{\frac{R}{4}} - \dfrac{GMm}{(R-\frac{R}{4})}$

$\Rightarrow U_1 = -\left(\dfrac{GM^2}{R} + \left(\dfrac{16}{3}\right)\dfrac{GMm}{R}\right) \cdots (1)$

Now at $r = \dfrac{R}{2}$, the potential energy of the system is,

$U_2 = -\dfrac{GM^2}{R} - \dfrac{GMm}{\frac{R}{2}} - \dfrac{GMm}{(R-\frac{R}{2})}$

$\Rightarrow U_2 = -\left(\dfrac{GM^2}{R} + 4\dfrac{GMm}{R}\right) \cdots (2)$

Now at $r = \dfrac{3R}{4}$, the potential energy of the system is,

$U_3 = -\dfrac{GM^2}{R} - \dfrac{GMm}{\frac{3R}{4}} - \dfrac{GMm}{(R-\frac{3R}{4})}$

$\Rightarrow U_3 = -\left(\dfrac{GM^2}{R} + \left(\dfrac{15}{3}\right)\dfrac{GMm}{R}\right) \cdots (3)$

Now from equations 1,2, and 3,

U_1 is less than U_2 and U_2 is greater than U_3, so the potential energy first increases and then decreases.

23(C). Given that in the strange planet acceleration due to gravity is twice as that on the surface of Earth

The expression for acceleration due to gravity on the surface of a planet is given by $g = \dfrac{GM}{r^2}$

Let g' is gravitational acc on the strange planet. The mass of it is M_s and the radius is R_s so

$g' = \dfrac{GM_s}{R_s^2}$

Let g is gravitational acc on earth. The mass of the earth is M and the radius is R so

$g = \dfrac{GM}{R^2}$

$\dfrac{g'}{g} = \dfrac{\frac{GM_s}{n_s^2}}{\frac{GM}{n^2}}$

$\dfrac{g'}{g} = \dfrac{M_s}{M}\dfrac{R^2}{R_s^2}$

The value of g on the other planet is double then

this will be satisfied by the only condition in option 3.

$\dfrac{g'}{g} = \dfrac{M_s/2}{M}\dfrac{R^2}{(R_s/2)^2}$

$\dfrac{g'}{g} = 2$

$g' = 2g$

24(B). Two times a two stage rocket should be fired to launch a satellite in its proper orbit. The two forces acting on the rocket immediately after leaving the launching pad are gravitational force and frictional force. The gravitational force acts downwards towards the earth and frictional force acts due to surrounding air.

25(B). Mass is independent of the place where it is measured. Weight can be different at different places with different gravitational field.
Mass of a body is constant that neither depends on the location of the body nor on the gravitational force exerted on the body. So mass of the body will remain unchanged on moon i.e., $M_m = M_e$

26(A). The gravitational force between two objects is F. If masses of both objects are halved without changing distance between them, then the gravitational force would become F/4.
Gravitational force between two objects varies directly as their masses and inversely as the square of the distance between them. So, when the masses of both objects are halved without changing the distance, the gravitational force between them would become one-fourth of the original value.

27(D). Initially the radius of the bubble is r. After reaching surface it becomes $2r$. The atmospheric pressure is given as,
$P_{atm} = Pcm$ of water
What we can conclude from this process is that the volume is changing in the air bubble but the temperature remains unchanged.
For isothermal process,
$P_1 V_1 = P_2 V_2$
Let the height of water surface be h.
$(P + h)\left(\frac{4}{3}\pi r^3\right) = P\left(\frac{4}{3}\pi 8r^3\right)$
$\Rightarrow h + P = 8P$
$\Rightarrow h = 7P$

28(A). Fluids offer resistance to motion due to internal friction, this property is called viscosity. The property of a fluid due to which it opposes the relative motion between its different layers is called viscosity (or fluid friction or internal friction) and the force between the layers opposing the relative motion is called viscous force.

29(A). $\eta = \dfrac{F}{A\left(\frac{dv}{dy}\right)}$

$\therefore \eta = \dfrac{10^{-2}}{(10^3 \times 10^{-4})\left(\frac{6\times 10^{-2}}{6\times 10^{-3}}\right)}$

$= \dfrac{10^{-2}\times 6\times 10^{-3}}{10^{-1}\times 6\times 10^{-2}}$

$\eta = 10^{-2} Nsm^{-2} = 0.1 \text{ poise}$

30(C). Given:
$r_1 = r; \ h_1 = h; \ r_2 = 2r$
Using rh = constant
$r_2 h_2 = r_1 h_1$
$(2\text{r})\text{h}_2 = \text{rh}$
$\Rightarrow \text{h}_2 = \dfrac{\text{h}}{2}$

Mass of the water in the capillary $M = \rho \left(\pi^2 h\right)$
where ρ is the density of the water
Mass of water that rises in the first capillary
$M_1 = 5\ \text{g}$
$\therefore 5 = \rho\pi r^2 h$ ....(1)
Mass of water that will rise in second capillary
$M_2 = \rho\left(\pi r_2^2\ h_2\right)$
$M_2 = \rho\pi(2r)^2\dfrac{h}{2} = 2 \times \rho\pi r^2\ h$
$\Rightarrow M_2 = 2 \times 5 = 10g$

31(A). **Concept:**
There are three methods of heat transfer between the two systems. They are conduction, convection, and radiation.
- **Conduction** is a method of heat transfer in solids and heat transfer takes place without the movement of particles.
- **Convection** is a method of heat transfer in fluids (gases and liquids) and heat transfer takes place due to the movement of particles.
- **Radiation** is a method of heat transfer where heat is transferred from one place to another without affecting the medium of heat transfer.

Both are at the same temperature, the metal will feel colder than the wood because of the thermal conductivity of the metal, compared to the wood is more.
Metal extract more heat from your hand than wood in a given time. Therefore, you perceive the metal as being colder than the wood.

32(C). The various temperature scales commonly used are Celsius (C) , Kelvin (K) , Fahrenheit (F) and Rankine (Ra) .
$^\circ F = \dfrac{9}{5}{}^\circ C + 32$
$^\circ F = \dfrac{9}{5} \times 200 + 32$
$= 360 + 32$
$= 392\,^\circ F$

33(C). In the presence of oxygen, the filament of the light bulb would burn up as a result of the high temperature. So the vacuum is maintained in the light bulb. Since there is no medium present in the light bulb, so the heat transfer takes place by radiation because the conduction and the convection require a material medium to transfer heat.

34(C). **Concept:**
Good Conductor of heat: The material that allows the heat to transfer through them easily is called a good conductor of heat. Examples: Copper, silver, iron, etc.
The bad conductor of heat or insulator: The material that doesn't allow the heat to transfer through them easily is called an insulator. Example: Wood, ice, glass, plastic, etc.
Heat transfer mainly takes place due to temperature differences.
Air changes temperature faster than water so, in winters, the air cools down before the water. The water on the surface is in direct contact with the air and therefore freezes first, before the water at the bottom.
Now since ice is less dense than water, it continues to float and doesn't sink. This ice sheet keeps getting thicker and acts as an insulator between the cold air and warm water at the bottom. This is why the water at the bottom stays liquid. So we can say that ice is a bad conductor of heat that's why the water at the bottom of the lake remains in the liquid state.

35(B). The following figure shows the cyclic process of gas. If an object returns to its initial position after one or more processes it went through.
$ABCDA$ is the cycle. The pressure at the points both D and C remain the same, which is $2P$. The volume at the point D is V and at the point C is $3V$. So, the work done by the gas from point D to point C, $W_{DC} = 2P(3V - V) = 4PV$
The pressures at the points C and B are $2P$ and P respectively. The volume at the points both C and B remain the same, which is $3V$. So, the work done by the gas from point C to point B,
$W_{CB} = P(3V - 3V) = 0$
The pressure at the points both B and A remain the same, which is P . The volume at the point B is $3V$ and at the point A is V ,
So, the work done by the gas from point B to point A, $W_{BA} = P(V - 3V) = -2PV$
The pressures at the points A and D are P and $2P$ respectively. The volume at the points both A and D remain the same, which is V .
So, the work done by the gas from point A to the point D, $W_{AD} = P(V - V) = 0$
Hence the total work done in the whole cycle,
$W = 4PV - 2PV = 2PV$
We know the heat rejected from the cycle is equal to the amount of total work done by the gas, so
$Q = W$
$Q = 2PV$

36(B). When the metal heated, the length, surface area, volume of the metal also increased. The increase in temperature which results in metal expands and this expansion is termed as the thermal expansion of metal i.e. expansion in metal due to the heating effect.
So, the iron blade has a ring in which the wooden handle is fixed. The ring is slightly smaller in size than a wooden handle. When the ring is heated which is made up of metal expands, after the ring cools, it tightly fits in the wooden handle.

37(B). Kirchhoff's Law describes the enthalpy of a reaction's variation with temperature changes. In general, enthalpy of any substance increases with temperature, which means both the products and the reactants' enthalpies increase. The overall enthalpy of the reaction will change if the increase in the enthalpy of products and reactants is different.
At constant pressure, the heat capacity is equal to change in enthalpy divided by the change in temperature.
$c_p = \dfrac{\Delta H}{\Delta T}$
Therefore, if the heat capacities do not vary with temperature then the change in enthalpy is a function of the difference in temperature and heat capacities. The amount that the enthalpy changes by is proportional to the product of temperature change and change in heat capacities of products and reactants.

38(C). Two bodies in contact are said to be in thermal equilibrium when no heat flow occurs between the two bodies.
Thermal equilibrium : Thermal equilibrium is a condition when two surfaces in physical contact

have no exchange of heat between them.
- Heat flows from an object of higher temperature to an object of lower temperature.
- So, temperature governs the direction of heat flow.
- When no heat flow occurs, it is to be inferred that the surfaces are at the same temperature.

39(D). Given:
$T_1 = 300K$ and $T_2 = 500K$
Mean time $\tau_1 = 6 \times 10^{-8}$
$\tau_2 = ?$

$$\tau = \frac{1}{\left(\sqrt{2}\pi\eta d^2 V_{Avg}\right)}$$

$$\eta = \left(\frac{\text{No. of molecules}}{\text{volume}}\right) = \frac{N}{V}$$

$$\tau = \frac{V}{\sqrt{2}\pi N d^2 V_{Avg}}$$

$$V_{Avg} = \sqrt{\frac{2RT}{MW}}$$

$$\tau \alpha \frac{V}{\sqrt{T}}$$

$$\tau \alpha \frac{\sqrt{T}}{p}$$

$$\frac{\tau_1}{\tau_2} = \sqrt{\frac{T_1}{T_2}}\left(\frac{p_2}{p_1}\right)$$

$$\tau_2 = \left(6 \times 10^{-8}\right)\sqrt{\frac{T_2}{T_1}}\left(\frac{p_1}{p_2}\right)$$

$$\tau_2 = \left(6 \times 10^{-8}\right)\sqrt{\frac{500}{300}}\left(\frac{p}{2p}\right)$$

$$\tau_2 = \left(3 \times 10^{-8}\right)\sqrt{\frac{5}{3}}$$

$$\tau_2 = 4 \times 10^{-8} \text{ sec.}$$

40(B). Given:
Density $= 4 Kg/m^3$
$P = 8 \times 10^4 N/m^2$
$U = \frac{5}{2}\mu RT$
For diatomic gases. (5 is the degrees of freedom as the gas is diatomic)
But $PV = \mu RT$
So,
$$U = \frac{5}{2}PV$$
$$V = \frac{\text{mass}}{\text{density}}$$
$$= \frac{1\ kg}{4\ kg/m^3}$$
$$= \frac{1}{4}\ m^3$$
$$P = 8 \times 10^4\ N/m^2$$
$$\therefore U = \frac{5}{2} \times 8 \times 10^4 \times \frac{1}{4}$$
$$= 5 \times 10^4\ J$$

41(C). A plotting compass is placed near the south pole of a bar magnet. The pointer of plotting compass point towards the south pole.
As you get closer to the magnetic South Pole, the field lines will curve to dive straight into the magnetic South Pole, running perpendicular to Earth's surface. "So quite often, compasses actually won't work," said Tom Jordan, a geophysicist with the British Antarctic Survey.

42(B). Induced current in a coil can be generated by changing magnetic field.
Induced Current: If a conducting loop is exposed to a changing magnetic field, A current can be induced in it. This current is known as induced current.
This change in the magnetic field may be produced in several ways; you can change the strength of the magnetic field, move the conductor in and out of

the field, alter the length of the distance between a magnet and the conductor, or by changing the area of a loop located in a stable magnetic field.
No matter how this change is achieved, the result, an induced current, is always the same.
The strength of the current will vary in proportion to the change of magnetic flux.

43(C). Force per unit length between two long current carrying wires is given by,
$$F_1 = \frac{\mu_0 I_1 I_2}{2\pi d}$$
When I_1 is changed to $2I_1$ and d is changed to $3d$
$$\therefore \quad F_2 = \frac{\mu_0 (2I_1)(I_2)}{2\pi(3d)}$$
$$= \frac{\mu_0 I_1 I_2}{2\pi d} \times \frac{2}{3}$$
$$= \frac{2F}{3}$$
As direction of current is reversed, the direction of the force will also get reversed.
$$\therefore F_2 = \frac{-2F}{3}$$
Here, negative sign indicates that the force is now repulsive in nature.

44(B). Curie temperature: Curie temperature is the temperature at which the magnetic properties of a material change. At this temperature, the magnetic materials lose their magnetic property.
When the temperature is greater than the Curie temperature, ferromagnetic material becomes paramagnetic material.

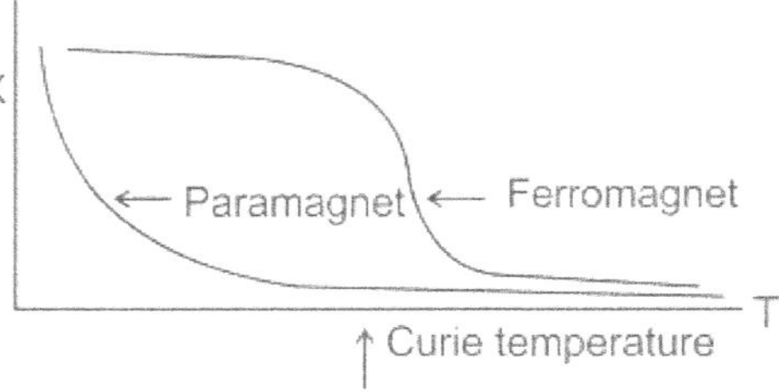

45(C). Given,
$B = 0.1$ tesla
The magnetic field at the centre of a circular coil is given by $B = \dfrac{\mu_0 NI}{2R} = 0.1$ tesla
If the number of turns is doubled and the radius is halved i.e.
Number of turns, $N' = 2\,N$ and radius $R' = \dfrac{R}{2}$
Then new magnetic induction is,
$$B' = \frac{\mu_o N' I}{2R'}$$
$$= \frac{\mu_o 2NI}{2\left(\frac{R}{2}\right)}$$
$$= \frac{4\mu_o NI}{2R}$$
$$\because B = \frac{\mu_o NI}{2R} = 0.1$$
$$= 4 \times 0.1 = 0.4T$$

46(A). Ferromagnetic substances are those which gets strongly magnetised when placed in an external magnetic field. They have strong tendency to move from a region of weak magnetic field to strong magnetic field, i.e., they get strongly attracted to a magnet.
The individual atoms (or ions or molecules) in a ferromagnetic material possess a dipole moment as in a paramagnetic material. However, they interact with one another in such a way that they spontaneously align themselves in a common

direction over a macroscopic volume called domain.

47(D). The volume of the cubic domain is:
$$V = \left(10^{-6}\,\text{m}\right)^3$$
$$= 10^{-18}\,\text{m}^3$$
$$= 10^{-12}\,\text{cm}^3$$
Its mass is volume $\times$ density
$$= 7.9\,\text{g}\,\text{cm}^{-3} \times 10^{-12}\,\text{cm}^3 = 7.9 \times 10^{-12}\,\text{g}$$
It is given that Avagadro number $\left(6.023 \times 10^{23}\right)$ of iron atoms have a mass of 55 g. Hence, the number of atoms in the domain is
$$N = \frac{7.9 \times 10^{-12} \times 6.023 \times 10^{23}}{55}$$
$$= 8.65 \times 10^{10}\,\text{atoms}$$
The maximum possible dipole moment $m_{\max}$ is achieved for the (unrealistic) case when all the atomic moments are perfectly aligned.
Thus,
$$m_{\max} = \left(8.65 \times 10^{10}\right) \times \left(9.27 \times 10^{-24}\right)$$
$$= 8.0 \times 10^{-13}\,\text{Am}^2$$
The consequent magnetisation is
$$M_{\max} = \frac{m_{\max}}{Domain\,volume}$$
$$= \frac{8.0 \times 10^{-13}\,\text{Am}^2}{10^{-18}\,\text{m}^3}$$
$$= 8.0 \times 10^5\,\text{Am}^{-1}$$

48(C). The effective length of magnet = 31.4 cm
Pole strength m = 0.8Am
Length of semi-circle $= \pi\dfrac{D}{2} = L$
where, D = diameter of circle
$$\Rightarrow D = \frac{2\,L}{\pi}$$
$$= \frac{2 \times 3.14 \times 10^{-2}}{3.14}$$
$$D = 20 \times 10^{-2}\,\text{m}$$
Now, the magnetic moment
$$= \text{ml} = \text{mD}$$
$$= 0.8 \times 20 \times 10^{-2}$$
$$= 16.0 \times 10^{-2}$$
$$= 0.16\,\text{Am}^2$$

49(A). When a ferromagnetic material is heated to Curie temperature, it disrupts the arrangements of the molecules and a weak magnetic behavior remains. This weak magnetic behavior is called Paramagnetic. Above this temperature, the paramagnetism property also decreases. Upon cooling, it regains its ferromagnetic behavior.

50(A). The electric current of an electromagnet is switched off then the magnetic property of the electromagnet will remain for few moment.
As the electromagnet is a temporary magnetic which is only working till when we give the current to it. Once the electric current is stopped the magnetic property of the electromagnet vanished. But there is a very small time duration, in which the magnetic property of the electromagnet exists after stopping the electric current in it. This is due to electromagnetic induction in the coil of the electromagnet.

51(B). Given that:
$$\phi = 3t^2 + 4t + 9$$
Number of turns is not given, so we will take is
$$N = 1$$
Time $(t) = 2\,\text{sec}$
We know that,
emf induced $(V) = -N\dfrac{d\varphi}{dt}$
Where N is the number of turns, ϕ is flux linked and

t is time
Here negative sign shows the direction of the induced emf.
Now,
$$(V) = -N\frac{d\varphi}{dt}$$
$$= -1 \times \frac{d\left(3t^2 + 4t + 9\right)}{dt}$$
$$= -(6t + 4 + 0)$$
$$= -(6t + 4)$$
$$= -(6 \times 2 + 4)$$
$$= -16V$$
Thus magnitude of emf induced \(=16 V \)

52(A). In the series LCR circuit, the power dissipation is through R.
The capacitor and inductor are the storage devices that store the energy in it. The inductor and capacitor can't dissipate energy. As the resistance opposes the flow of electric current. So the resistance of any circuit dissipates the power.

53(D). The concept of displacement current was proposed by Maxwell.
In electromagnetism, displacement current density is the quantity $\dfrac{\partial D}{\partial t}$ appearing in Maxwell's equations that is defined in terms of the rate of change of D, the electric displacement field. Displacement current density has the same units as electric current density, and it is a source of the magnetic field just as actual current is. However it is not an electric current of moving charges, but a time-varying electric field. In physical materials (as opposed to vacuum), there is also a contribution from the slight motion of charges bound in atoms, called dielectric polarization.
The electric displacement field is defined as:
$$D = \varepsilon_0 E + P$$
where:
ε_0 is the permittivity of free space
E is the electric field intensity
P is the polarization of the medium
Differentiating this equation with respect to time defines the displacement current density, which therefore has two components in a dielectric:
$$J_D = \varepsilon_0 \frac{\partial E}{\partial t} + \frac{\partial P}{\partial t}$$
The first term on the right hand side is present in material media and in free space
The second term on the right hand side, called polarization current density.
Thus, $I_D = \iint_S J_D \cdot \mathrm{d}S$
$$= \iint_S \frac{\partial D}{\partial t} \cdot \mathrm{d}S$$
$$= \frac{\partial}{\partial t} \iint_S D \cdot \mathrm{d}S$$
$$= \frac{\partial \Phi_D}{\partial t}$$

54(C). Given
Energy flux = $18\,W/cm^2$
Surface Area = $20\,cm^2$
Time period $(T) = 30\,min$
The total energy falling on the surface is,
$U = $ Energy flux $\times$ Surface Area $\times$ Time period
$$U = \left(18W/cm^2\right) \times \left(20cm^2\right) \times (30 \times 60s)$$
$$= 6.48 \times 10^5\,J$$
Therefore, the total momentum delivered (for complete absorption) is,
$$p = \frac{U}{c}$$

$$= \frac{6.48 \times 10^5 J}{3 \times 10^8 m/s}$$
$$= 2.16 \times 10^{-3} kg\,m/s$$

The average force exerted on the surface is,
$$F = \frac{p}{t}$$
$$= \frac{2.16 \times 10^{-3}}{0.18 \times 10^4}$$
$$[\because t = 30 \times 60s = 1800 = 0.18 \times 10^4]$$
$$= 1.2 \times 10^{-6} N$$

55(B). Given,
$$E_0 = 2 \text{ V m}^{-1}$$
$$\epsilon_0 = 8.85 \times 10^{-12}$$

Amplitude of electric field and magnetic field are related by the relation,
$$\frac{E_0}{B_0} = c$$
$$\Rightarrow B_0 = \frac{E_0}{c} \quad ....(i)$$

Average energy density of the magnetic field is,
$$U_B = \frac{1}{4} \frac{B_0^2}{\mu_0}$$

From equation (i), we get
$$U_B = \frac{1}{4} \frac{E_0^2}{\mu_0 c^2}$$

As we know,
$$c = \frac{1}{\sqrt{\mu_0 \epsilon_0}} \quad ....(ii)$$

Putting value of c from equation (ii), we get
$$U_B = \frac{1}{4} \epsilon_0 E_0^2$$
$$= \frac{1}{4} \times 8.854 \times 10^{-12} \times (2)^2$$
$$= 8.854 \times 10^{-12} \text{ J m}^{-3}$$
$$\approx 8.86 \times 10^{-12} \text{ J m}^{-3}$$

56(A). Given that:
Refractive index of the diamond $(\mu_d) = 2.5$
We know
The velocity of light in vacuum (c) $= 3 \times 10^8 m/s$
To find the velocity of light in diamond (v)
Now,
$$\mu_d = \frac{c}{v} \qquad \text{or,} \qquad 2.5 = \frac{3 \times 10^8}{v} \qquad \text{or,}$$
$$v = \frac{3 \times 10^8}{2.5} = 1.2 \times 10^8 m/s$$

57(D). Power of Lens: The inverse of the focal length is known as the power of the lens. It shows the bending strength for the light ray of the lens. The unit of power of a lens is Dioptre. when the focal length of the lens is taken in meter (m).
$$\Rightarrow P = \frac{1}{f(m)} = \frac{100}{f(cm)}$$

Where P is the power of the lens and f is the focal length of the lens.
Given,
$$f = 20 \text{ cm}$$
The power of the lens is written as,
$$P = \frac{100}{f(cm)}$$
$$\Rightarrow P = \frac{100}{20}$$
$$\Rightarrow P = 5 \text{ dioptre}$$

58(A). In the case of eye-piece lense
$$\frac{1}{v} - \frac{1}{u} = \frac{1}{f}$$
$$\Rightarrow \frac{1}{25} - \frac{1}{u} = \frac{1}{5}$$
$$\Rightarrow \frac{1}{u} = \frac{1}{25} - \frac{1}{5}$$
$$\Rightarrow u = \frac{-5}{4}$$
$$\Rightarrow u = -1.25 \text{ cm}$$
For objective the image distance

$$v = 20 - 1.25$$
$$= 18.75 \text{ cm}$$
Again, by the above formula-
$$\frac{1}{18.75} - \frac{1}{u} = \frac{1}{9.5}$$
$$\Rightarrow \frac{1}{u} = \frac{4}{75} - \frac{2}{19}$$
$$\Rightarrow \frac{1}{u} = \frac{76 - 150}{75 \times 19}$$
$$\Rightarrow u = \frac{75 \times 19}{-74}$$
$$\Rightarrow u = -19.25 \text{ cm}$$
Total magnification $m = m_1 \times m_2$
Here, $m = \frac{v}{u}$
$$\Rightarrow m = \frac{18.75}{19.25} \times \frac{25}{1.25}$$
$$\Rightarrow m = 19.6$$

59(C). The saturation photoelectric current is directly proportional to the intensity of incident radiation but it is independent of its frequency. Therefore, the saturation photoelectric current becomes doubled, when both the intensity and frequency of the incident light are doubled.

60(C). In the convex lens, the rays are converted to a point on the other side lens when the parallel rays are incident on the surface of the lens. If the central portion of the lens wrapped by black paper, the full image will be formed but with less brightness.

61(A).

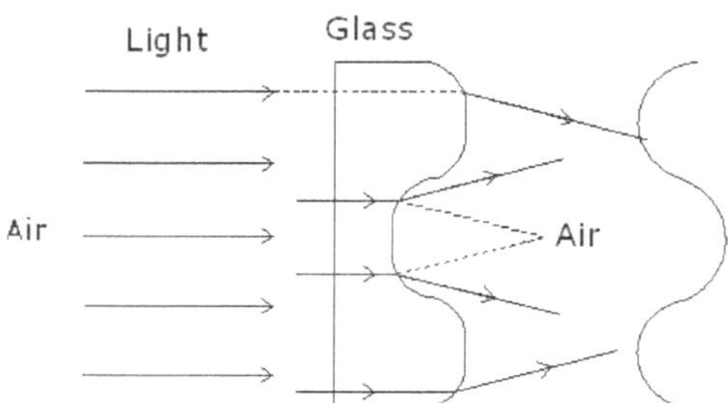

Concept: based on Huygens' principle.
Theory of wavefront → wave moves such that direction of propagation is perpendicular to the wavefront.
And as we can see that light ray will travel more in air than glass medium. And if the glass medium is more than wavefront will slack. So, the shape of the emergent wavefront will be:

62(B). The wave is in the $x - y$ plane, thus it is called a plane-polarized wave.

The wavefield displaces in the y-direction, thus it is called y-polarized or linearly polarised wave. When two orthogonal electric field component vectors are of equal magnitude and are out of phase by exactly $90°$, the wave is called circular polarized.

63(C). Sound is a mechanical wave. It requires a medium for transmission. There is no transmission of sound in a vacuum. The transmission of sound in the air is in the form of a longitudinal wave. The transmission of sound in the air is in the form of compression and deceleration caused by the vibration of air particles. So, the phenomenon of sound propagation in the air is also an adiabatic process.

64(A). Given,
$\lambda_1 = 600 \text{Å}$
$\lambda_2 = 400 \text{Å}$
The Photon energy formula is given by,
$E = \dfrac{hc}{\lambda} \quad \cdots (i)$
Where,
$E =$ Energy
$c =$ Speed of light $= \left(3 \times 10^8 \text{ m/s}\right)$
$\lambda =$ Wavelength
$h =$ Planck's constant $\left(6.6 \times 10^{-34} \text{Js}\right)$
By equation (i), we get
$E_1 = \dfrac{hc}{\lambda_1}$
$\Rightarrow E_1 = \dfrac{hc}{600} \quad \cdots (ii)$
$\Rightarrow E_2 = \dfrac{hc}{\lambda_2}$
$\Rightarrow E_1 = \dfrac{hc}{400} \quad \cdots (iii)$
By equation (ii) and equation (iii), we get,
$\dfrac{E_1}{E_2} = \dfrac{\frac{hc}{600}}{\frac{hc}{400}}$
$\Rightarrow \dfrac{E_1}{E_2} = \dfrac{400}{600}$
$\Rightarrow \dfrac{E_1}{E_2} = \dfrac{2}{3}$

65(B). Photoelectric effect
The photoelectric effect is a phenomenon where electrons are ejected from a metal surface when the light of sufficient frequency is incident on it. When a photon falls on the metal surface, the photon's energy is transferred to the electron.
Some part of the energy gets utilized in removing the electron from the metal surface, and the remaining goes into giving kinetic energy for the ejected electron.
Therefore, the total energy of photon = work function + maximum kinetic energy of the electron.
The energy of a photon is given by the equation:
$E = h\nu$
Where nν is the frequency of incident light and h is the Planck's constant.
Work function: It is the minimum amount of energy required to cause photo-emission of electrons from a metal surface when light is incident on it. The work function is also known as the threshold energy.
The photoelectric effect is said to have occurred when an electron is ejected from the metal surface with light incident on it.
For an electron to be emitted, it must acquire energy large enough to leave the metal surface. For this to happen, the electron should have an energy greater than the threshold energy. Since energy is directly proportional to frequency, the electron must acquire a frequency greater than the threshold frequency. Therefore, the frequency of incident light has to be greater than the threshold frequency for the photoelectric effect to occur.

66(C). We know that,
Energy incident Radiation = Work function + Kinetic energy ... (1)
Equation (1) becomes
$h\nu = h\nu_0 + E \ldots (2)$
Where v and v_0 are incident and threshold frequencies. When frequency of incident
radiation is doubled i.e $v = 2v$ then consider new kinetic energy is E_1 using equation
From (1) and (2)
Energy incident Radiation = work function + kinetic energy ... (1)
Equation (1) becomes
$h\nu = h\nu_0 + E \ldots (2)$
Where v and v_0 are incident and threshold frequencies. When frequency of incident
Radiation is doubled i.e $v = 2v$ then consider new kinetic energy is E_1 using equation
From (1) and (2)
Energy incident Radiation = work function + kinetic energy ... (1)
Equation (1) becomes
$h\nu = h\nu_0 + E \ldots (2)$
Where v and v_0 are incident and threshold frequencies. When frequency of incident
Radiation is doubled i.e $v = 2v$ then consider new kinetic energy is E_1 using equation
(1) an equation (2)
$h(2v) = h\nu_0 + E_1$
$2h\nu = (h\nu - E) + E_1$
$E_1 = -(h\nu - E) + 2h\nu$
$E_1 = E + h\nu$
$h(2v) = h\nu\nu_0 + E_1$
$2h\nu = (h\nu - E) + E_1$
$E_1 = -(h\nu - E) + 2h\nu$
$E_1 = E + h\nu$

67(B). The photoelectric effect is a phenomenon in which electrons are ejected from the surface of a metal when light is incident on it. These ejected electrons are called photoelectrons. It is important to note that the emission of photoelectrons and the kinetic energy of the ejected photoelectrons is dependent on the frequency of the light that is incident on the metal's surface. The process through which photoelectrons are ejected from the surface of the metal due to the action of light is commonly referred to as photoemission.

68(D). Given,
$E_1 = 2\phi$
$E_2 = 3\phi$
Kinetic energy $= \frac{1}{2}mV^2$
Kinetic energy = Energy of photon $-$ Work function
Kinetic energy of 1st photon $= 2\phi - \phi = \phi$ .... (i)
Kinetic energy of 2nd photon $= 3\phi - \phi = 2\phi$ .... (ii)
Dividing equation (i) by (ii), we get
$\dfrac{\frac{1}{2}mV_1^2}{\frac{1}{2}mV_2^2} = \dfrac{\phi}{2\phi}$
$\Rightarrow \dfrac{V_1^2}{V_2^2} = \dfrac{1}{2}$

$$\Rightarrow \frac{V_1}{V_2} = \frac{1}{\sqrt{2}}$$

$$V_1 : V_2 = 1 : \sqrt{2}$$

69(B). Given:

Distance between the free protons, $r = 1$ Å $= 1 \times 10^{-10}$ m

Initially kinectic energy of the proton is zero and electric potential energy is maximum.

At infinite separation, potential energy is zero and all the energy is converted into kinetic energy (using law of conservation of energy)

i.e., $2K = U$

Where, K is kinetic energy of each proton.

$$K = \frac{1}{2}U = \frac{1}{2}\frac{e^2}{4\pi\epsilon_0 I} \quad \text{.....(1)}$$

Where,

$e = 1.6 \times 10^{-19}$ C (charge on the proton)

$\epsilon_0 = 8.85 \times 10^{-12}$ C^2 N^{-1} m^{-2} (permittivity of free space)

Put all the given values in (1)

$$K = \frac{1}{2} \times \frac{\left(1.6 \times 10^{-19}\text{C}\right)^2}{\left(10^{-10}\text{ m}\right)} \times \frac{1}{4\pi\epsilon_0}$$

Also, $\frac{1}{4\pi\epsilon_0} = 9 \times 10^9$ Nm^{2}C^{-2}

$$\Rightarrow K = \frac{1}{2} \times \frac{\left(1.6 \times 10^{-19}\text{C}\right)^2}{\left(10^{-10}\text{ m}\right)} \times 9 \times 10^9 \text{Nm}^2\text{C}^{-2}$$

$$\Rightarrow K = 11.5 \times 10^{-19} \text{ J}$$

70(B). Given:

$T_{\frac{1}{2}} = 4.5 \times 10^9 y$

$= 4.5 \times 10^9 y \times 3.16 \times 10^7$ s/y

$= 1.42 \times 10^{17}$ s

One k mol of any isotope contains Avogadro's number of atoms, and so 1 g of $^{238}_{92}$U contains:

$$N = \frac{1}{238 \times 10^{-3}} \text{kmol} \times 6.025 \times 10^{26} \text{ atoms/kmol}$$

$N = 25.3 \times 10^{20}$ atoms

The decay rate R is:

$R = \lambda N$

$$= \frac{0.693}{T_{1/2}}N = \frac{0.693 \times 25.3 \times 10^{20}}{1.42 \times 10^{17}} \text{ s}^{-1}$$

$= 1.23 \times 10^4$ s^{-1}

$= 1.23 \times 10^4$ Bq

71(C). The atomic number of an electron of an element is the same as the number of protons of its atom this statement is correct.

The number of protons in the nucleus of the atom is equal to the atomic number (Z). The number of electrons in a neutral atom is equal to the number of protons. The mass number of the atom (M) is equal to the sum of the number of protons and neutrons in the nucleus. The number of neutrons is equal to the difference between the mass number of the atom (M) and the atomic number (Z).

72(A). As any type of nuclear reaction follows the laws of conservation of mass. Thus, we can say that the mass of reactants in the nuclear reaction is equal to the mass of the products. So the reaction will be:

$$_{92}U^{235} + _{0}n^1 \rightarrow _{q}X^P + _{36}Kr^{89} + 3_{0}n^1 + E$$

(energy)

Where we have considered X as the element which we have to find.

Sum of Atomic number on LHS $= 92 + 0 = 92$

Sum of Atomic number on RHS $= q + 36 + 3 \times 0$

Since, we know that nuclear reactions also follow the Law of conservation of mass. We can say that the total atomic mass of the reactants or LHS is equal to the total atomic masses of the products or

RHS.

$\therefore$ LHS=RHS

$92 = 36 + q$

$q = 56$

And, Sum of atomic mass number on LHS $= 235 + 1 = 236$

Sum of Atomic mass number on

RHS $= p + 89 + 3 \times 1$

As, LHS=RHS

$p + 92 = 236$

$\therefore p = 144$

So, the element is $_{56}Ba^{144}$.

73(B). $R = R_0(1 + \alpha t)$

$\therefore R_0(1 + 30\alpha) = 10\Omega$

and $R_0(1 + \alpha) = 11\Omega$

Therefore, $\frac{11}{10} = \frac{1 + \alpha t}{1 + 30\alpha}$

$\Rightarrow 11 + 330\alpha = 10 + 10\alpha t$

$\Rightarrow 11 + 330 \times 0.002 = 10 + 10 \times 0.002t$

$\Rightarrow 11.66 = 0.02t + 10$ Or $0.02t = 1.66$

$t = 83°C$

74(B). For full-wave rectifier, ripple frequency $= 2\times$ input frequency

$= 2 \times 50$

$= 100$ Hz

Note: A full-wave rectifier consists of two junction diodes, so, its efficiency is twice that of a half-wave rectifier.

75(C). Given,

$n_i = 1.5 \times 10^{16} m^{-3}$ and $n_h = 4.5 \times 10^{22} m^{-3}$

Now, we know that in an extrinsic semiconductor,

$n_e n_h = (n_i)^2$

$n_e \times 4.5 \times 10^{22} = \left(1.5 \times 10^{16}\right)^2$

$n_e = \frac{2.25 \times 10^{32}}{4.5 \times 10^{22}}$

$n_e = 5 \times 10^9$ m^{-3}

76(B). The increase in the width of the depletion region is due to the absence of the electrons and holes in the region. This occurs only in the case of the reverse bias only in a diode.

When we apply a negative voltage to the diode i.e. a positive terminal is connected towards the N-type and the negative terminal is towards the P-type, the junction width, or the width of the depletion layer is increased. It is called reverse bias.

77(D). For a transistor action, the junction must be lightly doped so that the base region is very thin. Also, the emitter junction must be reverse-biased.

78(D). $\ell = \left(\frac{FL}{AY}\right)$

i.e. $\ell = \left(\frac{FL}{AY}\right) \times \frac{L}{L} = \left(\frac{FL^2}{VY}\right)$ where $AL = V$

Given: volume is constant

F is same

Y is same

$\therefore \ell \propto L^2$

$\left(\frac{\ell_1}{\ell_2}\right) = \left(\frac{L_1}{L_2}\right)^2$

$\left(\frac{2}{\ell_2}\right) = \left(\frac{2}{8^2}\right)$

$\left(\frac{2}{\ell_2}\right) = \left(\frac{1}{16}\right)$

$\ell_2 = 32$ mm

$\ell_2 = 3.2$ cm

79(C). The breaking stress of a wire depends upon the material of the wire.

We know that the equation for the relation of stress

and strain is $\frac{\text{Stress}}{\text{Strain}} = \gamma$. This means that the stress on an object depends on γ . Now γ as we already know depends upon the material that makes up the wire.

Before starting the actual solution, it would be good to discuss stress, stress, and their relationship.

Stress – Stress is the force applied per unit area on a material.

Strain – Strain is the change in the dimensions of material when it is under stress.

The relation of stress-strain is given below:

$$\frac{\text{Stress}}{\text{Strain}} = \gamma$$

Here, $\gamma =$ The proportionality of linear expansion

By the stress-strain equation, i.e. $\frac{\text{Stress}}{\text{Strain}} = \gamma$, we can see that the strain of a body does not depend on the length of the wire, the shape of the cross-section of the wire, and the radius of the wire.

But stress does depend on γ . Now γ depends on the material of the wire, so the breaking stress also depends on the material of the wire.

In simple words, it means that two objects made of different material will have different breaking stress (the limit of strain the body can bear)

80(D). When the new mas is hanged to the wire, the force exerted on the wire is:

$F = mg$

The initial length of the wire is L and the new length is L_1 .

We know that the Young's modulus is given as:

$$Y = \frac{FL}{A\Delta l}$$

Here, $L_\circ$ is the initial length of wire and Δl is the change in length of wire.

Substitute the values:

$$Y = \frac{mg \times L}{A \times (L_1 - L)}$$

So, $Y = \frac{mgL}{A(L_1 - L)}$

1. Which of the following statement is correct?
(a) Torque and momentum have the same dimension but work has different dimension
(b) Torque and work have the same dimension but momentum have a different dimension
(c) Momentum and work have the same dimension but torque has a different dimension
(d) Torque, momentum, and work all have the same dimension

2. Which of the following standards do we currently use to measure time intervals?
(a) Earth's rotation period
(b) Atomic standard time
(c) Astronomical time standard
(d) All of the above

3. The accuracy in the measurement of the diameter of hydrogen atom as 1.06×10^{-10} m is:
(a) 0.01
(b) 106×10^{-10}
(c) $\frac{1}{106}$
(d) 0.01×10^{-10}

4. Which of the following method is used to measure the distance of a planet or star from Earth?
(a) Triangulation method
(b) Parallax method
(c) Echo method
(d) All of the above

5. The ratio of the distances travelled by a freely falling body in the $1^{st}, 2^{nd}, 3^{rd}$ and 4th second :
(a) $1:3:5:7$
(b) $1:1:1:1$
(c) $1:2:3:4$
(d) $1:4:9:16$

6. The displacement-time graphs of two moving particles make angles of $30°$ and $45°$ with the x-axis as shown in the figure. The ratio of their respective velocity is:

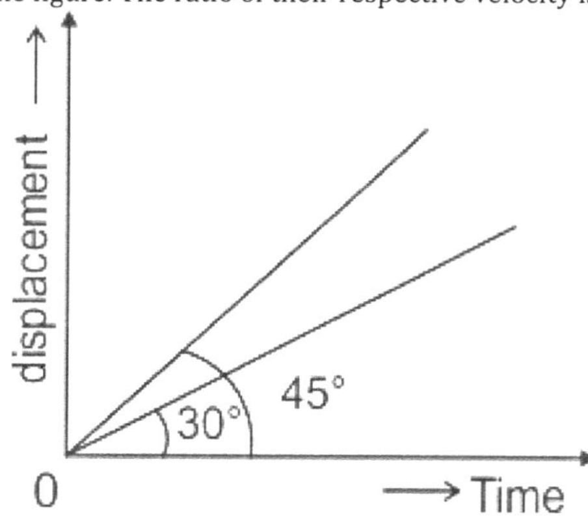

(a) $1:2$
(b) $1:\sqrt{3}$
(c) $\sqrt{3}:1$
(d) $1:1$

7. A stone dropped from the top of a tower reaches ground in 4 s. Height of the tower is $(g = 10 \text{ m/s}^2)$
(a) 20 m
(b) 40 m
(c) 80 m
(d) 160 m

8. A stone tied to the end of a string 80 cm long is whirled in a horizontal circle with a constant speed. If the stone make 14 revolutions in 25 sec, what is the magnitude of the acceleration of the stone?
(a) 9.89 m/s^2
(b) 3.30 m/s^2
(c) 8.90 m/s^2
(d) 6.90 m/s^2

9. Two bullets are fired simultaneously, horizontally and with different speeds from the same place. Which bullet will hit the ground first?
(a) The faster one
(b) Depends on their mass
(c) The slower one
(d) Both will reach simultaneously

10. The net acceleration of a particle in circular motion is _______.
(a) towards the centre
(b) always along the radius
(c) irregular
(d) circular in motion

11. A body of mass M is kept on a rough horizontal surface (friction coefficient $= \mu$). A person is trying to pull the body by applying a horizontal force but the body is not moving. The force by the surface on the body is F, where:
(a) $F = Mg$
(b) $F = \mu Mg$
(c) $Mg \leq F \leq Mg\sqrt{1 + \mu^2}$
(d) $Mg \geq F \geq Mg\sqrt{1 - \mu^2}$

12. Which one of the following has maximum inertia?
(a) An atom
(b) A molecule
(c) A one-rupee coin
(d) A cricket ball

13. A force produces an acceleration of 5.0 cm/s^2 when it acts on a body of mass 20 g. Find the force acting on the body.
(a) 2×10^{-3} N
(b) 4×10^{-3} N
(c) 1×10^{-3} N
(d) 6×10^{-3} N

14. A board is balanced on a rough horizontal semi-circular log. Equilibrium is obtained with the help of addition of a weight to one of the ends of the board when the board makes an angle θ with the horizontal. Coefficient of friction between the log and the board is:

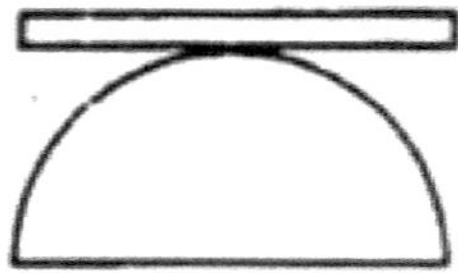

(a) $\tan \theta$
(b) $\cos \theta$
(c) $\cot \theta$
(d) $\sin \theta$

15. Which of the following is Kilowatt-hour a unit of?
(a) power
(b) force
(c) energy
(d) momentum

16. How much time is needed to perform 260 J of work at the rate of 10 W?
(a) 24 s
(b) 52 s
(c) 26 s
(d) 32 s

17. An electric generator converts:
(a) electrical energy into chemical energy

   (b)   chemical energy into electrical energy

   (c)   electrical energy into mechanical energy

   (d)   mechanical energy into electrical energy

18. What would be the expenditure in 30 days at the rate of 75 paise per unit, if a bulb of 100 W is used five hours per day?

   (a)   Rs. 10   (b)   Rs. 7.5

   (c)   Rs. 15   (d)   Rs. 11.25

19. The centre of mass of three particle s of masses $1\,kg, 2\,kg$, and $3\,kg$ is at $2, 2, 2$. The position of the fourth mass of $4\,kg$ to be placed in the system so that the new centre of mass is at $0, 0, 0$ is

   (a) $-3, -3, -3$ (b) $-3, 3, -3$

   (c) $2, 3, -3$ (d) $2, -2, 3$

20. The ratio of the radius of gyration of a thin uniform disc about an axis passing through its centre and normal to its plane to the radius of gyration of the disc about its diameter is :

   (a) $4 : 1$ (b) $1 : \sqrt{2}$

   (c) $2 : 1$ (d) $\sqrt{2} : 1$

21. Two objects of mass $10\,kg$ and $20\,kg$ respectively are connected to the two ends of a rigid rod of length $10\,m$ with negligible mass. The distance of the center of mass of the system from the $10\,kg$ mass is :

   (a) $10\,m$ (b) $5\,m$

   (c) $\frac{10}{3}\,m$ (d) $\frac{20}{3}\,m$

22. Critical velocity of a satellite is _______.

   (a)   The minimum velocity given to the satellite to escape from the gravitational pull

   (b)   The constant horizontal velocity given to the satellite to keep it in a stable orbit

   (c)   The constant horizontal velocity given to the satellite to keep its acceleration equal to zero

   (d)   The constant horizontal velocity given to the satellite to keep its acceleration equal to acceleration due to gravity

23. Two objects of different masses falling freely near the surface of moon would ______.

   (a)   Have different accelerations

   (b)   Undergo a change in their inertia

   (c)   Have same velocities at any instant

   (d)   Experience forces of same magnitude

24. The distance between two bodies becomes 6 times more than the usual distance. The the F becomes ______.

   (a)   36 times   (b)   6 times

   (c)   12 times   (d)   1/36 times

25. The weakest of the four fundamental interactions is the:

   (a)   Gravitational force   (b)   Electro-magnetic

   (c)   Strong nuclear force   (d)   Weak nuclear force

26. A woman whose mass is 60 kg on the earth surface is in a spacecraft at an altitude of two times the earth radius. Her mass there is:

   (a)   6.7 kg   (b)   15 kg

   (c)   20 kg   (d)   60 kg

27. If a liquid is heated in space under no gravity, the transfer of heat will take place by process of:

   (a)   Conduction   (b)   Convection

   (c)   Radiation   (d)   None of these

28. Boyle's law holds for an ideal gas during?

   (a)   Isobaric changes   (b)   Isothermal changes

   (c)   Isochoric changes   (d)   Adiabatic process

29. Which of the following substances has the least thermal conductivity?

   (a)   Water   (b)   Air

   (c)   Mercury   (d)   Brass

30. What is the relationship between the Celsius and Fahrenheit scale?

   (a) $C = \frac{9}{5}(F - 32)$ (b) $C = \frac{5}{9}(F - 32)$

   (c) $C = 5(F - 32)$ (d) $C = 9(F - 32)$

31. Which of the following is a thermodynamics law?

   (a)   Zeroth law of thermodynamics

   (b)   Faraday's Law of thermodynamics

   (c)   Ideal Gas Law of thermodynamics

   (d)   Boyle's Law of thermodynamics

32. Which of the following laws was expressed by Nernst?

   (a)   The first law of thermodynamics

   (b)   The second law of thermodynamics

   (c)   Third law of thermodynamics

   (d)   None of the above

33. The coolant in a chemical or a nuclear plant (i.e., the liquid used to prevent the different parts of a plant from getting too hot) should have:

   (a)   Low specific heat   (b)   High specific heat

   (c)   High Latent heat   (d)   None of the above

34. An electric heater supplies heat to a system at a rate of $100W$. If the system performs work at a rate of 75 Joules per second. At what rate is the internal energy increasing?

   (a) $25W$ (b) $20W$

   (c) $15W$ (d) $35W$

35. Two gases A and B have equal pressure P, temperature T, and volume V. The two gases are mixed together and the resulting mixture has the same temperature T and volume V as before. The ratio of pressure exerted by the mixture to either of the two gases is:

   (a) $1 : 1$ (b) $2 : 1$

   (c) $3 : 1$ (d) $1 : 2$

36. An ideal gas at $27°C$ is compressed adiabatically to $\frac{8}{27}$ of its original volume. The rise in its temperature is: $\left(\gamma = \frac{5}{3}\right)$

   (a) $225°C$ (b) $375°C$

   (c) $400°C$ (d) $450°C$

37. In a certain region of space there are only 5 molecules/cm^3 on an average. The temperature there is 3 K. The pressure of this dilute gas is $\left(k = 1.38 \times 10^{-23}\,\text{JK}^{-1}\right)$:

   (a) $20.7 \times 10^{-17}\,\text{Nm}^{-2}$ (b) $15.3 \times 10^{-13}\,\text{Nm}^{-1}$

   (c) $2.3 \times 10^{-10}\,\text{Nm}^{-1}$ (d) $3.5 \times 10^{-8}\,\text{Nm}^{-1}$

38. Two gases-argon (atomic radius 0.07 nm, atomic

weight 40) and xenon (atomic radius 0.1 nm, atomic weight 140) have the same number density and are at the same temperature. The ratio of their respective mean free times is closest to:

(a) 3.67 (b) 1.83
(c) 1.09 (d) 4.67

39. At what temperature is the root mean square speed of an atom in an argon gas cylinder equal to the r.m.s speed of a helium gas atom at -20^0C ? Given Atomic Mass is $Ar = 39.9$ and $He = 4.0$?

(a) $2523.7K$ (b) $2423.7K$
(c) $2223.7K$ (d) $3023.7K$

40. Two pendulums oscillate with a constant phase difference of 90°. If the time period of one of them is 2 sec., then the period of the other is:

(a) 2 sec (b) 4 sec
(c) 1 sec (d) 6 sec

41. Through which mode of propagation the radio waves can be sent from one place to another?

(a) Space wave propagation
(b) Sky wave propagation
(c) Ground wave propagation
(d) All of the above

42. Two sound waves traveling in the same direction, if the ratio of the average power and wavelength transmitted by both the waves is $1 : 2$, then the ratio of the amplitude of the pressure is ___.

(a) 1 (b) 2
(c) 4 (d) $\frac{1}{2}$

43. A ball of radius ' r ' is made to oscillate in a bowl of radius ' R '. The time period of its oscillation will be $(R > r)$:

(a) $2\pi\sqrt{\frac{r}{g}}$ (b) $2\pi\sqrt{\frac{R}{g}}$
(c) $2\pi\sqrt{\frac{R-r}{g}}$ (d) $2\pi\sqrt{\frac{R+r}{g}}$

44. Equation of motion of a particle is given by $a = -bx$, where a is the acceleration, x is the displacement from the mean position and b any constant. The time period of the particle is:

(a) $2\sqrt{\frac{\pi}{b}}$ (b) $\frac{2\pi}{b}$
(c) $\frac{2\pi}{\sqrt{b}}$ (d) $2\pi\sqrt{b}$

45. When the light pieces of paper which do not have any charge are kept close to a negatively charged comb, then there will be:

(a) Attraction (b) Repulsion
(c) No force (d) None of the above

46. Two small charged spheres A and B have charges $10\mu C$ and $940\mu C$, respectively, and are held at a separation of 90 cm from each other. At what distance from A would the electric intensity be zero?

(a) 22.5 cm (b) 18 cm
(c) 36 cm (d) 30 cm

47. Five identical charges R are placed equidistant on a semicircle as shown in the figure. Another point charge q is kept at the center of the circle of radius R . Calculate the electrostatic force experienced by the charge q .

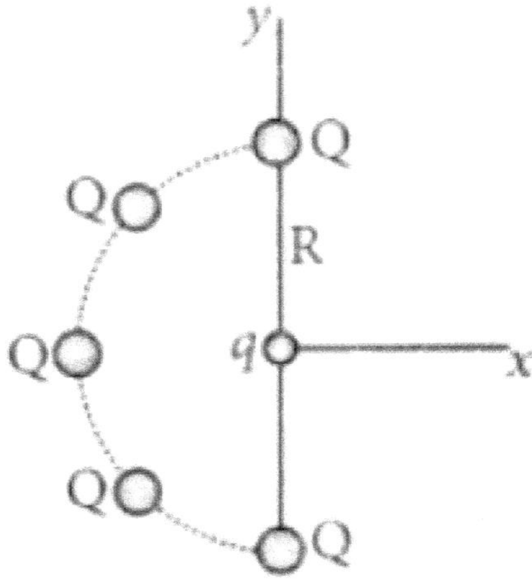

(a) $\vec{F} = \frac{1}{2\pi\varepsilon_0}\frac{qQ}{R^4}(1+\sqrt{2})N\hat{i}$

(b) $\vec{F} = \frac{1}{8\pi\varepsilon_0}\frac{qQ}{R^4}(1+\sqrt{4})N\hat{i}$

(c) $\vec{F} = \frac{1}{4\pi\varepsilon_0}\frac{qQ}{R^2}(1+\sqrt{2})N\hat{i}$

(d) $\vec{F} = \frac{1}{2\pi\varepsilon_0}\frac{qQ}{R^2}(1+\sqrt{4})N\hat{i}$

48. Consider two point charges q_1 and q_2 at rest as shown in the figure.

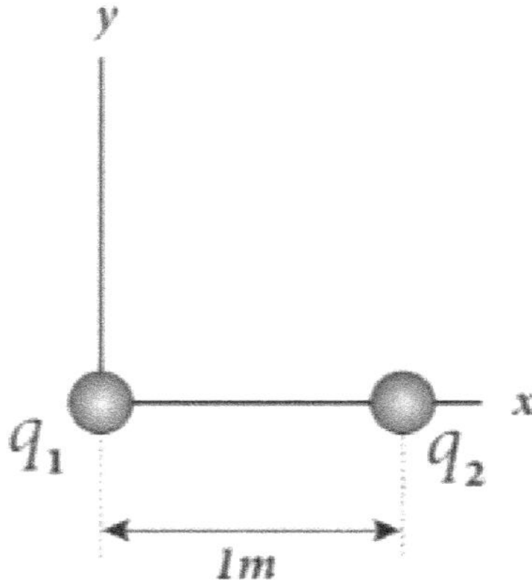

They are separated by a distance of 1 m . Calculate the force experienced by the two charges for the following case: $q_1 = +2\mu C$ and $q_2 = +3\mu C$

(a) $\vec{F}_{12} = -54 \times 10^{-3}\ N\hat{i}$
(b) $\vec{F}_{12} = -52 \times 10^{-5}\ N\hat{i}$
(c) $\vec{F}_{12} = -53 \times 10^{-4}\ N\hat{i}$
(d) $\vec{F}_{12} = -51 \times 10^{-3}\ N\hat{i}$

49. The electrostatic force between charges of $200\mu C$ and $500\mu C$ placed in free space is $5gf$. Find the distance between the two charges. Take $g = 10ms^{-2}$.

(a) 2.35×10^3 m (b) 1.34×10^3 m
(c) 1.34×10^2 m (d) 2.34×10^2 m

50. Calculate the force between an alpha particle and a proton separated by 5.12×10^{-15} m.

(a) 11.5 N (b) 15.5 N
(c) 17.5 N (d) 20.5 N

51. Which of the following effect is not related to the electromagnetic waves?

(a) Doppler effect   (b) Magnus effect
(c) Interference   (d) Diffraction

52. Which one of the following is the correct expression for displacement current (i_d) ?

(a) $i_d = \mu_0 \dfrac{d\phi_E}{dt}$

(b) $i_d = c^2 \dfrac{d\phi_E}{dt}$

(c) $i_d = \epsilon_0 \dfrac{d\phi_E}{dt}$

(d) None of the mentioned

53. A lens of large focal length and large aperture is best suited as an objective of an astronomical telescope since:

(a) A large aperture contributes to the quality and visibility of the images.

(b) A large area of the objective ensures better light gathering power.

(c) A large aperture provides a better resolution.

(d) All of the above

54. A convex lens 'A' of focal length 20 cm and a concave lens 'B' of focal length 5 cm are kept along the same axis with a distance 'd' between them. If a parallel beam of light falling on 'A' leaves 'B' as a parallel beam, then the distance 'd' in cm will be:

(a) 30   (b) 25
(c) 15   (d) 50

55. Find the value of the angle of emergence from the prism. Refractive index of the glass is $\sqrt{3}$.

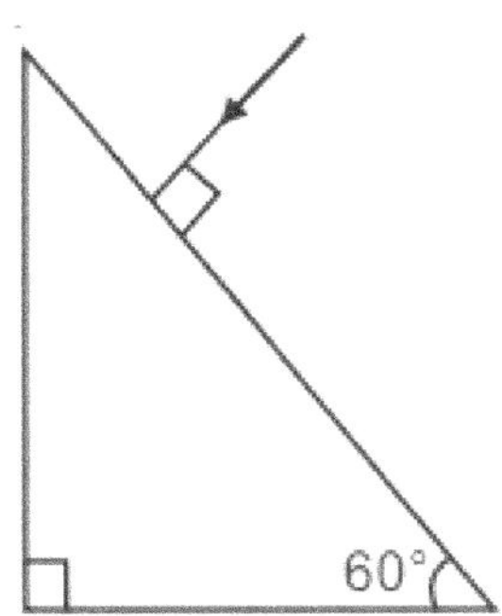

(a) 90°   (b) 60°
(c) 30°   (d) 45°

56. An equilateral triangular prism is made of glass $(\mu = 1.5)$. A ray of light is incident normally on one of its faces. The angle between the incident and emergent rays is:

(a) 180°   (b) 120°
(c) 60°   (d) 30°

57. Two identical coherent waves of intensity I_0 are superimposed at a point. If the resultant intensity at this point is three times of I_0 then find the phase difference between the two waves at this point.

(a) $\dfrac{\pi}{6}$ (b) $\dfrac{\pi}{4}$

(c) $\dfrac{\pi}{3}$ (d) None of these

58. A source emitting wavelengths 480 nm and 600 nm is used in Young's Double Slit Experiment. The separation between the slits is 0.25 mm. The interference is observed 1.5 m away from the slits. The linear separation between first maxima of the two wavelengths is :

(a) 0.72 mm   (b) 0.62 mm
(c) 0.76 mm   (d) 0.27 mm

59. Two waves having their intensities in the ratio of 9 : 1 produce interference. In the interference pattern, the ratio of maximum to minimum intensity is equal to:

(a) $\dfrac{4}{1}$ (b) $\dfrac{8}{4}$

(c) $\dfrac{2}{3}$ (d) $\dfrac{1}{2}$

60. The surface of a metal is illuminated with the light of 400 nm . The kinetic energy of the ejected photoelectrons was found to be 1.68eV . The work function of the metal is: $(hc = 1240\,\text{eVnm})$

(a) 3.09eV   (b) 1.42eV
(c) 1.51eV   (d) 1.68eV

61. When the wavelength of radiation falling on a metal is changed from 500 nm to 200 nm , the maximum kinetic energy of the photoelectrons becomes three times larger. The work function of the metal is close to:

(a) 0.62eV   (b) 0.52eV
(c) 0.81eV   (d) 1.02eV

62. What will be the kinetic energy of an electron having de-Broglie wavelength 2 Å?

(a) 37.5 eV   (b) 75 eV
(c) 150 eV   (d) 300 eV

63. Dual behaviour of matter proposed by de Broglie led to the discovery of electron microscope often used for the highly magnified images of biological molecules and other types of material. If the velocity of the electron in this microscope is $1.6 \times 10^{6}\,\text{ms}^{-1}$, calculate de Broglie wavelength associated with this electron.

(a) 4.55×10^{-10} m   (b) 4×10^{-10} m
(c) 6.5×10^{-10} m   (d) 4.55×10^{-12} m

64. Ratio of energies of two photons whose wavelengths are 600 Å and 400Å is:

(a) 2 : 3   (b) 3 : 2
(c) 1 : 5   (d) 5 : 1

65. Which curve may represent the speed of the electron in a Hydrogen atom as a function of the principal quantum number n ?

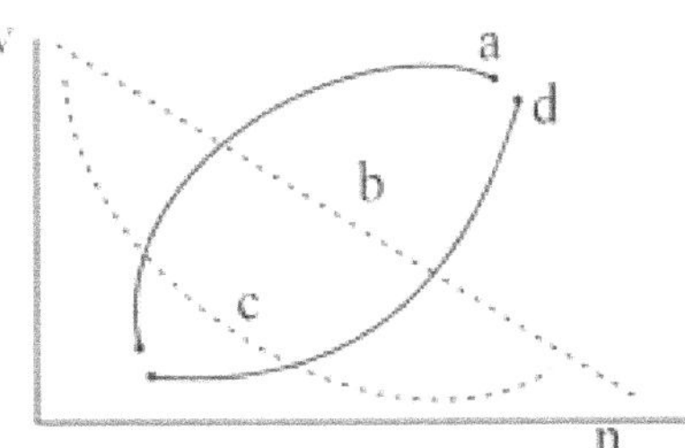

(a) a   (b) b
(c) c   (d) d

66. The rest mass of the photon is:

(a) 0
(b) ∞
(c) Between 0 and ∞
(d) Equal to that of an electron

67. The ratio of the specific charge of an α -particle to that of a proton is:

(a) $2:1$

(b) $1:1$

(c) $1:2$

(d) $1:3$

68. The first line of the Lyman series in a hydrogen spectrum has a wavelength of 1210 Å. The corresponding line of a hydrogenlike atom of $Z = 11$ is equal to:

(a) 4000 Å

(b) 100 Å

(c) 40 Å

(d) 10 Å

69. Which of the following option is incorrect regarding insulator?

(a) Low conductivity

(b) Large forbidden gap

(c) Very high resistivity

(d) Positive temperature coefficient

70. A semiconductor in its purest form is known as __________.

(a) Super conductor

(b) Extrinsic semiconductor

(c) Insulator

(d) Intrinsic semiconductor

71. What are the charge carriers in semiconductors?

(a) Electrons and holes

(b) Electrons

(c) Holes

(d) Charges

72. A forward biased PN junction diode has a resistance of the order of:

(a) Ω

(b) $k\Omega$

(c) $M\Omega$

(d) None of the above

73.

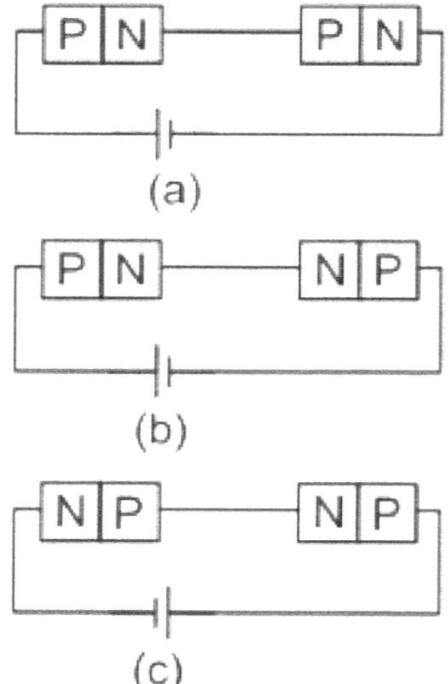

In the given circuits (a), (b) and (c), the potential drop across the two p-n junctions are equal in:

(a) Circuit (c) only

(b) Both circuits (a) and (c)

(c) Circuit (a) only

(d) Circuit (b) only

74. Steel and Copper wires of same length are stretched by the same weight one after the other. Young's modulus of Steel and Copper are $2.0 \times 10^{11} N/m^2$ and $1.2 \times 10^{11} N/m^2$. The ratio of increase in lengths will be:

(a) $\frac{2}{5}$

(b) $\frac{3}{5}$

(c) $\frac{5}{4}$

(d) $\frac{5}{2}$

75. **Direction:** Given below are two statements: One is labelled as Assertion (A) and the other is labelled as Reason (R).

Assertion (A):
The stretching of a spring is determined by the shear modulus of the material of the spring.

Reason (R):
A coil spring of copper has more tensile strength than a steel spring of same dimensions.

In the light of the above statements, choose the most appropriate answer from the options given below:

(a) (A) is true but (R) is false

(b) (A) is false but (R) is true

(c) Both (A) and (R) are true and (R) is the correct explanation of (A)

(d) Both (A) and (R) are true and (R) is not the correct explanation of (A)

76. An open-ended U-tube of uniform cross-sectional area contains water (density 10^3 kg m^{-3}) Initially the water level stands at 0.29 m from the bottom in each arm. Kerosene oil (a water-immiscible liquid) of density 800 kg m^{-3} added to the left arm until its length is 0.1 m , as shown in the schematic figure below. The ratio $\left(\frac{h_1}{h_2} \right)$ of the heights of the liquid in the two arms is:

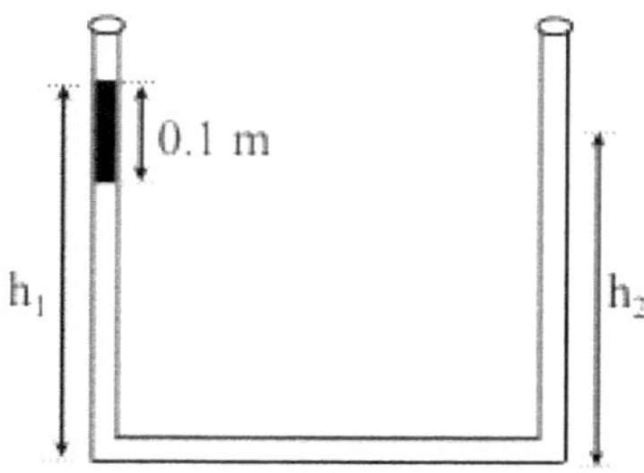

(a) $\frac{15}{14}$

(b) $\frac{35}{33}$

(c) $\frac{7}{6}$

(d) $\frac{5}{4}$

77. A metallic square plate EFGH is suspended vertically with a pair of sides horizontal by a light inelastic string (shown in the figure). A beaker of the water is brought below the plate and raised till the plate is completely immersed and the level of the water is above the plate. If the point of support is slowly raised vertically at a constant velocity, the graph of tension T in the string against the displacement s of the point support is represented by:

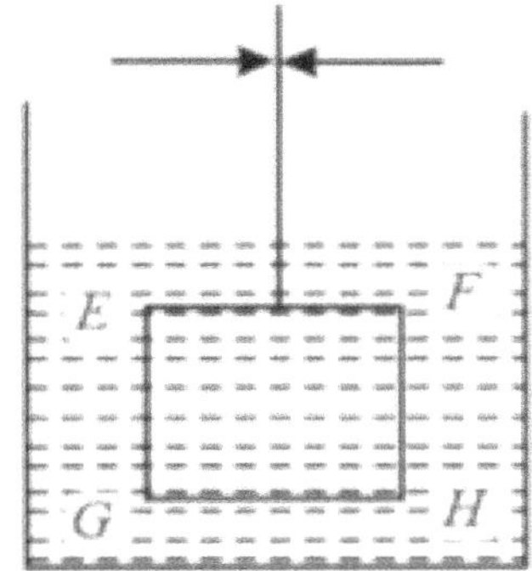

(a)

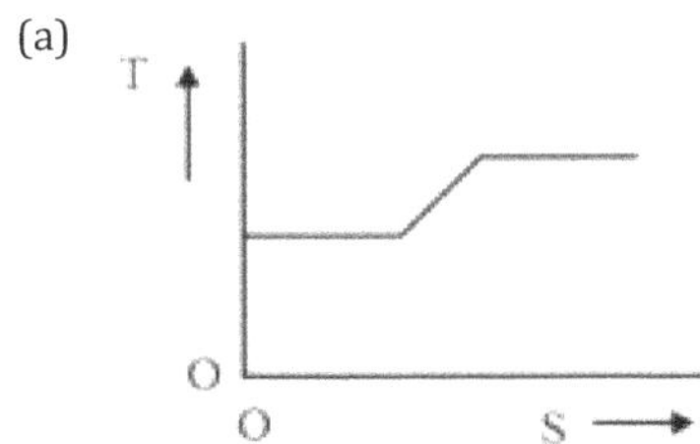

(b)

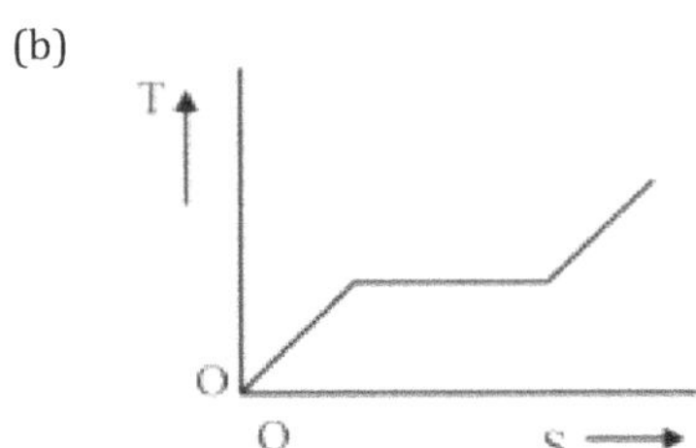

(c)

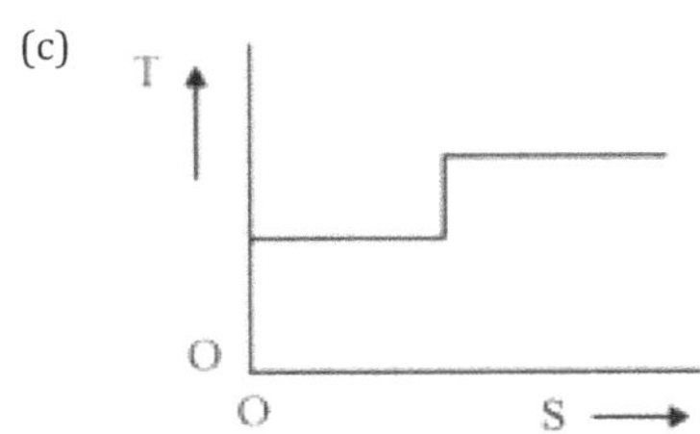

(d)

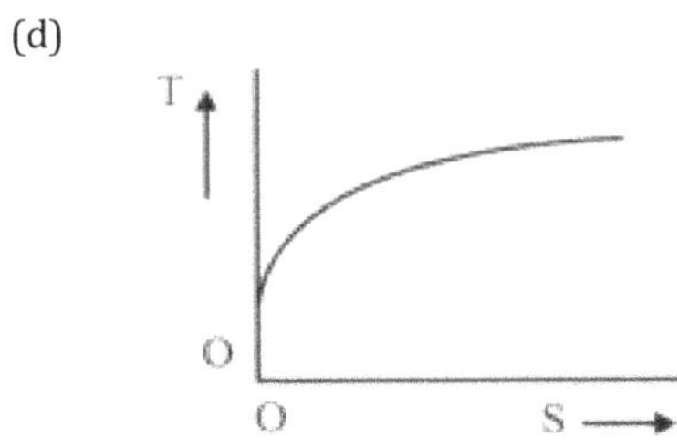

78. The velocity of a small ball of mass M and density d, when dropped in a container filled with glycerine becomes constant after some time. If the density of glycerine is $\frac{d}{2}$, then the viscous force acting on the ball will be:

(a) 2Mg

(b) $\frac{Mg}{2}$

(c) Mg

(d) $\frac{3}{2}Mg$

79. With the increasing molecular mass of a liquid, the viscosity:

(a) Decreases

(b) Increase

(c) Not affected

(d) None of these

80. A spherical ball is dropped in a long column of a highly viscous liquid. The curve in the graph shown, which represents the speed of the ball (v) as a function of time (t) is:

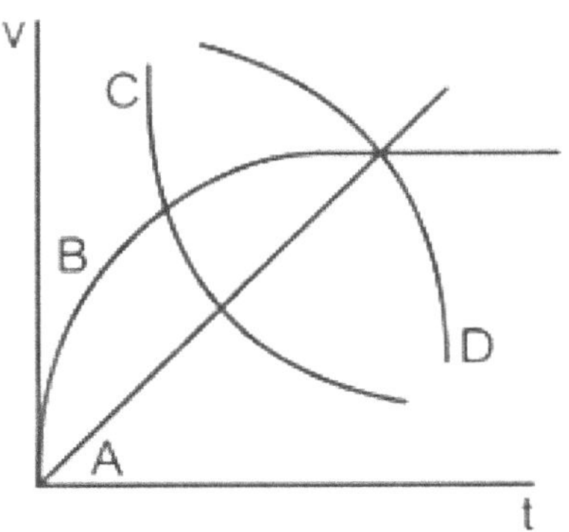

(a) C

(b) D

(c) A

(d) B

// Smart Answer Sheet //

Correct — Percentage of students who answered correctly.

Skipped — Percentage of students who skipped.

Q.	Ans.	Correct / Skipped	Q.	Ans.	Correct / Skipped	Q.	Ans.	Correct / Skipped
1	B	31.84% / 3.59%	2	B	82.88% / 0.0%	3	C	65.58% / 1.43%
4	B	68.72% / 1.2%	5	A	31.23% / 4.38%	6	B	83.2% / 0.0%
7	C	76.49% / 0.0%	8	A	64.02% / 1.23%	9	D	66.38% / 1.67%
10	A	88.83% / 0.0%	11	C	29.08% / 3.78%	12	D	81.95% / 0.0%
13	C	80.47% / 0.0%	14	A	15.51% / 4.75%	15	C	89.94% / 0.0%
16	C	62.07% / 1.69%	17	D	68.37% / 1.82%	18	D	11.08% / 4.24%
19	A	52.44% / 1.99%	20	D	51.89% / 1.47%	21	D	55.82% / 1.45%
22	B	83.27% / 0.0%	23	C	53.64% / 1.08%	24	D	40.22% / 1.63%
25	A	81.75% / 0.0%	26	D	13.22% / 3.11%	27	C	47.24% / 1.74%
28	B	87.31% / 0.0%	29	B	84.83% / 0.0%	30	B	76.29% / 0.0%
31	A	78.37% / 0.0%	32	C	68.82% / 1.09%	33	B	68.28% / 1.75%
34	A	83.14% / 0.0%	35	B	80.79% / 0.0%	36	B	47.06% / 1.78%
37	A	43.71% / 1.41%	38	C	53.73% / 1.1%	39	A	40.14% / 1.63%
40	A	58.16% / 1.02%	41	D	20.79% / 3.37%	42	A	26.82% / 4.0%
43	C	59.57% / 1.77%	44	C	62.69% / 1.0%	45	A	51.56% / 1.4%
46	D	48.44% / 1.04%	47	C	10.08% / 3.19%	48	A	63.66% / 1.55%
49	C	88.11% / 0.0%	50	C	45.81% / 1.28%	51	B	42.71% / 1.97%
52	C	79.81% / 0.0%	53	D	44.7% / 1.97%	54	C	50.81% / 1.28%
55	B	46.46% / 1.96%	56	C	67.96% / 1.14%	57	C	22.58% / 3.37%
58	A	67.27% / 1.05%	59	A	58.35% / 1.57%	60	B	81.02% / 0.0%

61	A	59.76% 1.41%	62	A	58.35% 1.77%	63	A	56.04% 1.43%
64	A	67.96% 1.5%	65	C	61.39% 1.84%	66	A	77.33% 0.0%
67	C	46.75% 1.46%	68	D	13.7% 4.3%	69	D	82.84% 0.0%
70	D	56.42% 1.26%	71	A	41.32% 1.16%	72	A	87.56% 0.0%
73	B	61.5% 1.15%	74	B	45.34% 1.47%	75	A	44.44% 1.16%
76	B	41.46% 1.88%	77	A	67.2% 1.76%	78	B	53.63% 1.01%
79	B	77.03% 0.0%	80	D	42.08% 1.95%			

// Hints and Solutions //

1(B). The amplitude of torque is as follows,

$$\Rightarrow [T] = [M^1 L^2 T^{-2}]$$

The dimension of the work is as follows,

$$\Rightarrow [T] = [M^1 L^2 T^{-2}]$$

The amplitude of the momentum is as follows,

$$\Rightarrow [T] = [M^1\, L^1\, T^{-1}]$$

From the above explanation, it is clear that torque and work have same dimension but momentum has a different dimension.

2(B). Time Standard is a specification for measuring time. It can be classified as the rate at which time is spent. At the present time, we use the atomic standard of time. The periodic vibrations produced in the cesium atom form the basis of the atomic standard of time. Just as the vibrations of the balance wheel control an ordinary wristwatch, the vibrations of the cesium atom control the rate of this cesium atomic clock. In the cesium atomic clock, one second is taken as the time required for $9,192,631,770$ vibrations of radiation to pass between two very fine levels of the basic state of the cesium-133 atom. This is called the cesium clock or atomic clock.

3(C). Given,

Measurement of the diameter of hydrogen atom,

$$d = 1.06 \times 10^{-10}$$

Least count, $\Delta d = 0.01 \times 10^{-10}$

$$\text{Accuracy} = \frac{\text{Least count}}{\text{Orginal measurement}}$$

$$= \frac{\Delta d}{d}$$

$$= \frac{0.01 \times 10^{-10}}{1.06 \times 10^{-10}}$$

$$= \frac{1}{106}$$

4(B). The parallax method is used to determine large distances, such as the distance from Earth to a planet or a star. Parallax is the projected shift in the position of one object with respect to another when we move the point observation slant. The distance between two points of observation is called the base (b). The distance of the object from the two points of view is D. The angle between the two directions along which the object is viewed is the parallax angle or displacement angle (θ).

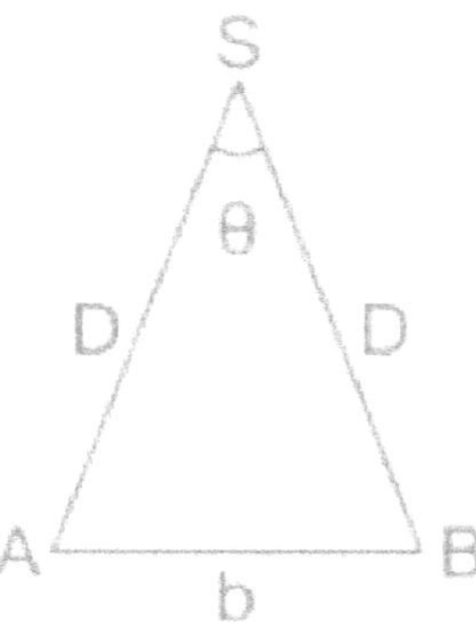

If S is the position of the object and AB is the two points of observation,

$$\theta = \frac{b}{D}$$

The triangulation method finds the angles in a triangle formed by three observation points. The other distances in a triangle are calculated using trigonometry and the measured length of just one side. It is used for geographic measurement and not astronomical distance.

The echo method uses the principle of reflection of sound or light. Knowing the speed of the wave and the time of reflection back to the source, the distance between the two points is calculated. This is not a very accurate method and therefore astronomical distances cannot be relied upon.

5(A). As we know that the equation of motion for the tth second is written as;

$$S_t = u + \frac{1}{2}g(2t - 1)$$

Here S is the distance, u is the initial velocity, a is the acceleration and t is the time.

According to the tth second, the equation of motion is

$$S_t = u + \frac{1}{2}g(2t - 1) \quad \cdots (1)$$

Here the initial velocity of the freely falling body is equal to zero, i.e. $u = 0$

$$S_t = 0 + \frac{1}{2}\,g(2t - 1)$$

$$\Rightarrow S_t = \frac{1}{2}\,g(2t - 1) \cdots (2)$$

Now for $t = 1$ second,

$$S_1 = \frac{1}{2}\,g(2 - 1)$$

$$\Rightarrow S_1 = \frac{1}{2}\,g \quad \cdots (3)$$

For $t = 2$ seconds,

$$S_2 = \frac{1}{2}\,g(4 - 1)$$

$$\Rightarrow S_2 = \frac{3}{2}\,g \quad \cdots (4)$$

Now for $t = 3$ seconds,

$$S_3 = \frac{1}{2}g(6 - 1)$$

$$\Rightarrow S_3 = \frac{5}{2}\,g \quad \cdots (5)$$

For $t = 4$ seconds,

$$S_3 = \frac{1}{2}\,g(8 - 1)$$

$$\Rightarrow S_3 = \frac{7}{2}\,g \quad \cdots (6)$$

Now to calculate the ratio of the distances traveled by a freely falling body in the $1^{\text{st}}, 2^{\text{nd}}, 3^{\text{rd}}$, and 4th second we divide the equations (3), (4), (5), and (6) we get;

$$S_1 : S_2 : S_3 : S_4 = \frac{1}{2}\,g : \frac{3}{2}\,g : \frac{5}{2}\,g : \frac{7}{2}\,g$$

$$\Rightarrow S_1 : S_2 : S_3 : S_4 = 1 : 3 : 5 : 7$$

6(B). Displacement- time graph is used to express the

displacement of a body with respect to time. The slope of Displacement- time graph is equal to velocity.

Slope $= \tan\theta =$ Velocity

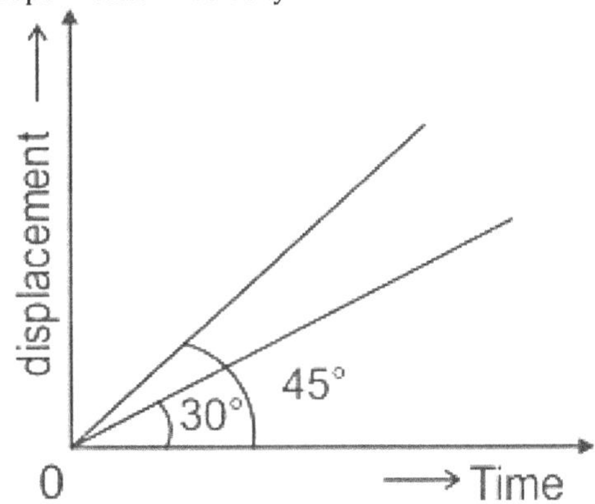

Angle made by first body, $\theta_1 = 30°$

Velocity of first body, $v_1 = \tan\theta_1 = \tan 30° = \dfrac{1}{\sqrt{3}}$

Angle made by second body, $\theta_2 = 45°$

Velocity of second body, $v_2 = \tan\theta_2 = \tan 45° = 1$

Ratio of Velocity $= \dfrac{v_1}{v_2} = \dfrac{\frac{1}{\sqrt{3}}}{1} = 1 : \sqrt{3}$

7(C). As,

$h = ut + \frac{1}{2}gt^2$

Here, $u = 0, g = 10ms^{-2}, t = 4s$

$\therefore h = 0 \times 4 + \frac{1}{2} \times 10 \times 4^2 = 80$ m

8(A). Given the length of the string is 80 cm $= 0.8$ m

It makes 14 revolutions in 25sec

Frequency is defined as the number of events that are occurring ina given period of time. Its formula is

f = No. of revolutions / time

Frequency of the string will be f $= \dfrac{14}{25}$

Now,

Angular speed is defined as the rate of change of angular displacement. In one rotation, angular distance is 2π and the time period is T

Angular speed is given by formula

$\Rightarrow \omega = \dfrac{2\pi}{t}$

We know that,

$\frac{1}{t} = $ f

$\Rightarrow \omega = 2 \times \pi \times$ f

Where ω is the angular speed f is the frequency

Substituting values in the above formula,

$\Rightarrow \omega = 2\pi \times \dfrac{14}{25}$

$\Rightarrow \omega = \dfrac{28\pi}{25}$ rad/sec

Also acceleration of a rotating body is given by

$a = \omega^2 r$

ω is the angular speed of the stone

r is the radius

$\Rightarrow a = 0.8 \times \left(\dfrac{28\pi}{25}\right)^2$

$\Rightarrow a = 0.8 \times \dfrac{784 \times 9.859}{625} = \dfrac{6183.564}{625}$

$\Rightarrow a = 9.89$ m/s^2

So The magnitude of the acceleration of the stone is 9.89 m/s^2 .

9(D). The projectiles' velocity has only a horizontal component at first, and the vertical component is zero. The bullets, on the other hand, have a downward acceleration, making their route semi-parabolic. As a result of their vertically downward

acceleration owing to gravity, both bullets will impact the ground.

There is no vertical component to velocity, only a horizontal component.The bullets are the same height because they are fired horizontally from the same location. Time is calculated using the formula:

$T = \sqrt{\dfrac{2h}{g}}$

Both bullets will hit the ground at the same time since their acceleration (g) is the same.As a result, the time it takes for the bullets to reach the ground is unaffected by their starting horizontal speed. As a result, both bullets fired in the horizontal direction from the same height will hit the ground at the same time.

10(A). The net acceleration of a particle in a circular motion is towards the centre only if its speed is constant. In uniform circular motion, the velocity vector changes at every instant of time, that is the direction of the velocity changes since it is tangent to the path. The circular motion is caused by the centripetal acceleration whose direction is towards the centre of the circular motion.

11(C). Free body diagram is given as,

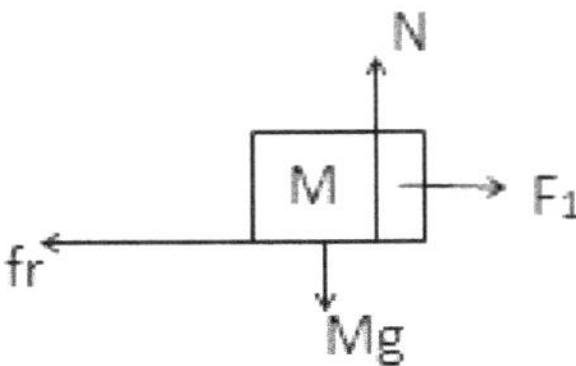

If $F_1 = 0$

So contact force will only have Normal which is equal to Mg .

So F will be Mg .

Now as F_1 increases f_r keeps increasing till it reaches limiting value i.e., $\mu N = \mu mg$.

So, in that case, contact force F will be,

$\sqrt{N^2 + f_r^2} = \sqrt{(Mg)^2 + (\mu Mg)^2}$

$F = Mg\sqrt{1 + \mu^2}$

This means contact force F will lie between $Mg \le F \le Mg\sqrt{1 + \mu^2}$.

12(D). The heavier the object is harder to move it or the greater the amount of force required to move it hence higher the inertia. Since higher mass has higher inertia. In all the above four options, a cricket ball has maximum mass so it will have maximum inertia.

According to Newton's first law of motion, an object will remain at rest or in uniform motion in a straight line unless acted upon by an external force. The inertia of rest: When a body is in rest, it will remain at rest until we apply an external force to move it. This property is called inertia of rest.

The inertia of motion: When a body is in a uniform motion, it will remain in motion until we apply an external force to stop it. This property is called inertia of motion.

13(C). Given,

Mass of the body, $m = 20$ g $= 0.02 kg$

Acceleration, $a = 5.0$ cm/s$^2 = 0.05 m/s^2$

As we know,

$F = ma$

$= 0.02 \times 0.05$

$= 1 \times 10^{-3}$ N

14(A). Free body diagram of the system when the weight is at one of the end of board,

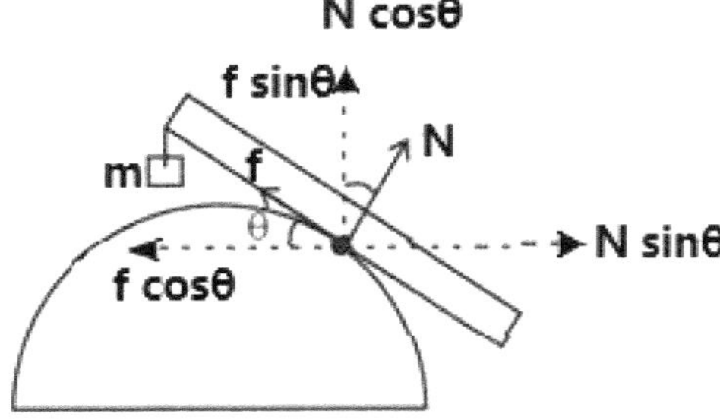

Now, as the net force on board is zero.
Net horizontal force $= 0$
$f\cos\theta - N sin\theta = 0$
$f = N tan\theta \ldots (1)$
As we know, frictional force is
$f = \mu N \ldots (2)$
From equation (1) and (2), we get
$\mu = \tan\theta$

15(C). The capacity to do work or power consumed in a given time is called energy. Power is the rate of doing work or the rate at which energy is spent. Kilowatt-hour is the unit of energy.

16(C). Given,
Work done $= W = 260\,J$
Power $= P = 10\,W$
Power is the rate of doing work,
$P = \dfrac{W}{t}$
or, $t = \dfrac{W}{P} = \dfrac{260}{10} = 26\,sec$
Therefore, the time needed to perform 260 J of work at the rate of 10 W is 26 s.

17(D). An electric generator is a device that is used to convert mechanical energy into electric energy. It is also known as a dynamo. An electric generator works on the Electromagnetic Induction Principle. The Principle of Electromagnetic Induction states that when a conductor is connected with a changing flux, it will induce an emf across it. The value of induced emf across the conductor depends on the rate of change of flux connected with the conductor.
An electric generator is generated by rotating a coil inside a magnetic field. When A coil is rotated in a magnetic field by magnetic energy, magnetic flux is changed through the coil and so, EMF is induced in the coil that produces current. So, Electric energy is generated.

18(D). 1 Unit of electricity $= 1kWh = 1000Watt-$ hour
$= 3.6 \times 10^6 J$
1 Kilo-watt $= 1000Watt$
$100W = 0.1kW \quad [\because 1kW = 1000W]$
In 30 days total consumption of the bulb $= 0.1kW \times 30$ days $\times 5$ hours / day $= 15kWh$
Given, cost of 1 unit $= 75$ paise
So total expenditure $= 75 \times 15 = 1125$ paise = Rs. 11.25

19(A). As the c.m. of three particles is at $2, 2, 2$
$\therefore$ The total mass $= 1 + 2 + 3 = 6$ kg
Now consider the 4 kg mass at the position (x, y, z)
Now centre of mass of total system at $0, 0, 0$
$\therefore \dfrac{6\times 2 + 4x}{10} = 0$
$\Rightarrow 12 = -4x$

$\Rightarrow x = -3$
Similarly, $\dfrac{6\times 2 + 4y}{12} = 0$
$\Rightarrow y = -3$
Similarly, $\dfrac{6\times 2 + 4z}{12} = 0$
$\Rightarrow z = -3$
From the above we can conclude that
$x = -3, y = -3, z = -3$

20(D). The radius of gyration is defined as the square root of the ratio of moment of inertia and mass and it is written as;
$k = \sqrt{\dfrac{I}{m}} \quad \cdots (1)$
Here k is the radius of gyration, I is the moment of inertia and m is the mass.
The figure of a thin uniform disc and disc is shown below;

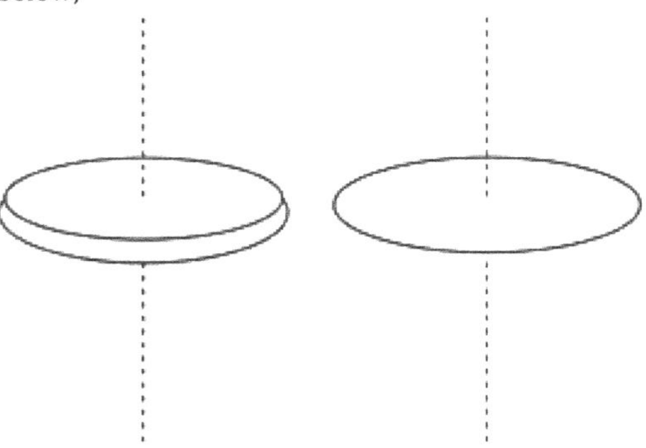

The radius of gyration of a thin uniform disc,
$k = \sqrt{\dfrac{I}{m}}$ and moment of inertia of the disc,
$I = \dfrac{mR^2}{4}$
Here we have R as the radius, m is the mass
Now, on putting the values in equation (1) we have;
The radius of gyration of the uniform disc;
$k_1 = \sqrt{\dfrac{\frac{mR^2}{2}}{m}}$
$k_1 = \sqrt{\dfrac{R^2}{2}} \quad \cdots (2)$
and the radius of gyration of the uniform disc;
$k_2 = \sqrt{\dfrac{mR^2}{4}}$
$k_2 = \sqrt{\dfrac{R^2}{4}} \quad \cdots (3)$
Now, on dividing equation (2) by equation (3) we have;
$\dfrac{k_1}{k_2} = \dfrac{\sqrt{\frac{R^2}{2}}}{\sqrt{\frac{R^2}{4}}}$
$\Rightarrow k_1 : k_2 = \sqrt{2} : 1$

21(D). Let a system of two particles of masses M_1 and M_2 located at points A and B respectively. Let X_1 and X_2 be the position of the particles relative to a fixed origin O. The position X of the center of mass of the system can be calculated using the formula:
Center of mass, $X = \dfrac{M_1 X_1 + M_2 X_2}{M_1 + M_2}$ ....(1)
Given,
$M_1 = 10\,kg, M_2 = 20\,kg$,
Length of rod $= 10\,m$
Let M_1 is at origin, then X_1 and X_2 is 0 and $10\,m$ respectively.
Putting the values in equation (1) we get,

$$X = \frac{10 \times 0 + 20 \times 10}{10 + 20} = \frac{200}{30} = \frac{20}{3}$$

Distance of the center of mass of the system from the 10 kg mass is $\frac{20}{3} m$.

22(B). Critical velocity of a satellite is the constant horizontal velocity given to the satellite to keep it in a stable orbit.

Critical velocity is defined as the speed at which a falling object reaches when both gravity and air resistance are equalized on the object. The other way of defining critical velocity is the speed and direction at which the fluid can flow through a conduit without becoming turbulent.

23(C). Two objects of different masses falling freely near the surface of moon would have same velocities at any instant.

When an object is under free fall, its acceleration depends only on the acceleration due to gravity and mass has no role to play. Due to this; irrespective of their masses, the object under free fall with have the same velocity at any instant.

24(D). The distance between two bodies becomes 6 times more than the usual distance. The the F becomes $1/36$ times.

Simply, new force will be reciprocal of square of given new distance. In the above question the distance becomes 6 times therefore, taking square of 6 and reciprocal it which is $1/36$. So, the new force will become $1/36$ times the previous force.

25(A). Gravitational Force is the weakest of all the four fundamental forces but has infinite range. It is always attractive in nature.

The electromagnetic force is the force between two charged particles or two poles of a magnet. It is stronger than Gravitational.

The strong nuclear force is the stronger version of nuclear force. It is the strongest force in nature.

The weak nuclear force is the weak force of attraction between the subatomic particles of the nucleus of an atom. Though the name suggests that it is weak, it is stronger than electromagnetic.

So, the weakest of the four fundamental interactions is the gravitational force.

26(D). The mass of an object will not change if the gravitational pull on the object changes; but the weight of the object will change.

"For instance, if you measure your mass on Earth and then measure your mass on the moon or somewhere else in space, your mass will remain the same."

The mass of a body is constant everywhere in the universe.

So, the mass of this 60 kg woman would be the same on the earth surface as well as in the spacecraft.

27(C). If a liquid is heated in space under no gravity the transfer of heat will take place by process of radiation.

In the case of conduction and convection, the presence of gravity is crucial for these processes to happen.

In the case of radiation, it does not need gravity hence heat transfer can happen only by the process of radiation.

28(B). Boyle's law holds for an ideal gas during isothermal changes.

According to Boyle's law, For a given mass of an ideal gas at a constant temperature, the volume of a gas is inversely proportional to its pressure i.e.

$V \propto \frac{1}{P}$ or $PV = $ constant

$P_1 V_1 = P_2 V_2$

29(B). Air has the least thermal conductivity.

The thermal conductivity of a material is a measure of the ability of the material to conduct heat. A high value for thermal conductivity indicates that the material is a good heat conductor, and a low value indicates that the material is a poor heat conductor or insulator. B rass and mercury are metals so they have a high value of conductivity, whereas air has the least.

i.e., K air $< K$ water $< K$ mercury $< K$ brass

30(B). **Concept:**

Celsius scale:

In this scale, LFP (ice point) is taken $0°$ and UFP (steam point) is taken $100°$. The temperature measured on this scale all in degree Celsius $(°C)$.

Farenheite scale:

This scale of temperature has LFP as $32°F$ and UFP as $212°F$. The change in temperature of $1°F$ corresponds to a change of less than $1°$ on the Celsius scale.

Kelvin scale:

The Kelvin temperature scale is also known as the thermodynamic scale. The triple point of water is also selected to be the zero of the scale of temperature. The temperatures measured on this scale are in Kelvin (K).

All these temperatures are related to each other by the following relationship.

$$\frac{F-32}{9} = \frac{C}{5} = \frac{K-273}{5}$$

Calculation:

Relationship between the Celsius and Fahrenheit scale is:

$$\frac{F-32}{9} = \frac{C}{5}$$

$$\Rightarrow C = \frac{5}{9}(F - 32)$$

31(A). Thermodynamics is primarily based on a set of four rules that are universally applicable when applied to systems that fall within their respective limitations. They are as follows:

- Zeroth law of thermodynamics
- First law of thermodynamics
- Second law of thermodynamics
- Third law of thermodynamics

32(C). The third law was developed by Walther Nernst during the years 1906–12, and is therefore often referred to as Nernst's theorem or Nernst's postulate. The third law of thermodynamics states that the entropy of a system at absolute zero is a well-defined constant. This is because a system at zero temperature exists in its ground state, so that its entropy is determined only by the degeneracy of the ground state.

In 1912 Nernst stated the law thus: "It is impossible for any procedure to lead to the isotherm $T = 0$ in a finite number of steps."

33(B). The coolant in a chemical or nuclear plant must have a high specific heat as it is known that higher the specific heat of the coolant, higher is its heat-absorbing capacity and vice-versa.

Thus, a liquid which has a high specific heat is the best coolant to be utilized in a nuclear or chemical plant. This prevents different parts of the plant from becoming too hot.

34(A). Heat is supplied to the system by an electric heater at a rate of $100W$.
Thus, heat supplied, $Q = 100J/s$
The system operates at a rate of $75J/s$.
Clearly, work done, $W = 75J/s$
Using the first law of thermodynamics,
$Q = U + W$
where,
$U = $ internal energy
$\Rightarrow U = Q - W$
$\Rightarrow U = 100 - 75$
$\Rightarrow U = 25J/s$
$\Rightarrow U = 25W$

35(B). Let P_1 and P_2 be the partial pressures of gases A and B, respectively. Under equal conditions of temperature and volume,
$P_1 = P_2$
Let P be the total pressure exerted by the mixture of two gases A and B. Using Dalton's law of partial pressures,
$P = P_1 + P_2$
$\Rightarrow P = 2P_1$
$\Rightarrow \dfrac{P}{P_1} = \dfrac{2}{1}$
$\Rightarrow P : P_1 = 2 : 1$

36(B). Let initial volume V_1 be V
Given:
Final volume, $V_2 = \dfrac{8}{27}V$
Initial temperature, $T_1 = 273 + 27 = 300K$
$\gamma = \dfrac{5}{3}$
We have to find the rise in temperature, say T_2.
For an adiabatic process:
$TV^{\gamma-1} = $ constant
Thus,
$T_1 V_1^{\gamma-1} = T_2 V_2^{\gamma-1}$
$\Rightarrow T_2 = T_1 \left(\dfrac{V_1}{V_2}\right)^{\gamma-1}$
$\Rightarrow T_2 = 300 \times \left(\dfrac{27}{8}\right)^{\frac{5}{3}-1}$
$\Rightarrow T_2 = 300 \times \left(\dfrac{27}{8}\right)^{\frac{2}{3}}$
$\Rightarrow T_2 = 300 \times \dfrac{9}{4} = 675K$
$\Rightarrow T_2 = 675 - 273 = 402°C$
Rise in temperature $= 402°C - 27°C = 375°C$

37(A). Given,
$\dfrac{n}{V} = 5$ molecules/ cm^3 = 5×10^6/m^3
T = 3 K
$k = 1.38 \times 10^{-23}$ JK^{-1}
From ideal gas equation,
$pV = nkT$
$p = \dfrac{n}{V}kT$
$= \left(5 \times 10^6 /\text{m}^3\right)\left(1.38 \times 10^{-23}/\text{JK}^{-1}\right) \times 3 \text{ K}$
$= 20.7 \times 10^{-17}$ Nm^{-2}

38(C). Mean free path of a gas molecule is given by:
$\lambda = \dfrac{1}{\sqrt{2}\pi d^2 n}$
Here, $n =$ number of collisions per unit volume $d =$ diameter of the molecule
If average speed of molecule is v then
Mean free time, $\tau = \dfrac{\lambda}{v}$

$\Rightarrow \tau = \dfrac{1}{\sqrt{2}\pi n d^2 v} = \dfrac{1}{\sqrt{2}\pi n d^2}\sqrt{\dfrac{M}{3RT}}$
$\left(\because v = \sqrt{\dfrac{3RT}{M}}\right)$
$\therefore \tau \propto \dfrac{\sqrt{M}}{d^2}$ and $\dfrac{\tau_1}{\tau_2} = \dfrac{\sqrt{M_1}}{d_1^2} \times \dfrac{d_2^2}{\sqrt{M_2}}$
$= \sqrt{\dfrac{40}{140}} \times \left(\dfrac{0.1}{0.07}\right)^2 = 1.09$

39(A). Let we know that, Vr.m.s. and V^1 r.m.s. are the root mean square speeds of Argon and helium
We have, Atoms at temperature T and T^1 respectively.
$R = $ Universal Gas constant
$T = $ Temperature
$M = $ Atomic Mass of Gas Now, Vr.m.s. $= \sqrt{\dfrac{3RT}{M}}$
$V^1 r \cdot m.s. = \sqrt{\dfrac{3RT^1}{M^1}}$
Given, $M = $ Mass of Argon $= 39.9$
$M^1 = $ Mass of Helium $= 4.0$
$T^1 = $ Temperature of helium $= -20^0 C$
$T^1 = 273 + (-20) = 253K$
$T = $ Temperature of Argon $= ?$
Now, Vr.m.s. $= V^1 r \cdot m.$
$\sqrt{\dfrac{3RT}{M}} = \sqrt{\dfrac{3RT^1}{M^1}}$
Squaring both side,
$\dfrac{T}{M} = \dfrac{T^1}{M^2} \Rightarrow T = \dfrac{T^1 M}{M^1}$
$T = \dfrac{253 \times 39.9}{4.0} = 2523.7K$

40(A). Two pendulums oscillate with a constant phase difference of $90°$. This can only be possible if their angular velocities and amplitude are the same.
$\omega_1 = \omega_2$, and
$A_1 = A_2$
So, $A_1\omega_1 = A_2\omega_2$
The longer the length of string, the longer the period, or back and forth swing of the pendulum.
The greater the amplitude, or angle, the farther the pendulum falls, the longer the period.
The longer the angular velocity of the pendulum, the shorter the time period.
So, the time period must be equal due to their oscillation in a constant phase difference of $90°$.
Therefore, the time period of the second pendulum must be equal to the first one $= 2$ sec

41(D). Radio Wave Propagation deals with the behavior of radio waves when the waves travel from one end to another. In order for electromagnetic (radio) waves to travel, a transmitting antenna and a receiving antenna is required. The path or mode in which the radio waves follow or can travel is termed radio wave propagation. There are three (3) modes of radio wave propagation as follows:
1. Ground wave or surface wave propagation
2. Space wave and line of sight (LOS) propagation
3. Skywave propagation

42(A). Given:
Average power transmitted, $P_1 : P_2 = 1 : 1$,
Wavelength, $\lambda_1 : \lambda_2 = 1 : 2$
The average power is given by, $P = \dfrac{1}{2}\rho\omega^2 A^2 Sv$
Since the average power transmitted by two waves in a cross section is equal.
$\dfrac{1}{2}\rho\omega_1^2 A_1^2 Sv = \dfrac{1}{2}\rho\omega_2^2 A_2^2 Sv$
$\Rightarrow \omega_1^2 A_1^2 = \omega_2^2 A_2^2$
$\Rightarrow \omega_1 A_1 = \omega_2 A_2$

Or, $\frac{A_1}{A_2} = \frac{\omega_2}{\omega_1}$ .... (1)

The relationship between angular frequency and wavelength is inversely proportional to each other, therefore, $\omega \propto \frac{1}{\lambda}$

$\frac{\omega_1}{\omega_2} = \frac{\lambda_2}{\lambda_1} = \frac{2}{1}$

From equation (1), $\frac{A_1}{A_2} = \frac{1}{2}$

Now, the pressure amplitude, $P = B_0 A K$

$\therefore \frac{P_1}{P_2} = \frac{A_1 \times K_1}{A_2 \times K_2}$

$= \frac{A_1 \times \lambda_2}{A_2 \times \lambda_1}$, यहाँ, $K = \frac{2\pi}{\lambda}$

$\Rightarrow \frac{P_1}{P_2} = \frac{1}{2} \times \frac{2}{1}$

$= 1$

43(C). This system of ball and bowl is similar to the simple pendulum system. The time period of a simple pendulum is given by:

$T = 2\pi\sqrt{\frac{l}{g}}$

Where $l =$ length and $g =$ acceleration due to gravity.

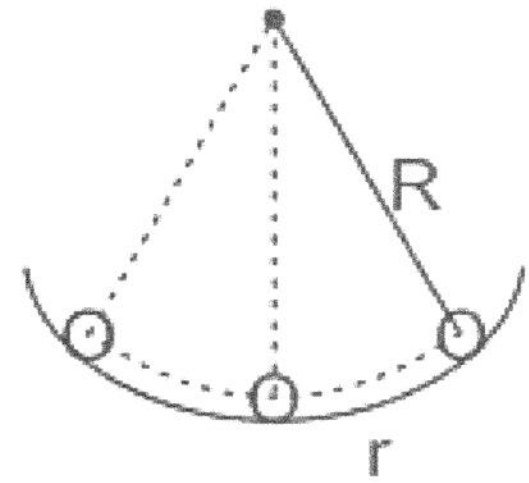

As per the diagram, we can see that the effective length of the system will be

$l_{\text{dff}} = R - r$

Thus the time period will be

$T = 2\pi\sqrt{\frac{l}{g}}$

$T = 2\pi\sqrt{\frac{R-r}{g}}$

44(C). Given:

Equation of motion is $a = -bx$,

Where a is the acceleration, x is the displacement from the mean position, and b any constant.

Compare it with the equation of acceleration

$a = -\omega^2 x$,

$\omega^2 = b$

$\omega = \sqrt{b}$

$T = \frac{2\pi}{\omega}$

$T = \frac{2\pi}{\sqrt{b}}$

45(A). When the light pieces of paper which do not have any charge are kept close to a negatively charged comb, then there will be attraction. A charged body may attract a neutral body. So when the light pieces of paper which do not have any charge are kept close to a negatively charged comb, there will be an attraction.

46(D).

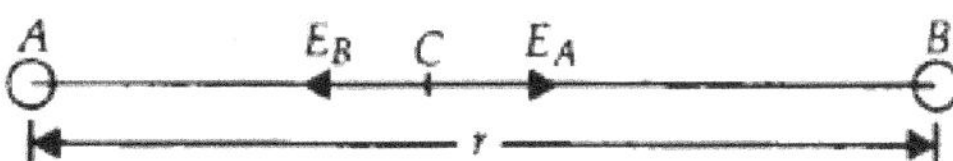

Here, $AB = r = 90$ cm $= 0.9$ m

$q_A = 10\mu C = 10 \times 10^{-6} C$

$q_B = 40\mu C = 40 \times 10^{-6} C$, $AC = ?$

At point C, $E_A = E_B$

$\frac{q_A}{4\pi\varepsilon_0 (AC)^2} = \frac{q_B}{4\pi\varepsilon_0 (BC)^2}$

$\frac{q_A}{(AC)^2} = \frac{q_B}{(r - AC)^2}$

$\frac{10 \times 10^{-6}}{(AC)^2} = \frac{40 \times 10^{-6}}{(0.9 - AC)^2}$

$\frac{1}{(AC)^2} = \frac{4}{(0.9 - AC)^2}$

$\frac{1}{AC} = \frac{2}{(0.9 - AC)}$

$0.9 - AC = 2AC$

$3AC = 0.9$

$AC = 0.3$ m $= 30$ cm

47(C). Force acting on q due to Q_1 and Q_5 are opposite direction, so cancel to each other. Force acting on q due to

Q_3 is $F_3 = \frac{1}{4\pi\varepsilon_0} \frac{qQ_3}{R^2}$

Force acting on q due to Q_2 and Q_4

Resolving in two component method:

(i) Vertical Component: $Q_2 \sin\theta$ and $Q_4 \sin\theta$ are equal and opposite direction, so they are cancel to each other.

(ii) Horizontal Component: $Q_2 \sin\theta$ and $Q_4 \cos\theta$ are equal and same direction, so they can get added.

$F_{24} = F_{q_2} + F_{q_4} = F_2 \cos 45° + F_4 \cos 45°$

$F_{24} = \frac{1}{4\pi\varepsilon_0} \frac{qQ_2}{R^2} \cos 45° + \frac{1}{4\pi\varepsilon_0} \frac{qQ_4}{R^2} \cos 45°$

Resultant net force F

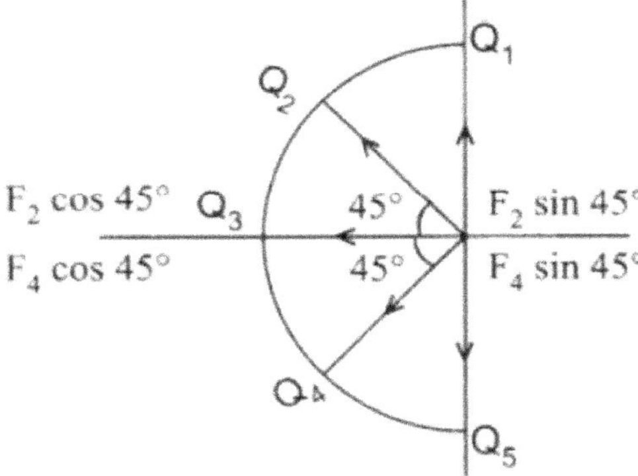

$F = F_3 + F_{24} + F_{15}$

$\cos 45° = \frac{1}{\sqrt{2}}$

$F = \frac{qQ}{4\pi\varepsilon_0 R^2}\left[1 + \frac{1}{\sqrt{2}} + \frac{1}{\sqrt{2}}\right]$

$= \frac{1}{4\pi\varepsilon_0} \frac{qQ}{R^2}\left[1 + \frac{2}{\sqrt{2}}\right]$

$F = \frac{1}{4\pi\varepsilon_0} \frac{qQ}{R^2}[1 + \sqrt{2}]N$

Vector form:

$\vec{F} = \frac{1}{4\pi\varepsilon_0} \frac{qQ}{R^2}(1 + \sqrt{2})N\hat{i}$

48(A).

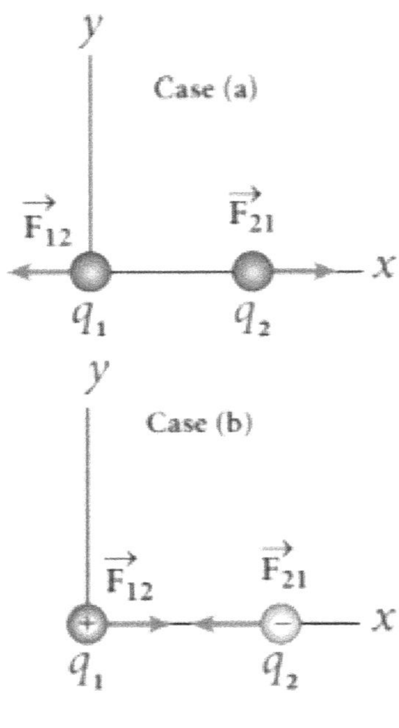

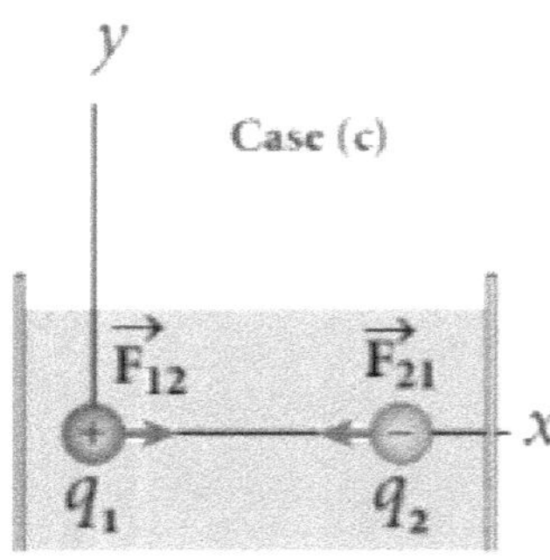

$q_1 = +2\mu C, q_2 = +3\mu C$, and r = 1 m.
Both are positive charges. so the force will be repulsive.
$$\vec{F}_{21} = \frac{1}{4\pi\varepsilon_\circ} \frac{q_1 q_2}{r^2} \hat{r}_{12}$$
Here $\hat{r}_{12}$ is the unit vector from q_1 to q_2 Since q_2 is located on the right of q_1, we have
$\hat{r}_{12} = \hat{i}$, so that
$$\vec{F}_{21} = \frac{9\times10^9 \times 2\times10^{-6}\times 3\times10^{-6}}{1^2}\hat{i}$$
$$\left[\frac{1}{4\pi\varepsilon_0} = 9\times 10^9\right]$$
$$= 54 \times 10^{-3} N\hat{i}$$
According to Newton's third law, the force experienced by the charge q_1 due to q_2 is
$$\vec{F}_{12} = -\vec{F}_{21}$$
$$\vec{F}_{12} = -\vec{F}_{21}$$
$$\vec{F}_{12} = -54 \times 10^{-3} \, N\hat{i}$$

49(C). Given:
Charge, $q_1 = 200 \times 10^{-6} C = 2 \times 10^{-4} C$
Charge, $q_2 = 500 \times 10^{-6} C = 5 \times 10^{-4} C$
Electrostatic force, $F = 5gf = 5 \times 10^{-3} kgf$
$$= 5 \times 10^{-3} \times 10 N$$
$$= 5 \times 10^{-2} N$$
We have to find the distance between two charges
i.e., r
Using the formula:
$$F = \frac{1}{4\pi\varepsilon_0} \frac{q_1 q_2}{r^2}$$
$$\Rightarrow 5 \times 10^{-2} = \frac{9\times10^9 \times 2\times10^{-4}\times 5\times10^{-4}}{r^2}$$
$$\Rightarrow r = 1.34 \times 10^2 \text{ m}$$

50(C). Given that:
Separation distance, $r = 5.12 \times 10^{-15}$ m
We know that:
Charge on an electron, $e = 1.6 \times 10^{-19}$
and, $\frac{1}{4\pi\epsilon_0} = 9 \times 10^9$
Charge on an alpha particle is $2e$.
∴ Using Coulomb's law,
$$F = \frac{1}{4\pi\epsilon_0} \frac{q_1 q_2}{r^2}$$
$$= \frac{1}{4\pi\epsilon_0} \frac{2\times1.6\times10^{-19}\times1.6\times10^{-19}}{\left(5.12\times10^{-15}\right)^2}$$
$$= 9 \times 10^9 \times 0.195 \times 10^{-8}$$
$$= 17.5 \text{ N}$$

51(B). The Magnus effect is not related to electromagnetic waves.
- The force exerted on a rapidly spinning cylinder or sphere moving through air or another fluid in a direction at an angle to the axis of spin is called the Magnus effect.
- This force is responsible for the swerving of balls when hit or thrown with spin.

The Doppler effect is the change in the observed frequency of an (electromagnetic) wave due to relative motion of the source and observer.
Interference occurs when several waves are added together provided that the phase differences between them remain constant over the observation time.
Diffraction takes place with sound; with electromagnetic radiation, such as light, X-rays, and gamma rays; and with very small moving particles such as atoms, neutrons, and electrons, which show wavelike properties.
Therefore, Magnus effect is our required answer.

52(C). The idea of displacement current was introduced to the current for making ampere circuital law consistent.
$$\oint \vec{B} \cdot d\vec{l} = \mu_0 (i_c + i_d) \quad \text{(Modified Ampere circuital law)}$$
Where, μ_0 is the permittivity of free space, i_d is the displacement current, and i_c is the conduction current. $\oint \vec{B} \cdot d\vec{l}$ is line integral of the magnetic field over the closed-loop.
The expression for displacement current is given by,
$$i_d = \epsilon_0 \frac{d\phi_B}{dt}$$
Where ϕ_E is the flux of the electric field through the area bounded by the closed curve, i_d is the displacement current, and ϵ_0 is the permittivity of free space.

53(D). With larger aperture of objective lens, the light gathering power in telescope is high.
Also, the resolving power or the ability to observe two objects distinctly also depends on the diameter of the objective. Thus, objective of large diameter is preferred.
Also, with large diameters fainter objects can be observed. Therefore, it also contributes to the better quality and visibility of images.

54(C).

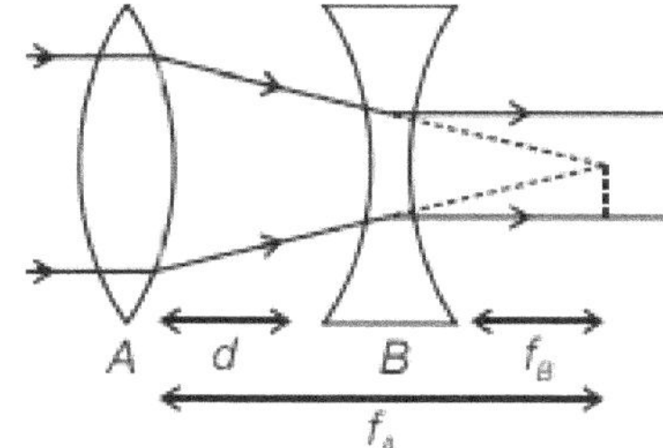

Parallel beam of light after refraction from convex lens converge at the focus of convex lens. In question it is given light after refraction pass through concave lens becomes parallel. Therefore, light refracted from convex lens virtually meet at focus of concave lens.

Given that:

$f_A = 20$ cm

And, $f_B = 5$ cm

According to above ray diagram,

$d = f_A - f_B$

$= 20 - 5$

$= 15$ cm

55(B). From the ray diagram shown in the figure. At point P, from Snell's law,

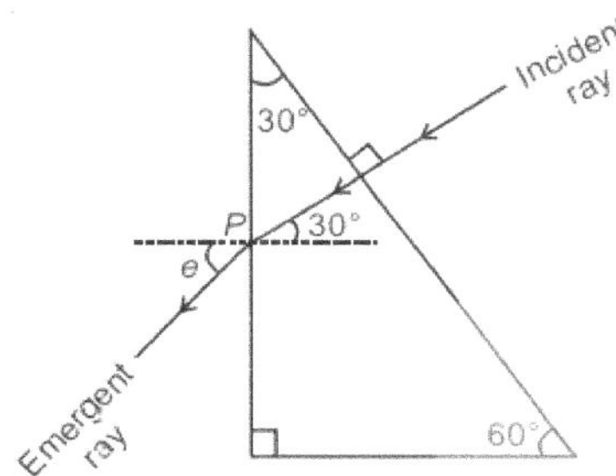

$\dfrac{\sin i}{\sin r} = \dfrac{\mu_{air}}{\mu_{Prism}}$

$\Rightarrow \dfrac{\sin 30°}{\sin e} = \dfrac{1}{\sqrt{3}}$ ($\angle r = \angle e$ emergent angle)

$\Rightarrow \sin e = \sqrt{3} \cdot \dfrac{1}{2}$

$\Rightarrow \angle e = 60°$

56(C). Angle of deviation $= \delta = i + e - A$

$i = 0,$

So, $r_1 = 0$

So, $r_2 = 60°$ (angle of incidence of second face)

$r_2 >$ critical angle for glass-air

$= \sin^{-1}\dfrac{1}{1.5} = 41.81°$

It will be totally internally reflected and fall on the base of prism at $90°$ to it. It will emerge with angle of emergence $e = 0°$

$\delta = 0 + 0 - 60°$

$= 60°$

57(C). Given:

Intensity $= I_0$, and Resultant intensity $I = 3I_0$, the resultant intensity at that point is given as,

$I = 4I_o \cos^2\left(\dfrac{\phi}{2}\right)$

$\Rightarrow 3I_o = 4I_o \cos^2\left(\dfrac{\phi}{2}\right)$

$\Rightarrow \cos\left(\dfrac{\phi}{2}\right) = \dfrac{\sqrt{3}}{2}$

$\Rightarrow \dfrac{\phi}{2} = \dfrac{\pi}{6}$

$\Rightarrow \phi = \dfrac{\pi}{3}$

58(A). First Maxima $= \dfrac{D\lambda}{d}$

$\beta_1 = \dfrac{1.5 \times 480 \times 10^{-9}}{0.25 \times 10^{-3}}$

$= 2.880 \times 10^{-3}$ m

$\beta_2 = \dfrac{1.5 \times 600 \times 10^{-9}}{0.25 \times 10^{-3}}$

$= 3.600 \times 10^{-3}$ m

So, $\beta_2 - \beta_1 = 0.72 \times 10^{-3}$ m

$= 0.72$ mm

59(A). Let the intensities of the two waves be I_1 and I_2.

Given,

$I_1 : I_2 = 9 : 1$

Ratio of maximum and minimum intensities

$\dfrac{I_{max}}{I_{min}} = \left(\dfrac{\sqrt{I_1} + \sqrt{I_2}}{\sqrt{I_1} - \sqrt{I_2}}\right)^2$

or,

$\dfrac{I_{max}}{I_{min}} = \left(\dfrac{\sqrt{\frac{I_1}{I_2}} + 1}{\sqrt{\frac{I_1}{I_2}} - 1}\right)^2$

or

$\dfrac{I_{max}}{I_{min}} = \left(\dfrac{\sqrt{9} + 1}{\sqrt{9} - 1}\right)^2$

$= \left(\dfrac{3+1}{3-1}\right)^2$

$\Rightarrow \dfrac{I_{max}}{I_{min}} = \dfrac{16}{4}$

$= \dfrac{4}{1}$

60(B). As we know that the Einstein's photo-electric equation is given by,

$K_{max} = h\nu - \phi_0 \ldots\ldots$ (i)

Also we know that the frequency of a light wave is given by $\nu = \dfrac{c}{\lambda} \ldots\ldots$ (ii)

Substituting the value from (ii) to (i), we get

$K_{max} = \dfrac{hc}{\lambda} - \phi_0$

So the work function of the metal is given by

$\phi_0 = \dfrac{hc}{\lambda} - K_{max} \ldots\ldots$ (iii)

According to the question,

$\lambda = 400$ nm, $K_{max} = 1.68$eV, $hc = 1240$eV nm

Putting these values in (iii), we get

$\phi_0 = \dfrac{1240}{400} - 1.68$

$\Rightarrow \phi_0 = 1.42$eV

Thus the work function of the metal comes out to be equal to 1.42eV.

61(A). Minimum energy required for emission of electrons

$\dfrac{hc}{\lambda} - \phi = (kE)_{max}$

$\lambda_1 = 500$ nm

$\lambda_2 = 200$ nm

$kE_1 = 3kE_2$ (given)

$\dfrac{hc}{\lambda_1} - \phi = kE_1 - (i)$

$\dfrac{hc}{\lambda_2} - \phi = 3kE_2 - (ii)$

From equation (i) and (ii),

$\dfrac{hc}{\lambda_1} - \phi = \dfrac{1}{3}\left(\dfrac{hc}{\lambda_2} - \phi\right)$

$\dfrac{hc}{\lambda_1} - \dfrac{1}{3} \times \dfrac{hc}{\lambda_2} = \dfrac{2\phi}{3}$

$hc\left(\dfrac{1}{\lambda_1} - \dfrac{1}{3\lambda_2}\right) = \dfrac{2\phi}{3}$

$\dfrac{1240\left(\frac{1}{500} - \frac{1}{600}\right)}{3000}$ (where $hc = 1240\ eV$)

$\dfrac{1240}{3000} = \dfrac{2\phi}{3}$

$\phi = 0.62$eV

62(A). The de-Broglie wavelength associated with electron

$\lambda_e = \frac{1.227}{\sqrt{V}}$ nm

We get,

$V = \frac{(12.27)^2}{\lambda_e^2} \times 10^{-2}$

$\Rightarrow V = \frac{150}{\lambda_e^2} \times 10^{-2}$

Where,

$\lambda_e = 0.2$ nm

$\Rightarrow V = \frac{150 \times 10^{-2}}{(0.2)^2}$

$\Rightarrow V = \frac{150 \times 10^{-2}}{4 \times 10^{-2}}$

$\Rightarrow V = 37.5$ volts

$\therefore$ Kinetic energy E = 37.5eV

63(A). Given,

The velocity of the electron in this microscope (v)

$= 1.6 \times 10^6$ ms^{-1}.

'h' = Plank's constant = 6.63×10^{-34} Hz^{-1}

Mass of electron (m) = 9.1×10^{-31} kg

The de Broglie wavelength,

$\lambda = \frac{h}{mv}$

$= \frac{6.63 \times 10^{-34}}{9.1 \times 10^{-31} 1.6 \times 10^6}$

$= 4.55 \times 10^{-10}$ m

64(A). Given,

$\lambda_1 = 600$ Å and $\lambda_2 = 400$ Å

The Photon energy formula is given by,

$E = \frac{hc}{\lambda}$ $\cdots (i)$

Where $E =$ energy,

c = speed of light (3×10^8 m/s), $\lambda =$ wavelength

and h = planck's constant (6.6×10^{-34} Js)

By equation (i),

$E_1 = \frac{hc}{\lambda_1}$

$\Rightarrow E_1 = \frac{hc}{600}$ $\cdots (ii)$

$\Rightarrow E_2 = \frac{hc}{\lambda_2}$

$\Rightarrow E_1 = \frac{hc}{400}$ $\cdots (iii)$

By equation (ii) and equation (iii),

$\frac{E_1}{E_2} = \frac{\frac{hc}{600}}{\frac{hc}{400}}$

$\Rightarrow \frac{E_1}{E_2} = \frac{400}{600}$

$\Rightarrow \frac{E_1}{E_2} = \frac{2}{3}$

65(C). The speed of an electron as a function of principle quantum number n is given by,

$v = \left(2.17 \times 10^7 \text{ m s}^{-1}\right) \times \frac{Z}{n}$

Where,

v is speed of electon

Z is atomic number

e is charge on electon

ϵ_0 is permittivity in free space

h is Planck's constant

We can write,

$v \propto \frac{1}{n}$

$v = \frac{Constant}{n}$

The above equation represents the rectangular hyperbola i.e., it is similar to the general equation of a rectangular hyperbola. The graph between speed and the principal quantum number is a rectangular hyperbola represented by graph c.

66(A). According to Einstein's quantum theory light propagates in the form of packets i.e. quanta of energy, which is called a photon.

The rest mass of photons is being zero. It can be shown, according to the relativity theory of light.

According to the relativistic theory equation, the mass of the photon is computed as:

$m = \frac{m_0}{\sqrt{1 - \frac{v^2}{c^2}}}$

$\Rightarrow m_0 = m\sqrt{1 - \frac{v^2}{c^2}}$

When $v = 0$

So, $m_0 = 0$

Where, m_0 is the rest mass of the Photon.

67(C). As we know,

Specific charge $= \frac{q}{m}$

Let the specific charge of proton be p.

Therefore specific charge of alpha particle = $2p$ ($\because \alpha$ -particle has 2 protons and 2 neutrons, neutrons have same mass ($m_p = m_\alpha$) as protons but charge is zero.)

Ratio $= \frac{\left(\frac{q}{m}\right)_\alpha}{\left(\frac{q}{m}\right)_p}$

Since the value of specific charge is given above that is $\frac{q}{m} = p$

Therefore on putting the value we get,

$= \frac{q_\alpha}{q_p} \times \frac{m_p}{m_\alpha}$

$= \frac{p}{2p}$

$= \frac{1}{2}$

$\therefore$ The ratio of the specific charge of an α -particle to that of a proton is 1: 2.

68(D). For first line of Lyman series,

$n_1 = 1$

$n_2 = 2$

$\therefore \frac{1}{\lambda} = Z^2 R \frac{3}{4}$

In the case of hydrogen atom,

$Z = 1$

$\frac{1}{\lambda} = R \frac{3}{4}$

For hydrogen-like atom,

$Z = 11$

$\frac{1}{\lambda'} = 121 R \frac{3}{4}$

$\Rightarrow \frac{\lambda'}{\lambda} = \frac{3R}{4} \times \frac{4}{121 R \times 3}$

$\Rightarrow \lambda' = \frac{\lambda}{121}$

$\Rightarrow \lambda' = \frac{1210}{121}$

$\Rightarrow \lambda' = 10$ Å

69(D). Insulators are materials in which valence electrons are not found to conduct electricity. That's why low conductivity is found in them.

Resistivity is the property of materials that opposes electric current. The resistivity of insulators is very high.

Insulators are materials that have a large band gap, or materials that have a high energy gap between the valence and conduction bands. This large energy difference makes it difficult for electrons to move into the conduction band through which they can flow and generate an electric current.

A negative coefficient of resistance of a material means that its resistance decreases with increase in temperature. Positive coefficients are found in conductors. Negative coefficient is found in insulators. So, option (D) is wrong.

70(D). A semiconductor in its purest form is known as

Intrinsic semiconductor.
An intrinsic (pure) semiconductor, also called an undoped semiconductor or i-type semiconductor, is a pure semiconductor without any significant dopant species present. The number of charge carriers is therefore determined by the properties of the material itself instead of the amount of impurities.

71(A). In semiconductors, both electrons and holes are charge carriers and will take part in conduction.
In n-type semiconductors they are electrons, while in p-type semiconductors they are holes. The less abundant charge carriers are called minority carriers in n-type semiconductors they are holes, while in p-type semiconductors they are electrons.

72(A). In forward bias, the resistance of a PN junction is of the order of Ω, approximately 100Ω Reverse bias PN junction has a resistance of the order of $M\Omega$. The ideal diode will acts as a short circuit in forward bias and open circuit in reverse bias condition. So, the forward resistance of the ideal diode is zero and reverse resistance of the ideal diode is infinity.

73(B). p-n junction is defined as the boundary between two semiconductor material types which is p-type and n-type. There are three biasing conditions and these conditions are based on the voltage applied. The basing conditions are shown below;
- Zero bias - Zero bias is defined as the condition in which no external voltage is applied externally to the p-n junction.
- Forward bias - In the positive terminal the battery is connected with p-type and the negative terminal of the battery is connected with n-type.
- Reversed bias - In the positive terminal the battery is connected with n-type and the negative terminal of the battery is connected with p-type.

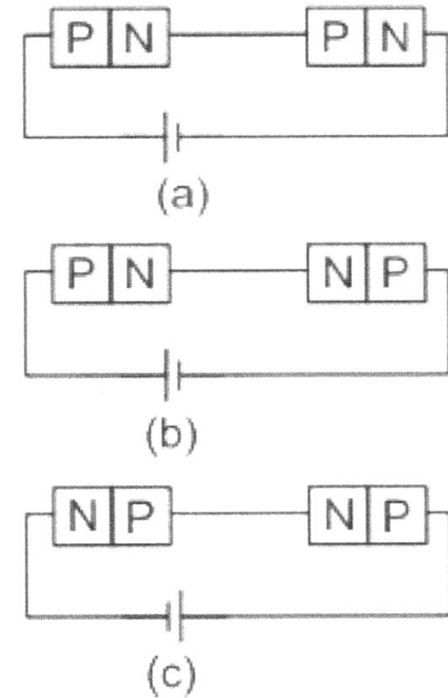

When we see in the circuit (a) the currents are flowing in the same direction. Therefore, its potential drop is equal. As we can see in circuit (b) the currents are opposite in direction. Therefore, its potential drop is not equal and in circuit (c) the currents are flowing in the same direction. Therefore, its potential drop is equal.

74(B). Let the length of the wire l,
They are stretched by a weight which produces Stress t in both the wires.
Let the increase in length be e for steel and c for copper.
Young's modulus for steel is given as,
$$\gamma = \frac{\text{stress}}{\text{strain}}$$
$$2 \times 10^{11} = \frac{t}{e/l}$$
$$2 \times 10^{11} = \frac{tl}{e}$$
Now,
Ratio of increase in lengths of steel and copper is,
$$ec = \frac{\frac{tl}{2\times10^{11}}}{\frac{tl}{1.2\times10^{11}}}$$
$$ec = \frac{tl}{tl} \times \frac{1.2}{2} \times \frac{10^{11}}{10^{11}}$$
$$ec = 0.6$$
$$ec = \frac{6}{10} = \frac{3}{5}$$
Therefore, the ratio of increase in length is $3 : 5$.

75(A). From the concept of Hook's law, we have-
Normal Stress $(\sigma) = E\epsilon$
where, $E =$ Young's Modulus of Elasticity and ϵ is strain which gives linear deformation of the object.
Also, Shear Stress $(\tau) = G\gamma$
where, $G =$ Shear Modulus of Elasticity of the material and γ is shear strain which gives angular deformation of the object.
When we stretch a spring, the length of the wire does not change but the coil experiences an angular twist. Hence shear modulus is used to determine the stretching of a spring.
$\therefore$ The assertion is True.
Also, we know that for a given dimension, Young's Modulus of Elasticity of steel is more than the Copper hence we can say that the tensile strength of Steel is more than that of Cu.
$\therefore$ The reason is False.

76(B). $h \Rightarrow 0.29$
Vertical colum $\Rightarrow$ initial $= 2 \times 0.29$
$\Rightarrow (h_1 - 0.1) + h_2 = 2 \times 0.29$
$\Rightarrow h_1 + h_2 = 0.58 + 0.1 = 0.68$ ....(i)

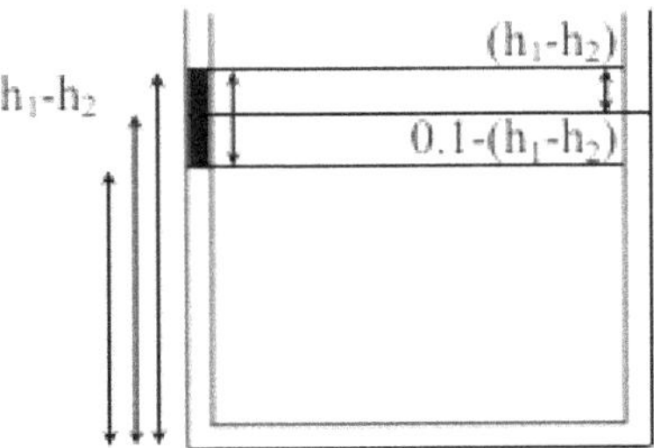

$P_{atm} + 800\,g \times 0.1 = (0.1 - (h_1 - h_2))1000 \times g$
$800\,g \times 0.1 = (0.1 - (h_1 - h_2))1000 \times g$
$(h_1 - h_2)1000\,g = 20$
$(h_1 - h_2) = \frac{20}{100}$
$h_1 - h_2 = 0.02$ ....(ii)
Adding equations (i) and (ii):
$\Rightarrow 2\,h_1 = 0.70$
Subtracting equation (ii) from equation (i):
$\Rightarrow 2\,h_2 = 0.66$
Dividing equation (iii) by equation (iv):
$\Rightarrow \frac{h_1}{h_2} = \frac{35}{33}$

77(A). It is given that a metallic plate having shape of a square is suspended with the help of string. When the plate is made to dip in water, the buoyant force will act on it. The amount of force is constant at that time and hence the tension in the string is constant. As the point X is slowly raised at constant velocity and as it come out of water, the tension in the string is balanced by the weight of metallic plate.

The tension is depend upon bouncy force. By applying equilibrium equation on metal block,

$T + \rho gh = mg$

$\Rightarrow T = mg - rgh$

Here, displacement is in term of height.

78(B). Let F_v be the viscous force and F_B be the Bouyant force acting on the ball.

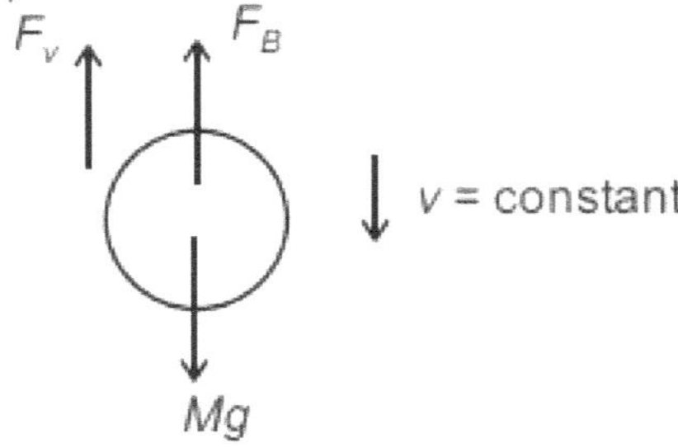

Then, when body moves with constant velocity,

$Mg = F_B + F_v \quad [a = 0]$

$F_v = Mg - F_B$

$= dVg - \dfrac{d}{2} \cdot Vg \quad (\because M = dVg)$ where V : volume of ball

$= \dfrac{d}{2} Vg$

$F_v = \dfrac{M}{2} g$

79(B). Kinetic viscosity is the ratio of the coefficient of viscosity to the fluid mass density.

With the increasing molecular mass of a liquid, the viscosity increases.

The flow of molecules is inversely proportional to their mass. Thus, liquids with high molecular mass possess greater viscosity.

80(D). Viscous force is the force of sliding friction between two solid surfaces in a fluid. Viscosity is frequently referred to as fluid friction because of this. Viscous forces, like other frictional forces, impede the relative motion of nearby fluid layers. When we drop a ball in a liquid that is highly viscous in nature and when it falls then initially gravitational force acts. As it goes inside liquid then viscous force increases so its speed will be constant with time after sometimes because gravitational force is balanced by drag or viscous force. When gravitational force is balanced by drag force then the acceleration of particle which can be measured by the slope of v and t graph initially becomes negative but after some time it becomes zero which means velocity becomes constant with time.

The $v - t$ graph can be shown by:

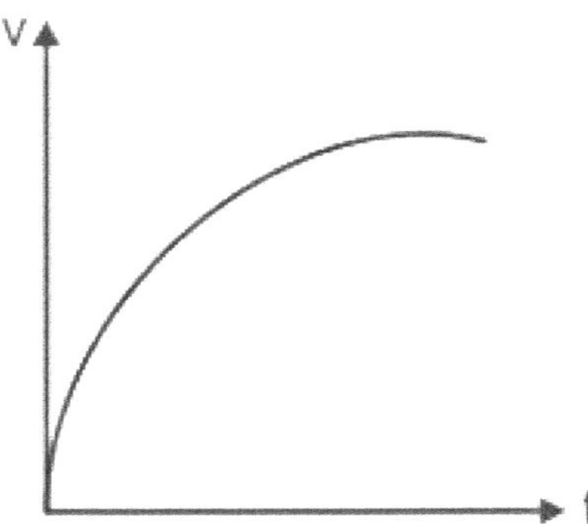

It shows motion as the B part of the graph.

1. Which of the following group has the correct units of fundamental quantities as per the SI system?
   (a) Meter, kilogram, second, coulomb, Kelvin, mole and candela
   (b) Meter, newton, second, coulomb, Kelvin, mole and candela
   (c) Meter, kilogram, second, ampere, Kelvin, mole and candela
   (d) Meter, kilogram, second, ampere, Kelvin, mole and lux

2. Candela is the unit of _______.
   (a) Acoustic Intensity   (b) Electric Intensity
   (c) Magnetic intensity   (d) Luminous intensity

3. What is the SI unit of surface tension of a fluid?
   (a) Newton   (b) Newton/Meter
   (c) Newton/Meter^2 (d) Newton/Meter^3

4. Which of the following pairs of physical quantities does not have same dimensional formula?
   (a) Work and torque
   (b) Angular momentum and Planck's constant
   (c) Tension and surface tension
   (d) Impulse and linear momentum

5. If the distance between the Earth and the Sun is half its present value, the number of days in a year will be
   (a) 64.5   (b) 129
   (c) 182.5   (d) 730

6. A man is standing on a weighing machine placed in a lift, when stationary, his weight is recorded as 40 kg .If the lift is accelerated upwards with an acceleration of $2\,\mathrm{m/s}^2$, then the weight recorded in the machine will be:
   (a) 48 kg   (b) 32 kg
   (c) 64 kg   (d) 80 kg

7. During the melting of solid, its temperature _______.
   (a) May increase or decrease depending on the nature of solid
   (b) Decreases
   (c) Increases
   (d) Does not change

8. The top of lake is frozen as the atmospheric temperature is $-10°C$. The temperature at the bottom of the lake is most likely to be _______.
   (a) $0°C$ (b) $-4°C$
   (c) $4°C$ (d) $-10°C$

9. A liquid with coefficient of cubical expansion γ is contained in α vessel having coefficient of linear expansion $\frac{\gamma}{3}$. When heated, what will happen to the level of the liquid in the vessel?
   (a) It falls
   (b) It rises
   (c) Not change
   (d) It may rise or fall depending upon the nature of the container

10. The temperature determines the direction of net change of:
    (a) Gross kinetic energy
    (b) Intermolecular kinetic energy
    (c) Gross potential energy
    (d) Intermolecular potential energy

11. A gas is compressed to half of its initial volume isothermally. The same gas is compressed again until the volume reduces to half through an adiabatic process. Then:
    (a) Work done during isothermal compression is more
    (b) Work done is independent of the processes used for compression
    (c) Work done is more during the adiabatic process
    (d) Work done is dependent on the atomicity of the gas

12. A point on $P - V$ diagram shows:
    (a) A thermodynamic process
    (b) The state of the system
    (c) Work done on or by the system
    (d) None of the above

13. Two bodies at different temperatures T_1 and T_2 if brought in thermal contact:
    (a) Do not settle settle down at mean temperature
    (b) Settle down at mean temperature
    (c) Settle down at any temperature
    (d) None of the above

14. A thermodynamic system is taken from an original state to an intermediate state by the linear process shown in figure below

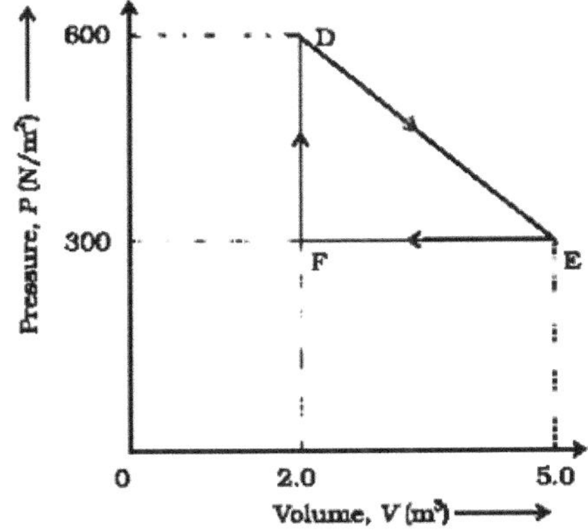

Its volume is then reduced to the original value from E to F by an isobaric process. Calculate the total work done by the gas from D to E to F .
   (a) $250J$ (b) $450J$
   (c) $350J$ (d) $550J$

15. A cylinder of fixed capacity 44.8 litres contains helium gas at standard temperature and pressure. What is the amount of heat needed to raise the temperature of the gas in the cylinder by $15.0°C$? $(R = 8.31\ \mathrm{J\ mol}^{-1}\,\mathrm{K}^{-1})$
   (a) 265 J   (b) 310.10 J
   (c) 373.95 J   (d) 387.97 J

16. Find the temperature at which root-mean-square

speed of an oxygen molecule will be sufficient to take it away from the surface of the earth. Given: escape speed from the surface of the earth $= 11.2\ km\ s^{-1}$, mass of an oxygen molecule $= 2.76 \times 10^{-26}\ kg$, Boltzmann constant $= 1.38 \times 10^{-23}\ J\ K^{-1}$

(a) $5.16 \times 10^4 K$ (b) $8.36 \times 10^4 K$

(c) $2.45 \times 10^4 K$ (d) $9.12 \times 10^4 K$

17. A gaseous mixture consists of 16 g of helium and 16 g of oxygen. The ratio C_P/C_V of the mixture is:

(a) 1.59   (b) 1.62

(c) 1.4   (d) 1.54

18. Two moles of an ideal gas with $\dfrac{C_P}{C_V} = \dfrac{5}{3}$ are mixed with 3 moles of another ideal gas with $\dfrac{C_P}{C_V} = \dfrac{4}{3}$. The value of $\dfrac{C_P}{C_V}$ for the mixture is:

(a) 1.45   (b) 1.50

(c) 1.47   (d) 1.42

19. Consider a mixture of n moles of helium gas and 2n moles of oxygen gas (molecules taken to be rigid) as an ideal gas. Its $\dfrac{C_P}{C_V}$ value will be:

(a) $\dfrac{19}{13}$ (b) $\dfrac{67}{45}$

(c) $\dfrac{40}{27}$ (d) $\dfrac{23}{15}$

20. If 1 L of gas A at 600 torr and 500 mL of gas B at 1000 torr are placed in 2 L flask, the final pressure will be:

(a) 500 torr   (b) 550 torr

(c) 1000 torr   (d) 1100 torr

21. Which of the following graph is correct representation between atomic number (Z) and magnetic moment of d -block elements? [Outer electronic configuration : $(n-1)d^x ns^{1\ or\ 3}$]

(a)

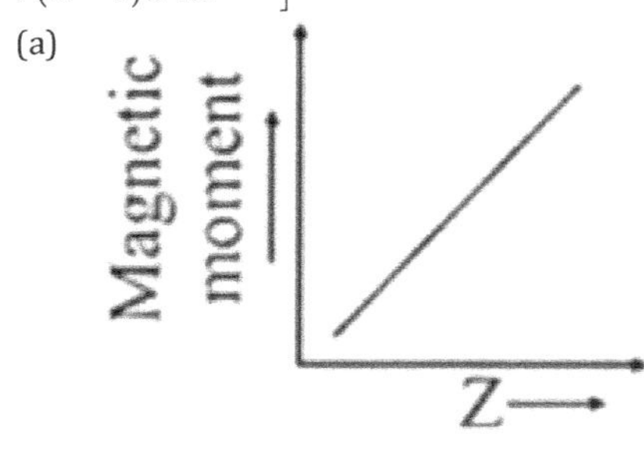

(b)

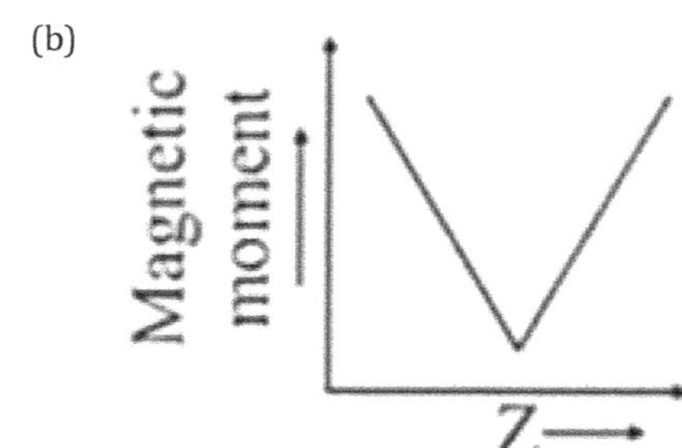

(c)

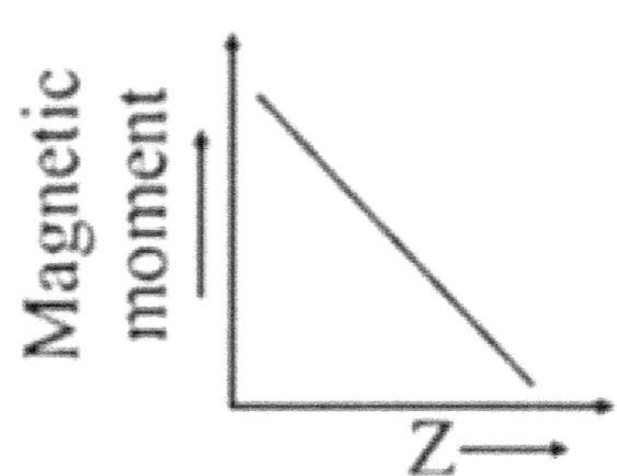

(d)

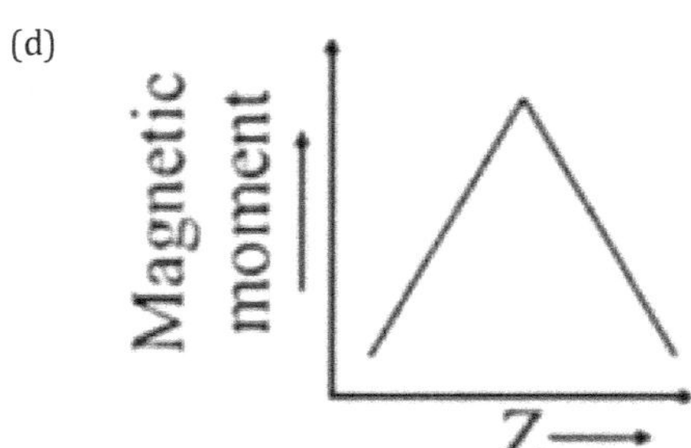

22. In mechanical oscillations a body oscillates about its mean position which is also its ________________.

(a) watt   (b) force

(c) motion   (d) equilibrium position

23. The IUPAC name for $CH_3CH = CHCH_2CHCH_2COOH$ with NH_2 on the fifth carbon is:

(a) 3− amino −5− heptenoic acid

(b) β− amino −δ

(c) 5− amino −2− heptenoic acid

(d) 5− amino-hex −2− enecarboxylic acid

24. Which of the following fertilizers has the highest nitrogen percentage?

(a) Ammonium sulphate   (b) Calcium cyanamide

(c) Urea   (d) Ammonium nitrate

25. The magnitude of the force on a charge Q in the electric field E is:

(a) $\dfrac{E}{Q}$ (b) $\dfrac{Q}{E}$

(c) EQ (d) $E^2 Q$

26. Which of the following statement is incorrect regarding charge on the body?

(a) Like the gravitational force between two masses, charges always attracts each other.

(b) Unlike charges attract each other

(c) Like charges repel each other

(d) All of the above are correct statements

27. A charge q is distributed uniformly on a ring of radius r. A sphere of equal radius r is constructed with its center at the periphery of the ring. The electric flux through the surface of the sphere is:

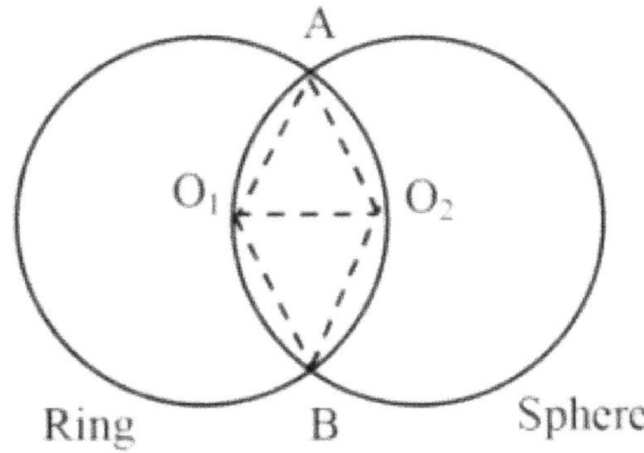

(a) $\dfrac{q}{\varepsilon_0}$

(b) $\dfrac{2q}{\varepsilon_0}$

(c) $\dfrac{q}{2\varepsilon_0}$

(d) $\dfrac{q}{3\varepsilon_0}$

28. Coulombs force between two point charges varies with distance 'r' in relation to ________.

(a) r

(b) $\dfrac{1}{r}$

(c) r^2

(d) $\dfrac{1}{r^2}$

29. In a certain region of space with volume $0.2\,\text{m}^3$, the electric potential is found to be 5 V throughout. The magnitude of electric field in this region is:

(a) Zero

(b) $0.5\,\text{N/C}$

(c) $1\,\text{N/C}$

(d) $5\,\text{N/C}$

30. The energy required to break one bond in DNA is $10^{-20}\,\text{J}$. This value in eV is nearly:

(a) 6

(b) 0.6

(c) 0.06

(d) 0.006

31. The capacitance of a parallel plate capacitor with air as medium is $6\mu\text{F}$. With the introduction of a dielectric medium, the capacitance becomes $30\mu\text{F}$. The permittivity of the medium is: $\left(\epsilon_0 = 8.85 \times 10^{-12}\,\text{C}^2\,\text{N}^{-1}\,\text{m}^{-2}\right)$

(a) $0.44 \times 10^{-13}\,\text{C}^2\,\text{N}^{-1}\,\text{m}^{-2}$

(b) $1.77 \times 10^{-12}\,\text{C}^2\,\text{N}^{-1}\,\text{m}^{-2}$

(c) $0.44 \times 10^{-10}\,\text{C}^2\,\text{N}^{-1}\,\text{m}^{-2}$

(d) $5.00\,\text{C}^2\,\text{N}^{-1}\,\text{m}^{-2}$

32. A short electric dipole has a dipole moment of $16 \times 10^{-9}\,\text{Cm}$. The electric potential due to the dipole at a point at a distance of $0.6\,\text{m}$ from the centre of the dipole, situated on a line making an angle of $60°$ with the dipole axis is: $\left(\dfrac{1}{4\pi\epsilon_0} = 9 \times 10^9\,\text{N m}^2/\text{C}^2\right)$

(a) 50 V

(b) 200 V

(c) 400 V

(d) Zero

33. Ohm's law is valid when the temperature of conductor is ________.

(a) Very low

(b) Very high

(c) Varying

(d) Constant

34. The potential gradient of a potentiometer is 3 mV/cm. It is used to measure the potential difference across a resistance of 20 Ω. If a length of 60 cm of the potentiometer wire is required to get the null point, then the current passing through the 20 Ω resistor is:

(a) 8 mA

(b) 9 mA

(c) 10 mA

(d) 11 mA

35. Find the current in the circuit shown below.

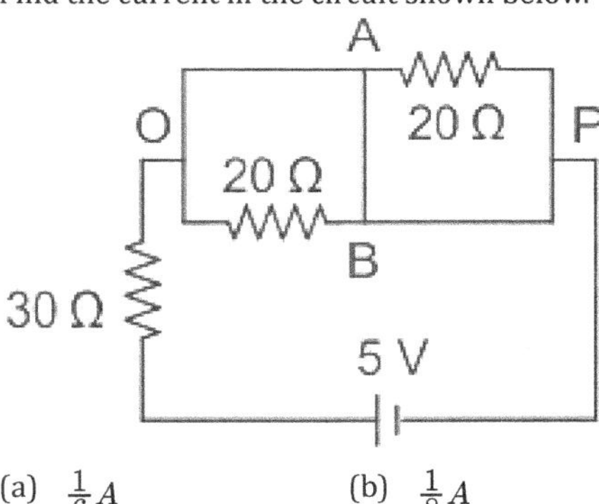

(a) $\dfrac{1}{6}A$

(b) $\dfrac{1}{8}A$

(c) $\dfrac{5}{70}A$

(d) $\dfrac{1}{3}A$

36. The SI unit of electric current is Ampere. One Ampere is defined as:

(a) Charge passing per minute

(b) 1 coulomb of charge flowing per second

(c) 2 coulomb of charge flowing per second

(d) Charge per second

37. Two long straight conductors with current I_1 and I_2 are placed along X and Y axes. The equation of locus of the point of zero magnetic induction is:

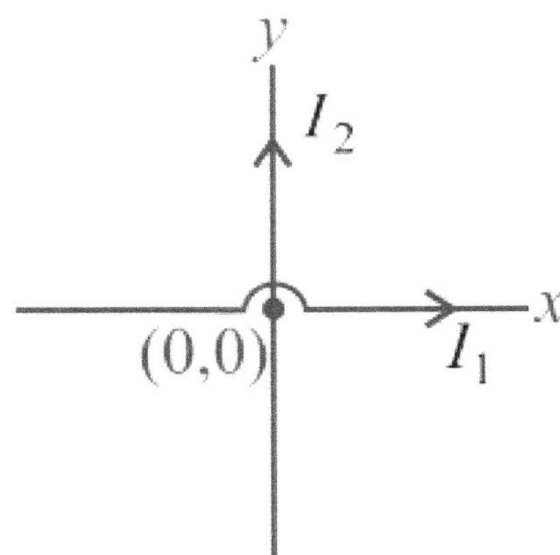

(a) $Y = X$

(b) $Y = \dfrac{I_2}{I_1}X$

(c) $Y = \dfrac{I_1}{I_2}X$

(d) $Y = \dfrac{X}{I_1 I_2}$

38. The magnetic field due to a small magnetic dipole of magnetic moment M, at distance r from the centre on the equatorial line is given by (in MKS system):

(a) $\dfrac{\mu_0}{4\pi} \times \dfrac{M}{r^2}$

(b) $\dfrac{\mu_0}{4\pi} \times \dfrac{M}{r^3}$

(c) $\dfrac{\mu_0}{4\pi} \times \dfrac{2M}{r^2}$

(d) $\dfrac{\mu_0}{4\pi} \times \dfrac{2M}{r^3}$

39. The negatively and uniformly charged non-conducting disc as shown is rotated clockwise. The direction of the magnetic field at point A in the plane of the disc is:

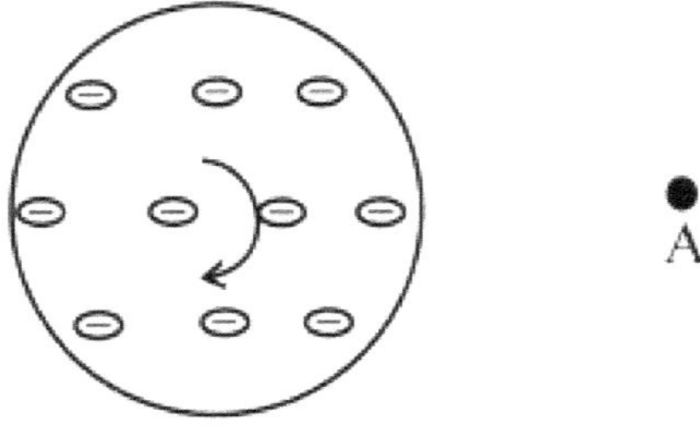

(a) Into the page

(b) Out of the page

(c) Upwards in the plane of the page

(d) Downwards in the plane of the page

40. A negative test charge is moving near a long straight wire carrying a current. The force acting on the test charge is parallel to the direction of the current. The motion of the charge is __________.

(a) away from the wire

(b) towards the wire

(c) parallel to the wire along the current

(d) parallel to the wire opposite to the current

41. A uniform magnetic field B of 0.3 T is along the positive Z-direction. A rectangular loop (abcd) of sides $10 \text{ cm} \times 5 \text{ cm}$ carries a current I of 12 A . Out of the following different orientations which one corresponds to stable equilibrium?

(a)

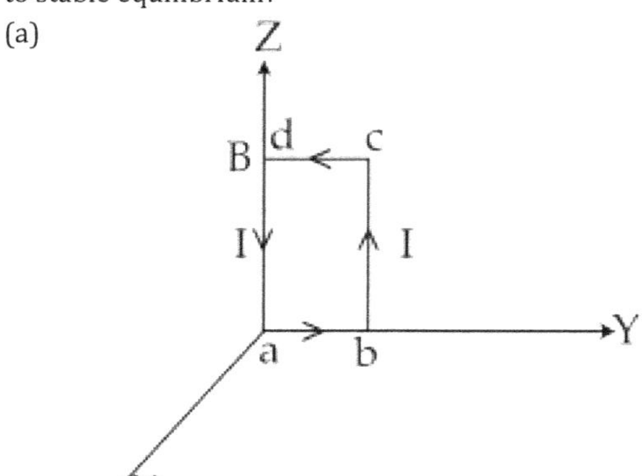

(b)

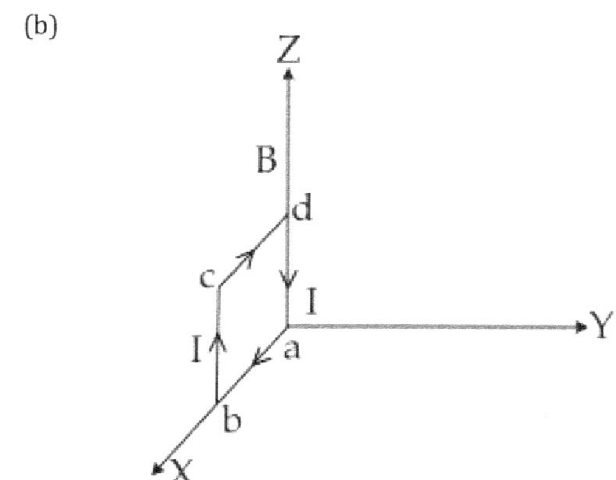

(c)

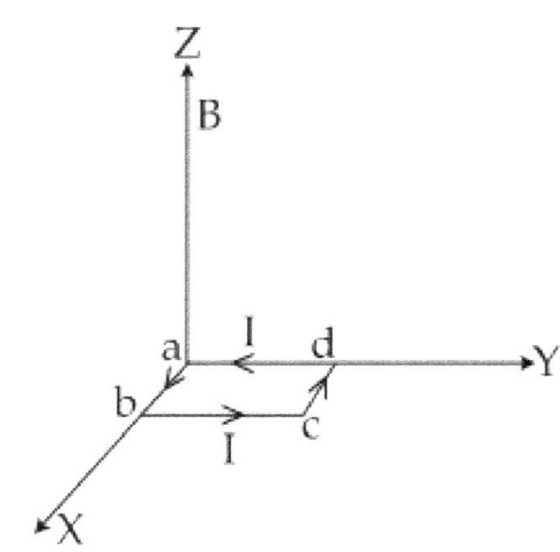

(d)

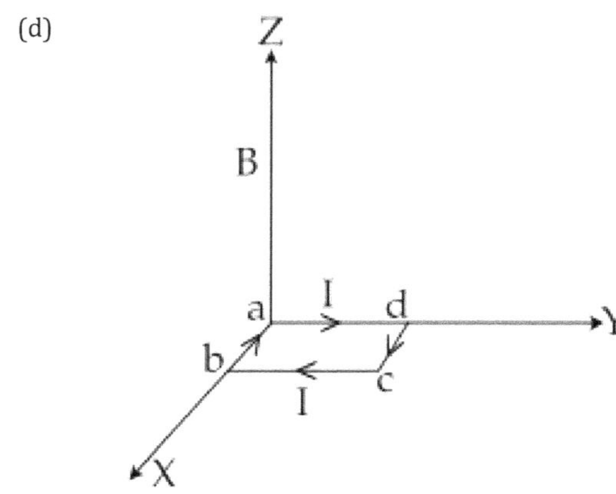

42. In a series LCR circuit the RMS voltages across the inductance, capacitance and resistance are respectively 4 V, 8 V and 5 V . The RMS voltage of the AC source in the circuit is:

(a) 17 V   (b) 13 V

(c) 5 V   (d) 6.4 V

43. Two different metals are joined end to end. One end is kept at constant temperature and the other end is heated to a very high temperature. The high depicting the thermo emf is

(a)

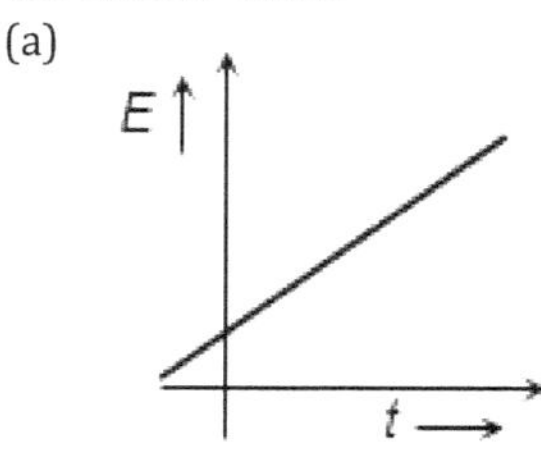

(b)

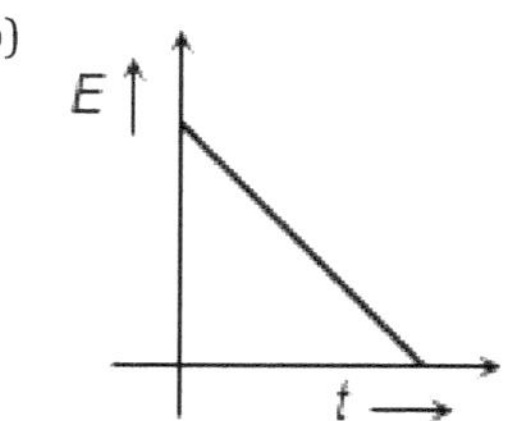

(c)

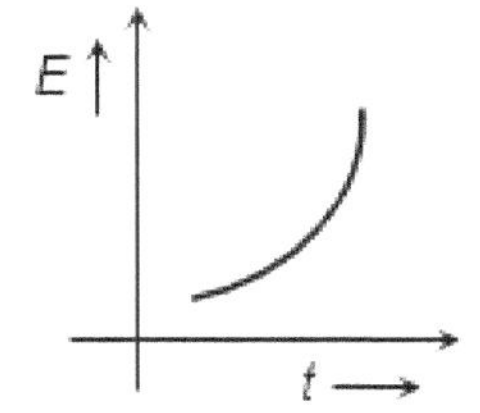

(d)

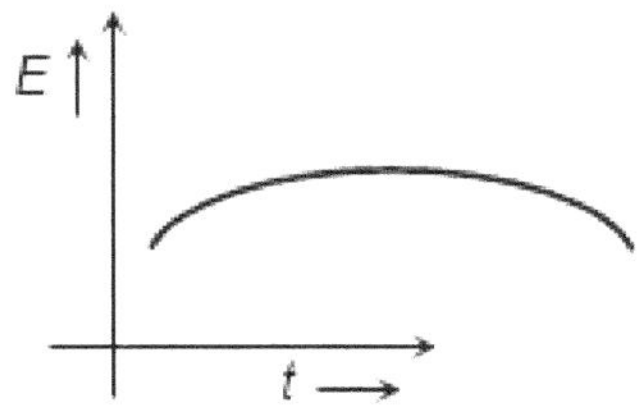

44. A sample of paramagnetic salt contains 2.0×10^{24} atomic dipoles each of dipole moment $1.5 \times 10^{-23} JT^{-1}$. The sample is placed under a homogeneous magnetic field of $0.64T$, and cooled to a temperature of $4.2K$. The degree of magnetic saturation achieved is equal to 15% . What is the total dipole moment of the sample for a magnetic field of $0.98T$ and a temperature of $2.8K$?

(a) $3 JT^{-1}$ (b) $6 JT^{-1}$

(c) $10 JT^{-1}$ (d) $12 JT^{-1}$

45. The magnetic flux of a 20 round coil is reduced to zero from 0.3 weber in one second then the induced e.m.f. between the terminal of coil.

(a) 2.5 V   (b) 6 V

(c) 3 V   (d) 1.5 V

46. Active power and apparent power are respectively measured in:

(a) kW and kVA   (b) kV and kWA

(c) kVA and kW   (d) kVW and kA

47. There is a uniform magnetic field directed perpendicular and into the pane of the paper. An irregular shaped conducting loop is slowly changing into a circular loop in the plane of the paper. Then_____

(a) AC is induced in the loop

(b) No current is induced in the loop

(c) Current is induced in the loop in the anti-clockwise direction

(d) Current is induced in the loop in the clockwise direction

48. 5.5×10^{-4} magnetic flux lines are passing through a coil of resistance 10 ohm and number of turns 1000. If the number of flux lines reduces to 5×10^{-5} in 0.1sec , find the current induced in the coil.

(a) $0.25A$ (b) $0.5A$

(c) $1.00A$ (d) $1.5A$

49. Choose the incorrect statements from the following regarding magnetic lines of field.

(a) The direction of magnetic field at a point is taken to be the direction in which the north pole of a magnetic compass needle points.

(b) Magnetic field lines are closed curves.

(c) If magnetic field lines are parallel and equidistant, they represent zero field strength.

(d) Relative strength of magnetic field is shown by the degree of closeness of the field lines.

50. In electromagnetic wave, the average energy density is associated:

(a) With electric field only

(b) With magnetic field only

(c) Equally with electric and magnetic fields

(d) None of these

51. The Electromagnetic Waves are:

(a) Longitudinal waves

(b) Transverse waves

(c) Both longitudinal and transverse waves

(d) It's nature depend upon medium

52. Which of the following statement is false for the properties of electromagnetic waves?

(a) These waves do not require any material medium for propagation

(b) Both electric and magnetic field vectors attains the maxima and minima at the same place and same time

(c) The energy in electromagnetic wave is divided equally between electric and magnetic vectors

(d) Both electric and magnetic field vectors are parallel to each other and perpendicular to the direction of propagation of wave

53. A ray is incident at an angle of incidence i on one surface of a small angle prism (with the angle of prism A) and emerges normally from the opposite surface. If the refractive index of the material of the prism is μ . Then the angle of incidence is nearly equal to:

(a) $\dfrac{\mu A}{2}$ (b) $\dfrac{A}{2\mu}$

(c) μA (d) $\dfrac{A}{\mu}$

54. A car is fitted with a convex side-view mirror of focal length 20 cm . A second car 2.8 m behind the first car is overtaking the first car at a relative speed of 15 ms^{-1} . The speed of the image of the second car as seen in the mirror of the first one is:

(a) $\dfrac{1}{10}$ ms^{-1} (b) $\dfrac{1}{15}$ ms^{-1}

(c) 10 ms^{-1} (d) 15 ms^{-1}

55. A light ray falls on a glass surface of refractive index $\sqrt{3}$, at an angle $60°$. The angle between the refracted and reflected rays would be:

(a) $90°$ (b) $120°$

(c) $30°$ (d) $60°$

56. A biconvex lens has radii of curvature, $20 \, cm$ each. If the refractive index of the material of the lens is 1.5 , the power of the lens is :

(a) $+5D$ (b) infinity

(c) $+2D$ (d) $+20D$

57. An observer is moving with half the speed of light towards a stationary microwave source emitting waves at frequency $10 GHz$. What is the frequency of the microwave measured by the observer? (speed of light $= 3 \times 10^8 ms^{-1}$)

(a) $10.1 GHz$ (b) $12.1 GHz$

(c) $17.3 GHz$ (d) $15.3 GHz$

58. In a Young's double slit experiment, slits are separated by $0.5mm$, and the screen is placed $150cm$ away. A beam of light consisting of two wavelengths, $650nm$ and $520nm$, is used to obtain interference fringes on the screen. The least distance from the common central maximum to the point where the bright fringes due to both the wave lengths coincide is:

(a) $1.56mm$ (b) $7.8mm$

(c) $9.75mm$ (d) $15.6mm$

59. A particle A of mass m and initial velocity v collides with a particle B of mass $\frac{m}{2}$ which is at rest. The collision is head on, and elastic. The ratio of the de-Broglie wave lengths λ_A to λ_B after the collision is:

(a) $\frac{\lambda_A}{\lambda_B} = \frac{1}{3}$ (b) $\frac{\lambda_A}{\lambda_B} = 2$

(c) $\frac{\lambda_A}{\lambda_B} = \frac{2}{3}$ (d) $\frac{\lambda_A}{\lambda_B} = \frac{1}{2}$

60. Monochromatic light of frequency 6.0×10^{14} Hz is produced by a laser. The power emitted is 2.0×10^{-3} W . What is the energy of a photon in the light beam?

(a) 3.98×10^{-19} J   (b) 5.98×10^{-19} J

(c) 6×10^{-19} J   (d) 2.98×10^{-19} J

61. The work function of caesium is 2.14eV . Find the wavelength of the incident light if the photocurrent is brought to zero by a stopping potential of 0.60 V .

(a) 454 nm   (b) 554 nm

(c) 450 nm   (d) 404 nm

62. What is the de Broglie wavelength associated with an electron moving with a speed of 5.4×10^6 m/s ?

(a) 5.135 nm   (b) 3.135 nm

(c) 0.135 nm   (d) 2.135 nm

63. Light of frequency 7.21×10^{14} Hz is incident on a metal surface. Electrons with a maximum speed of 6.0×10^5 m/s from the surface. What is the threshold frequency for photoemission of electrons?

(a) 5.74×10^{14} Hz   (b) 4.74×10^{14} Hz

(c) 6.74×10^{14} Hz   (d) 4×10^{14} Hz

64. In photoelectric effect, the momentum of incident photon of energy 3×10^{-19} J is :

(a) 9×10^{11}kgms^{-1} (b) 10^{-27}kgms^{-1}

(c) 3×10^{-11}kgms^{-1} (d) Zero

65. A solution containing active cobalt $^{60}_{27}$Co having activity of 0.8μCi and decay constant λ is injected in an animal's body. If 1 cm^3 of blood is drawn from the animal's body after 10 hrs of injection, the activity found was 300 decays per minute. What is the volume of blood that is flowing in the body ? $\left(1\text{Ci} = 3.7 \times 10^{10}\right.$ decays per second and at $t = 10$ hrs $\left. e^{-\lambda t} = 0.84\right)$

(a) 6 liters   (b) 7 liters

(c) 4 liters   (d) 5 liters

66. A proton is accelerating in a cyclotron where the applied magnetic field is 2 T . If the potential gap effectively 100kV then how many revolutions the proton has to make between the "dees" to acquire kinetic energy of 20MeV?

(a) 200   (b) 300

(c) 400   (d) 100

67. According to the Bore model, the velocity of the electron in the nth orbit is __________ proportional to the magnetic field at the center (at the nucleus) of the hydrogen atom.

(a) $\frac{1}{n^3}$ (b) $\frac{1}{n^5}$

(c) n^5 (d) n^3

68. The activation of a radioactive element decreases to one-third of the original intensity I_0 over a period of nine years. After the next nine years have passed, its activity will be:

(a) I_0 (b) $\frac{2}{3}I_0$

(c) $\frac{I_0}{9}$ (d) $\frac{I_0}{6}$

69. The electrical conductivity of a semiconductor increases when electromagnetic radiation of wavelength shorter than 2480 nm is incident on it. The band gap (in eV) for the semiconductor is

(a) 0.9   (b) 0.7

(c) 0.5   (d) 1.1

70. A junction diode has a resistance of 25Ω when forward-biased and 2500Ω when reverse-biased. The current in the arrangement shown in the figure will be

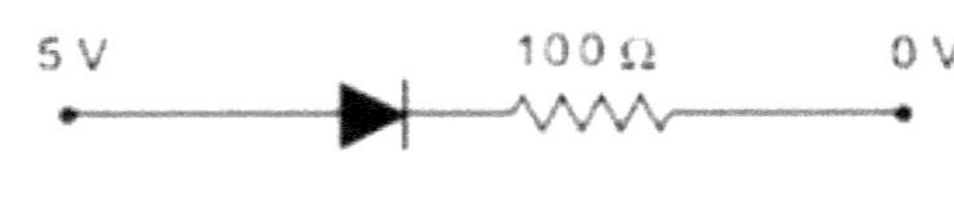

(a) $\frac{1}{10}A$ (b) $\frac{1}{25}A$

(c) $\frac{1}{520}A$ (d) $\frac{1}{480}A$

71. The circuit shown in the figure contains two diodes D_1 and D_2 , each with a forward resistance of 50 ohms and infinite backward resistance. If the battery voltage is 6 V, the current (in amperes) through the 100 ohm resistance is

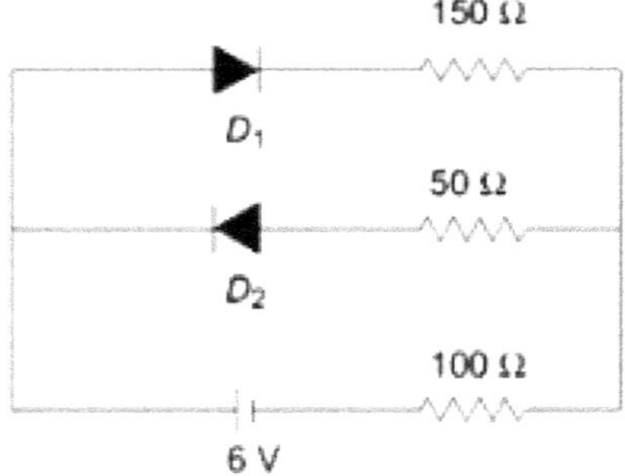

(a) zero   (b) $0.02A$

(c) $0.03A$ (d) $0.036A$

72. The input resistance of a common emitter transistor amplifier, if the output resistance is $500k\Omega$, the current gain $\alpha = 0.98$ and power gain is 6.0625×10^6 , is

(a) 198Ω (b) 300Ω

(c) 100Ω (d) 400Ω

73. In a p-n-p transistor, working as a common base amplifier, the current gain is 0.96 and the emitter current is 7.2 mA. The base current is:

(a) 0.20 mA   (b) 0.36 mA

(c) 0.29 mA   (d) 0.45 mA

74. Water from a tap emerges vertically downwards with

an initial speed of $1.0\,ms^{-1}$. The cross-sectional area of the tap is $10^{-4}m^2$. Assume that the pressure is constant throughout the stream of water and that flow is streamlined. The cross-sectional area of the stream, $0.15m$ below the tap would be:
(take $g = 110\,ms^{-2}$)

(a) $2 \times 10^{-5}m^2$ (b) $5 \times 10^{-5}m^2$

(c) $5 \times 10^{-4}m^2$ (d) $1 \times 10^{-5}m^2$

75. Two soap bubbles A and B are kept in a closed chamber where air is maintained at pressure $8N/m^2$. The radii of bubbles A and B are $2cm$ and $4cm$ respectively. Surface tension of the soap water used to make bubbles is $0.04N/m$. Find the ratio $\frac{n_B}{n_A}$, where n_A and n_B are the number of moles of air in bubbles A and B respectively. (neglect the effect of gravity)

(a) 2   (b) 9

(c) 8   (d) 6

76. Modulus of elasticity depends upon ___________.

(a) stress   (b) strain

(c) applied force   (d) None of these

77. A steel wire of cross-sectional area 3×10^{-6} m^2 can bear a maximum strain of 10^{-3}. Young's modulus of steel is 2×10^{11} N/m^2. The maximum mass this wire can hold is:

(a) 40 kg   (b) 60 kg

(c) 80 kg   (d) 100 kg

78. A wire elongates by l mm when a load W is hanged from it. If the wire goes over a pulley and two weights W each are hung at the two ends, the elongtion is ______.

(a) 1   (b) 2

(c) 0   (d) $\frac{l}{2}$

79. A wire can be broken by applying load of 200N. The force required to break another wire of the same length and same material, but double in diameter is ______.

(a) 200N   (b) 400N

(c) 600N   (d) 800N

80. Two wires of the same length and made of the same material, but having radii in the ratio 1 : 2 are stretched by two unequal forces to produce equal elongation. Find the ratio of the two forces.

(a) $1:4$ (b) $1:2$

(c) $2:1$ (d) $4:5$

// Smart Answer Sheet //

Correct — Percentage of students who answered correctly.

Skipped — Percentage of students who skipped.

Q.	Ans.	Correct / Skipped	Q.	Ans.	Correct / Skipped	Q.	Ans.	Correct / Skipped
1	C	41.89% / 1.55%	2	D	88.9% / 0.0%	3	B	46.84% / 1.66%
4	C	12.75% / 3.9%	5	B	59.97% / 1.64%	6	A	45.2% / 1.45%
7	D	79.55% / 0.0%	8	C	89.78% / 0.0%	9	C	41.07% / 1.46%
10	B	82.28% / 0.0%	11	C	65.85% / 1.38%	12	B	86.76% / 0.0%
13	A	69.4% / 1.6%	14	B	41.54% / 1.3%	15	C	56.49% / 1.93%
16	B	40.31% / 1.61%	17	B	27.67% / 4.48%	18	D	69.47% / 1.08%
19	A	56.73% / 1.05%	20	B	58.45% / 1.24%	21	D	69.78% / 1.78%
22	D	52.48% / 1.61%	23	A	59.29% / 1.24%	24	C	53.43% / 1.57%
25	C	47.6% / 1.25%	26	A	79.87% / 0.0%	27	D	63.88% / 1.21%
28	D	50.86% / 1.02%	29	A	78.06% / 0.0%	30	C	55.07% / 1.47%
31	C	67.99% / 1.99%	32	B	45.01% / 1.79%	33	D	60.91% / 1.37%
34	B	16.04% / 4.62%	35	A	63.66% / 1.12%	36	B	46.34% / 1.31%
37	C	67.48% / 1.59%	38	B	67.18% / 1.11%	39	A	51.21% / 1.94%
40	B	61.09% / 1.21%	41	C	57.42% / 1.48%	42	D	68.67% / 1.3%
43	D	41.87% / 1.07%	44	C	23.32% / 4.49%	45	B	54.72% / 1.56%
46	A	77.43% / 0.0%	47	C	47.43% / 1.53%	48	B	66.56% / 1.8%
49	C	52.46% / 1.05%	50	C	48.86% / 1.56%	51	B	85.06% / 0.0%
52	D	77.65% / 0.0%	53	C	40.55% / 1.27%	54	B	65.99% / 1.18%
55	A	25.46% / 4.99%	56	A	58.04% / 1.77%	57	C	51.38% / 1.82%
58	B	62.26% / 1.67%	59	B	54.54% / 1.73%	60	A	29.38% / 3.68%
61	A	32.66% / 4.87%	62	C	42.62% / 1.08%	63	B	19.62% / 4.99%
64	B	56.78% / 1.53%	65	D	32.88% / 4.66%	66	D	46.77% / 1.15%
67	B	56.35% / 1.35%	68	C	61.33% / 1.46%	69	C	64.98% / 1.79%
70	A	65.66% / 1.24%	71	B	55.59% / 1.17%	72	A	68.65% / 1.34%
73	C	62.91% / 1.99%	74	B	60.85% / 1.1%	75	D	23.13% / 4.38%
76	D	82.31% / 0.0%	77	B	52.14% / 1.92%	78	A	49.99% / 1.85%
79	D	68.04% / 1.75%	80	A	52.21% / 1.78%			

// Hints and Solutions //

1(C). Fundamental quantities are those quantities which cannot be expressed any other physical quantities. The seven fundamental quantities along as follows:

Fundamental quantity	Dimension	Unit
Time	T	second (s)
Mass	M	kilogram (kg)
Electric current	A	ampere (A)
Thermodynamic temperature	K	Kelvin (K)
Amount of substance	mol	mole (mol)
Luminous intensity	cd	Candela (cd)
Length	L	meter (m)

2(D). Candela is a unit of luminous intensity. In photometry, the wavelength-weighted power emanating from a light source in a particular direction, in a unit solid angle, is called luminous intensity. It is based on the optical formula, which is a standardized model of the sensitivity of the human eye.

3(B). Surface tension is the property of a fluid resisting an external force on its surface. Surface tension is caused by cohesive forces between the molecules of the fluid on the surface.

Mathematically,

Surface tension, $(S) = \dfrac{F}{l}$

Where, F = force, and l = length of the film of the fluid.

Surface tension is dimensionally equal to the ratio of force to length.

Therefore, the SI unit of surface tension is newton/metre.

4(C). Option (C):

Tension (force) $= \left[MLT^{-2}\right]$

Surface tension $= \dfrac{\text{force}}{\text{length}}$

$= \dfrac{\left[MLT^{-2}\right]}{[L]} = \left[ML^{0}T^{-2}\right]$

Option (A):

Work $= F \times \Delta x$

The dimension of force, $F = \left[MLT^{-2}\right]$

The dimension of distance, $\Delta x = \left[MLT^{-2}\right]$

$= \left[MLT^{-2}\right][L] = \left[ML^{2}T^{-2}\right]$

Torque = force $\times$ distance

$= \left[ML^{2}T^{-2}\right]$

Option (B):

Angular momentum $= mvr$

$= [M]\left[LT^{-1}\right][L] = \left[ML^{2}T^{-1}\right]$

Planck's constant $= \dfrac{E}{\nu}$

$= \dfrac{\left[ML^{2}T^{-2}\right]}{\left[T^{-1}\right]} = \left[ML^{2}T^{-1}\right]$

Option (D):

Impulse $= F \times \Delta t$

$= \left[MLT^{-2}\right][T] = \left[MLT^{-1}\right]$

Linear momentum $=$ mass $\times$ velocity

$= [M]\left[LT^{-1}\right] = \left[MLT^{-1}\right]$

So, among the above pairs only tension and surface tension does not have same dimensional formula. They both sound similar but they both have different meaning and different applications.

5(B). According to Kepler's law $\dfrac{T_1^2}{T_2^2} = \dfrac{R_1^3}{R_2^3}$

Here, $T_1 = 365$ days, $T_2 = ?, R_1 = R, R_2 = \dfrac{R}{2}$

$\Rightarrow rT_2 = T_1\left(\dfrac{R_2}{R_1}\right)^{\frac{3}{2}} = 365\left[\dfrac{\frac{R}{2}}{R}\right]^{\frac{3}{2}} = 129$ days

6(A). Mass of the man m $= 40$ kg

$g = 10\, m/s^2$

Acceleration of lift in upward direction a $= 2\ \text{m/s}^2$

Let the weight shown by machine be N.

Equation of motion for the body:

ma $=$ N $-$ mg

N $=$ m(a $+$ g)

$\therefore$ N $= (40)(2 + 10) = 480$ N

Thus weight of the man recorded by machine

W$' = \dfrac{N}{g}$

$\therefore$ W$' = \dfrac{480}{10}$

$= 48$ kg

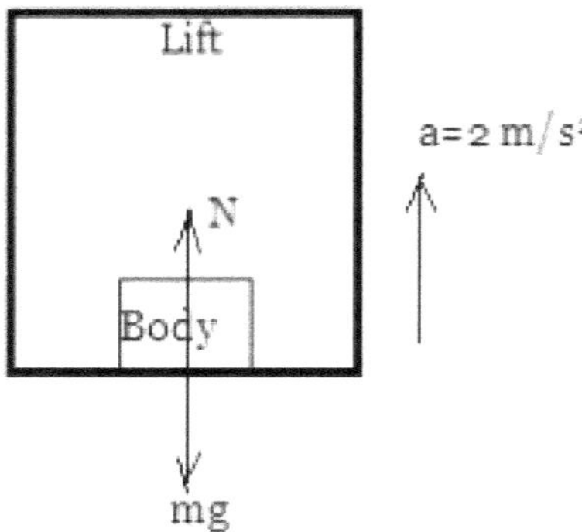

7(D). During the melting of solid, its temperature d oes not change.

During the melting of solid, all the heat given to the solid spend in the change of state from solid to liquid. That's why the temperature of the material does not change.

8(C). As we know, water can take a long time to warm up or cool down compared to the air. When water cools down to $0°C$, ice begins to form and floats on top of relatively warmer water; water at the bottom of a lake or river is typically $4°C$.

9(C). As the coefficient of cubical expansion of liquid equals the coefficient of cubical expansion of the vessel, the level of liquid will not change on heating.

If linear expansion is α, then $\gamma = 3\alpha$

Here, $\alpha = \dfrac{\gamma}{3}$ so $\gamma' = 3 \times \dfrac{\gamma}{3}$

Thus, $\gamma' = \gamma$.

10(B). The temperature determines the direction of net change of intermolecular kinetic energy.

On heating, the temperature rises, particles gain energy. As the kinetic energy increases, intermolecular space increases as they get separated from each other and the force of attraction decreases as the particles go far away from each other.

11(C). A gas is compressed to half of its initial volume isothermally. The same gas is compressed again until the volume reduces to half through an adiabatic process. Then work done is more during the adiabatic process.

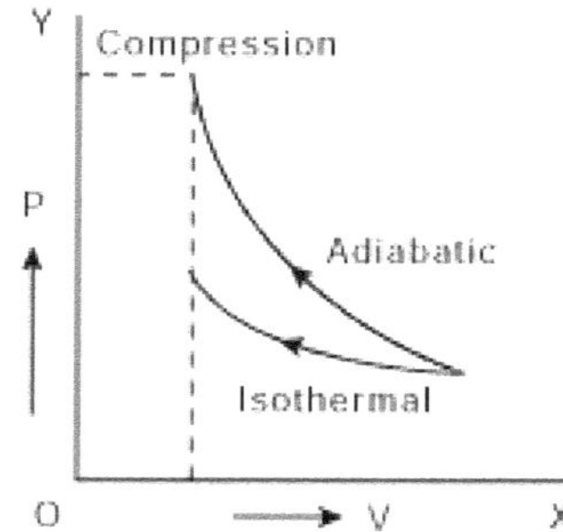

From the graph we can see that for compression of gas, area under the curve for adiabatic is more than isothermal process. Therefore, compressing the gas through adiabatic process will require more work to be done.

W_{ext} = negative of area with volume-axis

$W(\text{adiabatic}) > W(\text{isothermal})$

12(B). A point on $P - V$ diagram shows the state of the system. Each point on a $P - V$ diagram corresponds to a different state of the gas. The pressure is given on the vertical axis and the volume is given on the horizontal axis, as seen below.

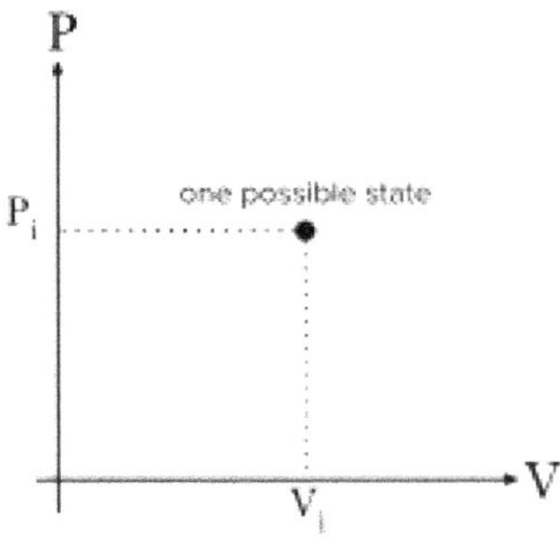

Every point on a $P - V$ diagram represents a different state for the gas (one for every possible volume and pressure).

13(A). If two bodies at different temperatures T_1 and T_2 are brought in thermal contact, heat is said to flow from the body at higher temperature to the body at lower temperature until an equilibrium is obtained, i.e., until a point at which the temperatures of both the bodies becomes the same. The equilibrium temperature turns out to be the same as the mean temperature, which can be denoted as $\frac{(T_1+T_2)}{2}$ only when thermal capacities of the two bodies are the same.

14(B). Considering the given linear process in a thermodynamic system, it can be understood that, Total work done by the gas from D to E to F is equal to the area of $\triangle DEF$.

Area of $\triangle DEF = \frac{1}{2} \times DF \times EF$

where,
DF = Change in pressure
$\Rightarrow DF = 600 N/m^2 - 300 N/m^2$
$\Rightarrow DF = 300 N/m^2$
FE = Change in volume $= 5 - 2 = 3 m^3$
Thus,
Area of $\triangle DEF = \frac{1}{2} \times 300 \times 3 = 450 J$

Clearly, the total work done by the gas from D to E to F is $450 J$.

15(C). The volume of 1 mole of He at $STP = 22.4$ litres
Total volume of He at $STP = 44.8$ litres
$\therefore$ No. of moles of He,
$n = \dfrac{\text{Total volume of He}}{\text{The volume of 1 mole of He}} = \dfrac{44.8}{22.4} = 2$
Molar specific heat of He (monoatomic gas) at constant volume,
$C_V = \frac{3}{2}R = \frac{3}{2} \times 8.31 \text{ J mol}^{-1} \text{ K}^{-1}$
$\Delta T = 15°C$
Heat required, $Q = nC_V\Delta T = 2 \times \frac{3}{2} \times 8.31 \times 15$
$Q = 373.95$ J

16(B). As we know, Kinetic energy $= \frac{3}{2}k_BT$
$\frac{3}{2}k_BT = \frac{1}{2}mv_{es}^2$
Temperature, $T = \dfrac{mv_{cn}^2}{3k_B}$ ... (i)
Here, escape velocity,
$v_{es} = 11.2 \, km/s = 11.2 \times 10^3 \, m/s$
$m = 2.76 \times 10^{-26}$ kg (mass)
$k_B = 1.38 \times 10^{-23} JK^{-1}$ (Boltzmann's constant)
Putting value in (i) so, we get,

$T = \dfrac{\left(11.2\times10^3\right)^2 \times 2.76\times 10^{-26}}{3\times1.38\times10^{-23}}$
or, $T = \dfrac{346.2144\times10^{-20}}{4.14\times10^{-21}}$
$\therefore T = 8.36 \times 10^4 K$

17(B). Given,
$M_{He} = 4$, $m_{He} = 16$ g
$M_{ox} = 32$, $m_{ox} = 16$ g
Specific heat of mixture at constant volume is given by,
$C_V = \dfrac{n_1 C_{V_1} + n_2 C_{V2}}{n_1 + n_2}$ $\quad\quad \dots\dots (1)$
For Helium gas,
Number of moles, $n_1 = \dfrac{m_{He}}{M_{He}}$
$n_1 = \dfrac{16}{4} = 4$
$\gamma_1 = \dfrac{5}{3}$
For Oxygen Gas,
Number of moles, $n_2 = \dfrac{m_{Ox}}{M_{Ox}}$
$n_2 = \dfrac{16}{32} = \dfrac{1}{2}$
$\gamma_2 = \dfrac{7}{5}$
And specific heat constant volume of helium gas,
$C_{V_1} = \dfrac{R}{\gamma_1 - 1} = \dfrac{R}{\frac{5}{3}-1} = \dfrac{3}{2}R$
The specific heat of oxygen at constant volume,
$C_{V_2} = \dfrac{R}{\gamma_2 - 1} = \dfrac{R}{\frac{7}{5}-1} = \dfrac{5}{2}R$
From equation (1),
$C_V = \dfrac{4\times\frac{3}{2}R + \frac{1}{2}\times\frac{5}{2}R}{4+\frac{1}{2}}$
$= \dfrac{6R + \frac{5}{4}R}{\frac{9}{2}}$
$= \dfrac{29R\times2}{9\times4} = \dfrac{29R}{18}$
Now, $C_V = \dfrac{R}{\gamma - 1}$
$\Rightarrow \gamma - 1 = \dfrac{R}{C_V}$
or $\gamma = \dfrac{R}{C_V} + 1 = \dfrac{R}{\frac{29}{18}R} + 1$
$\dfrac{C_p}{C_V} = \dfrac{18}{29} + 1$
$= \dfrac{18+29}{29} = 1.62$

18(D). Given that,
$n_1 = 2, \dfrac{C_{P_1}}{C_{V_1}} = \dfrac{5}{3}, n_2 = 3$ and $\dfrac{C_{P_2}}{C_{V_2}} = \dfrac{4}{3}$
We know that,
$\left(\dfrac{C_P}{C_V}\right)_{mix} = \dfrac{n_1 C_{P_1} + n_2 C_{P_2}}{n_1 C_{V_1} + n_2 C_{V_2}}$ $\quad\quad \dots\dots(1)$
And CP - CV = nR
$\Rightarrow \dfrac{C_P - 1}{C_V} = \dfrac{nR}{C_V}$
Rearranging the Eq.(1), we get,
$\dfrac{n_1}{\frac{C_{P_1}}{C_{V_1}}-1} + \dfrac{n_2}{\frac{C_{P_2}}{C_{V_2}}-1} = \dfrac{n_1 + n_2}{\left(\frac{C_P}{C_V}\right)_{mix}-1}$
$\Rightarrow \dfrac{2}{\frac{5}{3}-1} + \dfrac{3}{\frac{4}{3}-1} = \dfrac{5}{\left(\frac{C_P}{C_V}\right)_{mix}-1}$
$\Rightarrow \dfrac{2\times3}{2} + \dfrac{3\times3}{1} = \dfrac{5}{\left(\frac{C_p}{C_V}\right)_{mix}-1}$
$\Rightarrow 12 = \dfrac{5}{\left(\frac{C_P}{C_V}\right)_{mix}-1}$
$\Rightarrow \left(\dfrac{C_P}{C_V}\right)_{mix} - 1 = \dfrac{5}{12}$

$$\Rightarrow \left(\frac{C_P}{C_V}\right)_{\text{mix}} = \frac{5}{12} + 1$$
$$= \frac{17}{12}$$
$$= 1.42$$

19(A). Given that:
$$n_{He} = n, C_{V_H} = \frac{3R}{2}$$
$$C_{P_{He}} = \frac{5R}{2}$$
$$n_{O_2} = 2n$$
$$C_{V_{O_2}} = \frac{5R}{2}$$
$$C_{P_{O_2}} = \frac{7R}{2}$$
$$\frac{C_{P_{mit}}}{C_{V_{mit}}} = \frac{n_{He}C_{P_{He}} + n_{O_2}C_{P_{0_2}}}{n_{He}C_{V_{He}} + n_{O_2}C_{V_{0_2}}}$$
$$= \frac{n \times \left(\frac{5R}{2}\right) + 2n \times \left(\frac{7R}{2}\right)}{n \times \left(\frac{3R}{2}\right) + 2n \times \left(\frac{5R}{2}\right)} = \frac{\frac{19n}{2}}{\frac{13n}{2}} = \frac{19}{13}$$

20(B). The partial pressure of gas $A = \frac{P_1 V_1}{V_2}$
$$= \frac{600 \times 1000}{2000}$$
$$= 300 \text{ torr}$$
Similarly partial pressure of the gas B
$$= \frac{1000 \times 500}{2000}$$
$$= 250 \text{ torr}$$
So total pressure of the mixture = 300 torr + 250 torr
= 550 torr

21(D). Magnetic moment $= \sqrt{n(n+2)}$ BM
n : Number of unpaired e^-
As atomic number increases in d-block element number of unpaired e^- first increases upto middle then decreases.

22(D). In mechanical oscillations a body oscillates about its mean position which is also its equilibrium position. This position is when there is no net force acting on the body, it is in this position. The process of any quantity or measure fluctuating repeatedly about its equilibrium value in time is known as mechanical oscillation.

23(A). As - COOH group is the highest priority group, it is numbered one. So, the IUPAC name is 3– amino –5– heptanoic acid.
$$\overset{7}{C}H_3 - \overset{6}{C}H = \overset{5}{C}H - \overset{4}{C}H_2 - \overset{3}{C}H - \overset{2}{C}H_2 - \overset{1}{C}HOO$$
$$\qquad\qquad\qquad\qquad\qquad | $$
$$\qquad\qquad\qquad\qquad\quad NH_2$$

24(C). Urea has the highest nitrogen percentage i.e., (46.6%).
In other compounds are,
Ammonium sulphate $(NH_4)_2SO_4 = 21.2\%$
Calcium cyanamide $CaCN_2 = 35.0\%$
And Ammonium nitrate $NH_4NO_3 = 35.0\%$

25(C). The magnitude of electric force experienced by a charged particle in an electric field is given as,
$$F = Eq_0$$
Where E = electric field intensity, q_0 = charge on the particle.
Therefore when a charge Q is placed in the electric field E, the magnitude of the force on the charge Q will be:
$$F = EQ$$

26(A). A positive charge attracts a negative charge and repels the positive charge. A negative charge attracts a positive charge and repels a negative charge. It means Like charges repel each other and unlike charges attract each other. All the charges do not attract all the other charges always.

27(D).

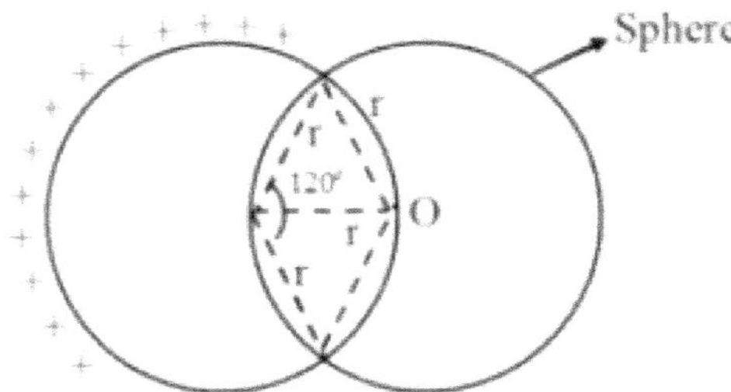

If angle at centre is 360° then charge is q.
If angle at centre is 120° then charge $= \frac{q}{360} \times 120$
So, $q_{eq} = \frac{q}{3}$
By Gauss's law,
$$\phi = \frac{q_{eq}}{\varepsilon_0}$$
$$\Rightarrow \phi = \frac{q}{3\varepsilon_0}$$

28(D). **Coulomb's law:** When two charged particles of charges q_1 and q_2 are separated by a distance r from each other then the electrostatic force between them is directly proportional to the multiplication of charges of two particles and inversely proportional to the square of the distance between them.

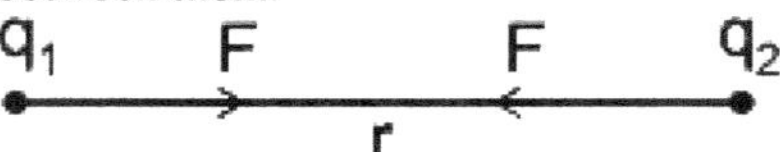

Force $(F) \propto q_1 \times q_2$
$$F \propto \frac{1}{r^2}$$
$$F = K\frac{q_1 \times q_2}{r^2}$$
Where K is a constant $= 9 \times 10^9 Nm^2/C^2$
From the above, it is clear that Coulomb's force between two point charges varies with distance 'r' in relation to $\frac{1}{r^2}$.

29(A). Given :
Volume $V = 0.2m^3, V = 5V$
The electric field in the form of potential can be written as;
$$E = -\frac{dV}{dr} \cdots (1)$$
Where V is the potential.
using equation (1) we have,
$$E = -\frac{dV}{dr}$$
$$\Rightarrow E = -\frac{d(5)}{dr}$$
$$\Rightarrow E = 0$$

30(C). The energy in electron volts is given as:
$$1eV = 1.602 \times 10^{-19} \text{ J}$$
The energy required to break the DNA bond is 10^{-20} J.
So, the energy in terms of eV will be:
$$10^{-20} \text{ J} = \frac{1}{1.602 \times 10^{-19}} \times 10^{-20}$$
$$eV = 0.062$$

31(C). Capacitance of air capacitor
$$C_0 = \frac{\varepsilon_0 A}{d} = 6\mu F \quad\ldots\ldots\ldots\ldots(i)$$
When a dielectric of permittivity ε_r and dielectric constant K is introduced between the plates, then
Capacitance, $C = \frac{K\varepsilon_0 A}{d} = 30\mu F \quad\ldots\ldots\ldots(ii)$

Dividing equation (ii) by (i), we get

$$\frac{C}{C_0} = \frac{\frac{K\epsilon_0 A}{d}}{\frac{\epsilon_0 A}{d}} = \frac{30}{6}$$

$\Rightarrow K = 5$

$\therefore$ permittivity of the medium $= \epsilon_0 K$

$= 8.85 \times 10^{-12} \times 5 = 0.44 \times 10^{-10} C^2\ N^{-1}\ m^{-2}$

32(B). Electric Potential at an angle of $60°$ is

$$V = \frac{KP \cos\theta}{r^2}$$

there $K = \dfrac{1}{4\pi\epsilon_0} = 9 \times 10^9 Nm^2/C^2$

$P = 16 \times 10^{-9} Cm$

$r = 0.6\ m$

$\therefore V = \dfrac{9 \times 10^9 \times 16 \times 10^{-9} \times \cos 60°}{(0.6)^2}$

$V = \dfrac{9 \times 16 \times 1}{0.6 \times 0.6 \times 2}$

$V = 200\ Vol$

33(D). Ohm's law is valid when the temperature of conductor is constant.

The resistance is dependent on resistivity and resistivity is variable at variable temperature, to keep resistance constant we have to consider resistivity as constant and to keep resistivity constant we have to keep temperature constant. Hence the ohm's law is said to be valid at constant temperature only.

so, $V \alpha I$ Or $I \alpha V$

And $I \alpha \dfrac{1}{R}$

$V = IR$

34(B). Given

$x = 3mV/cm = 0.3\ V/m$

$R = 20\Omega$

$I = 60\ cm = 0.6\ m$

Let the current in the 20Ω resistance be I.

So potential difference across 20Ω resistance is given as,

$\Rightarrow V = IR$ ....(1)

If the potential gradient is x and the null point comes at length l, then,

$\Rightarrow V = xl$ ....(2)

By equation 1 and equation 2,

$\Rightarrow I = \dfrac{xl}{R}$

$\Rightarrow I = \dfrac{0.3 \times 0.6}{20}$

$\Rightarrow I = 9 \times 10^{-3}\ A$

$\Rightarrow I = 9\ mA$

35(A). CALCULATION:

The given diagram is,

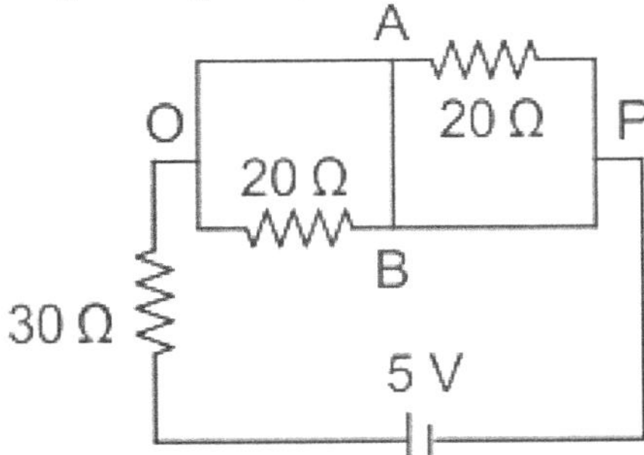

Since there is no resistance in the path O-A-B-P so the current will flow through this path and no current will flow in both 20 Ω resistance. So both 20 Ω resistance can be removed from the circuit. The above diagram can be drawn as,

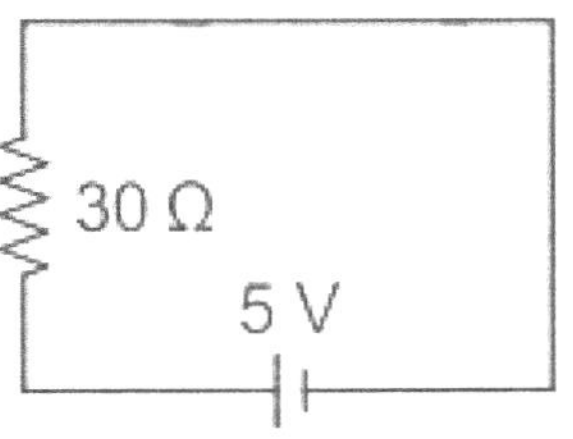

By Ohm's law,

$\Rightarrow I = \dfrac{V}{R}$

$\Rightarrow I = \dfrac{5}{30}$

$\Rightarrow I = \dfrac{1}{6} A$

36(B). CONCEPT:

Electric current: The flow of charge in a conductor under a potential difference maintained between the ends of the conductor constitutes an 'electric current' in the conductor. In other words, The rate of flow of charge is called 'electric current.

Thus, if in an electric circuit, an amount of charge Q flows in t second then the electric current (I) in the circuit is given by:

I = Q/t

- The SI unit of electric current is 'ampere' (A) Ampere is a fundamental unit in the S.I system. The ampere is defined on the basis of the force acting between two current-carrying, parallel conductors.

EXPLANATION:

If Charge (Q) = 1 coulomb (C) , t = 1 second (s) , then i = 1 ampere (A) , thus

1 ampere = 1 coulomb per second

$1A = 1\ Cs^{-1}$

37(C). Given,

Two long straight conductors with current I_1 and I_2 are placed along X and Y axes.

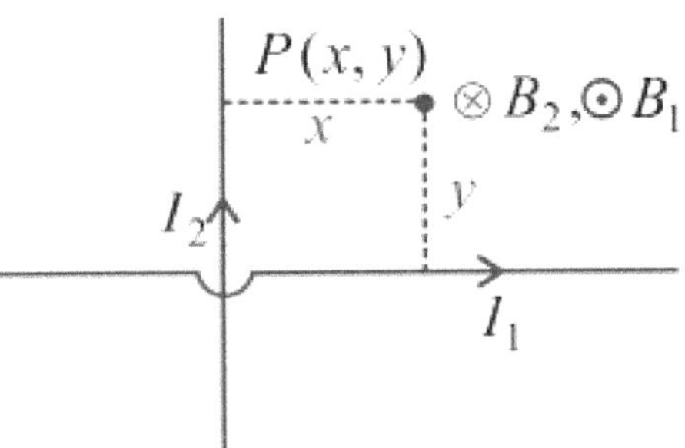

Magnetic field at point P,

$B_P = 0$

Magnetic fields by both currents have different direction. So,

$B_1 - B_2 = 0$

$\Rightarrow B_1 = B_2$

$\Rightarrow \dfrac{\mu_0 I_1}{2\pi Y} = \dfrac{\mu_0}{2\pi} \dfrac{I_2}{X}$

$\therefore Y = \dfrac{I_1}{I_2} X$

38(B). Magnetic diploe: It is a tiny magnet formed due to the flow of current through a closed-loop and acts like a tiny magnet having magnetic north and south poles.

Magnetic dipole moment:

The magnetic dipole moment is the product of current and area and is given by:

M = I × A

Where, I = Current and A = Area

The magnetic field on the equatorial line is given by:

$$B_e = \frac{\mu_0}{4\pi}\left(\frac{M}{r^3}\right)$$

39(A). The disc behaves made up of coils arranged in a plane in which current is flowing in an anticlockwise direction since the negative charge is rotating in a clockwise direction. The magnetic field at point A due to small elements of a ring will be into the plane of the page using Biot-Savart law.

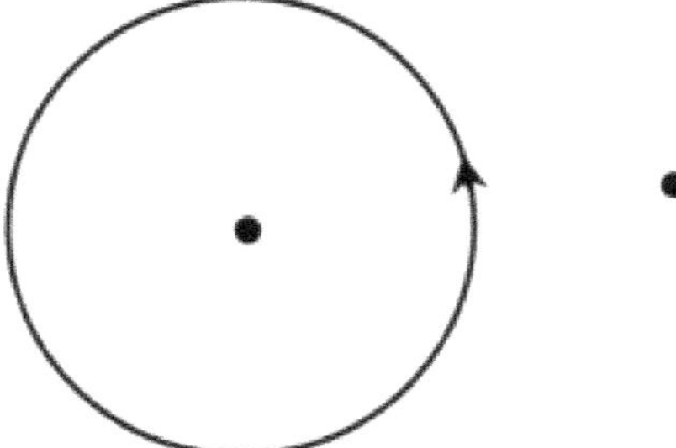

$$\vec{B} = \frac{\mu_0 \times i}{4\pi r^3}(\vec{dl} \times \vec{r})$$

By the right-hand rule, the direction of the magnetic field at point A in the plane of the disc is into the page.

40(B). A negative test charge is moving near a long straight wire carrying a current. The force acting on the test charge is parallel to the direction of the current. The motion of the charge is towards the wire.

It is given that a negative charge is moving near a long straight wire carrying a current. Let I be the current flowing through the wire along the y-axis and the charge is moving towards the wire along the x-axis. Let A be a point in the vicinity of the wire and the test charge. Then according to Fleming's left hand thumb rule the direction of the magnetic field at point A will be along the z-axis, that is out of the plane of the paper. The intensity of the magnetic field at A is given by $\vec{B} = B_0 \times \hat{k}$, where $\hat{k}$ is the unit vector along the z-axis. If is the velocity vector, then

The force acting on the test charge is given by,

$$\vec{F} = -q \times \vec{v} \times \vec{B}$$
$$\Rightarrow \vec{F} = -q \times v \times \hat{x} \times B_0 \times \hat{k}$$

As the vector product of $\hat{x} \times \hat{k}$ is $-\hat{j}$.

Therefore, $\vec{F} = +q \times v \times B_0 \times \hat{j}$

So, the particle will move towards the wire.

41(C). A uniform magnetic field B of 0.3 T is along the positive Z-direction. A rectangular loop (abcd) of sides 10 cm × 5 cm carries a current I of 12 A . The following different orientations one corresponds to stable equilibrium:

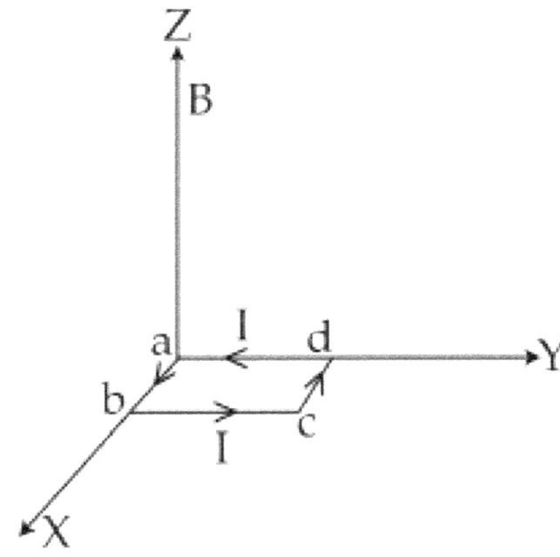

42(D). Given,
$V_L = 4$ V
$V_C = 8$ V
$V_R = 5$ V

Using $V = \sqrt{V_R^2 + (V_C - V_L)^2}$
$\Rightarrow V = \sqrt{5^2 + (8-4)^2}$
$\Rightarrow V = \sqrt{41}$
$\Rightarrow V = 6.4$ V

43(D). $E = \alpha t + \frac{1}{2}\beta t^2$,

The above equation is in the standard form of the parabola. According to this, the graph will be a parabola, such that first emf increases and then decreases.

The graph between E and t :

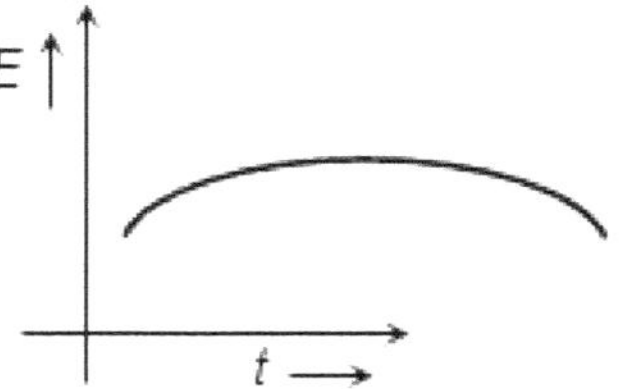

44(C). Total dipole moment of the atomic dipole $= n \times M$
$= 2 \times 10^{24} \times 1.5 \times 10^{-23}$
$= 30 JT^{-1}$

Magnetic saturation is achieved at 15%
$M_1 = \frac{15}{100} \times 30 = 4.5 JT^{-1}$

When magnetic field is $B_2 = 0.98T, T_2 = 2.8K$, its total dipole moment is M_2

According to Curie's Law, we have,
$$\frac{M_2}{M_1} = \frac{B_2}{B_1} \times \frac{T_1}{T_2}$$
$$\Rightarrow M_2 = 10.336 JT^{-1} \approx 10 JT^{-1}$$

45(B). Given,
$N = 20$
$\Phi = 0.3$ weber
$t = 1$ sec

$$\text{EMF induced} = \frac{\text{Net change of flux through the entire coil}}{\text{Time}}$$

$E = \frac{N\Phi}{t}$ (N = number of turns)
$E = 20 \times 0.3$
$= 6$ V

46(A). Active power and apparent power are respectively measured in kW and kVA.

Power factor of an AC circuit is defined as the ratio of the active power consumed by a circuit to the apparent power consumed by the same circuit. The power which is actually consumed or utilized in an AC Circuit is called active power. It is measured in kW or MW. The product of the root-mean-square value of voltage and current is known as apparent power. It is measured in kVA or MVA.

47(C). There is a uniform magnetic field directed perpendicular and into the pane of the paper. An irregular shaped conducting loop is slowly changing into a circular loop in the plane of the paper. Then current is induced in the loop in the anti-clockwise direction.

Due to changes in the shape of the loop, the area of the loop changes. So magnetic flux ϕ linked with the loop changes. So, By Faraday's Law, there will be induced emf in the loop so the current is induced in the loop in such a direction that it opposes the increases in flux.

48(B). Given,
Initial magnetic flux $(\phi_1) = 5.5 \times 10^{-4}$ Wb,
Final magnetic flux $(\phi_2) = 5 \times 10^{-5}$ Wb,
Resiatnace $(R) = 10\Omega$,
Number of turns $(N) = 1000$,
Change in time $(\Delta t) = 0.1$sec
Now,
Change in flux:
$$d\phi = (\phi_2 - \phi_1)$$
$$= \left(5 \times 10^{-5} - 5.5 \times 10^{-4}\right)$$
$$= -5 \times 10^{-4} \text{wb}$$
Induced emf in coils,
$$e = -N\frac{d\phi}{dt}$$
$$= -1000\frac{\left(-5 \times 10^{-4}\right)}{0.1}$$
$$= 5V$$
Induced current in the coil,
$$i = \frac{e}{R}$$
$$= \frac{5}{10}$$
$$= 0.5A$$

49(C). This statement is false about the magnetic field lines that if magnetic field lines are parallel and equidistant then they represent zero-field strength because if they are parallel and are at an equal distance then they have a uniform magnetic field and don't have zero magnetic field strength.

50(C). The energy in an electromagnetic wave is tied up in the electric and magnetic fields. In general, the energy per unit volume in an electric field is given by:

energy density in electric field $= \frac{1}{2}\epsilon_0 E^2$

In a magnetic field, the energy per unit volume is:

energy density in magnetic field $= \frac{1}{2}\frac{B^2}{\mu_0}$

An electromagnetic wave has both electric and magnetic fields, so the total energy density associated with an electromagnetic wave is

$$u = \frac{1}{2}\epsilon_0 E^2 + \frac{1}{2}\frac{B^2}{\mu_0}$$

It turns out that for an electromagnetic wave, the energy associated with the electric field is equal to the energy associated with the magnetic field, so the energy density can be written in terms of just one or the other:

$$u = \frac{1}{2}\epsilon_0 E^2 = \frac{1}{2}\frac{B^2}{\mu_0}$$

This also implies that in an electromagnetic wave, $E = cB$.

51(B). Electromagnetic waves are the transverse waves.
Transverse Waves:
Those waves whose direction of propagation and direction of disturbance is always perpendicular, are known as transverse waves.
These waves produced in a medium that can sustain shearing strain.
Example: Electromagnetic Waves, Ripples on the surface of water, Vibrations in a guitar string.

52(D). **CONCEPT:**
- Electromagnetic waves or EM waves: The waves that are formed as a result of vibrations between an electric field and a magnetic field and they are perpendicular to each other and to the direction of the wave is called an electromagnetic wave.
- The accelerating charged particle produces an electromagnetic (EM) wave.
- A charged particle oscillating about an equilibrium position is an accelerating charged particle.
- Electromagnetic waves do not require any matter to propagate from one place to another as it consists of photons. They can move in a vacuum.

Properties of electromagnetic waves:
- Not have any charge or we can say that they are neutral.
- Propagate as a transverse wave.
- They move with the velocity the same as that of light i.e 3×10^8 m/s.
- It contains energy and they also contain momentum.
- They can travel in a vacuum also.

From above it is clear that Electromagnetic waves do not require any matter to propagate from one place to another as it consists of photons. Therefore option (A) is correct.

In an electromagnetic wave, the electric field and magnetic field vary continuously with maxima and minima at the same place and same time. Therefore option (B) is correct.

The energy in an electromagnetic wave is divided equally between electric and magnetic fields. Therefore option (C) is correct.

An electromagnetic wave is a perpendicular variation in both the electric field(E) and Magnetic field(B). Therefore option (D) is incorrect.

53(C).

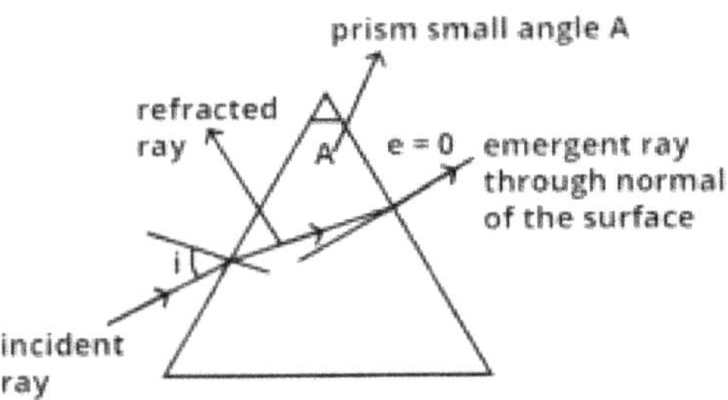

Given,
The angle of incident $= i$
Prism small angle $= A$
Refractive material of the prism $= \mu$
Let the angle of emergence $= e$
Now, it is given that the incident ray emerges normally from the opposite surface of the prism so the angle of emergence becomes zero.
$$\Rightarrow \angle e = 0 \ \text{......... } (i)$$
Let angle of deviation in the prime be δ
So, as we know the relation between the angle of

deviation (δ), small angle of prism (A) and the refractive index of the prism μ which is given as,
$$\Rightarrow \delta = (\mu - 1)A \quad\text{......... } (ii)$$
Now, as we know in a prism, a small angle of prism plus an angle of deviation in a prism is equal to the sum of angle of incidence and angle of emergence. Therefore, we have,
$$\Rightarrow \delta + A = i + e \quad\text{....... } (iii)$$
Now, substitute the value from equation (i) and (ii) in equation (iii) we have,
$$\Rightarrow (\mu - 1)A + A = i + 0$$
Now, simplify the above equation we have,
$$\Rightarrow \mu A - A + A = i$$
Now, cancel out the positive, negative same terms we have,
$$\Rightarrow i = \mu A$$
So, this is the required angle of incidence such that the prism has a small angle A and emerges normally from the opposite surface.

54(B). Given,
Focal length $= 20$ cm
Relative speed $= 15$ ms^{-1}
For the mirror, $\frac{1}{u} + \frac{1}{v} = \frac{1}{f}$
Differentiate this equation with respect to t, we get
$$\Rightarrow -\frac{1}{u^2}\frac{du}{dt} - \frac{1}{v^2}\frac{dv}{dt} = 0$$
$$\Rightarrow \frac{dv}{dt} = -\frac{v^2}{u^2}\left(\frac{du}{dt}\right)$$
But $\frac{v}{u} = \frac{f}{u-f}$
$$\therefore \frac{dv}{dt} = -\left(\frac{f}{u-f}\right)^2\left(\frac{du}{dt}\right)$$
$$= \left(\frac{0.2}{-2.8-0.2}\right)^2 \times 15$$
$$= \frac{1}{15}\ \text{ms}^{-1}$$

55(A). Given:
Refractive index of incidence, $n_1 = 1$
Refractive index of refraction, $n_2 = \sqrt{3}$
The angle of incidence, $\theta_1 = 60°$
and the angle of refraction, $\theta_2 = r$
A light ray falls on a glass surface of refractive index $\sqrt{3}$, at an angle of $60°$ as shown in the figure below,

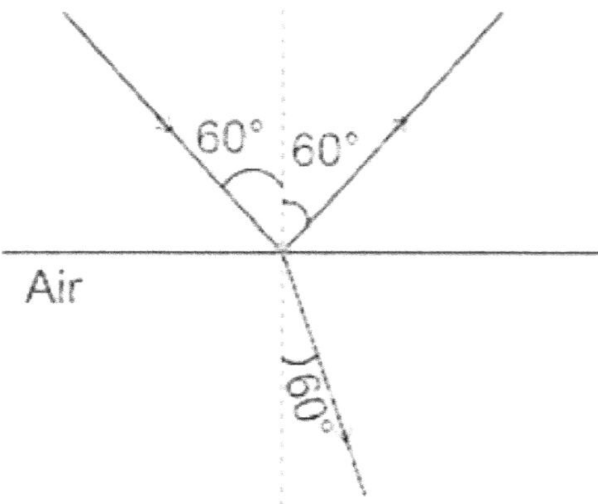

Now, according to Snell's law, we have;
$$n_1 \sin\theta_1 = n_2 \sin r \quad \cdots (1)$$
Now, on putting the given values in equation (1) we have;
$$1 \times \sin(60°) = \sqrt{3} \times \sin(r)$$
$$\Rightarrow \sin(r) = \frac{\sin(60°)}{\sqrt{3}}$$
$$\Rightarrow \sin(r) = \frac{\frac{\sqrt{3}}{2}}{\sqrt{3}}$$

$$\Rightarrow \sin(r) = \frac{1}{2}$$
$$\Rightarrow r = 30°$$
The angle of refraction. $r = 30°$
The angle between the refraction and reflection
$$= 60° + 30° = 90°$$

56(A). Given: Radii of curvature, $R_1 = +0.2\ m, R_2 = -0.2\ m$ refractive index, $\mu = 1.5$
The biconvex lens is shown below,

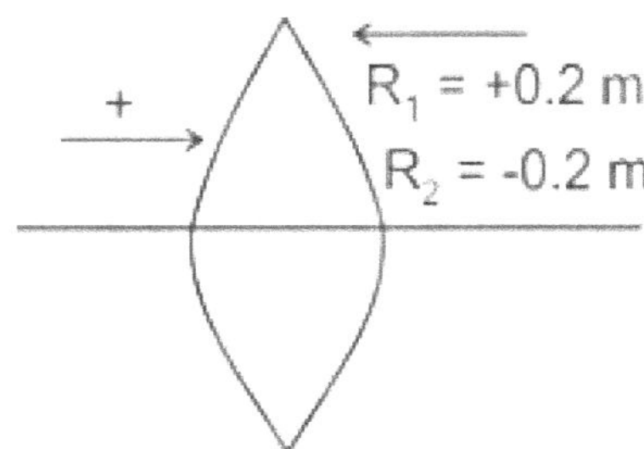

Now using the power of the biconvex which is
$$P = \frac{1}{f} = (\mu - 1)\left(\frac{1}{R_1} - \frac{1}{R_2}\right)$$
Now, on putting all the values we have;
$$P = (1.5 - 1)\left(\frac{1}{0.2} + \frac{1}{0.2}\right)$$
$$\Rightarrow P = 0.5 \times \frac{1}{0.1}$$
$$\Rightarrow P = +5D$$

57(C). Given,
Frequency of the light source, $f_0 = 10 GHz$
We know that speed of the observer, $v = \frac{C}{2}$
Using relativistic Doppler effect in case observer moves towards the stationary source.
Apparent frequency measured by observer,
$$f' = f_0\sqrt{\frac{C+v}{C-v}}$$
$$= f_0\sqrt{\frac{C+\frac{C}{2}}{C-\frac{C}{2}}}$$
$$= f_0\sqrt{\frac{\frac{3C}{2}}{\frac{C}{2}}}$$
$$= 10\sqrt{3}$$
$$= 10 \times 1.73$$
$$= 17.3 GHz$$
Thus, frequency of the microwave measured by the observer is 17.3GHz

58(B). Fringe width of pattern due to λ_1 wavelength only
$$= \frac{\lambda_1 D}{d} = \beta_1$$
Fringe width of pattern due to λ_2 wavelength only
$$= \frac{\lambda_2 D}{d} = \beta_2$$
Hence, the distance from central maximum to point where the bright fringes first meet must be the least integral multiple common to both.
$$n_1\beta_1 = n_2\beta_2$$
$$\Rightarrow n_1\frac{\lambda_1 D}{d} = n_2\frac{\lambda_2 D}{d}$$
$$\Rightarrow n_1(650) = n_2(520)$$
$$\Rightarrow n_1 = 4, n_2 = 5$$
Hence the required distance $= n_1\frac{\lambda_1 D}{d}$
$$= 4 \times \frac{(150\times10^{-2})\times(650\times10^{-9})}{(0.5\times10^{-3})}$$
$$= 7.8\ \text{mm}$$

59(B). From conservation of linear momentum,

$mv = mv_A + \frac{m}{2}v_B$

$v = v_A + \frac{v_B}{2}$

Also, by conservation of K.E,

$v^2 = v_A^2 + \frac{v_B^2}{2}$

$\left(v_A + \frac{v_B}{2}\right)^2 = v_A^2 + \left(\frac{v_B}{2}\right)^2$

$v_A v_B = \frac{v_B^2}{4}$

$\Rightarrow v_B = 4v_A$ and $m_B = \frac{m_A}{2}$

$P_A = m_A v_A$

$P_B = \frac{m_A}{2} \times 4v_A = 2P_A$

$\Rightarrow \frac{\lambda_A}{\lambda_B} = \frac{P_B}{P_A} = \frac{2P_A}{P_A} = 2$

60(A). Given,

Frequency of light, $v = 6.0 \times 10^{14}$ Hz

Power emitted by light, $P = 2.0 \times 10^{-3}$ W

We know that, $h = 6.63 \times 10^{-34}$ J s

The energy of a photon in the light beam,

$E = hv$

$= \left(6.63 \times 10^{-34} \text{Js}\right)\left(6.0 \times 10^{14} \text{ Hz}\right)$

$= 3.98 \times 10^{-19}$ J

61(A). Given,

The work function of caesium, $\phi_0 = 2.14$eV

Stopping potential $eV_0 = 0.60$ V

Planck's constant, $h = 6.63 \times 10^{-34}$ Js

Speed of light $c = 3 \times 10^8$ m/s

Einstein's Photoelectric equation is given as,

$eV_0 = hv - \phi_0 = \frac{hc}{\lambda} - \phi_0$

$\lambda = \frac{\left(6.63 \times 10^{-34} \text{ J s}\right) \times \left(3 \times 10^8 \text{ m/s}\right)}{(0.60\text{eV} + 2.14\text{eV})}$

$= \frac{19.89 \times 10^{-26} \text{ J m}}{(2.74\text{eV})}$

$\lambda = \frac{19.89 \times 10^{-26} \text{ J m}}{2.74 \times 1.6 \times 10^{-19} \text{ J}} = 454$ nm

62(C). Given,

For the electron:

Mass $m = 9.11 \times 10^{-31}$ kg

Speed $v = 5.4 \times 10^6$ m/s

Then, momentum,

$p = mv$

$= 9.11 \times 10^{-31}(\text{ kg}) \times 5.4 \times 10^6(\text{ m/s})$

$p = 4.92 \times 10^{-24}$ kg m/s

De Broglie wavelength, $\lambda = \frac{h}{p}$

$= \frac{6.63 \times 10^{-34} \text{Js}}{4.92 \times 10^{-24} \text{ kg m/s}}$

$\lambda = 0.135$ nm

63(B). Given,

$\nu = 7.21 \times 10^{14}$ Hz

$\nu_{\max} = 6 \times 10^5$ ms^{-1}

Planck's constant, $h = 6.62 \times 10^{-34}$ Js

Speed of light $c = 3 \times 10^8$ m/s

As we know,

$\nu_0 = \nu - \frac{mV_{\max}^2}{2h}$

$= 7.21 \times 10^{14} - \frac{9.1 \times 10^{-31} \times \left(6 \times 10^5\right)^2}{2 \times 6.62 \times 10^{-34}}$

$= 7.21 \times 10^{14} - 2.47 \times 10^{14}$

$= 4.74 \times 10^{14}$ Hz

64(B). Given,

The momentum of incident photon of energy,

$P = 3 \times 10^{-19}$ J

Speed of light $c = 3 \times 10^8$ m/s

Momentum of photon $P = \frac{E}{c}$

So, $P = \frac{3 \times 10^{-19}}{3 \times 10^8} = 10^{-27}$ kg m/s

65(D). The activity equation can be written as

$-\frac{dN}{dt} = \lambda N_\circ e^{-\lambda t}$

Given that

$\lambda N_0 = 0.8\mu\text{C}_i$

Putting the values,

$\lambda N_0 = 2.96 \times 10^4$

Let the volume of the blood flowing be V,

the activity would reduce by a factor of $\frac{10^{-3}}{V}$

Hence,

$\frac{\lambda N_0 10^{-3}}{V} e^{-\lambda t} = \frac{300}{60}$ (Both R.H.S. and L.H.S. are decay)

Putting the values of $e^{-\lambda t}$ and λN_0 we get

V = 5 liters

66(D). Given,

Magnetic field B = 2 T

Potential gap $\Delta V = 100$kV

We know that,

$r = \frac{mv}{qB}$

$\Rightarrow V = 100 \times 10^3 = 10^5$ volts

So, kinetic energy gained in each revolution

$= e(V) + e(V)$

$\Rightarrow 2e(V) = 2e \times 10^5$

Thus, number of revolution, $N = \frac{20 \times 10^6}{2 \times 10^5} = 100$ revolution

67(B). The center of the hydrogen atom, that is, the magnetic field on the nucleus,

$B = \frac{\mu_0 i}{2r};$

$i = \frac{e}{T} = ef \propto \frac{z^2}{n^3}$

or $r \propto \frac{n^2}{Z}$

or $B \propto \frac{i}{r} \propto \frac{Z^3}{n^5}$

To solve,

$B \propto \frac{1}{n^5}$

68(C). Original intensity $= I_0$

$t = 9$ years,

$\frac{I}{I_0} = \left(\frac{1}{2}\right)^{\frac{t}{T}}$

$\Rightarrow \frac{1}{3} = \left(\frac{1}{2}\right)^{\frac{9}{T}}$

After spending the next nine years,

$t = 18$ years,

$\Rightarrow \frac{I'}{I_0} = \left(\frac{1}{2}\right)^{\frac{18}{T}}$

$= \left\{\left(\frac{1}{2}\right)^{\frac{9}{T}}\right\}^2$

$\Rightarrow I' = \frac{I_0}{9}$

69(C). Band gap,

$E_g = \frac{hc}{\lambda}$

$= \frac{\left(6.63 \times 10^{-34}\right)\left(3 \times 10^8\right)}{2480 \times 10^{-9} \times 1.6 \times 10^{-19}} eV$

$= 0.5 \, eV$

70(A). The junction diode is forward biased. Therefore, the effective resistance

$= 25 + 100$

$= 2500\Omega$

$\therefore$ Current in diode

$\frac{5v}{100\Omega} = \frac{1}{10A}$

71(B). Given, $R = 50 + 150 + 100 = 300\,\Omega$
$V = 6\,V$
In the circuit diode D_1 is forward biased while D_2 is reverse biased.
Therefore current I will be,
$$I = \frac{V}{R}$$
$$= \frac{6}{300}$$
$$= 0.02\,A$$

72(A). Given: $\alpha = 0.98$,
According to formula:
Power gain = Voltage gain × Current gain ......(1)
Voltage gain $= A_V = \beta\dfrac{R_2}{R_1}$
Where $R_1 =$ Input resistance, $R_2 =$ Output resistance
Now, $A_V = (49)\left[\dfrac{500\times10^3}{R_1}\right]$
Also, current gain $\beta = \dfrac{\alpha}{1-\alpha} = \dfrac{0.98}{1-0.98} = 49$
From (1)
Power gain $= 49 \times \beta \times \dfrac{R_2}{R_1}$
$\Rightarrow$ Power gain
$= 6.0625 \times 10^6 = 49 \times \left[\dfrac{500\times10^3}{R_1}\right] \times .98$
$\therefore R_1 = 198\,\Omega$

73(C). Current gain $= \dfrac{I_C}{I_B}$
$I_C =$ collector current
$I_B =$ base current
So, $I_B = \dfrac{I_C}{\text{current gain}}$
$= \dfrac{7.2}{0.96}\,mA$
$= 7.5\,mA$
As $I_E = I_B + I_C$
So, $I_B = I_E - I_C$
$= (7.5 - 7.2)\,mA$
$= 0.3\,mA$
$\approx 0.29\,mA$

74(B). Let A_1, V_1 be the area and velocity of water emerging from the tap and A_2, V_2 be the area and velocity of water $0.15\,m$ below the tap.
Applying equation of motion for a fluid particle,
$V_2^2 = V_1^2 + 2gh$
$V_2 = \sqrt{1^2 + (2 \times 10 \times 0.15)}$
$V_2 = 2\,m/s$
Applying the continuity equation for incompressible flow,
$A_1 V_1 = A_2 V_2$
$10^{-4} \times 1 = A_2 \times 2$
$\Rightarrow A_2 = 5 \times 10^{-5}\,m^2$

75(D). As we know,
$$P = P_0 + \frac{4T}{r}$$
Where, P is pressure inside a bubble, 'P_0' is the outside pressure, 'T' is the surface tension and 'r' is the radius of the bubble.
$V = \frac{4}{3}\pi r^3$
Where, V is volume of the soap bubble
From the ideal gas equation, we know that
$PV = nRT$
Given, $P_0 = 8N/m^2$, $R_A = 2\,cm$, $R_B = 4\,cm$, $T = 0.04 N/m$
The ratio of the number of moles of air in bubbles B and A:
$$\frac{P_A V_A}{P_B V_B} = \frac{n_A R_A T}{n_B R_B T}$$

$\Rightarrow \dfrac{(16)\left(\frac{4}{3}\pi \times \left(2\times10^{-2}\right)^3\right)}{(12)\left(\frac{4}{3}\pi\left(4\times10^{-2}\right)^3\right)} = \dfrac{n_A R_A T}{n_B R_B T}$

$\Rightarrow \dfrac{(16)\left(2\times10^{-2}\right)^3}{(12)\left(4\times10^{-2}\right)^3} = \dfrac{n_A}{n_B}$

$\Rightarrow \dfrac{n_A}{n_B} = \dfrac{1}{6}$

$\Rightarrow \dfrac{n_B}{n_A} = 6$

76(D). Stress: Stress is the ratio of the load or force to the cross-sectional area of the material to which the load is applied. The standard unit of stress is N/m^2.
Strain: Strain is a measure of the deformation of the material as a result of the force applied. The strain is a unitless quantity.
Hooke's law states that within the elastic limit the stress applied on a body is directly proportional to strain produced.
$\Rightarrow$ Strain $\propto$ Stress
$\Rightarrow$ Strain = E × Stress
(Where $E =$ modulus of elalsticity)
$\Rightarrow \sigma = \dfrac{F(N)}{A(m^2)} \Rightarrow$ strain $= \dfrac{dl}{l} \Rightarrow \sigma =$ strain $\times E$
where $\sigma =$ stress,
F = applied force
A = cross-sectional area
dl = change in length
I = initial length and
E= young's modulus of elasticity
The young's modulus of elasticity is a proportionality constant and it depends on the material. So modulus of elasticity does not depend on stress and strain.

77(B). $A = 3 \times 10^{-6}\,m^2$
$\dfrac{\Delta l}{l} = 10^{-3}$
To find : maximun mass.
$\therefore \quad \dfrac{F}{A} = Y\dfrac{\Delta l}{l}$
$\Rightarrow \dfrac{mg}{A} = Y\dfrac{\Delta l}{l}$
$\Rightarrow m = Y\left(\dfrac{\Delta l}{l}\right)\dfrac{A}{g}$
$\Rightarrow m = \dfrac{2\times10^{11}\times10^{-3}\times3\times10^{-6}}{10} = 6 \times 10 = 60\,kg$

78(A). According to Hooke's law
Modules of elasticity, $E = \dfrac{W}{A} \times \dfrac{L}{1}$
where, $L =$ original length of the wire
$A =$ cross- sectional area of the wire
Elongation $\Delta = \dfrac{WL}{E}$
On either side of the wire, tension is W and length is $\frac{1}{2}$
$\Delta l = \dfrac{\frac{WL}{2}}{AE} = \dfrac{WL}{2AE} = \dfrac{1}{2}$
Total elongation in the wire $= \frac{1}{2} + \frac{1}{2} = 1$

79(D). Since the wires have same material, their modulus of elasticity must be same.
Thus, the ratio of longitudinal stress to longitudinal strain (which is Young's Modulus of Elasticity) must be same. Now, before breaking, the strains in both wires must be the same too.
Therefore, stress = Young's modulus × strain, must be same for both wires.
The second wire has diameter double that of the first wire, so area of cross section of second wire

is 4 times as large as that of first wire. Therefore, to develop the same stress, the force applied on second wire must be 4 times as large as the force applied on the first wire (since stress = force/cross section area).

Thus, force that needs to be applied to second wire to break it is $4 \times 200 = 800$ N

80(A). $Y = \dfrac{Fl}{a\Delta l}$

In the given problem, Y, l and Δl are constants.

$\Delta F \propto a$

$F \propto \pi r^2$

$F \propto r^2$

$\dfrac{F_1}{F_2} = \dfrac{r_1^2}{r_2^2} = \dfrac{1}{4}$

1. By which quantities of the following is pressure measured?

(a) Mass and Density   (b) Work done

(c) Force and Area   (d) Force and Distance

2. It is very difficult to measure a parallax angle less than 0.01 arcsec from Earth because of _______________.

(a) Variable intensity of sunlight

(b) The great distance between the earth and other celestial bodies

(c) Measurement error in the vacuum of outer space

(d) Effect of earth's atmosphere

3. What is the unit of work function of a metal used in photoelectric effect?

(a) Joule (J)   (b) Newton (N)

(c) Pascal (Pa)   (d) Hertz (Hz)

4. Which of the following units denotes the dimensions $\left[\dfrac{ML^2}{Q^2}\right]$, where Q denotes the electric charge?

(a) Wb/m^2 (b) H/m^2

(c) Weber (Wb) (d) Henry (H)

5. For motion in two or three dimensions, what is the angle between velocity and acceleration vectors?

(a) $0°$ (b) $180°$

(c) Between $0°$ to $180°$ (d) $90°$

6. How many variables are required to define the motion of a body in a plane?

(a) 3   (b) 2

(c) 1   (d) 4

7. A body is exhibiting circular motion. What kind of motion can this be termed as?

(a) Motion along a line   (b) Motion in a plane

(c) Motion along a point   (d) None of the above

8. A spring balance is attached to the ceiling of a lift. A man hangs his bag on the spring and the spring reads 49 N , when the lift is stationary. If the lift moves downward with an acceleration of $5\,\text{m/s}^2$, the reading of the spring balance will be:

(a) 24 N   (b) 74 N

(c) 15 N   (d) 49 N

9. A goalkeeper in a game of football pulls his hands backward after holding the ball shot at the goal. This enables the goalkeeper to-

(a) exert larger force on the ball

(b) reduce the force exerted by the ball on hands

(c) increase the rate of change of momentum

(d) decrease the rate of change of momentum

10. A car accelerates uniformly from 18 km/h to 36 km/h in 5 s . What is the acceleration in m/s^2 ?

(a) $0.5\,\text{m/s}^2$ (b) $3\,\text{m/s}^2$

(c) $1\,\text{m/s}^2$ (d) $2\,\text{m/s}^2$

11. Three equal weights A, B and C of mass 2 kg each are hanging on a string passing over a fixed frictionless pulley as shown in the figure. The tension in the string connecting weights B and C is:

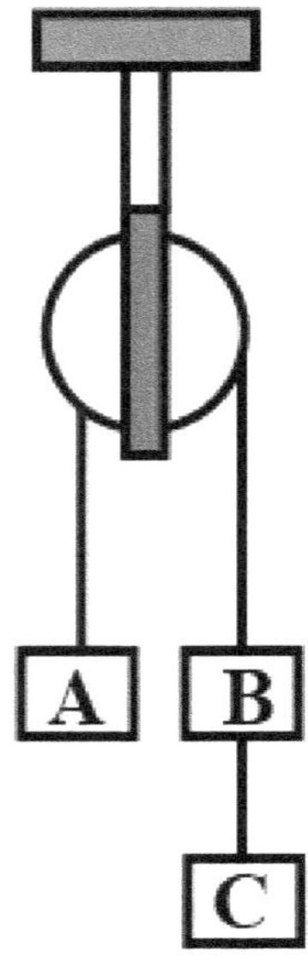

(a) Zero   (b) $13N$

(c) $3.3N$ (d) $19.6N$

12. An object of mass $40\,kg$ moving along a straight line with a horizontal velocity of $15\,ms^{-1}$ collides and sticks to a stationary wooden block of mass $10\,kg$. If the surface is smooth, the combined object (object and the wooden block) after collision moves along the same straight line with a velocity of:

(a) $9\,ms^{-1}$ (b) $10\,ms^{-1}$

(c) $12\,ms^{-1}$ (d) $12.5\,ms^{-1}$

13. The device used for converting mechanical energy into electrical energy is called a/an?

(a) Transformer   (b) Dynamo

(c) Cell   (d) Electric motor

14. A body is moved along a straight line by a machine delivering a constant power. The distance moved by the body in time t is proportional to:

(a) $t^{\frac{3}{4}}$ (b) $t^{\frac{3}{2}}$

(c) $t^{\frac{1}{4}}$ (d) $t^{\frac{1}{2}}$

15. A particle of mass m is driven by a machine that delivers a constant power k watts. if the particle starts from rest the force on the particle at time t is:

(a) $\sqrt{2mk}\ t^{-1/2}$ (b) $\frac{1}{2}\sqrt{mk}\ t^{-1/2}$

(c) $\sqrt{\dfrac{mk}{2}}\ t^{-1/2}$ (d) $\sqrt{mk}\ t^{-1/2}$

16. A stationary body of mass $3\,kg$ explodes into three equal pieces. Two of the pieces fly off at right angles to each other. One with a velocity of $2\hat{i}m/s$ and the other with a veloctiy of $3\hat{j}m/s$. If the explosion takes place in $10^{-5}s$, the average force actingon the third piece in newtons is:

(a) $(2\hat{i}+3\hat{j})\times 10^{-5}$ (b) $-(2\hat{i}+3\hat{j})\times 10^{5}$

(c) $(3\hat{i}+2\hat{j})\times 10^{-5}$ (d) $(2\hat{i}-3\hat{j})\times 10^{-5}$

17. A body is orbiting Earth at a mean radius 9 times as great as the orbit of a geostationary satellite. In how many days will it complete one revolution around Earth and what is its angular velocity?

(a) 20 days; $2.693 \times 10^{-9} \frac{rad}{sec}$

(b) 23 days; $2.693 \times 10^{-6} \frac{rad}{sec}$

(c) 27 days; $2.693 \times 10^{-6} \frac{rad}{sec}$

(d) 29 days; $2.693 \times 10^{-10} \frac{rad}{sec}$

18. What is the Moment of Inertia of a thin rod of mass 'M' and length 'L' about an axis perpendicular to the rod at its mid-point?

(a) $\frac{ML^2}{6}$

(b) $\frac{ML^2}{12}$

(c) $\frac{ML^2}{3}$

(d) $\frac{ML^2}{2}$

19. A stone is thrown upward with a speed of u, find maximum height it can get with this speed. (given g is the gravitational acceleration)

(a) $\frac{u^2}{2g}$

(b) $\frac{2u^2}{g}$

(c) $\frac{u}{g}$

(d) $\frac{u^2}{g}$

20. What is the intensity of the gravitational field at the center of a spherical shell of mass 'm' and radius 'r' ?

(a) $\frac{Gm}{r^2}$

(b) $\frac{Gm}{r}$

(c) Zero

(d) None of these

21. Satellite going round the earth in a circular orbit loses some energy due to collision. Its speed is v and distance from the earth is d _____.

(a) d will increase, v will increase.

(b) d will increase, v will decrease.

(c) d will decrease, v will decrease.

(d) d will decrease, v will increase.

22. The value of acceleration due to gravity __________.

(a) Is same on equator and poles

(b) Is least on poles

(c) Is least on equator

(d) Increases from pole to equator

23. A particle falls from infinity to the earth. Its velocity on reaching earth of radius R, is _______.

(a) 2Rg

(b) Rg

(c) $\sqrt{Rg}$

(d) $\sqrt{2Rg}$

24. Thermal equilibrium implies equality of:

(a) Energy

(b) Internal energy

(c) Kinetic energy

(d) Temperature

25. A metallic ball has a spherical cavity at its centre. If the ball is heated, what happens to the cavity?

(a) Its volume decreases

(b) Its volume increases

(c) Its volume remains unchanged

(d) Its volume may increase or decrease depending upon the nature of the metal

26. Two blocks of ice when pressed together join to form one block. This happens because:

(a) Melting point rises with pressure

(b) Melting point falls with pressure

(c) Heat is rejected to outside

(d) Heat is absorbed from outside

27. A liquid with coefficient of volume expansion γ is filled in a container of a material having coefficient of linear expansion α. If the liquid overflows on heating, then __________.

(a) $\gamma = 3\alpha$

(b) $\gamma > 3\alpha$

(c) $\gamma < 3\alpha$

(d) $\gamma = a^3$

28. Which of the following is an application of thermodynamics?

(a) Refrigerators

(b) Gas compressors

(c) Power plants

(d) All of the above

29. In the total work done by the system along the path ADC is $85J$ find the volume at point C.

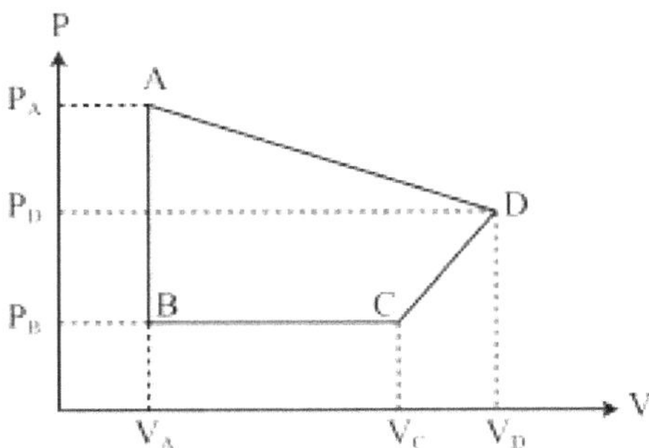

(a) 4.033 litres

(b) 1.003 litres

(c) 2.233 litres

(d) 1.233 litres

30. The translational kinetic energy of molecules of one mole of a monatomic gas is $U = \frac{3NkT}{2}$. The value of atomic specific heat of gas under constant pressure will be :

(a) $\frac{3}{2}R$

(b) $\frac{5}{2}R$

(c) $\frac{7}{2}R$

(d) $\frac{9}{2}R$

31. Why does mercury not evaporate at room temperature?

(a) Because melting point of mercury is higher

(b) Because boiling point of mercury is higher

(c) Because boiling point of mercury is lower

(d) Because boiling point of mercury is equal to room temperature

32. The respectively speeds of five molecules are 2,1,5,1.6,1.6 and 1.2 km/sec. The most probable speed in km/sec will be:

(a) 2

(b) 1.58

(c) 1.6

(d) 1.31

33. The molar specific heat of oxygen at constant pressure $C_p = 7.03 \text{ cal/mol}°C$ and $R = 8.32 \text{ J/mol}°C$. The amount of heat taken by 5 moles of oxygen when heated at constant volume from $10°C$ to $20°C$ will be approximately.

(a) 25 cal

(b) 50 cal

(c) 253 cal

(d) 500 cal

34. An enclosure of volume V contains a mixture of $8g$ of oxygen, $14g$ of nitrogen, and $22g$ of carbon- dioxide at absolute temperature T. The pressure of the mixture of gases is: (R is universal gas constant)

(a) $\frac{RT}{V}$

(b) $\frac{3RT}{2V}$

(c) $\frac{5RT}{4V}$

(d) $\frac{7RT}{5V}$

35. A given quantity of an ideal gas is at pressure P and absolute temperature T. The isothermal bulk modulus of the gas is

(a) $\frac{2}{3}P$

(b) P

(c) $\frac{3}{2}P$

(d) $2P$

36. Consider a gas of triatomic molecules. The molecules are assumed to the triangular and made of massless rigid rods whose vertices are occupied by atoms. The internal energy of a mole of the gas at temperature T is:

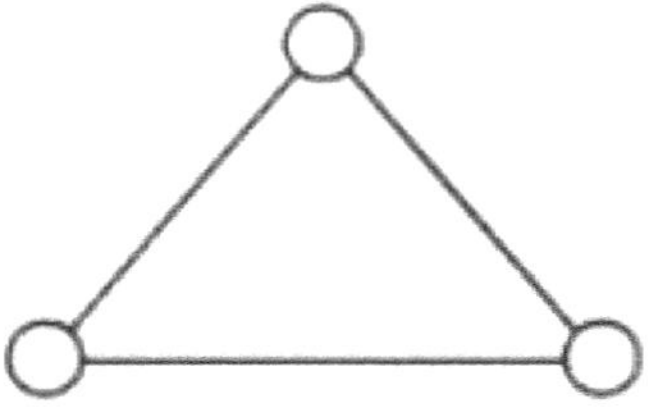

(a) $\frac{9}{2}RT$

(b) $\frac{3}{2}RT$

(c) $\frac{5}{2}RT$

(d) $3RT$

37. The period of oscillation of a simple pendulum of length L is _______.

(a) $2\pi\sqrt{(\frac{g}{L})}$

(b) $4\pi\sqrt{(\frac{L}{g})}$

(c) $2\pi\sqrt{(\frac{L}{g})}$

(d) $4\pi\sqrt{(\frac{g}{L})}$

38. The waves, in which the particles of the medium vibrate in a direction perpendicular to the direction of wave motion, is known as:

(a) Transverse waves

(b) Longitudinal waves

(c) Propagated waves

(d) None of these

39. Consider the wave $y = (5\,\text{mm})\sin\left[(1\,\text{cm}^{-1})\text{x} - (60\,\text{s}^{-1})\text{t}\right]$. Find the wave number.

(a) $10\,\text{cm}^{-1}$

(b) $2\,\text{cm}^{-1}$

(c) $0.1\,\text{cm}^{-1}$

(d) $1\,\text{cm}^{-1}$

40. For a stationary wave if frequency is equal to _______ then it is called second harmonic. (v is the speed of travelling waves on the string of length L).

(a) $\frac{V}{2\,L}$

(b) $\frac{2v}{L}$

(c) $\frac{V}{L}$

(d) $\frac{v}{4L}$

41. A spring block system having spring constant K and block has mass M. If we have to reduce the time period of SHM by 3 times then-new spring constant will be.

(a) 3K

(b) 9K

(c) 27K

(d) K

42. A long string with a charge of λ per unit length passes through an imaginary cube of edge a. The maximum flux of the electric field through the cube will be:

(a) $\frac{\lambda a}{\varepsilon_0}$

(b) $\frac{\sqrt{2}\lambda a}{\varepsilon_0}$

(c) $\frac{6\lambda a^2}{\varepsilon_0}$

(d) $\frac{\sqrt{3}\lambda a}{\varepsilon_0}$

43. Which of the following statements is not true about Gauss's law?

(a) Gauss's law is true for any closed surface.

(b) The term q on the right side of Gauss's law includes the sum of all charges enclosed by the surface.

(c) Gauss's law is not very useful in calculating electrostatic fields when the system has some symmetry.

(d) Gauss's law is based on the inverse square dependence on distance contained in the coulomb's law.

44. Charge separation is a process of exciting an electron. During the process of charge separation, there will be _______.

(a) creation of atom

(b) creation of charged particles

(c) creation of energy

(d) creation of neutrons

45. The electric field required to keep a water drop of mass m just remain suspended when charged with one electron is _______.

(a) $\frac{mg}{e}$

(b) mge

(c) $\frac{eg}{m}$

(d) $\frac{em}{g}$

46. A particle of mass m and charge q is placed at rest in a uniform electric field E and then released. The kinetic energy attained by the particle after moving distance y is:

(a) qEy^2

(b) qEy

(c) qE^2y

(d) q^2Ey

47. The potential difference between the two plates of a parallel plate capacitor is constant. When air between the plates is replaced by a dielectric material, the electric field intensity:

(a) Decreases

(b) Remains unchanged

(c) Becomes zero

(d) Increases

48. Dimensional formula and unit of potential difference:

(a) $ML^2T^{-3}A^{-1}$, Volt

(b) $MLT^{-2}A^{-1}$, Watt

(c) $ML^2T^{-2}A$, Volt

(d) $MLT^{-2}A$, Joule

49. Which of the following is not the property of equipotential surfaces?

(a) The electric field is always perpendicular to an equipotential surface.

(b) The direction of the equipotential surface is from low potential to high potential.

(c) Rate of change of potential with distance on them is zero

(d) In a uniform electric field, any plane normal to the field direction is an equipotential surface.

50. Find the value of current i?

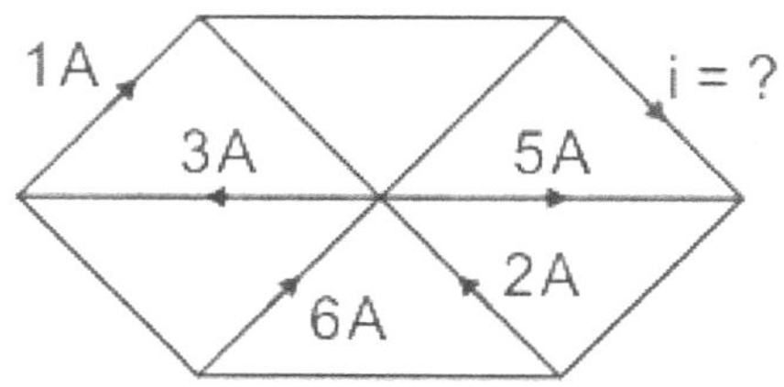

(a) 2 A

(b) 3 A

(c) 1 A

(d) 5 A

51. Value of mobility is:

(a) Positive only
(b) Negative only
(c) Both positive and negative
(d) None of the above

52. If resistance of a metal wire of length L and area of cross section A is given as R = $\dfrac{L}{\sigma A}$, then σ represents _____________ of the material.
(a) conductivity
(b) resistivity
(c) permittivity
(d) susceptibility

53. The equivalent emf of the given diagram is:

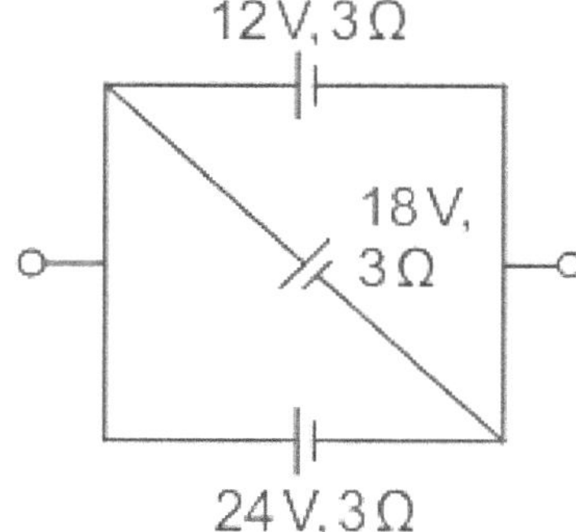

(a) 12 volts
(b) 18 volts
(c) 24 volts
(d) 16 volts

54. Gauss's law for magnetism states that, the net ______ through any closed surface is zero.
(a) magnetic susceptibility
(b) magnetic flux
(c) relative magnetic permeability
(d) magnetic intensity

55. At what temperature, a ferromagnetic material becomes paramagnetic material?
(a) Melting temperature
(b) Curie temperature
(c) Neel temperature
(d) None of the above

56. Which of the following gives the direction of the force acting on a current-carrying conductor in a magnetic field?
(a) Fleming's Right-hand rule
(b) Maxwell's Corkscrew Rule
(c) Fleming's Left-hand Rule
(d) None of the Above

57. A magnet of dipole moment $2Am^2$ is deflected through $30°$ from magnetic meridian. The required deflecting torque is $\left(B_H = 0.4 \times 10^{-4}T\right)$:
(a) 0.4×10^{-4} Nm
(b) 0.4Nm
(c) 0.2×10^{-4} Nm
(d) None of these

58. A long solenoid carrying a current produces a magnetic field B along its axis. If the current is doubled and the number of turns per cm is halved, then the new value of the magnetic field is:
(a) $\dfrac{B}{2}$
(b) B
(c) $2B$
(d) $4B$

59. Relative permittivity and permeability of a material are ϵ_r and μ_r , respectively. Which of the following values of these quantifies are allowed for a diamagnetic material?
(a) $\epsilon_r = 0.5, \mu_r = 0.5$
(b) $\epsilon_r = 1.5, \mu_r = 1.5$
(c) $\epsilon_r = 0.5, \mu_r = 1.5$
(d) $\epsilon_r = 1.5, \mu_r = 0.5$

60. Which of the following materials have higher retentivity of magnetism?
(a) Alnico
(b) Manganese
(c) Copper
(d) Bismuth

61. The magnetic field strength due to a short bar magnet directed along its axial line at a distance r is B. What is its value at the same distance along the equatorial line?
(a) B
(b) $\dfrac{2}{B}$
(c) $\dfrac{B}{2}$
(d) None of these

62. Magnetism at the center of a bar magnet is _____.
(a) half of the poles
(b) maximum
(c) minimum
(d) zero

63. The current through the capacitor is __________ of the applied voltage.
(a) $\dfrac{\pi}{2}$ ahead
(b) $\dfrac{\pi}{2}$ behind
(c) π ahead
(d) π behind

64. AC voltage is $V = 200 \sin 300t$ and if $R = 10\Omega$ and $L = 800$mH , the peak value of current is:
(a) 1.83 A
(b) 1.5 A
(c) 2.0 A
(d) 0.832 A

65. A coil of area 50 cm^2 has 1000 turns. Magnetic field of 0.2 weber /m^2 is perpendicular to the coil. The magnetic field is reduced to zero in 0.2 second. The induced emf in the coil is:
(a) $1V$
(b) $5V$
(c) $10V$
(d) $0V$

66. In an electromagnetic wave, the electric and magnetic fields are:
(a) Always in same phase
(b) Always in antiphase
(c) Always at 90 degree phase difference
(d) Always at 45 degree phase difference

67. Electromagnetic waves are produced by:
(a) Charge less particle
(b) A static charge
(c) A moving charge
(d) An acceleration charge

68. According to Maxwell's hypothesis, changing electric field gives rise to:
(a) Magnetic field
(b) Pressure gradient
(c) Charge
(d) Voltage

69. Which type of waves are used to communicate with the artificial satellite?
(a) X-rays
(b) Microwaves
(c) Ultraviolet waves
(d) Radio waves

70. Four students P, Q, R and S traced the path of a ray of light passing through a glass slab for an angle of incidence $40°$ and measured the angle of refraction. The values as measured them were $18°; 22° ; 25°$ and $30°$ respectively. The student who has performed the experiment methodically is:

(a) P (b) Q
(c) R (d) S

71. For a light of wavelength $250\,\text{nm}$, calculate the resolving power of a telescope whose objective lens has an aperture of $0.5\,\text{m}$.
(a) 3.28×10^6 (b) 1.64×10^6
(c) 6.4×10^6 (d) 1.64×10^{-6}

72. An eye specialist prescribes spectacles having a combination of a convex lens of focal length 40 cm in contact with a concave lens of focal length 25 cm. The power of this lens' combination is
(a) $+1.5\,D$ (b) $-1.5\,D$
(c) $+6.67\,D$ (d) $-6.67\,D$

73. A giant telescope in an observatory has an objective of focal length 19 m and an eye-piece of focal length 1.0cm. In normal adjustment, the telescope is used to view the moon. What is the diameter of the image of the moon formed by the objective? The diameter of the moon is 3.5×10^6m and the radius of the lunar orbit around Earth is 3.8×10^8m.
(a) $10\,cm$ (b) $12.5\,cm$
(c) $15\,cm$ (d) $17.5\,cm$

74. A car is moving towards a high cliff. The car driver sounds a horn of frequency f. The reflected sound heard by the driver has a frequency $2f$. If v is the velocity of sound, The velocity of the car in the same velocity units will be:
(a) $\dfrac{v}{\sqrt{2}}$ (b) $\dfrac{v}{3}$
(c) $\dfrac{v}{4}$ (d) $\dfrac{v}{2}$

75. In Young's experiment, one of the slit is covered with a transparent sheet of thickness 3.6×10^{-3} cm due to which position of central fringe shifts to a position originally occupied by 30 th bright fringe. The refractive index of the sheet, if $\lambda = 6000\,Å$ is
(a) 1.5 (b) 1.6
(c) 1.55 (d) 1.65

76. An observer moves towards a stationary source of sound with a velocity one-fifth the velocity of sound. The apparent increase in frequency is:
(a) 0 (b) 5%
(c) 20% (d) 0.1%

77. Light of wavelength $300\,nm$ is incident on a photo-sensitive surface. The stopping potential for emitted photoelectrons is $2.5V$. The wavelength of incident light is reduced to $150\,nm$. The stopping potential for emitted photoelectrons is:
(a) Exactly $5V$ (b) A little less than $5V$
(c) A little more than $5V$ (d) $2.5V$

78. What is quantization of photons?
(a) Photons are massless.
(b) Photons are discrete energy parcels
(c) Photons are stable.
(d) Photons carry energy

79. In a photoelectric experiment, if both the intensity and frequency of the incident light are doubled, then the saturation photoelectric current.

(a) Remains constant (b) Halved
(c) Doubled (d) Becomes four times

80. Monochromatic light of frequency $6.0 \times 10^{14}\,\text{Hz}$ is produced by a laser. The power emitted is $2.0 \times 10^{-3}\,\text{W}$. How many photons per second, on average, are emitted by the source?
(a) 3.0×10^{10} (b) 5.0×10^{15}
(c) 7.0×10^{12} (d) 9.0×10^{12}

// Smart Answer Sheet //

Correct — Percentage of students who answered correctly.

Skipped — Percentage of students who skipped.

Q.	Ans.	Correct	Skipped	Q.	Ans.	Correct	Skipped	Q.	Ans.	Correct	Skipped
1	C	56.38%	2.0%	2	D	87.12%	0.0%	3	A	76.96%	0.0%
4	D	32.58%	4.13%	5	C	85.35%	0.0%	6	B	54.86%	1.08%
7	B	82.64%	0.0%	8	A	43.52%	1.22%	9	D	25.23%	4.35%
10	C	49.3%	1.76%	11	B	43.11%	1.26%	12	C	62.54%	1.29%
13	B	77.11%	0.0%	14	B	57.98%	1.46%	15	C	45.46%	1.09%
16	B	63.87%	1.04%	17	C	44.42%	1.06%	18	B	57.03%	1.94%
19	A	29.41%	3.06%	20	C	26.85%	3.36%	21	D	53.73%	1.14%
22	C	82.19%	0.0%	23	D	27.29%	4.69%	24	D	80.46%	0.0%
25	B	53.28%	1.89%	26	B	88.14%	0.0%	27	B	87.35%	0.0%
28	D	64.94%	1.45%	29	D	11.45%	3.78%	30	B	47.91%	1.43%
31	B	49.84%	1.85%	32	D	63.61%	1.96%	33	C	27.79%	4.87%
34	C	63.95%	1.98%	35	B	41.86%	1.4%	36	D	77.15%	0.0%
37	C	84.44%	0.0%	38	A	51.24%	1.88%	39	D	59.26%	1.26%
40	C	58.47%	1.92%	41	B	55.27%	1.5%	42	D	85.47%	0.0%
43	C	45.87%	1.76%	44	B	84.9%	0.0%	45	A	69.39%	1.23%
46	B	80.69%	0.0%	47	A	55.35%	1.14%	48	A	78.2%	0.0%
49	B	45.88%	1.76%	50	C	65.68%	1.91%	51	A	82.71%	0.0%
52	A	46.36%	1.23%	53	B	49.52%	2.0%	54	B	88.98%	0.0%
55	B	51.51%	1.56%	56	C	49.42%	1.18%	57	A	78.9%	0.0%
58	B	52.91%	1.04%	59	D	48.29%	1.68%	60	A	88.22%	0.0%
61	C	57.29%	1.21%	62	D	86.15%	0.0%	63	A	89.9%	0.0%
64	D	13.76%	3.65%	65	B	25.08%	3.15%	66	A	83.41%	0.0%
67	D	28.64%	4.58%	68	A	57.47%	1.08%	69	B	87.79%	0.0%
70	C	21.1%	4.0%	71	B	58.88%	1.02%	72	B	60.85%	1.55%
73	D	63.17%	1.01%	74	B	47.95%	1.78%	75	A	47.79%	1.97%
76	C	40.19%	1.8%	77	C	51.03%	1.9%	78	B	81.75%	0.0%
79	C	81.88%		80	B	47.27%					

// Hints and Solutions //

1(C). Pressure is the force applied per unit area in a direction perpendicular to the surface of the object. The SI unit of pressure is the Pascal (Pa).

$$\text{Pressure } (P) = \frac{\text{Force}}{\text{Area}}$$

From the above information we can say that pressure is measured In the context of force and area.

2(D). Measuring a parallax angle less than 0.01 arcsec from Earth is very difficult due to the influence of the Earth's atmosphere. The parallax method is influenced by the path of light that travels from a distant planet to the points of observation on Earth. Light reaching an observer from a distant object passes through several layers of Earth's atmosphere. These layers of the atmosphere allow light to undergo multiple refractions and reduce the accuracy of the method. The parallax method is used to determine large distances, such as the distance from Earth to a planet or a star.

3(A). The unit of work function of a metal is used in photoelectric effect, is joule (J) . Work function is expressed in eV , and $1\text{eV} = 1.6 \times 10^{-19}$ J . Electron volt (eV) is the amount of energy gained (or lost) by the charge of a single electron moved across an electric potential difference of one volt. The minimum energy needed for an electron to escape from the metal surface is called work function.

4(D). Magnetic energy $= \frac{1}{2}LI^2$

$$= \frac{Lq^2}{2t^2} \quad [\text{as } I = \tfrac{q}{t}]$$

Where L = inductance, I = Current Energy has the dimensions $= [ML^2\,T^{-2}]$

Equate the dimensions, we have

$$[ML^2\,T^{-2}] = [\text{henry}] \times \frac{[Q^2]}{[T^2]}$$

$$[\text{Henry}] = \frac{[ML^2]}{[Q^2]}$$

5(C). For motion in one dimension, the velocity and acceleration are always along the same line either in the same direction or in opposite direction. For motion in two or three dimensions, the angle between velocity and acceleration vectors may have any value be tween $0°$ to $180°$.

6(B). The motion of a body in a plane can be defined by using 2 variables. These are the two defining axes of the co-ordinate system, X and Y. A body moving from one point to different points on the X and Y-axis is said to be executing motion in a plane. A plane comprises the X and Y-axis on which if we make the distance at the X-axis and the time at which a body moves along the vertical or Y-axis, then dividing the distance covered by the time taken we get the velocity.

7(B). Circular motion is a movement of an object along the circumference of a circle or rotation along a circular path. It can be uniform, with constant angular rate of rotation and constant speed. So if a body is exhibiting circular motion, this be termed as motion in a plane. Circular motion is an example of motion in a plane. As a circle is a 2 -dimensional entity, the body moving in a circle is also moving in a plane.

8(A). When the lift is stationary spring force balances weight:

$$kx = \text{mg} = 49 \text{ N}\ldots(1)$$

Where,

k = force constant of spring

x = elongation

True weight $= 49$ N

From equation (1), we get

$$k = \frac{49}{x}$$

$$\text{m} = \frac{49}{9.8} = 5 \text{ kg}$$

when lift moves with acceleration 5 m/s^2 downward we have:

$$kx_2 = \text{mg} - 5 \times \text{m}$$

Where,

Pseudo force in lift frame $= 5m$ upward

x_2 = new elongation

$$\Rightarrow \text{kx}_2 = 49 - 5 \times 5 = 24 \text{ N}$$

So new reading in spring balance $= 24$ N

9(D). A goalkeeper in a game of football pulls his hands backward after holding the ball shot at the goal. This enables the goalkeeper to decrease the rate of change of momentum.

According to Newton's Second law of motion:

$$\text{Force } (F) = \frac{\Delta p}{\Delta t}$$

When the ball comes toward the keeper, it has greater speed (as it is coming fast).

As momentum is the product of mass and velocity $(p = mv)$, the momentum of this ball is large.

(i) If the hands will be at rest position the velocity will be 0:

$$p = mv; p = 0 \text{ if } v = 0$$

- The hands will have no momentum, so when the ball will come towards them, the rate of change of momentum will be large and a large force will be exerted on the hands because:

$$F \propto \frac{dp}{dt}$$

- So, when the rate of change of momentum is large, the force will also be large

(ii) If the hands are moved backward from the rest position,

- The momentum of the hand increases as some velocity is provided.
- Now, when the ball will come towards them, the rate of change of momentum will be small and a lesser force will be exerted on the hands because:

$$F \propto \frac{dp}{dt}$$

- So, when the rate of change of momentum is small, the force will also be lesser.
- From this, it is clear that the goalkeeper pulls his hands backward while holding the ball shot at the goal to reduce the rate of change of momentum which in turn reduces the force exerted on the hands by the ball.

10(C). Given,

Initial velocity, $u = 18 \text{ km/h} = 18 \times \frac{5}{18} = 5 \text{ m/s}$

Final velocity, $v = 36 \text{ km/h}$ in

$$5 \text{ s} = 36 \times \frac{5}{18} = 10 \text{ m/s}$$

$$t = 5 \text{ s}$$

From the first equation of motion,

$$v = u + at$$

$$10 = 5 + a \times 5$$

$$a = 1 \text{ m/s}^2$$

11(B). The Free body diagram of the system is shown,

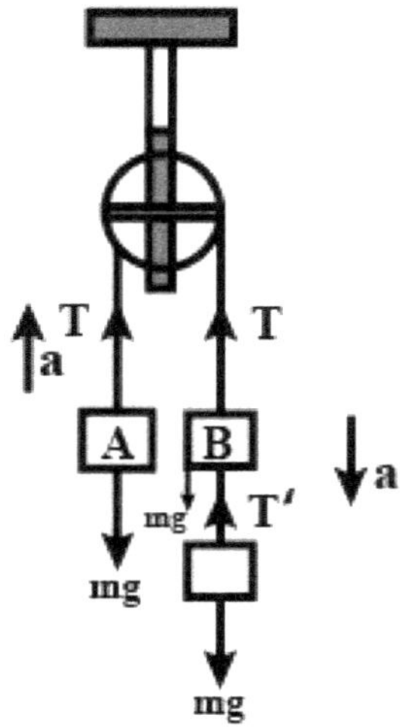

For block A :
$T - mg = ma$
$T - 2g = 2a$
$T = 2a + 2g$
For block $B + C$ system:
$mg + mg - T = (m + \text{m})a$
$2g + 2g - T = (2 + 2)a$
$4g - T = 4a$
$4g - 2a - 2g = 4a$
$2g = 6a$
$a = \frac{g}{3}$
For block C:
$mg - T' = ma$
$2g - T' = 2a$
$2g - T' = \frac{2g}{3}$
$T' = \frac{4g}{3}$
$= \frac{4 \times 10}{3} = 13$ N

12(C). Given,
Mass of the first object $= m_1 = 40\ kg$
Mass of the second object $= m_2 = 10\ kg$
The initial speed of the first object $= v_1 = 15\ ms^{-1}$
The initial speed of the second object $= v_2 = 0\ ms^{-1}$ (since wooden block is stationary)
From the conservation of linear momentum,
$m_1 v_1 + m_2 v_2 = (m_1 + m_2)v$
$v = \frac{m_1 v_1 + m_2 v_2}{m_1 + m_2}$
Now put the values,
$\Rightarrow v = \frac{40 \times 15 + 0}{40 + 10}$
$\Rightarrow v = 12\ ms^{-1}$
So, from the above points, we can clearly infer that the combined object will move with a velocity of $12\ ms^{-1}$.

13(B). Dynamo converts mechanical energy into electrical energy.
Its work is based on Faraday's law of Induction. The stator provides a magnetic field and armature (rotating windings) turns in a magnetic field. This magnetic field produces an electromotive force that pushes electrons thus generating current.

14(B). Let's consider a body is moved along a straight line by a machine delivering a constant power P . The distance moved by the body is S .

Power, $P = F.v \ldots \ldots (1)$
Force, $F = ma \ldots.(2)$
Where, $v = \frac{S}{t}$
Acceleration, $a = \frac{S}{t^2}$

m = mass
From equation (1) and equation (2), we get
$P = \frac{mS}{t^2} \times \frac{S}{t}$
$S^2 = \frac{Pt^3}{m}$
From the above equation, we get
$S^2 \propto t^3$
$S \propto t^{\frac{3}{2}}$
$\therefore$ The distance moved by the body in time t is proportional to $t^{\frac{3}{2}}$.

15(C). Constant power acting on the particle of mass m is k watt.
or $P = k$
$\frac{dW}{dt} = k;\quad dW = kdt$
Integrating both sides, $\int_0^W dW = \int_0^t kdt$
$\Rightarrow W = kt$ ...(i)
Using work energy theorem
$W = \frac{1}{2}mv^2 - \frac{1}{2}m(0)^2$
$kt = \frac{1}{2}mv^2$
[Using equation (i)]
$v = \sqrt{\frac{2kt}{m}}$
Acceleration of the particle, $a = \frac{dv}{dt}$
$a = \frac{1}{2}\sqrt{\frac{2k}{m}}\frac{1}{\sqrt{t}} = \sqrt{\frac{k}{2mt}}$
Force on the particle, $F = ma$
$= \sqrt{\frac{mk}{2t}} = \sqrt{\frac{mk}{2}}\ t^{-1/2}$

16(B). Since the body explodes into three equal parts, Therefore
$m_1 = m_2 = m_3 = \frac{m}{3} = 1\ Kg$
Let the velocity of the third part be $\vec{v}$.
According to the principle of conservation of the linear momentum-
Momentum of system before explosion = momentum of system after explosion
Or
$mv = m_1 v_1 + m_2 v_2 + m_3 v_3$
Or
$3 \times 0 = 1 \times 2i^2 + 3j^- + 1 \times \vec{v}$
Or
$v = -(2i + 3j°)m/s$
Average force acting on the third particle is
$\vec{F} = \frac{\overrightarrow{mv}}{t} = \frac{-1 \times (2\hat{i} + 3\hat{j})}{10^{-5}} = (2\hat{i} + 3\hat{j}) \times 10^5 N$

17(C). Given: $\left(\frac{T_1^2}{T_2^2}\right) = \left(\frac{R_1^3}{R_2^3}\right)$
$\Rightarrow T_2^2 = \left(\frac{R_2}{R_1}\right)T_1^2$
$\Rightarrow T_2 = \left(\frac{R_2}{R_1}\right)^{\frac{3}{2}} T_1$
For the geostationary satellite, $T_1 = 1$ day (24 hrs.)
$\therefore T_2 = \left(\frac{9R}{R}\right)^{\frac{3}{2}} = 27$ days
So it will complete one revolution in 27 days.
Now, $\omega = \frac{2\pi}{T_2} = \frac{2\pi}{27 \times 24 \times 3600}\ \frac{rad}{s}$
$= 2.693 \times 10^{-6} \frac{rad}{sec}$

18(B). **Moment of Inertia:** Moment of inertia plays the same role in rotational motion as mass plays in linear motion. It is the property of a body due to which it opposes any change in its state of rest or of uniform rotation.

The moment of inertia of a particle is,

$I = mrr^2$

For a uniform rod with negligible thickness, the moment of inertia about its centre of mass is:

$I_{cm} = \frac{1}{12}ML^2$

Where,

$M =$ mass of the rod

$L =$ length of the rod

$r =$ perpendicular distance of the particle from the rotational axis

From the above explanation, we can see that,

- Moment of inertia of the rod when the axis is perpendicular to it and passes through its centre is

$I_c = \frac{ML^2}{12}$

Hence, the correct option is (D).

19(A). When a body moves in a straight line under constant acceleration, it follows three equations of motion.

All unknowns are found by these equations.

$\Rightarrow v = u + at$

$\Rightarrow s = ut + (\frac{1}{2})at^2$

$\Rightarrow v^2 = u^2 + 2as$

Where u = initial velocity, v = final velocity, a = constant acceleration, t = time and s = displacement.

Given that the person throws balls into the air vertically upward with speed 'u'.

The height to which the ball will rise at this initial speed (at the highest point v will be zero)

Using the 3rd equation of motion:

$v = 0; u = u; a = -g; s = h$ (downward direction)

$\Rightarrow v^2 = u^2 + 2as$

$\Rightarrow 0^2 = u^2 - 2gh$

$\Rightarrow u^2 = 2gh$

$\Rightarrow h = \frac{u^2}{2g}$

20(C). Gravitational potential: Gravitational potential at any point inside the gravitational field is equal to work done in bringing a unit mass from infinite distance to a certain distance r from its center.

Thus, it can be expressed as:

$V = -\frac{GM}{r}$

Here V is gravitational potential, G is gravitational constant, M is mass of the planet and r is the distance between Mass M and some other object brought from an infinite distance.

- Inside the hollow sphere, the potential is equally distributed at every point of the surface in the gravitational field. So at any point, the potential will be zero.

21(D). Satellite going round the earth in a circular orbit loses some energy due to collision. Its speed is v and distance from the earth is d will decrease, v will increase.

Given that, the particle lost some energy due to a collision. So, it can no longer continue in that orbit as the earth's gravitational force is more than centripetal force. Due to this, the distance d decreases gradually and the particle moves towards earth at certain acceleration gaining speed. Thus distance d decreases and speed v

increases.

22(C). The value of acceleration due to gravity Is least on equator.

$g = \frac{GM}{R_e^2}$

Since radius R_e is maximum at the equator, value of acceleration due to gravity is least on the equator.

23(D). $P.E$ at infinity is zero and $K.E$ is also zero as the particle starts from rest at infinity.

Using conservation of mechanical energy at the surface of earth and at infinty,

$K \cdot E_R + P \cdot E_R = 0$

$\frac{1}{2}mv^2 + \left(-\frac{GMm}{R}\right) = 0$

$(\frac{1}{2})mv^2 = (\frac{GMm}{R})$

$v^2 = (\frac{2GM}{R})$

$v^2 = 2gR$ (since $g = \frac{GM}{R^2}$)

$\Rightarrow v = \sqrt{2gR}$

24(D). Thermal equilibrium implies equality of temperature which depends upon the average molecular kinetic energy.

Thermal equilibrium is defined as the state in which two objects connected by a permeable barrier don't have any heat transfer between them. Or in other words, two objects where heat isn't transferring between the objects even though they are connected. This happens when they have the same temperature.

25(B). The metal ball can be considered to be made up of several layers of thinner ones. On heating each of these layers will increase in radius. As the inner most layer also increases its radius, the volume inside it i.e. the volume of the hollow portion will also increase.

26(B). The melting point of ice is lowered on increasing the pressure.

When two blocks of ice are pressed against each other, the pressure applied on the blocks of ice increases and the melting point increases. Thus the two blocks of ice fuse together.

27(B). Volumetric coefficient of expansion of material is 3α.

As the system is heated liquid started flowing out of box, it means volumetric coefficient of expansion of liquid is greater then of the container. So, $\gamma > 3\alpha$.

28(D). The second law of thermodynamics applies to all refrigerators, deep freezers, industrial refrigeration systems, all forms of air-conditioning systems, heat pumps, and so on. Thermodynamic cycles govern the operation of all forms of air and gas compressors, blowers, and fans. The study of the feasibility of employing various forms of renewable energy sources for household and commercial purposes is an important topic area of thermodynamics.

29(D). Work done along $ADC =$ Work done along AD (expanding) - Work done along DC (contracting).

Work done along AD can be easily calculated by calculating area under line AD which comes out to be $88 J$

$85 = 88$ - Area under CD

Area under $CD = 3$

Let E be the intersection of lines from C and D and F and G be the x-intercepts from C and D respectively.

Area under $CD = \frac{1}{2} \times DE \times EC + CG \times EC$

$CD = \frac{1}{2}(P_D - P_B) \times (V_D - V_C) + P_B \times (V_D - V_C)3$

$= \frac{1}{2} \times 0.3 \times 10^5 \times (1.3 - V_C) + 0.3 \times 10^5 \times (1.3 - V_C)$

We know $10^{-3} m^3 = 1l$

Therefore, volume at point C is

$V_C = 1.3 - \dfrac{3}{45 \times 10^4}$

$= 1.3 - 0.66 \times 10^3$

$= 1.233$ litres

30(B). The value of atomic specific heat of gas under constant pressure is:

$C_P = C_V + R$

also value of atomic specific heat of gas under constant volume is by mathematical relation

$C_V = \frac{f}{2}R$.

For monoatomic gases, $f = 3$, as they have only translational degrees of freedom.

$C_V = \frac{f}{2}R = \frac{3}{2}R$

The value of atomic specific heat of gas under constant pressure is $C_P = C_V + R$

$C_P = C_V + R = \frac{3}{2}R + R = \frac{5}{2}R$

Since, The value of atomic number $N = 1$ specific heat of gas under constant pressure is $C_P = \frac{5}{2}R$.

31(B). When heat is given to particles, they gain energy. On gaining enough energy, particles start moving randomly to acquire kinetic energy and get mixed up with the particles present in air. It is a surface phenomenon.

We know that mercury does not evaporate at room temperature. It has its various applications like it is used in thermometers to check body temperatures also. We will see that mercury has a higher boiling point that is why it does not show the evaporation process at room temperature.

32(D). Given:

v_1, v_2, v_3, v_4, v_5 are $2, 1.5, 1.6, 1.6, 1.2$ respectivily.

RMS velocity of gas molecules is,

$v_{rms} = \sqrt{\left[\dfrac{(v_1^2 + v_2^2 + v_3^2 + v_4^2 + v_5^2)}{5}\right]}$

$v_{rms} = \sqrt{\left[\dfrac{(2^2 + 1.5^2 + 1.6^2 + 1.6^2 + 1.2^2)}{5}\right]}$

$v_{rms} = \sqrt{\dfrac{12.8}{5}}$

$v_{rms} = 1.6 \, m/s$

Most probable speed is,

$v_{mp} = \sqrt{\frac{2}{3}} \times v_{rms}$

$v_{mp} = 0.816 \times 1.6$

$v_{mp} = 1.306 \approx 1.31 \, km/s$

Therefore, the most probable speed of the gas is 1.31 km/s.

33(C). Molar heat is that amount of capacity in which heat is needed to raise the temperature of 1 mole of a substance by 1 kelvin or $1°C$ at constant volume. It is the amount of heat energy required per unit temperature. $C_p - C_v = R$.

Here R is the universal gas constant.

Now from the question:

Given $C_p = 7.03$ cal/mol°C

$R = 8.32$ J/mol°C $= \dfrac{8.32}{4.2}$ cal/mol°C (since 1 calorie=4.2 joule approx)

$T_1 = 10°C$ and $T_2 = 20°C$

Change in a temperature

$\Delta T = T_2 - T_1 = 20 - 10 = 10°C$

Molar heat capacity at constant volume,

$C_p - C_v = R$

$C_v = C_p - R$

$C_v = 7.03$ cal/mol°C $- \dfrac{8.32}{4.2}$ cal/mol°C

$C_v = 5.05$ cal/mol°C approx

Amount of heat absorbed $\Delta Q = nC_v\Delta T$

$= (5 \times 5.05)10$ cal

$= 252.5 = 253$ cal approx

34(C). Given:

Mass of oxygen, nitrogen and carbon-di-oxide are $8g, 14g, 22g$.

Molecular weight of oxygen, nitrogen and carbon-di-oxide are $32, 28, 44$.

The pressure exerted by a gas is given by

$P = \dfrac{nRT}{V}$

$= \dfrac{\text{mass}}{\text{molecular weight}} \times \dfrac{RT}{V}$

Pressure exerted by oxygen $P_1 = \dfrac{8RT}{32V}$

$= \dfrac{1RT}{4V}$

Pressure exerted by nitrogen $P_2 = \dfrac{14RT}{28V}$

$= \dfrac{1RT}{2V}$

Pressure exerted by carbon dioxide $P_3 = \dfrac{22RT}{44V}$

$= \dfrac{1RT}{2V}$

From Dalton's law of partial pressures, the total pressure exerted by the mixture is given by

$P = P_1 + P_2 + P_3$

$= \dfrac{1RT}{4V} + \dfrac{1RT}{2V} + \dfrac{1RT}{2V}$

$= \dfrac{5RT}{4V}$

35(B). Given:

An ideal gas is at pressure P and absolute temperature T.

We have to find the isothermal bulk modulus of the gas.

The equation of state for an ideal gas in an isothermal process is

PV = constant ....(i)

where,

P: pressure of the gas

V: volume occupied by the gas

Differentiating eq. (i), we have

P dV + VdP = 0

$\Rightarrow \left(\dfrac{dP}{dV}\right) = -\left(\dfrac{P}{V}\right)$ ......(ii)

Now, the bulk modulus of an ideal gas is

$B = -\left[\dfrac{dP}{\left(\frac{dV}{V}\right)}\right]$ ......(iii)

$\Rightarrow B = -\left(\dfrac{dP}{dV}\right)V$

Using eq. (ii) and eq. (iii), we get

$\Rightarrow B = -\left(\dfrac{-P}{V}\right)V$

$\Rightarrow B = P$

36(D). A triatomic (non-linear) gas molecule has 6 degrees of freedom (3 translational, 3 rotational and no vibrational) at room temperature. According to the law of equipartition of energy, the average energy per molecule of a triatomic gas at room temperature T is

$$E = \frac{1}{2}fRT$$
$$= \frac{1}{2}6RT = 3RT$$

37(C). Time Period and Energy of a Simple Pendulum:
The length of the wire is L, the mass of the body is m, and it is displaced by a small angle θ. Then
$$T - mg\cos\theta = mv^2 L$$
The torque tending to bring the mass to its equilibrium position,
$$\tau = mgL \times \sin\theta = mg\sin\theta \times L = I \times \alpha$$
For small angles of oscillations $\sin \approx \theta$,
Therefore, $I\alpha = -mgL\theta$
$$\alpha = -\frac{(mgL\theta)}{I}$$
From definition of SHM $\alpha = -\omega^2\theta$
$$-\omega^2\theta = -\frac{(mgL\theta)}{I}$$
$$\omega^2 = \frac{(mgL)}{I}$$
$$\omega = \sqrt{(\frac{mgL}{I})}$$
Using ML^2 [where I denote the moment of inertia of bob]
we get, $\omega = \sqrt{(\frac{g}{L})}$
So, the period of a simple pendulum of length L is given by,
$$T = \frac{2\pi}{\omega} = 2\pi \times \sqrt{(\frac{L}{g})}$$

38(A). Wave motion: The type of disturbance that travels through a medium due to repeated vibrations of the particles of the medium about their mean positions is called a wave motion.
There are two types of wave motion:
Longitudinal wave motion: It is that wave motion in which individual particles of the medium execute simple harmonic motion about their mean position along the same direction, in which the wave is propagated.
For example: Sound waves
Transverse wave motion: Vibration of particles in a medium and the propagation of wave are perpendicular to each other.
Example: Waves in the surface of the water, waves in a string.

39(D). Given,
The wave function,
$$y = (5\text{ mm})\sin\left[(1\text{ cm}^{-1})x - (60\text{ s}^{-1})t\right]$$
$$\Rightarrow y = A\sin(kx - \omega t) \Rightarrow y = (5mm)\sin\left[(1\text{ cm}^{-1})x - (60s^{-1})t\right]$$
$$\Rightarrow k = 1\text{ cm}^{-1}$$

40(C).

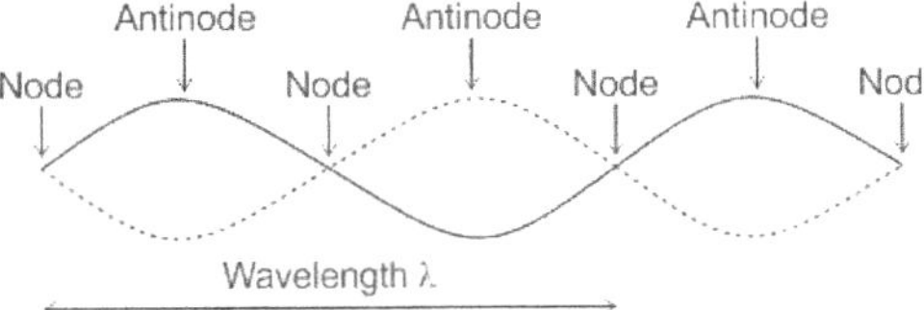

For second harmonic $n = 2$
Frequency of 2nd harmonic in standing wave,
$$\nu = \frac{nv}{2L}$$
$$\nu = \frac{2v}{2L}$$
$$\nu = \frac{v}{L}$$

41(B). For spring block system time-period is given by,
$$T = 2\pi\sqrt{\frac{m}{k}} \quad \left(\omega = \sqrt{\frac{k}{m}}\right)$$
Where m = inertial factor and k = spring factor
Given that, Time period (T_2) of the new system is $\frac{1}{3}^{rd}$ the given time period (T)
$$T_2 = \frac{T}{3}$$
We know, $T\alpha\frac{1}{\sqrt{k}}$
$$\Rightarrow \frac{T_2}{T} = \sqrt{\frac{k}{k_2}}$$
Where k = spring constant for first spring and k_2 = spring constant for second spring
$$\Rightarrow \sqrt{k_2} = \left(\frac{T}{T_2}\right)\sqrt{k}$$
By squaring both sides, we get
$$\Rightarrow k_2 = \left(\frac{T}{T_2}\right)^2 k$$
$$\Rightarrow k_2 = \left(\frac{T}{\left(\frac{T}{3}\right)}\right)^2 k$$
$$\Rightarrow k_2 = (3)^2 K$$
$$\Rightarrow k_2 = 9 K$$

42(D). The maximum flux will pass through the cube if the charge enclosed is the maximum (from Gauss' Law).
According to Gauss' law,
$$\phi = \frac{Q_{in}}{\epsilon_0}$$
So, in order to have maximum electric flux through the cube, we need to have maximum charge inside the cube, which is achieved by coinciding the wire with the space diagonal of the cube. The maximum length of the string which can fit into the cube is $\sqrt{3}a$, equal to its body diagonal. The total charge inside the cube is $\sqrt{3}a\lambda$
$$\phi = \frac{Q_{in}}{\epsilon_0} = \frac{\sqrt{3}\lambda a}{\epsilon_0}$$

43(C). According to Gauss's law, the total charge inside any closed surface is measured by the flow through it. As a result, the Gauss law holds true for closed surfaces. Only symmetric body charge distributions, such as spherical, cylindrical, and plane symmetry, are valid for Gauss's law. The sum of all charges encompassed by the surface is included in the term q on the right side of Gauss's law. The charges could be anywhere within the surface. The electrostatic field of a symmetric system can be calculated using Gauss's law. The inverse square dependence on distance inherent in Coulomb's law is the basis for Gauss's law. Any deviation from the inverse square law will be indicated by a violation of Gauss' law.
Gauss's law is often useful towards a much easier calculation of the electrostatic field when the system has some symmetry. This is facilitated by the choice of a suitable Gaussian surface.

44(B). There are only two types of charge available in an atom. One is known as positive and the second one is called negative. There will be repulsion which occurs in like charge particles and attraction occurs in unlike charges.
Electrons have the same magnitude of charge similar to protons but opposite in sign. Generally atoms are electrically neutral. But charge particles can be separated.
Charge separation is a process of exciting an

electron. Electrons are excited from lower energy level to higher energy level. After separation, electrons leave the atom and make the atom positively charged. So charged particles are created by charge separation.

45(A). If a charged particle is placed under the influence of gravity, for equilibrium gravitational force must be equal to the electrical force
$$\Rightarrow F_E = F_g$$
$$\Rightarrow qE = mg$$
For an electron, the above equation can be written as,
$$\Rightarrow eE = mg$$
$$\Rightarrow E = \frac{mg}{e}$$

46(B). It is given that,
The mass of the particle is m having charge q is placed at rest in uniform electric field E and then released.
We have to find the kinetic energy attained by the particle after moving a distance y.
Using the third equation of motion as:
$$v^2 - u^2 = 2as$$
Here, u = 0 (particle is initially at rest)
s = y (displacement)
$$v^2 = 2ay \ \dots\dots\dots (i)$$
Force on a particle in electric field is,
$$F = qE$$
Since, $F = ma$
So, $a = \dfrac{qE}{m}$ .... (ii)
Put the value of a in equation (i)
$$v^2 = 2\frac{qEy}{m} \ \dots\dots (iii)$$
We know that kinetic energy of a particle is given by,
$$E_k = \frac{1}{2}mv^2$$
Putting equation (iii) in above equation
$$E_k = qEy$$

47(A). In general capacitance of parallel plate, the capacitor is given by:
$$C = \frac{k\epsilon_0 A}{d}$$
Where C is capacitance, k is the relative permittivity of dielectric material, ϵ_0 is the permittivity of free space constant, A is an area of plates and d is the distance between them.
Therefore, the capacitance of parallel plates is increased by the insertion of a dielectric material. Further, the capacitance is inversely proportional to the electric field between the plates, and hence the presence of the dielectric decreases the effective electric field.

48(A). The mathematical expression for the potential difference is as defined as
$$V = \frac{W}{q}$$
Here, V is the potential, W is the work done and q is the charge.
Dimensional formula for work, W is ML^2T^{-2}
Dimensional formula for charge, q is AT^1
Dimensional formula for potential difference,
$$V = \frac{ML^2T^{-2}}{AT^1}$$
$$V = ML^2T^{-3}A^{-1} \text{ Volt}$$

49(B). Any surface over which the electric potential is same everywhere is called an equipotential surface. No work is required to move a charge from one point to another on the equipotential surface.

Properties of equipotential surface are:
- The electric field is always perpendicular to an equipotential surface.
- Two equipotential surfaces can never intersect.
- For a point charge, the equipotential surfaces are concentric spherical shells.
- For a uniform electric field, the equipotential surfaces are planes normal to the x-axis.
- The direction of the equipotential surface is from high potential to low potential.

50(C).

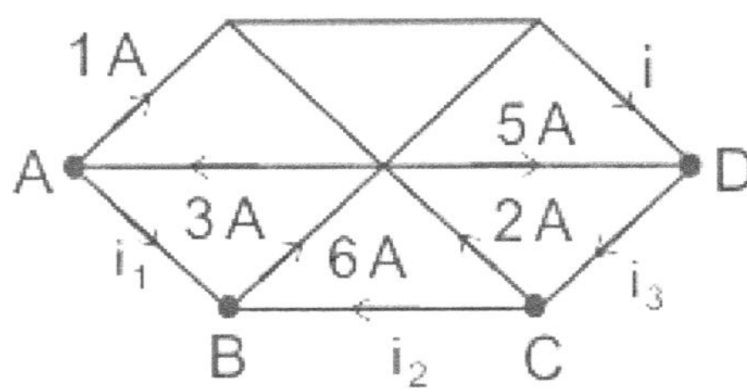

KCL at Node A
I₁ + 1A = 3A
I₁ = 2A
KCL at node B
I₂ + 2A = 6A
I₂ = 4 A
KCL at node C
I₃ = 4A + 2A
I₃ = 6A
KCL at node D
I = 6A - 5A = 1 A

51(A). Mobility: The magnitude of drift velocity per unit electric field is called mobility. It is denoted by μ.
$$\Rightarrow \mu = \frac{|v_d|}{E} \text{ where vd is the drift velocity, and E is the electric field.}$$
SI unit of mobility is m^2/ Vs.
Mobility is a positive quantity.

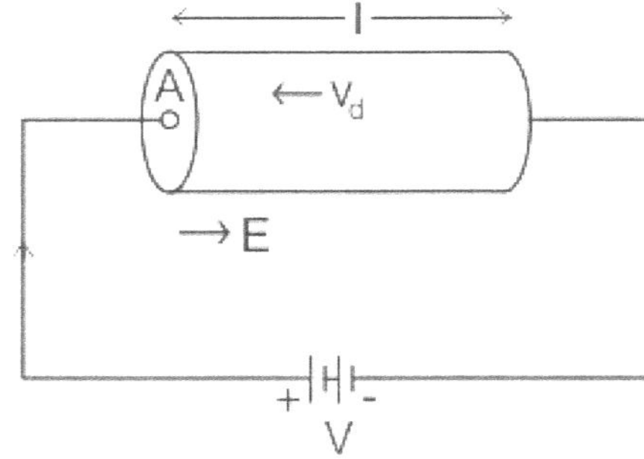

Drift velocity: Under the influence of the external electric field, drift velocity is the average velocity with which electrons get drifted towards the positive end of the conductor.
The drift velocity of electrons is of the order of 10^{-4} ms^{-1}.
$$\Rightarrow \mu = \frac{|v_d|}{E} = \frac{q\tau}{m}$$
Where, $v_d = \frac{qE\tau}{m}$ where, q is the charge, E is the electric field, and τ is the relaxation time.
Mobility is positive for positive current carriers as well as negative current carriers.

52(A). Resistance: The measure of the opposition to current flow in an electrical circuit is called its resistance.
The resistance of a wire depends on its length, area,

and metal resistivity.

Resistance is calculated by:

$$R = \rho\frac{l}{A}$$

$$R = \frac{l}{\sigma A}$$

Where l is its length, A area, and ρ is its metal resistivity, σ is conductivity.

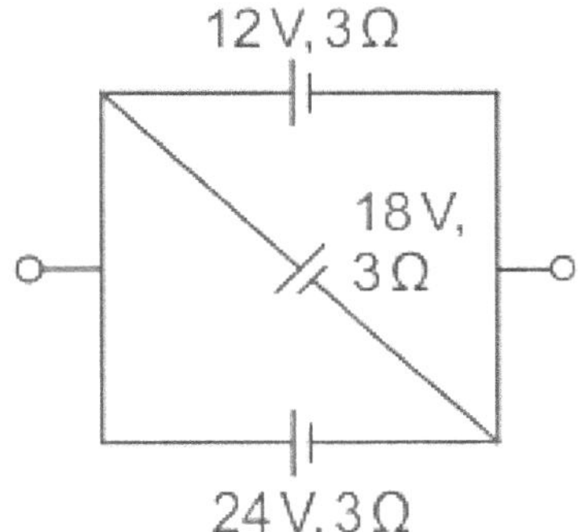

Resistance, $R = \dfrac{l}{\sigma A}$

Where l is its length, A area, and σ is conductivity.

53(B). Given,

$E_1 = 12$ volts, $r_1 = 3\Omega, E_2 = 18$ volts, $r_2 = 3\Omega, E_3 = 24$ volts, and $r_2 = 3\Omega$

The given diagram is,

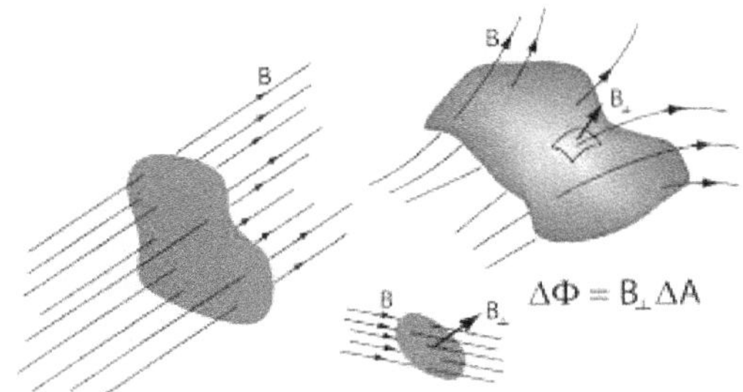

- From the above diagram, it is clear that this arrangement is a parallel combination of cells.
- The equivalent emf for the given arrangement is given as,

$$\Rightarrow E_{eq} = \frac{\frac{E_1}{r_1} + \frac{E_2}{r_2} + \frac{E_2}{r_2}}{\frac{1}{r_1} + \frac{1}{r_2} + \frac{1}{r_3}}$$

$$\Rightarrow E_{eq} = \frac{\frac{12}{3} + \frac{18}{3} + \frac{24}{3}}{\frac{1}{3} + \frac{1}{3} + \frac{1}{3}}$$

$$\Rightarrow E_{eq} = (4 + 6 + 8) \text{ volts}$$

$$\Rightarrow E_{eq} = 18 \text{ volts}$$

54(B). Gauss's law for magnetism: The net magnetic flux of the magnetic field must always be zero over any closed surface.

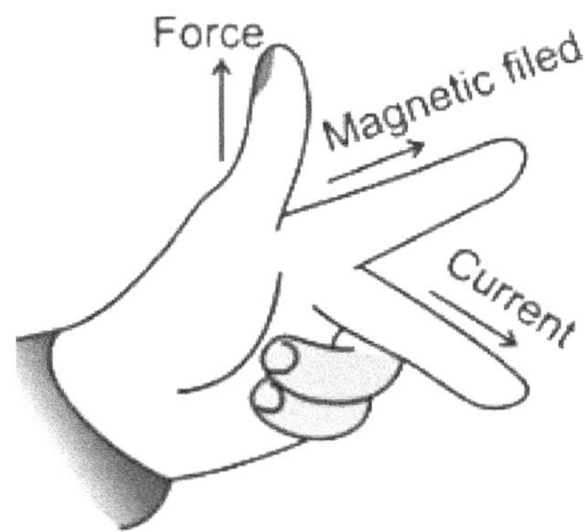

This means that as many field lines should seem to enter the surface as the number of lines leaving it.

Net magnetic flux $(\varnothing_B) = \sum B \cdot \Delta A = 0$

Integral form: $\int B.nds = 0$

Where B is the magnetic field and A is surface area.

55(B). Curie temperature is the temperature above which

a ferromagnetic material becomes paramagnetic material.

Curie Temperature is the temperature at which a magnetic material undergoes a sharp change in its magnetic properties. Above this temperature, some materials lose their magnetism. Above this temperature, ferromagnetic material becomes paramagnetic.

When a ferromagnetic material is heated to Curie temperature, it disrupts the arrangements of the molecules and a weak magnetic behaviour remains. This weak magnetic behaviour is called Paramagnetic.

56(C). Fleming's left-hand rule:

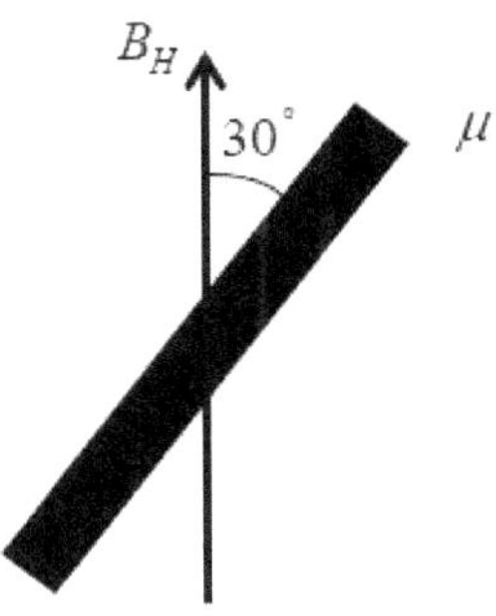

Stretch the thumb and the first two fingers of the left hand mutually perpendicular to each other.

If the forefinger points in the direction of the magnetic field, the central finger in the direction of the current, then the thumb gives the direction of the force on the charged particle.

57(A). As we know,

Torque, $\tau = \vec{\mu} \times \overrightarrow{B_H}$

Where μ is the magnets dipole moment and B_H is the horizontal component of Earth's magnetic field. We have been given that the dipole moment of the magnet, $\mu = 2Am^2$ and the horizontal component of the Earth's magnetic field is $B_H = 0.4 \times 10^{-4}T$. It is also given that the angle between the magnet and the magnetic meridian is $30°$.

So, we can illustrate the condition as follow,

Now, we can find the torque generated by using the formula,

$\tau = \vec{\mu} \times \overrightarrow{B_H} = \mu B_H \sin\theta$, where μ is the magnets dipole moment, B_H is the horizontal component of Earth's magnetic field and θ is the angle between the magnet and the magnetic meridian.

Therefore, $\tau = 2 \times 0.4 \times 10^{-4} \sin 30°$
$= \frac{0.8}{2} \times 10^{-4}$
$= 0.4 \times 10^{-4} Nm$

58(B). It is given that a solenoid carrying a current produces a magnetic field B along its axis.
We need to find the magnetic field when the current in the solenoid is doubled and the number of turns per cm is halved.
We know that the magnetic field in a solenoid depends directly on the current and number of turns.
The equation for finding magnetic field induction for a solenoid is given as
$B = \mu_0 n i$
Where, μ_0 is the permeability in free space, i is the current flowing through it and n is the number of turns of the coil.
Let the initial current be i_1 and the number of turns be n_1.
Then the magnetic field induction will be
$\Rightarrow B = \mu_0 n_1 i_1$
Now let us calculate the final magnetic field.
Let the new current be i_2 and the number of turns be n_2.
It is given that new current is twice that of initial current.
$\Rightarrow i_2 = 2i_1$
Number of turns is half the initial value.
$\Rightarrow n_2 = \frac{n_1}{2}$
So, the new magnetic field is given as
$\Rightarrow B' = \mu_0 n_2 i_2$
$\Rightarrow B' = \mu_0 \frac{n_1}{2} 2i_1$
$\Rightarrow B' = \mu_0 n_1 i_1$
This value is the same as that of the initial magnetic field.
$\Rightarrow B' = B$
This means there is no change in a magnetic field if you double the current and reduce the number of turns to half.

59(D). For a diamagnetic material, μ_r and ϵ_r should have following bounds $0 < \mu_r < 1$ and for any material $\epsilon_r > 1$. Diamagnetic materials create an induced magnetic field in a direction opposite to an external applied magnetic field and are repelled by applied magnetic field. Magnetic permeability of the diamagnetic materials is little less than unity.

60(A). Alnico has a higher retentivity of magnetism. The value of the intensity of magnetization of a material when the magnetizing field is reduced to zero is called retentivity. The materials that are suitable for electromagnets should have high retention.

61(C). We know that,
The magnetic field at any axial point is given as,
$B_a = \frac{2\mu_o}{4\pi r^3}$ ...(1)
The magnetic field at any equatorial point is given as,
$B_e = \frac{\mu_o}{4\pi r^3}$ ....(2)
Multiplying and Dividing equation (2) by 2, we get,
$B_e = \frac{1}{2} \frac{2\mu_o}{4\pi r^3}$
Putting the value of (1),
$B_e = \frac{B_a}{2}$ $[\because B_a = B]$
$B_e = \frac{B}{2}$

62(D). The magnetic field at the center of a bar magnet is zero in an ideal case.
- The field lines near the center is parallel to the bar magnet.
- The density of the field lines is maximum at the poles of the bar magnet and zero at the center which means that the magnitude of the magnetic field is small at the center.

63(A). The current through the capacitor is $\frac{\pi}{2}$ ahead of the applied voltage.
The alternating emf in the circuit is:
$e = e_o \sin \omega t$
Current in the capacitive circuit is:
$I = I_o \sin \left(\omega t + \frac{\pi}{2}\right)$
From above it is clear that electric current through the capacitor leads the applied voltage by $\frac{\pi}{2}$.

64(D). Given that:
$V = 200 \sin 300t$
$V_0 = 200$ V,
$\omega = 300 \text{rad/s} \ (\because V = V_0 \sin \omega t)$
$R = 10\Omega$
$L = 800 \text{mH}$
$= 800 \times 10^{-3} \text{H}$
Inductive reactance,
$X_L = L\omega = 800 \times 10^{-3} \times 300 \Omega$
We know that,
$Z = \sqrt{R^2 + (X_L - X_C)^2}$
Now,
$Z = \sqrt{R^2 + (X_L - 0)^2}$
$\Rightarrow Z = \sqrt{10^2 + \left(800 \times 10^{-3} \times 300\right)^2}$
$\Rightarrow Z = 240.2\Omega$
From Ohm's law,
$V_0 = I_0 R$
$\Rightarrow I_0 = \frac{V_0}{R}$
For an LCR circuit, the net resistance is the impedance Z.
$\therefore I_0 = \frac{V_0}{Z}$
$= \frac{200}{240.2}$
$= 0.832$ A

65(B). Given,
$\theta = 0$,
$A = 50 \text{ cm}^2$,
$N = 1000$,
$B_1 = 0.2 \text{ weber}/m^2$,
$B_2 = 0 \text{ weber}/m^2$,
$dt = 0.2 \text{sec}$
$A = 50 \text{ cm}^2$
$= 50 \times 10^{-4} \text{ m}^2$
The change in the magnetic field is:
$dB = B_2 - B_1$
$\Rightarrow dB = 0 - 0.2$
$\Rightarrow dB = -0.2 \text{ weber}/m^2$
When the magnetic field is changing and the area remains constant, the magnetic flux is:
$d\phi = A \times dB \times \cos\theta$
$\Rightarrow d\phi = A \times dB \times \cos 0$
$\Rightarrow d\phi = A \times dB$
$\Rightarrow d\phi = -50 \times 10^{-4} \times 0.2$
$\Rightarrow d\phi = -10 \times 10^{-4}$
$\Rightarrow d\phi = 10^{-3} \text{ weber}$ $...(i)$
By Faraday's law of electromagnetic induction, the magnitude of the induced emf in the coil is:

$$e = -N\frac{d\phi}{dt}$$
$$\Rightarrow e = -1000 \times \frac{(-10)^{-3}}{0.2}$$
$$\Rightarrow e = 5 \text{ V}$$

66(A). In an electromagnetic wave, the electric and magnetic fields are a lways in same phase.
Electromagnetic waves or EM waves are waves that are created as a result of vibrations between an electric field and a magnetic field. The electric field and magnetic field of an electromagnetic wave are perpendiculars (at right angles - 90°) to each other. They are also perpendicular to the direction of the EM wave. But they are in the same phase.

67(D). Electromagnetic waves are produced by an acceleration charge.
- As we know that the charged particle produces an electric field and it exerts a force on other charged particles. As the direction of the electric field is from positive charge to negative charge, therefore positive charges accelerate in the direction of the field and negative charges accelerate in the direction opposite to the field.
- From Hans Christian Oersted experiment we find that a moving charged particle produces a magnetic field. If a charged particle moves in the magnetic field then they experience a force. The force on these charges is always perpendicular to the direction of their velocity and therefore only changes the direction of the velocity, not the speed.
- An accelerating charged particle produces an electromagnetic (EM) wave.
- Basically, electromagnetic waves or EM waves are waves that are formed as a result of vibrations between an electric field and a magnetic field and they are perpendicular to each other and to the direction of the wave.
- A charged particle oscillating about an equilibrium position is an accelerating charged particle.

68(A). From Maxwell's Electromagnetic theory, the Electromagnetic Wave propagation contains electric and magnetic fields vibrating perpendicularly to each other. Thus, changing of electric field gives rise to magnetic field.
Then the Maxwell's equation,
$$\nabla \times \mathbf{B} = \mu_0 \left(\mathbf{J} + \epsilon_0 \frac{d\mathbf{E}}{dt}\right)$$
Using this equation of maxwell we can say changing electric field $\frac{d\mathbf{E}}{dt}$ induces magnetic field.

69(B). Microwaves are used to communicate with the artificial satellite.
Microwaves:
- In artificial satellites, mostly microwaves are used for communication.
- It is an electromagnetic wave with frequency ranges between $300\text{MHz}(0.3\text{GHz})$ and 300GHz in the electromagnetic spectrum.
- It is specially used in spacecraft communication, TV and long-distance telephone lines.

70(C). The student R has performed the experiment methodically. The reason can be explained using Snell's law.
According to Snell's law,
$$\frac{\sin i}{\sin r} = \mu_g$$
Here,

i = Angle of incidence
r = Angle of refraction
μ_g = Refractive index for glass
The angle of refraction measured by student R is most appropriate as it verifies the Snell's law.
Given,
$i = 40°$
The angle of refraction measured by student R,
$r = 25°$
Also,
$\sin 40° = 0.642$
$\sin 25° = 0.422$
Now,
$$\frac{\sin 40°}{\sin 25°} = \frac{0.642}{0.422} = 1.52$$
The refractive index for glass is 1.5 ; it verifies the result derived above.

71(B). Given,
Wavelength $= \lambda = 250 \text{ nm} = 2.5 \times 10^{-7} \text{ m}$
Aperture $= D = 0.5 \text{ m}$
As we know,
The resolving power of the telescope $= \dfrac{D}{1.22 \times \lambda}$
$$= \frac{0.5}{1.22 \times 2.5 \times 10^{-7}}$$
$$= 1.64 \times 10^6$$

72(B). Focal length of convex lens, $f_1 = +40\text{cm}$
Focal length of concave lens, $f_2 = -25\text{cm}$
And, as the lenses are in contact so separation between them is, $d = 0$
Power of the lens can be given as,
$$\text{Power} = \frac{100}{f(\text{ in } cm)}$$
Power of the combination can be given as:
$$P_{net} = P_1 + P_2 - dP_1P_2$$
$$\Rightarrow P_{net} = \frac{100}{40} - \frac{100}{25} - 0$$
$$\Rightarrow P_{net} = 2.5 - 4$$
$$\Rightarrow P_{net} = -1.5D$$

73(D). As, $u >> f_0$,
$$\Rightarrow v = f_0 = 19 \text{ m}$$
Now, $u = -3.8 \times 10^8 m$
Therefore, magnification produced by the objective is
$$m_0 = \frac{v}{u}$$
$$= -\frac{19}{3.8 \times 10^8}$$
$$= -0.5 \times 10^{-7}$$
$\therefore$ Diameter of the image of moon is
$$= 3.5 \times 10^6 \times 0.5 \times 10^{-7}$$
$$= 0.175 \text{ m}$$
$$= 17.5 \text{ cm}$$

74(B). Given,
v = Velocity of sound, v_s = Velocity of car
We have, $v = \dfrac{v+v_s}{v-v_s}v$
Or, $2f = \dfrac{v+v_s}{v-v_s}f$
Or, $2(v - v_s) = v + v_s$
Or, $2v - 2v_z = v + v_s$
$\therefore v = 3v_s$
Or, $v_s = \dfrac{v}{3}$

75(A). The position of 30 th bright fringe
$$y_{30} = \frac{30\lambda D}{d}$$
Now, position shift to central fringe is
$$my_0 = \frac{30\lambda D}{d}$$
But we know, $y_0 = \dfrac{D}{d}(\mu - 1)t$

$$\Rightarrow \frac{30\lambda D}{d} = \frac{D}{d}(\mu - 1)t$$

$$(\Rightarrow \mu - 1) = \frac{30\lambda}{t}$$

$$\Rightarrow \frac{30 \times 6000 \times 10^{-10}}{3.6 \times 10^{-5}} = 0.5$$

$$\Rightarrow \mu = 1.5$$

76(C). Let velocity of sound in air be v.

$\Rightarrow$ Velocity of the observer, V observer $= \frac{v}{5}$

Let v be the original frequency of the sound source and v be the apparent frequency heard by the moving observer.

Using Doppler effect when observer is moving towards the stationary source:

$$\mathrm{n}' = \left[\frac{\mathrm{v} + \mathrm{v_O}}{\mathrm{v}}\right]\mathrm{n} = \left[\frac{\mathrm{v} + \frac{v}{5}}{\mathrm{v}}\right]\mathrm{n} = \frac{6}{5}\mathrm{n} = 1.2\mathrm{n}$$

Increment in frequency $= 0.2\mathrm{n}$,

So, percentage change in frequency $= \frac{0.2\mathrm{n}}{\mathrm{n}} \times 100$

$= 20\%$

77(C). Using the formula,

$$e \times V_s = \frac{hc}{\lambda} - W \ (W = \text{work function})$$

$$\Rightarrow e \times 2.5 = \frac{hc}{300)} - W$$

$$\Rightarrow e \times 2.5 = \frac{1241.5 \times nm}{300} - W$$

$$\Rightarrow e \times 2.5 = \frac{1241.5}{300} - W$$

$$\Rightarrow e \times 2.5 = \frac{1241.5 \times (1.6 \times 10^{-19})}{300} - W$$

$$\Rightarrow e \times 2.5 = \frac{1241.5 \times e}{300} - W \ .....(i)$$

$$\Rightarrow e \times V_s = \frac{1241.5 \times e}{150} - W \ ....(ii)$$

Subtracting equation (i) and (ii)

$$e \times V_s - e \times 2.5 = \frac{1241.5 \times e}{150} - \frac{1241.5 \times e}{300}$$

$$\Rightarrow (V_s - 2.5) = \frac{1241.5}{150} - \frac{1241.5}{300}$$

$$\Rightarrow (V_s - 2.5) = \frac{1241.5}{150} - \frac{1241.5}{300} = \frac{1241.5}{300} = 4.138V$$

$$\Rightarrow V_s = 2.5 + 4.138 = 6.63V$$

78(B). The quantization of the photons means that photons are discrete energy parcels.
- These parcels are massless particles of definite energy, a definite momentum, and definite spin.
- The quantization of the photons means that photons are discrete energy parcels.
- Quantization means they exist in discrete particles with each discrete particle has a different energy, different momentum, etc.

79(C). The saturation photoelectric current is directly proportional to the intensity of incident radiation but it is independent of its frequency. Therefore the saturation photoelectric current becomes doubled when both the intensity and frequency of the incident light are doubled.

80(B). Given,

Frequency of light, $v = 6.0 \times 10^{14}$ Hz

Power emitted by light, $P = 2.0 \times 10^{-3}$ W

We know that, $h = 6.63 \times 10^{-34}$ J s

Each photon has energy,

$E = hv = \left(6.63 \times 10^{-34} \ \text{Js}\right)\left(6.0 \times 10^{14} \ \text{Hz}\right)$

$= 3.98 \times 10^{-19}$ J

If N is the number of photons emitted by the source per second, the power P transmitted in the beam equals N times the energy per photon E, so that P = N E. Then,

$$N = \frac{P}{E} = \frac{2.0 \times 10^{-3} \ \text{W}}{3.98 \times 10^{-19} \ \text{J}}$$

$= 5.0 \times 10^{15}$ photons per second.

1. Unit of surface tension is:
   (a) Dyne cm
   (b) Dyne cm^{-1}
   (c) Dyne cm^{-2}
   (d) None of these

2. How are the numerical value (n) and unit (u) of a physical quantity related:
   (a) $n \propto u$
   (b) $n \propto \sqrt{u}$
   (c) $n \propto \frac{1}{u}$
   (d) $n \propto \frac{1}{\sqrt{u}}$

3. Which one of the following is not a derived unit.
   (a) Frequency
   (b) Plank's constant
   (c) Gravitational constant
   (d) Electric current

4. If force (F), acceleration (A), Time (T) are used as fundamental units, the dimensional formula for length will be:
   (a) $[\mathrm{F^0 A T^2}]$
   (b) $[\mathrm{F A^0 T^2}]$
   (c) $[\mathrm{F A^0 T^0}]$
   (d) $[\mathrm{F A T}]$

5. What is the minimum number of co-planer vectors of different magnitudes which can give zero resultant?
   (a) 1
   (b) 4
   (c) 3
   (d) 6

6. A projectile fired from the ground follows a parabolic path. At what position will the speed of projectile be minimum?
   (a) At the top of the path
   (b) At the beginning of the path
   (c) While travelling along the path
   (d) Never

7. Which of the following is not true about projectile motion?
   (a) It is an example of motion in a plane
   (b) It is an example of motion along a curve
   (c) It is not an example of motion in space
   (d) The acceleration keeps changing in projectile motion

8. A body, under the action of a force $\vec{F} = 6\hat{i} - 8\hat{j} + 10\hat{k}$ acquires an acceleration of 1m/s^2. The mass of this body must be:
   (a) 10 kg
   (b) 20kg
   (c) $10\sqrt{2}$ kg
   (d) $2\sqrt{10}$ kg

9. An impulse is supplied to a moving object with the force at an angle of $120°$ with the velocity vector. The angle between the impulse vector and the change in momentum vector is:
   (a) $120°$
   (b) $0°$
   (c) $60°$
   (d) $240°$

10. A body of mass 4 kg accelerates from 15 m/s to 25 m/s in 5 seconds due to the application of a force on it. Calculate the magnitude of this force.
    (a) 32 N
    (b) 8 N
    (c) 16 N
    (d) 64 N

11. A player, trying to catch a cricket ball, usually pulls his hand back slowly. Which principle is this:
    (a) Newton's first law of motion
    (b) Newton's second law of motion
    (c) Newton's third law of motion
    (d) Newton's fourth law of motion

12. A body moves from a position $r_1 = (2\hat{i} - 3\hat{j} - 4\hat{k})m$ to a position, $r_2 = (3\hat{i} - 4\hat{j} + 5\hat{k})m$ under the influence of a constant force $\mathbf{F} = (4\hat{i} + \hat{j} + 6\hat{k})\mathrm{N}$. The work done by the force is:
    (a) 57 J
    (b) 58 J
    (c) 59 J
    (d) 60 J

13. A body of mass M splits into two parts α and $(1 - \alpha)M$ by an internal explosion which generates kinetic energy T. After explosion if the two parts move in the same direction as before, their relative speed will be -
    (a) $\sqrt{\dfrac{T}{(1-\alpha)M}}$
    (b) $\sqrt{\dfrac{2T}{\alpha(1-\alpha)M}}$
    (c) $\sqrt{\dfrac{T}{2(1-\alpha)M}}$
    (d) $\sqrt{\dfrac{2T}{(1-a)M}}$

14. An alpha-particle of mass m suffers 1-dimensional elastic collision with a nucleus at rest of unknown mass. It is scattered directly backwards losing, 64% of its initial kinetic energy. The mass of the nucleus is:
    (a) 1.5 m
    (b) 2 m
    (c) 3.5 m
    (d) 4 m

15. When we pull back the string of catapult (gulel) to throw a stone, it holds an energy. Which kind of energy is this?
    (a) Kinetic energy
    (b) Potential energy
    (c) Both (A) and (B)
    (d) None of the above

16. Two particles of mass 5 kg and 10 kg respectively are attached to the two ends of a rigid rod of length 1 m with negligible mass.
    The centre of mass of the system from the 5 kg particle is nearly at a distance of:
    (a) 33 cm
    (b) 50 cm
    (c) 67 cm
    (d) 80 cm

17. A uniform metal rod of length L and mass M is rotating with angular speed ω about an axis passing through one of the ends and perpendicular to the rod. If the temperature increases by $t°C$, then the change in its angular speed is proportional to
    (a) $\sqrt{\varpi}$
    (b) ω
    (c) w^2
    (d) $\frac{1}{\omega}$

18. The ratio of the radii of gyration of a circular disc about a tangential axis in the plane of the disc and a circular ring of the same radius about a tangential axis in the plane of the ring is:
    (a) $2 : 3$
    (b) $2 : 1$
    (c) $\sqrt{5} : \sqrt{6}$
    (d) $1 : \sqrt{2}$

19. Which of the following statement is true regarding the weight and mass of an object?
    (a) A body has the same weight and same mass on the moon as it has on the Earth
    (b) Only mass of a body is same on the Earth and on the Moon
    (c) Only weight of a body is same on the Earth and

on the Moon

(d) A body has different weight and different mass on the moon as it has on the Earth

20. Two spherical balls of mass 10 kg each are placed 10 cm apart. Determine the gravitational force of attraction between them.
   (a) $6.67 \times 10^{-7} N$
   (b) $4.67 \times 10^{-7} N$
   (c) $8.67 \times 10^{-14} N$
   (d) 3.67×10^{-6} N

21. Newton's law of gravitation is valid on:
   (a) Only for charged bodies
   (b) All bodies
   (c) Only heavy bodies
   (d) Only for small bodies

22. Planet A has double the radius than that of planet B. If mass of planet A is 4 times heavier than the mass of planet B, which of the following statements regarding weight of an object is correct?
   (a) Heavier on planet A than on planet B
   (b) Heavier on planet B than on planet A
   (c) Same on both the planets
   (d) Can't be measured on planet B

23. At a certain height H above the surface of the earth, the value of acceleration due to gravity equals that at a depth of 200 km into the surface. Then the distance H from the surface of Earth is:
   (a) 400 km
   (b) 300 km
   (c) 200 km
   (d) 100 km

24. The gas thermometer are more sensitive than liquid thermometers because gases __________.
   (a) Expand more than liquid
   (b) Are easily obtained
   (c) Are much lighter
   (d) None of these

25. When a solid ball of iron is heated, the largest percentage increase in _____ will occur.
   (a) Density
   (b) Surface area
   (c) Diameter
   (d) Volume

26. In the pressure cooker, the cooking is faster because the increase of vapour pressure:
   (a) Increases melting point
   (b) Increases boiling point
   (c) Decreases boiling point
   (d) Decreases melting point

27. Which of the following statement is wrong?
   (a) Bimetal is used in metal thermometer
   (b) Bimetals are used to generate electricity
   (c) Bimetals relays are used to open or close electric circuits
   (d) Bimetals is used in thermostats for regulating heating or cooling of rooms

28. Which of the following process is used to do maximum work done on the ideal gas if the gas is compressed to half of its initial volume?
   (a) Isothermal
   (b) Isochoric
   (c) Isobaric
   (d) Adiabatic

29. When a real gas expands adiabatically against a finite pressure, its:

(a) Internal energy increases
(b) Internal energy decreases
(c) Temperature always increases
(d) Internal energy remains constant

30. A refrigerator is to maintain eatables kept inside at $9°C$. If room temperature is $36°C$, calculate the coefficient of performance.
   (a) 10.44
   (b) 11.44
   (c) 9.04
   (d) 11.84

31. Two identical finite bodies of constant heat capacity at temperatures T_1 and T_2 are available to do work in a heat engine. The final temperature T_f reached by the bodies on delivery of maximum work is:
   (a) $T_F = \frac{T_1 + T_2}{2}$
   (b) $T_f = \sqrt{T_1 T_2}$
   (c) $T_f = T_1 = T_2$
   (d) $T_f = \sqrt{T_1^2 + T_2^2}$

32. Extension in length of a spring is 12cm when 5kg mass is suspended on it. If spring oscillate vertically, then its time period is:
   (a) 0.7 sec
   (b) 0.9 sec
   (c) 1.1 sec
   (d) 1.4 sec

33. For a simple pendulum the graph between L and T will be:
   (a) Hyperbola
   (b) Parabola
   (c) Straight line
   (d) Curved line

34. Two particles execute SHM of the same amplitude and frequency along the same straight line. If they pass each other when going in opposite directions, each time their displacement being half their amplitude, the phase difference between them is
   (a) $\frac{\pi}{2}$
   (b) $\frac{\pi}{6}$
   (c) $\frac{2\pi}{3}$
   (d) $\frac{2\pi}{7}$

35. A simple pendulum of length l has a brass bob attached at its lower end. Its period is T. If a steel bob of same size, having density x times that of brass, replaces the brass bob and its length is changed so that period becomes $2T$, then new length is
   (a) $2\,l$
   (b) $4\,l$
   (c) $4\,x$
   (d) $\frac{4\,l}{x}$

36. An observer is moving towards the stationary source of a sound, then
   (a) Apparent frequency will be less than the real frequency
   (b) Apparent frequency will be greater than the real frequency
   (c) Apparent frequency will be greater than the real frequency
   (d) Only the quality of sound will change

37. If number of neutrons become more than the number of electrons in the element then it will become:
   (a) Positively charged
   (b) Negatively charged
   (c) Neutral
   (d) Can't say

38. Positive charge can be generated on a body by:
   (a) Adding proton
   (b) Removing electron
   (c) Adding electron

(d)   By adding proton or removing electron

39. The potential difference between the two plates of a parallel plate capacitor is magnitude of charge on each plate of area A separated by a distance d):

(a) $Qd/(\varepsilon_0 \, A)$ (b) $d\varepsilon_o/AQ$

(c) $Ad/(\varepsilon_0 Q)$ (d) $QA/d\varepsilon_0$

40. An electron possesses a negative charge of:

(a) $1.6 \times 10^{+18}C$ (b) $1.6 \times 10^{-19}C$

(c) $1.6 \times 10^{-18}C$ (d) $1.6 \times 10^{-16}C$

41. An infinite line charge produces a field of $9 \times 10^4 N/C$ at distance of 2 cm. Calculate the linear charge density.

(a) $12\mu C/m$ (b) $10\mu C/m$

(c) $11\mu C/m$ (d) $9\mu C/m$

42. A uniformly charged conducting sphere of 2.4 m diameter has a surface charge density of 80.0 μC/m^2. What is the total electric flux leaving the surface of the sphere?

(a) $1.3 \times 10^8 \mathrm{Nm}^2/C$ (b) $1.6 \times 10^5 \mathrm{Nm}^3/C$

(c) $2.5 \times 10^8 \mathrm{Nm}^2/C$ (d) $1.6 \times 10^8 \mathrm{Nm}^2/C$

43. Determine the voltage (in V) of a battery connected to a parallel plate capacitor (filled with air) when the area of the plate is 10 square centimeters, the separation between the plates is 5 mm and the charge stored on the plates is 2 nC.

(a)   1230   (b)   1030

(c)   1130   (d)   1430

44. Electric potential at any point is $V = -5x + 3y + \sqrt{15}z$, then the magnitude of electric field is:

(a) $3\sqrt{2}$ (b) $4\sqrt{2}$

(c) $5\sqrt{2}$ (d)   7

45. Energy stored in a parallel plate capacitor is:

(a) $\dfrac{3q^2}{2C}$ (b) $\dfrac{q^2}{C}$

(c) $\dfrac{q^2}{2C}$ (d) $\dfrac{q^2}{3C}$

46. Five equal resistances each of value R are connected in a form shown in Fig. The equivalent resistance of the network

(a) between points B and D is $\dfrac{R}{2}$.

(b) between points A and C is R.

(c) between points B and D is R.

(d) between points A and C is $\dfrac{R}{2}$.

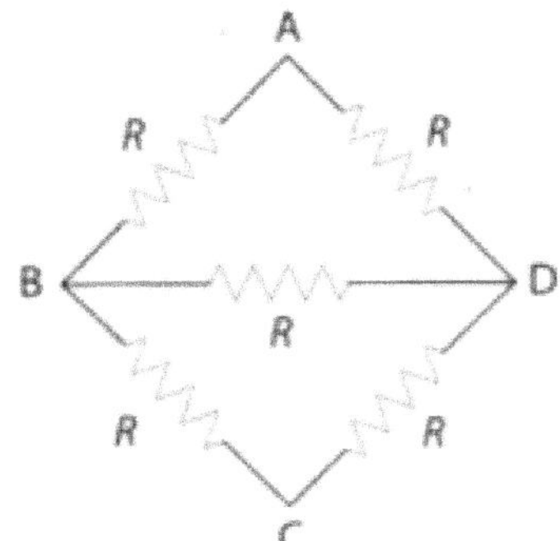

(a)   Only (a)   (b)   Only (b)

(c)   Both (a) and (b)   (d)   Both (a) and (c)

47. Three 2Ω resistors are connected to form a triangle. The resistance between any two corners is:

(a) $\dfrac{4}{3}\Omega$ (b) 6Ω

(c) 2Ω (d) $\dfrac{3}{4}\Omega$

48. An unknown resistance R_1 is connected in series with a resistance of 10Ω. This combination is connected to one gap of a metre bridge while a resistance R_2 is connected in the other gap. The balance point is at 50 cm. Now, when the 10Ω resistance is removed the balance point shifts to 40 cm. The value of R_1 is (in ohms):

(a)   20   (b)   10

(c)   60   (d)   40

49. The ____________ Law is an equation that describes the magnetic field created by a current-carrying wire and allows you to calculate its strength at various points.

(a)   Ampere's   (b)   Lorentz's

(c)   Biot-Savart's   (d)   Kirchhoff's

50. The electric field of a plane electromagnetic wave is given by $\vec{E} = E_0(\hat{x} + \hat{y})\sin(kz - \omega t)$
Its magnetic field will be given by:

(a) $\dfrac{E_0}{c}(\hat{x} - \hat{y})\cos(kz - \omega t)$

(b) $\dfrac{E_0}{c}(-\hat{x} + \hat{y})\sin(kz - \omega t)$

(c) $\dfrac{E_0}{c}(\hat{x} - \hat{y})\sin(kz - \omega t)$

(d) $\dfrac{E_0}{c}(\hat{x} + \hat{y})\sin(kz - \omega t)$

51. Which, among the following qualities, is not affected by the magnetic field?

(a)   Moving charge

(b)   Change in magnetic flux

(c)   Current flowing in a conductor

(d)   Stationary charge

52. Resultant force acting on a diamagnetic material in a magnetic field is in direction:

(a)   From stronger to the weaker part of the magnetic field

(b)   From weaker to the stronger part of the magnetic field

(c)   Perpendicular to the magnetic field

(d)   In the direction making 60° to the magnetic field

53. The electric current in a circular coil of two turns produced a magnetic induction of 0.2 T at its centre. The coil is unwound and then rewound into a circular coil of four turns. If same current flows in the coil, the magnetic induction at the centre of the coil now is:

(a)   0.2 T   (b)   0.4 T

(c)   0.6 T   (d)   0.8 T

54. Two circular coils 1 and 2 are made from the same wire, but the radius of the 1st coil is twice that of the 2nd coil. What is the ratio of potential differences applied across them, so that the magnetic field at their centres is the same?

(a)   3   (b)   4

(c) 6   (d) 2

55. A square metal wire loop of side 10cm and resistance 1Ω is moved with a constant velocity v in a uniform magnetic field $B = 2T$ as shown in the figure. The magnetic field is perpendicular to the plane of the loop and directed into the paper. The loop is connected to a network of resistors, each equal to 3Ω. What should be the speed of the loop, so as to have a steady current of 1mA in the loop?

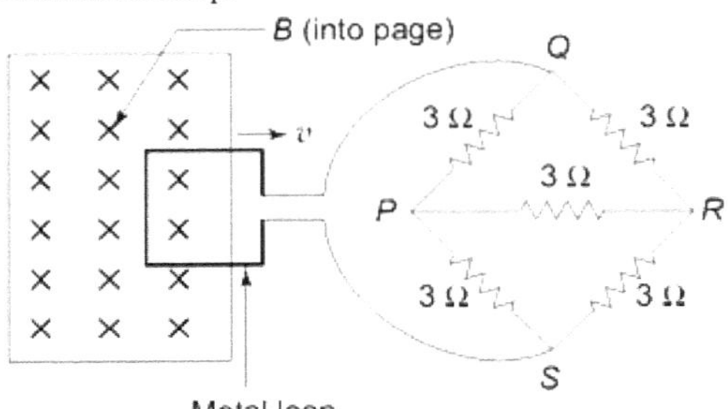

(a) $1 \, \text{cms}^{-1}$ (b) $2 \, \text{cms}^{-1}$
(c) $3 \, \text{cms}^{-1}$ (d) $4 \, \text{cms}^{-1}$

56. In an electromagnetic wave, the magnitude of electric and magnetic fields are 100 V/m and 0.265 A/m. The maximum energy flow is:
(a) $26.5 \, \text{W/m}^2$ (b) $36.5 \, \text{W/m}^2$
(c) $46.7 \, \text{W/m}^2$ (d) $765 \, \text{W/m}^2$

57. The magnetic flux ϕ (in weber) linked with a coil of resistance 10Ω varies with time t (in second) as $\phi = 8t^2 - 4t + 1$. The current induced in the coil at $t = 0.1$ sec is:
(a) 10 A   (b) 0.24 A
(c) 0.12 A   (d) 4.8 A

58. The eddy current loss in a transformer is reduced by:
(a) The reducing the resistance of core
(b) Using a laminated core
(c) It is not possible to reduce it
(d) Both (A) and (B)

59. Current in a coil changes from $4A$ to zero in 0.1 second and the emf induced is $100V$. The self inductance of the coil is:
(a) $4H$ (b) $2.5H$
(c) $0.4H$ (d) $0.25H$

60. A magnet NS is suspended from a spring and while it oscillates, the magnet moves in and out of the coil. The coil is connected to a galvanometer G. Then, as the magnet oscillates,

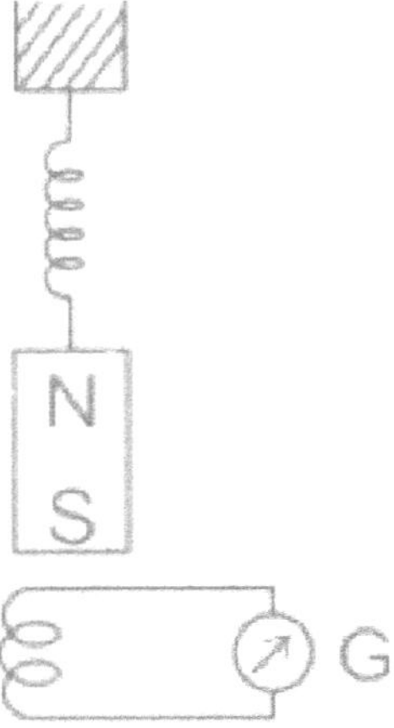

(a) G shows deflection to the left and right with constant amplitude
(b) G shows deflection on one side
(c) G shows no deflection
(d) G shows deflection to the left and right but the amplitude steadily decreases

61. The refractive index of the material of an equilateral prism is $\sqrt{3}$. What is the angle of minimum deviation?
(a) $30°$ (b) $45°$
(c) $60°$ (d) $75°$

62. In Young's double slit experiment, if the separation between coherent sources is halved and the distance of the screen from the coherent sources is doubled, then the fringe width becomes:
(a) Double   (b) Half
(c) Four times   (d) One-fourth

63. Assume that light of wavelength 600nm is coming from a star. The limit of resolution of telescope whose objective has a diameter of 2 m is:
(a) 3.66×10^{-7}rad   (b) 1.83×10^{-7}rad
(c) 7.32×10^{-7}rad   (d) 6.00×10^{-7}rad

64. The work function for sodium surface is 2.0eV and that for aluminum surface is 4.2eV. The two metals are illuminated with appropriate radiations, so as to cause photoemission. Then:
(a) The threshold frequency for sodium will be less than that for aluminum
(b) The threshold frequency of sodium will be more than that of aluminum
(c) Both sodium and aluminum will have the same threshold frequency
(d) None of the these

65. The energy flux of sunlight reaching the surface of the earth is $1.388 \times 10^3 \, \text{W/m}^2$. How many photons (nearly) per square metre are incident on the Earth per second? Assume that the photons in the sunlight have an average wavelength of 550 nm.
(a) 5.84×10^{21} (b) 9.84×10^{21}
(c) 3.84×10^{21} (d) 4.84×10^{21}

66. Which of the following phenomena can explain quantum nature of light?
(a) Photoelectric effect (b) Interference

(c) Diffraction (d) Polarization

67. The kinetic energy of the fastest moving photo electron from a metal of work function 2.8 eV is 2 eV. If the frequency of light is doubled, then find the maximum kinetic energy of photo electron.

(a) 6.8eV (b) 68eV
(c) -6.8eV (d) -68eV

68. Two radiations of photons energies 1eV and 2.5eV , successively illuminate a photosensitive metallic surface of work function 0.5eV . The ratio of the maximum speeds of the emitted electrons is:

(a) $1:4$ (b) $1:2$
(c) $1:1$ (d) $1:5$

69. An electron is moving in an orbit of a hydrogen atom at the 4th energy level. Find the number of spectral lines for a transition from here to the ground state.

(a) 8 (b) 3
(c) 6 (d) 10

70. When an electron in hydrogen atom is excited, from its 3rd to 4th stationary orbit, the change in angular momentum of electron is:

(a) 1.05×10^{-34} J/S (b) 3.14×10^{-34} J/s
(c) 6.64×10^{-34} J/S (d) 3.32×10^{-34} J/S

71. The angular momentum of an electron in the nth orbit is 3.17×10^{-34} J-s. Find n.

(a) n = 1 (b) n = 2
(c) n = 3 (d) n = 4

72. Electron volt (eV) is a unit of___________.

(a) Energy (b) Potential
(c) Current (d) Charge

73. Two different gases at the same temperature have equal root mean square velocities (C_{rms}). If M is the molecular mass of the gas, then:

(a) $C_{\text{rms}} \propto \sqrt{\dfrac{1}{M}}$ (b) $C_{\text{rms}} \propto \sqrt{M}$
(c) $C_{\text{rms}} \propto M$ (d) $C_{\text{rms}} = 0$

74. The gases Carbon monoxide and Nitrogen at the same temperature have kinetic energies E_1 and E_2 , respectively. Then,

(a) $E_1 = E_2$
(b) $E_1 > E_2$
(c) $E_1 < E_2$
(d) E_1 and E_2 cannot be compared

75. The distance travelled by a particle starting from rest and moving with an acceleration $\frac{4}{3}$ m s^{-2} in the third second is:

(a) 6 m (b) 4 m
(c) $\frac{10}{3}$ m (d) $\frac{19}{3}$ m

76. How many atoms of helium gas fill a spherical balloon of diameter 30.0 cm at 20.0°C and 1.00 atm?

(a) 4.493×10^{23} (b) 8.493×10^{23}
(c) 7.493×10^{23} (d) 3.493×10^{23}

77. Two different isotherms representing the relationship between pressure p and volume V at a given temperature of the same ideal gas are shown for masses m_1 and m_2 , then:

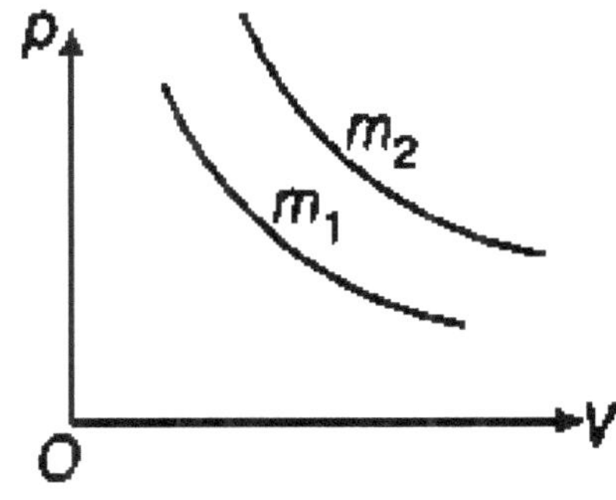

(a) $m_1 = m_2$
(b) $m_1 < m_2$
(c) $m_1 > m_2$
(d) Nothing can be predicted

78. If the ratio of the concentration of electrons to that of holes in semiconductors is $\frac{7}{5}$ and the ratio of currents is $\frac{7}{4}$, then the ratio of drift velocities is:

(a) $\frac{5}{8}$ (b) $\frac{4}{5}$
(c) $\frac{5}{4}$ (d) $\frac{4}{7}$

79. Which solid will have the weakest intermolecular forces?

(a) Ice (b) Phosphorus
(c) Naphthalene (d) Sodium fluoride

80. The full form of LED is:

(a) Light emitting diode
(b) Light emission diode
(c) Layer emission diode
(d) Layer electron device

// Smart Answer Sheet //

Correct — Percentage of students who answered correctly.

Skipped — Percentage of students who skipped.

Q.	Ans.	Correct / Skipped	Q.	Ans.	Correct / Skipped	Q.	Ans.	Correct / Skipped
1	B	84.4% / 0.0%	2	C	29.66% / 4.62%	3	D	66.53% / 1.08%
4	A	89.65% / 0.0%	5	C	51.99% / 1.47%	6	A	40.92% / 1.58%
7	D	86.1% / 0.0%	8	C	54.5% / 1.02%	9	B	76.45% / 0.0%
10	B	56.76% / 1.49%	11	B	58.82% / 1.61%	12	A	46.78% / 1.73%
13	B	43.87% / 1.9%	14	D	10.54% / 4.45%	15	B	65.97% / 1.62%
16	C	60.43% / 1.1%	17	B	44.94% / 1.28%	18	C	55.77% / 1.12%
19	B	21.72% / 4.18%	20	A	52.06% / 1.3%	21	B	76.75% / 0.0%
22	C	64.51% / 1.4%	23	D	78.84% / 0.0%	24	A	86.55% / 0.0%
25	D	46.99% / 1.96%	26	B	88.16% / 0.0%	27	B	57.17% / 2.0%
28	D	68.89% / 1.23%	29	B	60.4% / 1.14%	30	A	82.92% / 0.0%
31	B	31.46% / 3.09%	32	A	66.35% / 1.84%	33	B	50.54% / 1.4%
34	C	60.75%	35	B	66.54%	36	B	61.94%

No	Ans	%	No	Ans	%	No	Ans	%
		1.93%			1.64%			1.93%
37	D	60.95% 1.5%	38	B	67.58% 1.9%	39	A	51.07% 1.25%
40	B	57.62% 1.43%	41	B	46.55% 1.61%	42	D	52.14% 1.41%
43	C	64.8% 1.27%	44	D	61.73% 1.55%	45	C	21.64% 4.3%
46	C	23.94% 4.32%	47	A	69.88% 1.35%	48	A	67.05% 1.8%
49	C	60.29% 1.93%	50	B	68.88% 1.56%	51	D	69.28% 1.75%
52	A	54.24% 1.8%	53	D	15.98% 3.82%	54	B	66.55% 1.42%
55	B	53.43% 1.25%	56	A	62.05% 1.05%	57	B	60.76% 1.35%
58	B	56.0% 1.05%	59	B	58.0% 1.41%	60	D	49.45% 1.02%
61	C	68.74% 1.58%	62	C	58.16% 1.86%	63	A	52.91% 1.74%
64	A	62.57% 1.54%	65	C	62.01% 1.02%	66	A	65.78% 1.39%
67	A	47.43% 1.99%	68	B	45.61% 1.15%	69	C	86.92% 0.0%
70	A	68.1% 1.14%	71	C	64.26% 1.81%	72	A	81.12% 0.0%
73	A	60.76% 1.83%	74	A	53.74% 1.37%	75	C	54.28% 1.55%
76	D	47.75% 1.08%	77	B	44.25% 1.13%	78	C	21.87% 4.06%
79	A	88.96% 0.0%	80	A	47.43% 1.3%			

// Hints and Solutions //

1(B). Surface tension is the property by virtue of which liquid tries to minimize its free surface area.

In a spherical shape, the surface area is minimum and for this reason, the raindrops are spherical.

Surface tension is measured as the force acting per unit length of an imaginary line drawn on the liquid surface.

$$\text{Surface tension} = \frac{\text{Force}}{\text{length}}$$

$\therefore$ Unit of surface tension is Dyne/cm or Dyne cm^{-1}.

2(C). A quantity which can be measured and by which various physical phenomenon can be explained in the form of laws is called a physical quantity. For example length, mass, time, force etc.

Measurement is necessary to determine the magnitude of a physical quantity, to compare two similar physical quantities and to prove physical laws or equations.

Physical quantity (Q) = Magnitude $\times$ Unit = $n \times u$

Where n represents the numerical value and u represents the unit.

$nu = \text{constant}$

$n_1 u_1 = n_2 u_2 = \text{constant}$

$n \propto \dfrac{1}{u}$

3(D). Electric current: It is a physical quantity for measuring electric current. Its unit is Ampere (Å).

Frequency: The hertz (symbol: Hz) is the derived unit of frequency in the International System of Units (SI) and is defined as one cycle per second. It is named for Heinrich Rudolf Hertz.

Plank's constant: Planck's Constant relates the energy of light photons to their frequency. its value is 6.626×10^{-34} Js.

Gravitational acceleration: The acceleration produced in the motion of a body under the effect of gravity is called acceleration due to gravity, it is denoted by g.

The acceleration due to gravity on the surface of the earth is given by,

$$g = \frac{GM}{R^2}$$

Where G = universal gravitational constant, M = mass of the earth and R = radius of the earth.

So, electric current is not a derived quantity.

4(A). From the definition of acceleration,

$$A = \frac{dv}{dt} = \frac{d^2x}{dt^2}$$

$$\int dv = \int A\,dt$$

$$V = A \times T$$

$$\frac{x}{T} = AT$$

$$\Rightarrow X = AT^2$$

To write in the form of Dimensions,

$$\Rightarrow x = \left[F^0 AT^2 \right]$$

5(C). As the magnitude of the vectors is not equal so two vectors cannot give zero resultant. According to the Triangle Law of vector addition, a minimum of three vectors are needed to get zero resultant. The Triangle Law of vectors states that when two vectors are represented as the two sides of a triangle, then if we want to find the magnitude and direction then the third side of the triangle, should represent the magnitude and direction of the resultant vector. So the minimum number of co-planer vectors of different magnitudes which can give zero resultant is 3.

6(A). A projectile is any object upon which the only force is gravity, projectiles travel with a parabolic trajectory due to the influence of gravity, the speed of the projectile will be minimum at the top of the path. This is because a horizontal component of velocity will remain constant throughout the motion whereas the vertical component of the velocity is zero at the top.

7(D). Projectile refers to an object that is in flight after being thrown or projected. In a projectile motion, the only acceleration acting is in the vertical direction which is acceleration due to gravity (g). Equations of motion, therefore, can be applied separately in X-axis and Y-axis.

8(C). Given that,

$$\Rightarrow \vec{F} = 6\hat{i} - 8\hat{j} + 10\hat{k}$$

Resultant of force is given by

$$\Rightarrow |\vec{F}| = \sqrt{6^2 + (-8)^2 + 10^2} = 10\sqrt{2}$$

$$\Rightarrow m = \frac{|\vec{F}|}{a} = \frac{10\sqrt{2}}{1} = 10\sqrt{2} \text{ kg}$$

9(B). An impulse is supplied to a moving object with the force at an angle of $120°$ with the velocity vector. The angle between the impulse vector and the change in momentum vector is $0°$. Impulse of a force which is defined as force times its duration of action is equal to the change in the momentum of the body. So the direction of impulse will be along the direction of change in momentum.

10(B). Given,

The mass of the body, $m = 4$ kg

Final velocity, $v = 25$ m/s

Initial velocity, $u = 15$ m/s

Time, $t = 5$ s

From the first equation of motion,

$$25 = 15 + a \times 5$$

$10 = a \times 5$

$a = 2$

From the Newton's second law,

$F = ma$

$= 4 \times 2$

$= 8\,N$

11(B). The above principle is related to Newton's second law of motion.

A cricket player extends his hands backwards while catching so that the ball takes longer to stop, thus reducing the chances of injury.

The longer it takes to stop the ball, the less the impact of the ball on the hands and thus the less chance of injury and injury from the ball.

12(A). Given,

$r_1 = (2\hat{i} - 3\hat{j} - 4k)\,m$

$r_2 = (3\hat{i} - 4\hat{j} + 5\hat{k})\,m$

Net displacement, $r = r_2 - r_1 = \hat{i} - \hat{j} + 9\hat{k}$

$F = 4\hat{i} + \hat{j} + 6\hat{k}$

By using vector dot product.

Work done, $W = F.r$

$\Rightarrow W = (4\hat{i} + \hat{j} + 6\hat{k}) \cdot (\hat{i} - \hat{j} + 9\hat{k})$

$\Rightarrow W = 4 - 1 + 54$

$\Rightarrow W = 57\,J$

13(B). Let the speed of the body before explosion be u. After explosion, if the two parts move with velocities u_1 and u_2 in the same direction, then according to conservation of momentum,

Or $Mu_1 + (1 - \alpha)Mu^2 = Mu$

The kinetic energy T liberated during explosion is given

by $T = \frac{1}{2}\alpha Mu_1^2 + \frac{1}{2}(1 - \alpha)Mu_2^2 - \frac{1}{2}Mu^2$

$= \frac{1}{2}\alpha Mu_1^2 + \frac{1}{2}(1 - \alpha)Mu_2^2 - \frac{1}{2M}$

$[\alpha Mu_1 + (1 - \alpha)Mu_2]^2$

$= \frac{1}{2}M\alpha(1 - \alpha)\left[u_1^2 + u_2^2 - 2u_1u_2\right]$

$(u_1 - u_2)^2 = \dfrac{2T}{\alpha(1-\alpha)M}$

$\Rightarrow (u_1 - u_2) = \sqrt{\dfrac{2T}{\alpha(1-\alpha)M}}$

14(D). As we know,

$mv_0 = mv_2 - mv_1$

$\frac{1}{2}mV_1^2 = 0.36 \times \frac{1}{2}mv_0^2$

$v_1 = 0.6v_0$

$\frac{1}{2}MV_2^2 = 0.64 \times \frac{1}{2}mV_0^2$

$V_2 = \sqrt{\dfrac{m}{M}} \times 0.8\,V_0$

$mV = \sqrt{mM} \times 0.8\,V_0 - m \times 0.6\,V_0$

$\Rightarrow 1.6\,m = 0.8\sqrt{mM}$

$4\,m^2 = mM$

15(B). When we do work in stretching the rubber strings of a catapult (gulel), then the work done by us gets stored in the stretched rubber strings in the form of elastic potential energy.

The stretched strings of a catapult possess potential energy due to a change in their shape. This energy of the stretched strings of the catapult can be used to throw away a piece of stone with high speed.

16(C).

5 kg   X cm   10 kg

$x_1 = 0$ $x_2 = 1m$

Step 1: COM expression [Ref. Fig.]

$X_{COM} = \left(\dfrac{m_1x_1 + m_2x_2}{m_1 + m_2}\right)$ ....(1)

Step 2:

Masses $m_1 = 5\,kg$, $m_2 = 10\,kg$

Let the distance between the two masses be $d = 1\,m$ Considering point A as origin, So $B \equiv (d, 0)$

Using equation (1)

$X_{COM} = \left(\dfrac{m_1 \times 0 + m_2\,d}{m_1 + m_2}\right) = \dfrac{m_2\,d}{m_1 + m_2}$

The above result can be remembered for finding position of COM between two masses.

$X_{COM} = \dfrac{(10\,kg \times 1\,m)}{(5\,kg + 10\,kg)} = \dfrac{2}{3}\,m = 67\,cm$

17(B). The moment of inertia of a rod about an axis through one of its ends and perpendicular to the axis is $I = \frac{1}{3}ML^2$

As the temperature increases, the length of the rod expands.

Thus new length of the rod $L_f = L(1 + \alpha t)$

New moment of inertia of the rod

$I_f = \dfrac{ML_f^3}{3} = \frac{1}{3}ML^2(1 + \alpha t)^2$

Let the angular momentum decreases by $\Delta\omega$.

By the principle of conservation of angular momentum, we get $L_f = L$

$\Rightarrow I\omega = I_f(\omega - \Delta\omega)$

$\Rightarrow \Delta\omega = \dfrac{I_f - I}{I_f}\omega$

Thus, $\Delta\omega \propto \omega$

18(C). Moment of inertia of a circular disc about a tangential axis in the plane of disc

$I_1 = MK_1^2 = \frac{5}{4}MR^2$, $K_1 = \sqrt{\dfrac{5}{4}}R$

Moment of inertia of a circular ring of same radius about a tangential axis in the plane of the ring is

$I_2 = MK_2^2 = \frac{3}{2}MR^2$

$K_2 = \sqrt{\dfrac{3}{2}}R$

$\therefore \dfrac{K_1}{K_2} = \dfrac{\sqrt{5/4}R}{\sqrt{3/2}R}$

$= \sqrt{\dfrac{5}{4} \times \dfrac{2}{3}}$

$= \sqrt{\dfrac{5}{6}}$

$= \sqrt{5} : \sqrt{6}$

19(B).

Mass	Weight
Mass of a body is the measure of its inertia, greater the mass of the body greater will be the inertia.	The weight of a body at any place is the product of its mass and gravitational acceleration at that place. W = mg
Mass of the body always remains constant.	The weight of the body can slightly vary from place to place on the earth.
Its value can never be zero for any material particle.	At the pole, the weight of the body is maximum, whereas, at the equator, it is minimum.

- Mass of an object remains the same on the earth and on the moon.
- Weight is the measurement of the pull of gravity on an object.
- Since the gravity is different on the Earth and on

the moon, therefore the weight of an object is different on the earth and on the moon.

20(A). The gravitational force of attraction between the balls is given as by

$$F = \frac{Gm_1m_2}{r^2}$$

Given, $m_1 = m_2 = 10$ kg

$r = 10$ cm $= 0.10$ m

$$\therefore F = \frac{6.67 \times 10^{-11} \times 10 \times 10}{(0.10)^2}$$

$$= \frac{6.67 \times 10^{-11} \times 100}{0.01}$$

$$= 6.67 \times 10^{-11} \times 10^4$$

$$= 6.67 \times 10^{-7} \text{ N}$$

21(B). The gravitational constant is a scalar quantity. Its value is the same throughout the universe and is independent of the nature and size of the bodies as well as the nature of the medium between the bodies.

Thus, Newton's law of Gravitation holds good for two objects

1. Of any shape, size, and mass.
2. At all places
3. At all times throughout the universe.

22(C). Let the mass of planet B is M and the radius of planet B is R.

Given that:

Radius of planet $A(R_A) = 2 \times$ Radius of planet $B(R_B) = 2R$

Mass of planet $A(M_A) = 4 \times$ Mass of planet $B(M_B) = 4M$

Acceleration due to gravity on Planet $\mathbf{B}(g) = \frac{GM}{R^2}$

Weight of the object on planet $B(W_B) = mg$

Acceleration due to gravity on Planet $\mathbf{A}(g') = \frac{G(4M)}{(2R)^2} = \frac{GM}{R^2} = g$

Weight of the object on planet $A(W_A) = mg' = mg$

Therefore the weight of the object on both the planet is equal.

23(D). Given that:

At $h = H$ and $d = 200 \, km$, the acceleration due to gravity has the same value i.e. $g' = g''$

$$\Rightarrow g\left(1 - \frac{d}{R_e}\right) = g\left(1 - \frac{2H}{R_e}\right)$$

$$\Rightarrow (R_e - d) = (R_e - 2H)$$

$$\Rightarrow d = 2H$$

$$\Rightarrow 200 = 2H$$

$$H = 100 \text{ km}$$

24(A). The gas thermometers are more sensitive than liquid thermometers because gases expand more than liquids for a small rise in temperature, which will give better sensitivity in temperature measurement.

25(D). When a solid ball of iron is heated, the largest percentage increase in volume will occur.

Reason: Coefficient of areal expansion is twice that of linear expansion whereas coefficient of volume expansion is three times of linear expansion.

- Percentage increase in length is proportional to α
- Percentage increase in area is proportional to β
- Percentage increase in volume is proportional to γ

Now since $\alpha < \beta < \gamma$,

We get that percentage increase in volume will be maximum.

26(B). The steam transfers this thermal energy to the food that is being cooked. This heat is used up by the food to get cooked properly. Thus, in a pressure cooker since the boiling point increases, the steam has greater thermal energy which it can transfer to the food and hence the cooking is faster.

27(B). Bimetals are made of two different metals having different coefficient of expansion. A bimetallic strip is used to convert a temperature change into mechanical displacement. Bimetal has the property of bending when heated, so used for open or close circuits.

Thermostats can be constructed in many ways and may use a variety of sensors to measure the temperature, commonly a thermistor or bimetallic strip. The output of the sensor then controls the heating or cooling apparatus.

28(D). The $P - V$ diagram of adiabatic process, isothermal process and isobaric process.

Work done in process= area enclosed by $P - V$ diagram with volume axis. Since area under the curve is maximum for adiabatic process, so work done on the gas will be maximum for adiabatic process.

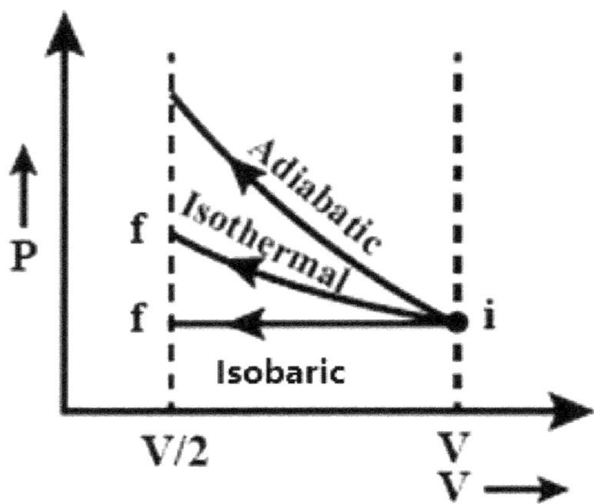

29(B). From the first law of thermodynamics,

$dU = q - W$

In adiabatic process no change of heat takes place.

So, $dU = -W$

Since, the gas is expanding, the work is done by the gas.

$dU = -W$.

Hence internal energy of the system decreases.

Again, $dU = C_v(T_2 - T_1) = W$

Since here W is negative, so $T_1 > T_2$.

So temperature will also decrease.

30(A). Here, the temperature inside the refrigerator can be provided as,

$T_1 = 9°C = 282K$

Room temperature is given as,

$T_2 = 36°C = 309K$

Coefficient of performance can be given by the relation,

$$COP = \frac{T_1}{(T_2 - T_1)}$$

$$\Rightarrow COP = \frac{282}{(309 - 282)}$$

$$\Rightarrow COP = 10.44$$

Clearly, the coefficient of performance of the mentioned refrigerator is 10.44.

31(B).

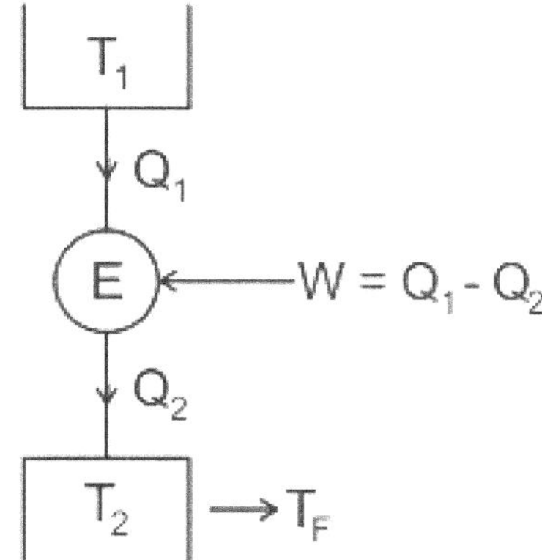

Assume $T_1 > T_2$

$Q_1 = C_p(T_1 - T_F)$

$Q_2 = C_p(T_F - T_2)$

$\therefore W = Q_1 - Q_2 = C_p(T_1 + T_2 - 2T_F)$

For 'w' to be maximum , T_{F} to be minimum

$\Delta S_1 = \int_{T_1}^{T_F} C_p \frac{dT}{T} = C_p \ln \frac{T_F}{T_1}$

$\Delta S_2 = \int_{T_1}^{T_F} C_p \frac{dT}{T} = C_p \ln \frac{T_F}{T_2}$

As,

$(\Delta S)_{\text{univ}} \geq 0 \setminus$

$C_p \ln \frac{T_F}{T_1} + C_p \ln \frac{T_F}{T_2} \geq 0$

$\therefore C_p \ln \left[\frac{T_F^2}{T_1 T_2}\right] \geq 0$

Now,

For T_F to be minimum

$\ln \frac{T_F^2}{T_1 T_2} = 0 \quad \therefore \ln \frac{T_F^2}{T_1 T_2} = \ln 1$

$\therefore T_F = \sqrt{T_1 T_2}$

32(A). Given,

Displacement $x = 12\,\text{cm} = 0.12\,\text{m}$ and mass $m = 5\,\text{kg}$

We know that when the spring-mass system oscillates, there will be simple harmonic motion and the time period is given as,

$T = 2\pi\sqrt{\frac{m}{k}} \quad \cdots(i)$

Where k = spring constant

$k = \frac{F}{x} \quad \cdots(ii)$

Here,

F = mg

Where g = gravitational acceleration $\approx 10\,\text{m/s}^2$

$\Rightarrow F = 5 \times 10 = 50\,\text{N}$

By equation (ii),

$\Rightarrow k = \frac{50}{0.12}$

By equation (i),

$\Rightarrow T = 2\pi\sqrt{\frac{5}{\frac{50}{0.12}}}$

$\Rightarrow T = 2\pi\sqrt{\frac{5 \times 0.12}{50}}$

$\Rightarrow T = 0.7 sec$

33(B). An ideal simple pendulum consists of a heavy point mass body (bob) suspended by a weightless, inextensible and perfectly flexible string from rigid support about which it is free to oscillate.

For a simple pendulum, the time period of swing of a pendulum depends on the length of the string and acceleration due to gravity.

The time period of a simple pendulum is given by:

$T = 2\pi\sqrt{\frac{l}{g}}$

The above formula is only valid for small angular displacements only.

T = Time period of oscillation,

l = length of the pendulum,

g = gravitational acceleration.

For a simple pendulum, the time period of swing of a pendulum depends on the length of the string and acceleration due to gravity.

$T = 2\pi\sqrt{\frac{l}{g}}$

Squaring both side.

$T^2 = 4\pi^2 \frac{l}{g}$

$l = \frac{g}{4\pi^2} \times T^2$

Thus, we can say that the relation between the time period of oscillation and the length of the pendulum will be: $T^2 \propto l$

This means the graph of the time period of oscillation with respect to the length of the pendulum will be a parabolic orbit as shown below.

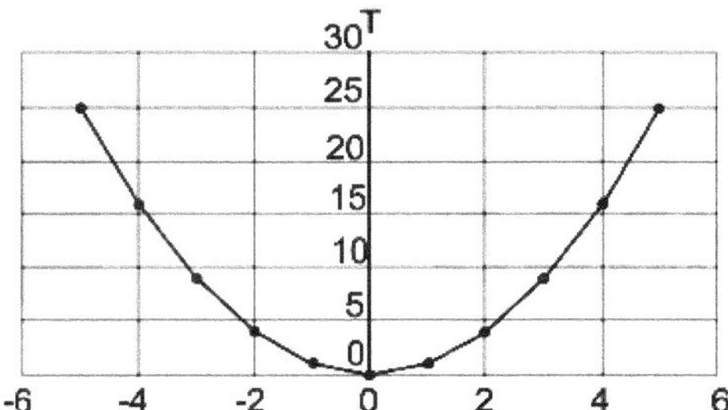

34(C). Equation of simple harmonic wave is

$y = A\sin(\omega t + \phi)$

Here, $y = \frac{A}{2}$

$\therefore A\sin(\omega t + \phi) = \frac{A}{2}$

So, $\quad \delta = \omega t + \phi = \frac{\pi}{6}$ or $\frac{5\pi}{6}$

So, the phase difference of the two particles when they are

crossing each other at $y = \frac{A}{2}$ in opposite directions are

$\delta = (\delta_1 - \delta_2)$

$= \left(\frac{5\pi}{6} - \frac{\pi}{6}\right)$

$= \left(\frac{2\pi}{3}\right)$

35(B). $T \propto \sqrt{l}$

Time period depends only on effective length. Density has no effect on time period. If length made 4 times then time period becomes 2 times.

36(B). When an observer is moving towards the stationary source of sound, then the apparent frequency will be greater than the real frequency. Then the apparent frequency heard in this situation.

$\nu' = \left[\frac{(v - v_m) - v_o}{(v + v_m) - v_s}\right]\nu^o$

As the source is stationary and medium is constant, then $v_m = 0$ and $v_s = 0$

$\nu' = \left[\frac{v - (-v_o)}{v}\right]\nu^o = \left[\frac{v + v_o}{v}\right]\nu^o$

37(D). Positive charge: A body having a deficiency of electrons and the number of protons becomes more than the number of electrons.

Negative charge: A body having an excess of electrons and the number of electrons becomes more than the number of protons.

Neutron is not responsible for the charge on the

element.
The number of neutrons becomes more than the number of electrons in the element, by this statement, we can't predict whether the number of protons is more than, less than, or equal to the number of electrons in the element.
So we can't predict the type of charge on the element. Hence, option 4 is correct.

38(B). Positive charge: A body having a deficiency of electrons.
We know that the proton is present in the nucleus so we can't add or remove protons in the element but we can add or remove electrons from the element.
So the body can be positively charged by removing electrons and negatively charged by adding electrons.
A charge cannot be generated by adding or removing protons.

39(A). **Capacitance** : The ability of an electric system to store an electric charge is known as capacitance.
where Q is the charge on it, V is the voltage, and C is the capacitance of it.
For the parallel plate capacitor, the capacitance is given by:
$$C = \frac{KA\varepsilon_0}{d}$$
where A is the area of the plate, d is the distance between plates, K is the dielectric constant of material and ϵ is constant.
K = 1 for air or vacuum.
Given that parallel plate capacitor
$$C = \frac{A\varepsilon_0}{d}$$
and $C = Q/V$
$V = Q/C$
$V = Qd/(\varepsilon_0 A)$

40(B). Atoms are the smallest particle of the matter which is indivisible in nature i.e. cannot be further divided.
- Atoms consist of three fundamental particles - 1. Proton 2. Neutron 3. Electron.
- Proton and Neutron are present in the Nucleus of an Atom.
- While Electron revolves in the orbit of an atom.
- Proton discovered by E. Goldenstein and having Charge (+1.6 × 10-19) and Mass (1.67 × 10-27 Kg).
- Electron discovered by J.J Thomson and having Charge (-1.6 × 10-19) and Mass (9.1 × 10-31 Kg).
- Neutron discovered by James Chadwick and it is Neutral in nature i.e. zero charge or no charge and Mass (1.67 × 10-27 kg).

41(B). Given,
Electric field, $E = 9 \times 10^4 N/C$
Distance, $r = 2 \times 10^{-2}$ m
$$E = \frac{\lambda}{2\pi r \varepsilon_0}$$
$\lambda = E \cdot 2\pi r \cdot \varepsilon_0$
where, λ is a linear charge density, and, $\epsilon_0 = 8.854 \times 10^{-12}$
Then, put allthe given value in above formula:
$\lambda = 9 \times 10^4 \times 2\pi \times 2 \times 10^{-2} \times 8.854 \times 10^{-12}$
$= 10 \times 10^{-6}$
Therefore,
Linear charge density, $\lambda = 10\mu C/m$

42(D). Given:
Diameter of the sphere = 2.4
$\therefore$ Radius of sphere, $r = \frac{2.4}{2} = 1.2$ m
Surface charge density of conducting sphere,
$\sigma = 80 \times 10^{-6} C/m^2$
Therefore,
Charge on sphere will be:
$q = \sigma A = \sigma 4\pi r^2$
$q = 80 \times 10^{-6} \times 4 \times 3.14 \times (1.2)^2$
$q = 1.45 \times 10^{-3} C$
Then, the total electric flux leaving the surface of the sphere will be calculated using the gauss formula, i.e.,
$$\phi = \frac{q}{\varepsilon_0}$$
$\phi = \frac{1.45 \times 10^{-3}}{8.854 \times 10^{-12}} \quad (\because \epsilon_0 = 8.854 \times 10^{-12})$
$\phi = 1.6 \times 10^8 Nm^2/C$

43(C). Given:
Charge, $(Q) = 2nC$
Separation between the plates, $(d) = 5$ mm
Area of the plate, $(A) = 10$ sq.cm.
Relative permeability of air $(\epsilon_r) = 1$
We know that:
Capacitance, $C = \frac{\epsilon_0 \epsilon_r A}{d}$
Put all the given value in above formula:
$C = \frac{8.85 \times 10^{-12} \times 1 \times 10 \times 10^{-4}}{5 \times 10^{-3}}$
$C = 1.77 pF$
Also, we know that:
$Q = CV$
$V = \frac{Q}{C}$
$= \frac{2 \times 10^{-9}}{1.77 \times 10^{-12}}$
$V = 1130$ V

44(D). $V = -5x + 3y + \sqrt{(15)}z$
as $E_x = [\frac{-dv}{dx}] = [\frac{-d}{dx}][-5x + 3y + \sqrt{(15)}z] = 5$
$Ey = [\frac{-dv}{dy}] = [\frac{-d}{dy}][-5x + 3y + \sqrt{(15)}z] = -3$
$Ez = [(-dV)/dz] = [(-d)/dz][-5x + 3y + \sqrt{(15)}z] = -\sqrt{(15)}$
$\therefore E = \sqrt{(Ex^2 + Ey^2 + Ez^2)}$
$= \sqrt{(5)^2 + (-3)^2 + \{-\sqrt{(15)}\}^2}.$
$= \sqrt{(25 + 9 + 15)}$
$E = 7N/C$

45(C). The capacitor is a charge storage device work has to be done to store the charges in a capacitor. This work done is stored as electrostatic potential energy in the capacitor.
Let q be the charge and V be the potential difference between the plates of the capacitor. If dq is the additional charge given to the plate,
Work done is,
dw = V dq dw
$= \frac{q}{C} dq \quad (\because V = \frac{q}{C})$
Total work done to charge a capacitor is,
w = $\int$ dw
$= \int_0^q \frac{q}{C} dq$
$= \frac{1}{2} \frac{q^2}{C}$
This work done is stored as electrostatic potential energy (U) in the capacitor.
$U = \frac{1}{2} \frac{q^2}{C} = \frac{1}{2} CV^2 \quad (\because q = CV)$

$$U = \frac{q^2}{2C}$$

46(C).

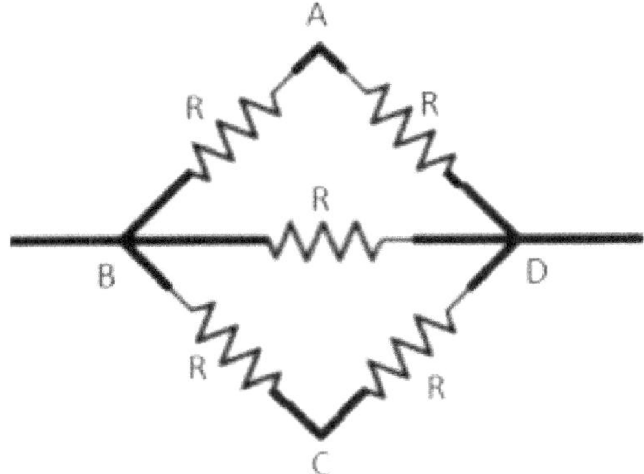

For Resistance between B and D

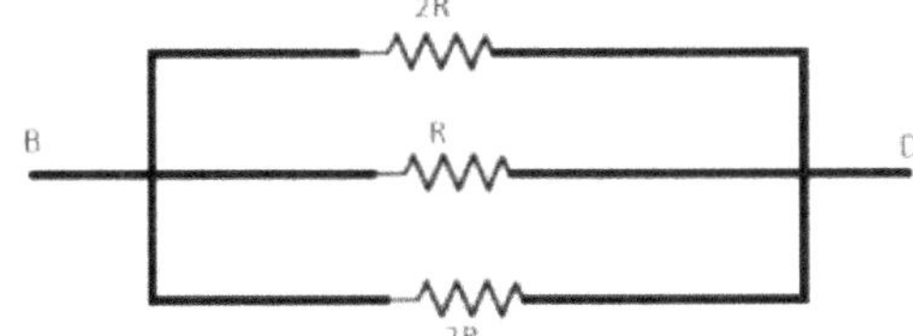

$$= \frac{1}{2R} + \frac{1}{R} + \frac{1}{2R}$$
$$= \frac{1+2+1}{2R}$$
$$R_{BD} = \frac{R}{2}$$

Resistance between A and C

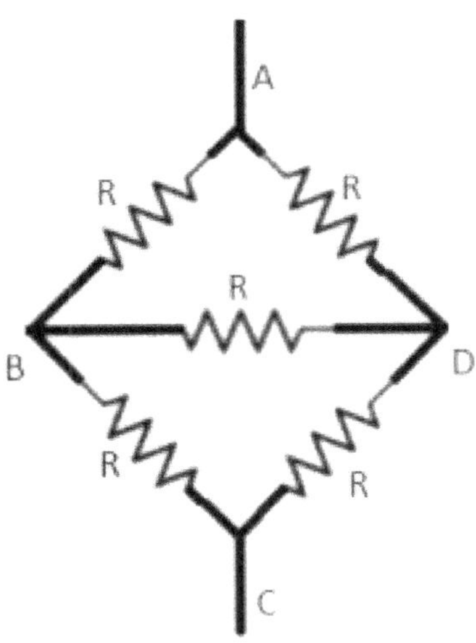

It is a balanced whealstone bridge
$\therefore$ Resistance between B and D will not be considered. The circuit diagram can be drawn as

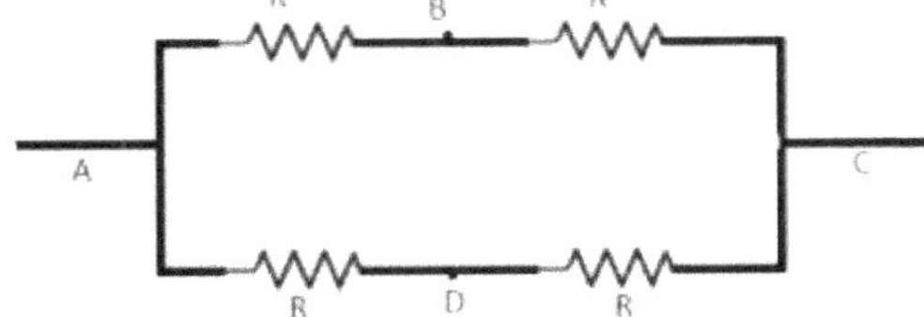

$$\therefore R_{AC} = 2R \| 2R$$
$$\frac{1}{R_{AC}} = \frac{1}{2R} + \frac{1}{2R}$$
$$R_{AC} = R$$

So, both options (a) and (b) are correct.

47(A).

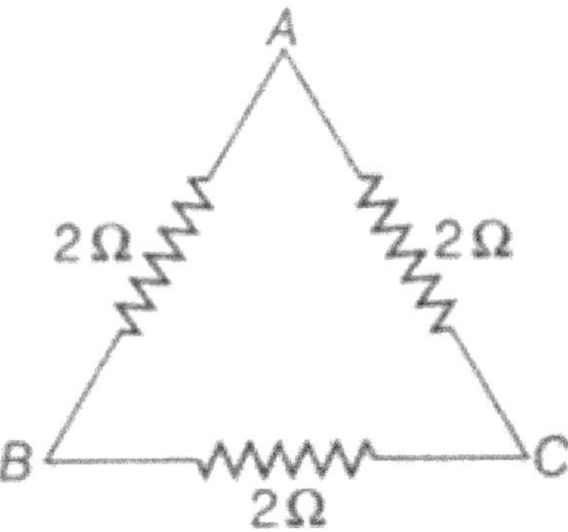

It is given that, three 2Ω resistors are connected to form a triangle. So, from the above figure, it is clear that resistors R_1 and R_2 are in series.
Therefore, their equivalent resistance will be-
$$R = R_1 + R_2$$
$$R = 2\Omega + 2\Omega$$
$$R = 4\Omega$$
Now resistors R_3 and R are in parallel with each other.
Therefore, their equivalent resistance will be,
$$\frac{1}{R'} = \frac{1}{R_3} + \frac{1}{R}$$
$$\frac{1}{R'} = \frac{1}{2} + \frac{1}{4}$$
$$\frac{1}{R'} = \frac{3}{4}$$
$$R' = \frac{4}{3}\Omega$$

48(A). Balanced condition in meter bridge experiment is given by
$$\frac{R}{S} = \frac{L}{100-L} \quad ......(i)$$
Where R and S are the equivalent resistances attached between the two gaps.
Case-1:
Balance point is at $L = 50$ cm :
$R = R_1 + 10$ and $S = R_2$
Substituting values in eq. (i), we get
$$\frac{R_1+10}{R_2} = \frac{50}{50} = 1$$
$$\Rightarrow R_1 + 10 = R_2 \quad ......(ii)$$
Case-2:
When only resistance R_1 is used and balance point shifted to $L = 40$ cm :
$R = R_1$ and $S = R_2$
$$\Rightarrow \frac{R_1}{R_2} = \frac{40}{60}$$
Substituting value of R_2 from eq. (ii), we get
$$\Rightarrow \frac{R_1}{R_1+10} = \frac{40}{60}$$
$$\Rightarrow 60R_1 = 40R_1 + 400$$
$$\Rightarrow R_1 = \frac{400}{20}\Omega = 20\Omega$$

49(C). Biot-Savart Law: The law that gives the magnetic field generated by a constant electric current is the Biot-savart law.
Let us take a current-carrying wire of current I and we need to find the magnetic field at a distance r from the wire then it is given by:
$$dB = \frac{\mu_0 I}{4\pi}\left(\frac{\vec{dl}\times\hat{r}}{r^2}\right)$$
Where $\mu_0 = 4\pi \times 10^{-7} T.m/A$ is the permeability of free space/vacuum, dl = a small element of wire, and $\hat{r}$ is the unit position vector of the point where we need to find the magnetic field.

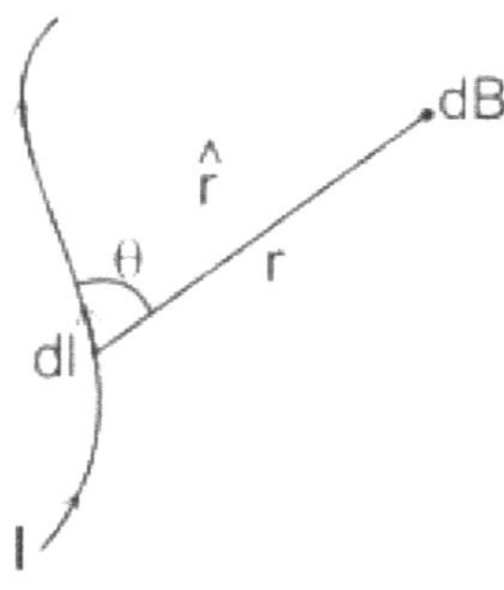

50(B). The electric field of a plane electromagnetic wave is given by
$$\vec{E} = E_0(\hat{x} + \hat{y})\sin(kz - \omega t)$$
direction of propagation $= +\hat{k}$
$$\hat{E} = \frac{\hat{i} + \hat{j}}{\sqrt{2}}$$
$$\hat{k} = \hat{E} \times \hat{B}$$
$$\hat{k} = \left(\frac{\hat{i} + \hat{j}}{\sqrt{2}}\right) \times \hat{B}$$
$$\Rightarrow \hat{B} = \frac{-\hat{i} + \hat{j}}{\sqrt{2}}$$
$$\hat{B} = \frac{E_0}{c}(-\hat{x} + \hat{y})\sin(kz - \omega t)$$

51(D). A stationary charge is not affected by a magnetic field because stationary charges do not have any velocity. Magnetic field cannot occur in a particle having zero velocity.

52(A). Resultant force acting on a diamagnetic material in a magnetic field is in direction from stronger to the weaker part of the magnetic field. Diamagnetic substances are those which have tendency to move from stronger to the weaker part of the external magnetic field. In other words, unlike the way a magnet attracts metals like iron, it would repel a diamagnetic substance.

53(D). When there are two turns in the coil.
Then, $l = 2 \times 2\pi r_1$
$$r_1 = \frac{l}{4\pi}$$
$$B_1 = \frac{\mu_0 N_1 I}{2r_1}$$
$$\Rightarrow B_1 = \frac{\mu_0 \times 2 \times I}{2 \times (\frac{1}{4}\pi)}$$
$$\Rightarrow B_1 = \frac{\mu_0 4\pi I}{l} \quad ....(i)$$
When there are four turns in the coil.
Then, $l = 4 \times 2\pi r_2$
$$r_2 = \frac{1}{8\pi}$$
$$B_2 = \frac{\mu_0 N_2 I}{2r_2}$$
$$\Rightarrow B_2 = \frac{\mu_0 \times 4 \times I}{2 \times (\frac{1}{8}\pi)}$$
$$\Rightarrow B_2 = \frac{\mu_0 16\pi I}{l} \quad ...(ii)$$
By dividing both equations, we get
$$\frac{B_1}{B_2} = \frac{4}{16}$$
$$\Rightarrow \frac{B_1}{B_2} = \frac{1}{4}$$
$$\Rightarrow B_2 = 4B_1$$
$$\Rightarrow B_2 = 4 \times 0.2\,T$$
$$\Rightarrow B_2 = 0.8\,T$$

54(B). Magnetic field due to the first coil and the second coil is same at the centre.
Then magnetic field B at centre is,

$$B = \frac{\mu_0 I_1}{2(2r)} = \frac{\mu_0 I_2}{2(r)} = \frac{I_1}{I_2} = 2$$
As we know that Resistance of coil is related as,
$R = \rho\frac{l}{A}$ where $\rho =$ resistivity , $l =$ length , $A =$ area of cross section.
ρ and A is same for both coil but $l_1 = 2\pi(2r)$ and $l_2 = 2\pi(r')$
If V_1 and V_2 applied across first and second coil then,
$$I_1 = \frac{V_1}{R_1} \text{ and } I_2 = \frac{V_2}{R_2} \quad ....(1)$$
$$I_1 = \frac{V_1}{\rho\frac{l_1}{A}} \quad ....(2) \text{ and } I_2 = \frac{V_2}{\rho\frac{l_2}{A}} \quad .....(3)$$
From (1), (2), (3)
$$\frac{V_1}{l_1} \times \frac{l_2}{V_2} = 2$$
$$\frac{V_1}{V_1} \times \frac{l_2}{l_1} = 2$$
$$\frac{V_1}{V_2} \times \frac{1}{2} = 2$$
$$\frac{V_1}{V_2} = 4$$
$$V_1 = 4V_2$$

55(B). We know,
$$\varepsilon = Blv = 2 \times 10^{-1} \times v$$
$$= 0.2v$$
$$I = \frac{\varepsilon}{R} = 10^{-3}$$
$$\Rightarrow \frac{0.2v}{4} = 10^{-3}$$
[Since effective resistance R of bridge is $R = \frac{6\times6}{6+6} = 3\Omega$
so total resistance $= 1 + 3 = 4\Omega$]
$$\Rightarrow v = 2\,\text{cms}^{-1}$$

56(A). Given,
Electrical field $E = 100\,$V/m
Magnetic field $B = 0.265\,$A/m
The energy flow is given by the Poynting vector
$$\vec{S} = \vec{E} \times \vec{B}$$
$$\Rightarrow S = EB\sin\phi$$
$$\Rightarrow S = EB\,(\phi = 90°, \text{ as } E \text{ and } B \text{ are perpendicular to each other})$$
$$\Rightarrow S = 100 \times 0.265$$
$$\Rightarrow S = 26.5\,\text{W/m}^2$$

57(B). Given,
Resistance of coil $= 10\Omega$
$\phi = 8t^2 - 4t + 1$
We have,
$$E = -\frac{d\phi}{dt}$$
$$\Rightarrow E = -\frac{d(8t^2 - 4t + 1)}{dt}$$
By differentiating, we get
$$\Rightarrow E = -16t + 4$$
At 0.1 sec,
$$E = -1.6 + 4 = 2.4\,V$$
$$i = \frac{E}{R}$$
$$\Rightarrow i = \frac{2.4}{10}$$
$$\Rightarrow i = 0.24\,A$$

58(B). The eddy current loss in a transformer is reduced by using a laminated core.
Eddy current losses due to joule heating in the core that are proportional to the square of the transformer's applied voltage. Eddy current losses can be reduced by making the core of a stack of plates electrically insulated from each other, rather than a solid block; all transformers operating at low frequencies use laminated or similar cores.

59(B). Given,

Change in current, $di = (0 - 4)\mathrm{A}$

Here, the current is changing from 4 A to 0 A i.e. current is falling.

Therefore,

Change in current = (final − initial)

Current = $(0 - 4)\mathrm{A}$

Time interval, $dt = 0.1\ \mathrm{s}$

Induced emf, $e = 100\ \mathrm{V}$

Now by using,

$$e = -L\frac{di}{dt}$$

$$\Rightarrow 100 = -L\left(\frac{0-4}{0.1}\right)$$

$$\Rightarrow L = \frac{10}{4}$$

So, Self-inductance, $\mathrm{L} = 2.5\mathrm{H}$

60(D). A magnet NS is suspended from a spring and while it oscillates, the magnet moves in and out of the coil. The coil is connected to a galvanometer G. Then, as the magnet oscillates G shows deflection to the left and right but the amplitude steadily decreases.

When the magnet oscillates in and out of the spring, it induces an EMF, the direction in which EMF is getting induced will be different. Due to the induced EMF, a current will be set up in the coil which will deflect the pointer in the galvanometer in the opposite directions, as the magnet oscillates in and out of the spring an eddy current is set up in it decreases the amplitude of oscillation. In short, the EMF will be induced in opposite directions, i.e., Left and Right, as the magnet oscillates in and out of the spring also the eddy current will reduce the amplitude of oscillation as the time goes on (Damping).

61(C). Refractive index of prism,

$$\mu = \sqrt{3}$$

Angle of prism,

$$A = 60°$$

Now using the prism formula,

$$\frac{\sin\frac{(A+\delta_m)}{2}}{\sin\frac{A}{2}}$$

$$\sqrt{3} = \frac{\sin\frac{\delta_m+60°}{2}}{\sin\frac{60°}{2}}$$

$$\sqrt{3} \times \sin 30° = \sin\left(\frac{\delta_m+60°}{2}\right)$$

$$\sin\left(\frac{\delta_m+60°}{2}\right) = \sqrt{3} \times \frac{1}{2} = \sin 60°$$

$$\frac{\delta_m+60°}{2} = 60°$$

$$\delta_m + 60° = 120°$$

$\delta_m = 60°$ is the required minimum angle of deviation.

62(C). Fringe width in Young's double slit experiment is given by,

$$\beta = \frac{\lambda D}{d}$$

If the separation between coherent sources is halved and the distance of the screen from the coherent sources is doubled, then the fringe width,

$$\beta' = \frac{\lambda 2D}{d/2} = \frac{4\lambda D}{d} = 4\beta$$

So, new fringe width is four times.

63(A). Diameter of objective of telescope,

$$\mathrm{D} = 2\ \mathrm{m} = 100 \times 2 = 200\ \mathrm{cm}$$

The wavelength of light is:

$$\lambda = 600\ \mathrm{nm} = 6 \times 10^{-5}\ \mathrm{cm}$$

Limit of resolution of telescope,

$$\mathrm{d}\theta = \frac{1.22\lambda}{\mathrm{D}}$$

$$= \frac{1.22 \times 6 \times 10^{-5}}{200}$$

$$= 3.66 \times 10^{-7}\ \mathrm{rad}$$

64(A). As work function,

$$W = hf_0$$

Where,

f_0 is the threshold frequency.

Greater the work function, greater is the threshold frequency. Therefore, the threshold frequency for sodium will be lesser than that for aluminum.

65(C). Given,

Energy flux of sunlight reaching the surface of earth,

$$\phi = 1.388 \times 10^3\ \mathrm{W/m^2}$$

Thus, power of sunlight per square metre,

$$\mathrm{P} = 1.388 \times 10^3\ \mathrm{W}$$

Speed of light,

$$c = 3 \times 10^8\ \mathrm{m/s}$$

Planck's constant,

$$h = 6.626 \times 10^{-34}\ \mathrm{Js}$$

Average wavelength of photons present in sunlight,

$$\lambda = 550\ \mathrm{nm} = 550 \times 10^{-9}\ \mathrm{m}$$

Number of photons per square metre incident on earth per second = n

Thus, the equation for power can be written as,

$$P = nE$$

$$\therefore n = \frac{P}{E}$$

As we know,

$$\mathrm{E} = \frac{hc}{\lambda}$$

Then,

$$\frac{P\lambda}{hc} = \frac{1.388 \times 10^3 \times 550 \times 10^{-9}}{6.626 \times 10^{-34} \times 3 \times 10^8}$$

$$= 3.84 \times 10^{21}\ \mathrm{photons\ /m^2/s}$$

66(A). Photoelectric effect phenomena can explain the quantum nature of light.

The emission of free electrons from a metal surface when the light is shone on it, it is called the photoemission or the photoelectric effect.

This effect led to the conclusion that light is made up of packets or quantum of energy.

67(A). Given:

$$\phi = 2.8\mathrm{eV}, \mathrm{E} = 2\mathrm{eV}$$

We know that Maximum kinetic energy $(\mathrm{E}) = \mathrm{h}\nu - \phi$

Put the given values in above formula.

$$2 = \mathrm{h}\nu - 2.8$$

$$\Rightarrow \mathrm{h}\nu = 4.8\mathrm{eV}$$

New frequency $\nu = 2\nu$

So, $E' = h\nu' - \phi$

$$\Rightarrow E' = 2\ \mathrm{h}\nu - \phi$$

Put the given values in above formula.

$$= 2 \times 4.8 - 2.8$$

$$= 6.8\mathrm{eV}$$

68(B). Given, Photon energy

$$\mathrm{E}_1 = \mathrm{h}v_1 = 1\mathrm{eV}, \mathrm{E}_2 = 2.5\mathrm{eV}, \mathrm{W} = 0.5\mathrm{eV},$$

Let v_1 and v_2 be the speed of the emitted electrons

Using Einstein's Photoelectric equation

$$\mathrm{K.E} = \mathrm{E} - \Phi$$

$$\Rightarrow \frac{1}{2}mv_1^2 = 1 - 0.5 \Rightarrow v_1 = \sqrt{\frac{2 \times 0.5}{m}}$$

$$\Rightarrow \frac{1}{2}mv_2^2 = 2.5 - 0.5 \Rightarrow v_2 = \sqrt{\frac{2 \times 2}{m}}$$

$$\Rightarrow \frac{v_1}{v_2} = \frac{1}{2}$$

Hence, the ratio of the maximum speeds of the

emitted electrons is $1 : 2$.

69(C). Given that transition is from n = 4 to n = 1 (ground state). So transition spectral lines

$$N = \frac{n(n-1)}{2}$$

$$N = \frac{4(4-1)}{2} = 6$$

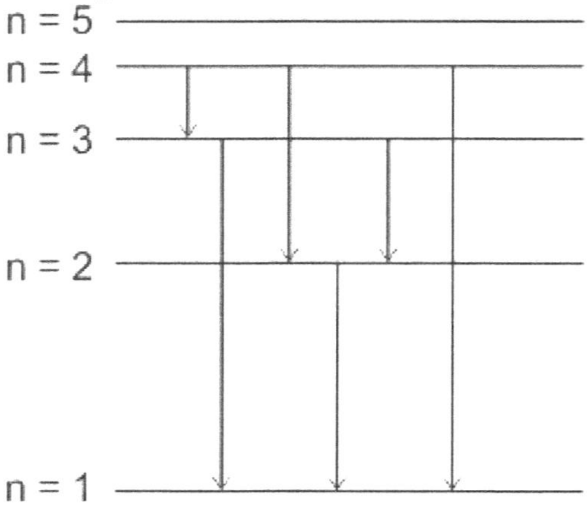

n = 5 ———————————————

n = 4 ———————————————

n = 3 ———————————————

n = 2 ———————————————

n = 1 ———————————————

70(A). Given:

$n_1 = 3$ and $n_2 = 4$

The magnitude of the electron's angular momentum in 3rd orbit is:

$$L_1 = \frac{3h}{2\pi}$$

The magnitude of the electron's angular momentum in 4th orbit is:

$$L_2 = \frac{4h}{2\pi}$$

Change in angular momentum

$$\Delta L = L_2 - L_1$$

$$= \frac{h}{2\pi}(4-3)$$

$$\Rightarrow \Delta L = \frac{6.64 \times 10^{-34}}{2 \times 3.14}(4-3)$$

$$= 1.05 \times 10^{-34} J/S$$

71(C). Angular momentum $= \frac{nh}{2\pi}$

$$\therefore n = \frac{3.17 \times 10^{-13} \times 2 \times 3.14}{(6.63 \times 10^{-34})}$$

n = 3

72(A). It is the amount of energy gained by the charge of a single electron moved across an electric potential difference of one volt. Electron volt, a unit of energy commonly used in atomic and nuclear physics, equal to the energy gained by an electron (a charged particle carrying unit electronic charge) when the electrical potential at the electron increases by one volt. The electron volt equals 1.602×10^{-12} erg or 1.602×10^{-19} joule.

73(A). Root mean square velocity is given by,

$$C_{\text{rms}} = \sqrt{\frac{3RT}{M}}$$

For a particular temperature,

$$C_{\text{rms}} \propto \sqrt{\frac{1}{M}}$$ i.e., C_{rms} will have different values for different gases.

74(A). The degree of freedom of diatomic gas is 5.

The law of equipartition of energy states that the energy of each degree of freedom is $\frac{1}{2}kT$.

Carbon monoxide (CO) and Nitrogen (N_2) gases are diatomic. So, both have equal kinetic energy $\left(\frac{5}{2}kT\right)$ i.e., $E_1 = E_2$.

75(C). Distance travelled in the nth second is given by,

$$S_n = u + \frac{a}{2}(2n-1)$$

By putting,

$u = 0$

$a = \frac{4}{3}$ m s^{-2}

$n = 3$

$\therefore$ Distance $= 0 + \frac{4}{3 \times 2}(2 \times 3 - 1)$

$= \frac{4}{6} \times 5$

$= \frac{10}{3}$ m

76(D). Given,

Diameter $(d) = 30$ cm

Radius $(r) = \frac{d}{2} = 15$ cm $= 0.15$ m

$T = 20°C = 293$ K

$P = 1$ atm $= 10^5$ N/m^2

The volume of helium gas in the balloon,

$$V = \frac{4}{3}\pi r^3$$

$$= \frac{4}{3}\pi(0.150 \text{ m})^3$$

$$= 1.41 \times 10^{-2} \text{ m}^3$$

Number of moles can be obtained from ideal gas equation,

$$PV = nRT$$

$$\Rightarrow n = \frac{PV}{RT}$$

$$\Rightarrow n = \frac{(10^5 \text{ N/m}^2)(1.41 \times 10^{-2} \text{ m}^3)}{(8.314 \text{ N·m/mol−K})(293 \text{ K})} = 0.588 \text{ mol}$$

The number of molecules of helium gas,

$N = nN_A = (0.588 \text{ mol})(6.02 \times 10^{23}$ molecules/mol$)$

$$\Rightarrow N = 3.493 \times 10^{23}$$

77(B).

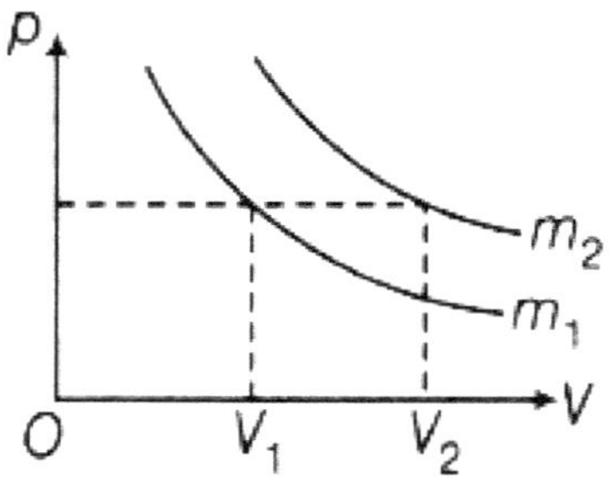

$\therefore \text{pV} = \text{nRT} = \frac{\text{m}}{\text{M}}\text{RT}$

For $m_1, P = \frac{m_1}{M} \cdot \frac{RT}{V_1}$ ..... (i)

For $m_2, P = \frac{m_2}{M} \cdot \frac{RT}{V_2}$ .... (ii)

From eqs. (i) and (ii) we get,

$$\frac{m_1}{M} \cdot \frac{RT}{V_1} = \frac{m_2}{M} \cdot \frac{RT}{V_2}$$

$$\Rightarrow \frac{m_1}{V_1} = \frac{m_2}{V_2}$$

Thus, $V \propto m$

$\therefore V_2 > V_1$

$\therefore m_2 > m_1$

78(C). The drift velocity of charge carriers in the material of constant cross-sectional area A is given as:

$$v = \frac{I}{nAq}$$

(Here I is the current flowing through the material, n is the charge-carrier density, and q is the charge on the charge-carrier).

We have the ratio of I as $\frac{7}{4}$ and ratio of n as $\frac{7}{5}$.

Thus, we get the ratio of v as $\frac{5}{4}$.

79(A). Molecules in liquids are held to other molecules by intermolecular interactions, which are weaker than the intramolecular interactions that hold molecules and polyatomic ions together.

Ice has the lowest melting point out of the given solids, hence it has the weakest intermolecular forces.

80(A). The full form of LED is Light Emitting Diode.

The LED is a PN-junction diode that produces light as it passes via an electric current in the forward path. Recombining the charge carrier occurs in the LED. The N-side electron and the P-side hole are mixed and provide the energy in the form of light and heat. The LED is produced from the colourless semiconductor substance, and the light is radiated via the diode junction. Depending on the semiconductor material used and the doping quantity, a colored light will be emitted at a specified spectral wavelength when LEDs is biased forward.

1. The SI Unit of Charge is:
   (a) Ampere
   (b) Volt
   (c) Coulomb
   (d) Ohm

2. The unit Nautical mile per hour is used to measure the speed of which of the following?
   (a) Maglev
   (b) Ship
   (c) Bullet Train
   (d) None of these

3. In the relation $\alpha = \beta t + \lambda$, α and λ is measured in meter (m) and t is measured in second (s). The SI unit of β must be:
   (a) m
   (b) m s
   (c) s
   (d) ms^{-1}

4. The dimensions of power are:
   (a) ML^2T^{-2}
   (b) ML^2T^{-3}
   (c) M^2LT^{-3}
   (d) M^2LT^{-2}

5. Motion of the tip of second hand of the clock is an example for _________.
   (a) Uniform circular motion
   (b) Projectile motion
   (c) Motion in a plane with uniform velocity
   (d) Motion in a plane with constant acceleration

6. A passenger arriving in a new town wishes to go from the station to a hotel located 10 km away on a straight road from the station. A dishonest cabman takes him along a circuitous path 23 km long and reaches the hotel in 28 min, what is the average velocity of the taxi?
   (a) 21.43 km/h
   (b) 75 km/h
   (c) 49.3 km/h
   (d) 21 km/h

7. The ceiling of a long hall is 25 m high. What is the maximum horizontal distance that a ball thrown with a speed of 40 m/s can go without hitting the ceiling of the hall?
   (a) 150.5 m
   (b) 125.5 m
   (c) 360.5 m
   (d) 750.5 m

8. A bullet of mass 20 g has an initial speed of $1\ ms^{-1}$, just before it starts penetrating a mud wall of thickness 20 cm. If the wall offers a mean resistance of 2.5×10^{-2} N, the speed of the bullet after emerging from the other side of the wall is close to:
   (a) $0.3\ ms^{-1}$
   (b) $0.4\ ms^{-1}$
   (c) $0.1\ ms^{-1}$
   (d) $0.7\ ms^{-1}$

9. What is the mass of an object that requires a force of 90 N to accelerate at a rate of $2.6\ m/s^2$?
   (a) 44.6 kg
   (b) 34.6 kg
   (c) 54.6 kg
   (d) 48 kg

10. Find the acceleration of B.

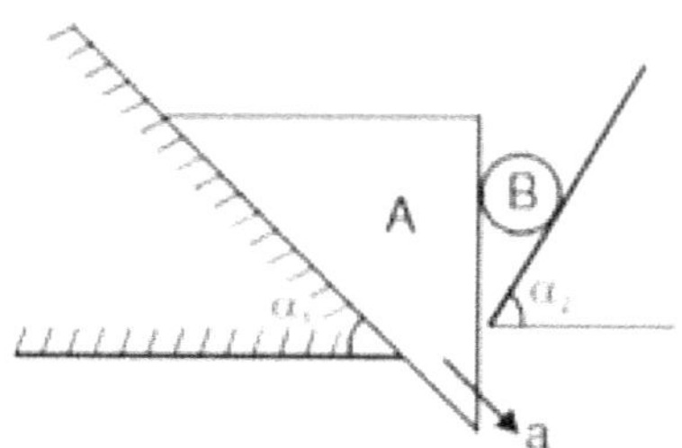

   (a) $\dfrac{a\cos\alpha_1}{\cos\alpha_2}$
   (b) $\dfrac{a\sin\alpha_1}{\cos\alpha_2}$
   (c) $\dfrac{a\cos_2}{\cos\alpha_1}$
   (d) $\dfrac{\cos\alpha_1}{\cos\alpha_2}$

11. A man getting down a running bus falls forward because:
   (a) Due to inertia of rest
   (b) Due to inertia of motion
   (c) Due to inertia of direction
   (d) None of these

12. A force $F = -K(y\hat{i} + a\hat{j})$ (where K is a positive constant) acts on a particle moving in the xy-plane. Starting from the origin, the particle is taken along the positive x-axis to the point $(a, 0)$ and then parallel to the y-axis to the point (a, a). The total work done by the force F on the particles is:
   (a) $-2Ka^2$
   (b) $2Ka^2$
   (c) $-Ka^2$
   (d) Ka^2

13. A cannon and a supply of cannon balls are inside a sealed rail road car. The cannon fires to the right, and the car recoils to the left. The cannon balls remain in the car after hitting the far wall. Find the maximum distance by which the rail road car move assuming it starts from the rest:
   (a) $\dfrac{L}{2}$
   (b) L
   (c) 0
   (d) Can't determine

14. A body is moved along a straight line by a machine delivering a constant power. The distance moved by the body in time t proportional to:
   (a) $\sqrt{t}$
   (b) $t^{\frac{3}{4}}$
   (c) $t^{\frac{3}{2}}$
   (d) t^2

15. A uniform force of $(3\hat{i} + \hat{j})N$ acts on a particle of mass 2 kg. Hence the particle is displaced from position $(2\hat{i} + \hat{k})m$ to position $(4\hat{i} + 3\hat{j} - \hat{k})m$. The work done by the force on the particle is:
   (a) 9 J
   (b) 6 J
   (c) 13 J
   (d) 15 J

16. A solid cylinder and a solid sphere, having same mass M and radius R, roll down the same inclined plane from top without slipping. They start from rest. The ratio of velocity of the solid cylinder to that of the solid sphere, with which they reach the ground, will be:
   (a) $\sqrt{\dfrac{5}{3}}$
   (b) $\sqrt{\dfrac{4}{5}}$
   (c) $\sqrt{\dfrac{3}{5}}$
   (d) $\sqrt{\dfrac{14}{15}}$

17. A football of radius R is kept on a hole of radius r (r < R) made on a plank kept horizontally. One end of the plank is now lifted so that it gets tilted making an angle θ from the horizontal as shown in the figure below. The maximum value of θ so that the football does not start rolling down the plank satisfies (figure is schematic and not drawn to scale)

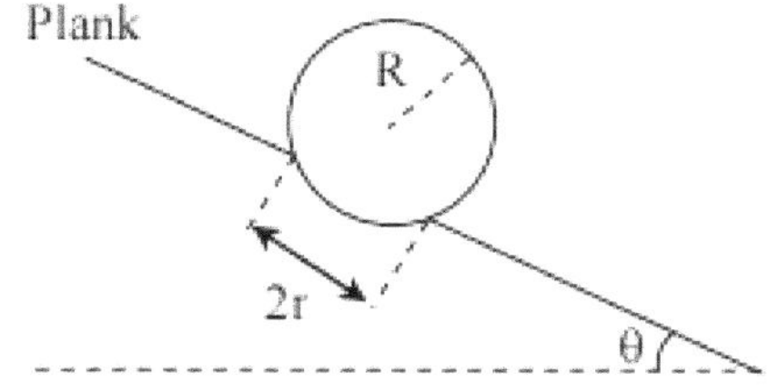

(a) $\sin\theta = \frac{r}{R}$ (b) $\tan\theta = \frac{r}{R}$

(c) $\sin\theta = \frac{r}{2R}$ (d) $\cos\theta = \frac{r}{2R}$

18. The gravitational potential energy of an object at a point above the ground is defined as the work done in _______.

(a) keeping it at the centre

(b) applying gravitational force on it

(c) raising it from the ground to that point against gravity

(d) allowing it to stand on the ground against gravity

19. A weightless bag is filled with 5 kg of water and then weighed in water. The reading of spring balance is:

(a) 5 kgf   (b) 2.5 kgf

(c) 1.25 kgf   (d) Zero

20. A particle is projected vertically with speed V from the surface of the earth. Maximum height attained by the particle, in terms of the radius of earth R, V and g is (V escape velocity, g is the acceleration due to gravity on the surface of the earth).

(a) $\dfrac{3RV^2}{2gR-2V^2}$ (b) $\dfrac{2RV^2}{3gR-V^2}$

(c) $\dfrac{RV^2}{2gR-V^2}$ (d) $\dfrac{RV^2}{gR-V^2}$

21. Variation of acceleration due to gravity (g) with distance x from the centre of the Erath is best represented by ($R \to$ Radius of the Earth):

(a)

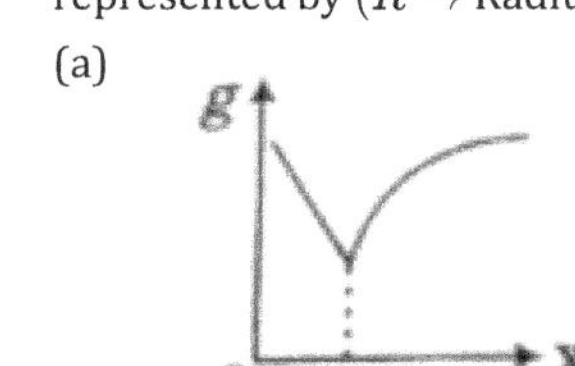

(b)

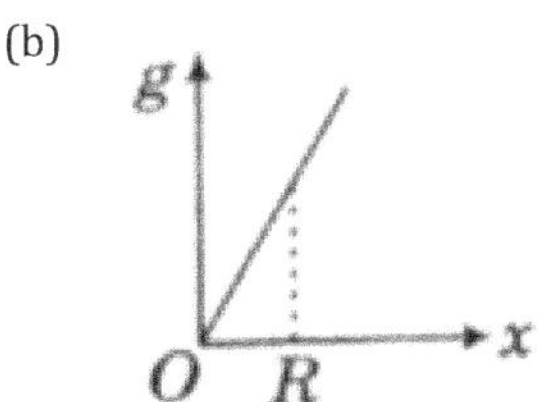

(c)

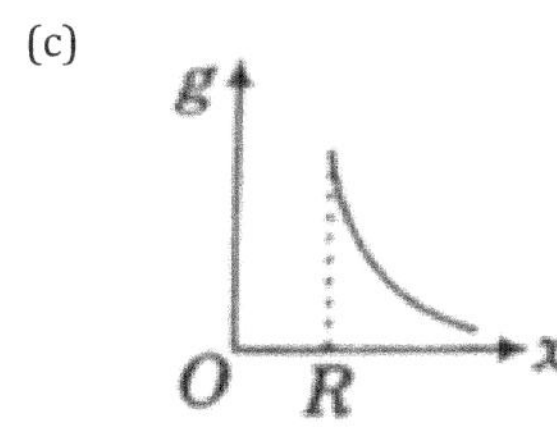

(d)

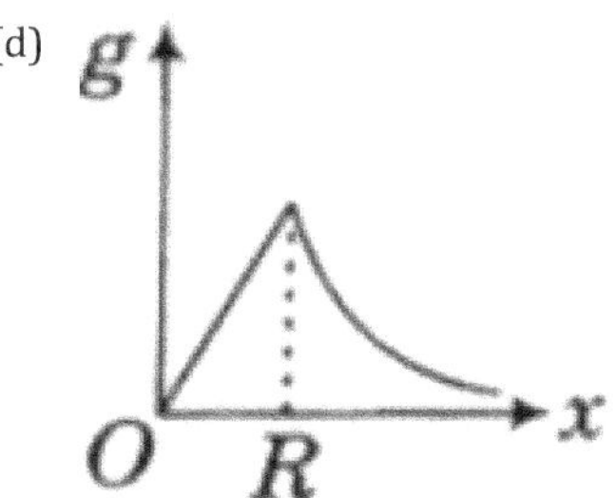

22. A block of mass m is placed on a smooth wedge of inclination θ. The whole system is accelerated horizontally so that the block does not slip on the wedge. The force exerted by the wedge on the block (g is the acceleration due to gravity) will be -

(a) $\dfrac{mg}{\cos\theta}$ (b) $mg\cos\theta$

(c) $mg\sin\theta$ (d) $\dfrac{mg}{\sin\theta}$

23. The coefficient of linear expansion of any material depends on _________.

(a) Temperature difference

(b) Length of material

(c) Shape of material

(d) None of these

24. The presence of ______, a bad conductor of heat, between the walls of the thermos flask, maintains the temperature of the liquid inside the flask.

(a) Wood   (b) Cloth

(c) Water   (d) Vacuum

25. The temperature of a block of iron is $140°F$. Its temperature on the celsius scale is:

(a) $32°C$ (b) $60°C$

(c) $108°C$ (d) $140°C$

26. The entropy of an isolated system continuously ___ and becomes a ___ at the state of equilibrium.

(a) decreases, minimum   (b) increases, maximum

(c) increases, minimum   (d) decreases, maximum

27. Which of the following processes exhibit external mechanical Irreversibility?

(a) Isothermal dissipation of work

(b) Adiabatic dissipation of work

(c) Both (A) and (B)

(d) None of the above

28. In a reversible process, the entropy of a system _______.

(a) First increases and then decreases

(b) Increases

(c) Remains the same

(d) Decreases

29. From Brewster's law of polarisation, it follows that the angle of polarisation depends upon:

(a) The wavelength of light

(b) Plane of polarisation's orientation

(c) Plane of vibration's orientation

(d) None of these

30. The speed 'v' of transverse waves on a stretched string of linear mass density 'μ' and tension 'T' is equal to?

(a) $\sqrt{(\mu/T)}$ (b) $\sqrt{(T/\mu)}$

(c) $(T/\mu)^2$ (d) $(\mu/T)^2$

31. In longitudinal wave motion, compression is a region where:

(a) Pressure increases while volume decreases

(b) Pressure decreases while volume increases

(c) Pressure and volume both increases

(d) Pressure and volume both decreases

32. Two tuning forks have frequencies 200 Hz and x. When they are sounded together 4 $\frac{beats}{sec}$ are heard. The value of x is?

(a) 196 Hz or 204 Hz   (b) 200 Hz only

(c) 205 Hz or 201 Hz   (d) 200 Hz or 198 Hz

33. Which of the following statements are INCORRECT about ultrasonic waves?

(a) The sound frequency of ultrasonic waves is above 20,000Hz

(b) Ultrasounds can be used to detect cracks and flaws in metal blocks

(c) The frequency range of ultrasonic waves is below 20Hz

(d) Ultrasound is generally used to clean parts located in hard-to-reach places.

34. An electric dipole is placed at an angle of $60°$ with an electric field of intensity $10^5 NC^{-1}$. It experiences a torque equal to $8\sqrt{3}Nm$. If the dipole length is 2 cm then the charge on the dipole is c.

(a) -8×10^3 (b) 8.54×10^{-4}

(c) 8×10^{-3} (d) 0.85×10^{-6}

35. Suppose a charge +q on Earth's surface and another +q charge is placed on the surface of the Moon. Calculate the value of q required to balance the gravitational attraction between Earth and Moon.
(Take $m_E = 5.9 \times 10^{24}$ kg, $m_M = 7.9 \times 10^{22}$ kg)

(a) $q = 5.86 \times 10^{13}C$ (b) $q = 4.50 \times 10^{11}C$

(c) $q = 4.18 \times 10^{13}C$ (d) $q = 7.48 \times 10^{13}C$

36. A point charge of $+10\mu C$ is placed at a distance of 20 cm from another identical point charge of $+10\mu C$. A point charge of $-2\mu C$ is moved from point a to b as shown in the figure. Calculate the change in potential energy of the system?

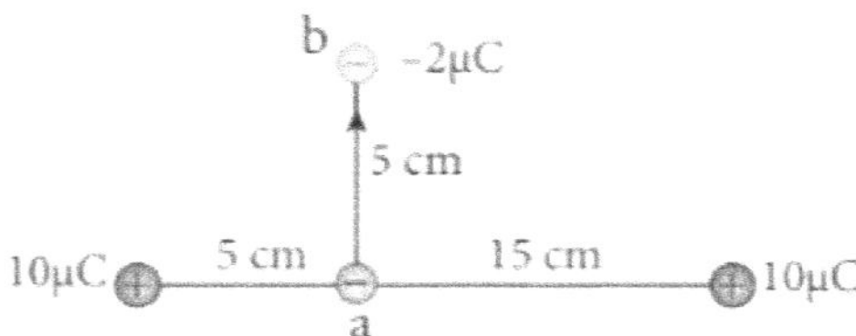

(a) W = 3.1172 J   (b) W = 2.1172 J

(c) W = 1.1172 J   (d) W = 4.1172 J

37. Calculate the Coulomb force between 2 alpha particles separated by 3.2×10^{-15} m

(a) $60N$ (b) $50N$

(c) $90N$ (d) $70N$

38. A point charge of 10^{-7} coulomb is situated at the center of a cube of 1 m side. Calculate the electric flux through its surface.

(a) $0.13 \times 10^4 Nm^2C^{-1}$ (b) $1.1 \times 10^4 Nm^2C^{-1}$

(c) $13 \times 10^4 Nm^2C^{-1}$ (d) $1.13 \times 10^4 Nm^2C^{-1}$

39. The potential at a point P , which is forming a corner of a square of side $93mm$ with charges $Q_1 = 33nC$, $Q_2 = -51nC$, $Q_3 = 47nC$ located at the other three corners, is nearly:

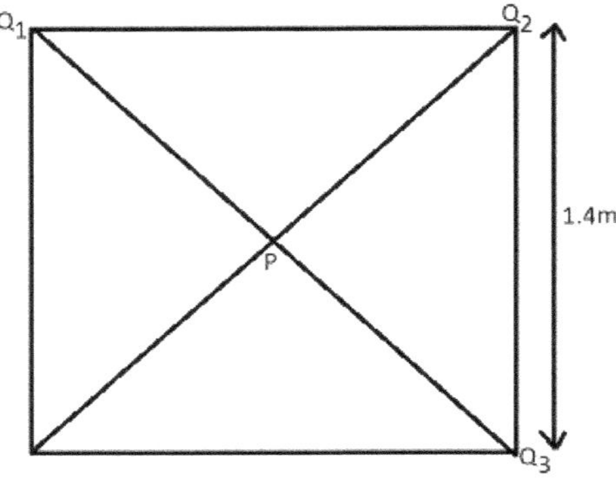

(a) 16kV   (b) 4kV

(c) 400kV   (d) 160kV

40. **Direction:** In the given figure, a hollow spherical capacitor is shown. The electric field will not be zero at

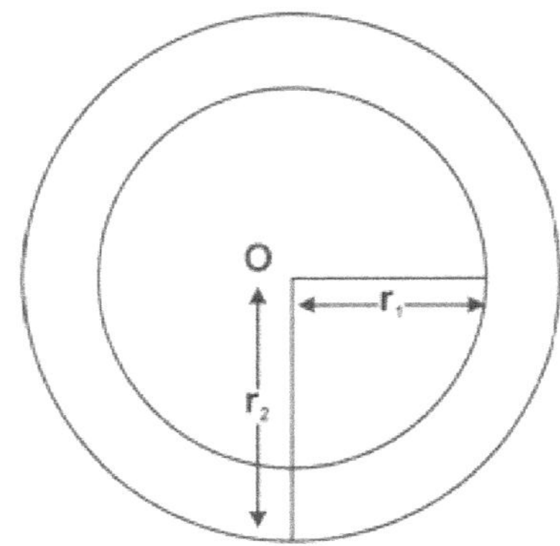

(a) $r < r_1$ (b) $r > r_2$

(c) $r < r_2$ (d) $r_1 < r < r_2$

41. In the given circuit diagram when the current reaches steady state in the circuit, the charge on the capacitor of capacitance C will be:

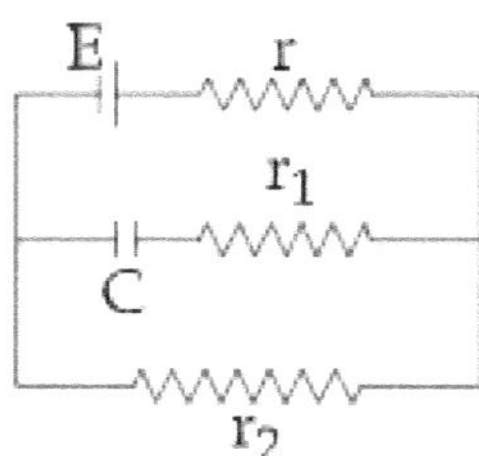

(a) CE (b) $CE \dfrac{r_1}{(r_2+r)}$

(c) $CE \dfrac{r_2}{(r+r_2)}$ (d) $CE \dfrac{r_1}{(r_1+r)}$

42.

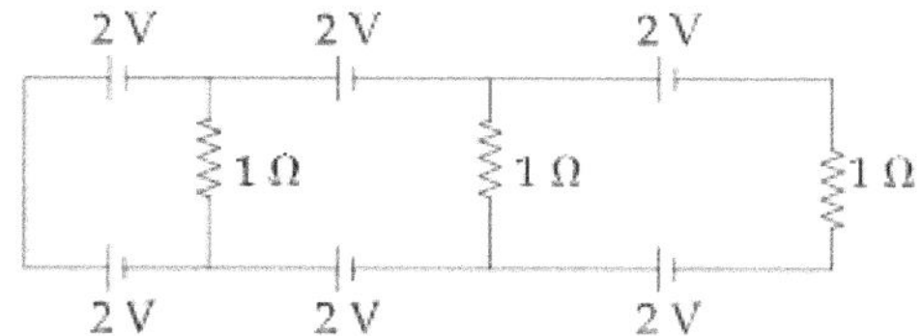

In the above circuit the current in each resistance is:
(a) 1 A
(b) 0.25 A
(c) 0.5 A
(d) 0 A

43. When a current of $5mA$ is passed through a galvanometer having a coil of resistance 15Ω, it shows full scale deflection. The value of the resistance to be put in series with the galvanometer to convert it into a voltmeter of range $0 - 10V$ is:
(a) $1.985 \times 10^3 \Omega$
(b) $2.045 \times 10^3 \Omega$
(c) $2.535 \times 10^3 \Omega$
(d) $4.005 \times 10^3 \Omega$

44. Which of the following statements is false?
(a) Wheat stone bridge is the most sensitive when all the four resistances are of the same order of magnitude
(b) In a balanced wheat stone bridge if the cell and the galvanometer are exchanged, the null point is disturbed
(c) A rheostat can be used as a potential divider
(d) Kirchhoff's second law represents energy conservation

45. A long insulated copper wire is closely wound as a spiral of 'N' turns. The spiral has an inner radius 'a' and an outer radius 'b'. The spiral lies in the X-Y plane and a steady current 'I' flows through the wire. The Z-component of the magnetic field at the center of the spiral is:

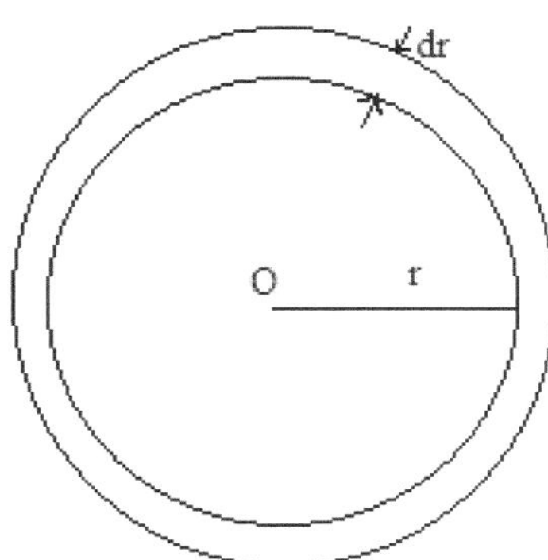

(a) $\frac{\mu_0 NI}{2(b-a)}\ln\left(\frac{b}{a}\right)$
(b) $\frac{\mu_0 NI}{2(b-a)}\ln\left(\frac{b+a}{b-a}\right)$
(c) $\frac{\mu_0 NI}{2b}\ln\left(\frac{b}{a}\right)$
(d) $\frac{\mu_0 NI}{2b}\ln\left(\frac{b+a}{b-a}\right)$

46. The coercivity of a small magnet where the ferromagnet gets demagnetized is 3×10^3 A m^{-1}. Find the current (in Amper) required to be passed in a solenoid of length 10 cm and the number of turns 100, so that the magnet gets demagnetized when inside the solenoid.
(a) $30mA$
(b) $60mA$
(c) $3A$
(d) $6A$

47. An electron is moving on a circular path of radius r with speed v in a transverse magnetic field B, then $\frac{e}{m}$ will be:
(a) Bvr
(b) $\frac{B}{rv}$
(c) $\frac{v}{Br}$
(d) $\frac{vr}{B}$

48. The magnetic field intensity on the equatorial line of a bar magnet of length l at a distance r from the centre of the magnet is B. If the magnetic is divided into two equal parts such that the width of each part is half that of the initial one, then the magnetic field intensity on the equatorial line at a distance r of any part will be: (l $<<$ r).
(a) $\frac{B}{2}$
(b) B
(c) 2B
(d) $\frac{B}{4}$

49. A beam of protons with speed 4×10^5 ms^{-1} enters a uniform magnetic field of 0.3 T at an angle of $60°$ to the magnetic field. The pitch of the resulting helical path of protons is close to : (Mass of the proton $= 1.67 \times 10^{-27}$ kg , charge of the proton $= 1.69 \times 10^{-19}$C)
(a) 2 cm
(b) 5 cm
(c) 4 cm
(d) 12 cm

50. An iron rod of susceptibility 599 is subjected to a magnetising field of 1200Am^{-1}. The permeability of the material of the rod is $(\mu_0 = 4\pi \times 10^{-7}TmA^{-1})$
(a) $2.4\pi \times 10^{-4}$TmA^{-1}
(b) 8.0×10^{-5}TmA^{-1}
(c) $2.4\pi \times 10^{-5}$TmA^{-1}
(d) $2.4\pi \times 10^{-7}$TmA^{-1}

51. Given the mass of the iron nucleus as 55.85 u and A = 56, find the nuclear density.
(a) 2.29×10^{17} kg/m^3
(b) 4.29×10^{17} kg/m^3
(c) 5.30×10^{17} kg/m^3
(d) 8.39×10^{17} kg/m^3

52. Find the energy equivalent of one atomic mass unit.first in Joules and then in MeV. Using this, express the mass defect of $^{16}_{8}$O in MeV/C^2.
(a) $1.49 \times 10^{-10}J$, 14905.6 MeV/C^2
(b) $5.49 \times 10^{-10}J$, 15805.6 MeV/C^2
(c) $1.50 \times 10^{-10}J$, 13205.6 MeV/C^2
(d) $2.49 \times 10^{-10}J$, 15605.6 MeV/C^2

53. If alpha, beta and gamma rays carry the same momentum, which has the longest wavelength?
(a) Alpha rays
(b) Beta rays
(c) Gamma rays
(d) All have the same wavelength

54. Which one of the following graphs is not correct for ideal gas?

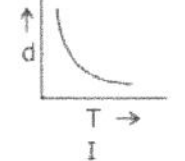
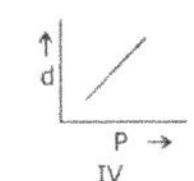

d = Density, P = Pressure, T = Temperature
(a) I
(b) II
(c) III
(d) IV

55. A gas mixture consists of 3 moles of oxygen and 5 moles of argon at temperature T. Assuming the gases to be ideal and the oxygen bond to be rigid, the total internal energy (in units of RT) of the mixture is:

(a) 11   (b) 13
(c) 15   (d) 20

56. An ideal gas undergoes a four step cycle as shown in the $P - V$ diagram below. During this cycle, heat is absorbed by the gas in:

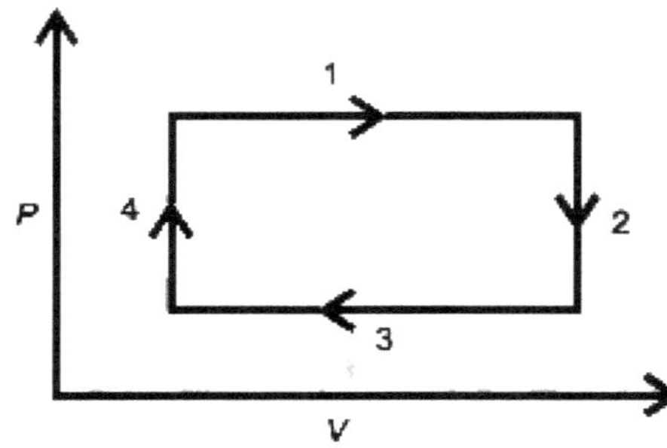

(a) steps 1 and 2   (b) steps 1 and 3
(c) steps 1 and 4   (d) steps 2 and 4

57. The volume occupied by the molecules contained in 4.5 kg water at STP, if the intermolecular forces vartish away is:
(a) $5.6 \times 10^{-3} m^3$ (b) $5.6 m^3$
(c) $5.6 \times 10^{6} m^3$ (d) $5.6 \times 10^{3} m^3$

58. In the circuit, the logical value of $A = 1$ or $B = 1$ when potential at A or B is $5V$ and the logical value of $A = 0$ or $B = 0$ when potential at A or B is $0V$.

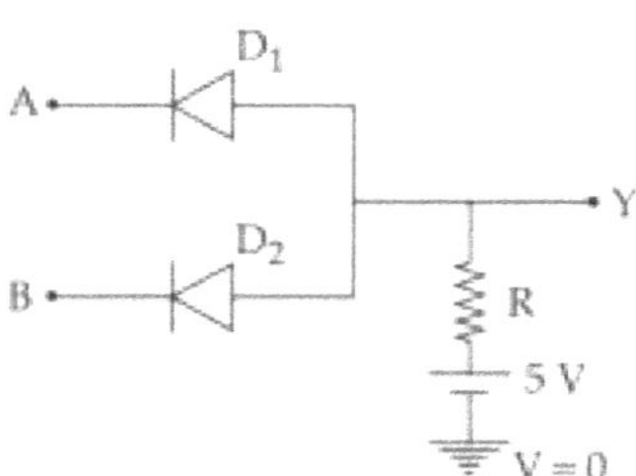

The truth table of the given circuit will be:

(a)

A	B	Y
0	0	0
1	0	0
0	1	0
1	1	1

(b)

A	B	Y
0	0	0
1	0	1
0	1	1
1	1	1

(c)

A	B	Y
0	0	0
1	0	0
0	1	0
1	1	0

(d)

A	B	Y
0	0	1
1	0	1
0	1	1
1	1	0

59. What type of material is obtained when an intrinsic semiconductor is doped with trivalent impurity?
(a) Extrinsic semiconductor
(b) Insulator
(c) n -type semiconductor
(d) p -type semiconductor

60. In the given circuit, the potential difference across PQ will be nearest to

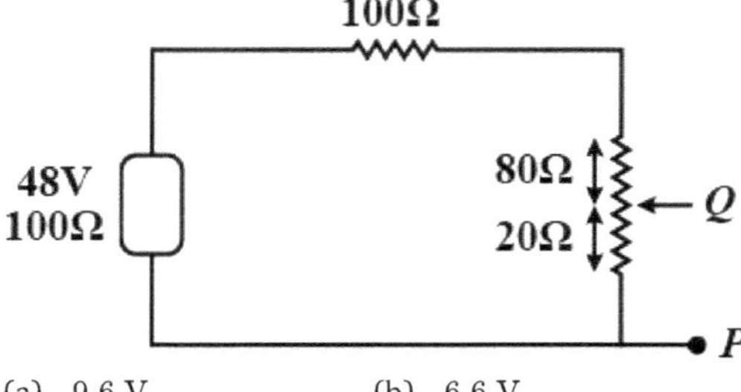

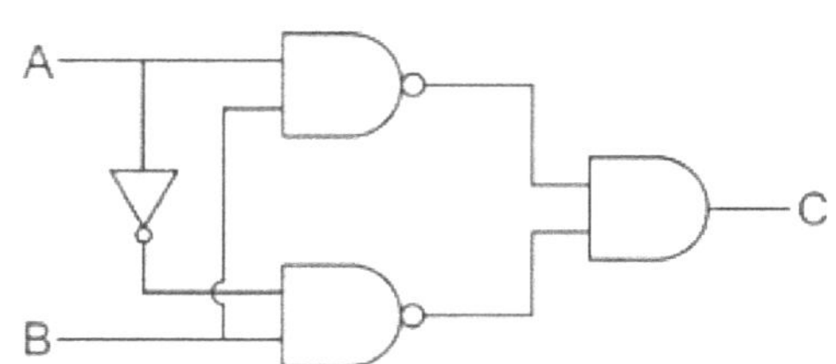

(a) 9.6 V   (b) 6.6 V
(c) 4.8 V   (d) 3.2 V

61.

The truth table for the given logic circuit is :

(a)

A	B	C
0	0	1
0	1	0
1	0	1
1	1	0

(b)

A	B	C
0	0	0
0	1	1
1	0	0
1	1	1

(c)

A	B	C
0	0	0
0	1	1
1	0	1
1	1	0

(d)

A	B	C
0	0	1
0	1	0
1	0	0
1	1	1

62. What force is required to stretch a wire of 1 cm^2 in cross-section to double its length? Given $Y = 2 \times 10^{11} \text{ N/m}^2$
(a) $2 \times 10^7 \text{ N}$ (b) $2 \times 10^8 \text{ N}$
(c) $2 \times 10^{11} \text{ N}$ (d) None

63. Two wires A and B are stretched by the same load. If the area of cross-section of wire 'A' is double that of 'B', then the stress on 'B' is:
(a) Equal to that on A (b) Twice that on A
(c) Half that on A (d) Four times that on A

64. Which of the following statement is not correct for an object moving along a straight path in an accelerated motion?

(a) Its speed keeps changing

(b) Its velocity always changes

(c) It always goes away from the earth

(d) A force is always acting on it

65. A car, initially at rest travels $20\,\mathrm{m}$ in 4 sec along a straight line with constant acceleration. Find the acceleration of car?

(a) $4.9\,\mathrm{m/s^2}$ (b) $2.5\,\mathrm{m/s^2}$

(c) $0.4\,\mathrm{m/s^2}$ (d) $1.6\,\mathrm{m/s^2}$

66. Rain drops are spherical because of:

(a) viscosity

(b) air resistance

(c) surface tension forces

(d) atmospheric pressure

67. A fluid is one which can be defined as a substance that:

(a) has same shear stress at all points

(b) can deform indefinitely under the action of smallest shear force

(c) has the small shear stress in all directions

(d) is practically incompressible

68. In the isothermal condition, the isothermal bulk modulus of an ideal gas is equal to _____.

(a) constant   (b) pressure

(c) temperature   (d) viscosity

69. The difference of pressure between the inside and outside of a liquid drop is _____.

(a) $p = T \times r$ (b) $p = \dfrac{T}{r}$

(c) $p = \dfrac{T}{2r}$ (d) $p = \dfrac{2T}{r}$

70. A body starts from rest and travels with a uniform acceleration of $20\,\mathrm{m/s^2}$. Calculate the time taken by the body to cover a distance of $90\,\mathrm{m}$.

(a) $6\,s$ (b) $3\,s$

(c) $13\,s$ (d) $12\,s$

71. The slope of an acceleration-time graph gives:

(a) velocity   (b) impulse

(c) force   (d) jerk

72. In which one of the following devices, the light energy is converted into the electrical energy?

(a) Light-emitting diode   (b) Laser diode

(c) Solar cell   (d) Transistor

73. An object is made of two equal parts by volume; one part has density ρ_0, and the other part has density $2\rho_0$. What is the average density of the object?

(a) $3\rho_0$ (b) $\dfrac{3}{2}\rho_0$

(c) ρ_0 (d) $\dfrac{1}{2}\rho_0$

74. The molecule of a monatomic gas has only three translational degrees of freedom. Thus, the average energy of a molecule at temperature $'T'$ is _________.

(a) $3\mathrm{k}_B T$ (b) $\left(\dfrac{3}{4}\right)\mathrm{k_B}T$

(c) $\left(\dfrac{1}{3}\right)\mathrm{k_B}T$ (d) $\left(\dfrac{3}{2}\right)\mathrm{k_B}T$

75. The minimum electrostatic force between two charged particles placed at a distance of $1\,m$ is,

(a) $2.3 \times 10^{-28}\,\mathrm{N}$ (b) $6.2 \times 10^{-34}\,\mathrm{N}$

(c) $1.02 \times 10^{-26}\,\mathrm{N}$ (d) $4.2 \times 10^{-27}\,\mathrm{N}$

76. These materials are repelled by a magnetic field. An applied magnetic field creates an induced magnetic field in them in the opposite direction, causing a repulsive force. What is the name of this type of material?

(a) Paramagnetic   (b) Diamagnetic

(c) Ferromagnetic   (d) Ferrimagnetism

77. If the moment of inertia of a rotating body is increased then what will be the effect on the angular velocity?

(a) It will increase

(b) It will decrease

(c) There will be no effect

(d) First increase and then decrease

78. If a gas at $27°C$ is allowed to expand to thrice its original volume and pressure is halved then what will be its new temperature (in $°C$) ?

(a) 227   (b) 450

(c) 550   (d) 177

79. An ideal gas heat engine operates in Carnot's cycle between $227°C$ and $127°C$ It absorbs 6×10^4 J at high temperature. The amount of heat converted into work is _______.

(a) $4.8 \times 10^4 \times J$ (b) $3.5 \times 10^4 \times J$

(c) $1.6 \times 10^4 \times J$ (d) $1.2 \times 10^4 \times J$

80. Relative permittivity of a material is ϵ_r. Which of the following values of these quantifies is allowed for a diamagnetic material?

(a) $\epsilon_r = 0$ (b) $\epsilon_r = 1.5$

(c) $\epsilon_r = 0.5$ (d) None of these

// Smart Answer Sheet //

Correct — Percentage of students who answered correctly.

Skipped — Percentage of students who skipped.

Q.	Ans.	Correct / Skipped	Q.	Ans.	Correct / Skipped	Q.	Ans.	Correct / Skipped
1	C	82.47% / 0.0%	2	B	50.24% / 1.25%	3	D	68.79% / 1.47%
4	B	55.5% / 1.31%	5	A	83.15% / 0.0%	6	A	51.5% / 1.17%
7	A	32.99% / 3.95%	8	D	17.14% / 4.49%	9	B	85.24% / 0.0%
10	A	69.37% / 1.94%	11	B	40.28% / 1.55%	12	C	51.52% / 1.41%
13	B	65.85% / 1.38%	14	C	66.3% / 1.3%	15	A	48.99% / 1.29%
16	D	63.74% / 1.5%	17	A	66.74% / 1.78%	18	C	64.54% / 1.27%
19	D	65.31% / 1.33%	20	C	54.51% / 1.22%	21	D	41.64% / 1.76%
22	A	66.76% / 1.77%	23	D	53.62% / 1.97%	24	D	23.59% / 4.39%
25	B	62.42% / 1.25%	26	B	76.04% / 0.0%	27	C	80.69% / 0.0%
28	C	62.83% / 1.32%	29	A	64.11% / 1.24%	30	B	57.23% / 1.8%
31	A	46.71% / 1.95%	32	A	57.62% / 1.25%	33	C	48.04% / 1.93%
34	C	49.56% / 1.37%	35	A	66.95% / 1.02%	36	C	27.29% / 3.61%
37	C	69.13%	38	D	52.96%	39	B	21.31%

		1.63%			1.65%			3.87%
40	D	41.41%	41	C	58.47%	42	D	18.35%
		1.91%			1.38%			4.67%
43	A	77.08%	44	B	83.79%	45	A	18.89%
		0.0%			0.0%			3.05%
46	C	28.13%	47	C	70.0%	48	A	64.02%
		4.54%			1.21%			1.24%
49	C	19.54%	50	A	55.24%	51	A	13.22%
		3.17%			1.16%			4.84%
52	A	51.67%	53	D	77.99%	54	B	83.09%
		1.09%			0.0%			0.0%
55	C	67.03%	56	C	54.09%	57	B	82.99%
		1.21%			1.08%			0.0%
58	A	54.1%	59	D	50.41%	60	D	21.05%
		1.29%			1.64%			4.79%
61	A	18.95%	62	A	51.98%	63	B	52.42%
		3.62%			2.0%			1.91%
64	C	51.41%	65	B	48.19%	66	C	51.16%
		1.26%			1.35%			1.89%
67	B	50.65%	68	B	45.67%	69	D	47.86%
		1.49%			1.33%			1.32%
70	B	64.4%	71	D	83.82%	72	C	82.41%
		1.56%			0.0%			0.0%
73	B	41.47%	74	D	67.76%	75	A	67.3%
		1.57%			1.56%			1.9%
76	B	64.75%	77	B	65.86%	78	D	69.85%
		1.26%			1.58%			1.02%
79	D	42.17%	80	B	52.9%			
		1.67%			1.67%			

// Hints and Solutions //

1(C). Coulomb:
- The SI Unit of Charge is Coulomb.
- It is denoted as C.
- The coulomb is defined as the quantity of electricity transported in one second by a current of one ampere.

2(B). The unit Nautical mile per hour is used to measure the speed of the Ship.
Nautical Miles:
- It is based on the circumference of the planet Earth.
- A minute of arc out of 360 on the planet Earth is 1 nautical mile.
- It is also equal to one minute of latitude.
- The nautical mile per hour is called Knots.
- 1 knot = 1.15 miles per hour
- 1 knot = 1.852 km/h

3(D). Given: $\alpha = \beta t + \lambda$
$\Rightarrow$ meter = (β × time) + meter
$\Rightarrow$ (meter-meter) = (β × time)
$\Rightarrow \beta$ = meter/time $\Rightarrow$ m t$^{-1} \Rightarrow$ m s^{-1}
SI Unit: It is an abbreviation from the French name Le Systeme International d'Unites.

4(B). Concept:
- The rate of work done is called power.
- It is denoted by P. The SI unit of power is the watt (W).

Power $(P) = \dfrac{W}{t}$

W = work done
t = time
Dimensions of force is MLT^{-2}.
Energy or Work done = Force × Distance
Dimensions of energy is ML^2T^{-2}.
The dimensions of power
$= \dfrac{\text{Dimension of work}}{\text{Time } (t)} = \dfrac{ML^2T^{-2}}{T} = ML^2T^{-3}$

5(A). In a uniform circular motion, the object moves with uniform speed along the circumference of a circle. But the velocities are different at different points due to the change in the direction of velocity. If an object is moving with uniform speed if it covers equal distances in equal intervals of time. If a particle moves along a circular path with a constant speed then its motion is said to be a uniform circular motion. So, the motion of the tip of the second hand of a clock is an example for uniform circular motion.

6(A). Total distance traveled = 23 km
Total time taken = 28 min = $\dfrac{28}{60}$ h

Now,
Average speed of the taxi = Total Distance Travelled / Total Time Taken
$= \dfrac{23}{\frac{28}{60}}$
$= 23 \times \dfrac{60}{28}$
$= 49.29$ km/h
Now,
Distance between the hotel and the station = 10 km = Displacement of the car
So, Average velocity $= \dfrac{10}{\frac{28}{60}}$
$= 10 \times \dfrac{60}{28}$
$= 21.43$ km/h

7(A). Given,
Height of the wall (H) = 25 m,
Speed of ball $(u) = 40$ m/s
Now,
Suppose that the ball is thrown at an angle θ with the horizontal distance.
We know,
$H = \dfrac{u^2 \sin^2 \theta}{2g}$
$\therefore 25 = \dfrac{(40)^2 \sin^2 \theta}{2 \times 9.8}$
or $\sin^2 \theta = \dfrac{25 \times 2 \times 9.8}{(40)^2}$
or $\sin \theta = \dfrac{\sqrt{490}}{40} = 0.5534$
or $\theta = 33.6°$
Now, $R = \dfrac{u^2 \sin 2\theta}{g}$
$= \dfrac{(40)^2 \sin 2(33.6°)}{9.8}$
$= \dfrac{(40)^2 \sin 67.2°}{9.8}$
$= \dfrac{(40)^2 \times 0.9219}{9.8}$
$= 150.5$ m

8(D). Given,
$m = 20$ g $= 20 \times 10^{-3}$ kg
Initial speed $m = 1$ ms^{-1}
Thickness, $s = 20$ cm $= 20 \times 10^{-2}$ m
Resistance offered by the wall, $F = -2.5 \times 10^{-2}$ N
So, deacceleration of bullet,
$F = ma$
$a = \dfrac{F}{m}$
$= \dfrac{-2.5 \times 10^{-2}}{20 \times 10^{-3}}$
$= -\dfrac{5}{4}$ ms^{-2}
Now, using the equation of motion,
$v^2 = u^2 + 2as$
$v^2 = 1 + 2\left(-\dfrac{5}{4}\right)\left(20 \times 10^{-2}\right)$

$v^2 = \frac{1}{2}$

$v = \frac{1}{\sqrt{2}} = 0.7 \text{ ms}^{-1}$

9(B). Given,
Force, $F = 90$ N
Acceleration, $a = 2.6 \text{ m/s}^2$
The force required to accelerate a body of mass m with acceleration a is given by,
$F = ma$
$90 = m \times 2.6$
$m = \frac{90}{2.6}$
$m = 34.6$ kg

10(A). Free body diagram of the system,

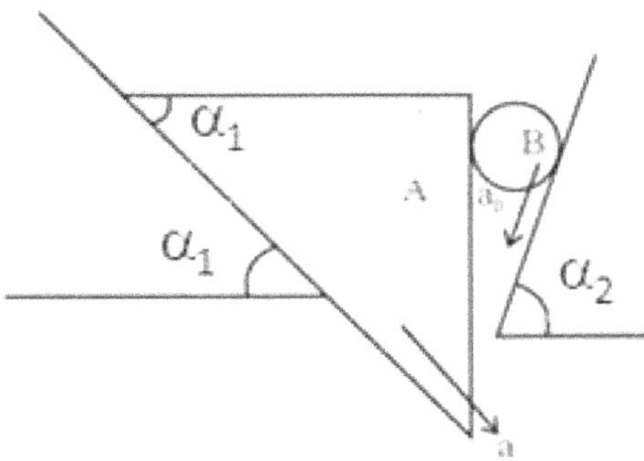

for B.

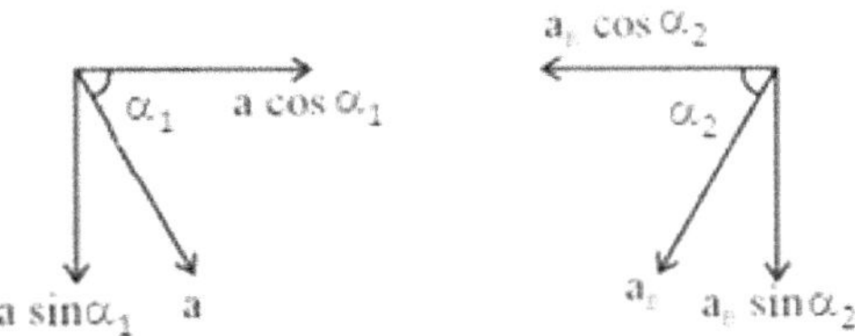

As the acceleration along normal to surface in contact shall be same.
$a \cos \alpha_1 = a_B \cos \alpha_2$
$a_B = \frac{a \cos \alpha_1}{\cos \alpha_2}$

11(B). A man getting down a running bus falls forward because due to inertia of motion.
Newton's first law defines inertia and is rightly called the law of inertia. A body continues to be in its state of rest or of uniform motion along a straight line unless it is acted upon by some external force to change the state. The inertia of motion is the inability of a body to change by itself its state of uniform motion i.e., a body in uniform motion can neither accelerate nor retard on its own.
When a man getting down from a running bus, he falls forward because the lower part of his body comes to rest with the ground but the upper part tends to continue its motion due to inertia of motion.

12(C). While moving from $(0, 0)$ to $(a, 0)$
Along positive x-axis, $y = 0$
$\therefore \vec{F} = -Kx\hat{j}$
i.e. force is in negative y-direction while displacement is in positive $x-$ direction.
$\therefore W_1 = 0$
Because force is perpendicular to the displacement.
Then particle moves from $(a, 0)$ to (a, a) along a line parallel to y-axis ($x = +a$) during this,
$\vec{F} = -K(y\hat{i} + a\hat{j})$

The first component of force, $-Ky\hat{i}$ will not contribute any work because this components is along negative x-direction $(-\hat{i})$ while displacement is in positive y-direction $(a, 0)$ to (a, a).
The second component of force i.e. $-Ka\hat{j}$
$\therefore W_2 = (-Ka\hat{j})(a\hat{j}) = (-Ka)(a) = -Ka^2$
So net work done on the particle is,
$W = W_1 + W_2$
$= 0 + (-Ka^2) = -Ka^2$

13(B).

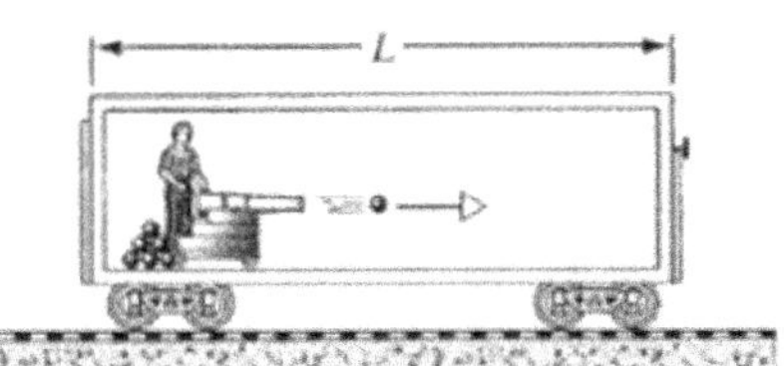

Initially, the whole system is at rest, so
$v_{CM} = 0$.
As there is no external force acting on the system,
$v_{CM} = \text{constant} = 0$
So the position of the center of mass of the system remains fixed.
$x_{CM} = \frac{mx_1 + Mx_2}{m + M}$ ....(i)
where m is mass of the cannon balls and M that of the (car + cannon) system.
As $\Delta x_{CM} = 0$
$m\Delta x_1 + M\Delta x_2 = 0$ ....(ii)
As cannon balls cannot leave the car, so maximum displacement of the balls relative to the car is L and in doing so the car will shift a distance $\Delta x_2 = D$ (say) relative to the ground, opposite to the displacement of the balls; then the displacement of balls relative to ground will be
$\Delta x_1 = L - D$ ....(iii)
Substituting the value of Δx_1 from Equation (iii) in Equation (ii), we get
$m(L - D) - MD = 0$
$\Rightarrow D = \frac{mL}{M + m}$
$= \frac{L}{1 + \frac{M}{m}}$
$\Rightarrow D$ i.e., rail road car cannot travel more than L.

14(C). $\text{Power} = \frac{\text{K.E}}{\text{time}} = \frac{\frac{1}{2}mv^2}{t} = \text{Constant}$
So, $\frac{v^2}{t} = \text{Constant}$
$v = \sqrt{Ct}$
$\Rightarrow v = Kt^{\frac{1}{2}}$
$\Rightarrow \frac{dx}{dt} = Kt^{\frac{1}{2}}$
$\Rightarrow dx = Kt^{\frac{1}{2}}dt$
Integrating both side
$x = \int Kt^{\frac{1}{2}} dt$
$\Rightarrow x = \frac{Kt^{\frac{3}{2}}}{\frac{3}{2}} + C$
$\Rightarrow x \propto t^{\frac{3}{2}}$

15(A). Given that,
A uniform force, $\vec{F} = (3\hat{i} + \hat{j})$
Mass, $m = 2$ kg
Initial position of particle, $\vec{r_1} = (2\hat{i} + \hat{k})$m
Final position of particle, $\vec{r_2} = (4\hat{i} + 3\hat{j} - \hat{k})$m
Net Displacement of particle,

$\vec{\Delta r} = \vec{r_2} - \vec{r_1} = (2\hat{i} + 3\hat{j} - 2\hat{k})\,\text{m}$

Work done by the force on the particle,

$W = \vec{F} \cdot \vec{\Delta r}$

$\Rightarrow W = 6 + 3$

$\Rightarrow W = 9\ \text{J}$

16(D). $a = \dfrac{g\sin\theta}{1+\frac{K^2}{R^2}}$

$v = \sqrt{\dfrac{2Sg\sin\theta}{1+\frac{K^2}{R^2}}}$

$\Rightarrow \dfrac{v_c}{v_{ss}} \sqrt{\dfrac{1+\frac{K_{Ss}^2}{R^2}}{1+\frac{K_c^2}{R^2}}}$

$= \sqrt{\dfrac{1+\frac{2}{5}}{1+\frac{1}{2}}}$

$\Rightarrow \sqrt{\dfrac{\frac{7}{5}}{\frac{3}{2}}}$

$= \sqrt{\dfrac{14}{15}}$

17(A). Let us draw the free body diagram for given case, where the normal reaction will act on point of contact. So,

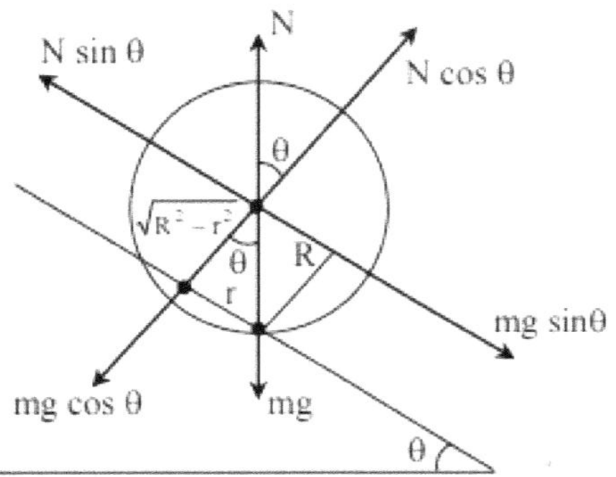

Writing the torque balancing equations for the components of weight:

$mg\sin\theta\sqrt{R^2-r^2} = mg\cos\theta\, r$

$\tan\theta = \dfrac{r}{\sqrt{R^2-r^2}}$

And, $\sin\theta = \dfrac{r}{R}$

18(C). The gravitational potential energy of an object at a point above the ground is defined as the work done in raising it from the ground to that point against gravity.

- Gravitational energy, such as elevating objects against the gravity of the Earth, is the potential energy correlated with gravitational force.
- If an object falls within a gravitational field from one point to another point, the gravity force will do positive work on the object, and the gravitational potential energy will decrease by the same amount.
- Near the surface of the Earth, the product mgh is the work performed in raising an object through a height h, so U = mgh
- The Newton's law of gravitation: This law states that every point mass in the universe attracts every other point mass with a force that is directly proportional to the product of its masses and inversely proportional to the distance between them in the square.

19(D). Since the weight of the bag with water is equal to the weight of the water displaced, the spring balance reading is zero.

The spring balance is a type of balance (scales). It consists of a spring, one end of which is fixed and the other end is hung by a hook, whose weight is to be determined. It works on Hooke's law.

20(C). By the law of conservation of energy,

$\dfrac{1}{2}mV^2 - \dfrac{GMm}{R} = \dfrac{-GMm}{R+h}$

$\Rightarrow \dfrac{1}{2}V^2 - \dfrac{GM}{R^2}\cdot R = \dfrac{-Gm}{R^2}\dfrac{R^2}{(R+h)}$

$\Rightarrow \dfrac{1}{2}V^2 - gR = \dfrac{-gR^2}{(R+h)}$

$\Rightarrow R + h = \dfrac{-2gR^2}{V^2-2gR}$

$\Rightarrow h = \dfrac{-2gR^2}{V^2-2gR} - R$

$\Rightarrow h = \dfrac{-RV^2}{V^2-2gR}$

$\Rightarrow h = \dfrac{RV^2}{2gR-V^2}$

21(D). The value of g is maximum at the surface of the Earth and $g = 0$ at centre of the Earth. If one goes away from the Earth's surface, again the value of g decreases.

Thus, the graph (D) is showing the correct variation of g.

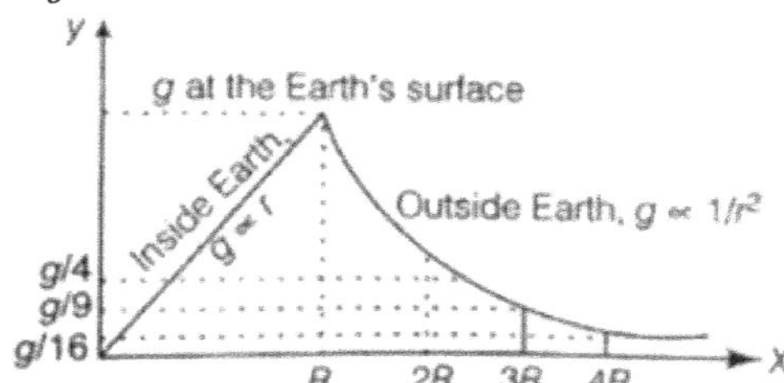

22(A).

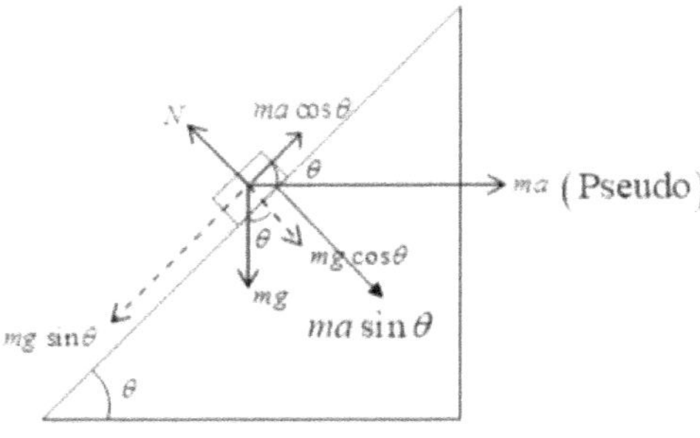

$N = ma\sin\theta + mg\cos\theta \ .....(i)$

Also, $mg\sin\theta = ma\cos\theta \ .....(ii)$

Substituting the value of a from (i) and (ii), we get

$a = g\tan\theta$

$\therefore N = mg\dfrac{\sin^2\theta}{\cos\theta}(+mg\cos\theta)$

$\therefore N = \dfrac{mg}{\cos\theta}(\sin^2\theta + \cos^2\theta) = \dfrac{mg}{\cos\theta}$

or, $N = \dfrac{mg}{\cos\theta}$

23(D). From the below explanation, we can see that, we can predict the amount of linear expansion by the relation:

$\Delta L = L\alpha\Delta T$, in this L and ΔL is original length and change in length respectively.

Whereas ΔT and α are changed in temperature and constant known as coefficients of linear expansion, which only depends on the material of an object.

The coefficient of linear expansion is independent of temperature difference, length of material, and shape of the material.

24(D). The presence of Vacuum between the walls of the Thermo flask maintains the temperature of the liquid inside the flask. A Thermo flask is a container used to maintain the temperature of the liquid for an extended period of time.

In a Thermo flask, hot liquids remain hot and cold liquids remain cold. Vacuum is a bad conductor of heat. Vacuum is used between the walls of the thermos flask to reduce loss of heat through convection and conduction.

As a result presence of the vacuum between the walls of the thermos flask helps in maintaining the liquid at an optimum temperature for long hours without much of a change.

25(B). Concept:

Temperature can be measured in three different units Fahrenheit, Celsius, and Kelvin. $°F$, $°C$, and K are used to represent Fahrenheit, Celsius, and Kelvin units respectively. There are different formulae for their conversions.

Calculation:

In the given problem temperature is given in $°F$. It has to covert in $°C$. The formula for this conversion is,

$$°C = \frac{5}{9}(°F - 32)$$

$$T°C = \frac{5}{9}(140°F - 32) = 0.556 \times 108$$

$$T°C = 60°C$$

Temperature $140°F$ is $60°C$ on a Celsius scale.

26(B). The entropy of an isolated system continuously decreases and becomes a minimum at the state of equilibrium.

If an isolated system's entropy differs from some parameter, then that parameter has a certain value that maximizes the entropy.

27(C). Isothermal dissipation of work and adiabatic dissipation of work exhibit external mechanical Irreversibility.

In the isothermal compression of a gas there is work done on the system to decrease the volume and increase the pressure. The work done in adiabatic process derivation can be derived from the first law of thermodynamics relating to the change in internal energy dU to the work dW done by the system and the heat dQ added to it. The work done dW for the change in volume V by dV is given as PdV.

28(C). If the system is isolated, there is no change in the entropy of the surroundings and $\Delta S \geq 0$, for an isolated system.

Therefore the entropy of an isolated system either increases or, in the limit, remains constant. The equality sign holds good when the process undergone by the system is reversible, the inequality sign holds good if there is any irreversibility present in the process. This statement is usually called the principle of entropy increase.

Irreversible or spontaneous processes can occur only in that direction for which the entropy of the universe or that of an isolated system, increases. These processes cannot occur in the direction of decreasing entropy.

For an isolated system,

- $\Delta S < 0$, for irreversible processes
- $\Delta S = 0$, for reversible processes
- $\Delta S > 0$, the process is impossible

But for reversible process, $\Delta S = 0$ (i.e. entropy remains constant.)

29(A). Brewster Law,

$$\tan i_p = \mu$$

But $\mu \propto \dfrac{1}{\lambda}$

$$\therefore \tan i_p \propto \frac{1}{\lambda}$$

Where i_p, μ and λ are angle of polarisation (incidence), refractive index of material and wavelength of light respectively. Thus, from Brewster's law of polarisation, it follows that the angle of polarisation depends upon the wavelength of light.

30(B). CONCEPT:

Simple Harmonic Motion (SHM): Simple harmonic motion is a special type of periodic motion or oscillation where the restoring force is directly proportional to the displacement and acts in the direction opposite to that of displacement.

- Example: Motion of an undamped pendulum, undamped spring-mass system.

The speed of a transverse wave on a stretched string is given by:

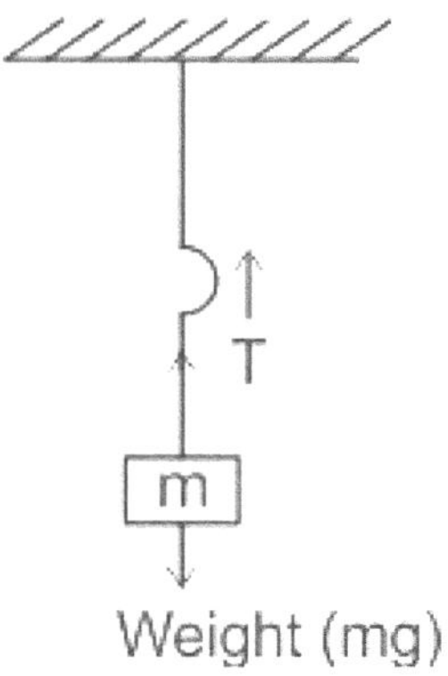

$$v = \sqrt{\frac{T}{\mu}}$$

Where

v = the velocity of the wave,

T = the tension in the string;

μ = mass per unit length.

EXPLANATION:

The speed of transverse waves on a stretched string is given by

$$v = \sqrt{\frac{T}{\mu}}$$

31(A). Longitudinal wave motion is that wave motion in which individual particles of the medium execute simple harmonic motion about their mean position along the same direction, in which the wave is propagated.

It travels in the form of compression (C) and rarefaction (R).

Compression is a region of the medium in which particles are compressed i.e. particles come closer i.e. distance between the particles becomes less than normal distance between them.

Thus, there is a temporary decrease in volume and consequently a temporary increase in pressure in the medium in the region of compression.

32(A). If n_1 and n_2 are the frequency of two sources, then the difference in frequencies of two sources
$\Rightarrow m = (n_1 - n_2)$ or $(n_2 - n_1)$
Where m = beat frequency
CALCULATION:
Given – m = 4, n_1 = 200 Hz and n_2 = x
The beat frequency can be calculated as
$\Rightarrow m = (n_1 \pm n_2)$
$\Rightarrow x = 200 - 4 = 196$ HZ
$\Rightarrow m = (n_2 - n_1)$
$\Rightarrow x = 200 + 4 = 204$ HZ

33(C). The types of sound waves whose frequencies are higher than the upper audible limit of human hearing are called ultrasound. The sound frequency of ultrasonic waves is above 20,000Hz. Thus option (A) is correct.
Ultrasounds can be used to detect cracks and flaws in metal blocks. Thus, option (B) is correct.
The frequency range of infrared waves is below 20Hz. Thus option (C) is incorrect.
Ultrasound is generally used to clean parts located in hard-to-reach places. Thus option (D) is correct.

34(C). Given:
$\theta = 60°, E = 10^5 NC^{-1}, T = 8\sqrt{3} Nm$
Electric field strength $= E = [\dfrac{T}{(P \sin \theta)}]$

Where P is dipole moment
$\therefore 10^5 = [\dfrac{(8\sqrt{3})}{(P \sin 60°)}]$
$\therefore P = \left[\dfrac{(8\sqrt{3})}{\{(\sqrt{3}/2)\times 10^5\}}\right] = 16 \times 10^{-5} c - m$
As $P = q \cdot (2\ell)$
Here 2ℓ = length of dipole $= 2 \times 10^{-2}$ m
$\therefore q = (\dfrac{P}{2\ell})$
$= \left[\dfrac{(16 \times 10^{-5})}{(2 \times 10^{-2})}\right] = 8 \times 10^{-3} c$

35(A). Given:
$m_E = 5.9 \times 10^{24} Kg$
$G = 6.626 \times 10^{-11} Nm^2 Kg^{-2}$
$m_M = 7.9 \times 10^{22} Kg$
$K = 9 \times 10^9 Nm^2 C^{-2}$
$F_G = \dfrac{Gm_E m_M}{r^2}$
$F_e = \dfrac{Kq^2}{r^2}$
$\therefore \dfrac{Kq^2}{r^2} = \dfrac{Gm_E m_M}{r^2}$
$q^2 = \dfrac{Gm_E m_M}{K} =$
$\dfrac{6.626 \times 10^{-11} \times 5.9 \times 10^{24} \times 7.9 \times 10^{22}}{9 \times 10^9}$
$q^2 = 34.31 \times 10^{26}$
$q = 5.86 \times 10^{13} C$

36(C). Given:
$q_1 = 10\mu C, q_2 = 10\mu C, q_3 = -2\mu C$
$r_{13} = 20$ cm $= 0.2$ m
$r_{12} = 5$ cm $= 0.05$ m
$r_{23} = 15$ cm $= 0.15$ m
$r'_{13} = 5\sqrt{2}$ m; $r'_{12} = 0.05$ m
$r'_{23} = \sqrt{15^2 + 5^2} = \sqrt{225 + 25} = \sqrt{250}$
$r'_{23} = 5\sqrt{10} \times 10^{-2}$ m
Initial Potential Energy,
$U_i = \dfrac{1}{4\pi\varepsilon_0}\left[\dfrac{q_1 q_2}{r_{12}} + \dfrac{q_2 q_3}{r_{23}} + \dfrac{q_1 q_3}{r_{13}}\right]$

$= 9 \times 10^9$
$\left[\dfrac{10\times 10^{-6}\times(-2\times 10^{-6})}{0.05} + \dfrac{(-2\times 10^{-6}\times 10\times 10^{-6})}{0.15}\right.$
$\left. + \dfrac{10\times 10^{-6}\times 10\times 10^{-6}}{0.2}\right]$
$= 9 \times 10^9$
$\left[\dfrac{-20\times 10^{-12}}{5\times 10^{-2}} + \dfrac{(-20\times 10^{-12})}{15\times 10^{-2}} + \dfrac{100\times 10^{-12}}{20\times 10^{-2}}\right]$
$= 9 \times 10^9 \left[-4 \times 10^{-10} - \dfrac{4}{3} \times 10^{-10} + 5 \times 10^{-10}\right]$
$= 9 \times 10^9 \left[\dfrac{(-12-4+15)}{3} \times 10^{-10}\right]$
$= 3 \times 10^9 \times [-1 \times 10^{-10}]$
$U_i = -0.3$ J
Final potential Energy
$U_F = \dfrac{1}{4\pi\varepsilon_0}\left[\dfrac{q_1 q_2}{r'_{12}} + \dfrac{q_2 q_3}{r'_{23}} + \dfrac{q_1 q_3}{r'_{13}}\right]$
$= 9 \times 10^9$
$\left[\dfrac{10\times 10^{-6}\times(-2\times 10^{-6})}{\sqrt{2}\times 5\times 10^{-2}} + \dfrac{(-2\times 10^{-6}\times 10\times 10^{-6})}{5\sqrt{10}\times 10^{-2}}\right.$
$\left.\right]$
$+ \dfrac{10\times 10^{-6}\times 10\times 10^{-6}}{20\times 10^{-2}}$
$U_F = 9 \times [0.0908]$
$U_F = 0.8172$ J
$\therefore$ Workdone $= U_F - U_i = -0.8172 - (0.3)$
W = 1.1172 J
A positive sign indicates that external work is required to move $-2\mu C$ charge from a to b.
$\Delta U = -3.246$ J , the negative sign implies that to move the charge $-2\mu C$ no external work is required. The system spends its stored energy to move the charge from point a to point b.

37(C). Given:
Charge on an alpha particle $q_1 = q_2 = +2e$
Distance between the particles $(r) = 3.2 \times 10^{-15}$ m
We know that:
Charge on an electron $(e) = 1.6 \times 10^{-19}$
$\dfrac{1}{4\pi\epsilon_0} = 9 \times 10^9$
Now, using coulomb's law, Force acting on the particles is given by,
$F = \dfrac{1}{4\pi\epsilon_0}\dfrac{q_1 q_2}{r^2}$
Put all the given values in above formula:
$F = \dfrac{9\times 10^9 \times 2\times 1.6\times 10^{-19}\times 2\times 1.6\times 10^{-19}}{3.2\times 10^{-15}\times 3.2\times 10^{-15}}$
$F = 90 N$

38(D). Given:
A point charge of 10^{-7} coulomb is situated at the center of a cube of 1 m side.

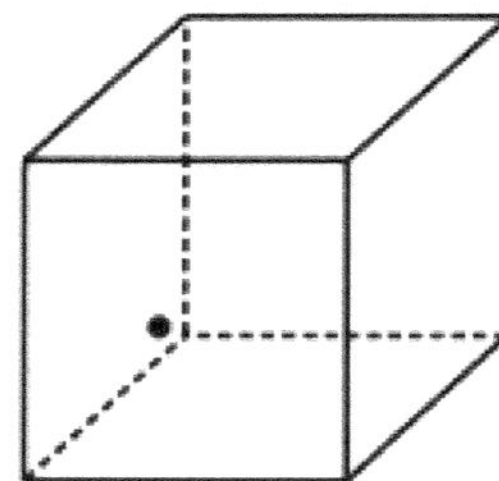

Electric flux through the surfaces of cube
$= \dfrac{\text{charge enclosed}}{\epsilon_0}$
$= \dfrac{10^{-7}}{8.854\times 10^{-12}}$
$= 1.13 \times 10^4 Nm^2 C^{-1}$

39(B). Given,
Corner of a side of a square $= 93\ mm$

$\therefore a = 93 \times 10^{-3}$

Potential at a point P = Potential at a point Q_1+ Potential at a point Q_2+ Potential at a point Q_3.

$$V = \frac{1}{4\pi\varepsilon_0}\left(\frac{Q_1}{r_1} + \frac{Q_2}{r_2} + \frac{Q_3}{r_3}\right)$$

$$= \frac{1}{4\pi\varepsilon_0}\left(\frac{33 \times 10^{-9}}{93 \times 10^{-3}} - \frac{51 \times 10^{-9}}{\sqrt{2} \times 93 \times 10^{-3}} + \frac{47 \times 10^{-9}}{93 \times 10^{-3}}\right)$$

$$= \frac{1}{4\pi\varepsilon_0} \times \frac{10^{-9}}{93 \times 10^{-3}}\left(33 - \frac{51}{\sqrt{2}} + 47\right)$$

$$\approx 4 \times 1000 \text{ V}$$

$$= 4\text{kV}$$

40(D). The electric field of a hollow spherical capacitor is localized in between the inner and outer surfaces of the spherical conductor. Therefore, at point $r_1 < r < r_2$, the electric field will not be zero.

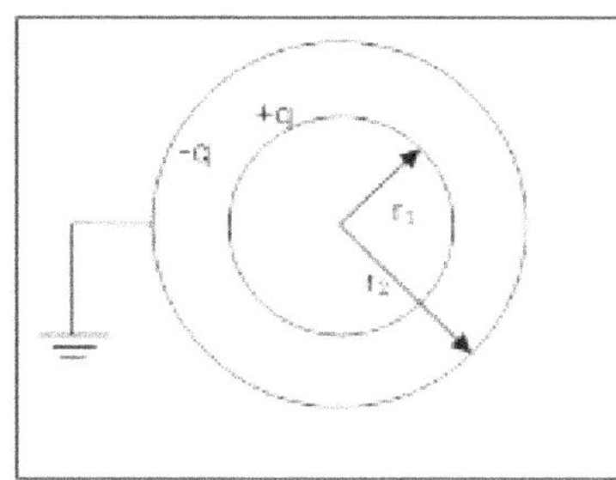

41(C). At the steady-state, the current through the capacitor is zero

Since the capacitor behaves as an open circuit, then the current through r_1 is 0 , therefore

Current through the circuit is given by

$$I = \frac{E}{r+r_2},\ldots\ldots(1)$$

Now calculate the voltage across the capacitor V_C and remove resistance r_1 since no current flows through it.

The voltage across the capacitor is obtained by

$$V_C = I \cdot r_2 - - - (\text{ From } 1)$$

$$V_C = \left(\frac{E}{r+r_2}\right)r_2$$

$$V_C = \frac{Er_2}{r+r_2} - - - -(2)$$

Use the formula $Q = CV$ to find the charge stored in the capacitor $Q = CV_C - - - (\text{ From } 2)$

$$Q = C \cdot \frac{Er_2}{r+r_2}$$

$$= CE\left(\frac{r_2}{r+r_2}\right)$$

42(D). The given circuit can be split into 3 loops , loop 1 consisting of two 2V source and 1 ohm resistor and the second loop consisting of two 2V source and two 1 ohm resistors and the final loop similar as the second loop.

To identify the current at each loop we can use Kirchhoff's Voltage rule and grounding method.

Applying KVL at node 1,

Now, current at loop1 is assumed as i_1 , current at loop2 is assumed as i_2 and current at loop3 is assumed as i_3 .

$$2 - 2 + (i_1 - i_2) \times 1 = 0$$

$$\Rightarrow i_1 = i_2$$

Applying KVL at node 2 ,

$$2 + ((i_1 - i_2) \times 1) - 2 + ((i_2 - i_3) \times 1) = 0$$

Since, $i_1 = i_2$

$$2 - 2 + ((i_2 - i_3) \times 1) = 0$$

$$\Rightarrow i_2 = i_3$$

Applying KVL at loop 3 ,

$$2 + ((i_2 - i_3) \times 1) - 2 + (i_3 \times 1) = 0$$

Since $i_2 = i_3$

$$\Rightarrow 2 - 2 + (i_3 \times 1) = 0$$

$$\Rightarrow i_3 = 0$$

Therefore since $i_2 = i_3$, the value of $i_2 = 0$

And since the value of $i_1 = i_2$

The current value in loop 1 is also equal to 0 .

It is found that the value of current across all the resistors to be zero.

43(A). According to Ohm's law

$$V = IR$$

Where, V is the potential difference across the circuit, I is the current through the circuit and R is the resistance of the circuit.

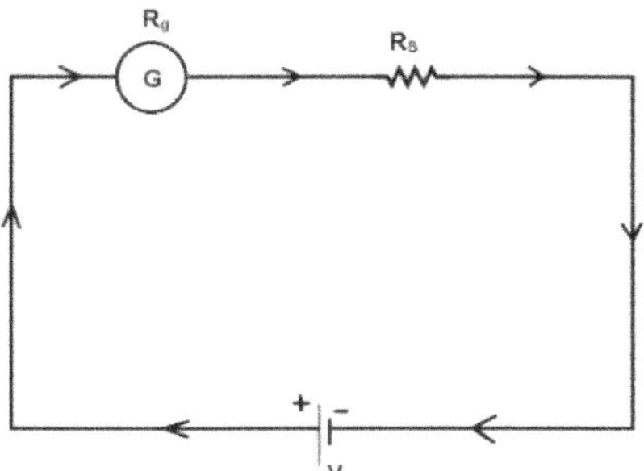

Here,

$V = 10\ V$

$I = I_g = 5\ mA = 5 \times 10^{-3}\ A$

$R_g = 15\Omega$

Now,

R_g and R_S are in series.

Thus, the total resistance will be $(R_g + R_S)$.

Now,

$V = I_g\left(R_g + R_S\right)$

Putting in the values, we get

$10 = \left(5 \times 10^{-3}\right)(15 + R_S)$

Further, we get

$15 + R_S = \dfrac{10}{5 \times 10^{-3}}$

Also, we get

$15 + R_S = 2 \times 10^3$

$R_S = 2000 - 15$

$R_S = 1985\Omega = 1.985 \times 10^3\Omega$

44(B). A Wheatstone bridge is an electrical circuit used to measure an unknown electrical resistance by balancing two legs of a bridge circuit, one leg of which includes the unknown component. The primary benefit of the circuit is its ability to provide extremely accurate measurements Its operation is similar to the original potentiometer.

A galvanometer is an electromechanical measuring instrument for electric current. Early galvanometers were uncalibrated, but improved versions, called ammeters, were calibrated and could measure the flow of current more precisely.

In a balanced Wheatstone bridge, there is no effect on the position of the null point, we exchange the battery and galvanometer.

The balanced condition is given by $\dfrac{P}{Q} = \dfrac{R}{S}$; When battery and Galvanometer are exchanged, it become $\dfrac{P}{R} = \dfrac{Q}{S}$

45(A). Let us consider an elementary ring of radius r and thickness dr in which current I is flowing.

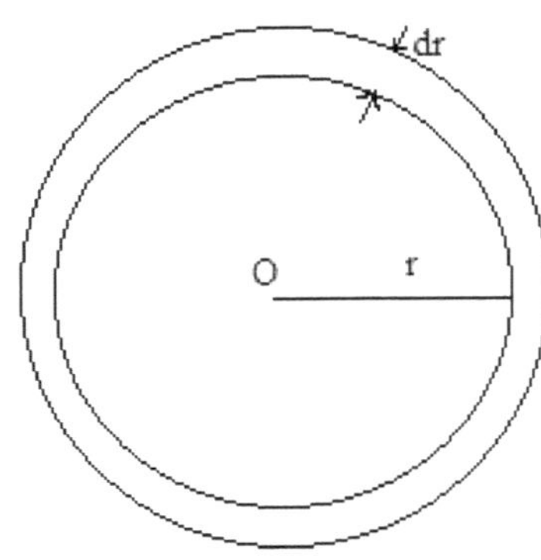

Number of turns in this elementary ring

$$dN = \frac{N}{b-a} dr$$

We know that the magnetic field at the centre of a ring is given by:

$$B = \frac{\mu_0 N I}{2r}$$

Where,

μ_0 is the permeability of free space.

N is the number of terms.

L is currently flowing.

r is the radius of the ring.

Thus magnetic field at the centre O due to this ring

$$dB = \frac{\mu_0 dN I}{2r}$$

Putting the value of dN, we get:

$$dB = \frac{\mu_0 N I dr}{2(b-a)r}$$

To get the net magnetic field at the centre of the spiral, we will integrate the above equation from 'a' to 'b'.

$$\int_0^B dB = \int_a^b \frac{\mu_0 N I dr}{2(b-a)r} = \frac{\mu_0 N I}{2(b-a)} \int_a^b \frac{dr}{r} = \frac{\mu_0 N I}{2(b-a)}$$

$$[\ln r]_a^b$$

$$\Rightarrow B = \frac{\mu_0 N I}{2(b-a)} \ln \frac{b}{a}$$

Therefore, the required magnetic field is

$$\Rightarrow B = \frac{\mu_0 N I}{2(b-a)} \ln \frac{b}{a}$$

46(C). The particular intensity of the magnetic field at which the magnet is demagnetized is called the coercivity of the magnet.

The coercivity of the magnet can be written as

$$H = \frac{B}{\mu_0}$$

For a solenoid, the magnetic field will be,

$$B = \mu_0 n I$$

where B is the magnetic field, n is the number of turns per unit length, μ_0 is the permeability of free space, and I is the current through each turn,

$$\therefore \frac{B}{\mu_0} = H = nI$$

The coercivity of the small magnet is given by,

$$H = 3 \times 10^3 \, Am^{-1}$$

The length of the solenoid is given by,

$$L = 10 \text{ cm} = 0.1 \text{ m}$$

The number of turns of the solenoid is given by,

$$N = 100$$

The number of turns per unit length can be written as,

$$n = \frac{100}{0.1}$$

From this we get,

$$I = \frac{H}{n}$$

It is given that, $H = 3 \times 10^3 Am^{-1}$ and $n = \frac{100}{0.1}$

Substituting the values in the above equation, we get

$$I = \frac{3 \times 10^3}{\frac{100}{0.1}} = \frac{300}{100} = 3A$$

Therefore the current required to be passed in a solenoid of length 10 cm and number of turns 100, so that the magnet gets demagnetized when inside the solenoid is $3A$.

47(C). Given:

m = mass of the electron, q = e (charge on the electron), r = radius, v = speed, and B = magnetic field

When the velocity of a charged particle is perpendicular to a magnetic field, it describes a circle and the radius of the circle is given by:

$$r = \frac{mv}{qB} \quad \text{......(1)}$$

$$r = \frac{mv}{eB}$$

$$\Rightarrow \frac{e}{m} = \frac{v}{rB}$$

48(A). We know that the magnetic field intensity at a distance r on the equatorial line of the bar magnet is given as,

$$B = \frac{\mu_o}{4\pi} \frac{m \times 2l}{(r^2+l^2)^{\frac{3}{2}}} \quad \text{.....(1)}$$

Where, μ = permeability, m = pole strength, and $2l$ = length of the magnet

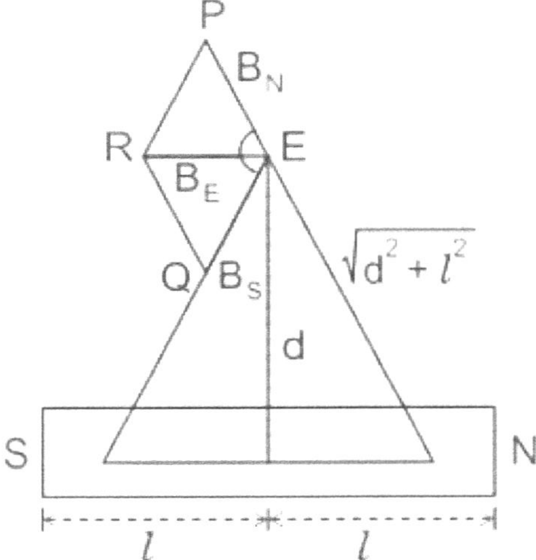

When the magnet is cut long its width in two equal parts, its pole strength becomes half.

So, the pole strength of each part will be,

$$m' = \frac{m}{2} \quad \text{.....(2)}$$

So, the magnetic field intensity at a distance r on the equatorial line of any part of the bar magnet is given as,

$$B' = \frac{\mu_o}{4\pi} \frac{m' \times 2l}{(r^2+l^2)^{\frac{3}{2}}}$$

$$= \frac{\mu_o}{4\pi} \frac{m \times 2l}{2(r^2+l^2)^{\frac{3}{2}}}$$

$$= \frac{1}{2} \times \frac{\mu_o}{4\pi} \frac{m \times 2l}{(r^2+l^2)^{\frac{3}{2}}}$$

$$= \frac{B}{2}$$

49(C). Given:

velocity of beam of proton $= 4 \times 10^5 \, ms^{-1}$

mass of proton $= 1.67 \times 10^{-27} \, kg$

angle of magnetic field $= 60°$

As we know,

When a charged particle is projected at an angle θ to a magnetic field, the component of velocity parallel to the field is $v\cos\theta$ while perpendicular to the field is $v\sin\theta$, so the particle will move in a circle of radius

$$r = \frac{m(v\sin\theta)}{qB}$$

$$= \frac{(1.67\times10^{-27})\times(4\times10^5\times\sin 60°)}{1.6\times10^{-19}\times0.3}$$

$$= \frac{(1.67\times10^{-27})\times\left(4\times10^5\times\frac{\sqrt{3}}{2}\right)}{1.6\times10^{-19}\times0.3}$$

$$= \frac{2\times10^{-2}}{\sqrt{3}}$$

Time period: $T = \frac{2\pi r}{v\sin\theta}$

$$= \frac{2\pi\times\frac{2\times10^{-2}}{\sqrt{3}}}{4\times10^5\times\sin 60^0}$$

$$= \frac{2\pi\times\frac{2\times10^{-2}}{\sqrt{3}}}{4\times10^5\times\frac{\sqrt{3}}{2}}$$

$$= \frac{2\pi}{3}\times10^{-7}$$

Pitch: $P = v\cos\theta T$

$$= (4\times10^5)\times\cos 60^0\times\frac{2\pi}{3}\times10^{-7}$$

$$= \frac{4\pi}{3}\times10^{-2}$$

$$= 4.35\times10^{-2}\text{ m}$$

$$= 4\text{ cm}$$

50(A). Given,

susceptibility (γ_m) = 599

We know that,

$(\mu_r) = 1 + (\gamma_m)$

So, $\mu_r = 599 + 1 = 600$

Now,

permeability of the material of the rod (μ) is $= \mu_0\mu_r$

$\mu = 600\times4\pi\times10^{-7}$

$= 2.4\pi\times10^{-4}\text{TmA}^{-1}$

51(A). Given,

The mass of the iron nucleus = 55.85 u

The mass number of the iron, A = 56

Where,

$r_0 = 1.2\times10^{-15}$ m

And A is the mass number of the nucleus.

Substitute the given values in the above equation to find the value of the nucleus of the iron. we get,

$r_0 = 1.2\times10^{-15}m$

According to Rutherford's relation, the radius of the nucleus is given by the formula,

$r' = r_0\times A^{\frac{1}{3}}$

$r' = 1.2\times10^{-15}\times(56)^{\frac{1}{3}}$

$\Rightarrow r' = 1.2\times10^{-15}\times 3.8258$

$\Rightarrow r' = 4.59\times10^{-15}$ m

Therefore, the value of the nucleus of the iron is 4.59×10^{-15} m.

Now compute the value of the mass of the iron nucleus. We know that,

$1U = 1.67\times10^{-27}$ kg

Therefore, the mass of the iron nucleus is,

$= 55.85\times1.67\times10^{-27}$ kg

$= 9.327\times10^{-26}$ kg

Finally, compute the nuclear density of the iron nucleus. The density is given by the formula,

$\rho = \frac{m}{V}$

Where m is the mass and V is the volume.

The volume is given by the formula,

$V = \frac{4}{3}\pi r^3$

Where r is the radius of the nucleus.

Substitute the values in the above equation to find the value of the density of the iron nucleus. we get,

$\rho = \frac{m}{V}$

$\Rightarrow \rho = \frac{m}{\frac{4}{3}\pi(r')^3}$

$\Rightarrow \rho = \frac{9.372\times10^{-26}}{\frac{4}{3}\times\frac{22}{7}\times(4.59\times10^{-15})^3}$

$\Rightarrow \rho = 2.3\times10^{17}\text{ kg/m}^3$

The nuclear density of the iron nucleus is $2.29\times10^{17}\text{ kg/m}^3$.

52(A). Given,

1 amu $= 1.66\times10^{27}$ kg

C = Speed of light $= 3\times10^8$ m/s

$E = mC^2$

$= 1.66\times10^{27}(3\times10^8)^2$

$= 1.49\times10^{-10}$ J

1 meV $= 1.6\times10^{-13}$ J

$E = \frac{1.49\times10^{-10}}{1.6\times10^{-13}} = 931.6$ MeV

O_8^{16} = Mass number = 16

Energy for 16 amu $= 16\times931.6$

$= 14905.6$ MeV

Mass defect $= \frac{\text{Energy}}{C^2}$

$= 14905.6\text{ MeV}/C^2$

53(D). On the basis of dual nature of light, Louis de Broglie suggested that the dual nature is not only of light, but each moving material particle has the dual nature. He assumed a wave to be associated with each moving material particle which is called the matter wave. The wavelength of this wave is determined by the momentum of the particle.

If, p is the momentum of the particle, the wavelength of the wave associated with it is,

$\lambda = \frac{h}{p}$

Where, h is the Planck's constant.

Since, it is given that, alpha, beta and gamma rays carry the same momentum, so, they will have the same wavelength.

54(B). We know the relation $d = \frac{[P\times M]}{RT}$. So by using this we can draw the relation given below:

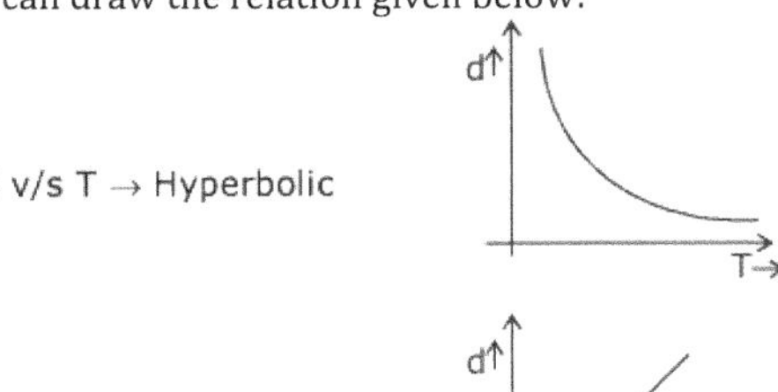

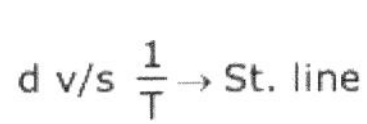

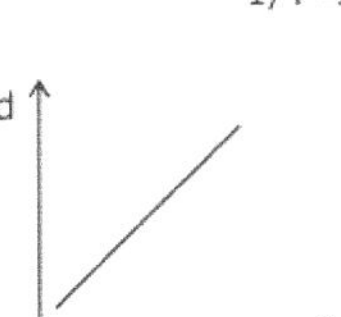

$\therefore$ Graph II is incorrect.

55(C). The internal energy of the system is the measure of its kinetic energy. Kinetic energy is different for different gas molecules. It is different for monoatomic gas while it is different for diatomic gas. The internal energy of a gas is given by:

$$U = n\frac{f}{2}RT$$

where n = no. of moles
f = degree of freedom
T = temperature
R = universal gas constant
Moles of oxygen= 3
Moles of argon=5
Oxygen is a diatomic gas and for a diatomic molecule:
Degree of freedom of translational motion of a diatomic molecule = 3
Degree of freedom of rotational motion = 2
Total degrees of freedom = 5

$$\Rightarrow U_{\text{oxygen}} = 3\frac{5}{2}RT$$

$$\Rightarrow U_{\text{oxygen}} = \frac{15}{2}RT$$

Argon is monoatomic gas and for a monatomic gas:
Degree of freedom of translational motion= 3
Degree of freedom of rotational motion=0
Total degrees of freedom=3

$$\Rightarrow U_{\text{argon}} = 5\frac{3}{2}RT$$

$$\Rightarrow U_{argon} = \frac{15}{2}RT$$

The internal energy will be the summation of the two internal energies.

$$\Rightarrow U_{\text{system}} = U_{\text{oxygen}} + U_{\text{argon}}$$

$$\Rightarrow U_{\text{system}} = \frac{15}{2}RT + \frac{15}{2}RT$$

$$\therefore U_{\text{system}} = 15RT$$

56(C). Given $P - V$ diagram

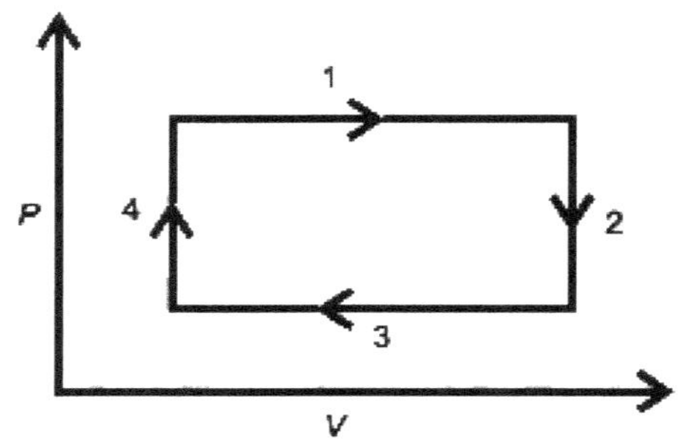

Process-1
P = constant, Volume increases and temperature also increases
$\Rightarrow W$ = positive, ΔU = positive
$\Rightarrow$ Heat is positive and supplied to gas
Process -2
V = constant, Pressure decrease
$\Rightarrow$ Temperature decreases
$W = \int pdV = 0$
ΔT is negative and $\Delta U = \frac{f}{2}nR\Delta T$
$\Rightarrow \Delta U$ in negative
$\Delta Q = \Delta U + W$
$\therefore \Delta Q \rightarrow$ Heat is negative and rejected by gas
Process-3
P = constant, Volume decreases
$\Rightarrow$ Temperature also decreases
$W = P\Delta V$ = negative
$\Delta U = \frac{f}{2}nR\Delta T$ = negative
$\Delta Q = W + \Delta U$ = negative
Heat is negative and rejected by gas.
Process-4
V = constant, Pressure increases
$W = \int pdV = 0$
$PV = nRT \Rightarrow$ Temperature increase

$\Rightarrow \Delta U = \frac{f}{2}nRAT$ is positive

57(B). Given:
Weight of water $= 4.5\ Kg$
When intermolecular forces vanish, we know the liquid is changed to liquid vapours.
Molecular mass of water vapours $= 18g = 18 \times 10^{-3}Kg$
We know that volume occupied by one mole of water at STP $= 22.4$ litre $= 22.4 \times 10^{-3}m^3$
$\therefore$ The volume occupied by $4.5Kg$ of water molecules is: $\dfrac{\text{Weight of water}}{\text{Molecular mass of water}}$

$$= \frac{22.4\times10^{-3}\times4.5}{18\times10^{-3}} = 5.6m^3$$

58(A). Given circuit is equivalent to an AND gate.
$\therefore$

A	B	Y
0	0	0
0	1	0
1	0	0
1	1	1

59(D). p -type semiconductor is obtained by doping an intrinsic semiconductor with trivalent impurity. The p stands for Positive, which means the semiconductor is rich in holes or Positive charged ions. When we dope intrinsic material with Pentavalent impurities we get n -Type semiconductor, where n stands for Negative.

60(D). The potential difference across PQ
i.e., potential difference across the resistance of 20Ω which is $V = i \times 20$

$$i = \frac{48}{100+100+80+20}$$
$$= 0.16 \text{ A}$$
$$V = 0.16 \times 20$$
$$= 3.2 \text{ V}$$

61(A). Here we have used concept of AND, and NAND gate concepts.

If two inputs A, B are connected in And gate then the output can be written as: $Y = A.B \ \cdots (1)$

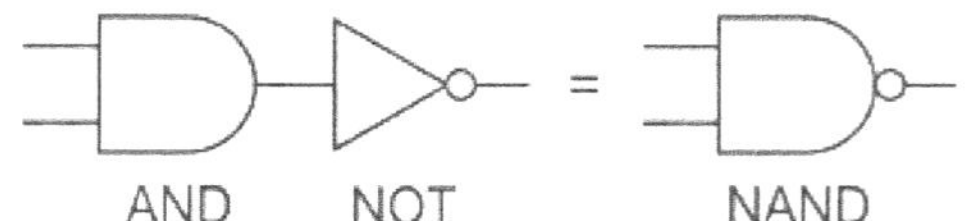

In the case of the NAND gate when we connect two inputs A and b then output is: $Y = \overline{A \cdot B} \ \cdots (2)$
Given:

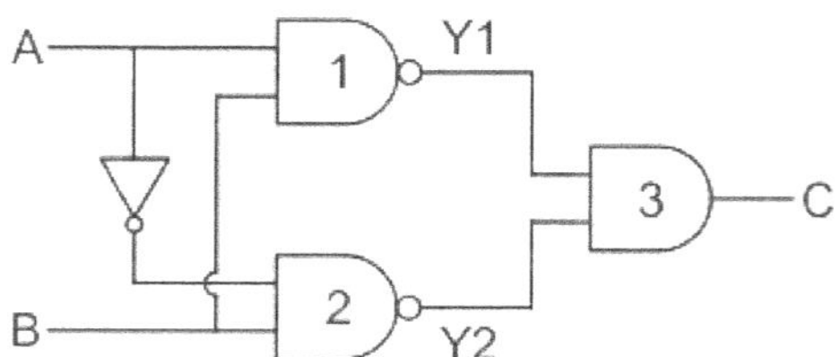

Here in this circuit, we have labeled it as $1, 2, 3$ part of circuit having outputs $Y1, Y2$, and C.
$Y1$ = solution of first two input NAND gate, $Y2 =$

solution of second two input NAND gate

$C =$ solution of third AND gate connecting both NAND gates as two inputs From the circuit diagram, we can see that $Y1 = \overline{A.B}$ $\cdots (3)$

And $Y2 = \overline{\bar{A} \cdot B}$ $\cdots (4)$

Here output

$C = \overline{Y2 \cdot Y1} = \overline{\overline{\bar{A} \cdot B} \cdot \overline{\bar{A} \cdot B}} = \bar{A} \cdot B + AB$ (By De Morgan's theorem)

This can be written as: $(\bar{A} + A)B = \bar{1} + \bar{B} = \bar{B}$ (Where $A + \bar{A} = 1$)

So, we can write the truth table as $C = \bar{B}$

When $B = 0$ then $C = 1$, $B = 1$ then $C = 0$ so that solution is completely independent on A.

So, the truth table is:

A	B	C
0	0	1
0	1	0
1	0	1
1	1	0

62(A). Concept:
- If a wire is under force, there will be an increase or decrease in length due to the developed stress and strain in it.
- Stress is calculated by Force (F) divided by the cross-section area (A) on which it is applied.
- Stress $= \dfrac{F}{A}$
- The strain is the change in length of wire (x) divided by the original length (L) of the wire.
- Strain $= \dfrac{x}{L}$
- Hook's Law of elasticity Young's modulus $= \dfrac{stress}{strain}$

$$\Rightarrow Y = \dfrac{Fl}{A\Delta l}$$

Where $F =$ Force applied, $A =$ area of cross-section, $I =$ original length and $\Delta I =$ change in length

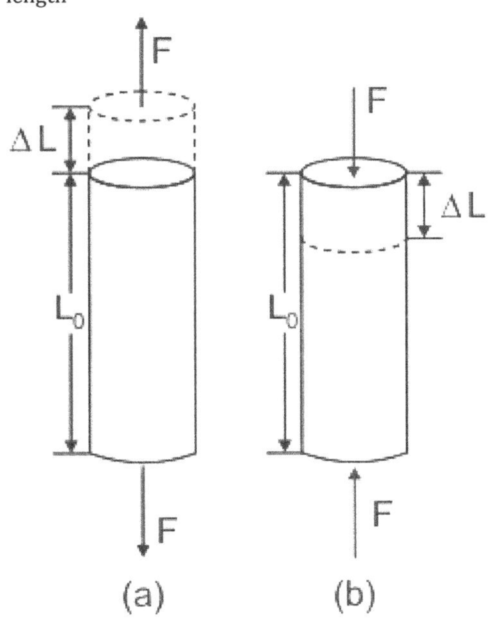

Given

Area $(A) = 1 \text{ cm}^2 = 10^{-4} \text{ m}^2$, $L_1 = I, L_2 = 2I$

$\Delta I = L_2 - L_1 = I$

As we know, the Young modulus is

$$\Rightarrow Y = \dfrac{Fl}{A\Delta l}$$
$$\Rightarrow F = \dfrac{YA\Delta l}{l}$$
$$\Rightarrow F = \dfrac{2\times10^{11}\times10^{-4}\times l}{l} = 2 \times 10^7 \text{ N}$$

63(B). Given that:

Force /load (F) on both the wires is the same.

Let the cross-sectional area of wire B is equal to A. Cross-sectional area of wire A $(A_1) = 2\times$ Cross-sectional area of wire B $(A_2) = 2A$

Stress on wire $A(S) = \dfrac{\text{Force } (F)}{\text{Area of wires } A(A_1)} = \dfrac{F}{2A}$

Stress on wire $B(S') = \dfrac{\text{Force } (F)}{\text{Area of wires } B(A_2)} = \dfrac{F}{A}$

On dividing equations 1 and 2, we get

$$\Rightarrow \dfrac{\text{Stress on wire } A(S)}{\text{Stress on wire } B(S')} = \dfrac{1}{2}$$

$\Rightarrow$ Stress on wire B $(S') = 2\times$ Stress on wire $A(S)$

64(C). The motion is accelerated, or velocity is changing, which means either speed or direction is changing or both are changing.
- A body is travelling in a straight line and the motion is accelerated.
- So, the direction is not changing and hence speed is changing.
- Now, an example of such kind of motion can be a free fall, where the object is just dropped with zero initial velocity and hence it is acted upon by g, acceleration due to the gravity of the earth.
- It is falling toward earth.
- So, the statement 'It always goes away from the earth' is wrong.
- Also, if there is acceleration, there is unbalanced force, so the statement 'A force is acting on it is the correct statement.

So, the correct option here is 'It always goes away from the earth'.

65(B). Concept:

Equation of motion: The mathematical equations used to find the final velocity, displacements, time, etc of a moving object without considering force acting on it are called equations of motion.

These equations are only valid when the acceleration of the body is constant and they move on a straight line.

There are three equations of motion:

$V = u + at$

$V^2 = u^2 + 2aS$

$S = ut + \dfrac{1}{2}at^2$

Where, $V =$ final velocity, $u =$ initial velocity, $s =$ distance traveled by the body under motion, $a =$ acceleration of body under motion, and $t =$ time taken by the body under motion.

Given that:

Initial velocity (u) $= 0$

Distance (S) $= 20 \text{ m}$

Time (t) $= 4\text{sec}$

Use $S = ut + \dfrac{1}{2}at^2$

$20 = 0 + \dfrac{1}{2} \times a \times 4^2$

Acceleration $= a = \dfrac{20}{8} = 2.5 \text{ m/s}^2$

66(C). Rain drops are spherical because of surface tension forces.

- The property of a fluid due to which it opposes the relative motion between its different layers is called viscosity (or fluid friction or internal friction). Therefore option (A) is incorrect.
- A small liquid drop has a spherical shape, as due to surface tension the liquid surface tries to have the minimum surface area and for a given volume, the sphere has a minimum surface area. Therefore option (C) is correct.

67(B). A fluid is one which can be defined as a substance that can deform indefinitely under the action of smallest shear force.
- Substance in liquid or gaseous phase is called fluid.
- They are capable of deforming continuously under the action of shear stress.
- In case of fluid, stress is proportional to strain rate.
- Fluids flow under the action of shear (tangential) forces. That is, they do not resist the shear stresses as solids do.

68(B). In the isothermal condition, the isothermal bulk modulus of an ideal gas is equal to pressure.
Compressibility is the reciprocal of the bulk modulus of elasticity.
Compressibility $(p) = \frac{1}{K}$, and K = bulk modulus of Elasticity
$$K = \frac{\text{Increase of pressure}}{\text{Volumetric strain}} = \frac{dP}{\frac{-dv}{v}} = \frac{-dP}{dv} \times V$$
........(i)
For isothermal process:
$\frac{P}{\rho} = \text{Constant} \Rightarrow P \times V = \text{constant}$ .... (ii)
Differentiating equation (ii),
$PdV + Vdp = 0$
$\Rightarrow PdV = -Vdp$
$\Rightarrow P = \frac{-VdP}{dV}$ ....(iii)
From equation (i) & (iii), we have
$K = P$

69(D). Let T = surface tension of the liquid
p = pressure intensity inside the droplet (in excess of the outside pressure intensity).
d = Dia of droplet
r = radius of droplet

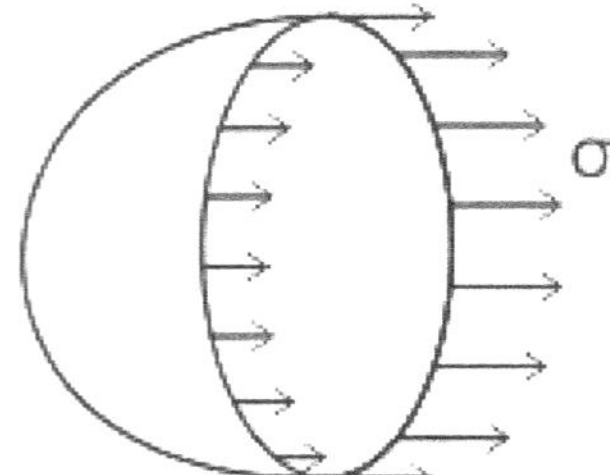

(liquid droplet cat into two halves)
Tensile force due to surface tension $= T \times \pi d$
Pressure force on the area $\frac{\pi}{4} d^2 = p \times \frac{\pi}{4} \times d^2$
From equilibrium conditions:
$T \times d = p \times \frac{\pi}{4} \times d^2$
$p = \frac{4\,T}{d} = \frac{4\,T}{2r} = \frac{2\,T}{r}$
Important Formulas to remember:
Press diff in (a) Hollow bubble $= \frac{4\,T}{r}$
(b) Liquid jet $= \frac{2\,T}{d} = \frac{T}{r}$

70(B). Given that:
Acceleration $(a) = 20 \text{ m/s}^2$

Distance traveled $(S) = 90 \text{ m}$
Initial Velocity $(u) = 0$
To find the time taken (t) to cover 90 m .
Equation of motion states that:
$S = ut + \frac{1}{2}at^2$
$90 = 0 \times t + \frac{1}{2} \times 20 \times t^2$
$t^2 = 9$
Time taken $(t) = 3 \text{ sec}$

71(D). The slope of an acceleration time graph equals the ratio of change in acceleration for the time interval considered.
Slope $= \frac{\Delta a}{\Delta t}$ = rate of change of acceleration = jerk

72(C). A solar cell is a P-N junction device that converts solar energy into electrical energy.
- Solar Cell works on the principle of photovoltaic effect. The photovoltaic effect is the process of generation of EMF due to the absorption of ionizing radiation from sunlight.
- In solar cells, various types of semiconductor materials are used such as GaAs, CdSe, etc but the most common semiconductor material used is silicon.
- About 90% of solar cells are composed of silicon.
- When two pieces of semiconductor material (silicon) containing N-type and P-type impurities are connected by some means then a P-N junction is created.
- The light energy is converted into electrical energy from the solar cells.

73(B). Given data for the first part density $= \rho_0$ and for the second part density $= 2\rho_0$, and volume is the same for both parts $= v$
Mass of First part $= m_1 = \rho_0 \times v$ ......(1)
Mass of second part $= m_2 = 2\rho_0 \times v \cdots$ (2)
Total volume $= v + v = 2v$ ......(3)
The average density of objects $= \frac{\text{total mass}}{\text{total volume}}$
From equation 1, 2, and 3
$\Rightarrow \rho = \frac{\rho_0 \times v + 2\rho_0 \times v}{2v}$
$\Rightarrow \rho = \frac{3}{2}\rho_0$

74(D). Concept:
According to kinetic energy theory, if we increase the temperature of a gas, it will increase the average kinetic energy of the molecule, which will increase the motion of the molecules.
This increased motion increases the outward pressure of the gas.
The average kinetic energy (KE) or energy (E) of translation per molecules of the gas is related to temperature by the relationship:
$KE = \frac{3}{2}k_B T$ (degree of freedom of a monoatomic gas = 3)
Where KE = kinetic energy, k_B = Boltzmann constant and T = temperature.
The average energy of a molecule is given by:
$KE = E = (\frac{3}{2})k_B T$

75(A). Given,
Distance, $r = 1$ m
Minimum charge on particle
$q_1 = q_2 = ne = 1 \times e = 1.6 \times 10^{-19} \text{C}$
Now, $F_E = K\frac{q_1 q_2}{r^2}$

$$\Rightarrow F_E = 9 \times 10^9 \times \frac{\left(1.6 \times 10^{-19}\right)^2}{1^2}$$

$$\Rightarrow F_E = 2.3 \times 10^{-28} \text{ N}$$

76(B). Diamagnetic materials are repelled by a magnetic field;

- An applied magnetic field creates an induced magnetic field in them in the opposite direction, causing a repulsive force.
- Diamagnetism is a property of all materials, and always makes a weak contribution to the material's response to a magnetic field
- Substances, where the diamagnetic behaviour is the strongest effect, are termed diamagnetic materials, or diamagnets.
- Diamagnetics include water, wood, most organic compounds such as petroleum and some plastics,

77(B). If there is no external torque acting on system then initial angular momentum (L $_{initial}$) of system is equal to final momentum (L $_{final}$).

So, the angular momentum in a closed system is a conserved.

$\therefore I\omega = \text{constant}$

$\Rightarrow I \propto \frac{1}{\omega}$

i.e. Moment of inertia is inversely proportional to the angular velocity.

So, if the moment of inertia of a rotating body is increased then the angular velocity decreases.

78(D). Given that

$V_2 = 3V_1; P_2 = \frac{P_1}{2}; T_1 = 27^\circ\text{C} = 273 + 27 = 300$ $K; T_2 = ?$

Ideal gas equation

$PV = nRT$

$n = \frac{PV}{RT}$

During the whole process, no. of moles will not change. So,

n1 = n2

$$\frac{P_1 V_1}{RT_1} = \frac{P_2 V_2}{RT_2}$$

$$\frac{P_1 V_1}{300R} = \frac{\left(\frac{P_1}{2}\right)(3V_1)}{RT_2}$$

$$\frac{1}{300} = \frac{3}{2T_2}$$

$$T2 = 450 \text{ K} = 450 - 273 = 177^\circ\text{C}$$

79(D). Given:

$T_1 = 227 + 273 = 500 \text{ K}$

$T_2 = 127 + 273 = 400 \text{ K}$

Heat absorbed by the engine is $Q_1 = 6 \times 10^4$ J .

The efficiency of the heat engine is given by:

$$\Rightarrow \eta = \frac{W}{Q_1} = 1 - \frac{T_2}{T_1}$$

$$\Rightarrow \frac{W}{6 \times 10^4} = 1 - \frac{400}{500}$$

$$\Rightarrow \frac{W}{6 \times 10^4} = 1 - \frac{4}{5}$$

$$\Rightarrow \frac{W}{6 \times 10^4} = \frac{1}{5}$$

$$\Rightarrow W = \frac{6 \times 10^4}{5} = 1.2 \times 10^4 \text{ J}$$

80(B). For a diamagnetic material, ϵ_r should have following bounds $0 < \epsilon_r < 1$ and for any material $\epsilon_r > 1$. Diamagnetic materials create an induced magnetic field in a direction opposite to an external applied magnetic field and are repelled by applied magnetic field. Magnetic permeability of the diamagnetic materials is little less than unity.

1. The nearest star to our solar system is 4.29 light-years away. How much is this distance in terms of parsec? How much parallax would this star (named Alpha Centauri) show when viewed from two locations of the Earth six months apart in its orbit around the Sun?
   (a) 1.32 parsec and 1.52 radian
   (b) 2.32 parsec and 2.52 radian
   (c) 3.32 parsec and 3.52 radian
   (d) 4.32 parsec and 4.52 radian

2. The dimensional formula of the coefficient of thermal conductivity is :
   (a) $\left[M^1 L^1 T^{-3} K^{-1}\right]$ (b) $\left[M^3 L^{-1} T^{-3} K\right]$
   (c) $\left[M^1 L^{-3} T^{-1} K^{-1}\right]$ (d) $\left[M^1 L^1 T^{-3} K\right]$

3. Newton-second is the unit of
   (a) Velocity   (b) Angular momentum
   (c) Momentum   (d) Energy

4. Which of the following is not equal to watt
   (a) Joule/second   (b) Ampere $\times$ volt
   (c) (Ampere)$^2 \times$ ohm   (d) Ampere/volt

5. The velocity-time graph of a moving train is depicted in the figure below. The average velocity during time OD was

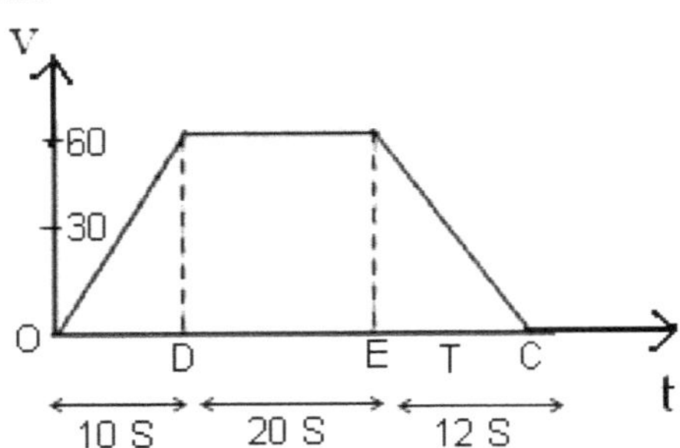

   (a) 30 m/s   (b) 60 m/s
   (c) 45 m/s   (d) 23 m/s

6. Displacement y (in m) of a body varies with time t (in sec) as: $y = \frac{-2}{3}t^2 + 16t + 2$. How long does the body take to come to rest?
   (a) 8 sec (b) 10 sec
   (c) 12 sec (d) 16 sec

7. At $t = 0$, an arrow is fired vertically upwards with a speed of $100 ms^{-1}$. A second arrow is fired vertically upwards with the same speed at $t = 5\ s$. Then,
   (a) The two arrows will be at the same height above the ground at $t = 20\ s$
   (b) The two arrows will reach back to their starting points at $t = 20\ s$ and $t = 25\ s$
   (c) The ratio of the speed of the first arrow and that of the second arrow at $t = 20\ s$ will be $2 : 1$
   (d) The maximum height attained by either arrow will be 980 m

8. A man can swim with a speed of 4.0 km/h in still water. How long does he take to cross a river 1.0 km wide if the river flows steadily at 3 km/h and he makes his strokes normal to the river current? How far does he go in the river when he reaches the other bank of the river?
   (a) 450 m   (b) 690 m
   (c) 750 m   (d) 455 m

9. Which of the following is not an example of motion in a plane?
   (a) A car moving in a rectangular path
   (b) A bicycle moving in a circular path
   (c) Motion of a train on a straight railway track
   (d) A truck moving in an infinite spiral

10. A body executing uniform circular motion has at any instant is velocity vector and acceleration vector __________.
   (a) Along the same direction
   (b) In opposite direction
   (c) Normal to each other
   (d) Not related to each other

11. What is the direction of force of friction acting on a body moving on a fixed surface?
   (a) Along the different of motion
   (b) Opposite to the direction of motion
   (c) Independent of Motion
   (d) Both (A) and (B)

12. A smooth sphere of mass m strikes a second sphere of mass $2m$ which is at rest. After the collision their directions of motion are at right angles. Then the coefficient of restitution is:
   (a) 0   (b) $\frac{1}{2}$
   (c) $-\frac{1}{2}$ (d) 1

13. A ball balanced on a vertical rod is an example of:
   (a) Stable equilibrium   (b) Unstable equilibrium
   (c) Neutral equilibrium   (d) Perfect equilibrium

14. l One end of a string of length m is tied to a particle of mass and the other end to a peg on a smooth horizontal table. If the particle moves in a circle with a speed v , then the net force on the particle (directed towards the centre) is:
   (a) T   (b) $T - \frac{mv^2}{l}$
   (c) $T + \frac{mv^2}{l^2}$ (d) 0

15. A mass M is dragged by a pulley on a horizontal plane by a force anti-parallel to its displacement. The work done in pulling the mass M is
   (a) zero   (b) positive
   (c) infinite   (d) negative

16. Body A of mass $4m$ moving with speed u collides with another body B of mass $2m$, at rest. The collision is head-on and elastic in nature. After the collision the fraction of energy lost by the colliding body A is:
   (a) $\frac{1}{9}$ (b) $\frac{8}{9}$
   (c) $\frac{4}{9}$ (d) $\frac{5}{9}$

17. A disc of radius $2m$ and mass $100kg$ rolls on a horizontal floor. Its centre of mass has a speed of $20cm/s$. How much work is needed to stop it?

(a) $3J$ (b) $30J$
(c) $2J$ (d) $1J$

18. A force $F = 20 + 10y$ acts on a particle in y-direction where F is in newton and y in meter. Work done by this force to move the particle from $y = 0$ to $y = 1m$ is:
(a) $30J$ (b) $5J$
(c) $25J$ (d) $20J$

19. The angular momentum of a particle performing uniform circular motion is L. If the kinetic energy of the particle is doubled and frequency is halved, then angular momentum becomes:
(a) $\dfrac{L}{2}$ (b) $2\,L$
(c) $\dfrac{L}{4}$ (d) $4\,L$

20. A body of M.I. of $3\,\text{kg} - \text{m}^2$, rotating with an angular velocity of $2\text{rad}/s$, has the same K.E. as a mass of 12 kg moving with a velocity of:
(a) $8\,\text{m/s}$ (b) $4\,\text{m/s}$
(c) $2\,\text{m/s}$ (d) $1\,\text{m/s}$

21. Calculate the M.I. of a thin uniform ring about an axis tangent to the ring and in a plane of the ring, if its M.I. about an axis passing through the centre and perpendicular to plane is 4kgm^2.
(a) 12kgm^2 (b) 3kgm^2
(c) 6kgm^2 (d) 9kgm^2

22. F_g and F_e represent gravitational and electrostatic force respectively between electrons situated at a distance 0.1 m. $\dfrac{F_g}{F_e}$ is of the order:
(a) 10^{-41} (b) 10^{-45}
(c) 10^{40} (d) 10^{-42}

23. A thief stole a box with valuable article of weight W and jumped down a wall of height h. Before he reach the ground he experienced a load of-
(a) zero   (b) $\dfrac{W}{2}$
(c) W (d) $2\,W$

24. Acceleration due to gravity $'g'$ and the mean density of the earth $'\rho'$ are related by which of the following relations where G is the gravitational constant and R_e is the radius of the earth:
(a) $\rho = \left(\dfrac{g}{G}\right)\dfrac{4\pi}{3}R_e^3$ (b) $\rho = \dfrac{\left(\frac{g}{G}\right)}{\left(\frac{4\pi}{3}R_e\right)}$
(c) $\rho = \dfrac{g}{G}\dfrac{4\pi}{3}R_e^2$ (d) $\rho = \dfrac{\left(\frac{g}{G}\right)}{\left(\frac{4\pi}{3}R_e^3\right)}$

25. A geostationary satellite is orbiting the earth at a height 6R above the earth's surface, where R is radius of earth. The time period of another satellite at a height 2.5R from earth's surface would be:
(a) $24\,\text{h}$ (b) $\dfrac{6}{2.5}\,\text{h}$
(c) $\dfrac{25}{6}\,\text{h}$ (d) $6\sqrt{2}\,\text{h}$

26. A particle moving with uniform acceleration has its final velocity $(v = \sqrt{150 + 8x})\text{m/s}$ where x is the distance travelled by the body. Then the acceleration is:
(a) $+4\,\text{m/s}^2$ (b) $-4\,\text{m/s}^2$
(c) $+8\,\text{m/s}^2$ (d) $-8\,\text{m/s}^2$

27. A parachute helps a parachuter, while jumping from aeroplanes, to:
(a) Protect him from frictional forces of the air
(b) To protect him from the attack of birds
(c) To reduce his speed of descent due to upward thrust of the air on the open parachute
(d) To reduce his speed of descent controlling the air currents

28. ______is the property of fluid by virtue of which an internal force of friction comes into play when a fluid is in motion and which opposes the relative motion between its different layers.
(a) Surface Tension
(b) Viscosity
(c) Coefficient Of Viscosity
(d) None of the above

29. Viscosity of a liquid ______ with the increase in temperature.
(a) decreases
(b) increases
(c) may decrease or increase
(d) independent of temperature

30. If we place a needle slowly on a water surface, it may float. Which of the following fluid property is responsible for this phenomenon?
(a) Law of Floatation
(b) Adhesive Force
(c) Surface Tension
(d) Equal Pressure distribution in fluids

31. If a liquid is heated in weightlessness the heat is transmitted through:
(a) Conduction   (b) Convection
(c) Radiation   (d) None of these

32. Thermal expansion of solids are:
(a) 2 types   (b) 3 types
(c) 4 types   (d) 5 types

33. Heat is flowing through a conductor of length I from $x = 0$ to $x = 1$. If its thermal resistance per unit length is uniform, which of the following graph is correct?
(a)

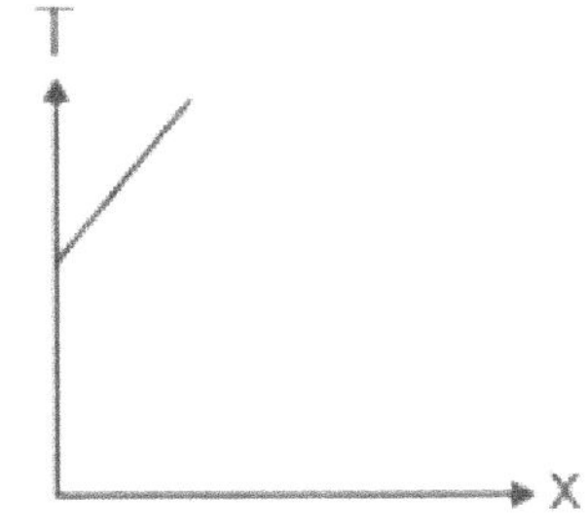

(b)

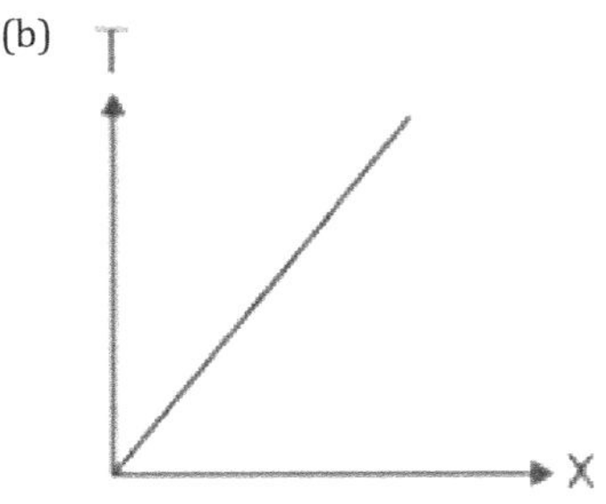

(c)

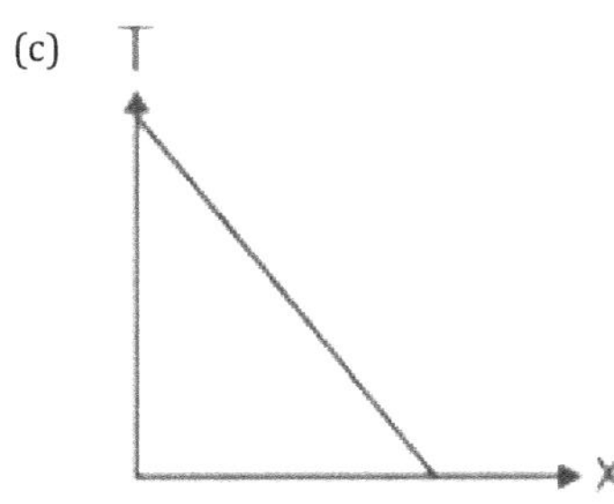

(d)

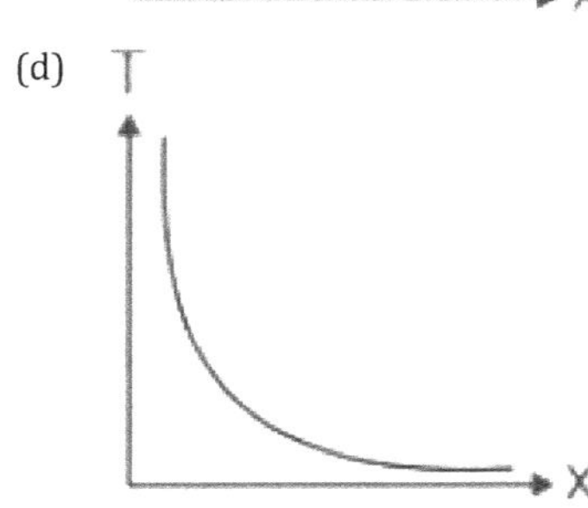

34. A black body at $2000K$ emits maximum energy at a wavelength of $1.56\mu m$. At what temperature will it emit maximum energy at a wavelength of $1.8\mu m$?

(a) $1153K$ (b) $1353K$

(c) $1733K$ (d) $1533K$

35. Which of the following is a thermodynamics law?

(a) Zeroth law of thermodynamics

(b) Faraday's Law of thermodynamics

(c) Ideal Gas Law of thermodynamics

(d) Boyle's Law of thermodynamics

36. Consider a spherical shell of radius R at temperature T. The black body radiation inside it can be considered as an ideal gas of photons with internal energy per unit volume $u = \dfrac{U}{V}\alpha T^4$ and pressure $P = \dfrac{1}{3}\left(\dfrac{U}{V}\right)$. If the shell now undergoes an adiabatic expansion the relation between T and R is:

(a) $T\alpha e^{-R}$ (b) $T\alpha e^{-3R}$

(c) $T\alpha \dfrac{1}{R}$ (d) $T\alpha \dfrac{1}{R^3}$

37. Changes in enthalpy in an exothermic reaction is __________.

(a) positive   (b) negative

(c) constant   (d) neutral

38. A steam engine delivers $5.4 \times 10^8 J$ of work per minute and services $3.6 \times 10^9 J$ of heat per minute from its boiler. What is the efficiency of the engine? How much heat is wasted per minute?

(a) $5.06 \times 10^{-9} J$ (b) $3.06 \times 10^9 J$

(c) $8.06 \times 10^{19} J$ (d) $1.05 \times 10^8 J$

39. If the mean free path of atoms is doubled then the pressure of gas will become

(a) $\dfrac{P}{4}$ (b) $\dfrac{P}{2}$

(c) $\dfrac{P}{8}$ (d) P

40. A gas cylinder containing cooking gas can withstand a pressure of 14.9atm. The pressure gauge of cylinder indicates 12 atm at 27 $°$ C. Due to sudden fire in building the temperature starts rising. The temperature at which the cylinder explodes is:

(a) $42.5\,°C$ (b) $67.8\,°C$

(c) $99.5\,°C$ (d) None of these

41. On increasing the temperature of solids, the kinetic energy of the particles _______.

(a) first increases and then decreases

(b) is constant

(c) increases

(d) decreases

42. If the ideal gas inside a cylindrical tank is kept at 54° C. If the pressure remains constant but its volume decreases from 10 m^3 to 6 m^3 What is the ratio of the initial and final temperature?

(a) $4:3$ (b) $3:4$

(c) $3:5$ (d) $5:3$

43. The number of Degree of freedom for a diatomic molecule is _______. (Assume molecules are rigid)

(a) 2   (b) 3

(c) 5   (d) 6

44. $Al^{3+}(aq) + 3e^- \to Al(s); E° = -1.66\,V$

$Cu^{2+}(aq) + 2e^- \to Cu(s); E° = +0.34\,V$

What voltage is produced under standard conditions by combining the half-reaction with these standard electrode potentials?

(a) 1.32 V   (b) 2.00 V

(c) 2.30 V   (d) 4.34 V

45. For vaporization of water at 1 atmospheric pressure, the values of ΔH and ΔS are 40.63 kJmol^{-1} and 108.8 JK^{-1} mol^{-1} respectively. The temperature when Gibbs energy change (ΔG) for this transformation will be zero, is:

(a) 293.4 K   (b) 273.4 K

(c) 393.4 K   (d) 373.4 K

46. The solution of which of the following will be non-conducting?

(a)

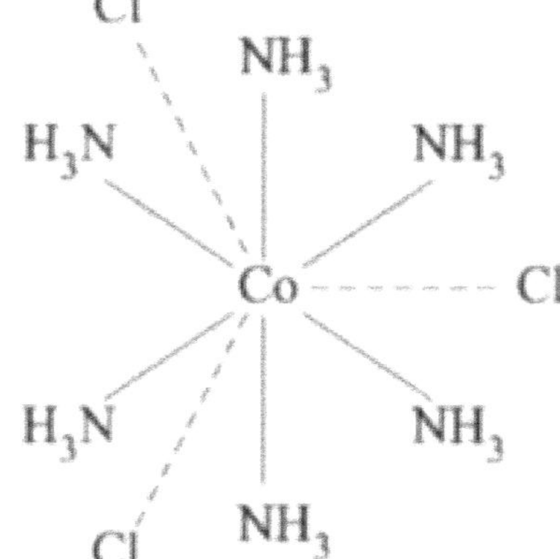

(b)

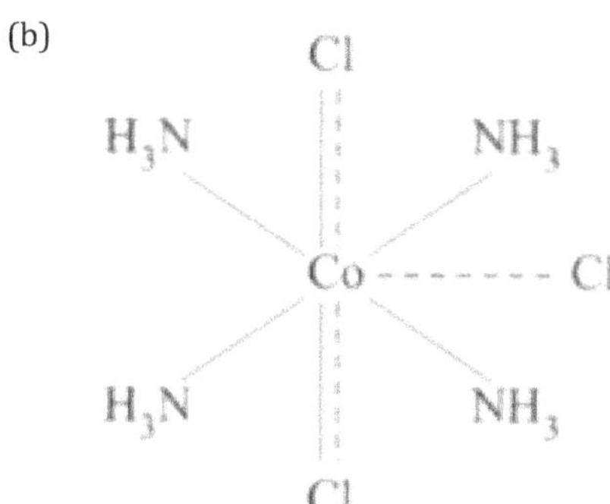

(c)

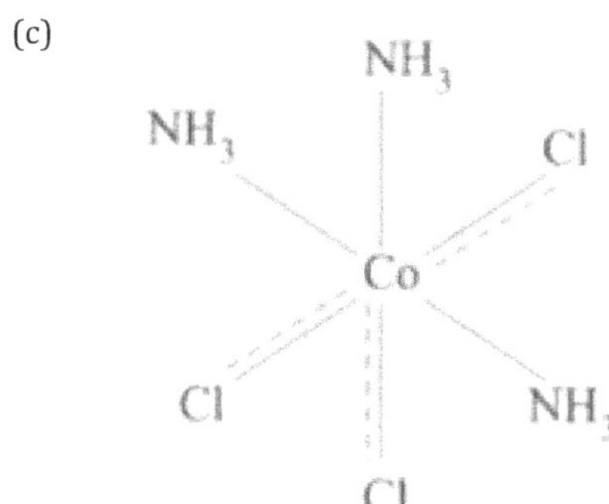

(d)

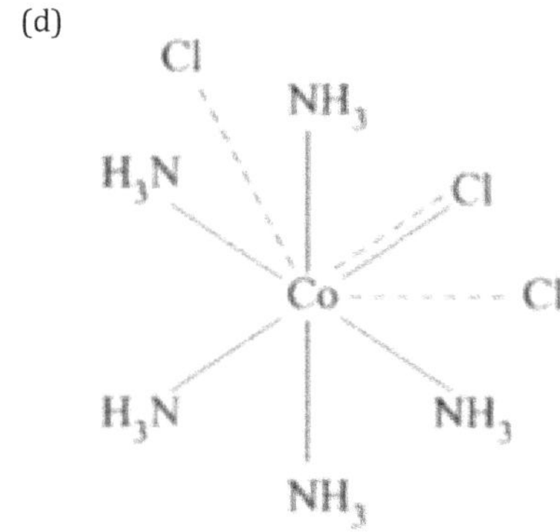

47. Which one given below is a non-reducing sugar?

(a) Glucose　　　　(b) Sucrose

(c) Maltose　　　　(d) Lactose

48. In which of the following compounds there is more than one kind of hybridization (sp, sp^2, sp^3) for carbon?

(a) $CH_2 = CH - CH = CH_2$

(b) $H - C \equiv C - H$

(c) $CH_3CH_2CH_2CH_3$

(d) $CH_3 - CH = CH - CH_3$

49. The total number of electrons in the human body is typically in the order of 10^{28} . Suppose, due to some reason, you and your friend lost 1% of this number of electrons. Calculate the electrostatic force between you and your friend separated at a distance of $1\,m$. Compare this with your weight. Assume mass of each person is 60 kg and use point charge approximation.

(a) $F_e = 8 \times 10^{65} N, W = 428N$

(b) $F_e = 8 \times 10^{41} N, W = 368N$

(c) $F_e = 9 \times 10^{61} N, W = 588N$

(d) $F_e = 9 \times 10^{51} N, W = 648N$

50. Two conducting spheres of radius $r_1 = 8\,cm$ and $r_2 = 2\,cm$ are separated by a distance much larger than 8 cm and are connected by a thin conducting wire as shown in the figure. A total charge of $Q = +100nC$ is placed on one of the spheres. After a fraction of a second, the charge Q is redistributed and both the spheres attain electrostatic equilibrium.

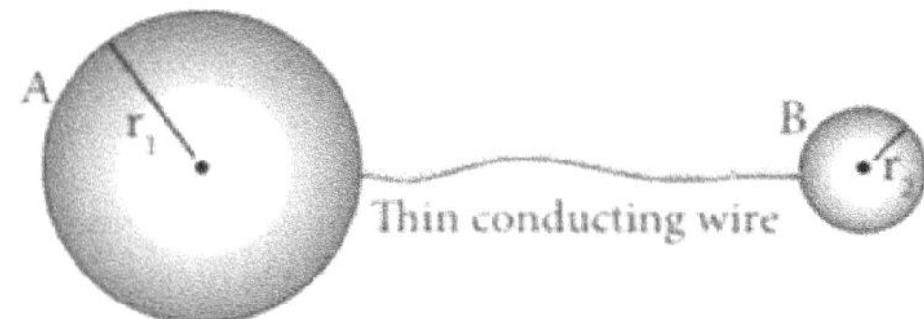

Calculate the charge and surface charge density on each sphere.

(a) $4kV$　　　　　　(b) $5kV$

(c) $9kV$　　　　　　(d) $7kV$

51. Two small charged spheres A and B have charges $10\mu C$ and $940\mu C$, respectively, and are held at a separation of 90 cm from each other. At what distance from A would the electric intensity be zero?

(a) 22.5 cm　　　　(b) 18 cm

(c) 36 cm　　　　　(d) 30 cm

52. Two particles X and Y , having equal charges, after being accelerated through the same potential difference, enter a region of uniform magnetic field and describe circular paths of radii R_1 and R_2 , respectively. The ratio of mass of X to that of Y is

(a) $\left(\dfrac{R_1}{R_2}\right)^{\frac{1}{2}}$　　　　(b) $\dfrac{R_2}{R_1}$

(c) $\left(\dfrac{R_1}{R_2}\right)^{2}$　　　　(d) $\dfrac{R_1}{R_2}$

53. Two identical charges (Q each) are separated by a certain distance. A third charge q is placed on the line joining the two charges, such that all the three charges are in equilibrium. What is the magnitude of the third charge?

(a) $q = 0$　　　　　(b) $q = \dfrac{Q}{4}$

(c) $q = \dfrac{Q}{2}$　　　　(d) $q = \dfrac{Q}{3}$

54. Twenty seven drops of same size are charged at 200 V each. They combine to form a bigger drop. Calculate the potential of the bigger drop.

(a) 1980 V　　　　(b) 660 V

(c) 1320 V　　　　(d) 1520 V

55. A copper sphere of mass 2 g contains nearly 2×10^{22} atoms. The charge on the nucleus of each atom is 29 e. What fraction of the electrons must be removed from the sphere to give it a charge of $+2\mu C$?

(a) 2.16×10^{-12}　　　　(b) 3.15×10^{-11}

(c) 3.15×10^{-12}　　　　(d) 2.16×10^{-11}

56. A table tennis ball that has been covered with a conducting point is suspended by a light thread so that it hangs between two metal p.a.es. One plate is earthed, while the other is attached to a high voltage generator, the ball

(a) Hangs without moving

(b) Swings backward & forward hitting each plate in turn

(c) Is attracted to the high voltage plate and stays

there

(d) Is repelled by an earthed plate and stays there

57. An electric bulb is connected to 220 V generator. The current drawn is 600 mA. What is the power of the bulb?

(a) 132 W   (b) 13.2 W

(c) 1320 W   (d) 13200 W

58. Which one of the following solutions is not capable of conducting electricity?

(a) Copper sulphate   (b) Sodium chloride

(c) Sugar   (d) Sodium hydroxide

59. A current of 0.6 A is drawn by an electric bulb for 10 minutes. Which one of the following is the amount of electric charge that flows through the circuit?

(a) 6 C   (b) 0.6 C

(c) 360 C   (d) 36 C

60. Which one of the following terms cannot represent electrical power in a circuit?

(a) VI (b) $\dfrac{I^2}{R}$

(c) I^2R (d) $\dfrac{V^2}{R}$

61. A circular loop of radius r, carrying current I, lies in the x-y plane with its centre at the origin. The total magnetic flux through x-y plane is:

(a) Directly proportional to I

(b) Directly proportional to R

(c) Inversely proportional to R

(d) Zero

62. In the formula, $X = 3YZ^2$, X and Z have dimensions of capacitance and magnetic field respectively. What are the dimensions of Y in the MKSQ system?

(a) $[\mathrm{M^{-3}\,L^{-1}\,T^3Q^4}]$ (b) $[\mathrm{M^{-3}\,L^{-2}\,T^4Q^4}]$

(c) $[\mathrm{M^{-2}L^{-2}\,T^4Q^4}]$ (d) $[\mathrm{M^{-3}\,L^{-2}\,T^4Q}]$

63. The ratio of intensity of magnetisation to the magnetisation force is known as:

(a) flux density   (b) susceptibility

(c) relative permeability   (d) none of the above

64. The galvanometer deflection, when key K_1 is closed but K_2 is open, equals θ_0 (see figure). On closing K_2 also and adjusting R_2 to 5Ω, the deflection in galvanometer becomes $\dfrac{\theta_0}{5}$. The resistance of the galvanometer is, then, given by [Neglect the internal resistance of battery]:

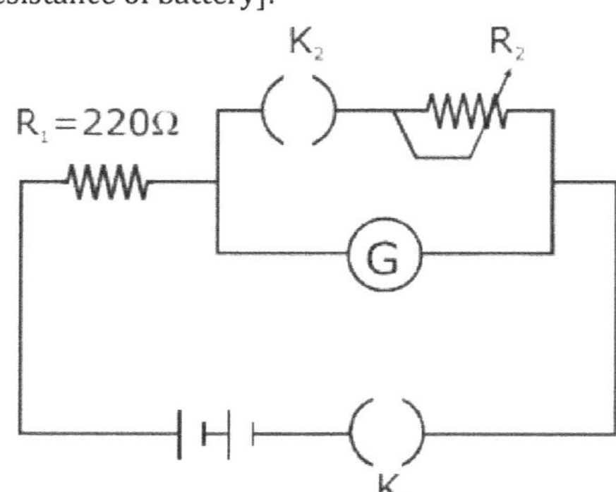

65. A paramagnetic sample shows a net magnetisation of 6 A/m when it is placed in an external magnetic field of $0.4T$ at a temperature of $4K$. When the sample is placed in an external magnetic field of $0.3T$ at a temperature of $24K$, then the magnetisation will be:

(a) $4A/m$ (b) 0.75 A/m

(c) 2.25 A/m   (d) 1 A/m

66. A circular coil of wire consisting of 100 turns, each of radius 8.0 cm carries a current of 0.40 A. What is the magnitude of the magnetic field B at the centre of the coil?

(a) 3.14×10^{-4} T   (b) 5.20×10^{-4} T

(c) 4.14×10^{-4} T   (d) 6.14×10^{-4} T

67. At a place of Earth, the vertical component of Earth's magnetic field is $\sqrt{3}$ times its horizontal component. The angle of dip at this place is:

(a) 60°   (b) 30°

(c) 45°   (d) 0°

68. The magnetic field lines:

(a) Do not form any closed loops

(b) Form continuous closed loop

(c) Can't say

(d) None of these

69. A bar magnet is placed on table where lot of iron fillings are present. Which of the following observation is correct?

(a) Iron nails were uniformly attracted to every part of magnet

(b) The two ends of magnet have larger concentration of iron nails as compared to center

(c) The Center has larger concentration of magnet as compared to the sides of the magnet

(d) The iron nails are randomly distributed over the magnet without any proper pattern

70. The core of transformer is laminated because:

(a) The weight of the transformer may be reduced

(b) Rusting of the core may be prevented

(c) Ratio of in primary and secondary may be increases

(d) Energy losses due to eddy currents may be minimised

71. Two long solenoids S_1 and S_2 have equal lengths and the solenoid S_1 is placed co-axially inside the solenoid S_2. If the radius of the inner solenoid is halved, then the mutual inductance of both the solenoids will become:

(a) Half   (b) One-fourth

(c) Double   (d) None of these

72. Which of the following is correct regarding Faraday's Law?

(a) Change in magnetic flux can cause a voltage to be induced

(b) The induced emf can not generate the current

(c) Increase in number of turns in a coil will decrease induced emf

(d) All of these

73. A 4.5 cm long needle is placed 12 cm away from a convex mirror of focal length 15 cm. Give the location of the image and the magnification.

   (a) 6.7 cm; 0.56   (b) 7.6 cm; 0.23

   (c) 8.3 cm; 0.12   (d) 9.2 cm; 0.92

74. A small hole P is made in a piece of cardboard. The hole is illuminated by a torch as shown in the figure. The ray of light coming out of the hole falls on a mirror.

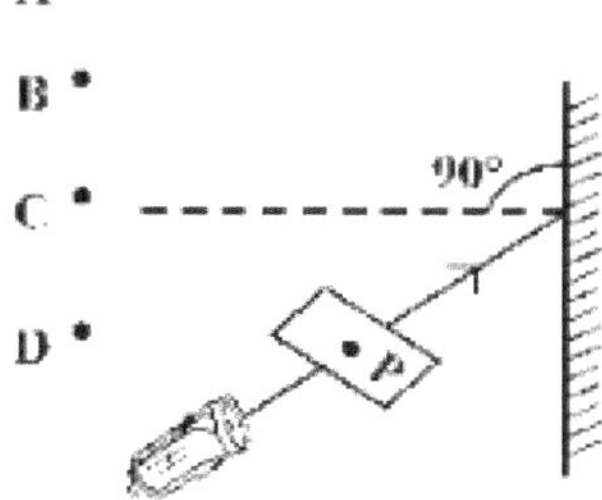

At which point should the eye be placed, so that the hole can be seen?

   (a) A   (b) B

   (c) C   (d) D

75. A person can see clearly only upto a distance of 25 cm. He wants to read a book placed at a distance of 50 cm from his eyes. What is the power of the lens of his spectacles?

   (a) -1.0D   (b) -1.33D

   (c) -1.67D   (d) -2D

76. Which of the following is used in optical fibres?

   (a) Total internal reflection

   (b) Scattering

   (c) Diffraction

   (d) Refraction

77. In Young's experiment, 70 fringes are observed in a field of vision if yellow light $\lambda = 5800$ Å is used. How many fringes would be observed in the same field of vision if violet light $\lambda = 5800$ Å is used?

   (a) 70   (b) 90

   (c) 53   (d) 84

78. In Young's double slit experiment the 10th maximum, of wavelength λ_1 is at a distance of y_1 from the central maximum. When the wavelength of the source is changed to λ_2, 5th maximum is at a distance of y_2 from its central maximum. The ratio $\frac{y_1}{y_2}$

   (a) $\frac{2\lambda_1}{\lambda_2}$ (b) $\frac{2\lambda_2}{\lambda_1}$

   (c) $\frac{\lambda_1}{2\lambda_2}$ (d) $\frac{\lambda_2}{2\lambda_1}$

79. If the electron in the hydrogen atom jumps from the third orbit to the second orbit, the wavelength of the emitted radiation in term of Rydberg constant is:

   (a) $\frac{6}{5R}$ (b) $\frac{36}{5R}$

   (c) $\frac{64}{7R}$ (d) $\frac{36}{7R}$

80. Ultrasonic waves are used for stirring liquid solutions because they

   (a) Can produce a perfectly homogeneous solution

   (b) Are easy to produce

   (c) Do not produce noise during the operation

   (d) Do not produce chemical reactions in the solution

// Smart Answer Sheet //

Correct — Percentage of students who answered correctly.

Skipped — Percentage of students who skipped.

Q.	Ans.	Correct / Skipped	Q.	Ans.	Correct / Skipped	Q.	Ans.	Correct / Skipped
1	A	11.94% / 86.23%	2	A	67.12% / 31.73%	3	C	47.15% / 37.0%
4	A	56.51% / 42.44%	5	A	66.04% / 30.35%	6	C	51.47% / 35.59%
7	C	55.8% / 43.23%	8	C	54.92% / 44.87%	9	C	40.65% / 54.26%
10	C	82.22% / 13.78%	11	B	79.57% / 19.51%	12	B	65.38% / 30.55%
13	B	79.93% / 15.51%	14	A	46.17% / 42.65%	15	D	47.59% / 43.68%
16	B	68.13% / 30.21%	17	A	50.43% / 36.17%	18	C	52.19% / 43.61%
19	D	65.79% / 30.98%	20	D	45.21% / 47.91%	21	C	48.65% / 33.74%
22	D	43.89% / 34.15%	23	A	80.55% / 11.88%	24	B	62.3% / 36.45%
25	D	42.52% / 35.49%	26	A	67.57% / 31.72%	27	C	64.94% / 30.04%
28	B	62.74% / 30.86%	29	A	57.82% / 36.02%	30	C	43.48% / 53.62%
31	A	63.91% / 35.21%	32	B	21.74% / 67.0%	33	C	57.79% / 35.65%
34	C	10.78% / 83.65%	35	C	76.62% / 13.67%	36	C	13.6% / 77.65%
37	B	84.62% / 12.2%	38	B	57.5% / 40.75%	39	B	62.46% / 33.33%
40	C	48.9% / 31.02%	41	C	51.58% / 37.05%	42	D	48.41% / 36.62%
43	C	41.35% / 57.16%	44	B	19.66% / 70.01%	45	D	13.36% / 74.67%
46	C	45.36% / 48.68%	47	B	51.02% / 48.02%	48	D	47.42% / 32.69%
49	C	40.3% / 42.39%	50	C	64.52% / 34.85%	51	D	68.03% / 31.29%
52	C	78.75% / 15.75%	53	B	25.05% / 68.62%	54	A	13.23% / 75.82%
55	D	21.5% / 74.67%	56	B	58.02% / 37.16%	57	A	79.44% / 19.0%
58	C	46.21% / 38.24%	59	C	59.16% / 32.48%	60	B	85.76% / 13.02%
61	D	80.35% / 14.49%	62	B	22.58% / 74.65%	63	B	45.83% / 46.64%
64	A	32.06% / 67.37%	65	B	62.55% / 31.09%	66	A	46.45% / 51.82%
67	A	60.4% / 38.32%	68	B	55.56% / 31.95%	69	B	56.83% / 39.23%
70	D	48.45% / 35.78%	71	B	41.17% / 49.1%	72	A	44.35% / 51.72%
73	A	47.38% / 41.65%	74	A	55.78% / 39.23%	75	D	84.2% / 10.04%
76	A	51.19% / 39.39%	77	D	59.47% / 38.92%	78	A	54.57% / 30.01%
79	B	50.77% / 38.81%	80	A	84.98% / 10.45%			

// Hints and Solutions //

1(A). Given:

Distance of the star from the solar system $= 4.29$ ly
As we know,
1 light year $=$ Speed of light $\times 1$ year
$= 3 \times 10^8 \times 365 \times 24 \times 60 \times 60$
$= 94608 \times 10^{11}$ m
$\Rightarrow 4.29\text{ly} = 4.29 \times 94608 \times 10^{11}$ m
$= 405868.32 \times 10^{11}$ m
$[\because 1 \text{ parsec} = 3.08 \times 10^{16} \text{ m}]$
$\therefore 4.29\text{ly} = \dfrac{405868.32 \times 10^{11} \text{ m}}{3.08 \times 10^{16} \text{ m}}$
$= 1.32$ parsec
Now, using the Young's Double Slit Experiment,
$\theta = \dfrac{d}{D}$
Where,
d $=$ diameter of Earth's orbit $= 3 \times 10^{11}$ m
D $=$ Distance of star from the Earth
$= 405868.32 \times 10^{11}$ m
$\Rightarrow \theta = \dfrac{3 \times 10^{11} \text{ m}}{405868.32 \times 10^{11} \text{ m}}$
$= 7.39 \times 10^{-6}$ radian
But, 1 sec $= 4.85 \times 10^{-6}$ radian
$\therefore 7.39 \times 10^{-6} \text{ radian} = \dfrac{7.39 \times 10^{-6}}{4.85 \times 10^{-6}}$
$= 1.52$ radian

2(A). The dimensional formula of the coefficient of thermal conductivity is
$\left[\text{M}^1\,\text{L}^1\,\text{T}^{-3}\,\text{K}^{-1}\right]$

3(C). Newton-second is the unit of Momentum.
Impulse $=$ change in momentum $= F \times t$.
So the unit of momentum will be equal to Newton - sec.

4(A). We know that the unit of power is watt and it is also represented as:
Watt=Joule/second
Also, watt=Ampere×volt
And watt=Ampere×Ohm
So, option D is not the unit of power i.e. watt.

5(A). The velocity-time graph of a moving train is depicted in the question figure. The average velocity during time OD was 30 m/s by the formula,
i.e., $v = \dfrac{d}{t}$

6(C). The displacement is given as:
$y = ut + \dfrac{1}{2}at^2$
where, u is the initial velocity and a is the acceleration.
Comparing with given expression:
$y = 16t - \dfrac{2t^2}{3} + 2$,
We get,
$u = 16\,m/s$, and $a = -\dfrac{4}{3}\,m/s^2$
As, $v = u + at$, where v is final velocity.
Taking $v = 0$, the time taken for body to come to rest.
$0 = 16 - \dfrac{4}{3}t$
$\Rightarrow t = 12sec$

7(C). Let them meet at height after time t.
$h = 100t - \dfrac{1}{2gt^2} \rightarrow$ for the first arrow
$= 100(t-5) - 12g(t-5)^2 \rightarrow$ for the second arrow
$\Rightarrow t = -12.5\,s$ (after solving).
Time of flight of the first arrow:
$T = \dfrac{2u}{g} = 2 \times \dfrac{100}{10} = 20s$
The second arrow will reach after $5s$ of reaching the first.

$(v_1 = 100 - 10 \times 20 = -100 ms^{-1})$,
$(v_2 = 100 - 10 \times 15 = -50 ms^{-1})$
Ratio: $\dfrac{v_1}{v_2} = 2 : 1$

8(C). Speed of man $= 4.0$ km/h
Distance travelled $= 1.0$ km
Speed of river $= 3 kmh^{-1}$
Then, Time $(t) =$ Distance/ Speed
$\dfrac{1 \text{ km}}{4 \text{ km}}$
$= \dfrac{1}{4}$ h
$= \dfrac{60}{4}$ min
$= 15$ min
The man is carried down by stream with velocity of river water.
$\therefore$ Distance travelled by man in 15 min (or $\dfrac{1}{4}$ h) is
$= 3 \times \dfrac{1}{4}$ h
$= 3000 \times \dfrac{15}{60}$
$= 750$ m

9(C). Motion of a train on a straight railway track is an example of 3 -dimensional motion. Since motion of a train on a straight line, hence, it cannot be out in the category of motion in a plane. The truck moving in an infinite spiral is also an example of motion in a plane as spiral is a 2 -dimensional entity. A car moving in a rectangular path and a bicycle moving in a circular path both are also the examples of motion in a plane as they have 2 -dimensional motion.

10(C). The centripetal acceleration vector points toward the center of the circular path of motion and is an acceleration in the radial direction. In uniform circular motion the magnitude of centripetal acceleration remain constant but its direction always get changed due to change in position of object. So centripetal acceleration is a constant vector. So a body executing uniform circular motion at any instant has velocity vector and acceleration vector normal to each other.

11(B). When we try to slide a body on a surface, the motion of the body is opposed by a force called the force of friction. The frictional force arises due to intermolecular interaction.

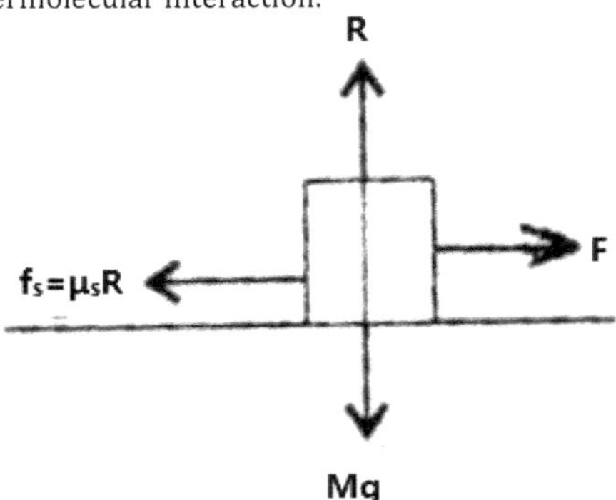

When an external force (F) is applied to move the body and the body does not move, then the frictional force acts opposite to applied force F and is equal to the applied force i.e., $F - f = 0$. When the body remains at rest, the frictional force is called the static friction. Static friction is a self-adjusting force.
Friction force, $f_s = \mu mg$
Where,
$\mu_s =$ coefficient of friction.

Thus, friction force act opposite to the direction of motion.

12(B). Given,

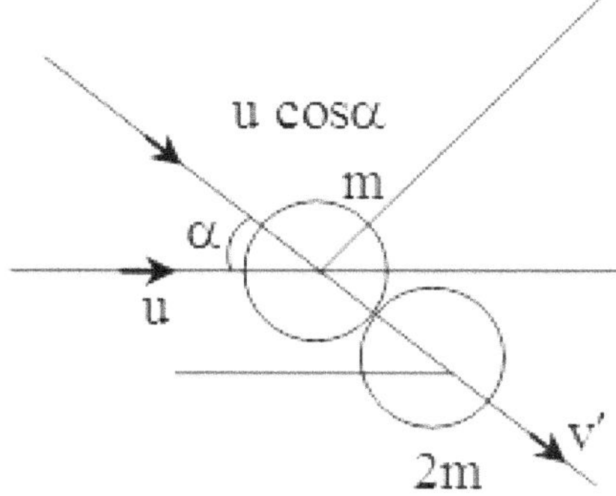

At equilibrium,
$$mu \cos \alpha = 2mv'$$
$$\Rightarrow v' = \frac{u \cos \alpha}{2}$$
$$\Rightarrow \frac{1}{2} = \frac{v'}{u \cos \alpha} \dots \dots (1)$$

As we know that,
The coefficient of restitution,
$$e = \frac{v'}{u \cos \alpha} \dots (2)$$
From equation (1) and (2), we get
$$e = \frac{1}{2}$$

13(B). A ball balanced on a vertical rod is an example of unstable equilibrium. A system is in unstable equilibrium if, when displaced from equilibrium, it experiences a net force or torque in the same direction as the displacement from equilibrium.

If a ball is placed on vertical rod, it is in unstable equilibrium because once it is displaced from its place, it will experience the net force in the direction of displacement and never come back to its original position. The potential energy of the ball is maximum at this point.

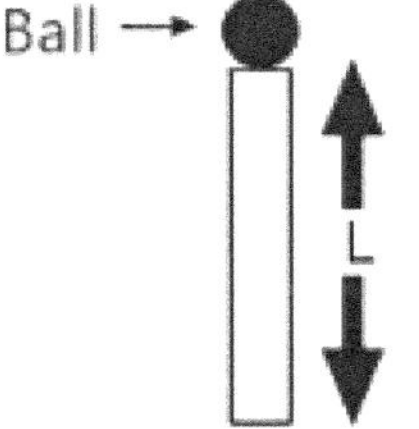

14(A). Given,

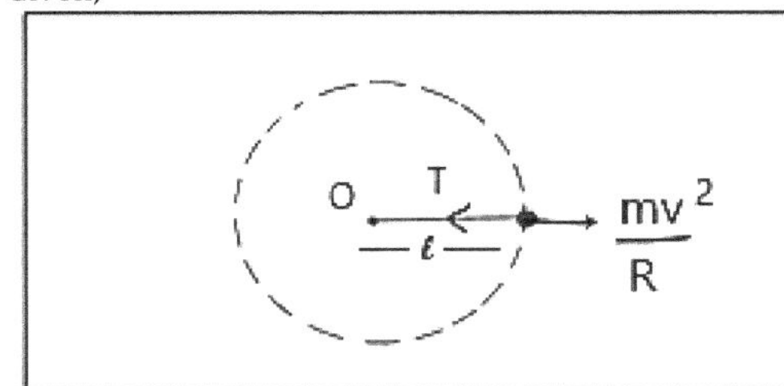

Radius, $R = l$
From the figure we can write,
$$T = \frac{mv^2}{R}$$
$$T = \frac{mv^2}{l}$$

15(D). Work (W) is said to be done by a force when the force acting on it causes the object to displace. Mathematically it is given by,
$$W = \vec{F} \cdot \vec{d} = Fd \cos \theta \quad \dots (i)$$
Where F = The magnitude of the force vector, d = The magnitude of the displacement vector
Given,
The pull force F is applied in the antiparallel direction to the displacement of the mass on the plane.
Referring to the diagram,

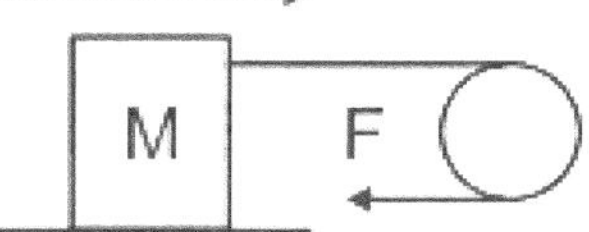

So, the displacement and pulling force vectors will be in the antiparallel direction to each other as the angle between them will be $180°$.
$$\because \theta = 180° \Rightarrow \cos 180° = -1$$
So, using equation (i),
The work done in pulling the mass M will be negative as the magnitude of the force and displacement vector can not be negative.

16(B). Given: mass $m_1 = 4m$
mass, $m_2 = 2m$
Body A is having mass m_1 having initial velocity, $u_1 = u$, and body B have mass m_2 is having zero initial velocity, i.e, $u_2 = 0$.
Let us take the final velocity of body A as v_1 and the final velocity of body A as v_2.
When body A with speed u is collide with body B and it is having an elastic collision after the collision is shown in the figure below,

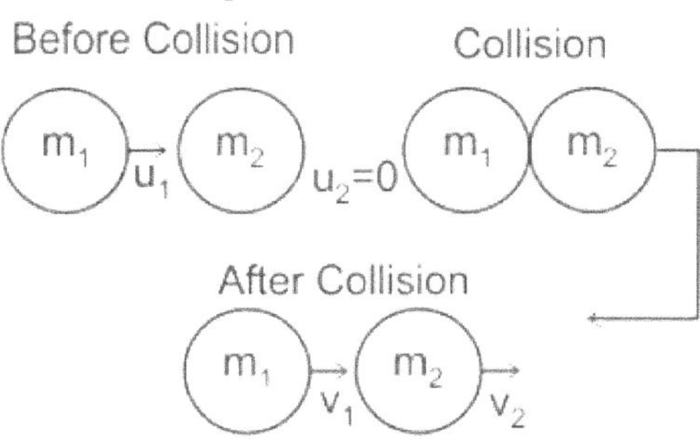

Now, The final velocity of the body B in the elastic collision is written as;
$$v_2 = \frac{m_2 - m_1}{m_1 + m_2} u_2 + \frac{2m_1 u_1}{m_1 + m_2}$$
$$\Rightarrow v_2 = \frac{2-4}{4+2} \times 0 + \frac{2 \times 4u}{4+2}$$
$$\Rightarrow v_2 = \frac{2 \times 4u}{4+2}$$
$$\Rightarrow v_2 = \frac{4u}{3}$$

Body A after the collision will transfer some kinetic energy to the body B therefore fractional loss of Kinetic energy of the colliding body is written as;
$$\frac{\text{Kinetic energy of Body B}}{\text{Kinetic energy of Body A}} = \frac{\frac{1}{2} m_2 v_2^2}{\frac{1}{2} m_1 v_1^2}$$

Now, on putting the values of masses m_1 and m_2 and finial velocities v_1 and v_2, we get;
$$\frac{\text{Kinetic energy of Body B}}{\text{Kinetic energy of Body A}} = \frac{\frac{1}{2} \times 2 \times \left(\frac{4u}{3}\right)^2}{\frac{1}{2} \times 4 \times u_1^2}$$
$$\Rightarrow \frac{\text{Kinetic energy of Body B}}{\text{Kinetic energy of Body A}} = \frac{\left(\frac{4u}{3}\right)^2}{2 \times u^2}$$
$$\Rightarrow \frac{\text{Kinetic energy of Body B}}{\text{Kinetic energy of Body A}} = \frac{8}{9}$$

17(A). Work done to stop the disc = change in total kinetic energy of disc

Final $KE = 0$

Initial KE = Translational $K.E$ + Rotational $K.E$

$= \frac{1}{2}mv^2 + \frac{1}{2}I\omega^2$

$= \frac{1}{2}mv^2 + \frac{1}{2} \times \frac{mR^2}{2} \times \left(\frac{v}{R}\right)^2$

$= \frac{1}{2}mv^2 + \frac{1}{4}mv^2 = \frac{3}{4}mv^2$

$= \frac{3}{4} \times 100 \times \left(20 \times 10^{-2}\right)^2 = 3J$

$|\Delta KE| = 3J$

18(C). Given that,

Force $F = 20 + 10y$

Where limits of y are, $0 < y < 1$

Hence work done on a particle is given as:

$W = \int_0^1 F \cdot dy = \int_0^1 20 + 10y$

$\therefore W = \left[20y + \frac{10y^2}{2}\right]_0^1 = 20 + 5 = 25J$

19(D). Angular momentum, $L = I\omega$ ....(i)

Where, I is the moment of inertia

Kinetic energy $K = \frac{1}{2}I\omega^2$

$\Rightarrow K = \frac{1}{2}(I \times \omega)\omega$

(From eq. (i))

$\Rightarrow K = \frac{1}{2}L\omega$

$L = \frac{2K}{\omega}$

Now, given angular frequency is halved, so, let $\omega' = \frac{\omega}{2}$

And the kinetic energy is doubled, so, $K' = 2K$ If L' is the new angular momentum, then we can write,

$L' = \frac{2K'}{\omega'}$

$\Rightarrow L' = \frac{2(2K)}{\frac{\omega}{2}}$

$\Rightarrow L' = 4\frac{2K}{\omega}$

$\Rightarrow L' = 4L$

So, angular momentum becomes four times its original value.

20(D). Given:

Moment of inertia $(I) = 3 \text{ kg} - m^2$

Angular Velocity $(\omega) = 2\text{rad/s}$

Mass (m) $= 12$ kg

To Find velocity (v)

The velocity is given as,

$\frac{1}{2}I\omega^2 = \frac{1}{2}mv^2$

$\frac{1}{2} \times 3(2)^2 = \frac{1}{2} \times 12 \times v^2$

$v = 1 \text{ m/s}$

Thus, the speed of the body is 1 m/s.

21(C). Given, M.I. of a thin uniform ring about an axis passing through the centre and perpendicular to plane is $4\text{kgm}^2 = mr^2$

Using Perpendicular axix theorem,

M.I. of a thin uniform ring about an axis passing through the centre and in the plane of the ring is

$2\text{kgm}^2 = \frac{1}{2}mr^2$

Now, Using Parallel axix theorem,

M.I. of ring about an axis tangent to the ring and in a plane of the ring

$\frac{1}{2}mr^2 + md^2 = \frac{3}{2}mr^2$

$= \frac{3}{2}mr^2 = \left(\frac{3}{2}\right)4\text{kgm}^2$

$= 6\text{kgm}^2$

22(D). F_g and F_e represent gravitational and electrostatic force respectively between electrons situated at a distance $= 0.1m$

$F_e = \frac{1}{4\pi\epsilon_0}\frac{\mathbf{q}^2}{\mathbf{d}^2}$

$F_g = \mathbf{G}\frac{\mathbf{m}^2}{\mathbf{d}^2}$

$\frac{1}{4\pi\epsilon_0} = 9\times10^9$

$G = 6.67\times10^{-11}$

$q = 1.6\times10^{-19}$

$m = 9.1\times10^{-31}$

let, us take the ratio $\dfrac{\mathbf{F}_e}{\mathbf{F}_g} = \dfrac{\frac{1}{4\pi\epsilon_0}\frac{q^2}{d^2}}{\mathbf{G}\frac{\mathbf{m}^2}{\mathbf{d}^2}}$

$\dfrac{\mathbf{F}_e}{\mathbf{F}_g} = \frac{1}{4\pi\epsilon_0} \times \frac{1}{\mathbf{G}} \times \frac{\mathbf{q}^2}{\mathbf{m}^2}$

$\dfrac{\mathbf{F}_e}{\mathbf{F}_g} = 9 \times 10^9 \times \frac{1}{6.67\times10^{-11}} \times \frac{\left(1.6\times10^{-19}\right)^2}{\left(9.1\times10^{-31}\right)^2}$

$\Rightarrow \dfrac{\mathbf{F}_e}{\mathbf{F}_g} = 4.17 \times 10^{42}$

or, $\dfrac{\mathbf{F}_e}{\mathbf{F}_g}$ is of the order of 10^{-42}.

23(A). While the thief along with the box was in air, the box and the thief experienced same amount of acceleration due to gravity g in downward direction. Thus the box did not exert any force on the thief due to which he did not experience any load due to the box.

24(B). The gravitational acceleration on the earth's surface is $g = \dfrac{GM}{R_e^2}$

Now, Density $\rho = \text{mass/volume} = \dfrac{M}{V}$

or $M = \rho V = \rho \times \left(\frac{4}{3}\right)\pi R_e^3$

Thus, $\rho = \dfrac{G_p\left(\frac{4}{3}\right)\pi R_e^3}{R_e^2}$

or $\rho = \dfrac{\left(\frac{g}{G}\right)}{\left(\frac{4}{3}\right)\pi R_e}$

25(D). For geostationary satellite : $r_1 = R + 6R = 7R$, $T_1 = 24h$

For second satellite : $r_2 = R + 2.5R = 3.5R$

Time period of satellite: $T = 2\pi\sqrt{\dfrac{r^3}{GM}}$ where, r is the radius of orbit

$\Rightarrow \dfrac{T_2}{T_1} = \sqrt{\dfrac{r_2^3}{r_1^3}}$

$\therefore \dfrac{T_2}{24} = \sqrt{\dfrac{(3.5R)^3}{(7R)^3}}$

$= \dfrac{1}{2\sqrt{2}}$

$\Rightarrow T_2 = \dfrac{24}{2\sqrt{2}}$

$= 6\sqrt{2}\text{ h}$

26(A). Given:

$v = \sqrt{150 + 8x}$

On squaring,

$v^2 = 150 + 8x$

On differentiating,

$\frac{d}{dt}\left(v^2\right) = \frac{d}{dt}(150 + 8x)$

$2v\frac{dv}{dt} = \frac{d}{dt}(8x)$

$\because 8\frac{dx}{dt} = 8v$

So,

$2v\frac{dv}{dt} = 8v$

$$\frac{dv}{dt} = a = \frac{8}{2} = 4$$

27(C). A parachute helps a parachuter, while jumping from aeroplanes, to reduce his speed of descent due to upward thrust of the air on the open parachute.
- When parachuter jumps from airplanes , his velocity goes on increasing due to gravity. Therefore, the opposing viscous drag which acts upwards also goes on increasing .
- Parachute dramatically reduces the terminal velocity of the parachuter by increasing the air resistance as he falls.
- The air resistance is increased by opening the parachute and creating a large surface area of material with a huge amount of drag .
- Thus, a stage reaches when the true weight of the body is just equal to the sum of the upward thrust due to buoyancy and the upward viscous drag . At this stage, there is no net force to accelerate the body .
- Hence, you hit the ground at a relatively low speed .

28(B). Viscosity is the property of fluid by virtue of which an internal force of friction comes into play when a fluid is in motion and which opposes the relative motion between its different layers.
- Viscosity is like friction which converts kinetic energy into heat energy.
- Viscosity is considered an internal resistance that comes into play when fluid is in motion.

29(A). Viscosity of a liquid decreases with the increase in temperature.
- Effect of temperature on viscosity: When a liquid is heated, the kinetic energy of its molecules increases and the intermolecular attraction becomes weaker.
- Hence the viscosity of a liquid decreases with the increases in its temperature.

30(C). Surface Tension: The tendency of a liquid to reduce its surface area is called surface tension.
The water molecules at the surface are pulled in by the cohesive force between themselves and molecules inside the bulk and thus have higher potential energy than those insides.
If carefully placed on the surface, a small needle can be made to float on the surface of the water even though it is several times as dense as water. This is due to surface tension even if the density of iron nail is much higher than water.

31(A). In weightlessness, there is no interaction between molecules.
Convection: In convection, gravity plays an important role. When liquid is heating the density of the lower molecules decreases. More dense molecules come down. In this example, there is no gravity so the molecule won't perform this motion.
Radiation: It is the transfer of thermal energy in form of an electromagnetic wave.
It does not require a medium to transfer heat. Here heat is transferred by conduction. the vessel will conduct heat and transfer it to liquid.
Conduction: In this process, heat is transferred due to temperature differences in neighbouring molecules.

32(B). **Concept:**
Thermal Expansion: Whenever the solids, liquids, and gases are heated at some temperature, they start changing their shape and that process is known as thermal expansion.
Thermal expansions are of mainly three types.
Calculation:
Thermal expansion of solids can be further classified into three types based on their change in dimension.
1 . **Linear Expansion:** When the expansion of solid is linear when heated, such expansion is known as linear expansion and coefficient of linear expansion,
$$\alpha = \frac{\text{Increase in length}}{\text{Original length} \times \text{change in temperature}} = \frac{\Delta L}{L \times \Delta T}$$
2 . **Areal/Superficial Expansion:** When the expansion of solid expands along two dimensions, i.e., in case of expansion of lamina both length and breadth will expand when heated such expansion is known as Superficial expansion.
Coefficient of Superficial expansion,
$$\beta = \frac{\Delta A}{A \times \Delta T}$$
3 . **Volumetric Expansion or Cubical Expansion:** When the expansion of solids expands along three dimensions, i.e., in the case of expansion of lamina, both length, height, and breadth will expand when heated, such expansion is known as Volumetric expansion or Cubical Expansion.
Coefficient of Volumetric expansion,
$$\gamma = \frac{\Delta V}{V \times \Delta T}$$
Relationship between α, β, and γ
Using error theorem, we can say that, $\beta = 2\alpha, y = 3\alpha$, and $\alpha : \beta : y = 1 : 2 : 3$

33(C). **Concept:**
Thermal conductivity is the rate of flow of heat at a given temperature difference.
The flow of heat is directly proportional to the temperature difference $(T_C - T_0)$ and area of the cross-section (A).
The flow of heat is inversely proportional to length (L).
$$H = \frac{K(T_C - T_0)A}{L} \quad \dots (1)$$
Calculation:
Thermal resistance per unit length is uniform.
$$R_T = \frac{L}{KA}$$
Substitute it in equation (1)
$$H = \frac{(T_C - T_0)}{R_T}$$
$$HR_T = \delta T$$
Differentiate with respect to x
$$H\frac{dR_T}{dx} = \frac{dT}{dx}$$
As $\frac{dR_T}{dx} = \text{uniform}$
In options (A), (B) and (C) slope is uniform.
We know that if the distance is increasing temperature will decrease.

34(C). Wein's displacement law: Emitted wavelength peak is inversely proportional to the temperature of a blackbody.
As the temperature of a blackbody increases the highest peak of radiated wavelength moves towards a shorter wavelength.

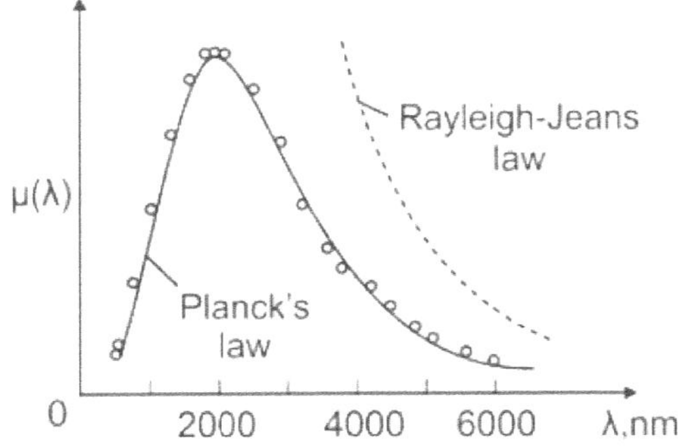

$\lambda_{max} \propto \dfrac{1}{T}$

$\lambda_{max} = \dfrac{b}{T}$

b is Wein's displacement constant

In given condition $\lambda_{max1} = 1.56\mu m$ at $T_1 = 2000K$

$\lambda_{max2} = 1.8\mu m$ $T_2 = ?$

$\dfrac{\lambda_{max1}}{\lambda_{max2}} = \dfrac{T_2}{T_1}$

$\dfrac{1.56\times10^{-6}}{1.8\times10^{-6}} = \dfrac{T_2}{2000}$

$T_2 = \dfrac{2000\times1.56}{1.8} = \dfrac{3120}{1.8}$

$T_2 = 1733K$

35(C). Thermodynamics is primarily based on a set of four rules that are universally applicable when applied to systems that fall within their respective limitations. They are as follows:
- Zeroth law of thermodynamics
- First law of thermodynamics
- Second law of thermodynamics
- Third law of thermodynamics

36(C). In a spherical shell, the internal energy per unit volume is given by $\dfrac{U}{V}\alpha T^4$

$\Rightarrow U = CVT^4$

Here C is a constant

Next the value of P,

$= \dfrac{1}{3}\left(\dfrac{U}{V}\right) = \dfrac{1}{3}\left(\dfrac{CVT^4}{V}\right)$

From adiabatic expansion, $dQ = 0$ and $dU = -dW$

$d(CVT)^4 = -PdV$

We get,

$\Rightarrow 4VdT = -\dfrac{4}{3}TdV$

$\Rightarrow \dfrac{dT}{T} = \dfrac{dV}{3V}$

On integrating,

$\Rightarrow TV^{\frac{1}{3}} = C^1$

$\Rightarrow T\left(\dfrac{4}{3}\pi R^3\right)^{\frac{1}{3}} = C^1$

$TR = \text{Constant}$

$\Rightarrow T\alpha\dfrac{1}{R}$

37(B). Changes in enthalpy in an exothermic reaction is negative. So if a reaction releases more energy than it absorbs, the reaction is exothermic and enthalpy will be negative. If a reaction absorbs or uses more energy than it releases, the reaction is endothermic, and enthalpy will be positive.

38(B). Work done by the steam engine per minute, $W = 5.4 \times 10^8 J$

Heat supplied from the boiler, $H = 3.6 \times 10^9 J$

Efficiency of the engine $= \dfrac{\text{Output Energy}}{\text{Input Energy}}$

$\Rightarrow \eta = \dfrac{W}{H}$

$\Rightarrow \eta = \dfrac{5.4\times10^8}{3.6\times10^9}$

$\Rightarrow \eta = 0.15$

Thus, the percentage efficiency of the engine is 15 .

Amount of heat wasted $= 3.6 \times 10^9 - 5.4 \times 10^8$

$= 30.6 \times 10^8$

$= 3.06 \times 10^9 J$

Clearly, the amount of heat wasted per minute is $3.06 \times 10^9 J$.

39(B). Mean free path, $\lambda = \dfrac{\mu}{P}\sqrt{\dfrac{\pi RT}{2M}}$

Where, μ = Viscosity

P = Pressure

R = Gas constant

T = Tempreture

M = Molecular weight

$\Rightarrow \lambda \propto \dfrac{1}{p}$

$P \propto \dfrac{1}{\lambda}$

If we double the mean free Path, the pressure will be $1/2$.

40(C). Given,

$P_1 = 12$ atm

$T_1 = 300$ K

$P_2 = 14 \cdot 9$ atm

As we know,

$\dfrac{P_1}{T_1} = \dfrac{P_2}{T_2}$

$\dfrac{12}{300} = \dfrac{14.9}{T_2}$

$T_2 = 372 \cdot 5k$

$T_2 = 372 - 273 = 99 \cdot 5°C$

41(C). Increase the temperature, the randomness will increase, and hence the kinetic energy of the molecules increases.
- The energy of a molecule in the solid is due to its randomness.
- If there is a change in the temperature of the solid, the randomness of the molecules will change.

Kinetic energy: The energy possessed by a body due to its motion is called.

42(D). Ideal gas: It is a hypothetical gas, consisting of molecules that are having negligible volume and their collision is perfectly elastically (means no loss of energy) and obeys gas law.

Boyle's law- It allows to set up the relationship between the changes in pressure and volume under constant temperature-

$P_1 V_1 = P_2 V_2$ [P_1 and P_2 are pressure of gases and V_1 and V_2 are volume]

Pressure is constant so we can apply Charles's law

$V_1 = 10\,\text{m}^3, V_2 = 6\,\text{m}^3$

$\Rightarrow \dfrac{V_1}{T_1} = \dfrac{V_2}{T_2}$

$\Rightarrow \dfrac{10}{T_1} = \dfrac{6}{T_2} \Leftrightarrow \dfrac{T_1}{T_2} = 5 : 3$

43(C). A diatomic molecule has a degree of freedom = 5, because

It can move in translational motion in x y and z-direction.

So the degree of freedom due to translational motion = 3

Also due to rotational motion, degree of freedom = 2

So total degree of freedom = 3 + 2 = 5

44(B). Given,

$Al^{3+}(aq) + 3e^- \rightarrow Al(s); E° = -1.66$ V

$Cu^{2+}(aq) + 2e^- \rightarrow Cu(s); E° = +0.34\ V$
The cell will be,
$Al(s)\left|Al^{3+}(aq)\right|\left|Cu^{2+}(aq)\right|Cu(s)$
$E°_{cell} = E°_{cathode} - E°_{anode}$
$= E°_{Cu^{2+}/Cu} - E°_{Al^{3+}/A}$
$= +0.34 - (-1.66)$
$= +2.00\ V$

45(D). $H_2O(l) \overset{1atm}{\rightleftharpoons} H_2O(g)$
Given,
$\Delta H = 40.630\ J\ mol^{-1}$
$\Delta S = 108.8\ JK^{-1}\ mol^{-1}$
$\Delta G = \Delta H - T\Delta S$
When, $\Delta G = 0$
$\Delta H - T\Delta S = 0$
$T = \dfrac{\Delta H}{\Delta S}$
$\Rightarrow T = \dfrac{40630}{108.8}$
$\Rightarrow T = 373.4\ K$

46(C). Using Werner's theory in this complex all the chlorine atoms are showing secondary valency so they cannot be precipitated. So, the second structure of the solution will be non-conducting.

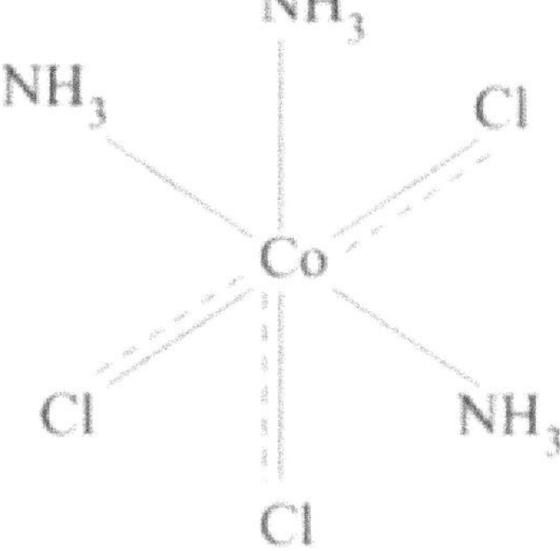

47(B). All monosaccharides whether aldoses or ketoses are reducing sugars. Disaccharides such as sucrose in which the two monosaccharide units are linked through their reducing centres i.e., aldehydic or ketonic groups are non-reducing. This is why sucrose is non-reducing sugar. The linkage between the glucose and fructose units in sucrose, which involves aldehyde and ketone groups, is responsible for the inability of sucrose to act as a reducing sugar.

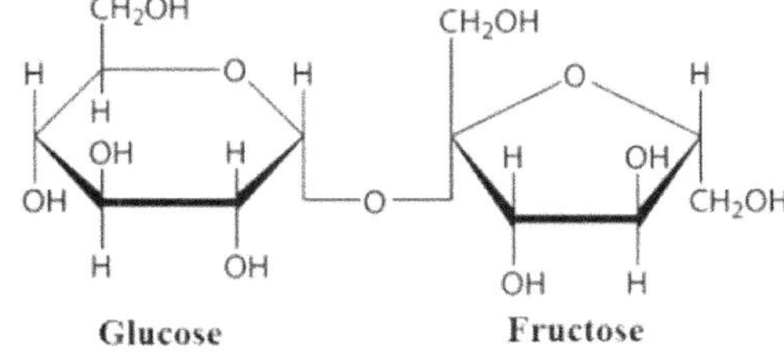

48(D). In $CH_3 - CH = CH - CH_3$, there is more than one kind of hybridization are shown:
$CH_3 - CH = CH - CH_3$
$\ \ \ sp^3 \quad sp^2 \quad sp^2 \quad sp^3$

49(C). Given:
$n = 10^{28}$ (No.of electrons)
$r = 1\ m$
Loss in electrons = 1% i.e., 10^{26} electrons lost
$\therefore$ Charge on each person $= 10^{26} \times 1.6 \times 10^{-19} C$
$M = 60\ kg$

$Fe = \dfrac{1}{4\pi\varepsilon_0}\dfrac{q_1 q_2}{r^2}$
$= \dfrac{9\times10^9\times10^{26}\times1.6\times10^{-19}\times1.6\times10^{-19}\times10^{26}}{1}$
$Fe = 23.04 \times 10^{23}\ N$
Weight $W = mg = 60 \times 9.8 = 588\ N$
$F_e = 9 \times 10^{61} N, W = 588N$

50(C). The electrostatic potential on the surface of the sphere A is $V_A = \dfrac{1}{4\pi\varepsilon_0}\dfrac{q_1}{r_1}$
The electrostatic potential on the surface of the sphere A is $V_B = \dfrac{1}{4\pi\varepsilon_\circ}\dfrac{q_2}{r_2}$
Since $V_A = V_B$. We have
$\dfrac{q_1}{r_1} = \dfrac{q_2}{r_2}$
$\Rightarrow q_1 = \left(\dfrac{r_1}{r_2}\right)q_2$
But from the conservation of total charge,
$Q = q_1 + q_2$,
we get $q_1 = Q - q_2$.
By substituting this in the above equation,
$Q - q_2 = \left(\dfrac{r_1}{r_2}\right)q_2$
so that
$q_2 = Q\left(\dfrac{r_2}{r_1+r_2}\right)$
Therefore,
$q_2 = 100 \times 10^{-9} \times \left(\dfrac{2}{10}\right) = 20nC$
and $q_1 = Q - q_2 = 80nC$
The electric charge density for sphere A is
$\sigma_1 = \dfrac{q_1}{4\pi r_1^2}$
The electric charge density for sphere B is
$\sigma_2 = \dfrac{q_2}{4\pi r_2^2}$
Therefore,
$\sigma_1 = \dfrac{80\times10^{-9}}{4\times64\times10^{-4}} = 0.99 \times 10^{-6} Cm^{-2}$
and
$\sigma_2 = \dfrac{20\times10^{-9}}{4\pi\times4\times10^{-4}} = 3.9 \times 10^{-6} Cm^{-2}$
The potential on both spheres is the same. So we can calculate the potential on any one of the spheres.
$V_A = \dfrac{1}{4\pi\varepsilon}\dfrac{q_1}{r_1}$
$= \dfrac{9\times10^9\times80\times10^{-9}}{8\times10^{-2}}$
$= 9kV$

51(D). $E_A = \dfrac{kq_A}{x^2}$ rightward
And,
$E_B = \dfrac{kq_B}{(1-x)^2}$ leftward
since,
There is no field at P
$E = E_A - E_B = 0$
$\Rightarrow kq\left(\dfrac{q_A}{x^2} - \dfrac{q_B}{(1-x)^2}\right) = 0$
$\Rightarrow \left(\dfrac{1-x}{x}\right)^2 = \dfrac{q_B}{q_A}$
$\Rightarrow \dfrac{-x}{x} = \sqrt{\dfrac{40}{10}} = 2$
$\Rightarrow -x = 2x$
$\Rightarrow x = \dfrac{1}{3} = \dfrac{90}{3}\ cm$
$\Rightarrow x = 30\ cm$

52(C). Radius of circular path traced by a particle $r = \dfrac{mv}{Bq}$
Kinetic energy $K = \frac{1}{2}mv^2 = eV$
$r = \dfrac{\sqrt{m^2v^2}}{Bq} = \dfrac{\sqrt{2mK}}{Bq}$

Or $r = \dfrac{\sqrt{2meV}}{Bq}$

$\Rightarrow m \propto r^2$

Thus we get the ratio of masses of X to Y $\dfrac{m_1}{m_2} = \left[\dfrac{r_1}{r_2}\right]^2$

53(B). Two identical point charges Q are kept at a distance r from each other. A third point charge is placed on the line joining these two charges such that all the three charges are in equilibrium. i.e.,

$AO = x$, $OB = r - x$

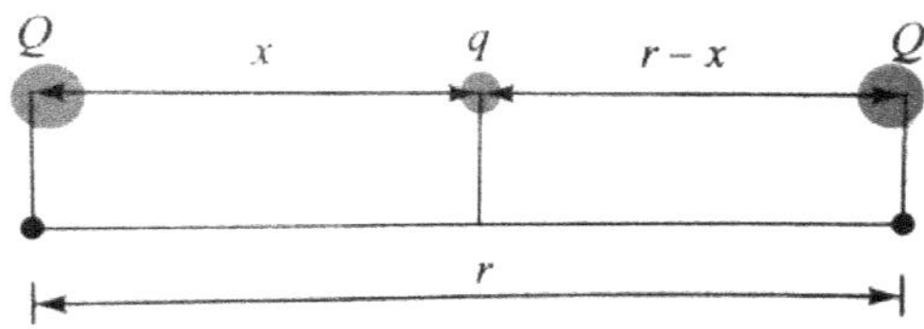

Now, using Coulomb's law,

$\dfrac{1}{4\pi\varepsilon_0}\dfrac{Qq}{x^2} = \dfrac{1}{4\pi\varepsilon_0}\dfrac{qQ}{(r-x)^2}$

$\Rightarrow x^2 = (r - x)^2$

$\Rightarrow x = \pm(r - x)$

$\Rightarrow x = \dfrac{r}{2}$

the position of the third charge is at $x = \dfrac{r}{2}$

Now, to find the magnitude of the charge we will consider the case where charge $+Q$ at A or $+Q$ at B are in equilibrium.

i.e., $\dfrac{1}{4\pi\varepsilon_0}\dfrac{Qq}{(\frac{r}{2})^2} = \dfrac{1}{4\pi\varepsilon_0}\dfrac{QQ}{r^2}$

$\Rightarrow q = \dfrac{Q}{4}$

54(A). Electric potential due to a charged sphere $= \dfrac{kQ}{R}$

$k = 9 \times 10^9\ \text{N} - \dfrac{\text{m}^2}{\text{C}^2}$

Q : charge on sphere

R : Radius of sphere

Let charge and radius of smaller drop is q and r respectively,

For smaller drop, $V = \dfrac{kq}{r}$

$= 220\ \text{V}$

Let R be radius of bigger drop,

As volume remains the same,

$\left(\dfrac{4}{3}\pi r^3\right) \times 27 = \dfrac{4}{3}\pi R^3$

$\Rightarrow R = \sqrt[3]{27}r = 3r$

Now, using charge conservation,

$\Rightarrow Q = 27q$

$V_{\text{bigdrop}} = \dfrac{kQ}{R}$

$= \dfrac{k(27q)}{3r}$

$= 9\left(\dfrac{kq}{r}\right)$

$= 9 \times 220$

$= 1980\ \text{V}$

55(D). Given a mass of copper sphere $= 2$ g contains 2×10^{22} atoms.

We have to find the fraction of electrons that must be removed from sphere to give it $+2\mu$ C charge.

Charge on nucleus of each atom $= 29$ e

$\therefore$ Net charge on 2 gm sphere $= (29)e \times \left(2 \times 10^{22}\right) = 5.8 \times 10^{23}$ ec

$\therefore$ No of electrons on sphere $= 5.8 \times 10^{23}$

$\therefore$ Number of electrons removed to give $2\mu c$ charge $= \dfrac{q}{e}$

$= \dfrac{2\times10^{-6}}{1.6\times10^{-19}}$

$= 1.25 \times 10^{13}$

Fraction of electrons removed

$= \dfrac{1.25\times10^{13}}{\text{Total number of electrons in sphere}}$

$= \dfrac{1.25\times10^{13}}{29\times2\times10^{22}}$

$= 2.16 \times 10^{-11}$

56(B). By induction, the tennis ball gets -ve charge and gets attracted to the +ve plate and touches it. Charges are then shared, as charges repel and hence ball moves away & touches the earthed plate which gives its charge and goes to initial position & process repeats.

57(A). Given data, Voltage = 220 V, Current = 600mA = 0.6A

Power, P = V × I = 220 × 0.6 = 132 W

58(C). When sugar is added to water, it does not produce ions to facilitate electrical conductivity, Thus we can say Sugar is not capable of conducting electricity.

59(C). Given data: Current, $i = 0.6$ A ; Time $\Delta t = 10$ minutes $= 10 \times 60 = 600$ seconds

$\Rightarrow \Delta Q = i \times \Delta t$

$\Rightarrow \Delta Q = 0.6 \times 600 = 360$C

60(B). Power is given by formula, $P = VI$ ...(i) and $V = IR$ ...(ii).

Therefore, $P = I^2 R$ and $P = \dfrac{V^2}{R}$ {from (i) and (ii)}

61(D). Since the current loop is in the x-y plane, the magnetic lines of force will be perpendicular to the x-y plane i.e. in the z-direction.

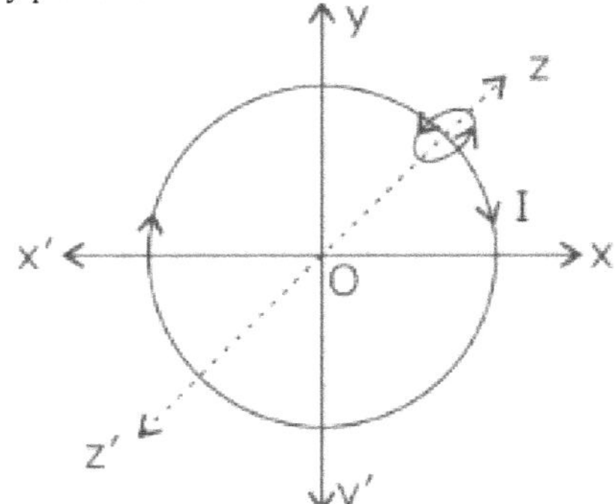

Magnetic flux is given by

$\Phi_m = \oint \vec{B} \cdot \vec{dA}$

The number of magnetic lines of force going towards the positive z-direction through the circular loop is equal to the number of magnetic lines of force going towards the negative z-direction through the x-y plane outside the circular loop. This is true because the magnetic lines of forces form a closed loop. Thus, the net magnetic flux through the x-y plane is zero.

62(B). The magnetic force (F) experienced by a moving charged particle (q) in a uniform magnetic field (B) is given by

$F = qvB\sin\theta$

$\Rightarrow B = \dfrac{F}{qv\sin\theta}$

where, θ is angle between the magnetic field and the velocity of the particle.

The dimensions of charge, force and velocity are
$[q] = [Q]$
$[F] = [MLT^{-2}]$
$[v] = [LT^{-1}]$
$\sin\theta$ is a dimensionless quantity. Now, the dimension of magnetic field is
$$[B] = \frac{[F]}{|q||v|\sin\theta} = \frac{[MLT^{-2}]}{[Q][LT^{-1}]} = [MT^{-1}Q^{-1}]$$
The energy stored in a capacitor is given by
$$E = \frac{q^2}{2C}$$
where, C is capacitance.
The dimension of energy is
$[E] = [ML^2T^{-2}]$
Thus, the dimension of capacitance is
$$[C] = \frac{[q^2]}{[E]}$$
$$\Rightarrow [C] = \frac{[Q^2]}{[ML^2T^{-2}]}$$
$$\Rightarrow [C] = [M^{-1}L^{-2}T^2Q^2]$$
Given: $X = 3YZ^2$ where, X and Z have the dimensions of capacitance and magnetic field respectively. Thus, $[X] = [C] = [M^{-1}L^{-2}T^2Q^2]$
$[z] = [B] = [MT^{-1}Q^{-1}]$

Therefore, the dimension of Y is $[Y] = \dfrac{[X]}{[Z]^2}$
$$\Rightarrow [Y] = \frac{[M^{-1}\,L^{-2}\,T^2Q^2]}{[MT^{-1}Q^{-1}]^2}$$
$$\Rightarrow [Y] = \frac{[M^{-1}L^{-2}T^2Q^2]}{[M^2T^{-2}Q^{-2}]}$$
$$\Rightarrow [Y] = [M^{-3}L^{-2}T^4Q^4]$$

63(B). The ratio of intensity of magnetisation to the magnetisation force is known as susceptibility.
In electromagnetism, the magnetic susceptibility is one measure of the magnetic properties of a material. The susceptibility indicates whether a material is attracted into or repelled out of a magnetic field.

64(A). Case 1 : In the first case, it is given that, when the key K_1 is closed but K_2 is open then deflection in the galvanometer equals θ_0.
Let the current flowing in the galvanometer is i_g and the deflection in the galvanometer is given by θ_0. We know that the current in the galvanometer is proportional to the deflection in the galvanometer.
Thus, $i_g \propto \theta_0$
After removing proportional sign we get a constant C,
$i_g = C\theta_0$ ......(1)
Let us assume the emf of the battery is E.
We know that the current flowing in the circuit is equal to the ratio of emf of the battery to the total resistance in the circuit.
So, $i_g = \dfrac{E}{220+R_g}$ ......(2)
From equation (1) and (2), we get
$\dfrac{E}{220+R_g} = C\theta_0$ ......(3)
Now, according to the second condition when K_2 is closed and adjusting R_2 to 5Ω, the deflection in the galvanometer becomes $\dfrac{\theta_0}{5}$.
We know that the current in the galvanometer is proportional to the deflection in the galvanometer.
Here deflection is $\dfrac{\theta_0}{5}$

$i_g = C\dfrac{\theta_0}{5}$ ....(4)
We know that the current flowing in the circuit is equal to the ratio of emf of the battery to the total resistance in the circuit.
$$i_g = \left(\frac{E}{220+\frac{5R_g}{5+R_g}}\right) \times \left(\frac{5}{R_g+5}\right) \quad\text{..........(5)}$$
From equation (4) and (5), we get
$$\left(\frac{E}{220+\frac{5R_g}{5+R_g}}\right) \times \left(\frac{5}{R_g+5}\right) = C\frac{\theta_0}{5}$$
On further solving this, we get
$$\Rightarrow \frac{5E}{225R_g+1100} = \frac{C\theta_0}{5} \quad\text{......(6)}$$
Now finally solving equation (3) and (6) from case 1 and 2 respectively, we get,
$$\Rightarrow \frac{225R_g+1100}{1100+5R_g} = 5$$
On further solving, we get
$\Rightarrow 5500 + 25R_g = 225R_g + 1100$
$\Rightarrow 200R_g = 4400$
On finally solving this, we get
$R_g = 22\Omega$
Thus, the resistance of the galvanometer is 22Ω.

65(B). Given:
$T_1 = 4K, T_2 = 24K$
For paramagnetic material,
According to curies law,
$M = \chi H$, $\left(\chi = \dfrac{C}{T}\right)$
where,
$\chi > 0$ is the (volume) magnetic susceptibility,
M is the magnitude of the resulting magnetization (A/m),
H is the magnitude of the applied magnetic field (A/m)
T is absolute temperature (K),
C is a material-specific Curie constant (K).
$\chi \propto \dfrac{1}{T}$
$\Rightarrow \chi_1 T_1 = \chi_2 T_2$
$\Rightarrow \dfrac{6}{0.4} \times 4 = \dfrac{I}{0.3} \times 24$
$I = \dfrac{0.3}{0.4} = 0.75 A/m$

66(A). Given,
Number of turns in a circular coil, N=100
The radius of each turn, r = 8.0 cm = 0.08 m
Current flowing in the coil, I = 0.4 A
We know that the magnitude of the magnetic field B at the centre of the coil is given by,
$$B = \frac{\mu_0 NI}{2r}$$
Where,
μ_0 represents the permeability of free space and is numerically equal to $4\pi \times 10^{-7} m/A$.
N represents the number of turns per unit length.
r represents the radius of the circular coil.
$$\Rightarrow B = \frac{4\pi\times10^{-7}\times0.4\times100}{2r\times0.08}$$
$\Rightarrow B = 3.14 \times 10^{-4}T$
So, the magnitude of the magnetic field is $B = 3.14 \times 10^4 T$.

67(A). Given,
At a place of Earth, the vertical component of Earth's magnetic field is $\sqrt{3}$ times its horizontal component.
As, vertical component of Earth's magnetic field,
$B_V = \sqrt{3}\, B_H$

Angle of dip at any place is given as,
$$\tan\delta = \frac{B_V}{B_H}$$
$$\tan\delta = \frac{\sqrt{3}\,B_H}{B_H} = \sqrt{3}$$
$$\Rightarrow \delta = \tan^{-1}(\sqrt{3}) = 60°$$

68(B). A magnetic field line is an imaginary line such that tangent to it at any point gives the direction of the magnetic field at that point in space.
- Magnetic field lines are drawn to represent the magnetic fields.
- Magnetic field lines can be drawn with the help of a magnetic compass.
- Magnetic field lines are also called magnetic lines of force.

69(B). The density of field lines is near poles of magnet hence strength of the magnet is more near poles.
- A bar magnet consists of two equal and opposite magnetic poles separated by a small distance.
- The poles of a bar magnet are near the endpoints of a bar magnet.
- A magnet has two poles, the north pole, and the south pole.
- Like poles attract and unlike poles repel each other.

70(D). The core of transformer is laminated because energy losses due to eddy currents may be minimised.
The core of the transformer is laminated to reduce these to a minimum as they interfere with the efficient transfer of energy from the primary coil to the secondary one. The eddy currents cause energy to be lost from the transformer as they heat up the core - meaning that electrical energy is being wasted as heat.

71(B). We know that,
If there are two solenoids of equal length and one solenoid is placed coaxially inside the other solenoid then the mutual inductance of solenoid 1 with respect to solenoid 2 will be equal to the mutual inductance of solenoid 2 with respect to solenoid 1 .
The mutual inductance of both the solenoids is given as,
$$M_{12} = M_{21} = \mu_o n_1 n_2 \pi r_1^2 l \quad \ldots(i)$$
Where $n_1 =$ number of turns per unit length of solenoid 1, $n_2 =$ number of turns per unit length of solenoid 2, $r_1 =$ radius of the inner solenoid, and $I =$ length of both the solenoids
When the radius of the inner solenoid is halved, $\left(r_1' = \frac{r_1}{2}\right)$, the mutual inductance is given as,
$$M_{12}' = M_{21}' = \mu_o n_1 n_2 \pi \left(\frac{r_1}{2}\right)^2 l$$
$$\Rightarrow M_{12}' = M_{21}' = \frac{\mu_o n_1 n_2 \pi r_1^2 l}{4} \quad \ldots(ii)$$
By equation (i) and equation (ii),
$$M_{12}' = \frac{M_{12}}{4}$$
$$\Rightarrow M_{21}' = \frac{M_{21}}{4}$$

72(A). "Change in magnetic flux can cause a voltage to be induced" is correct regarding Faraday's Law.
Any change in the magnetic flux of wire will cause a voltage (induced emf) to be "induced" in the coil. This change can be produced by changing the magnetic field strength, moving the coil into or out of the magnetic field, moving a magnet toward or away from the coil, rotating the coil relative to the magnet, etc.

73(A). Given: Height of the needle, $h_1 = 4.5\ cm$
Object distance, $u = -12\ cm$
The focal length of the convex mirror, $f = 15\ cm$
Image distance, v
The value of v can be obtained using the mirror formula. $\frac{1}{v} + \frac{1}{u} = \frac{1}{f}$
$$\Rightarrow \frac{1}{v} + \frac{1}{-12} = \frac{1}{15}$$
$$\Rightarrow \frac{1}{v} = \frac{1}{12} + \frac{1}{15}$$
$$\Rightarrow \frac{1}{v} = \frac{9}{60}$$
$$\therefore v \approx 6.7\ cm$$
Hence, the image of the needle is $6.7\ cm$ away from the mirror. Also, it is on the other side of the mirror. The image size is given by the magnification formula.
$$m = \frac{h'}{h} = -\frac{v}{u}$$
$$h' = \frac{6.7 \times 4.5}{12}$$
$$\Rightarrow h' = +2.5\ cm$$
So, $m = \frac{2.5}{4.5}$
$$\Rightarrow m = 0.56$$
The height of the image is $2.5\ cm$. The positive sign indicates that the image is erect, virtual, and diminished. If the needle is moved farther from the mirror, the size of the image will reduce gradually.

74(A). According to law of reflection we know in case of plane mirror the angle of reflection is equal to the angle of incidence. So,if we place the eye on point A the hole can be seen.

75(D). For correcting myopia, a concave lens is used and for the lens.
$$\frac{1}{f} = \frac{1}{v} - \frac{1}{u}$$
$$\Rightarrow \frac{1}{f} = \frac{1}{-25} - \frac{1}{(-50)}$$
$$\Rightarrow f = -50\ cm$$
So power,
$$P = \frac{100}{f}$$
$$= \frac{100}{-50}$$
$$= -2D$$

76(A). In optical fibers total internal reflection property of light waves are used, so as to confine the light rays inside the fiber.
When light traveling in an optically dense medium hits a boundary at a steep angle (larger than the critical angle for the boundary), the light is completely reflected. This is called total internal reflection. This effect is used in optical fibers to confine light in the core.

77(D). Given, $\lambda_1 = 5893\ \text{Å}$, $n_1 = 62$, $\lambda = 4358\ \text{Å}$
As field of view in case of both the wavelengths is same,
Therefore,
$$n_1 \beta_1 = n_2 \beta_2$$
As, $n_1 \left(\frac{D\lambda_1}{d}\right) = n_2 \left(\frac{D\lambda_2}{d}\right)$
Or $n_2 = n_1 \left(\frac{\lambda_1}{\lambda_2}\right)$
$$\Rightarrow 62 \times \frac{5893}{4358} = 84$$

78(A). Position fringe from central maxima:
$$y_1 = \frac{n\lambda_1 D}{d}$$
Given, $n = 10$

$$\therefore y_1 = \frac{10\lambda_1 D}{d} \ldots (i)$$

For second source:

$$y_2 = \frac{5\lambda_2 D}{d} \ldots (ii)$$

$$\therefore \frac{y_1}{y_2} = \frac{\frac{10\lambda_1 D}{d}}{\frac{5\lambda_2 D}{d}}$$

$$\Rightarrow \frac{y_1}{y_2} = \frac{2\lambda_1}{\lambda_2}$$

79(B). As given, in the hydrogen atom jumps from the third orbit to the second orbit

$$n_1 = 2$$
$$n_2 = 3$$

By this relation,

$$\frac{1}{\lambda} = R\left(\frac{1}{n_1^2} - \frac{1}{n_2^2}\right)$$

$$\frac{1}{\lambda} = R\left(\frac{1}{2^2} - \frac{1}{3^2}\right)$$

$$\Rightarrow \frac{1}{\lambda} = R\left(\frac{1}{4} - \frac{1}{9}\right)$$

$$\Rightarrow \frac{1}{\lambda} = R\left(\frac{9-4}{36}\right)$$

$$\Rightarrow \frac{1}{\lambda} = \frac{5R}{36}$$

$$\Rightarrow \lambda = \frac{36}{5R}$$

80(A). Ultrasound having a frequency different from a frequency of a standing wave generated from the ultrasound vibrators symmetrically arranged on the walls at both sides of the channel to stir and mix the sample fluids. Ultrasonic vibrators are used to produce a perfectly homogeneous solution as these vibrations symmetrically arranged on the walls at both sides of the channel to stir and mix the sample fluids.

1. Which of these relations is wrong?
   (a) 1 cal = 4.18 J
   (b) $1\,\text{Å} = 10^{-10}$ m
   (c) $1\,\text{MeV} = 1.6 \times 10^{-13}$ J
   (d) $1\,\text{N} = 10^{-5}$ dyne

2. Dimensions of torque is:
   (a) $[\text{M}^1\,\text{L}^2\,\text{T}^{-2}]$
   (b) $[M^2L^2T^2]$
   (c) $[\text{M}^{-1}\text{LT}^{-1}]$
   (d) $[\text{M}^{-2}\,\text{L}^{-2}\,\text{T}^{-2}]$

3. Unit of magnetic flux is:
   (a) Ampere/metre^2
   (b) Weber
   (c) Gauss
   (d) Orested

4. Dimension of Planck's constant is similar to:
   (a) Linear momentum
   (b) Angular momentum
   (c) Torque
   (d) Velocity

5. A stone is thrown vertically upward with an initial velocity of $40\,\text{ms}^{-1}$. Taking $g = 10\,\text{ms}^{-2}$, the maximum displacement and distance covered by the stone on reaching the ground is:
   (a) Displacement = zero; distance = 80 m
   (b) Displacement = zero; distance covered = 160 m
   (c) Displacement = 80 m; distance = 160 m
   (d) Displacement and distance = 180 m

6. The area under the velocity-time graph between any two instants $t = t_1$ and $t = t_2$ gives the displacement in time $\delta t = t_2 - t_1$:
   (a) Only if the particle moves with a uniform velocity
   (b) Only if the particle moves with a uniform acceleration
   (c) Only if the particle moves with an acceleration increasing at a uniform rate
   (d) In all cases irrespective of whether the motion is one of uniform velocity, or of uniform acceleration or of variable acceleration

7. For a body moving with uniform acceleration a, initial and final velocities in a time interval t are u and v respectively. Then, its average velocity in the time interval t is:
   (a) $\left(v + \frac{at}{2}\right)$
   (b) $\left(u + \frac{at}{2}\right)$
   (c) $(v - at)$
   (d) None of these

8. Three particles A, B and C are projected from the same point with the same initial speed making angles 30°, 45° and 60° respectively with the horizontal. Which of the following statements is correct?
   (a) A, B and C have unequal ranges
   (b) Ranges of A and C are equal and less than that of B
   (c) Ranges of A and C are equal and greater than that of B
   (d) A, B and C have equal ranges

9. A bullet fired at an angle of 30° with the horizontal hits the ground 3.0 km away. By adjusting its angle of projection, find maximum range (R_{max}) is achieved by the bullet? Assume the muzzle speed to be fixed, and neglect air resistance.
   (a) 2.222 km
   (b) 4.576 km
   (c) 3.464 km
   (d) 6.245 km

10. A cricketer can throw a ball to a maximum horizontal distance of 100 m. How much high above the ground can the cricketer throw the same ball?
    (a) 60 m
    (b) 50 m
    (c) 80 m
    (d) 75 m

11. "When a hanging carpet is beaten with a stick, dust particles start coming out of it". This phenomenon is best example of:
    (a) Newton's First Law of motion
    (b) Newton's Second Law of motion
    (c) Newton's Third Law of motion
    (d) Newton's Law of gravitation

12. A ball of mass 2 kg was initially in the hand of a girl. The girl throws the ball with 20 m/s then find the impulse imparted to the ball.
    (a) 10 kg m/s
    (b) −20 kg m/s
    (c) 40 kg m/s
    (d) −40 kg m/s

13. The momentum of a body of mass 0.5 kg dropped from a certain height (h), when reaches the ground is 10 N s. The value h is:
    ($g = 10\,\text{ms}^{-2}$)
    (a) 20 m
    (b) 40 m
    (c) 10 m
    (d) 80 m

14. N bullets, each of mass $m\,kg$, are fired with a velocity $v\,ms^{-1}$ at the rate of n bullets per second upon a wall. The reaction offered by the wall to the bullets is given by:
    (a) nmv
    (b) $\frac{Nmv}{n}$
    (c) $n\frac{Nm}{v}$
    (d) $n\frac{Nv}{m}$

15. A body of mass 2 kg is driven by an engine delivering a constant power of 1 J/s. The body starts from rest and moves in a straight line. After 9 seconds, the body has moved a distance (in m):
    (a) 20
    (b) 19
    (c) 18
    (d) 16

16. A mass 'm' moves with a velocity 'v' and collides inelastically with another identical mass. After collision the 1st mass moves with velocity $\frac{v}{\sqrt{3}}$ in a direction perpendicular to the initial direction of motion. Find the speed of the 2nd mass after collision.

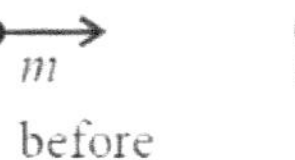

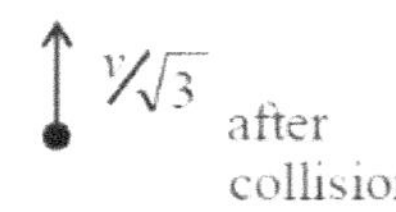

   (a) $\sqrt{3}v$
   (b) v
   (c) $\frac{v}{\sqrt{3}}$
   (d) $\frac{2}{\sqrt{3}}v$

17. A 100-gram ball is kept on the top of a building of 70 m height. Find the potential energy of the ball (assume g = 10 m/s^2)
    (a) 70 J
    (b) 80 J
    (c) 50 J
    (d) 60 J

18. A force $\vec{F} = (5\hat{i} + 3\hat{j})$ newton displaces a body by $(2\hat{i} - \hat{j})$ metre. The work done by the force is:

(a) Zero   (b) 12 Joules

(c) 7 Joules   (d) 13 Joules

19. An athlete throws a discus from rest to a final angular velocity of 15 rad/s in $0.270\ s$ before releasing it. During acceleration, the discus moves a circular arc of radius $0.810\ m$. The acceleration of the discus before it is released is ___ ms^{-2}.

(a) 45   (b) 182

(c) 187   (d) 192

20. The moment of inertia of a uniform semicircular disc of mass M and radius r, about a line perpendicular to the plane of the disc through the centre, is

(a) $\frac{1}{4}Mr^2$ (b) $\frac{2}{5}Mr^2$

(c) Mr^2 (d) $\frac{1}{2}Mr^2$

21. A uniform cylindrical rod of mass m and length L is rotating with an angular velocity ω. The axis of rotation is perpendicular to its axis of symmetry and passes through one of its edges faces. If the room temperature increases by t and the coefficient of linear expansion is α, the change in its angular velocity is :

(a) $\sqrt{\omega}$ (b) $2\omega\alpha t$

(c) ω^2 (d) $\frac{1}{\omega}$

22. Newton's law of gravitation is applicable in the case of _______.

(a) Planets and stars only

(b) Point masses only

(c) Big bodies onlyy

(d) All bodies in the universe

23. Law of gravitation gives the gravitational force between _______.

(a) The Earth and a point mass only

(b) The Earth and Sun only

(c) Any two bodies having mass

(d) Two charged bodies only

24. What is the intensity of gravitational field of the centre of a spherical shell?

(a) Variable   (b) Minimum

(c) Maximum   (d) Zero

25. A missile is launched with a velocity less than the escape velocity. The sum of its kinetic and potential energy is _______.

(a) Positive

(b) Negative

(c) Zero

(d) May be positive or negative depending upon its initial velocity

26. The approximate height of a geostationary satellite from the earth's surface is _______.

(a) 36000 km   (b) 42000 km

(c) 30000 km   (d) 46000 km

27. A soap bubble, having radius of $1mm$, is blown from a detergent solution having a surface tension of $2.5 \times 10^{-2} N/m$. The pressure inside the bubble equals at a point Z_0 below the free surface of water in a container. Taking $g = 10m/s^2$, density of water $= 10^3 kg/m^3$, the value of Z_0 is:

(a) $100cm$ (b) $10cm$

(c) $1cm$ (d) $0.5cm$

28. A small hole of area of cross-section $2mm^2$ is present near the bottom of a fully filled open tank of height $2m$. Taking $g = 10m/s^2$, the rate of flow of water through the open hole would be nearly

(a) $12.6 \times 10^{-6} m^3/s$ (b) $8.9 \times 10^{-6} m^3/s$

(c) $2.23 \times 10^{-6} m^3/s$ (d) $6.4 \times 10^{-6} m^3/s$

29. The surface of a liquid acts like a stretched elastic membrane under tension. This is mainly due to _______.

(a) viscosity   (b) surface tension

(c) velocity of flow   (d) capillarity

30. The pressure of water in a pipe when water is not flowing is $3 \times 10^5 Pa$ and when the water flows the pressure falls to $2.5 \times 10^5 Pa$. Find the speed of flow of water (in m/s) ?

(a) 5   (b) 10

(c) 20   (d) 1

31. The point at which the solid, liquid and gaseous from of a substance co- exist is called its?

(a) Boiling point   (b) Freezing point

(c) Melting point   (d) Triple point

32. By what process is heat transmitted from the filament of an evacuated electric bulb to the glass?

(a) Convection

(b) Radiation

(c) Conduction

(d) Heat cannot be transmitted through vacuum

33. One end of a brass rod $2\ m$ long and $1\ cm$ radius is maintained at $250°C$. When a steady state is reached, the rate of heat flow across any cross-section is $0.5\ cals\ s^{-1}$. What is the temperature of the other end? $\left(k = 0.26\ cals\ s^{-1}{}°C^{-1}cm^{-1}\right)$

(a) $127.6°C$ (b) $187.2°C$

(c) $197.5°C$ (d) $210.7°C$

34. A solid copper sphere (density ρ and specific heat capacity c) of radius r at an initial temperature $200K$ is suspended inside a chamber whose walls are at almost $0K$. The time required (in μs) for the temperature of the sphere to drop to $100K$ is

(a) $\frac{72}{7}\frac{r\rho c}{\sigma}$ (b) $\frac{7}{72}\frac{r\rho c}{\sigma}$

(c) $\frac{27}{7}\frac{r\rho c}{\sigma}$ (d) $\frac{7}{27}\frac{r\rho c}{\sigma}$

35. In changing the state of a gas adiabatically from an equilibrium state A to another equilibrium state B, an amount of work equal to $22.3J$ is done on the system. If the gas is taken from state A to B via a process in which the net heat absorbed by the system is $9.35cal$, how much is the net work done by the system in the latter case? (Take $1cal = 4.19J$)

(a) $12.39J$ (b) $12.08J$

(c) $15.88J$ (d) $16.88J$

36. A diatomic gas does $80\ J$ of work when compressed isobarically. The heat given to the gas during this process is:

(a) $700\ J$ (b) $350\ J$

(c) $280\ J$ (d) $300\ J$

37. Which option is correct about the specific heat of gas?

(a) It has any positive value from zero to infinity.

(b) It may have negative value.

(c) Its exact value depends on mode of heating of gas.

(d) All of the above

38. What is the value of specific heat capacity for an isothermal process?

(a) 0 (b) $\frac{3}{2}R$

(c) ∞ (d) None of the above

39. Cooking gas containers are kept in a lorry moving with uniform speed. The temperature of the gas molecules inside will __________

(a) Increase

(b) Decrease

(c) Remain the same

(d) Decreases for some, while the increase for others

40. The behavior of real gases approaches that of ideal gas in which of these following conditions?

(a) Low pressure & low temperature

(b) High Pressure & high temperature

(c) Low pressure & high temperature

(d) High pressure & low temperature

41. If the pressure of a gas is increased then its mean free path becomes __________.

(a) zero   (b) less

(c) more   (d) infinity

42. A cylinder contains hydrogen gas at a pressure of $249 kPa$ and a temperature of $27^\circ C$. What is its density?
$R = 8.3\ Jmol^{-1}K^{-1}$

(a) $0.2 kg/m^3$ (b) $0.1 kg/m^3$

(c) $0.02 kg/m^3$ (d) $0.5 kg/m^3$

43. 1 mole of H_2 gas is contained in a box of volume $V = 1.00 m^3$ at $T = 300K$. The gas is heated to a temperature of $T = 3000K$ and the gas gets converted to a gas of hydrogen atoms. The final pressure would be (considering all gases to be ideal):

(a) Same as the pressure initially

(b) 2 times the pressure initially

(c) 10 times the pressure initially

(d) 20 times the pressure initially

44. Positive Beilstein shows that:

(a) Halogens are definitely present

(b) Halogens are absent

(c) Halogens may be present

(d) None of these

45. 2-Methyl-2-butene will be represented as:

(a)
$$CH_3 - \overset{\overset{\displaystyle CH_3}{|}}{CH} - CH_2CH_3$$

(b) $CH_3 - \underset{\underset{\displaystyle CH_3}{|}}{C} = CH - CH_3$

(c) $CH_3 - CH_2 - \underset{\underset{\displaystyle CH_3}{|}}{C} = CH$

(d) $CH_3 - \underset{\underset{\displaystyle CH_3}{|}}{CH} - CH = CH$

46. Ammonia forms the complex $[Cu(NH_3)_4]^{2+}$ with copper ions in alkaline solution but not in acidic solution. The reason for this is:

(a) In alkaline solution $Cu(OH)_2$ is precipitated which is soluble in excess of alkali

(b) Copper hydroxide is amphoteric substance

(c) In acidic solution hydration protects Cu^{2+} ions

(d) In acidic solution protons are coordinated with ammonia molecules forming NH_4^+ ions

47. SO_2Cl_2 (sulphuryl chloride) reacts with water to given a mixture of H_2SO_4 and HCl. What volume of $0.2MBa(OH)_2$ is needed to completely neutralize 25 mL of $0.2MSO_2Cl_2$ solution:

(a) 25 mL   (b) 100 mL

(c) 200 mL   (d) 50 mL

48. A mixture contains 5.4 g of Al, 1.2 g of Mg and 4.6 g of C_2H_5OH. The ratio of their moles is:
(Atomic weights of $Al = 27u, Mg = 24u, C = 12u, O = 16u, H = 1u$)

(a) $4:1:2$ (b) $2:1:5$

(c) $2:1:4$ (d) $2:3:4$

49. A body can be negatively charged by _______________.

(a) giving some electrons to it

(b) removing some electrons from it

(c) giving some protons to it

(d) removing some neutrons to it

50. What happens to the plates of the apparatus if we measure alternating charge using a Gold-leaf oscilloscope?

(a) It doesn't diverge at all

(b) It diverges momentarily

(c) The plates give a proper divergence

(d) The degree of divergence increases and decreases repeatedly

51. A system has two charges $q_A = 2.5 \times 10^{-7}C$ and $q_B = -2.5 \times 10^{-7}C$ located at points $A : (0, 0, -15cm)$ and $B : (0, 0, +15cm)$ respectively. What are the total charge and electric dipole moment of the system?

(a) $8.5 \times 10^8 Cm$ (b) $7.5 \times 10^{18} Cm$

(c) $4.5 \times 10^{-8} Cm$ (d) $7.5 \times 10^{-8} Cm$

52. What is the force between two small charged spheres of charges $2 \times 10^{-7}C$ and $3 \times 10^{-7}C$ placed $30cm$ apart in the air?

(a) $5 \times 10^3 N$ (b) $4 \times 10^{-13} N$

(c) $6 \times 10^{-3} N$ (d) None of the above

53. Two charges, one of $+5\mu C$ and another of $-5\mu C$ are kept 1 mm apart. Find the dipole moment.

(a) 2×10^{-5} cm   (b) 5×10^{-9} cm

(c) 8×10^{-4} cm   (d) 7×10^{-9} cm

54. A particle of mass m carrying charge $+q_1$ is revolving around a fixed charge $-q_2$ in a circular path of radius r. Calculate the period of revolution.

(a) $4\pi r\sqrt{\dfrac{\pi\epsilon_0 mr}{q_1 q_2}}$

(b) $8\pi r\sqrt{\dfrac{\pi^3\epsilon_0 mr^3}{q_1 q_2}}$

(c) $\sqrt{\dfrac{q_1 q_2}{16\pi^3\epsilon_0 mr^3}}$

(d) Zero

55. An electric dipole, when held at $30°$ with respect to a uniform electric field of 10^4N/C experiences a torque of 9×10^{-26}Nm . Calculate the dipole moment of the dipole.

(a) 1.8×10^{-19}Cm

(b) 2.7×10^{-18}Cm

(c) 1.7×10^{-14}Cm

(d) 3.8×10^{-20}Cm

56. Which of the following material has the highest relative permittivity?

(a) Water

(b) Transformer Oil

(c) Epoxy Resin

(d) Mica

57. A lead-acid battery of a car has an e.m.f of 12V. If the internal resistance of the battery is 0.5 ohm, the maximum current that can be drawn from the battery will be:

(a) 30 A

(b) 20 A

(c) 6 A

(d) 24 A

58. A battery of emf 10 V and internal resistance 3 ohm is connected to a resistor. If the current in the resistor is 0.5 A, what is the resistance of the resistor? What is the terminal voltage of the battery when the circuit is closed?

(a) 17Ω and $8.5V$

(b) 18Ω and $8.5V$

(c) 19Ω and $8.5V$

(d) 15Ω and $8.5V$

59. Six similar bulbs are connected as shown in the figure with a DC source of emf E and zero internal resistance. The ratio of power consumption by the bulbs when (i) all are glowing and (ii) in the situation when two from section A and one from section B are glowing, will be:

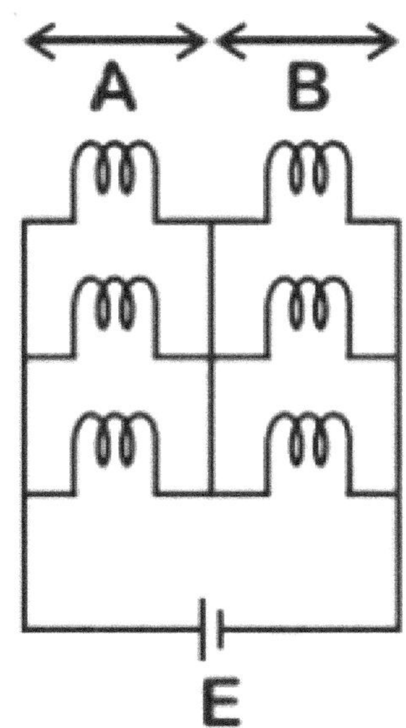

(a) $4 : 9$

(b) $9 : 4$

(c) $1 : 2$

(d) $2 : 1$

60. In the circuits shown below, the readings of voltmeters and the ammeters will be

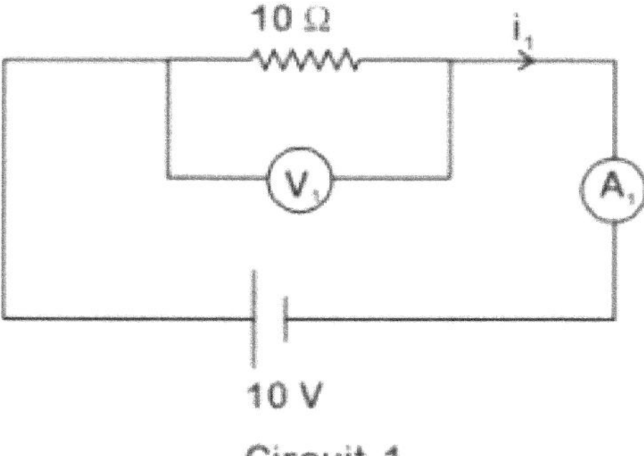

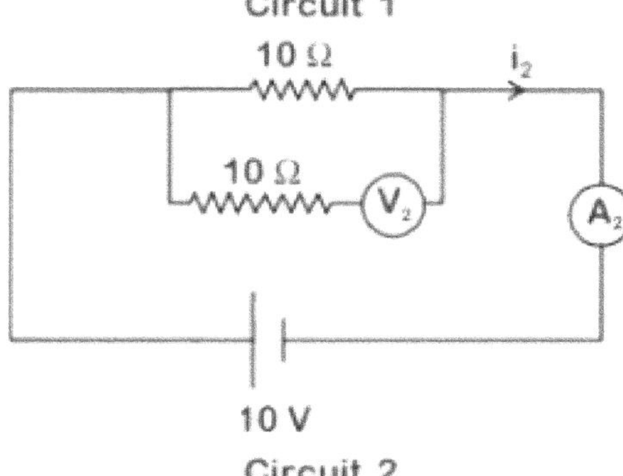

(a) $V_2 > V_1$ and $i_1 = i_2$

(b) $V_1 = V_2$ and $i_1 > i_2$

(c) $V_1 = V_2$ and $i_1 = i_2$

(d) $V_2 > V_1$ and $i_1 > i_2$

61. A moving coil galvanometer can be converted into a ammeter by connecting to the moving coil galvanometer:

(a) A low resistance in series

(b) A low resistance in parallel

(c) A high resistance in parallel

(d) A high resistance in series

62. What happens to the strength of electromagnet if the soft iron core is put into it?

(a) It will increase

(b) It will decrease

(c) It will remain constant

(d) Initially, it will increase and then decrease.

63. A straight wire of length L and radius a has a current I . A particle of mass m and charge q approaches the wire moving at a velocity v in a direction anti parallel to the current. The line of motion of the particle is at a distance r from the axis of the wire. Assume that r is slightly larger than a so that the magnetic field seen by the particle is similar to that caused by a long wire. Neglect end effects and assume that speed of the particle is high so that it crosses the wire quickly and suffers a small deflection θ in its path. Calculate θ .

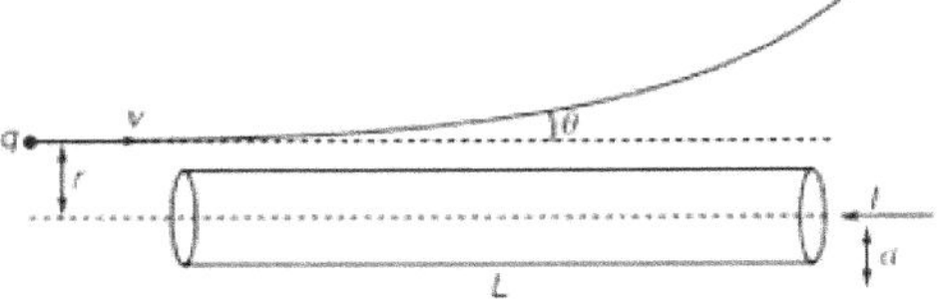

(a) $\dfrac{\mu_0 IqL}{7\pi rmV}$

(b) $\dfrac{\mu_0 IqL}{5\pi rmV}$

(c) $\dfrac{\mu_0 IqL}{1\pi rmV}$

(d) $\dfrac{\mu_0 IqL}{2\pi rmV}$

64. On heating a ferromagnetic substance above Curie

temperature:

(a) Becomes paramagnetic

(b) Becomes diamagnetic

(c) Remains ferromagnetic with constant magnetic susceptibility

(d) Becomes electromagnetic

65. A particle of charge +q has velocity v in the positive x-direction. A magnetic field B exist in the positive y-direction. The trajectory of the charged particle will be:

(a) A straight line

(b) A circle in the x-y plane

(c) A circle in the y-z plane

(d) A circle in the x-z plane

66. One proton enters in a magnetic field of 2500 of N / Amp- m intensity with velocity 4×10^5 m/sec in parallel of field. The force exerted on proton will be:

(a) 4.8×10^{-10} N   (b) 0.48×10^{-10} N

(c) 0 N   (d) 4.8×10^{10} N

67. Let $\vec{E}$ and $\vec{B}$ denote the electric and magnetic fields in a certain region of space. A proton moving with a velocity along a straight line enters the region and is found to pass through it undeflected. Indicate which of the following statements are consistent with the observations:

(a) $\vec{E} = 0$ and $\vec{B} = 0$

(b) $\vec{E} \neq 0$ and $\vec{B} = 0$

(c) $\vec{E} \neq$ and $\vec{B} \neq 0$ and both $\vec{E}$ and $\vec{B}$ are parallel to $\vec{v}$

(d) All of above

68. Polar molecules are the molecules:

(a) Having a permanent electric dipole moment.

(b) Having zero dipole moment.

(c) Acquire a dipole moment only in the presence of electric field due to displacement of charges.

(d) Acquire a dipole moment only when magnetic field is absent.

69. The magnetic field of Earth at a given point is $0.5 \times 10^{-5} Wb/m^2$. This field is to be neutralised by magnetic induction at the centre of a circular conducting loop of radius 5.0 cm. The current required to be passed through the loop is nearly

(a) 0.2 A   (b) 0.4 A

(c) 4 A   (d) 40 A

70. A cylindrical bar magnet is placed axially along the axis of a circular coil. If the coil is rotated about its axis, then:

(a) Only an e.m.f. will get induced in the coil

(b) Only a current will induce in the coil

(c) Both the current and the e.m.f. will induce in the coil

(d) Neither e.m.f. nor current will induce in the coil

71. Faraday's law says that:

(a) An emf is induced in a loop when it moves through an electric field

(b) The induced emf produces a current whose

magnetic field opposes the original change

(c) The induced emf is proportional to the rate of change of magnetic flux

(d) The induced emf is inversely proportional to the rate of change of magnetic flux

72. A coil and a magnet are moved in the same direction and with same speed. What will happen?

(a) The coil will experience a force

(b) The magnet will experience a force

(c) Electric current will be induced in the coil

(d) Electric current will not be induced in the coil

73. A spherical surface of radius of curvature R separates air (refractive index 1.0) from glass (refractive index 1.5). The centre of curvature is in the glass. A point object P placed in air is found to have a real image Q in the glass. The line PQ cuts the surface at point O and $PO = OQ$. The distance PO is equal to

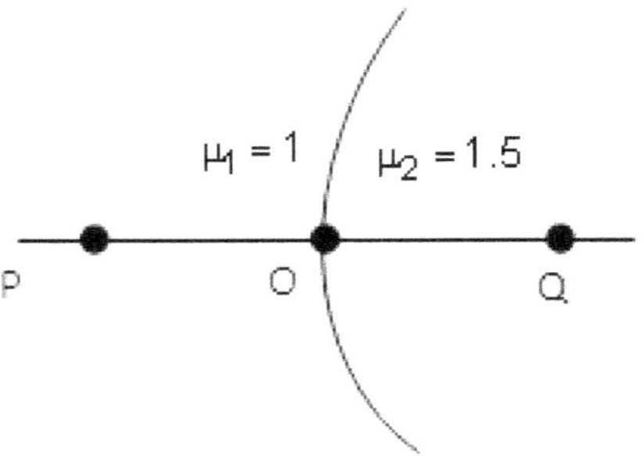

(a) $5R$ (b) $3R$

(c) $2R$ (d) $1.5R$

74. A small telescope has an objective lens of focal length 150 cm and an eyepiece of focal length 5 cm . if this telescope is used to view 100 m high towers 3 km away. Find the height of the final image when it is formed 25 cm away from the eyepiece.

(a) $-30\ cm$ (b) $-24\ cm$

(c) $28\ cm$ (d) $32\ cm$

75. A ray is incident at an angle of incidence i on one surface of a small angle prism (with angle of prism A) and emerges normally from the opposite surface. If the refractive index of the material of the prism is μ, then the angle of incidence is nearly equal to

(a) $\dfrac{A}{2\mu}$ (b) $\dfrac{2A}{\mu}$

(c) μA (d) $\dfrac{\mu A}{2}$

76. Unpolarised light is incident from air on a plane surface of a material of refractive index $'\mu'$. At a particular angle of incidence $'i'$, it is found that the reflected and refracted rays are perpendicular to each other. Which of the following options is correct for this situation?

(a) $i = \sin^{-1}\left(\dfrac{1}{\mu}\right)$

(b) Reflected light is polarised with its electric vector perpendicular to the plane of incidence

(c) Reflected light is polarised with its electric vector parallel to the plane of incidence

(d) $i = \tan^{-1}\left(\dfrac{1}{\mu}\right)$

77. Two coherent waves are $y_1 = a\cos(\omega t)$ and $y_2 = 2a\cos(\omega t)$. If the two waves undergo constructive interference, then the resultant amplitude will be:

(a) a　　　　　　　　(b) $5a$

(c) $3a$　　　　　　　　(d) None of these

78. A beam of light of wavelength 600 mm from a distant source falls on a single slit 1.0 mm wide and the resulting diffraction pattern is observed on a screen 2 m away. The distance between the first dark fringes on either side of the central bright fringe is:

(a) 1.2 cm　　　　　　(b) 1.2 mm

(c) 2.4 cm　　　　　　(d) 2.4 mm

79. In the figure given below, PQ represents a plane wavefront and AO and BP represent the corresponding extreme rays of monochromatic light of wavelength λ. The value of angle θ for which the ray BP and the reflected ray OP interfere constructively is given by:

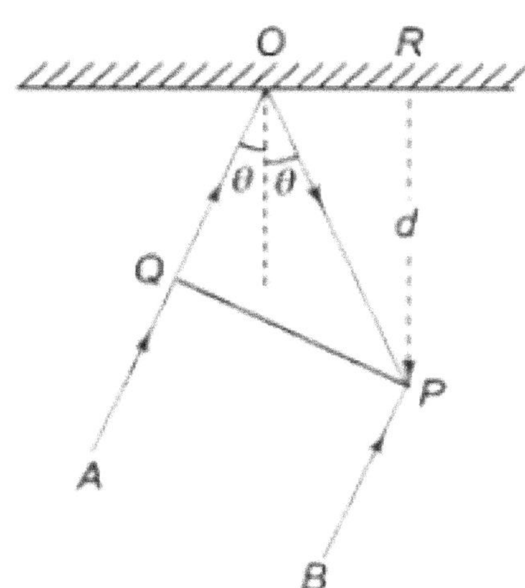

(a) $\cos\theta = \dfrac{\lambda}{2d}$　　　　(b) $\cos\theta = \dfrac{\lambda}{4d}$

(c) $\sec\theta = \dfrac{\lambda}{3d}$　　　　(d) $\sec\theta = \dfrac{2\lambda}{3d}$

80. Two bodies of masses 4 kg and 5 kg are acted upon by the same force if acceleration of lighter body is 3m/s^2

(a) 1.4 m/sec^2　　　　(b) 2.4 m/sec^2

(c) 3.4 m/sec^2　　　　(d) 4.4 m/sec^2

// Smart Answer Sheet //

	Correct	Percentage of students who answered correctly.
	Skipped	Percentage of students who skipped.

Q.	Ans.	Correct / Skipped	Q.	Ans.	Correct / Skipped	Q.	Ans.	Correct / Skipped
1	D	16.53% / 82.0%	2	A	54.51% / 31.46%	3	B	52.77% / 33.31%
4	B	20.4% / 71.06%	5	B	47.25% / 32.25%	6	D	43.19% / 31.31%
7	B	64.3% / 33.9%	8	B	47.51% / 49.95%	9	C	59.78% / 39.72%
10	B	26.02% / 70.3%	11	A	86.37% / 11.92%	12	C	40.62% / 45.27%
13	A	46.05% / 43.11%	14	A	58.06% / 35.37%	15	C	56.5% / 41.99%
16	D	64.63% / 35.01%	17	A	62.79% / 36.29%	18	C	47.05% / 51.57%
19	A	58.92% / 39.27%	20	D	26.8% / 68.13%	21	B	69.87% / 30.08%
22	D	76.18% / 13.59%	23	C	89.2% / 10.65%	24	D	79.94% / 18.38%
25	B	84.09% / 14.47%	26	A	89.57% / 10.13%	27	C	61.9% / 35.72%
28	A	45.22% / 32.02%	29	B	86.14% / 13.55%	30	B	16.86% / 73.01%
31	D	62.01% / 35.92%	32	B	53.46% / 43.93%	33	A	31.79% / 68.05%
34	B	65.84% / 33.09%	35	D	54.44% / 36.66%	36	C	85.2% / 11.03%
37	D	50.97% / 36.27%	38	C	40.23% / 34.34%	39	C	62.03% / 32.07%
40	C	43.78% / 48.64%	41	B	84.77% / 11.47%	42	A	44.5% / 46.19%
43	D	23.38% / 68.04%	44	C	69.24% / 30.63%	45	B	64.31% / 34.25%
46	D	55.69% / 37.0%	47	D	69.92% / 30.07%	48	A	54.12% / 36.59%
49	A	77.44% / 18.4%	50	C	62.46% / 36.11%	51	D	18.53% / 67.8%
52	C	57.74% / 31.95%	53	B	85.05% / 10.13%	54	A	81.14% / 12.32%
55	A	69.67% / 30.17%	56	A	77.0% / 14.28%	57	D	64.83% / 34.47%
58	A	64.77% / 32.46%	59	B	48.58% / 46.33%	60	C	40.56% / 58.12%
61	B	59.41% / 39.54%	62	A	68.95% / 30.08%	63	D	50.25% / 31.99%
64	A	29.96% / 68.68%	65	D	48.35% / 30.21%	66	C	17.12% / 79.63%
67	D	49.94% / 45.86%	68	A	85.19% / 12.67%	69	B	65.67% / 31.94%
70	D	62.74% / 36.85%	71	C	82.84% / 14.65%	72	D	48.63% / 44.03%
73	A	14.98% / 69.3%	74	A	64.15% / 33.13%	75	C	54.74% / 39.97%
76	B	76.36% / 18.53%	77	C	65.33% / 32.24%	78	D	76.09% / 13.89%
79	B	15.93% / 82.61%	80	B	40.14% / 58.07%			

// Hints and Solutions //

1(D). Both Dyne and Newton are units of force in the CGS and S.I system.

Newton and dyne can also be written as,

$(1\ N = kgm/s^2)$ and $(1\ dyne = gmcm/s^2)$

$\Rightarrow 1\ dyne = 1gmcm/s^2$ and $1\ newton = 1\ kgm/s^2$

$\Rightarrow 1\ kg = 1000gm$

$\Rightarrow 1\ m = 100\ cm$

$\Rightarrow 1\ kgm/s^2 = 1000gm \times 100\ cm/s^2$

$\Rightarrow 10^5 gmcm/s^2 = 10^5\ dyne$

$\Rightarrow 1\ dyne = 10^{-5}\ kgm/s^2$

$\Rightarrow 10^{-5}\ N$

$\Rightarrow 1\ N = 10^5\ dyne$

2(A). Torque is a physical computation with the dimension of force times distance. Its SI unit is a newton meter. It also has a unit as joule per radian.

We know that,

Torque $(T) = rF\sin\theta$

As we know, that the dimension of force $(F) = \left[MLT^{-2}\right]$

The dimension of $r = [L]$

$\therefore$ The dimensions of torque (T) is

$\Rightarrow T = \left[M^1\,L^2\,T^{-2}\right]$

3(B). Unit of magnetic flux is weber.

Magnetic flux is a measurement of the total magnetic field which passes through a given area. It is a useful tool for helping describe the effects of the magnetic force on something occupying a given area.

Since magnetic flux $(\varphi) = \mathrm{BA}$

Where, B = megnatic field and A = area

The SI unit of magnetic flux = SI unit of magnetic field × SI unit of area = tesla meter ^{2} = $\mathrm{Tm^2}$

Since, 1 Weber = 1 $\mathrm{Tm^2}$

Thus the SI unit of magnetic flux is $\mathrm{Tm^2}$ and which is equal to weber (Wb).

4(B). The dimension of Planck's constant is similar to angular momentum.

It is a physical constant that is the quantum of electromagnetic action. It relates the energy carried by a photon to its frequency by, $\mathrm{E} = \mathrm{h}\nu$

$\Rightarrow h = \dfrac{\mathrm{E}}{\nu}$

Where, E = energy, ν = frequency and h = Planck's constant.

Now,

Dimensional formula of energy $(\mathrm{E}) = \left[\mathrm{ML^2\,T^{-2}}\right]$

Dimensional formula of frequency $(\nu) = \left[\mathrm{T^{-1}}\right]$

The dimension of the Planck's constant is (h)

$\Rightarrow h = \dfrac{[ML^2T^{-2}]}{[T^{-1}]} = [ML^2T^{-1}]$

Angular momentum:

It is the rotational equivalent of linear momentum.

$\Rightarrow \mathrm{L} = \mathrm{r} \times \mathrm{p}$

Where, L = angular momentum, r = distance and p = linear momentum.

Now,

Dimensional formula of $(\mathrm{r}) = [\mathrm{L}]$

Dimensional formula of $(\mathrm{p}) = \left[\mathrm{MLT^{-1}}\right]$

Therefore, the dimensional formula of L is

$\Rightarrow \mathrm{L} = [L] \times \left[MLT^{-1}\right]$

$\Rightarrow \mathrm{L} = \left[ML^2T^{-1}\right]$

5(B). Given,

Initial velocity, $u = 40\,\mathrm{m/s}$

Final velocity, $\mathrm{v} = 0\,\mathrm{m/s}$

Acceleration due to gravity, $\mathrm{g} = 10\,\mathrm{m/s^2}$ (downward motion)

Maximum height, $\mathrm{s} = \mathrm{H}$

As the body is thrown upward $a = -g$ the relation

$\mathrm{v}^2 = \mathrm{u}^2 - 2as$

$\mathrm{v}^2 = \mathrm{u}^2 - 2a\mathrm{H}$

We have,

$\mathrm{H} = \dfrac{\mathrm{u}^2 - \mathrm{v}^2}{2\,\mathrm{g}}$

$= \dfrac{40\,\mathrm{m/s}^2 - 0^2}{2(10\,\mathrm{m/s^2})}$

$= \dfrac{1600}{20} = 80\,\mathrm{m}$

If a stone is thrown vertically upward, it returns to its initial position after achieving maximum height. So, the net displacement = Difference of positions between initial and final positions = 0

Total distance covered = $80\,\mathrm{m} + 80\,\mathrm{m} = 160\,\mathrm{m}$

6(D). In general the area under the velocity-time graph gives the displacement happening in given time. The area under the velocity-time graph between any two instants $t = t_1$ and $t = t_2$ gives the displacement in time $\delta t = t_2 - t_1$. This holds good for objects in uniform velocity, uniform acceleration, variable acceleration.

7(B). Given a body is moving with uniform acceleration 'a', initial velocity is u and final velocity is v, time is t.

We have to find the average velocity.

From the equations of motion we know

$s = ut + \dfrac{1}{2}at^2$

and $v = u + at$

If an object velocity is increasing at a constant rate then it is called as uniform acceleration.

We know Average velocity can be calculated using the formula

Average velocity

$= \dfrac{\text{Total displacement}}{\text{Total Time}} = \dfrac{ut + \frac{1}{2}a^2}{t}$

Average velocity $= u + \dfrac{1}{2}\,at$

8(B). All of the particles A, B and C are projected from the same point with the same initial speed making angles $30°$, $45°$ and $60°$ respectively with the horizontal. According to the law of projectile motion, if two bodies thrown at same speed at angles such that their sum is equal to $\pi/2$ then both of them will have the same range, so A and C will have same range. Also the range is maximum when angle of projection is $45°$. So the ranges of A and C are equal and less than that of B.

9(C). Horizontal Range $(\mathrm{R}) = 3\,\mathrm{km}$

Angle of projection $(\theta) = 30°$

Acceleration due to gravity $(\mathrm{g}) = 9.8\,\mathrm{m/s^2}$

Horizontal range for the projection velocity $\mathrm{u_0}$, is given by the relation:

$\mathrm{R} = \dfrac{\mathrm{u_0^2}\sin 2\theta}{\mathrm{g}}$

$3 = \dfrac{\mathrm{u_0^2}\sin 60°}{\mathrm{g}}$

$\dfrac{\mathrm{u_0^2}}{\mathrm{g}} = 2\sqrt{3} \quad \dots\dots (i)$

The maximum range $\mathrm{R_{max}}$ is achieved by the bullet when it is fired at an angle of $45°$ with the horizontal, that is

$\mathrm{R_{max}} = \dfrac{\mathrm{u_0^2}}{\mathrm{g}} \quad \dots\dots (ii)$

On comparing equations (i) and (ii), we get:

$\mathrm{R_{max}} = 2 \times 1.732$

$\mathrm{R_{max}} = 3.464\,\mathrm{km}$

10(B). Here,

Maximum horizontal distance $(\mathrm{R_{max}}) = 100\,\mathrm{m}$

The cricketer will only be able to throw the ball to the maximum horizontal distance when the angle of projection is $45°$, i.e., $\theta = 45°$

The horizontal range for a projection velocity v, is given by the relation:

$\mathrm{R_{max}} = \left(\mathrm{u}^2\sin 2\theta\right)/\mathrm{g}$

$100 = \left(\mathrm{u}^2\sin 90°\right)/\mathrm{g}$

$\mathrm{u}^2/\mathrm{g} = 100 \dots (i)$

The ball will achieve the maximum height when it is thrown vertically upward. For such motion, the final velocity v is zero at the maximum height H.

Acceleration $(\mathrm{a}) = -\mathrm{g}$

Using the third equation of motion:

$\mathrm{v}^2 - \mathrm{u}^2 = -2\mathrm{gH}$

$\mathrm{H} = \mathrm{u}^2/2\,\mathrm{g}$

$\mathrm{H} = 100/2 = 50\,\mathrm{m}$

So the cricketer will throw the same ball from $50\,\mathrm{m}$ high above the ground.

11(A). If a carpet is beaten with a stick then the carpet begins to move. But, the particles of dust are trying to resist their state of rest. The concept is based on Newton's first law of motion.

Newton's First Law: A body continues to be in its

state of rest or of uniform motion along a straight line unless it is acted upon by some external force to change the state.

12(C). Given,
Mass of the ball, $m = 2$ kg
Initial velocity of ball, $u = 0$
Final velocity of ball, $v = 20$ m/s
Impulse imparted to the ball $= P_2 - P_1$
$= mv - mu$
$= 2 \times 20 - 2 \times 0$
40 kg m/s

13(A). Given,
Mass of a body, $m = 0.5$ kg
The momentum of a body, $p = 10$ N s
Initial velocity, $u = 0$
Momentum of the body on reaching the ground,
P $=$ mv
$10 = 0.5 \times v$
$v = 20$ m/s
Using equation of motion,
$v^2 = u^2 + 2gh$
$400 = 2 \times 10 \times h$
$h = 20$ m

14(A). Number of bullet $= N$
Mass of each bullet $= m$
The velocity of each bullet $= v$
Time $= 1sec$
Acceleration of each bullet = velocity per unit time
$= v$
Force applied by the bullet $= ma = m \times v$
Force applied by N number of bullets $= nmv$
By Newton's third law of motion, the action equals the reaction.
Therefore, the reaction applied by the wall is equalled to the action produced by the bullet
$= nmv$

15(C). Given, Mass of the body, $m = 2$ kg Power delivered by engine, $P = 1$ J/s
Time, $t = 9$ seconds
Power, $P = Fv$
$\Rightarrow P = mav \quad [\because F = ma]$
$\Rightarrow m\frac{dv}{dt}v = P \quad (\because a = \frac{dv}{dt})$
$\Rightarrow vdv = \frac{P}{m}dt$
Integrating both sides we get
$\Rightarrow \int_0^v vdv = \frac{P}{m}\int_0^t dt$
$\Rightarrow \frac{v^2}{2} = \frac{Pt}{m} \Rightarrow v = (\frac{2Pt}{m})^{1/2}$
$\Rightarrow \frac{dx}{dt} = \sqrt{\frac{2P}{m}}t^{1/2} \quad (\because v = \frac{dx}{dt})$
$\Rightarrow \int_0^x dx = \sqrt{\frac{2P}{m}}\int_0^t t^{1/2}dt$
$\therefore$ Distance, $x = \sqrt{\frac{2P}{m}}\frac{t^{3/2}}{3/2} = \sqrt{\frac{2P}{m}} \times \frac{2}{3}t^{3/2}$
$\Rightarrow x = \sqrt{\frac{2\times 1}{2}} \times \frac{2}{3} \times 9^{3/2} = \frac{2}{3} \times 27 = 18$

16(D). Considering conservation of momentum along x -direction,
$mv = mv_1\cos\theta \quad .....(1)$
where v_1 is the velocity of second mass In y -direction,
$0 = \frac{mv}{\sqrt{3}} - mv_1\sin\theta$
or $mv_1\sin\theta = \frac{mv}{\sqrt{3}} \quad .....(2)$

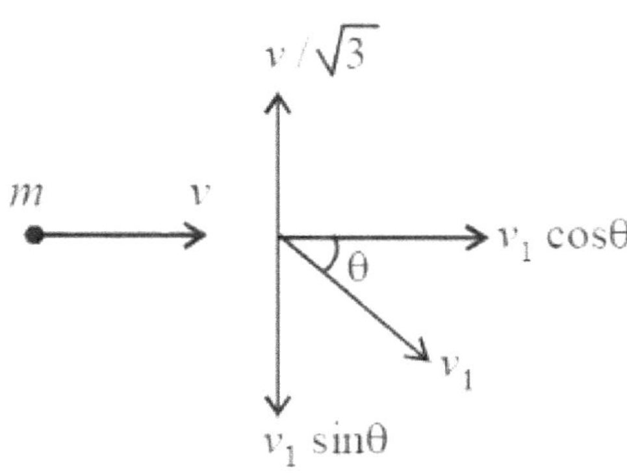

Squaring and adding eqns. (1) and (2) we get
$v_1^2 = v^2 + \frac{v^2}{\sqrt{3}} \Rightarrow v_1 = \frac{2}{\sqrt{3}}v$

17(A). Given that:
Mass (m) = 100 gram = 0.1 kg
Height (h) = 70 m
Gravity (g) = 10 m/s^2
We know that,
Potential energy (PE) = mgh
Potential energy (PE) = 0.1 × 10 × 70
Potential energy = 70 J

18(C). Given:
$\vec{F} = (5\hat{i} + 3\hat{j})$ and $\vec{x} = (2\hat{i} - \hat{j})$
The work done by the force is:
$W = \vec{F} \cdot \vec{x}$
$W = (5\hat{i} + 3\hat{j}) \cdot (2\hat{i} - \hat{j})$
$W = 10 - 3$
$W = 7$ Joules

19(A). $\omega = \omega_0 + \alpha t$
$\Rightarrow \omega = 0 + \alpha t$
$\Rightarrow \alpha = \frac{15}{0.270} rad/s^2$
Now, $a = r, \alpha = 0.81 \times \frac{15}{0.270} = 45ms^{-2}$

20(D). The mass of the complete (circular) disc is
$M + M = 2M$
The moment of inertia of the disc is
$I = \frac{2Mr^2}{2}$
$= Mr^2$
Let the moment of inertia of semicircular disc is I_1

The disc may be assumed as a combination of two semicircular parts.
Thus, $I_1 = I - I_2$
$I_1 = \frac{I}{2} = \frac{Mr^2}{2}$
$= \frac{1}{2}Mr^2$

21(B). If the temp is increased by $t, 1' = 1(1 + \alpha t)$
Initial $MlI = \frac{ml^2}{3}$
Final $MlI' = \frac{ml'^2}{3}$
From the conservation of angular momentum,
$I\omega = I'\omega'$
$\Rightarrow \frac{ml^2}{3}\omega = \frac{ml'^2}{3}\omega' = \frac{ml^2(1+\alpha t)^2}{3}\omega'$
$\Rightarrow \frac{\omega'}{\omega} = (1 + \alpha t)^{-2}$
$\Rightarrow \omega' = \omega(1 - 2\alpha t)$
Neglecting $2nd$ order term as it is negligible
$\Delta\omega = -2\omega\alpha$
Angular velocity decreases since I increase.

22(D). Newton's law of gravitation is applicable in the case of all bodies in the universe.

Newton's law of universal gravitation states that any two bodies in the universe attract each other with a force that is directly proportional to the product of their masses and inversely proportional to the square of the distance between them. Since any two bodies can be there so it doesn't matter whether they are small or large.

23(C). The universal law of gravitation gives the gravitational force between any two bodies having some mass.

The gravitational force between any two bodies having some mass can be determined from Newton's law of gravitation.

The force of attraction between bodies is directly proportional to the product of their masses and inversely proportional to the square of the distance between them.

This force is applied in the direction of the line joining the two bodies.

$$F = G\frac{Mm}{r^2}$$

Here, G is called the universal gravitational constant.

24(D). Zero is the intensity of the gravitational field at the center of a spherical shell.

It's because the pull from every direction is exactly the same. This is obvious from the center, but as you move to one side, you're closer to that side, which increases its pull, but this is exactly offset by the fact that there's now MORE mass on the other side.

25(B). A missile is launched with a velocity less than the escape velocity. The sum of its kinetic and potential energy is negative.

The sum of kinetic energy and potential energy is negative. This is because for the velocity less than escape velocity the missile is bounded due to gravitational field of the earth. so, its total energy is negative.

26(A). The approximate height of a geostationary satellite from the earth's surface is 36000 km.

- The approximate height of a geostationary satellite from the earth's surface is 36000 km.
- A geostationary orbit is a circular orbit.
- It is 35,786 km above the earth's equator.
- A satellite in a geostationary orbit appears stationary.
- A geostationary satellite follows an orbit parallel to the equator and rotates with the same period of 24 hours as the earth. As a result, it appears to be motionless in relation to the earth's surface.

27(C). As we known that the surface tension, the pressure which is outside the bubble is equal the the inside the bubble and it is written as;

$$P_0 + \frac{4T}{R} = P_0 + \rho g Z_0 \cdots (1)$$

Given: Tension, $T = 2.5 \times 10^{-2} N/m$

$g = 10 m/s^2$

Density of water, $\rho = 10^3 kg/m^3$

radius, $R = 1mm$

As we know that the pressure inside the surface is equal to below the free surface of water in a container therefore,the equation (1) becomes,

$$\frac{4T}{R} = \rho g Z_0$$

$$\Rightarrow Z_0 = \frac{4T}{R\rho g}$$

Now, on putting all the given values we have;

$$Z_0 = \frac{4 \times 2.5 \times 10^{-2}}{10^{-3} \times 1000 \times 10} m$$

$$\Rightarrow Z_0 = 10^{-2} m$$

$$\Rightarrow Z_0 = 1cm$$

28(A). Given that,

A hole at the bottom of the tank of area $= 2mm^2 = 2 \times 10^{-6} m$

Height at which liquid is filled $= 2m$

Gravitational acceleration $= 10 m/s^2$

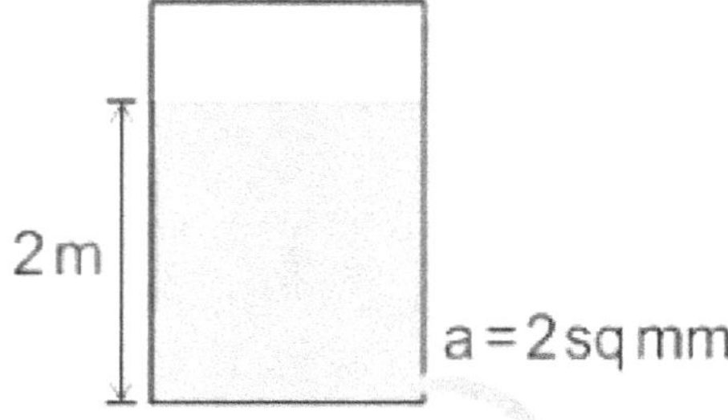

Now the rate of flow (Q) can be given as

$$Q = A \times v = A\sqrt{2gh}$$

$$= 2 \times 10^{-6} \times \sqrt{2 \times 10 \times 2}$$

Rate of flow $Q = 12.6 \times 10^{-6} m^3/s$

29(B). The surface of a liquid acts like a stretched elastic membrane under tension. This is mainly due to surface tension.

When a liquid is exposed to the air, it behaves like a stretched membrane as the water molecules are attracted to each other. This property of liquid is also called Surface tension.

At liquid-air interfaces, surface tension results from the attraction of water molecules to each other, which is a cohesive force, then to the molecules in the air, which is an adhesive/repulsive force.

The combined effect of these two forces is an inward force at the surface of the liquid which causes the surface to behave as if it were covered with a stretched elastic membrane.

30(B). Given:

Initial velocity $(v_1) = 0 m/s$, Initial pressure $(P_1) = 3 \times 10^5 Pa$, and Final pressure $(P_2) = 2.5 \times 10^5 Pa$

According to Bernoulli's principle

$$\Rightarrow P_1 + \frac{1}{2}\rho v_1^2 = P_2 + \frac{1}{2}\rho v_2^2$$

$$\Rightarrow P_1 = P_2 + \frac{1}{2}\rho v_2^2$$

The above equation can be written as

$$\Rightarrow v_2^2 = \frac{2(P_1 - P_2)}{\rho}$$

$$\Rightarrow v_2^2 = \frac{2(3 \times 10^5 - 2.5 \times 10^5)}{10^3} = 10^2 m^2/s^2$$

$$\Rightarrow v_2 = 10 m/s$$

31(D). The point at which the solid, liquid and gaseous from of a substance co- exist is called its t riple point.

In thermodynamics, the triple point of a substance is the temperature and pressure at which the three phases (gas, liquid, and solid) of that substance coexist in thermodynamic equilibrium. It is the temperature and pressure at which the sublimation curve, fusion curve, and vaporization curve meet. For example, the triple point of mercury occurs at a temperature of -38.83440 °C (-37.90192 °F) and a pressure of 0.165 mPa. Helium-4 is a special case that presents a triple point involving two different fluid phases (lambda point).

32(B). Radiation is heat transmitted from the filament of an evacuated electric bulb to the glass.
Radiation is the emission or transmission of energy in the form of waves or particles through space or through a material medium.
Since there is no medium present in the light bulb, so the heat transfer takes place by radiation because the conduction and the convection require a material medium to transfer heat.

33(A). Given, $\frac{Q}{t} = 0.5\ cals^{-1}$
Value of $K = 0.26\ cals^{-1}cm^{-1}°C^{-1}$
The unit of K is given in the CGS system.
So, we first need to convert the units of all the given quantities into a CGS system.
Length of rod $= 2\ m = 200\ cm$
$\Delta x = 200\ cm$
Radius $= 1\ cm$
Cross-sectional area of the other end of the brass rod will be a circle.
$\therefore$ Area of circle $= \pi r^2$
$= 3.14 \times (1)^2$
$= 3.14\ cm^2$
We have to find the temperature of the other end T_2
We know the temperature of the first end
$T_1 = 250°C$
Now use formula, $\frac{Q}{t} = \frac{K(T_1 - T_2)A}{\Delta x}$
Where, Q is the amount of heat transferred.
t is time taken
T is temperature
A is area of cross section
Δx is the change in length.
$T_1 - T_2 = \frac{\Delta x Q}{KAt}$
Substitute the values in the above equation
$\Rightarrow T_1 - T_2 = \frac{200 \times 0.5}{3.14 \times 0.26}$
By simplifying the fraction, we get
$T_1 - T_2 = \frac{100}{0.8164}$
$= 1.224 \times 100$
$\Rightarrow T_1 - T_2 = 122.4°C$
But it is given that $T_1 = 250°C$
Therefore, the equation
$T_1 - T_2 = 122.4°C$
which can be rearranged as
$T_2 = T_1 - 122.4°C$
will give
$T_2 = 250°C - 122.4°C$
$\Rightarrow T_2 = 127.6°C$

34(B). $\frac{dT}{dt} = \frac{\sigma A}{mcJ}\left(T^4 - T_0^4\right)$
In the given problem, fall in temperature of body $dT = (200 - 100) = 100K$,
Temperature of surrounding $T_0 = 0K$
Initial temperature of body $T = 200K$
$\Rightarrow \frac{100}{dt} = \frac{\sigma 4\pi r^2}{\frac{4}{3}\pi r^3 \rho cJ}\left(200^4 - 0^4\right)$
$\Rightarrow dt = \frac{r\rho cJ}{48\sigma} \times 10^{-6}s$
$= \frac{r\rho c}{\sigma} \cdot \frac{4.2}{48} \times 10^{-6}$

$= \frac{7}{80}\frac{r\rho c}{\sigma}\mu s \approx \frac{7}{72}\frac{r\rho c}{\sigma}\mu s$ [As $J = 4.2$]

35(D). It is provided that the work done (W) on the system when the gas transforms from state A to state B is $22.3J$.
This is an adiabatic process. Thus, the change in heat is zero.
$\Rightarrow \Delta Q = 0$
(As the work is done on the system)
Using the first law of thermodynamics,
$\Delta Q = \Delta U + \Delta W$
where,
$\Rightarrow \Delta W = -22.3J$
on putting the above value we get,
$\Rightarrow \Delta U = 22.3J$
$\Delta U =$ change in the internal energy of the gas
When the gas transforms from state A to state B via a process, the net heat absorbed by the system is given by
$\Delta Q = 9.35cal = 9.35 \times 4.19J = 39.1765J$
Heat absorbed can be given by the equation,
$\Delta Q = \Delta U + \Delta W$
$\Rightarrow \Delta W = \Delta Q - \Delta U = 39.1765 - 22.3 = 16.8765\ J$
Clearly, $16.88J$ of work is done by the system.

36(C). We know that,
Isobaric Process (Constant Pressure): Work done in an isobaric process is given by:
$\Delta W = P\Delta V$
Where W is Work done, P is the pressure and ΔV is change in volume.
The ideal gas equation is given by:
$PV = nRT$
Where P is pressure, V is volume, n is the number of moles, R is gas constant and T is temperature.
According to the first law of Thermodynamics:
$\Delta Q = \Delta W + \Delta U$
Where $\Delta Q =$ Heat supplied to the system, $\Delta W =$ work done by the system, and $\Delta U =$ change in internal energy of the system
The change in internal energy (ΔU) is given by:
$\Delta U = nC_v\Delta T$
Where $C_v = \frac{fR}{2} =$ molar-specific heat capacity at the constant volume, f is the degree of freedom.
For diatomic molecule,
$Y = \frac{7}{5}$, and $CV = \frac{R}{(Y-1)} = \frac{5R}{2}$
$\therefore \Delta U = nC_V\Delta T = n\left(\frac{5R}{2}\right)\Delta T = 5nR\Delta\frac{T}{2}$
Given that:
For isobaric process:
Work done $(\Delta W) = 80\ J = P\Delta V$
Since $PV = nRT$
So $P\Delta V = nR\Delta T$
$\Delta U = 5nR\Delta\frac{T}{2} = \frac{5(P\Delta V)}{2} = 5 \times \frac{80}{2} = 200\ J$
Applying first law of thermodynamics:
$\Delta Q = \Delta W + \Delta U = 80 + 200 = 280\ J$
Heat given to the gas $= 280\ J$

37(D). Specific heat is the amount of heat that is required to raise the temperature of 1 gram of a substance by 1 degree celcius.
Specific heat C
$C = \frac{\delta Q}{\Delta T \Delta m}$ kJ/kgK
For an isothermal process, $\Delta T = 0$
So, $C = \infty$
For an isothermal process, $\partial Q = 0$
So, $C = 0$

So, It has any positive value from zero to infinity. When heat is absorbed by the system, q is positive. So, specific heat will be positive. When heat is absorbed from the system, q is negative. So, specific heat will be negative.

Thus, Specific heat of gas can be positive, negative or zero in between 0 to ∞.

38(C). Specific heat $S = \dfrac{\Delta Q}{\Delta T}$

We know that for an isothermal process $\Delta T = 0$

$S = \dfrac{\Delta Q}{\Delta T} = \dfrac{\Delta Q}{0} = \infty$

The Specific heat for the isothermal process is infinity (∞).

39(C). The centre of mass of the gas molecules moves with uniform speed along with the lorry. As there is no change in relative motion, the translational kinetic energy and hence the temperature of the gas molecules will remain the same.

40(C). Ideal gas is based on the assumptions of kinetic theory of gases(KTG). At low pressure and high temperature the intermolecular forces become less significant and the size of molecules becomes less as compared to separation between them. These are two postulates of KTG and hence in these conditions real gas behavior is similar to that of ideal gases.

41(B). As gas pressure increases mean free path of the gas decreases.

Mean free path is the distance traveled by a gas molecule between two successive collisions.

So, as pressure increases number of collisions increase. Hence, mean free path decreases.

42(A). Given,
$P = 249 kPa = 249 \times 10^3\ \text{Pa}$
$T = 27^\circ C = 27 + 273 = 300 K$
$R = 8.3\ Jmol^{-1}K^{-1}$
As we know that,
$PV = nRT$
$\Rightarrow \therefore PV = \left(\dfrac{m}{M}\right) RT$
$\Rightarrow PM = \dfrac{m}{V} RT$
$\Rightarrow \rho = \dfrac{PM}{RT}$
$\Rightarrow \rho = \dfrac{249 \times 10^3 \times 2 \times 10^{-3}}{8.3 \times 300}$
$\Rightarrow \rho = 0.2 kg/m^3$

43(D). As we know,
$PV = nRT$
When R and n are constant we can write it as;
$\dfrac{PV}{T} = \text{constant}$
Now, we can write
$\dfrac{P_2 V_2}{T_2} = \dfrac{P_1 V_1}{T_1}$
$\Rightarrow \dfrac{P_2}{P_1} = \dfrac{V_1}{V_2} \dfrac{T_2}{T_1}$
Given: $T_1 = 3000K$ and $T_2 = 300K$
$\Rightarrow \dfrac{P_2}{P_1} = \dfrac{V_1}{V_2} \times \dfrac{300}{3000}$
When H_2 splits into hydrogen atoms we have volume as $\dfrac{V_1}{2}$, therefore,
$\Rightarrow \dfrac{P_2}{P_1} = \dfrac{V_1}{\frac{V_1}{2}} \times \dfrac{300}{3000}$
$\Rightarrow P_2 = 20 P_1$

44(C). Positive Beilstein shows that halogens may be present. A positive Beilstein's test for halogens does not always indicate the presence of halogen since

some halogen-free compounds viz. urea, thiourea, amides etc. also respond this test. The reason being the fact that these halogen-free compounds form cuprous cyanide which is volatile and decomposes to copper which burns with green flame.

45(B). 2-Methyl-2-butene will be represented as:

$$\overset{\displaystyle CH_3}{\underset{\displaystyle |}{{}^1CH_3 - {}^2C} = {}^3CH - {}^4CH_3}$$

CH$_3$ is numbered first and in this, the Methyl group has been added so we will name Methyl.

46(D). Ammonia acts as a ligand as it donates its lone pair of electrons to Cu^{2+} ions to form $[Cu(NH_3)_4]^{2+}$ complex. This is possible in basic medium. In acidic medium, the lone pair of electrons present on ammonia is donated to proton to form ammonium ion which is not a ligand and cannot form a complex with Cu^{2+} ions.

$Cu^{2+}(aq) + 4\,NH_3 \overset{OH^-}{\rightleftharpoons} [Cu(NH_3)_4]^{2+}$

$Cu^{2+}(aq) + 4\,NH_3 \overset{H^+}{\rightleftharpoons} Cu^{2+} + 4\,NH_4^+$

47(D). The reaction is as follows:
$SO_2Cl_2 + 2H_2O \rightarrow H_2SO_4 + 2HCl$
Millimoles of H_2SO_4 produced = 5
Millimoles of HCl produced = 10
Millimoles of $Ba(OH)_2$ required $= 5\,(\text{ for }$
$H_2SO_4) + \dfrac{10}{2}\,(\text{ for HCl})$
$= 10$
$\therefore M \times V = 10$
$0.2 \times V = 10$
Therefore, $V = 50\ \text{mL}$

48(A). Applying the formula,
$\text{Moles} = \dfrac{\text{Given mass (in grams)}}{\text{Molar mass }\left(\text{in gmol}^{-1}\right)}$
Moles of Al $= \dfrac{5.4}{27} = 0.2$
Moles of Mg $= \dfrac{1.2}{24} = 0.05$
Molar mass of $C_2H_5OH = (2 \times 12) + (6 \times 1)$
$+ (1 \times 16) = 46\ g$
Thus, moles of $C_2H_5OH = \dfrac{4.6}{46}$
$= 0.1$
Then, the ratio of their moles $= 0.2 : 0.05 : 0.1$
$= 4 : 1 : 2$

49(A). A body can be negatively charged by giving some electrons to it.
A body having an excess of electrons. Protons are positively charged particles so giving a proton to a body will make it positively charged. Neutrons have no charge so removing neutrons from a body will not charge it. So a body can be negatively charged by giving some electrons to it.

50(C). The divergence of the plates of the Gold-leaf oscilloscope depends only on the presence of a charge, not on the quality of charge i.e. positive or negative. So, if the charge changes from positive to negative and vice versa the degree of divergence of the plates remains the same.

51(D). The figure given below represents the system mentioned in the question:

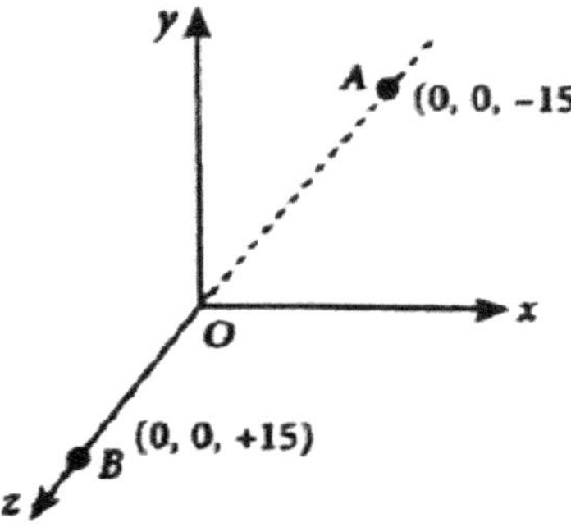

The charge at point A, $q_A = 2.5 \times 10^{-7} C$
The charge at point B, $q_B = -2.5 \times 10^{-7} C$
Then, the net charge
$q = q_A + q_B = 2.5 \times 10^{-7} C - 2.5 \times 10^{-7} C = 0$
The distance between two charges at A and B would be,
$d = 15 + 15 = 30 cm$
$d = 0.3 m$
The electric dipole moment of the system could be given by,
$P = q_A \times d = q_B \times d$
$P = 2.5 \times 10^{-7} \times 0.3$
$P = 7.5 \times 10^{-8} Cm$ along the $+z$ axis.
Therefore, the electric dipole moment of the system is found to be $7.5 \times 10^{-8} Cm$ and it is directed along the positive z-axis.

52(C). Repulsive force of magnitude, $F = 6 \times 10^{-3} N$
Charge on the first sphere, $q_1 = 2 \times 10^{-7} C$
Charge on the second sphere, $q_2 = 3 \times 10^{-7} C$
Distance between the two spheres,
$r = 30 cm = 0.3 m$
Electrostatic force between the two spheres is given by Coulomb's law as, $F = \dfrac{1}{4\pi\varepsilon_0} \dfrac{q_1 q_2}{r^2}$

Where, ε_0 is the permittivity of free space and,
$\dfrac{1}{4\pi\varepsilon_0} = 9 \times 10^9 Nm^2 C^{-2}$

Now on substituting the given values, Coulomb's law becomes.
$F = \dfrac{9 \times 10^9 \times 2 \times 10^{-7} \times 3 \times 10^{-7}}{(0.3)^2}$
$F = 6 \times 10^{-3} N$
Therefore, we found the electrostatic force between the given charged spheres to be $F = 6 \times 10^{-3} N$. Since the charges are of the same nature, we could say that the force is repulsive.

53(B). Given:
Charge on dipole is $\pm 5\mu C = \pm 5 \times 10^{-6} C$
Distance between the charges $= 1$ mm $= 10^{-3}$ m
We know that:
Dipole moment is given by:
$P = q(2a) = qd$
$= 5 \times 10^{-6} \times 10^{-3}$
$= 5 \times 10^{-9}$ Cm

54(A). Since the particle carrying positive charge is revolving around another charge,
Electrostatic force $=$ Centripetal force
$\Rightarrow \dfrac{1}{4\pi\varepsilon_0} \dfrac{q_1 q_2}{r^2} = mr\omega^2$
$\Rightarrow \dfrac{1}{4\pi\varepsilon_0} \dfrac{q_1 q_2}{r^2} = \dfrac{4\pi^2 mr}{T^2}$
$\Rightarrow T^2 = \dfrac{(4\pi\varepsilon_0) r^2 (4\pi^2 mr)}{q_1 q_2}$
$\Rightarrow T = 4\pi r \sqrt{\dfrac{\pi\varepsilon_0 mr}{q_1 q_2}}$

55(A). Given,

Electric field, $E = 10^4 \text{N/C}$
Torque,
$T = 9 \times 10^{-26} \text{Nm}$
$\theta = 30°$
When electric dipole is placed at an angle θ with the direction of the electric field, torque acting on the dipole is given by,
$T = pE \sin\theta$
$\therefore$ The electric moment of the dipole,
$p = \dfrac{T}{E \sin\theta}$
$= \dfrac{9 \times 10^{-26}}{10^4 \times \sin 30°}$
$= \dfrac{9 \times 10^{-26}}{10^4 \times \frac{1}{2}}$
$= \dfrac{9 \times 10^{-26}}{10^4 \times 0.5}$
$= 1.8 \times 10^{-19} \text{Cm}$

56(A). The relative permittivity of the water is highest among the other materials given.
Permittivity describes the amount of charge needed to generate one unit of electric flux in a particular medium. Accordingly, a charge will yield more electric flux in a medium with low permittivity than in a medium with high permittivity. Thus, permittivity is the measure of a material's ability to resist an electric field.
Relative permittivity is the ratio of its absolute permittivity 'ϵ' to free space (empty of matter) permittivity 'ϵ_0' i.e.,
$\epsilon_r = \dfrac{\epsilon}{\epsilon_0}$

57(D). The internal resistance is the resistance which is present within the battery that tries to resist the current flow when connected to a circuit. As a result of this resistance, a voltage drop occurs when current flows through the battery. This resistance in the battery is due to the electrolyte and electrodes which are the part of the battery.
This resistance due to the electrolyte and electrodes present in the battery is called internal resistance of the battery which causes a small voltage drop inside the battery.

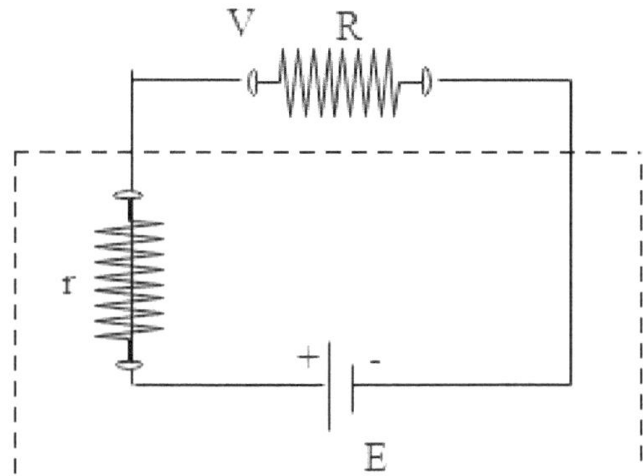

As we know that the potential difference across a battery is given by the following expression:
$V = \varepsilon - Ir$
Here V represents the potential difference across the battery, ε is the e.m.f. produced by the battery while r is the internal resistance of the battery and I is the amount of current that can be drawn from the battery.
Now, for the given battery if we consider that it is not yet connected to the car then V = 0. Then we have

$\varepsilon - \mathrm{I}r = 0$

We are already given the values of e.m.f. and the internal resistance of the battery, therefore, we have

$I = \dfrac{\varepsilon}{r}$

$= \dfrac{12}{0.5}$

$= 24A$

58(A). In the question, we are given a simple circuit. We have a battery of emf 10 V and internal resistance 3ohm and it is further connected to a resistor of some unknown resistance R. We are also told that a current of 0.5 A is measured across the resistor.

By Ohm's law, the current in a circuit with a battery of emf E and internal resistance r and resistor of resistance R is given by,

$I = \dfrac{E}{R+r}$

$\Rightarrow R = \dfrac{E}{I} - r$

Substituting the given values into the equation, we get

$R = \dfrac{10}{0.5} - 3$

$\Rightarrow R = 20 - 3$

$\therefore R = 17\Omega \ldots \ldots (1)$

Now, when the circuit is closed, the terminal voltage is V. We could again apply Ohm's law to get

$V = I \times R$

$\Rightarrow V = 0.5 \times 17$

$\therefore V = 8.5V$

Thereby, we have calculated the resistance of the resistor and also the terminal voltage V whose value is respectively given by:

$R = 17\Omega$

$V = 8.5V$

59(B). (i) All bulbs are glowing

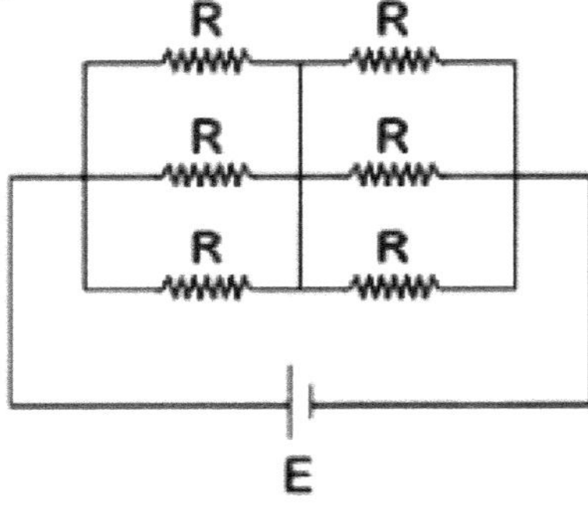

$R_{eq} = \dfrac{R}{3} + \dfrac{R}{3} = \dfrac{2R}{3}$

Power $(P_i) = \dfrac{E^2}{R_{eq}} = \dfrac{3E^2}{2R}$

(ii) Two from section A and one from section B are glowing

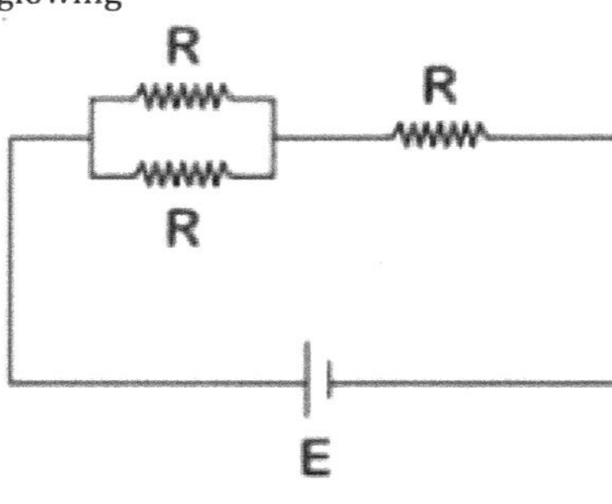

$R_{eq} = \dfrac{R}{2} + R = \dfrac{3R}{2}$

Power $(P_f) = \dfrac{2E^2}{3R}$

$\dfrac{P_i}{P_f} = \dfrac{3E^2 3R}{4RE^2} = 9 : 4$

60(C).

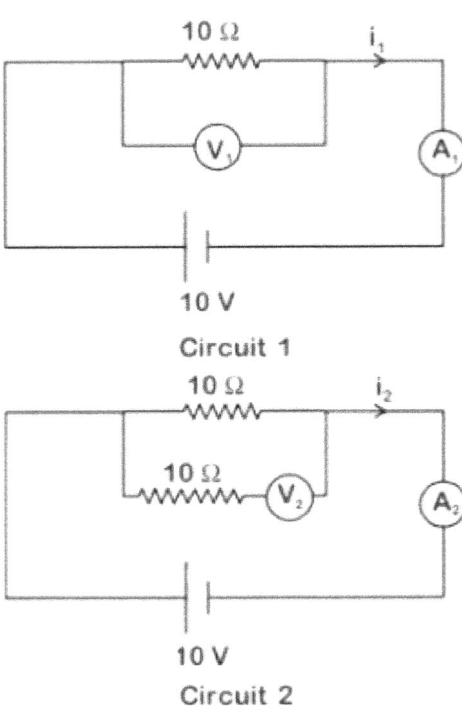

For circuit 1, $R_{\text{eff}} = 10\Omega, i_1 = 1A$ and $V_1 = 10V$

For circuit 2, voltmeter is connected in series combination with 10 Ω in lower branch.

So, that branch draws no current because of infinite resistance of voltmeter.

So, $R_{\text{eff}} = 10\Omega, i_2 = 1A$

$\therefore V_1 = V_2, i_1 = i_2$

61(B). A moving coil galvanometer can be converted into a ammeter by connecting a low resistance in parallel to the moving coil galvanometer.

A galvanometer can be converted into an ammeter by connecting a shunt resistance in parallel to it. The shunt resistance should have very low resistance. So, the ammeter (the parallel combination of galvanometer and shunt resistance) will have low resistance.

62(A). When a soft iron core is inserted inside the solenoid then the strength of the magnetic field becomes very large because the iron core gets magnetized by induction.

The soft iron core helps in concentrating the magnetic lines of forces through the solenoid so that the magnetic field is almost uniform at the end face of the core.

Thus, the strength of the magnetic field increases when a soft iron core is inserted inside a solenoid.

63(D). Given,

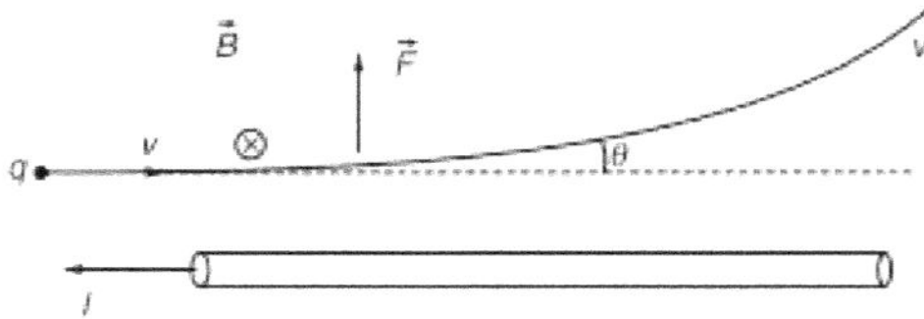

$$B = \frac{\mu_0 I}{2\pi r}$$

Force on the particle is $F = qvB = \frac{\mu_0 Iqv}{2\pi r}(\uparrow)$

This force is always perpendicular to the velocity. Since deflection is small, the force is nearly in ($\uparrow$) direction always.

Impulse is:

$$F\Delta t = \frac{\mu_0 Iqv\Delta t}{2\pi r} = \frac{\mu_0 IqL}{2\pi r}$$

$$\therefore \Delta P = \frac{\mu_0 IqL}{2\pi r}(\uparrow)$$

$$\theta = \frac{\Delta P}{P} = \frac{\mu_0 IqL}{2\pi rmV}$$

64(A). On heating a ferromagnetic substance above Curie temperature becomes paramagnetic.
When a ferromagnetic material is heated to Curie temperature, it disrupts the arrangements of the molecules and a weak magnetic behavior remains. This weak magnetic behavior is called Paramagnetic. Above this temperature, the paramagnetism property also decreases. Upon cooling, it regains its ferromagnetic behavior.

65(D). A particle of charge +q has velocity v in the positive x-direction. A magnetic field B exist in the positive y-direction. The trajectory of the charged particle will be a circle in the x-z plane.
The velocity v of the particle is in the x-direction. The magnetic field B is in the y-direction. The force on the moving charged particle due to the magnetic field is

$$\Rightarrow F_B = q(v \times B)$$

$$\Rightarrow F_B = q(v\hat{\imath} \times B\hat{\jmath}) = qvB(\hat{\imath} \times \hat{\jmath}) = qvB\hat{k}$$

Since the acceleration is in the z-plane, the motion will be in the x-z plane. The magnetic field in the y-direction will always be perpendicular to the motion of the particle (x-z plane). Hence no work will be done by this force. But this force changes the direction of motion of the particle.

66(C). Given,
$B = 2500$ N / Amp-m
$v = 4 \times 10^5$ m/s
q = Charge on proton
$= 1.6 \times 10^{-19}$ Culomb
The proton enters parallel to the magnetic field.
$\therefore \theta = 180°$
$F = q \cdot v \cdot B \cdot \sin\theta$
$= 1 \cdot 6 \times 10^{-19} \times 4 \times 10^5 \times 2500 \times \sin 180°$
$= 1 \cdot 6 \times 10^{-19} \times 4 \times 10^5 \times 2500 \times 0$
$(\because \sin 180° = 0)$
$= 0$

67(D).
(A). When both $\vec{E}$ and $\vec{B}$ are zero, the particle is undeflected.

(B). When $\vec{E} \neq 0$ and $\vec{B} = 0$, the particle will move in the direction of $\vec{E}$ and remains undeflected provided $\vec{E} \parallel \vec{v}$.

(C). $\vec{E} \neq 0, \vec{B} \neq 0, \vec{E} \parallel \vec{v}$ and $\vec{B} \parallel \vec{v}$. Thus, there is no deflection due to magnetic field and particle will accelerate or decelerate in the direction of $\vec{v}$.

68(A). Polar molecules are the molecules having a permanent electric dipole moment.

- In polar molecules, the centre of positive charges does not coincide with the centre of negative charges.
- Therefore, these molecules have a permanent electric dipole moment of their own.

69(B). The magnetic field at the center of a circular loop carrying current is given by,
$$B = \frac{\mu_0 I}{2r}$$
Where r is the radius of the circular loop.
Given,
$r = 5.0$cm $= 0.05$m
Earth's magnetic field
$B_E = 0.5 \times 10^{-5}$ Wb/m^2
B_E is annulled by B
$$\frac{\mu_0 I}{2r} = B_E = 0.5 \times 10^{-5}$$
$$I = \frac{0.5 \times 10^{-5} \times 2 \times 0.05}{\mu_0}$$
$$\Rightarrow \frac{0.5 \times 10^{-5} \times 0.1}{4\pi \times 10^{-7}}$$
$$= 0.3978 \approx 0.4 \text{ A}$$

70(D). A cylindrical bar magnet is placed axially along the axis of a circular coil. If the coil is rotated about its axis, then neither e.m.f. nor current will induce in the coil.
When a cylindrical bar magnet is placed axially along the axis of a circular coil and if the coil is rotated about its axis, then the distance and the orientation of the coil with respect to the magnet will remain the same. Since the distance and the orientation of the coil with respect to the magnet are not changing, so the magnetic flux associated with the coil will remain constant. Since the flux associated with the coil is not changing, so neither e.m.f. nor current will induce in the coil.

71(C). Faraday's law says that the induced emf is proportional to the rate of change of magnetic flux. According to Faraday's second law of electromagnetic induction, the induced emf in a coil is directly proportional to the rate of change of flux linked with the coil. Therefore, t he induced emf is proportional to the rate of change of magnetic flux.

72(D). A coil and a magnet are moved in the same direction and with same speed. Then electric current will not be induced in the coil.
When a bar magnet is pushed toward the coil, the magnetic field linked with the coil increases, hence induced current/ induced e.m.f. is set up in the coil. So, galvanometer deflects right. When the bar magnet is pulled away from the coil, the magnetic field linked with the coil decreases, So, induced current/ induced e.m.f. is set up in the coil. So, galvanometer deflects left. When the bar magnet held stationary inside the coil there is no change in the magnetic field, So no induced current. Such that galvanometer doesn't show any deflection. When the coil and a magnet are moved in the same direction and at the same speed, then there is no change in the magnetic field across the coil and hence no induced current.

73(A). Given, $PO = OQ$
$\Rightarrow u = v$
We know
$$\frac{\mu_2}{v} - \frac{\mu_1}{u} = \frac{\mu_2 - \mu_1}{R}$$
$$\Rightarrow \frac{\mu_2}{v} - \frac{\mu_1}{u} = \frac{\mu_2 - \mu_1}{R}$$

$$\Rightarrow \frac{\mu_2+\mu_1}{V} = \frac{\mu_2-\mu_1}{R}$$
$$\Rightarrow \frac{1.5+1}{v} = \frac{1.5-1}{R}$$
$$\Rightarrow \frac{2.5}{v} = \frac{0.5}{R}$$
$$\Rightarrow v = \frac{2.5R}{0.5}$$
$$v = 5R$$
$$OP = OQ = u = v = 5R$$

74(A). The Magnifying power of a telescope is defined as the ratio of the angle subtended at the eye by the image formed at least distance of distinct vision to angle subtended at the eye by the object lying in infinity.

$$M = -\frac{f_o}{f_e}\left(1 + \frac{f_e}{D}\right)$$

fo = focal length of the object = 150 cm fe= focal length of the eyepiece=5cm

D = least distance of the distinct vision = 25 cm

$$M = \frac{-150}{5}\left(1 + \frac{5}{25}\right) = -36$$

$$M = \frac{\beta}{\alpha} = \frac{\tan\beta}{\tan\alpha} \ (as \text{ we know angles are small })$$

$$\tan\alpha = \frac{H}{u} = \frac{100}{3000}$$
$$= \frac{1}{30}$$

Where H = height of the object and u = distance of the object from the objective.

$$M = \frac{\tan\beta}{\left(\frac{1}{30}\right)} = \frac{-36}{30}$$
$$= \frac{H'}{D}$$

H' = the height of the image and D = distance of the image formation

Thus,

$$H' = \frac{-36\times25}{30} = -30 \text{ cm}$$

Therefore, the negative sign indicates that we get an inverted image.

75(C). Given data:
The angle of incidence = i
The angle of the prism = A
The angle of emergence = e
the refractive index of the material of the prism is μ

.
For a small angle prism, angle of deviation,
$\delta = (\mu - 1)A$ ....(i)
Since, the ray emerges normally, $\therefore e = 0$
By the relation,
$A + \delta = i + e$
We have, i = A + δ
or $\delta = (i - A)$ ....(ii)
From Equation (i) and (ii)
$(i - A) = (\mu - 1)A$
$\Rightarrow$ i = μA

76(B). The Reflected ray of light, when the angle of incidence is Brewster angle, would comprise of only the other component of light wave which is oscillating in a direction perpendicular to vibration of electric field vectors:

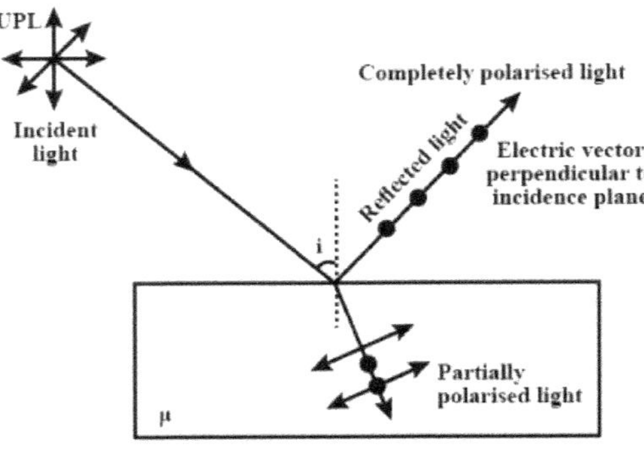

77(C). Given:
$y_1 = a \cdot \cos(\omega t)$ and $y_2 = 2a \cdot \cos(\omega t)$
If the two waves undergo constructive interference, then the resultant displacement is given as,
$y = y_1 + y_2$
$\Rightarrow y = a\cos(\omega t) + 2a\cos(\omega t)$
$\Rightarrow y = 3a \cdot \cos(\omega t)$ ...(1)
By equation (1), the amplitude 'A' of the resultant wave is given as,
$A = 3a$

78(D). For a dark fringe to form,
$$\frac{dy}{D} = \lambda$$
$$y = \frac{D\lambda}{d}$$
$$= \frac{2\times600\times10^{-9}}{10^{-3}}$$
$$= 1.2 \text{ mm}$$
Distance between the first dark fringes on either side of central bright fringe $= 2 \times y = 2.4\text{ mm}$

79(B). In this figure Q and P are at the same phase. Therefore, at P point the path difference between ray BP and reflected ray OP.
We can say, angles of QO and OP are the same.
In triangle $POR, OP = \frac{PR}{cos\theta} = \frac{d}{cos\theta}$
In triangle $QOP, QO = OP\sin(90° - 2\theta) = OP\cos 2\theta$
$\Delta = OP\cos 2\theta + OP$
$= OP(\cos 2\theta + 1)$
$= 2OP\cos^2\theta$
$= 2 \times \frac{d}{\cos\theta} \times \cos^2\theta$
$= 2d\cos\theta$
Now, path difference is $\frac{\lambda}{2}$
Due to reflection at point P
$\Delta = \frac{\lambda}{2}, \frac{3\lambda}{2} \dots\dots\dots\dots\dots$
$2d\cos\theta = \frac{\lambda}{2}, \frac{3\lambda}{2} \dots\dots\dots$
$\cos\theta = \frac{\lambda}{4d}, \frac{3\lambda}{4d} \dots\dots\dots\dots$

80(B). For lighter body
$F = M \times a$
$F = 4 \times 3 = 12N$
For heavier body, since the force is same
$12 = 5 \times a$
$a = \frac{12}{5}$
$a = 2.4 \text{ m/sec}^2$